7th Workshop on Representation Learning for NLP (RepL4NLP-2022)

Dublin, Ireland
26 May 2022

ISBN: 978-1-7138-6750-0

Printed from e-media with permission by:

Curran Associates, Inc.
57 Morehouse Lane
Red Hook, NY 12571

Some format issues inherent in the e-media version may also appear in this print version.

Printed with permission by Curran Associates, Inc. (2023)

Association for Computational Linguistics
209 N. Eighth Street
Stroudsburg, Pennsylvania 18360

Phone: 1-570-476-8006
Fax: 1-570-476-0860

acl@aclweb.org

Additional copies of this publication are available from:

Curran Associates, Inc.
57 Morehouse Lane
Red Hook, NY 12571 USA
Phone: 845-758-0400
Fax: 845-758-2633
Email: curran@proceedings.com
Web: www.proceedings.com

ACL 2022

The 7th Workshop on Representation Learning for NLP (RepL4NLP 2022)

Proceedings of the Workshop

May 26, 2022

The ACL organizers gratefully acknowledge the support from the following sponsors.

Gold

Silver

Introduction

The 7th Workshop on Representation Learning for NLP (RepL4NLP 2022) will be hosted by ACL 2022 and held on 26 May 2022. The workshop is being organised by Spandana Gella, He He, Burcu Can, Maximilian Mozes, Eleonora Giunchiglia, Sewon Min, Samuel Cahyawijaya, Xiang Lorraine Li and Bodhisattwa Prasad Majumder; and advised by Isabelle Augenstein, Anna Rogers, Kyunghyun Cho, Edward Grefenstette, Chris Dyer and Laura Rimell. The workshop is organised by the ACL Special Interest Group on Representation Learning (SIGREP).

The 7th Workshop on Representation Learning for NLP aims to continue the success of the Repl4NLP workshop series, with the 1st Workshop on Representation Learning for NLP having received about 50 submissions and over 250 attendees – the second most attended collocated event at ACL'16 after WMT. The workshop was introduced as a synthesis of several years of independent *CL workshops focusing on vector space models of meaning, compositionality, and the application of deep neural networks and spectral methods to NLP. It provides a forum for discussing recent advances on these topics, as well as future research directions in linguistically motivated vector-based models in NLP. The workshop will take place in a hybrid setting, and, as in previous years, feature interdisciplinary keynotes, paper presentations, posters, as well as a panel discussion.

Organizing Committee

Workshop Organizers

Spandana Gella, Amazon AI
He He, New York University
Bodhisattwa Prasad Majumder, University of California San Diego
Burcu Can, University of Wolverhampton
Eleonora Giunchiglia, University of Oxford
Samuel Cahyawijaya, Hong Kong University of Science and Technology
Sewon Min, University of Washington
Maximilian Mozes, University College London
Xiang Lorraine Li, University of Massachusetts Amherst

Senior Advisors

Isabelle Augenstein, University of Copenhagen
Anna Rogers, University of Copenhagen
Kyunghyun Cho, New York University
Edward Grefenstette, Facebook AI Research
Laura Rimell, DeepMind
Chris Dyer, DeepMind

Program Committee

Program Committee

Aleksandr Drozd, RIKEN
Ankur Padia, University of Maryland, Baltimore County
Anna Tigunova, Saarland Informatics Campus, Max-Planck Institute
Ashutosh Modi, IIT Kanpur
Daichi Mochihashi, The Institute of Statistical Mathematics
Dong Zhou, Hunan University of Science and Technology
Eraldo Rezende Fernandes, Leuphana Universität Lüneburg
Federico Bianchi, Bocconi University
Frank Rudzicz, University of Toronto
Hai Wang, JD Finance America Corp
Haiqin Yang, International Digital Economy Academy
Hong Yu, Apple
Hongyu Gong, Facebook
Imed Zitouni, Google
Izzeddin Gur, Google
Jey Han Lau, The University of Melbourne
Jingjing Xu, Peking University
John P. Lalor, University of Notre Dame
Kang Min Yoo, NAVER
Kimberly Mai, University College London, University of London
Lijun Wu, Microsoft Research
Lili Mou, University of Alberta
Lin Chen, University of Illinois at Chicago
Mareike Hartmann, German Research Center for AI
Matthieu Labeau, Télécom ParisTech
Menno van Zaanen, North-West University
Minhao Cheng, Hong Kong University of Science and Technology
Mladen Karan, Queen Mary University London
Muhammad Abdul-Mageed, University of British Columbia
Nadi Tomeh, Université Sorbonne Paris Nord
Nicholas Andrews, Johns Hopkins University
Peng Qi, JD AI Research
Pranava Madhyastha, City, University of London
Qinliang Su, SUN YAT-SEN UNIVERSITY
Robin Jia, University of Southern California
Rodrigo Wilkens, UCL
Sergey Feldman, Allen Institute for Artificial Intelligence
Shankar Kumar, Google
Shuai Tang, Amazon Web Services
Sneha Mehta, Virginia Tech
Sung Ju Hwang, Korea Advanced Institute of Science and Technology
Surangika Ranathunga, University of Moratuwa
Tao Li, School of Computing, University of Utah
Tingting Mu, University of Manchester
Tsuyoshi Okita, Kyushu Institute of Technology
Tsvetomila Mihaylova, Instituto de Telecomunicações, Portugal

Vipul Raheja, Grammarly
Vladimir Eidelman, FiscalNote, Inc.
Xia Cui, University of Manchester
Yitong Li, Huawei Technologies Co., Ltd.
Yue Chen, Microsoft

Invited Speakers

Been Kim, Google Brain
Emma Strubell, Carnegie Mellon University
Monojit Choudhury, Microsoft Research, India
Percy Liang, Stanford University
Sebastian Riedel, University College London and Facebook AI Research

Table of Contents

Distributionally Robust Recurrent Decoders with Random Network Distillation

Antonio Valerio Miceli Barone
University of Edinburgh
amiceli@ed.ac.uk

Alexandra Birch
University of Edinburgh
a.birch@ed.ac.uk

Rico Sennrich
Universität Zürich
sennrich@cl.uzh.ch

Abstract

Neural machine learning models can successfully model language that is similar to their training distribution, but they are highly susceptible to degradation under distribution shift, which occurs in many practical applications when processing out-of-domain (OOD) text. This has been attributed to "shortcut learning": relying on weak correlations over arbitrary large contexts. We propose a method based on OOD detection with Random Network Distillation to allow an autoregressive language model to automatically disregard OOD context during inference, smoothly transitioning towards a less expressive but more robust model as the data becomes more OOD, while retaining its full context capability when operating in-distribution. We apply our method to a GRU architecture, demonstrating improvements on multiple language modeling (LM) datasets.

1 Introduction

Neural language models have become the main component of modern natural language processing systems, with larger and larger models being used as feature extractors for downstream tasks (Devlin et al., 2019), as probability estimators for ranking and ensembling (Gulcehre et al., 2015) or as language generators (Bahdanau et al., 2015; Vaswani et al., 2017; Brown et al., 2020).

Despite their success, neural machine learning models can suffer large performance degradation when they are applied to out-of-domain data which is substantially different than their training data (Lapuschkin et al., 2019; Hupkes et al., 2019; Recht et al., 2019).

Unlike the older statistical language models, Recurrent LMs (RNNLMs) (Mikolov et al., 2010) and their successors Transformers LMs (Vaswani et al., 2017) can consider the entire prefix of a sentence when predicting or generating the next token. By being able to relate a very high-dimensional input to the output, these models can learn many subtle correlations which are highly useful as long as the input is in-distribution, unfortunately these correlations tend to be brittle to distribution shift, causing a model that depends on them to go astray. This phenomenon is known as "shortcut learning" (Geirhos et al., 2020) and it has been found to also occur in humans and animals, but it is especially prevalent in artificial neural networks. Research on this problem has explored models invariant or equivariant w.r.t. certain transformations by means of compositional representations (Sabour et al., 2017; Soulos et al., 2019; Liu et al., 2020), causal modeling (Schölkopf et al., 2021), or both (Arjovsky et al., 2019; Krueger et al., 2020), but these works focus on classification tasks often on synthetic datasets and can't be straightforwardly applied to black-box language models. Approaches specific to LMs have focused on robustness where the data domains are known and represented in the training data (Oren et al., 2019; Gerstenberger et al., 2020).

In this work we propose a method that uses Random Network Distillation (RND) (Burda et al., 2018) to dynamically adapt the amount of context that the model relies upon during inference based on an estimate of how much this context is out-of-distribution (OOD). This way the model can still make use of all available context when operating within a familiar context space, exploiting long-distance weak correlations, but it reduces to a less expressive and more robust model when operating OOD, relying only on the strongest correlations. As a proof of concept we implement our approach on a GRU recurrent language model (Cho et al., 2014). While Transformer decoders outperform RNNs when trained on large training sets, RNNs remain competitive on smaller datasets ($< 10^7$ tokens) where OOD phenomena are easier to measure, furthermore they are easier to optimize, simplifying architecture and hyperparameter

Proceedings of the 7th Workshop on Representation Learning for NLP, pages 1 - 8

search. We evaluate our method on language modeling tasks on English datasets, obtaining improvements when evaluating on eight OOD domains.We report additional preliminary sequence-to-sequence results on Transformer-RNN models (Zhang et al., 2018) in appendix A. We leave extensions of our method to full Transformers as future research.

2 Background

Recurrent Language Model Given a sequence $x(t)$ of tokens encoded as one-hot vectors, an autoregressive causal recurrent language model estimates at each step t a probability distribution $\Pr(x(t+1)|x(0),\ldots,x(t)) = y(t+1)$ over the next token conditional on the observed prefix which is summarized as a fixed-dimensional state $h(t+1) \in \mathcal{R}^d$ computed according to the recurrence relation:

$$u(t) = \text{Emb}(x(t), \theta) \quad (1)$$
$$h(0) = 0^{\otimes d} \quad (2)$$
$$h(t+1) = \text{RNN}(h(t), u(t), \theta) \quad (3)$$
$$y(t+1) = \text{Proj}(h(t+1), \theta) \quad (4)$$

where Emb is an embedding layer, RNN is a recurrent cell (in our case, a GRU), Proj is a readout layer (we use a mixture-of-softmaxes layer (Yang et al., 2018)) and θ represents all the trainable parameters. The initial state $h(0)$ is fixed at zero.

An interesting property of this model is that close to the beginning of the sequence the state vector $h(t)$ has a small norm, and the entropy of the predicted token distribution is usually high because many tokens are plausible, while as more and more tokens are observed the state norm grows (token embeddings are approximately "added" to the state (Levy et al., 2018)) up to a point, and at the same time the entropy of the predicted token distribution decreases as the model becomes more confident of its prediction due to the larger observed context (Figure 1). Indeed, in a softmax readout layer:

$$\text{Proj}(h) = \text{softmax}(W \cdot h + b)$$

where W is the output projection matrix and b is the output bias vector, increasing the norm of the state vector h will usually cause the probability distribution to become sharper unless $W \cdot h$ happens to approximately cancel out the bias vector b, which in high dimensions requires a rather specific alignment. A mixture-of-softmaxes readout also

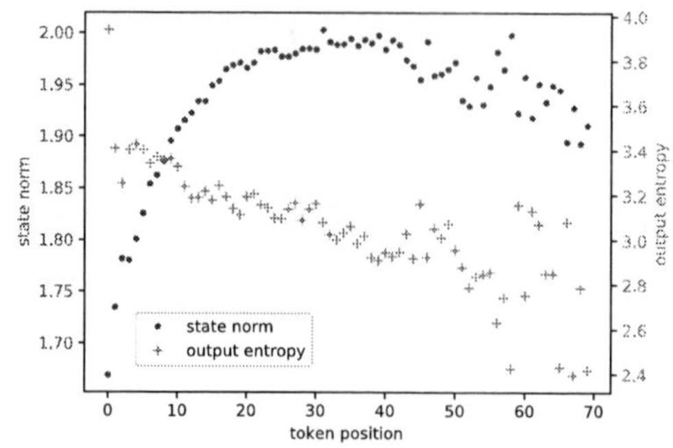

Figure 1: L2-norm of top GRU state (blue dots) and output softmax entropy (red crosses) over BPE token position, averaged over in-domain test set (Penn Treebank). Sentences are evaluated independently starting from the zero state. Norm and entropy correlate at -0.58. Model trained on Penn Treebank (sec. 4).

exhibits this property. Furthermore, it has been observed that the state of a RNN is usually dominated by the most recently observed inputs as the contribution of past inputs decreases exponentially over time (Jaeger, 2001; Pascanu et al., 2013; Levy et al., 2018; Zhang and Sennrich, 2019). Therefore, we hypothesize that the norm of the state vector corresponds to the amount of context that the model is considering for its future predictions, and this in turn controls the confidence of the model in its predictions.

Random Network Distillation In order to estimate how much the state of our RNNLM has deviated from the training distribution we choose the Random Network Distillation (RND) approach (Burda et al., 2018; Ciosek et al., 2020). Given a representation h, we define an OOD detector as

$$\text{OOD}(h) = |T(h) - S(h, \phi)|^2 \quad (5)$$

where $T(h)$ is a randomly initialized and frozen feed-forward teacher network that pseudorandomly maps the state h to a high-dimensional output and $S(h, \phi)$ is a feed-forward student network with parameters ϕ trained to copy the teacher by minimizing eq. 5 on the training set. At inference time the distillation error of eq. 5 provides an OOD estimate of h. This works by deliberately exploiting the fragility of neural networks w.r.t. distribution shift: while in principle the student could learn to copy the teacher for all possible inputs, in practice it only learns to do so on the training set (in-domain by definition) and becomes increasingly uncorrelated to it as the input becomes more OOD.

See Ciosek et al. (2020) for an extensive analysis. We chose this method because it can be applied to internal representations, is completely unsupervised and does not require any OOD tuning data. RND has been proposed initially in the context of reinforcement learning where the OOD signal can be used as a "curiosity" reward to stimulate exploration, and it has been subsequently studied in the context of OOD estimation for image classification. To our knowledge, we are the first to apply it to NLP, and to use it to actively compensate for distribution shift rather than just measure it.

3 Proposed approach

Our approach consists of estimating how much out-of-distribution the state of the model is and scaling it towards the all-zero initial state accordingly, effectively purging the OOD context out of the memory of the model and forcing it to rely only on the strongest, usually short-distance, correlations that survive the purge. As the state is pushed towards zero, the model also becomes more conservative in its predictions, avoiding the typical overconfidence of neural networks in OOD conditions. Specifically, for our language modeling experiments, we train a GRU RNNLM as usual, then we freeze it and train a RND OOD estimator on the RNNLM states on the same training set. Then during inference we modify the recurrence relation (eq. 3) to

$$\tilde{h} = \mathrm{RNN}(h(t), u(t), \theta) \tag{6}$$

$$h(t+1) = \tilde{h} \cdot \alpha \exp(-\beta \cdot \mathrm{OOD}(\tilde{h})) \tag{7}$$

where we use a simple exponential scaling with α and β hyperparameters[1] which we set to 1. When the OOD signal is zero the model behaves like the baseline RNNLM, when it is high instead it behaves more like a unigram language model. This way, we can retain the expressivity of "shortcut learning" when it is beneficial, and hopefully avoid its influence when it is detrimental.

4 Experiments

Setup For all our language modelling experiments we use two-layer stacked GRUs, with a PyTorch implementation based on code by Zhang and Sennrich (2019)[2]. We train separate models on the Penn Treebank and Wikitext-2 corpora using the default hyperparameters provided by the codebase. We also train models on BPE subtokenized (Sennrich et al., 2016) versions of the corpora using SentencePiece[3]. These models are used both as baselines and to provide the initial models for our approach. For our approach we train one RND OOD model for each layer of the RNNLM, the teachers are 2-layer LeakyReLU MLPs (Maas et al., 2013) with layer normalization (Ba et al., 2016) and the students are like the teachers followed by 4 Resnet blocks (He et al., 2016) with 2 LeakyReLU MLP layers each. All hidden dimensions are set to match the RNNLM state dimension. For consistency with the original codebase, we use SGD with decaying learning rate and early stopping to train the baseline RNNLMs, while we switch to Adam (Kingma and Ba, 2015), with constant learning rate and early stopping when training the RND OOD estimator. GRU hyperparameters are the default ones from the reported Penn Treebank and Wikitext-2 models of the baseline implementation. The code to run the experiments is available.[4]

Perplexity estimation We investigate OOD performance with two standard corpora, Penn Treebank and Wikitext2. We evaluate each of the models both in-distribution, on the default test set of its training corpus, and out-of-distribution, on the test set of the other corpus. We also use additional test sets adapted from machine translation robustness evaluations, specifically the English sides of the De-En test sets of Müller et al. (2020), which is a collection of corpora from diffent domains (I.T., Koran, law, medical and movie subtitles) and the English sides of the MTNT Ja-En and Fr-En test sets of Michel and Neubig (2018), which are corpora scraped from Reddit and have been used for the WMT-19 robustness shared task (Li et al., 2019).

We report the results in tables 1 and 2. We find that for the word-level models trained on Penn Treebank our approach improves the perplexity consistently both in-distribution and out-of-distribution for all the test sets we considered. For the word-level models trained on Wikitext-2 our approach preserves perplexity in-distribution and improves it on most OOD test sets, namely the Penn Treebank test set, the Ja-En test set of the MTNT corpus and all the tests sets of Müller et al. (2020) except

[1] α can also be tuned by SGD on the training set, but we found this to be unnecessary.

[2] https://github.com/bzhangGo/lrn

[3] https://github.com/google/sentencepiece

[4] https://github.com/Avmb/lm-robustness

	in-domain		(Müller et al., 2020)					MTNT	
	Penn	WT-2	IT	Koran	Law	Med	Sub	fr-en.en	ja-en.en
				word-level					
Baseline	68.04	55.73	59.37	50.12	64.12	35.10	47.81	76.75	66.08
RND	67.86	**55.00**	**58.18**	**49.12**	**62.94**	**34.67**	**47.01**	**75.33**	**64.73**
RND (abl.)	**67.84**	55.41	59.02	49.76	63.67	34.99	47.55	76.25	65.64
				BPE-level					
Baseline	**27.85**	1371.16	5657.39	5493.64	4123.78	5657.54	4048.14	2837.97	4051.66
RND	28.16	**1197.07**	**4828.55**	**4774.78**	**3552.22**	**4520.38**	**3558.99**	**2519.75**	**3551.63**
RND (abl.)	27.93	1287.26	5178.40	5159.36	3815.87	4898.91	3792.19	2675.51	3794.22

Table 1: Perplexity of language models trained on the Penn Treebank dataset.

	in-domain		(Müller et al., 2020)					MTNT	
	WT-2	Penn	IT	Koran	Law	Med	Sub	fr-en.en	ja-en.en
				word-level					
Baseline	**64.69**	361.84	162.01	159.02	178.92	103.87	**96.65**	**177.73**	184.69
RND	**64.69**	**333.52**	**156.73**	156.59	**171.42**	**102.33**	100.46	175.34	**180.54**
RND (abl.)	**64.69**	338.33	157.96	**155.75**	172.94	102.74	98.82	174.20	180.91
				BPE-level					
Baseline	**29.39**	190.91	648.84	**694.86**	339.46	355.74	**563.92**	**495.39**	**497.27**
RND	29.73	**183.23**	637.63	712.93	335.86	348.16	656.86	530.45	526.30
RND (abl.)	29.46	185.48	**632.52**	695.54	**334.37**	**347.75**	624.27	515.16	512.96

Table 2: Perplexity of language models trained on the Wikitext-2 dataset.

			(Müller et al., 2020)					MTNT	
Training	WT-2	Penn	IT	Koran	Law	Med	Sub	fr-en.en	ja-en.en
WT-2	**0.0240***	0.1137	0.0735	0.1155	0.0767	0.0485	0.0936	0.1070	0.0896
Penn	0.0237	0.0252*	0.0244	**0.0233**	0.0244	0.0234	0.0236	0.0240	0.0238
WT-2 (BPE)	**0.0220***	0.0534	0.1054	0.1824	0.0697	0.0657	0.1472	0.1328	0.1196
Penn (BPE)	**0.0256**	0.0257*	0.0321	0.0279	0.0313	0.0359	0.0300	0.0308	0.0302

Table 3: OOD estimates, averaged over GRU layers and tokens in each test set. * denotes the in-domain test sets.

the subtitles test set. The Penn Treebank results are somewhat anomalous in that the perplexity of some OOD test sets is lower than the perplexity of the in-distribution test sets (and in fact the perplexity of the Wikitext-2 test set is even lower that the perplexity of the same test set evaluated by its own in-domain model). This effect is caused by the limited vocabulary of the Penn Treebank training set which causes many of the tokens of the OOD test sets to be replaced by UNKs, which are easy to predict. To avoid this artifact, we evaluate BPE-level models, which are open vocabulary and hence do not introduce any UNKs. For the BPE-level models we find that for both the baselines and the RND approach the perplexities on the OOD datasets are much higher than the perplexities on the in-domain test sets. Comparing our approach to the baselines, we observe a minimal degradation of perplexity in-distribution and substantial improvements on all OOD test sets when training on Penn Treebank, while when training on Wikitext-2 we observe more mixed results.

In order to analyse if the model is learning sensible values for scaling the out-of-distribution states, we compute the OOD scores estimated by the RND OOD detectors, averaged over the two GRU layers and over all the tokens in each test set. We report these scores in table 3. The models trained on Wikitext-2 (both the word-level and BPE-level versions) always estimate the lowest OOD scores on the in-domain test set, as expected. The Penn Treebank word-level model performs poorly, estimating similar scores for all the test sets, consistent with the aforementioned vocabulary collapse to UNKs, the BPE-level model instead is generally able to distinguish in-domain and out-of-domain test sets, albeit by a small margin and fails on one test set (Wikitext-2).

Ablation One could hypothesize that the improvements obtained by our model are due to just increasing the entropy of the output distribution rather than dropping unnecessary context from the RNN state. We evaluate a variant of our model where we apply the OOD scaling only on the output of the top-layer RNN but not to the internal states. This increases the output entropy without affecting the context remembered by the model between time steps. This ablation generally improves over the baseline but performs worse than our full model except for the model trained on Wikitext-2 BPE where the results are mixed.

5 Conclusions and future work

We proposed a method to improve the robustness of language models to distribution shift caused by train/test domain mismatch. Our model contracts the RNN state based on an unsupervised out-of-distribution estimator in order to reduce the model dependency on weak long-distance correlations, which are useful in-distribution but tend to be spurious in out-of-distribution conditions. We obtain perplexity improvements on multiple out-of-domain test sets without substantial degradation on in-domain test sets.

While our approach is based on Recurrent decoders, its general principles may be applicable to other neural architectures. For instance, the self-attention heads of a Transformer might modulated by an OOD detector in order to avoid attending to out-of-distribution parts of a sentence. We anticipate that extending our method to these kind of models will be a promising research direction.

Broader impact and ethical concerns

This work provides improvements for language model technology on application domains not well represented in the training data.

We expect that our approach might promote an increased deployment and usage of such technology. We do not expect our approach to introduce any bias against any specific group of users. Our approach adds only small computational costs over baseline language models and therefore is unlikely to prevent users with limited computational budgets from benefiting from the technology.

Acknowledgments

This project received funding from the European Union's Horizon 2020 research and innovation programme under grant agreement 825299 (GoURMET), the European Research Council (ERC StG BroadSem 678254; ERC CoG TransModal 681760) and funding by the UK Engineering and Physical Sciences Research Council (EPSRC) fellowship grant EP/S001271/1 (MTStretch).

References

Martin Arjovsky, Léon Bottou, Ishaan Gulrajani, and David Lopez-Paz. 2019. Invariant risk minimization. *arXiv preprint arXiv:1907.02893*.

Jimmy Lei Ba, Jamie Ryan Kiros, and Geoffrey E. Hinton. 2016. Layer normalization.

Dzmitry Bahdanau, Kyunghyun Cho, and Yoshua Bengio. 2015. Neural machine translation by jointly learning to align and translate. In *3rd International Conference on Learning Representations, ICLR 2015, San Diego, CA, USA, May 7-9, 2015, Conference Track Proceedings*.

Tom B. Brown, Benjamin Mann, Nick Ryder, Melanie Subbiah, Jared Kaplan, Prafulla Dhariwal, Arvind Neelakantan, Pranav Shyam, Girish Sastry, Amanda Askell, Sandhini Agarwal, Ariel Herbert-Voss, Gretchen Krueger, Tom Henighan, Rewon Child, Aditya Ramesh, Daniel M. Ziegler, Jeffrey Wu, Clemens Winter, Christopher Hesse, Mark Chen, Eric Sigler, Mateusz Litwin, Scott Gray, Benjamin Chess, Jack Clark, Christopher Berner, Sam McCandlish, Alec Radford, Ilya Sutskever, and Dario Amodei. 2020. Language models are few-shot learners.

Yuri Burda, Harrison Edwards, Amos Storkey, and Oleg Klimov. 2018. Exploration by random network distillation. *arXiv preprint arXiv:1810.12894*.

Mauro Cettolo, Jan Niehues, Sebastian Stüker, Luisa Bentivogli, and Marcello Federico. 2014. Report on the 11th iwslt evaluation campaign, iwslt 2014. In *Proceedings of the International Workshop on Spoken Language Translation, Hanoi, Vietnam*, volume 57.

Mia Xu Chen, Orhan Firat, Ankur Bapna, Melvin Johnson, Wolfgang Macherey, George F. Foster, Llion Jones, Niki Parmar, Mike Schuster, Zhifeng Chen, Yonghui Wu, and Macduff Hughes. 2018. The best of both worlds: Combining recent advances in neural machine translation. *CoRR*, abs/1804.09849.

Kyunghyun Cho, Bart van Merriënboer, Caglar Gulcehre, Dzmitry Bahdanau, Fethi Bougares, Holger Schwenk, and Yoshua Bengio. 2014. Learning phrase representations using RNN encoder–decoder for statistical machine translation. In *Proceedings of the 2014 Conference on Empirical Methods in*

Natural Language Processing (EMNLP), pages 1724–1734, Doha, Qatar. Association for Computational Linguistics.

Kamil Ciosek, Vincent Fortuin, Ryota Tomioka, Katja Hofmann, and Richard Turner. 2020. Conservative uncertainty estimation by fitting prior networks. In *International Conference on Learning Representations*.

Jacob Devlin, Ming-Wei Chang, Kenton Lee, and Kristina Toutanova. 2019. BERT: Pre-training of deep bidirectional transformers for language understanding. In *Proceedings of the 2019 Conference of the North American Chapter of the Association for Computational Linguistics: Human Language Technologies, Volume 1 (Long and Short Papers)*, pages 4171–4186, Minneapolis, Minnesota. Association for Computational Linguistics.

Robert Geirhos, Jörn-Henrik Jacobsen, Claudio Michaelis, Richard Zemel, Wieland Brendel, Matthias Bethge, and Felix A Wichmann. 2020. Shortcut learning in deep neural networks. *arXiv preprint arXiv:2004.07780*.

Alexander Gerstenberger, Kazuki Irie, Pavel Golik, Eugen Beck, and Hermann Ney. 2020. Domain robust, fast, and compact neural language models. In *ICASSP 2020 - 2020 IEEE International Conference on Acoustics, Speech and Signal Processing (ICASSP)*, pages 7954–7958.

Caglar Gulcehre, Orhan Firat, Kelvin Xu, Kyunghyun Cho, Loic Barrault, Huei-Chi Lin, Fethi Bougares, Holger Schwenk, and Yoshua Bengio. 2015. On Using Monolingual Corpora in Neural Machine Translation. *arXiv e-prints*, page arXiv:1503.03535.

K. He, X. Zhang, S. Ren, and J. Sun. 2016. Deep residual learning for image recognition. In *2016 IEEE Conference on Computer Vision and Pattern Recognition (CVPR)*, pages 770–778.

Dieuwke Hupkes, Verna Dankers, Mathijs Mul, and Elia Bruni. 2019. The compositionality of neural networks: integrating symbolism and connectionism. *CoRR*, abs/1908.08351.

Herbert Jaeger. 2001. The "echo state" approach to analysing and training recurrent neural networks-with an erratum note. *Bonn, Germany: German National Research Center for Information Technology GMD Technical Report*, 148(34):13.

Diederik P. Kingma and Jimmy Ba. 2015. Adam: A method for stochastic optimization. In *3rd International Conference on Learning Representations, ICLR 2015, San Diego, CA, USA, May 7-9, 2015, Conference Track Proceedings*.

David Krueger, Ethan Caballero, Jörn-Henrik Jacobsen, Amy Zhang, Jonathan Binas, Rémi Le Priol, and Aaron C. Courville. 2020. Out-of-distribution generalization via risk extrapolation (rex). *CoRR*, abs/2003.00688.

Sebastian Lapuschkin, Stephan Wäldchen, Alexander Binder, Grégoire Montavon, Wojciech Samek, and Klaus-Robert Müller. 2019. Unmasking clever hans predictors and assessing what machines really learn. *CoRR*, abs/1902.10178.

Omer Levy, Kenton Lee, Nicholas FitzGerald, and Luke Zettlemoyer. 2018. Long short-term memory as a dynamically computed element-wise weighted sum. In *Proceedings of the 56th Annual Meeting of the Association for Computational Linguistics (Volume 2: Short Papers)*, pages 732–739, Melbourne, Australia. Association for Computational Linguistics.

Xian Li, Paul Michel, Antonios Anastasopoulos, Yonatan Belinkov, Nadir Durrani, Orhan Firat, Philipp Koehn, Graham Neubig, Juan Pino, and Hassan Sajjad. 2019. Findings of the first shared task on machine translation robustness. In *Proceedings of the Fourth Conference on Machine Translation (Volume 2: Shared Task Papers, Day 1)*, pages 91–102, Florence, Italy. Association for Computational Linguistics.

Qian Liu, Shengnan An, Jian-Guang Lou, Bei Chen, Zeqi Lin, Yan Gao, Bin Zhou, Nanning Zheng, and Dongmei Zhang. 2020. Compositional generalization by learning analytical expressions. *arXiv preprint arXiv:2006.10627*.

Thang Luong, Hieu Pham, and Christopher D. Manning. 2015. Effective approaches to attention-based neural machine translation. In *Proceedings of the 2015 Conference on Empirical Methods in Natural Language Processing*, pages 1412–1421, Lisbon, Portugal. Association for Computational Linguistics.

Andrew L. Maas, Awni Y. Hannun, and Andrew Y. Ng. 2013. Rectifier nonlinearities improve neural network acoustic models. In *in ICML Workshop on Deep Learning for Audio, Speech and Language Processing*.

Paul Michel and Graham Neubig. 2018. Mtnt: A testbed for machine translation of noisy text. In *Proceedings of the 2018 Conference on Empirical Methods in Natural Language Processing*.

Tomáš Mikolov, Martin Karafiát, Lukáš Burget, Jan Černockỳ, and Sanjeev Khudanpur. 2010. Recurrent neural network based language model. In *Eleventh annual conference of the international speech communication association*.

Mathias Müller, Annette Rios, and Rico Sennrich. 2020. Domain robustness in neural machine translation. In *Proceedings of the 14th Conference of the Association for Machine Translation in the Americas (Volume 1: Research Track)*, pages 151–164, Virtual. Association for Machine Translation in the Americas.

Yonatan Oren, Shiori Sagawa, Tatsunori B. Hashimoto, and Percy Liang. 2019. Distributionally robust language modeling. In *Proceedings of the 2019 Conference on Empirical Methods in Natural Language Processing and the 9th International Joint Conference on Natural Language Processing (EMNLP-IJCNLP)*, pages 4227–4237, Hong Kong, China. Association for Computational Linguistics.

Myle Ott, Sergey Edunov, Alexei Baevski, Angela Fan, Sam Gross, Nathan Ng, David Grangier, and Michael Auli. 2019. fairseq: A fast, extensible toolkit for sequence modeling. In *Proceedings of NAACL-HLT 2019: Demonstrations*.

Razvan Pascanu, Tomas Mikolov, and Yoshua Bengio. 2013. On the difficulty of training recurrent neural networks. In *Proceedings of the 30th International Conference on International Conference on Machine Learning - Volume 28*, ICML'13, page III–1310–III–1318. JMLR.org.

Benjamin Recht, Rebecca Roelofs, Ludwig Schmidt, and Vaishaal Shankar. 2019. Do imagenet classifiers generalize to imagenet? *CoRR*, abs/1902.10811.

Sara Sabour, Nicholas Frosst, and Geoffrey E. Hinton. 2017. Dynamic routing between capsules. In *Proceedings of the 31st International Conference on Neural Information Processing Systems*, NIPS'17, page 3859–3869, Red Hook, NY, USA. Curran Associates Inc.

Bernhard Schölkopf, Francesco Locatello, Stefan Bauer, Nan Rosemary Ke, Nal Kalchbrenner, Anirudh Goyal, and Yoshua Bengio. 2021. Toward causal representation learning. *Proceedings of the IEEE*, 109(5):612–634.

Rico Sennrich, Barry Haddow, and Alexandra Birch. 2016. Neural machine translation of rare words with subword units. In *Proceedings of the 54th Annual Meeting of the Association for Computational Linguistics (Volume 1: Long Papers)*, pages 1715–1725, Berlin, Germany. Association for Computational Linguistics.

Paul Soulos, Tom McCoy, Tal Linzen, and Paul Smolensky. 2019. Discovering the compositional structure of vector representations with role learning networks. *CoRR*, abs/1910.09113.

Ashish Vaswani, Noam Shazeer, Niki Parmar, Jakob Uszkoreit, Llion Jones, Aidan N Gomez, Ł ukasz Kaiser, and Illia Polosukhin. 2017. Attention is all you need. In *Advances in Neural Information Processing Systems*, volume 30, pages 5998–6008. Curran Associates, Inc.

Zhilin Yang, Zihang Dai, Ruslan Salakhutdinov, and William W. Cohen. 2018. Breaking the softmax bottleneck: A high-rank RNN language model. In *International Conference on Learning Representations*.

Biao Zhang and Rico Sennrich. 2019. A lightweight recurrent network for sequence modeling. In *Proceedings of the 57th Annual Meeting of the Association for Computational Linguistics*, pages 1538–1548, Florence, Italy. Association for Computational Linguistics.

Biao Zhang, Deyi Xiong, and Jinsong Su. 2018. Accelerating neural transformer via an average attention network. In *Proceedings of the 56th Annual Meeting of the Association for Computational Linguistics (Volume 1: Long Papers)*, pages 1789–1798, Melbourne, Australia. Association for Computational Linguistics.

Appendices

A Sequence-to-sequence experiments

We performed additional experiments on sequence-to-sequence (seq2seq) tasks. We obtained negative results, which we report here.

Architecture Our models use a Transformer-GRU architecture. The encoder is a standard bidirectional Transformer while the decoder is a two-layer stacked GRU (sec. 2). The recurrent cell also accesses contextual embeddings of a source sentence tokens via an attention mechanism implemented as in Luong et al. (2015), except that instead of a single attention head we use a Transformer multihead attention layer, similar to Chen et al. (2018). The RND OOD model has the same architecture as in the LM experiments, although for simplicity we train it jointly with the MT models rather than in a separate stage, we make sure not to propagate gradients between the RND OOD model and the translation model hence there is no tradeoff between their training objectives. The implementation is based on the Fairseq (Ott et al., 2019) Transformer and LSTM architectures, using the hyperparameters for their default IWSLT14 configuration.

Machine translation We trained De→En translation models on the IWSLT14 training set (Cettolo et al., 2014) with the standard Fairseq preprocessing pipeline[5]. We used on the standard test set produced by the preprocessing script as our in-domain test set and the Müller et al. (2020) test sets as our OOD test sets. We report BLEU scores in table 4. The baseline and the RND model have nearly identical scores on the in-domain test set, while they deviate up to about 1 BLEU point on the OOD test sets, although in a non-systematic way.

	in-domain	(Müller et al., 2020)				
	IWSLT14	IT	Koran	Law	Med	Sub
Base	32.95	11.03	**5.72**	11.35	13.76	**19.19**
RND	**32.97**	**12.07**	5.13	**12.02**	**13.93**	18.71

Table 4: Machine translation results

Sentence reversal We considered a synthetic task intended to elicit the RND OOD activity. The source segments consist each of a number of concatenated sentences separated by a separator token, the target segments are made of the same sentences, where each sentence is reversed at token level, but the sentences are concatenated in the same order as the source. Since reversing a sentence does not depend on the previous sentences in the segment, the previous sentences become distractors that pollute the decoder GRU state with irrelevant information. The model can learn to compensate in in-domain conditions where the test set is sampled from the same distribution of the training set, but we hypothesize that in OOD scenarios with longer segments composed by a higher number of sentences this spurious information will greatly decrease accuracy. We test whether the RND OOD mechanism is effective at discarding this spurious information.

We consider two versions of the task, in one we sample the source segments from a synthetic vocabulary of 256 tokens, with uniform probability per token, 32 tokens per sentence, 8 sentences per training segment. We test in-domain at 8 sentences and OOD at 10 and 12 sentences per segment. In the second version, we train on concatenations of 4 consecutive sentences of the English side of the IWSLT14 De-En training set, and we test at $4, 6, 8, 10$ and 12 sentences per segment. We use the same hyperparameters of our translation experiments, during inference we constrain the decoder to match the source length.

All the models achieve near perfect (> 99.9) BLEU scores in-domain, while OOD the scores quickly decrease as the number of sentences per segment increases, as expected. Unfortunately we find no systematic difference between baseline and RND OOD models.

Discussion Unlike our language modeling experiments, we did not observe systematic improvements from using the RND out-of-distribution detector to contract the state of the GRU decoder in our sequence-to-sequence results. There are multiple possible hypotheses for this discrepancy, such as encoder effects, generating outputs by beam search rather than scoring natural text, or the target distribution being more peaked around the mode. We plan to investigate this effect in the future.

[5]prepare-iwslt14.sh

Q-Learning Scheduler for Multi Task Learning Through the use of Histogram of Task Uncertainty

Kourosh Meshgi, Maryam Sadat Mirzaei & Satoshi Sekine
RIKEN Center for Advanced Intelligence Project (AIP)
Tokyo, Japan
{kourosh.meshgi, maryam.mirzaei, satoshi.sekine}@riken.jp

Abstract

Simultaneous training of a multi-task learning (MTL) network on different domains or tasks is not always straightforward. It could lead to inferior performance or generalization compared to the corresponding single-task networks. An effective training scheduling method is deemed necessary to maximize the benefits of multi-task learning. Traditional schedulers follow a heuristic or prefixed strategy, ignoring the relation of the tasks, their sample complexities, and the state of the emergent shared features. We proposed a deep Q-Learning Scheduler (QLS) that monitors the state of the tasks and the shared features using a novel histogram of task uncertainty, and through trial-and-error, learns an optimal policy for task scheduling. Extensive experiments on multi-domain and multi-task settings with various task difficulty profiles have been conducted, the proposed method is benchmarked against other schedulers, its superior performance has been demonstrated, and results are discussed.

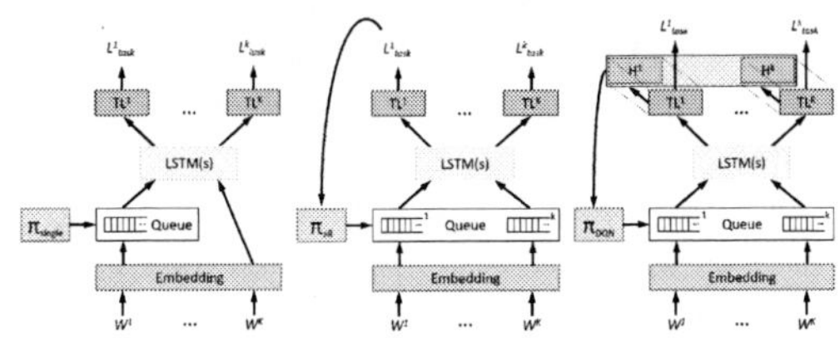

(a) Single Task Scheduler (b) All Tasks Scheduler (c) Proposed Scheduler

Figure 1: Different schedulers for multi-task learning **(a)** Single scheduler that adjusts the training priority of one task compared to others, **(b)** All scheduler that dynamically adjusts the relative importance of each task compared to others using key performance indicators (e.g., validation loss) of tasks, **(c)** Proposed scheduler that learns an optimal scheduling policy by employing deep Q-learning on task uncertainties. Similar scheduling effect can be achieved via adjusting learning rate and gradient manipulation, and training queue is depicted as an example of scheduling methods. In this figure, TL denotes task layer, π denotes the (trained) policy, and L^i_{task} indicates the loss of the specific task i.

1 Introduction

Multi-task learning aims to jointly improve the generalization of several classification and regression tasks. It does so by sharing the domain-centric information of each task, reducing trainable parameters, focusing attention on relevant features amid noisy or high dimensional data, regularizing other tasks, and exploiting the relations among tasks (Ruder, 2017; Zamir et al., 2018). The tasks can be defined as applying the same model on different data (also known as multi-domain learning) (Nam and Han, 2016; Liu et al., 2017a), or on various problems in a linear (Zamir et al., 2020) or hierarchical manner (e.g., named entity recognition, entity mention detection, and relation extraction in hierarchical MTL-HMTL (Sanh et al., 2019). Typical MTL is trained with mini-batches of every task intermittently, while the order of the training is usually uniform or related to the tasks' database size (Kiperwasser and Ballesteros, 2018). This simplistic approach leads to unnecessary computations, due to redundancy in tasks and samples (Lin et al., 2017), or due to the fact that some tasks are prerequisites for learning others (Ruder et al., 2017). Additionally, task imbalances deteriorate appropriate training because they lead to imbalances between back-propagated gradients (Chen et al., 2018b). Therefore, researchers have proposed methods to train the tasks and samples in a certain order, a process called "MTL Scheduling".

Effective scheduling increases accuracy, reduces overfitting across multiple tasks, avoids catastrophic forgetting, improves the low-resource task accuracy. Meanwhile, it keeps the high resource task accuracy intact, provides extensive control over the training dynamics of MTL, and exploits task relations to learn required features for upsteam tasks. Early scheduling approaches include non-adaptive heuristics and fixed strategies to order

Proceedings of the 7th Workshop on Representation Learning for NLP, pages 9 - 19
May 26, 2022

the training. Such scheduling was applied to one target task (single scheduling, Figure 1(a)) or was used by scaling per-task learning rates (Jean et al., 2019). As these methods were not adequate to handle more complicated MTL systems (e.g., UberNet (Kokkinos, 2017)), more flexible and adaptive scheduling methods started to emerge. They use learning progress signals such as training loss (Kiperwasser and Ballesteros, 2018), validation loss (Jean et al., 2019), and uncertainty (Kendall et al., 2018) to tailor the schedule accordingly (Figure 1(b)). Advanced schedulers are expected to monitor task learning progress, emergent shared feature representation, and sample complexity of each task to be able to provide a suitable strategy for task orders. Additionally, when the underlying multi-task models learn to improve the performance of harder tasks, they may hit a plateau; as a result, simpler (or data-poor) tasks can be overtrained (overfitted). Needless to say that some tasks may be forgotten if the schedule is improper (catastrophic forgetting). Using a prefixed model to handle all these factors (model bias problem) without considering instantaneous feedback from the network (lack of temporal monitoring) is the main challenge for many of the current schedulers.

To address the challenges, we propose using reinforcement learning (RL) method to learn a potentially complex strategy. This allows for handling different states of the MTL training and avoids catastrophic forgetting. It also enables learning long-term temporal effects of task selection on the network's performance using the intrinsic delayed reward handling mechanism of RL. Moreover, it uncovers task relations with no explicit modeling (model-free), merely based on trial-and-error and receiving (delayed) feedback from the MTL training (Figure 1(c)). We use deep Q-Net (DQN) (Mnih et al., 2013) to map the state of the MTL to the desired actions (i.e., *which task to train on next?*), and propose the *histogram of task uncertainty* to describe the MTL state for the algorithm. Our contributions are:

- Introducing histogram of task uncertainty for the descriptive signal of the MTL;
- Proposing the use of deep Q-learning to learn the MTL scheduling to *(i)* handle temporal progress in MTL, *(ii)* provide sufficiently complex strategy for marginal cases, *(iii)* avoid catastrophic forgetting actively, and *(iv)* consider sample and task complexity;
- Extensive tests to investigate the performance and generalization of MTL's learned features;
- Experiments on multi-task and multi-domain learning problems with homo- or heterogeneous tasks, with various inter-task relations.

Note that in our experiments we focus on the performance of our Q-learning scheduler compared with other scheduling methods. We used LSTM instead of variations of transformers to make a fair comparison with other methods that used LSTM. In the future, we will incorporate QLS with transformers to benchmark the addition of such scheduling.

2 Related Works

Multi-Task Learning: To leverage from correlations of different tasks, MTL could be performed on tasks such as: those derived from different subsets of a shared data pool (Meyerson and Miikkulainen, 2018), adversarial tasks (Ganin and Lempitsky, 2015), auxiliary tasks which provide hints or attention for the main task (Yu and Jiang, 2016; Caruana, 1997), tasks arranged in an easy-to-hard hierarchy (Sanh et al., 2019), those which explicitly perform representation learning for a more complex application (Rei, 2017; Subramanian et al., 2018), or those which facilitate training for a quickly-plateauing main task (Bingel and Søgaard, 2017). Also, it can be helpful to learn the inter-task relations to enable efficient transfer learning or task grouping (Ruder et al., 2017; Bingel and Søgaard, 2017; Zamir et al., 2018; Standley et al., 2019).

In the hard parameter sharing architectures, shared parameters provide a global feature representation, while task-specific layers further process these features or provide a complimentary feature set for a specific task. MTL methods assume that learning easy tasks is the prerequisite for learning complex ones (Ruder, 2017), hence put tasks in hierarchies (Hashimoto et al., 2017; Sanh et al., 2019) or group similar tasks to form group-specific shared layers (Liu et al., 2017b).

Scheduling MTL: To train a deep neural network on a battery of tasks simultaneously, the tasks are sampled uniformly or in proportion to their dataset size (Jean et al., 2019). Since this may offer limited control over the performance trade-offs (e.g., accuracy vs. overfitting), task scheduling methods were proposed to improve the MTL's performance compared to single-task networks, static heuristics, and grid search methods. Thus, non-adaptive (fixed strategy) and adaptive methods were used, and various classes of scheduling emerged, such as:

Sample schedulers try to over-sample tasks with worse results compared to the baseline (Kiperwasser and Ballesteros, 2018) or down-weight easier samples to focus on harder ones for training (Lin et al., 2017). Yet, such strategies fail if a task is highly over-sampled or datasets are imbalanced.

Task difficulty schedulers are usually built upon the notion of curriculum learning that favors smaller and easier tasks to learn first (Pentina et al., 2015), aligned with the training of natural intelligence in human babies. This idea falls into two forms, task hierarchies (e.g., (Sanh et al., 2019)) and task prioritization (Pentina et al., 2015; Graves et al., 2017; Zaremba and Sutskever, 2014). In the latter case, if the data of the tasks are coming from significantly different distributions (e.g., domain adaptation (Luo et al., 2017; Glorot et al., 2011; Tzeng et al., 2015)), the assumptions of curriculum learning do not hold (Bengio et al., 2009), and prefixed schedulers might not be effective.

Task weighting is another approach for scheduling problem. MTL is sensitive to the task weights (Kendall et al., 2018). These weights scale the loss term of each task in the total loss of the network. Static task weights can be selected by hyperparameter tuning (Kokkinos, 2017; Sermanet et al., 2013), yet this approach is suboptimal in the presence of less important or redundant tasks/samples (Lin et al., 2017). Non-adaptive weighting schemes fetch tasks intermittently early in training and gradually weigh more on a specific task (Jean et al., 2019). Adaptive schedulers dynamically prioritize different tasks by monitoring measures such as performance (Jean et al., 2019) and homoscedastic uncertainty (Kendall et al., 2018). Another method is to dynamically tune the gradient magnitudes (Chen et al., 2018b). Here, we use Q-learning scheduler which can dynamically schedule the learning of long-term temporal effects of task selection. As a result of scheduling, QLS selects the task to draw samples for the next training episodes.

3 Multi-task Classification

We selected text classification, in which a document needs to be assigned to a set of classes. The solutions range from hand-crafting good features to be used in convolutional neural networks (NNs) for word-level (Kim, 2014) and character-level encoding (Zhang et al., 2015), recurrent NNs (Liu et al., 2016) and convolutional recurrent NNs (Lai et al., 2015). Here, we address the problem of text classification using long-short term memory networks (LSTM) with a variant explored in (Jozefowicz et al., 2015) to facilitate further analysis of the effects of the proposed method in the representation. Generally, this method can be applied to any encoder-decoder-based NLP task that uses LSTM as the encoder. The text sequence of words $\mathbf{w} = \{w_1, w_2, \ldots, w_T\}$ is converted to a sequence of word embeddings $\mathbf{x}_i$ and is given to an LSTM layer. Each cell of LSTM layer at time t, includes input, forget and output gates, a memory and a hidden state $\mathbf{h}_t$. The LSTM memory chain updates as

$$\mathbf{h}_t = \mathrm{LSTM}\left(\mathbf{h}_{t-1}, \mathbf{x}_t, \theta_p\right) \tag{1}$$

where the output of the last unit $\mathbf{h}_T$ represents the whole sequence, and θ_p encapsulates the weights and biases of the LSTM. This is then fed to the task-specific output layers. The network is then trained on a training corpus with N samples $(\mathbf{w}_i, y_i)$ using cross-entropy loss function

$$L(\hat{y}, y) = -\sum_{i=1}^{N}\sum_{j=1}^{C} y_i^j \log\left(\hat{y}_i^j\right) \tag{2}$$

where y_i^j is the groundtruth in $\{1..C\}$ and $\hat{y}_i^j$ is the predicted probability of label j for document i. By exploiting commonalities and differences among tasks, multi-task learning aims to improve the learning efficiency and prediction accuracy for all tasks by learning from them in parallel. To this end, a learner shares some of its parameters between tasks while keeping some of them specific to each task. Considering our baseline classifier, the shared features are the hidden states of the LSTM at the end of the input sequence. There are several ways to implement the MTL using this baseline for classification. The most popular idea is to use a fully-shared model, in which all tasks are using the extracted features of the shared LSTM layer, and then differentiate using a final task layer.

We denote different datasets D_k as datasets with N_k examples for task k, $D_k = \left\{\left(w_i^{\langle k\rangle}, y_i^{\langle k\rangle}\right)\right\}_{i=1}^{N_k}$. Given task k, the final task-specific softmax layer for classification, converts the shared feature $\mathbf{h}_T^{(k)}$ into probability distribution $\hat{y}^{(k)}$. The parameters of the network are trained by minimizing the cross-entropy of true distribution of the task $y^{(k)}$ and the predicted distribution $\hat{y}^{(k)}$, using the loss

$$L_{task} = \sum_{k=1}^{K} \alpha_k L\left(\hat{y}^{\langle k\rangle}, y^{\langle k\rangle}\right). \tag{3}$$

Here, α_k is the importance of each task k and $L(\hat{y}, y)$ is defined in eq(2). A scheduler, when applied to this MTL frameworks, adopts one of the following modifications: change the task weight (α_k), modify its gradient in the back-propagation, re-weight the samples ($\mathbf{x}_t$), or select a task to draw samples for the next training episodes. Here, for simplicity, we select the latter case to focus more on the idea. Yet, the extension of the proposed idea to all different approaches is straightforward.

4 Proposed Method

4.1 Progress Signal for Learning Strategy

Graves et al. (Graves et al., 2017) employ accuracy as a learning progress signal to find a policy for task curriculum learning (Oudeyer et al., 2007). A syllabus of curriculum learning is selected using this learning progress signal to maximize the overall training progress. Progress signals are typically used in RL problems as reward signals to encourage exploration (Schmidhuber, 1991; Itti and Baldi, 2006; Houthooft et al., 2016). Similarly, Routing Networks (Rosenbaum et al., 2017) select different network submodules, based on the task and rewards via a multi-agent formulation. An ambitious idea is to train an agent that is capable of designing the entire network architecture in neural architecture search (Zoph and Le, 2016) using accuracy as the signal. DTP (Guo et al., 2018) scheduler uses prediction gain (Bellemare et al., 2016) to dynamically compute task weights/priority during training.

Here, we use overall task uncertainty and validation loss as the progress signal of the network. Together, these metrics give a comprehensive view of the state of the MTL.

4.2 Proposed Histogram of Task Uncertainty

Task uncertainty measures what the model does not know or what cannot be inferred from the data (Kendall and Gal, 2017). In MTL, we need to learn multiple tasks simultaneously, while the uncertainty of each task varies. In a fully-shared MTL setting, each task contributes to the loss function based on the errors it make, and since one task is being trained at a time, minimizing this error may negatively change the shared parameters for other tasks. Using uncertainty instead of task accuracy provides an additional signal to train the model.The classifiers suffer from uncertainty when choosing the label. However, adding model uncertainty to the loss helps classifiers to make more determined decisions.This helps by reflecting the internal state of the classifiers. The model uncertainty can be obtained via Monte Carlo dropout sampling (Kendall et al., 2015), as a function of the samples' variance to be used as an estimation of the error (Kendall and Cipolla, 2016). Another way is to compute the standard deviation over the softmax outputs and average them over all classes to obtain a single value (Kampffmeyer et al., 2016). Moreover, Kendall et al. (2018) calculated homoscedastic uncertainty (the uncertainty of the entire task itself not dependent on input data) and used this to learn a weighting for each loss term in a multi-task setting.

To calculate the uncertainty of a multi-class classifier, uncertainty sampling methods could be applied. Thus, we proposed the uncertainty loss term as using margin uncertainty (Scheffer et al., 2001)

$$\zeta_M = 1 - P_k\left(\hat{y}^{(1)}|x\right) + P_k\left(\hat{y}^{(2)}|x\right), \quad (4)$$

where $\hat{y}^{(j)}$ ($j = 1, 2$) is the label with jth largest predicted probability. For each task k all validation data are given to the MTL, and their label uncertainty is calculated using margin uncertainty. The final histogram of task uncertainties, $\mathcal{H}_t^{(k)}$, is formed by concatenating all histograms.

4.3 Q-Learning Scheduler

In our method, QLS monitors the state of the tasks to measure the task uncertainty, generates the task uncertainty histogram, and then uses Q learning to schedule tasks. We formulate a Q-learning agent to adjust the histogram of task uncertainty for the proposed MTL scheduler. At time t, the agent takes an action a_t based on the state S_t of the MTL environment, and the environment gives the reward $r(S_t, a_t)$ and updates its state to S_{t+1}. The agent chooses its action w.r.t its policy $\pi(a_t|S_t)$ to maximize the cumulative reward $R_t = \sum_{i=t}^{T} \gamma^{i-t} r(S_i, a_i)$. Here, $0 < \gamma \leq 1$ is the discount factor to weigh more on earlier rewards. Q-learning calculates Q-values, which is the expected max scores for each action a_t in state S_t, as

$$Q(S_t, a_t) = r(S_t, a_t) + \gamma Q(S_{t+1}, a_{t+1}) \quad (5)$$

State: The state $S_t \in \mathbf{S}_t$ of the environment is explained using the concatenation of n_b-bin histogram of uncertainty measurements of the main classifier for all samples $\mathbf{x}_t$, for all tasks. To eliminate the effect of the stochastic sampling on the uncertainty histogram, a deterministic sampling approach is used, which obtains the batch hard samples (Hermans et al., 2017) from the validation set of each task. The histogram of task uncertainty, $\mathcal{H}_t^{(k)}$, forms the input of the DQN network.

Action: Actions $a_t \in \mathbf{A}_t$ are K one-hot vectors, each indicating the task that is to be trained next.

Reward: During training time, the reward is defined as the $-L_{task}$ on all of the validation samples which includes the summation of losses of all tasks (eq(3)).If the average accuracy of the MTL drops under 95% of the single-task network, a big punishment (manually set to -10) is fed back to the scheduling learner agent to punish the use of chosen policy.

Policy: During the training time, we use Boltzmann-Gumbel exploration (Cesa-Bianchi et al., 2017) to exploit all the information present in the estimated Q-values with an additional temperature parameter, which is annealed over time. This parameter controls the spread of the softmax distribution so that at the start of the training, the equal chance is assigned to each action while actions are sparsely distributed by the end of the training.

4.4 Implementation Details

Our proposed method, QSL-MTL, used LSTM of length 128, GloVe (Pennington et al., 2014) word embedding (300d version on 840B Common Crawl data), and Xavier initialization for the parameters. The mini-batch size is set to 16, including samples of the same task. Other than these, we follow the training procedure and hyper-parameter settingin (Søgaard and Goldberg, 2016). The Q-learning parameters are then set to fixed values of $n_b = 20$ and $\gamma = 0.99$, and the Q-values are randomly initialized.

We used different uncertainty measures such as using least confidence (Settles and Craven, 2008), margin (Scheffer et al., 2001), and Shanon's entropy to calculate the histogram of uncertainty. We also experimented with accuracy for the initial phase to find the best performance according to the preliminary results. We used 10K iterations for our initial testing to explore the best practice and found the margin loss has the best performance.

The proposed scheduler is trained on the training data of all tasks. The rest ofhyper-parameters are tuned over the validation sets. For each of the 1M training episodes, we randomly sample a minibatch from one of K tasks, and reset the MTL modelevery 10K training episode to enable exploring other cases in the MTL. We used GeForce GTX 1080 GPU. During run-time, the scheduler greedily selects the action a_t^* which yields the highest expected reward, $a_t^* = \text{argmax}_{a_t' \in \mathbf{A}_t} Q(S_t, a_t')$. In experiments, we run our system three times and report the average. Note that unlike other methods that randomly fill minibatches with samples, our proposed method learns the policy for sample selection. Although training time takes longer, our method saves a lot of time by finding the best learning policy by itself using q-learning hence eliminates human feature selection procedure and is able to discover surprisingly good features which may not be straightforward for human.

5 Experiment

Our proposed scheduling method is benchmarked under three different scenarios: *(i)* A multi-domain setting, in which a similar task is performed on different datasets, *(ii)* a simple multi-task setting, where the network does three different but slightly related tasks, and *(iii)* a complex multi-task setting in which task relations are complex (e.g., one task can be a prerequisite for another, improving one may hamper the performance of another, etc.). We have conducted an extensive analysis of the first task to clarify our proposed method's internal mechanism and advantages.

5.1 Multiple Domains

In this experiment, we consider text classification as the learning task and 16 different datasets as domains of the task. Each domain consists of around 2000 comments about a class of products labeled as positive or negative reviews and 2000 unlabeled comments. We have applied various MTL scheduling methods on the fully-shared MTL (hereafter, the baseline) and compared the performance of our proposed method to the competitors and their performance on unseen data.

Dataset: Fourteen product review datasets for different products from (Blitzer et al., 2007) have been obtained as domains, with their labels as positive (4+ stars) or negative (2- stars), omitting the borderline 3-star comments. IMDB and MR movie review datasets from (Maas et al., 2011) and (Pang and Lee, 2005) with binary labels (subjective/objective and positive/negative) are also used as two additional domains. Table 1 shows domain statistics.

Competitor Models: We compared our algorithm with several scheduling strategies that are implemented on top of Fully-Shared MTL with a pretrained word embedding and shared LSTM layers

Domain	Books	Elecs	DVD	Kitchen	Apparel	Camera	Health	Music	Toys	Video	Baby	Mags	Soft	Sports	IMDB	MR
Train	⋆	1398	⋆	⋆	⋆	1397	⋆	⋆	⋆	⋆	1300	1370	1315	⋆	⋆	⋆
Dev	— All 200 —														200	200
Test	— All 400 —														400	400
Len	159	101	173	89	57	130	81	136	90	156	104	117	129	94	269	21
Vocab	62K	30K	69K	28K	21K	26K	26K	60K	28K	57K	26K	30K	26K	30K	44K	12K

Table 1: Datasets' statistics (i.e., domains) for multi-domain text classification experiment. (⋆ = 1400)

(baseline). *Uniform*: All tasks have the same importance from beginning to the end of training; *Hand Crafted*: Tasks received a fixed importance coefficient for all training obtained by grid search; *Random*: A random task is selected for the next training episode; *Greedy*: The task with the highest loss is selected for the next training episode; *Loss Exponentiation*: Loss outputs are magnified by the power of 1.15 (found by a grid search). In this way, larger losses (for the tasks needing more changes in the shared space) are magnified; *Homoscedastic Uncertainty* (Kendall et al., 2018): Calculates the task uncertainty using loss magnitude and use it to weigh different tasks; *Self Paced* (Li et al., 2017): Introduces task weights as learnable parameters and employs a regularization that favors training on easy tasks earlier in the training process; *Focal Loss* (Lin et al., 2017): Sample-level scheduler that down-weights easier samples and focuses on hard samples during training; *DTP* (Guo et al., 2018): Uses learning progress signals to automatically compute a priority level at both a task-level and example-level.; *Grad Norm* (Chen et al., 2018b): Scales task gradients based on the magnitude of the gradients and training losses; *Adaptive* (Jean et al., 2019): Oversamples tasks with poorer results compared to their baseline; *QLS*: Our proposed fully-trained Q-learning-based scheduling method.

Task-Specific Output Layer: The obtained shared representation is fed to the task-specific output classifiers composed of a fully connected layer followed by a softmax layer to predict the labels.

Performance Evaluation and Discussion: We perform the multi-domain learning on all 16 tasks to compare the task-specific and overall performance of the proposed method. All schedulers are added on top of untrained FS-MTL (baseline), and the training is governed by the scheduling strategy. Based on Table 2, in most of the cases, our learned strategy outperforms other strategies. An in-depth analysis revealed that in the early stages of the training, for instance, the performance of the `Kitchen` domain was higher, while other domains were still trying to improve their performances. Additionally, hand-crafted domain weights are working well for most of the domains. Yet, these weights are fixed, resulting in the suboptimal performance of this strategy. The uncertainty weighting by (Kendall et al., 2018) also ignores some categories since the early emergent features in the shared space are suboptimal for the task. Although these measures keep the tasks' homoscedastic uncertainty low, they fail to guarantee high performance. This finding calls for better uncertainty measures in such an approach. One of the shortcomings of the GradNorm algorithm was observed in cases that a very noisy minibatch from a task was selected. By largely redirecting the gradients to the corresponding task, GradNorm magnifies the label noise in the training of the task, causing some confusion in updating the feature space. Moreover, we observed that by using Q-Learning, our method *(i)* enables the discovery of more latent features (especially when two or more tasks have a mutual tacit feature that assists those tasks to have better overall performance), *(ii)* easily switches between hard and easy tasks periodically to learn the policies and *(iii)* finds longer sequences as features that work well in the run phase. We also found two groups of mistakes by our model: *(i)* sentences with complicated structures such as when two negative words are separated by two or more words and *(ii)* sentences that require reasoning or external references (e.g., to pop culture) that conveys a particular sentiment, analogies (e.g., "The actors really are made of cardboard") or other types of inferences, out of the dataset's scope.

Shared Knowledge Transfer: One of the reasons for using MTL methods is to obtain a better-shared representation between tasks that cancels out the systematic noise of each individual task and provides a generalizable feature set that performs well out-of-the-box on unseen data. We hypothesize that by properly scheduling the MTL, more generalizable and useful features emerge early in the feature space. Therefore, the training procedure focuses more on improving such features rather than using some inefficient or suboptimal features and discarding them later. To test this hypothesis, we perform a leave-one-out experiment in which the proposed classifier is trained on 15 tasks and tested on one task which was excluded from training (e.g., we train on all tasks/categories except ϕ `(Book)` then we test on ϕ `(Book)` category, we then do the

Domain	Uniform (baseline)	Hand Crafted	Random	Greedy	Loss Exponen.	Homos. Unc.	Self Paced	Focal Loss	DTP	Grad Norm	Adaptive	QLS (ours)
Books	82.5	89.1	83.3	83.0	83.4	87.8	88.1	87.0	90.3	89.3	89.1	90.4
Electronics	85.7	91.1	87.2	86.0	86.6	90.7	90.7	90.6	92.8	92.4	92.3	92.8
DVD	83.5	89.8	84.4	83.8	84.4	88.6	88.4	88.8	90.9	90.2	90.0	90.9
Kitchen	86.0	93.1	86.8	86.0	86.9	90.1	91.6	93.1	87.2	92.7	92.6	93.2
Apparel	84.5	88.8	85.8	85.0	85.3	89.1	89.0	88.4	90.9	91.2	90.9	91.3
Camera	86.5	91.3	89.4	86.8	87.3	91.4	91.3	90.8	93.3	93.2	92.9	93.2
Health	88.0	91.9	88.4	88.1	88.9	91.6	91.6	91.7	90.3	92.6	92.5	92.6
Music	81.2	87.8	81.9	81.4	82.0	86.6	86.5	86.9	89.0	87.9	87.6	89.1
Toys	84.5	90.4	85.0	84.7	85.4	89.6	89.1	88.8	91.8	91.4	91.2	92.2
Video	83.7	89.9	84.6	83.7	84.6	88.9	88.6	89.4	91.3	90.5	90.2	91.9
Baby	88.0	90.0	89.1	88.2	88.9	92.0	91.9	89.4	93.1	94.7	94.7	94.6
Magazines	92.5	92.6	93.1	92.5	93.4	92.2	91.9	90.7	93.0	94.0	93.6	94.2
Software	86.2	90.1	87.3	86.3	87.1	90.8	90.3	88.2	92.6	92.9	92.6	93.1
Sports	85.5	88.6	86.7	85.8	86.3	89.8	89.9	86.8	91.3	92.2	91.9	92.2
IMDB	82.5	89.7	83.5	82.8	83.4	87.9	87.9	89.0	90.5	89.2	89.1	91.3
MR	74.7	78.8	78.7	74.7	75.6	79.3	79.6	76.9	81.0	81.3	81.3	81.4
AVG	84.7	89.6	86.0	84.9	85.6	89.2	89.2	88.5	90.6	91.0	90.8	91.5

Table 2: Accuracy of different scheduling methods on 16 domains, compared to its Fully-Shared-MTL baseline (First, second, and third ranks). Our QLS method outperforms others in almost all of tasks.

same for the next category). We freeze the weights of the trained shared model, perform 5-fold cross-validation on the left-out task, and report the result in Table 3. For each unseen domain, new task layers are made on top of the shared feature space. The task layer israndomly initialized, and trained on a new domain.

5.2 Multiple Tasks with Simple Relations

This experiment considers a heterogeneous multi-task learning scenario in which three different tasks (part-of-speech tagging, chunking, and named entity recognition) on various datasets are considered. Despite their differences, these tasks are related, but none of them could benefit from the output of others. We trained FS-MTL with different strategies and compared their performance on these different tasks (Table 5). We excluded pre-training from our model to provide a fair comparison (as in the modern Transformer sense).

Domain	Hand Craft	Loss Exp.	Homos Unc.	Self Paced	Focal Loss	DTP	Grad Norm	Adapt.	QLS (ours)
ϕ (Books)	86.3	81.8	85.9	82.2	81.7	86.5	86.3	86.4	86.6
ϕ (Elec.)	86.2	83.6	86.1	85.0	84.1	86.4	86.1	86.1	86.3
ϕ (DVD)	86.8	84.5	86.7	85.6	85.0	86.6	87.0	86.8	[illegible]
ϕ (Kitchen)	86.5	84.1	86.4	84.7	84.8	86.7	86.7	86.5	[illegible]
ϕ (Apparel)	86.3	84.7	86.2	85.1	84.7	86.2	86.3	86.2	86.3
ϕ (Camera)	87.3	86.2	87.3	86.9	86.2	87.3	87.1	87.1	87.3
ϕ (Health)	89.0	84.4	88.7	85.3	85.1	89.0	[illegible]	89.0	89.3
ϕ (Music)	85.6	79.7	85.0	80.2	80.2	[illegible]	[illegible]	[illegible]	86.1
ϕ (Toys)	[illegible]	83.7	86.1	84.1	84.1	85.6	[illegible]	86.0	86.4
ϕ (Video)	[illegible]	85.0	[illegible]	86.1	85.7	85.7	85.9	85.8	85.9
ϕ (Baby)	86.1	82.9	85.9	83.8	83.1	86.3	86.2	86.2	86.3
ϕ (Mags)	90.5	88.8	90.5	89.9	89.4	90.5	90.3	90.4	90.6
ϕ (Soft)	87.3	84.0	87.0	84.0	84.0	86.6	[illegible]	87.2	87.6
ϕ (Sports)	85.9	83.2	85.7	84.2	83.8	86.1	86.0	85.9	86.0
ϕ (IMDB)	87.7	86.8	87.7	87.5	87.1	87.5	87.6	87.5	87.6
ϕ (MR)	[illegible]	73.7	75.6	74.3	74.0	[illegible]	75.4	75.4	75.8
ϕ (AVG)	86.2	83.5	86.0	84.3	83.9	86.2	86.2	86.2	86.4

Table 3: Accuracy of fully shared representation learned with different strategies on all-but-one domains tested on the remaining unseen domain. ϕ(DOMAIN) means we transfer the knowledge of other 15 tasks to the target DOMAIN. Using the proposed scheduling of all tasks while training, we improved overall accuracy of MTL classifier on unseen data by 2.2% compared to baseline.

Task-Specific Output Layer: Inspired by (Ma and Hovy, 2016), obtained shared representation is fed to a conditional random field (Lafferty et al., 2001) for sequence tagging. Baseline has a pre-trained embedding, fully-shared LSTM(s), and a CRF.

Dataset: For sequence tagging task, we use Wall Street Journal (WSJ) subset of Penn Treebank (Marcus et al., 1993), CoNLL 2000 chunking, and CoNLL 2003 English NER dataset as in Table 4.

Datasets	Task	Train	Dev	Test
WSJ	POS Tagging	912,344	131,768	129,654
CoNLL 2000	Chunking	211,727	-	47,377
CoNLL 2003	NER	204,567	51,578	46,666

Table 4: Statistics of datasets for multi-task sequence tagging experiment.

Competitor Models: We compare our method with Huang et al. (2015) that uses a BiLSTM encoding and CRF output layer, text classifier of (Collobert et al., 2011), and multi-task text classifier with Meta-LSTM (Chen et al., 2018a). We trained the baseline MTL with different strategies such as DTP (Guo et al., 2018), Grad Norm (Chen et al., 2018b), and Adaptive scheduler (Jean et al., 2019) that performed best in the previous task. We also used Hand Crafted (worked well by finding fixed task weights) and uncertainty-based loss weighting (Kendall et al., 2018) to compare with our QLS.

Results and Discussion: Table 5 shows that our model consistently outperforms others. It is robust and has good generalization among related tasks. However, the task prioritization of Homoscedastic uncertainty and Grad Norm works well for some tasks but not others. One reason lies in the differences in task complexities: the emergent features are not always successful in handling the complexity of all tasks. Grad Norm aggressively decreases the relative weight of Chunking loss leading to a higher error rate in this task, and Homoscedastic uncertainty favors NER that made fewer mistakes early in training. While DTP works well, adaptive scheduling shows a mediocre performance.

5.3 Multiple Tasks with Complex Relations

In this experiment, we use different tasks (two easy and one complex [translation]) to investigate the effect of scheduling on the target task. We selected neural machine translation (NMT) as the target task and chose POS tagging and Parsing as the other tasks in MTL. As Table 6 shows, our method outperforms other static and dynamic scheduling methods. Compared to the baseline single-task NMT (with 19.30 BLEU score), our scheduled ML gains +2.6 points improvement in BLEU points.

Task-Specific Output Layer: NMT has an LSTM encoder and a seq2seq decoder (Sutskever et al., 2014; Bahdanau et al., 2014). Here, to be consistent with the literature, we perform POS tagging as a translation between source language and sequence of POS tags, similar to (Niehues and Cho, 2017). We also used the decoder in (Kiperwasser and Ballesteros, 2018) for dependency parsing.

Dataset: For translation setting, we use WMT'14 parallel corpus (Buck et al., 2014) including 4.5M training sentence pairs, 3000 sentences of *newstest2013* as the development set, and *newstest2014* for test set. English POS tagging, dependency heads and labels are from the Penn tree-bank with Stanford Dependencies (Training:02-21, Dev:22, Test:23) and German ones from TIGER tree-bank

	Chunking (CoNLL2000)	NER (CoNLL2003)	POS Tagging (WSJ)
BiLSTM+CRF	93.67	89.91	97.25
Meta-BiLSTM+CRF	93.71	90.08	97.30
(Collobert et al., 2011)	94.32	89.59	97.29
Meta-MTL + CRF	95.11	90.72	97.45
FS-MTL + CRF⋆	94.18	89.99	97.14
+ Hand Crafted	94.16	89.42	97.33
+ Homos. Unc.	95.05	90.24	97.42
+ DTP	95.46	90.73	97.38
+ Grad Norm	95.07	90.30	97.38
+ Adaptive	94.97	90.18	97.46
+ **QLS** (ours)	95.91	91.02	97.46

Table 5: Accuracy rates of the models for chunking and NER tasks using F1-score (%) and for POS tagging using Accuracy (%). Our QLS method outperforms others in most of the tasks. (⋆: baseline)

	Prior. Easy	Prior. Hard	Hand Crafted	Sigmoid	Exponential	Homo. Unc.	DTP	Grad Norm	Ada.	**QLS** (ours)
MT+POS	18.9	19.1	20.9	19.2	20.0	19.2	21.3	20.5	20.9	21.7
MT+Par.	18.7	18.6	20.5	19.1	18.9	18.9	18.9	20.4	21.1	21.4
MT+POS+Par.	19.0	18.3	20.9	19.3	18.0	19.0	20.8	20.7	21.5	21.9

Table 6: BLEU score of target machine translation with POS tagging and parsing (written as par.) as auxiliary tasks in multi-task framework trained with different scheduling strategies. The BLEU score of baseline Neural MT system (without auxiliary tasks) is 19.30. QLS shows superior performance among schedulers.

(Hajič et al., 2009). Translation quality is measured with case-sensitive BLEU (Papineni et al., 2002).

Competitor Models: We have included three types of schedulers: *(i)* all-task schedulers such as DTP (Guo et al., 2018), Grad Norm (Chen et al., 2018b), Adaptive (Jean et al., 2019), Homoscedastic Uncertainty (Kendall et al., 2018), and ours; *(ii)* one-task scheduler which tunes the weight of the target task over training episodes while keeping the rest of the weights intact; and *(iii)* constant schedules that assign each task a fixed weight for the entire training. Second category contains *exponential schedule* and *sigmoid schedule* (Kiperwasser and Ballesteros, 2018), and third category includes *prioritize hard/easy* strategies that assign the weight of 0.98 to the hardest/easiest task and 0.01 to others.

Results and Discussion: We selected NMT that is significantly harder than other tasks. Thus, the syntax representations learned by POS and Parsing tasks are required to process the input better and generate more meaningful sentences. As the table shows, merely plugging different tasks in the MTL framework does not guarantee better results as *(i)* some task combinations are not compatible (e.g., NMT and Parsing), which is aligned with the findings of (Zamir et al., 2020), and *(ii)* unified task weights can be damaging to the overall performance of a target model, while it might increase the overall performance of all tasks. It can be seen that even a carefully selected task's weighting (although static) could significantly improve this situation. Another observation is that single task schedulers are not always successful (only NMT + POS + Exponential scheduler improves the results in Table 6). DTP, Grad Norm, and homoscedastic uncertainty weighting suppress the performance of the NMT task, either because of its high initial error rate or due to favoring easier tasks that show better improvement during training. Among these, DTP sometimes covers difficult tasks better in the cost of performance of the overall tasks, depending on its KPI. On the other hand, adaptive scheduling handles catastrophic forgetting better and improves overall performance. However, we see that a tailored strategy (that our RL scheduler achieved through numerous trial-and-errors) works a lot better in handling such task difficulty imbalance. Yet, our method may not perform the best in handling balanced tasks or complex tasks that can benefit from sufficient amount of related easy ones.

6 Conclusion

We augment the fully-shared MTL framework with a reinforcement-learning-based scheduling scheme that obtains an optimal scheduling policy for tasks through trial and error. The scheduler detects the task states through a novel state definition: histogram of task uncertainty. It adjusts the scheduling policy to improve the training and validation accuracy of the MTL, enhances generalization of the emergent shared features, and handles different relationships among tasks. The proposed method is also capable of leveraging unlabeled data, obtaining highly-nonlinear strategies, and tackling different sources of task uncertainty.

References

Dzmitry Bahdanau, Kyunghyun Cho, and Yoshua Bengio. 2014. Neural machine translation by jointly learning to align and translate. *arXiv preprint arXiv:1409.0473*.

Marc Bellemare, Sriram Srinivasan, Georg Ostrovski, Tom Schaul, David Saxton, and Remi Munos. 2016. Unifying count-based exploration and intrinsic motivation. In *Advances in neural information processing systems*, pages 1471–1479.

Yoshua Bengio, Jérôme Louradour, Ronan Collobert, and Jason Weston. 2009. Curriculum learning. In *Proceedings of the 26th annual international conference on machine learning*, pages 41–48.

Joachim Bingel and Anders Søgaard. 2017. Identifying beneficial task relations for multi-task learning in deep neural networks. In *ACL'15*, pages 164–169.

John Blitzer, Mark Dredze, and Fernando Pereira. 2007. Biographies, bollywood, boom-boxes and blenders: Domain adaptation for sentiment classification. In *Proceedings of the 45th annual meeting of the association of computational linguistics*, pages 440–447.

Christian Buck, Kenneth Heafield, and Bas Van Ooyen. 2014. N-gram counts and language models from the common crawl. In *LREC*, volume 2, page 4. Citeseer.

Rich Caruana. 1997. Multitask learning. *Machine learning*, 28(1):41–75.

Nicolò Cesa-Bianchi, Claudio Gentile, Gábor Lugosi, and Gergely Neu. 2017. Boltzmann exploration done right. In *NIPS'17*, pages 6284–6293.

Junkun Chen, Xipeng Qiu, Pengfei Liu, and Xuanjing Huang. 2018a. Meta multi-task learning for sequence modeling. In *Thirty-Second AAAI Conference on Artificial Intelligence*.

Zhao Chen, Vijay Badrinarayanan, Chen-Yu Lee, and Andrew Rabinovich. 2018b. Gradnorm: Gradient normalization for adaptive loss balancing in deep multitask networks. In *International Conference on Machine Learning*, pages 794–803.

Ronan Collobert, Jason Weston, Léon Bottou, Michael Karlen, Koray Kavukcuoglu, and Pavel Kuksa. 2011. Natural language processing (almost) from scratch. *Journal of machine learning research*, 12(Aug):2493–2537.

Yaroslav Ganin and Victor Lempitsky. 2015. Unsupervised domain adaptation by backpropagation. In *ICML'15*, pages 1180–1189.

Xavier Glorot, Antoine Bordes, and Yoshua Bengio. 2011. Domain adaptation for large-scale sentiment classification: A deep learning approach. In *ICML*.

Alex Graves, Marc G Bellemare, Jacob Menick, Remi Munos, and Koray Kavukcuoglu. 2017. Automated curriculum learning for neural networks. *arXiv preprint arXiv:1704.03003*.

Michelle Guo, Albert Haque, De-An Huang, Serena Yeung, and Li Fei-Fei. 2018. Dynamic task prioritization for multitask learning. In *Proceedings of the European Conference on Computer Vision (ECCV)*, pages 270–287.

Jan Hajič, Massimiliano Ciaramita, Richard Johansson, Daisuke Kawahara, Maria Antònia Martí, Lluís Màrquez, Adam Meyers, Joakim Nivre, Sebastian Padó, Jan Štepánek, et al. 2009. The conll-2009 shared task: Syntactic and semantic dependencies in multiple languages.

Kazuma Hashimoto, Yoshimasa Tsuruoka, Richard Socher, et al. 2017. A joint many-task model: Growing a neural network for multiple nlp tasks. In *EMNLP'17*, pages 1923–1933.

Alexander Hermans, Lucas Beyer, and Bastian Leibe. 2017. In defense of the triplet loss for person reidentification. *arXiv preprint arXiv:1703.07737*.

Rein Houthooft, Xi Chen, Yan Duan, John Schulman, Filip De Turck, and Pieter Abbeel. 2016. Vime: Variational information maximizing exploration. In *Advances in Neural Information Processing Systems*, pages 1109–1117.

Zhiheng Huang, Wei Xu, and Kai Yu. 2015. Bidirectional LSTM-CRF models for sequence tagging. *arXiv preprint arXiv:1508.01991*.

Laurent Itti and Pierre F Baldi. 2006. Bayesian surprise attracts human attention. In *Advances in neural information processing systems*, pages 547–554.

Sébastien Jean, Orhan Firat, and Melvin Johnson. 2019. Adaptive scheduling for multi-task learning. *arXiv preprint arXiv:1909.06434*.

Rafal Jozefowicz, Wojciech Zaremba, and Ilya Sutskever. 2015. An empirical exploration of recurrent network architectures. In *ICML'15*, pages 2342–2350.

Michael Kampffmeyer, Arnt-Borre Salberg, and Robert Jenssen. 2016. Semantic segmentation of small objects and modeling of uncertainty in urban remote sensing images using deep convolutional neural networks. In *Proceedings of the IEEE conference on computer vision and pattern recognition workshops*, pages 1–9.

Alex Kendall, Vijay Badrinarayanan, and Roberto Cipolla. 2015. Bayesian segnet: Model uncertainty in deep convolutional encoder-decoder architectures for scene understanding. *arXiv preprint arXiv:1511.02680*.

Alex Kendall and Roberto Cipolla. 2016. Modelling uncertainty in deep learning for camera relocalization. In *2016 IEEE international conference on Robotics and Automation (ICRA)*, pages 4762–4769. IEEE.

Alex Kendall and Yarin Gal. 2017. What uncertainties do we need in bayesian deep learning for computer vision? In *Advances in neural information processing systems*, pages 5574–5584.

Alex Kendall, Yarin Gal, and Roberto Cipolla. 2018. Multi-task learning using uncertainty to weigh losses for scene geometry and semantics. In *CVPR'18*, pages 7482–7491.

Yoon Kim. 2014. Convolutional neural networks for sentence classification. In *EMNLP'14*, pages 1746–1751.

Eliyahu Kiperwasser and Miguel Ballesteros. 2018. Scheduled multi-task learning: From syntax to translation. *Transactions of the Association for Computational Linguistics*, 6:225–240.

Iasonas Kokkinos. 2017. Ubernet: Training a universal convolutional neural network for low-, mid-, and high-level vision using diverse datasets and limited memory. In *Proceedings of the IEEE Conference on Computer Vision and Pattern Recognition*, pages 6129–6138.

John Lafferty, Andrew McCallum, and Fernando CN Pereira. 2001. Conditional random fields: Probabilistic models for segmenting and labeling sequence data.

Siwei Lai, Liheng Xu, Kang Liu, and Jun Zhao. 2015. Recurrent convolutional neural networks for text classification. In *AAAI'15*.

Changsheng Li, Junchi Yan, Fan Wei, Weishan Dong, Qingshan Liu, and Hongyuan Zha. 2017. Self-paced multi-task learning. In *Thirty-First AAAI Conference on Artificial Intelligence*.

Tsung-Yi Lin, Priya Goyal, Ross Girshick, Kaiming He, and Piotr Dollár. 2017. Focal loss for dense object detection. In *Proceedings of the IEEE international conference on computer vision*, pages 2980–2988.

Pengfei Liu, Xipeng Qiu, and Xuanjing Huang. 2016. Recurrent neural network for text classification with multi-task learning. *arXiv preprint arXiv:1605.05101*.

Pengfei Liu, Xipeng Qiu, and Xuanjing Huang. 2017a. Adversarial multi-task learning for text classification. In *ACL'17*, pages 1–10.

Sulin Liu, Sinno Jialin Pan, and Qirong Ho. 2017b. Distributed multi-task relationship learning. In *ACM SIGKDD'17*, pages 937–946. ACM.

Zelun Luo, Yuliang Zou, Judy Hoffman, and Li F Fei-Fei. 2017. Label efficient learning of transferable representations acrosss domains and tasks. In *Advances in Neural Information Processing Systems*, pages 165–177.

Xuezhe Ma and Eduard Hovy. 2016. End-to-end sequence labeling via bi-directional LSTM-CNNs-CRF. *arXiv preprint arXiv:1603.01354*.

Andrew L Maas, Raymond E Daly, Peter T Pham, Dan Huang, Andrew Y Ng, and Christopher Potts. 2011. Learning word vectors for sentiment analysis. In *Proceedings of the 49th annual meeting of the association for computational linguistics: Human language technologies-volume 1*, pages 142–150. Association for Computational Linguistics.

Mitchell Marcus, Beatrice Santorini, and Mary Ann Marcinkiewicz. 1993. Building a large annotated corpus of english: The penn treebank.

Elliot Meyerson and Risto Miikkulainen. 2018. Pseudo-task augmentation: From deep multitask learning to intratask sharing—and back. *ICML'18*.

Volodymyr Mnih, Koray Kavukcuoglu, David Silver, Alex Graves, Ioannis Antonoglou, Daan Wierstra, and Martin Riedmiller. 2013. Playing atari with deep reinforcement learning. *arXiv preprint arXiv:1312.5602*.

Hyeonseob Nam and Bohyung Han. 2016. Learning multi-domain convolutional neural networks for visual tracking. In *ICPR'16*, pages 4293–4302.

Jan Niehues and Eunah Cho. 2017. Exploiting linguistic resources for neural machine translation using multi-task learning. *arXiv preprint arXiv:1708.00993*.

Pierre-Yves Oudeyer, Frdric Kaplan, and Verena V Hafner. 2007. Intrinsic motivation systems for autonomous mental development. *IEEE transactions on evolutionary computation*, 11(2):265–286.

Bo Pang and Lillian Lee. 2005. Seeing stars: Exploiting class relationships for sentiment categorization with respect to rating scales. In *Proceedings of the 43rd annual meeting on association for computational linguistics*, pages 115–124. Association for Computational Linguistics.

Kishore Papineni, Salim Roukos, Todd Ward, and Wei-Jing Zhu. 2002. Bleu: a method for automatic evaluation of machine translation. In *Proceedings of the 40th annual meeting of the Association for Computational Linguistics*, pages 311–318.

Jeffrey Pennington, Richard Socher, and Christopher Manning. 2014. Glove: Global vectors for word representation. In *EMNLP'14*, pages 1532–1543.

Anastasia Pentina, Viktoriia Sharmanska, and Christoph H Lampert. 2015. Curriculum learning of multiple tasks. In *Proceedings of the IEEE Conference on Computer Vision and Pattern Recognition*, pages 5492–5500.

Marek Rei. 2017. Semi-supervised multitask learning for sequence labeling. In *ACL'17*, pages 2121–2130.

Clemens Rosenbaum, Tim Klinger, and Matthew Riemer. 2017. Routing networks: Adaptive selection of non-linear functions for multi-task learning. *arXiv preprint arXiv:1711.01239*.

Sebastian Ruder. 2017. An overview of multi-task learning in deep neural networks. *arXiv preprint arXiv:1706.05098*.

Sebastian Ruder, Joachim Bingel, Isabelle Augenstein, and Anders Søgaard. 2017. Sluice networks: Learning what to share between loosely related tasks. *stat*, 1050:23.

Victor Sanh, Thomas Wolf, and Sebastian Ruder. 2019. A hierarchical multi-task approach for learning embeddings from semantic tasks. In *AAAI'19*, volume 33, pages 6949–6956.

Tobias Scheffer, Christian Decomain, and Stefan Wrobel. 2001. Active hidden markov models for information extraction. In *Advances in Intelligent Data Analysis*, pages 309–318, Berlin, Heidelberg. Springer Berlin Heidelberg.

Jürgen Schmidhuber. 1991. A possibility for implementing curiosity and boredom in model-building neural controllers. In *Proc. of the international conference on simulation of adaptive behavior: From animals to animats*, pages 222–227.

Pierre Sermanet, David Eigen, Xiang Zhang, Michaël Mathieu, Rob Fergus, and Yann LeCun. 2013. Overfeat: Integrated recognition, localization and detection using convolutional networks. *arXiv preprint arXiv:1312.6229*.

Burr Settles and Mark Craven. 2008. An analysis of active learning strategies for sequence labeling tasks. In *EMNLP'08*, pages 1070–1079. Association for Computational Linguistics.

Anders Søgaard and Yoav Goldberg. 2016. Deep multi-task learning with low level tasks supervised at lower layers. In *ACL'16*, pages 231–235.

Trevor Standley, Amir R Zamir, Dawn Chen, Leonidas Guibas, Jitendra Malik, and Silvio Savarese. 2019. Which tasks should be learned together in multi-task learning? *arXiv preprint arXiv:1905.07553*.

Sandeep Subramanian, Adam Trischler, Yoshua Bengio, and Christopher Pal. 2018. Learning general purpose distributed sentence representations via large scale multi-task learning. *arXiv preprint arXiv:1804.00079*.

Ilya Sutskever, Oriol Vinyals, and Quoc V Le. 2014. Sequence to sequence learning with neural networks. In *Advances in neural information processing systems*, pages 3104–3112.

Eric Tzeng, Judy Hoffman, Trevor Darrell, and Kate Saenko. 2015. Simultaneous deep transfer across domains and tasks. In *Proceedings of the IEEE International Conference on Computer Vision*, pages 4068–4076.

Jianfei Yu and Jing Jiang. 2016. Learning sentence embeddings with auxiliary tasks for cross-domain sentiment classification. In *EMNLP'16*, pages 236–246.

Amir R Zamir, Alexander Sax, Nikhil Cheerla, Rohan Suri, Zhangjie Cao, Jitendra Malik, and Leonidas J Guibas. 2020. Robust learning through cross-task consistency. In *Proceedings of the IEEE/CVF Conference on Computer Vision and Pattern Recognition*, pages 11197–11206.

Amir R. Zamir, Alexander Sax, William Shen, Leonidas J Guibas, Jitendra Malik, and Silvio Savarese. 2018. Taskonomy: Disentangling task transfer learning. In *CVPR'18*, pages 3712–3722.

Wojciech Zaremba and Ilya Sutskever. 2014. Learning to execute. *arXiv preprint arXiv:1410.4615*.

Xiang Zhang, Junbo Zhao, and Yann LeCun. 2015. Character-level convolutional networks for text classification. In *NIPS'15*, pages 649–657.

Barret Zoph and Quoc V Le. 2016. Neural architecture search with reinforcement learning. *arXiv preprint arXiv:1611.01578*.

PARADISE: Exploiting Parallel Data for Multilingual Sequence-to-Sequence Pretraining

Machel Reid
The University of Tokyo
machelreid@weblab.t.u-tokyo.ac.jp

Mikel Artetxe
Facebook AI Research
artetxe@fb.com

Abstract

Despite the success of multilingual sequence-to-sequence pretraining, most existing approaches rely on monolingual corpora, and do not make use of the strong cross-lingual signal contained in parallel data. In this paper, we present PARADISE (**PARA**llel & **D**enoising **I**ntegration in **SE**quence-to-sequence models), which extends the conventional denoising objective used to train these models by (i) replacing words in the noised sequence according to a multilingual dictionary, and (ii) predicting the reference translation according to a parallel corpus instead of recovering the original sequence. Our experiments on machine translation and cross-lingual natural language inference show an average improvement of 2.0 BLEU points and 6.7 accuracy points from integrating parallel data into pretraining, respectively, obtaining results that are competitive with several popular models at a fraction of their computational cost.

1 Introduction

Multilingual sequence-to-sequence pretraining has achieved strong results both in cross-lingual classification (Xue et al., 2021) and machine translation (Liu et al., 2020). These models are usually pretrained on combined monolingual corpora in multiple languages using some form of denoising objective. More concretely, they noise each sequence x with a noising function g_ϕ, and maximize the probability of recovering x given $g_\phi(x)$:

$$\ell_{\text{mono}}(x) = -\log P\big(x|g_\phi(x)\big) \qquad (1)$$

Common noising functions include sentence-permutation and span masking (Lewis et al., 2020; Liu et al., 2020).

While these methods obtain strong cross-lingual performance without parallel data, they are usually trained at a scale that is prohibitive for most NLP practitioners. At the same time, it has been argued that the strict unsupervised scenario is not realistic (Artetxe et al., 2020), and parallel data could provide a stronger signal and make training more efficient.

Motivated by this, we propose PARADISE, a pretraining method for sequence-to-sequence models that exploits both word-level and sentence-level parallel data. The core idea of our approach is to augment the conventional denoising objective introduced above by (i) replacing words in the noised sequence according to a bilingual dictionary, and (ii) predicting the reference translation rather than the input sequence. Despite their simplicity, we find that both techniques bring substantial gains over conventional pretraining on monolingual data, as evaluated both in machine translation and zero-shot cross-lingual transfer. Our results are competitive with several popular models, despite using only a fraction of the compute providing strong support for the importance of the inclusion of parallel information in smaller-scale multilingual pre-training methods.

2 Proposed method

As illustrated in Figure 1, we propose two methods for introducing parallel data into pretraining: dictionary denoising and bitext denoising.

Dictionary denoising. Our first method encourages learning similar representations at the word-level by introducing anchor words through multilingual dictionaries (Conneau et al., 2020b). Let $D_l(w)$ denote the translation of word w into language $l \in L$ according to the dictionary D. Given the source sentence $x = (x_1, x_2, \dots, x_n)$, we define its noised version $g_\psi(x) = (\tilde{x}_1, \tilde{x}_2, \dots, \tilde{x}_n)$, where $\tilde{x}_i = D_l(x_i)$ with probability $\frac{p_r}{|L|}$ and $\tilde{x}_i = x_i$ otherwise (i.e. we replace each word with its translation into a random language with probability p_r). We set $p_r = 0.4$. Given the dictionary-noised sentence, we train our model using the denoising

Proceedings of the 7th Workshop on Representation Learning for NLP, pages 20 - 28

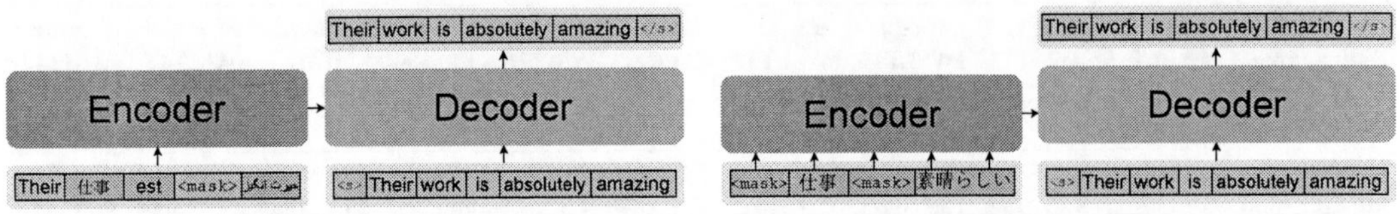

(a) Dictionary Denoising

(b) Bitext Denoising

Figure 1: Our proposed techniques for integrating parallel data into sequence-to-sequence pretraining.

auto-encoding objective in Eq. 1:

$$\ell_{\text{dict}}(x) = -\log P\big(x|g_\phi(g_\psi(x))\big) \tag{2}$$

Bitext denoising. Our second approach encourages learning from both monolingual and parallel data sources, by including translation data in the pretraining process. Given a source-target bitext pair (x, y) in the parallel corpus, assumed to be semantically equivalent, we model the following:

$$\ell_{\text{bitext}}(x, y) = -\log P\big(y|g_\phi(x)\big) \tag{3}$$

in which we optimize the likelihood of generating the target sentence y conditioned on the noised version of the source sentence, $g_\phi(x)$.[1]

Combined objective. Our final objective combines ℓ_{mono}, ℓ_{dict} and ℓ_{bitext}.[2] Given that our corpus contains languages with varying data sizes, we sample sentences using the exponential sampling technique from Conneau and Lample (2019). We use $\alpha_{\text{mono}} = 0.5$ to sample from the monolingual corpus, and $\alpha_{\text{bitext}} = 0.3$ to sample from the parallel corpus. To prevent over-exposure to English on the decoder side when sampling from the parallel corpus, we halve the probability of to-English directions and renormalize the probabilities. In addition, given that we have fewer amounts of parallel data (used for ℓ_{bitext}) than monolingual data (used for ℓ_{mono} and ℓ_{dict}), we sample between each task using $\alpha_{\text{task}} = 0.3$.

3 Experimental Settings

We pretrain our models on 20 languages (English, French, Spanish, German, Greek, Bulgarian, Russian, Turkish, Arabic, Vietnamese, Thai, Chinese, Hindi, Swahili, Urdu, Japanese, Basque, Romanian, Sinhala and Nepalese), and evaluate them on machine translation and cross-lingual classification.

3.1 Pretraining

Data. We use Wikipedia as our monolingual corpus, and complement it with OSCAR (Ortiz Suárez et al., 2020), and CC100 (Conneau et al., 2020a) for low-resource languages. For a fair comparison with monolingually pretrained baselines, we use the same parallel data as in our downstream machine translation experiments (detailed in §3.2). In addition, we train a separate variant (detailed below) using additional parallel data from ParaCrawl (Esplà et al., 2019), UNPC (Ziemski et al., 2016), CCAligned (El-Kishky et al., 2020), and OpenSubtitles (Lison and Tiedemann, 2016).[3] We tokenize all data using SentencePiece (Kudo and Richardson, 2018) with a joint vocabulary of 125K subwords. We use bilingual dictionaries from FLoRes[4] (Guzmán et al., 2019) for Nepalese and Sinhala, and MUSE[5] (Lample et al., 2018) for the rest of languages. Refer to Appendix A for more details.

Models. We use the same architecture as BART-base (Lewis et al., 2020), totaling ~196M parameters, and train for 100k steps with a batch size of ~520K tokens. This takes around a day on 32 NVIDIA V100 16GB GPUs. As discussed before, we train two variants of our full model: **PARADISE**, which uses the same parallel data as the machine translation experiments, and **PARADISE++**, which uses additional parallel data. To better understand the contribution of each objective, we train two additional models without dictionary denoising, which we name **PARADISE (w/o dict.)** and **PARADISE++ (w/o dict.)**. Finally, we train a baseline system using the monolingual objective alone, which we refer to as **mBART (ours)**. This follows the original mBART work (Liu et al., 2020), but is directly comparable to the rest of our models in terms of data and hyperparameters.

[1] To make our pretraining sequence length consistent with ℓ_{mono} and ℓ_{dict}, we concatentate randomly sampled sentence pairs from the same language pair to fit the maximum length.

[2] We use the same noising function g_ϕ used by Lewis et al. (2020) and Liu et al. (2020).

[3] We cap the size of each language pair to 2GB.

[4] https://github.com/facebookresearch/flores

[5] https://github.com/facebookresearch/MUSE

Languages	En-Vi		En-Tr		En-Ja		En-Ar		En-Ne		En-Ro		En-Si		En-Hi		En-Es		En-Fr	
Data Source	IWSLT15		WMT17		IWSLT17		IWSLT17		FLoRes		WMT16		FLoRes		IITB		WMT13		WMT14	
Size	133K		207K		223K		250K		564K		608K		647K		1.56M		15M		41M	
Direction	←	→	←	→	←	→	←	→	←	→	←	→	←	→	←	→	←	→	←	→
Random init.	23.6	24.8	12.2	9.5	10.4	12.3	27.5	16.9	7.6	4.3	34.0	34.3	7.2	1.2	10.9	14.2	32.1	31.4	37.0	38.9
mBART (ours)	29.1	31.5	21.3	15.8	15.7	17.3	32.1	19.2	10.3	6.1	34.3	34.9	11.0	2.7	20.2	19.0	29.8	30.4	36.0	38.2
PARADISE	**30.0**	**32.6**	**23.5**	**17.2**	**17.2**	**19.2**	**35.3**	**21.1**	**13.7**	**7.9**	**35.9**	**36.5**	**14.0**	**3.7**	**23.6**	**20.7**	**32.6**	**32.7**	**37.8**	**39.8**

Table 1: Machine translation results. Random initialization numbers taken from Liu et al. (2020).

Lang. pair (En-XX)	Tr	Ro	Si	Hi	Es	Avg_Δ
mBART (ours)	15.8	34.9	2.7	19.0	30.4	$20.6_{\pm 0.0}$
PARADISE (w/o dict.)	16.8	36.2	3.2	20.5	32.4	$21.8_{+1.2}$
PARADISE	17.2	36.5	3.7	20.7	32.7	$22.2_{+1.6}$
PARADISE++	19.0	37.3	4.2	20.7	33.0	$\mathbf{22.8}_{+2.2}$

Lang. pair (XX-En)	Tr	Ro	Si	Hi	Es	Avg_Δ
mBART (ours)	21.3	34.3	11.0	20.2	29.8	$23.3_{\pm 0.0}$
PARADISE (w/o dict.)	23.2	35.6	13.2	22.3	31.6	$25.2_{+1.9}$
PARADISE	23.5	35.9	14.0	23.6	32.6	$25.9_{+2.6}$
PARADISE++	24.9	36.8	15.1	23.5	32.9	$\mathbf{26.6}_{+3.3}$

Table 2: Ablation results on machine translation.

3.2 Downstream Settings

Machine translation. Following Liu et al. (2020), we evaluate our models on sentence-level machine translation from and to English using the following datasets: IWSLT (Cettolo et al., 2015, 2017) for Vietnamese, Japanese and Arabic, WMT (Callison-Burch et al., 2009a,b; Bojar et al., 2016, 2017) for Spanish, French, Romanian and Turkish, FLoRes (Guzmán et al., 2019) for Sinhala and Nepalese, and IITB (Kunchukuttan et al., 2018) for Hindi. We report performance in BLEU as detailed in Appendix C.

Cross-lingual classification. We evaluate our models on zero-shot cross-lingual transfer on XNLI (Conneau et al., 2018) and PAWS-X[6] (Yang et al., 2019), where we finetune on English data and test performance on other languages. We develop a new approach for applying sequence-to-sequence models for classification: feeding the sequence into both the encoder and decoder, and taking the concatenation of the encoder's <s> representation and the decoder's </s> representation as the input of the classification head. We provide an empirical rationale for this in Appendix E. We finetune all models with a batch size of 64 and a learning rate of 2×10^{-5} for a maximum of 100k iterations, performing early stopping on the validation set.

[6]Following Hu et al. (2021), we use English, German, Spanish, French and Chinese for PAWS-X.

4 Results

4.1 Machine Translation

As shown in Table 1, PARADISE consistently outperforms our mBART baseline across all language pairs. Note that these two models have seen the exact same corpora, but mBART uses the parallel data for finetuning only, whereas PARADISE also uses it at the pretraining stage. This suggests that incorporating parallel data into pretraining helps learn better representations, which results in better downstream performance.

Table 2 reports additional ablation results on a subset of languages. As can be seen, removing dictionary denoising hurts, but is still better than our mBART baseline. This shows that both of our proposed approaches—dictionary denoising and bitext denoising—are helpful and complementary. Finally, PARADISE++ improves over PARADISE, indicating that a more balanced corpus with more parallel data is helpful.

4.2 Cross-lingual Classification

We report XNLI results in Table 3 and PAWS-X results in Appendix F. Our proposed approach outperforms mBART in all languages by a large margin. To our surprise, we also observe big gains in English. We conjecture that this could be explained by bitext denoising providing a stronger training signal from all tokens akin to ELECTRA (Clark et al., 2020), whereas monolingual denoising only gets effective signal from predicting the masked portion. In addition, given that we are using parallel data between English and other languages, PARADISE ends up seeing much more English text compared to mBART—yet a similar amount in the rest of languages—which could also contribute to its better performance in this language. Finally, we observe that all of our different variants perform similarly in English, but incorporating dictionary denoising and using additional parallel data both reduce the cross-lingual transfer gap.

Model	en	zh	es	de	ar	ur	ru	bg	el	fr	hi	sw	th	tr	vi	avg
mBART (ours)	77.5	68.0	70.7	68.8	66.7	62.2	68.6	72.1	69.6	70.1	63.4	62.6	66.6	65.0	69.7	68.1
PARADISE	**83.4**	73.8	77.6	76.0	**72.4**	65.1	74.0	74.4	73.2	**77.7**	**70.6**	66.2	70.4	72.1	75.3	73.5
PARADISE++ (w/o dict.)	83.3	72.9	77.2	75.7	64.4	**66.9**	73.4	74.8	75.7	**77.7**	68.5	67.4	71.0	73.3	75.0	73.1
PARADISE++	83.0	**74.0**	**79.0**	**76.5**	68.5	66.8	**74.3**	**76.0**	**76.4**	**77.7**	70.2	**70.5**	**72.3**	**74.2**	**75.4**	**74.3**

Table 3: Accuracy of zero-shot crosslingual classification on the XNLI dataset.

Model	**#Langs**	**Task**	**Params.**	**Est. GPU Days**	**Data (GB)**	**XNLI**	**PAWS-X**	**MT**
mBERT (Devlin et al., 2019)†	104	MLM	179M (0.9x)	—	60	65.4	86.2	—
MMTE (Siddhant et al., 2019)†	102	Translation	375M (1.9x)	—	5000	67.4	85.6	—
mT5-small (Xue et al., 2021)	101	Eq. 1	300M (1.5x)	—	27000	67.5	85.8	—
mT6 (Chi et al., 2021a)	94	SC+PNAT+TSC	300M (1.5x)	40 (1.3x)	2120	64.7	86.6	—
AMBER (Hu et al., 2021)	104	MLM+TLM	179M (0.9x)	1000 (31x)	100	71.6	89.2	—
XLM-15 (Conneau and Lample, 2019)‡	15	MLM+TLM	250M (1.3x)	450 (14x)	100	72.6	88.0	—
XLM-R-base (Conneau et al., 2020a)‡	100	MLM	270M (1.4x)	13K (406x)	2400	73.4	87.4	—
mBART (Liu et al., 2020)	25	Eq. 1	680M (3.5x)	4.5K (140x)	2400	—	—	23.5
mBART (ours)	20	Eq. 1	196M (1.0x)	32 (1.0x)	72	68.1	85.4	21.1
PARADISE	20	Eq. 1, 2, 3	196M (1.0x)	32 (1.0x)	81	73.5	89.0	23.1
PARADISE++	20	Eq. 1, 2, 3	196M (1.0x)	32 (1.0x)	95	**74.3**	**89.2**	**23.8**

Table 4: Comparison with prior work. † denotes results taken from Hu et al. (2020). ‡ denotes results taken from Hu et al. (2021). 1 GPU day = 1 day on an NVIDIA V100 GPU.

4.3 Comparison with prior work

So as to put our results into perspective, we compare our models with several popular systems from the literature. As shown in Table 4, our proposed approach obtains competitive results despite being trained at a much smaller scale. Just in line with our previous results, this suggests that incorporating parallel data makes pretraining more efficient given that we outperform XLM-R base, mT5, and mBART despite using less data/compute/model size. Interestingly, our method also outperforms XLM-15, MMTE, and mT6 which also use parallel data, as well as AMBER, showing evidence contrary to Hu et al. (2021)'s suggestion that using dictionaries may hurt performance. Detailed per-language results for each task can be found in Appendix F.

5 Related Work

Most prior work on multilingual pretraining uses monolingual data only (Pires et al., 2019; Conneau et al., 2020a; Song et al., 2019; Liu et al., 2020; Xue et al., 2021). There have been several proposals to incorporate parallel data into encoder-only models (Lample and Conneau, 2019; Huang et al., 2019; Hu et al., 2021; Chi et al., 2021b), with some approaches replacing words according to a bilingual dictionary, similar to our dictionary denoising objective (Conneau et al., 2020b; Chaudhary et al., 2020; Dufter and Schütze, 2020). In contrast, we focus on sequence-to-sequence models, which we believe are more flexible and provide a more natural way of integrating parallel data. In that spirit, Siddhant et al. (2019) showed that vanilla machine translation models are already competitive in cross-lingual classification. Closer to our work, Chi et al. (2021a) incorporated parallel corpora into sequence-to-sequence pretraining by feeding concatenated parallel sentences to the encoder and using different masking strategies. In contrast, our approach feeds a noised sentence into the encoder, and tries to recover its translation in the decoder side, obtaining better results with a similar computational budget. Concurrent to our work, Kale et al. (2021) extended T5 to incorporate parallel corpora using a similar approach to our bitext denoising.

6 Conclusions

In this work, we proposed PARADISE, which introduces two new objectives to integrate parallel data into sequence-to-sequence pretraining. Experimental results on machine translation and cross-lingual classification show that PARADISE provides significant improvements over mBART-style pretraining on monolingual corpora, obtaining results that are competitive with several popular models at a much smaller scale. Given these findings, we encourage use of parallel data in smaller-scale multilingual pre-training work. In the future, we look to see if our improvements also hold at a larger scale.

References

Mikel Artetxe, Sebastian Ruder, Dani Yogatama, Gorka Labaka, and Eneko Agirre. 2020. A Call for More Rigor in Unsupervised Cross-lingual Learning. *ArXiv*.

Ondřej Bojar, Rajen Chatterjee, Christian Federmann, Yvette Graham, Barry Haddow, Shujian Huang, Matthias Huck, Philipp Koehn, Qun Liu, Varvara Logacheva, Christof Monz, Matteo Negri, Matt Post, Raphael Rubino, Lucia Specia, and Marco Turchi. 2017. Findings of the 2017 conference on machine translation (WMT17). In *Proceedings of the Second Conference on Machine Translation*, pages 169–214, Copenhagen, Denmark. Association for Computational Linguistics.

Ondřej Bojar, Rajen Chatterjee, Christian Federmann, Yvette Graham, Barry Haddow, Matthias Huck, Antonio Jimeno Yepes, Philipp Koehn, Varvara Logacheva, Christof Monz, Matteo Negri, Aurélie Névéol, Mariana Neves, Martin Popel, Matt Post, Raphael Rubino, Carolina Scarton, Lucia Specia, Marco Turchi, Karin Verspoor, and Marcos Zampieri. 2016. Findings of the 2016 conference on machine translation. In *Proceedings of the First Conference on Machine Translation: Volume 2, Shared Task Papers*, pages 131–198, Berlin, Germany. Association for Computational Linguistics.

Chris Callison-Burch, Philipp Koehn, Christof Monz, and Josh Schroeder. 2009a. Findings of the 2009 Workshop on Statistical Machine Translation. In *Proceedings of the Fourth Workshop on Statistical Machine Translation*, pages 1–28, Athens, Greece. Association for Computational Linguistics.

Chris Callison-Burch, Philipp Koehn, Christof Monz, and Josh Schroeder. 2009b. Findings of the 2009 Workshop on Statistical Machine Translation. In *Proceedings of the Fourth Workshop on Statistical Machine Translation*, pages 1–28, Athens, Greece. Association for Computational Linguistics.

M. Cettolo, Marcello Federico, L. Bentivogli, Niehues Jan, Stüker Sebastian, Sudoh Katsuitho, Yoshino Koichiro, and Federmann Christian. 2017. Overview of the iwslt 2017 evaluation campaign.

M. Cettolo, J. Niehues, S. Stüker, L. Bentivogli, R. Cattoni, and Marcello Federico. 2015. The iwslt 2015 evaluation campaign.

Aditi Chaudhary, Karthik Raman, Krishna Srinivasan, and Jiecao Chen. 2020. Dict-mlm: Improved multilingual pre-training using bilingual dictionaries.

Zewen Chi, Li Dong, Shuming Ma, Shaohan Huang Xian-Ling Mao, Heyan Huang, and Furu Wei. 2021a. mt6: Multilingual pretrained text-to-text transformer with translation pairs. *arXiv preprint arXiv:2104.08692*.

Zewen Chi, Li Dong, Furu Wei, Nan Yang, Saksham Singhal, Wenhui Wang, Xia Song, Xian-Ling Mao, Heyan Huang, and Ming Zhou. 2021b. InfoXLM: An information-theoretic framework for cross-lingual language model pre-training. In *Proceedings of the 2021 Conference of the North American Chapter of the Association for Computational Linguistics: Human Language Technologies*, pages 3576–3588, Online. Association for Computational Linguistics.

Kevin Clark, Minh-Thang Luong, Quoc V. Le, and Christopher D. Manning. 2020. ELECTRA: Pre-training Text Encoders as Discriminators Rather Than Generators. *arXiv:2003.10555 [cs]*.

Alexis Conneau, Kartikay Khandelwal, Naman Goyal, Vishrav Chaudhary, Guillaume Wenzek, Francisco Guzmán, Edouard Grave, Myle Ott, Luke Zettlemoyer, and Veselin Stoyanov. 2020a. Unsupervised cross-lingual representation learning at scale. In *Proceedings of the 58th Annual Meeting of the Association for Computational Linguistics*, pages 8440–8451, Online. Association for Computational Linguistics.

Alexis Conneau and Guillaume Lample. 2019. Cross-lingual language model pretraining. In *Advances in Neural Information Processing Systems 32: Annual Conference on Neural Information Processing Systems 2019, NeurIPS 2019, December 8-14, 2019, Vancouver, BC, Canada*, pages 7057–7067.

Alexis Conneau, Ruty Rinott, Guillaume Lample, Adina Williams, Samuel Bowman, Holger Schwenk, and Veselin Stoyanov. 2018. XNLI: Evaluating cross-lingual sentence representations. In *Proceedings of the 2018 Conference on Empirical Methods in Natural Language Processing*, pages 2475–2485, Brussels, Belgium. Association for Computational Linguistics.

Alexis Conneau, Shijie Wu, Haoran Li, Luke Zettlemoyer, and Veselin Stoyanov. 2020b. Emerging cross-lingual structure in pretrained language models. In *Proceedings of the 58th Annual Meeting of the Association for Computational Linguistics*, pages 6022–6034, Online. Association for Computational Linguistics.

Jacob Devlin, Ming-Wei Chang, Kenton Lee, and Kristina Toutanova. 2019. BERT: Pre-training of deep bidirectional transformers for language understanding. In *Proceedings of the 2019 Conference of the North American Chapter of the Association for Computational Linguistics: Human Language Technologies, Volume 1 (Long and Short Papers)*, pages 4171–4186, Minneapolis, Minnesota. Association for Computational Linguistics.

Philipp Dufter and Hinrich Schütze. 2020. Identifying elements essential for BERT's multilinguality. In *Proceedings of the 2020 Conference on Empirical Methods in Natural Language Processing (EMNLP)*, pages 4423–4437, Online. Association for Computational Linguistics.

Ahmed El-Kishky, Vishrav Chaudhary, Francisco Guzmán, and Philipp Koehn. 2020. CCAligned: A massive collection of cross-lingual web-document pairs. In *Proceedings of the 2020 Conference on Empirical Methods in Natural Language Processing (EMNLP)*, pages 5960–5969, Online. Association for Computational Linguistics.

Miquel Esplà, Mikel Forcada, Gema Ramírez-Sánchez, and Hieu Hoang. 2019. ParaCrawl: Web-scale parallel corpora for the languages of the EU. In *Proceedings of Machine Translation Summit XVII Volume 2: Translator, Project and User Tracks*, pages 118–119, Dublin, Ireland. European Association for Machine Translation.

Francisco Guzmán, Peng-Jen Chen, Myle Ott, Juan Pino, Guillaume Lample, Philipp Koehn, Vishrav Chaudhary, and Marc'Aurelio Ranzato. 2019. The FLoRes Evaluation Datasets for Low-Resource Machine Translation: Nepali-English and Sinhala-English. *arXiv:1902.01382 [cs]*.

Junjie Hu, Melvin Johnson, Orhan Firat, Aditya Siddhant, and Graham Neubig. 2021. Explicit Alignment Objectives for Multilingual Bidirectional Encoders. *arXiv:2010.07972 [cs]*.

Junjie Hu, Sebastian Ruder, Aditya Siddhant, Graham Neubig, Orhan Firat, and Melvin Johnson. 2020. XTREME: A Massively Multilingual Multi-task Benchmark for Evaluating Cross-lingual Generalization. *arXiv:2003.11080 [cs]*.

Haoyang Huang, Yaobo Liang, Nan Duan, Ming Gong, Linjun Shou, Daxin Jiang, and Ming Zhou. 2019. Unicoder: A universal language encoder by pre-training with multiple cross-lingual tasks. In *Proceedings of the 2019 Conference on Empirical Methods in Natural Language Processing and the 9th International Joint Conference on Natural Language Processing (EMNLP-IJCNLP)*, pages 2485–2494, Hong Kong, China. Association for Computational Linguistics.

Mihir Kale, Aditya Siddhant, Noah Constant, Melvin Johnson, Rami Al-Rfou, and Linting Xue. 2021. nmt5 – is parallel data still relevant for pre-training massively multilingual language models? *arXiv preprint arXiv:2106.02171*.

Taku Kudo and John Richardson. 2018. SentencePiece: A simple and language independent subword tokenizer and detokenizer for neural text processing. In *Proceedings of the 2018 Conference on Empirical Methods in Natural Language Processing: System Demonstrations*, pages 66–71, Brussels, Belgium. Association for Computational Linguistics.

Anoop Kunchukuttan, Pratik Mehta, and Pushpak Bhattacharyya. 2018. The IIT Bombay English-Hindi parallel corpus. In *Proceedings of the Eleventh International Conference on Language Resources and Evaluation (LREC 2018)*, Miyazaki, Japan. European Language Resources Association (ELRA).

Guillaume Lample and Alexis Conneau. 2019. Cross-lingual Language Model Pretraining. *arXiv:1901.07291 [cs]*.

Guillaume Lample, Alexis Conneau, Marc'Aurelio Ranzato, Ludovic Denoyer, and Hervé Jégou. 2018. Word translation without parallel data. In *6th International Conference on Learning Representations, ICLR 2018, Vancouver, BC, Canada, April 30 - May 3, 2018, Conference Track Proceedings*. OpenReview.net.

Mike Lewis, Yinhan Liu, Naman Goyal, Marjan Ghazvininejad, Abdelrahman Mohamed, Omer Levy, Veselin Stoyanov, and Luke Zettlemoyer. 2020. BART: Denoising sequence-to-sequence pre-training for natural language generation, translation, and comprehension. In *Proceedings of the 58th Annual Meeting of the Association for Computational Linguistics*, pages 7871–7880, Online. Association for Computational Linguistics.

Pierre Lison and Jörg Tiedemann. 2016. OpenSubtitles2016: Extracting large parallel corpora from movie and TV subtitles. In *Proceedings of the Tenth International Conference on Language Resources and Evaluation (LREC'16)*, pages 923–929, Portorož, Slovenia. European Language Resources Association (ELRA).

Yinhan Liu, Jiatao Gu, Naman Goyal, Xian Li, Sergey Edunov, Marjan Ghazvininejad, Mike Lewis, and Luke Zettlemoyer. 2020. Multilingual denoising pre-training for neural machine translation. *Transactions of the Association for Computational Linguistics*, 8:726–742.

Paulius Micikevicius, Sharan Narang, Jonah Alben, Gregory F. Diamos, Erich Elsen, David García, Boris Ginsburg, Michael Houston, Oleksii Kuchaiev, Ganesh Venkatesh, and Hao Wu. 2018. Mixed precision training. In *6th International Conference on Learning Representations, ICLR 2018, Vancouver, BC, Canada, April 30 - May 3, 2018, Conference Track Proceedings*. OpenReview.net.

Pedro Javier Ortiz Suárez, Laurent Romary, and Benoît Sagot. 2020. A monolingual approach to contextualized word embeddings for mid-resource languages. In *Proceedings of the 58th Annual Meeting of the Association for Computational Linguistics*, pages 1703–1714, Online. Association for Computational Linguistics.

Myle Ott, Sergey Edunov, Alexei Baevski, Angela Fan, Sam Gross, Nathan Ng, David Grangier, and Michael Auli. 2019. fairseq: A fast, extensible toolkit for sequence modeling. In *Proceedings of the 2019 Conference of the North American Chapter of the Association for Computational Linguistics (Demonstrations)*, pages 48–53, Minneapolis, Minnesota. Association for Computational Linguistics.

Telmo Pires, Eva Schlinger, and Dan Garrette. 2019. How multilingual is multilingual BERT? In *Pro-*

ceedings of the 57th Annual Meeting of the Association for Computational Linguistics, pages 4996–5001, Florence, Italy. Association for Computational Linguistics.

Matt Post. 2018. A call for clarity in reporting BLEU scores. In *Proceedings of the Third Conference on Machine Translation: Research Papers*, pages 186–191, Brussels, Belgium. Association for Computational Linguistics.

Rico Sennrich, Barry Haddow, and Alexandra Birch. 2016. Edinburgh neural machine translation systems for WMT 16. In *Proceedings of the First Conference on Machine Translation: Volume 2, Shared Task Papers*, pages 371–376, Berlin, Germany. Association for Computational Linguistics.

Aditya Siddhant, Melvin Johnson, Henry Tsai, Naveen Arivazhagan, Jason Riesa, Ankur Bapna, Orhan Firat, and Karthik Raman. 2019. Evaluating the cross-lingual effectiveness of massively multilingual neural machine translation.

Kaitao Song, Xu Tan, Tao Qin, Jianfeng Lu, and Tie-Yan Liu. 2019. MASS: Masked Sequence to Sequence Pre-training for Language Generation. *arXiv:1905.02450 [cs]*.

Linting Xue, Noah Constant, Adam Roberts, Mihir Kale, Rami Al-Rfou, Aditya Siddhant, Aditya Barua, and Colin Raffel. 2021. mT5: A massively multilingual pre-trained text-to-text transformer. *arXiv:2010.11934 [cs]*.

Yinfei Yang, Yuan Zhang, Chris Tar, and Jason Baldridge. 2019. PAWS-X: A cross-lingual adversarial dataset for paraphrase identification. In *Proceedings of the 2019 Conference on Empirical Methods in Natural Language Processing and the 9th International Joint Conference on Natural Language Processing (EMNLP-IJCNLP)*, pages 3687–3692, Hong Kong, China. Association for Computational Linguistics.

Michał Ziemski, Marcin Junczys-Dowmunt, and Bruno Pouliquen. 2016. The United Nations parallel corpus v1.0. In *Proceedings of the Tenth International Conference on Language Resources and Evaluation (LREC'16)*, pages 3530–3534, Portorož, Slovenia. European Language Resources Association (ELRA).

A Data

We list data sources used for pretraining PARADISE++ in Table 9 (monolingual data) and Table 10 (parallel data).

B Pretraining hyperparameters

We use the Adam optimizer ($\epsilon = 10^{-6}, \beta = (0.9, 0.98)$), and warm up the learning rate to a peak of 7×10^{-4} after 10K iterations and then proceed to decay the learning rate with the polynomial decay schedule up until 100K iterations. All code and experiments are performed with `fairseq` (Ott et al., 2019). Following Liu et al. (2020), we add an additional layer-normalization layer on top of both the encoder and decoder to stabilize training with FP16 precision (Micikevicius et al., 2018). All models are trained on 32 V100 16GB GPUs and takes 24 hours to finish training.

C Machine translation evaluation

Following Liu et al. (2020), we use detokenized SacreBLEU (Post, 2018) for all languages unless specified otherwise next. For Japanese we use KyTea[7], for Nepalese, Sinhala, and Hindi we use Indic-NLP[8], for Arabic we use the QCRI Arabic Normalizer[9,10], and for Romanian we use Moses tokenization and script normalization following Sennrich et al. (2016); Liu et al. (2020).

D Machine Translation Finetuning

We finetune our models using the same setup as mBART, warming up the learning rate to 3×10^{-5} over 2500 iterations and then decaying with a polynomial schedule. We use 0.3 dropout and label smoothing $\epsilon = 0.2$.

E Comparison of finetuning approaches

Model	avg	Δ
PARADISE++ (*encoder-decoder*)	74.3	—
decoder-only	73.8	-0.5
encoder-only	72.0	-2.3

Table 5: Ablation of finetuning methods on XNLI.

Table 5 compares our proposed finetuning approach, which combines the representations from both the encoder and the decoder (see §3), to using either of them alone.[11] While prior work either minimally used the decoder if at all (Siddhant et al., 2019; Xue et al., 2021), or only added a classification head on top of the decoder (Lewis et al., 2020), we find that combining them both works best.

F Additional results

We list detailed results by language in this section with results on XNLI in Table 8, PAWS-X in Table 6, and our machine translation ablation (with mBART (Liu et al., 2020) results included) in Table 7. We note that on XNLI that mBART underperforms XLM-R-large, however that may be attributed to the fact that XLM-R was trained for much longer rather than the architectural design.

Model	de	en	es	fr	zh	Avg
mBERT	85.7	94.0	87.4	87.0	77.0	86.2
MMTE	85.1	93.1	87.2	86.9	75.9	85.6
mT5-small	86.2	92.2	86.1	86.6	77.9	85.8
AMBER	89.4	**95.6**	89.2	**90.7**	80.9	89.2
XLM-15	88.5	94.7	89.3	89.6	78.1	88.0
XLM-100	85.9	94.0	88.3	87.4	76.5	86.4
XLM-R-base	87.0	94.2	88.6	88.7	78.5	87.4
XLM-R-large	**89.7**	94.7	**90.1**	90.4	**82.3**	**89.4**
PARADISE++	89.1	94.3	89.6	90.6	**82.3**	89.2

Table 6: Accuracy of zero-shot cross-lingual classification on PAWS-X. Bold numbers highlight the highest scores across languages on the existing models (upper part) and PARADISE variants (bottom part). We source baseline results from Hu et al. (2020, 2021); Xue et al. (2021).

[7] http://www.phontron.com/kytea/

[8] https://github.com/anoopkunchukuttan/indic_nlp_library

[9] https://github.com/qntfy/gomosesgo

[10] https://alt.qcri.org/tools/arabic-normalizer/

[11] For *decoder-only*, we feed the input sequence to both the encoder and the decoder, but add a classification head on top of the decoder only, following Lewis et al. (2020).

Lang. Pair	En-Tr	En-Ro	En-Si	En-Hi	En-Es	Tr-En	Ro-En	Si-En	Hi-En
mBART (ours)	15.8	34.9	2.7	19.0	30.4	21.3	34.3	11.0	20.2
PARADISE (w/o dict.)	16.8	36.2	3.2	20.5	32.4	23.2	35.6	13.2	22.3
PARADISE	17.2	36.5	3.7	20.7	32.7	23.5	35.9	14.0	**23.6**
PARADISE++	**19.0**	37.3	**4.2**	20.7	33.0	**24.9**	36.8	**15.1**	23.5
mBART	17.8	**37.7**	3.3	**20.8**	**34.0**	22.5	**37.8**	13.7	23.5

Table 7: Ablation results on machine translation. Note that mBART is trained with 140x more compute and 3.5x more parameters.

Models	en	zh	es	de	ar	ur	ru	bg	el	fr	hi	sw	th	tr	vi	avg
mBERT	80.8	67.8	73.5	70.0	64.3	57.2	67.8	68.0	65.3	73.4	58.9	49.7	54.1	60.9	69.3	65.4
MMTE	79.6	69.2	71.6	68.2	64.9	60.0	66.2	70.4	67.3	69.5	63.5	61.9	66.2	63.6	69.7	67.5
mT5-small	79.6	65.8	72.7	69.2	65.2	59.9	70.1	71.3	68.6	70.7	62.5	59.7	66.3	64.4	66.3	67.5
AMBER	84.7	71.6	76.9	74.2	70.2	61.0	73.3	74.3	72.5	76.6	66.2	59.9	65.7	73.2	73.4	71.6
XLM-15 (MLM+TLM)	84.1	68.8	77.8	75.7	70.4	62.2	75.0	75.7	73.3	78.0	67.3	67.5	70.5	70.0	73.0	72.6
XLM-100	82.8	70.2	75.5	72.7	66.0	59.8	69.9	71.9	70.4	74.3	62.5	58.1	65.5	66.4	70.7	69.1
XLM-R-base	83.9	73.6	78.3	75.2	71.9	65.4	75.1	76.7	75.4	77.4	69.1	62.2	72.0	70.9	74.0	73.4
mBART	87.7	76.4	81.5	79.8	75.5	—	78.9	—	—	80.6	73.0	—	—	76.1	77.4	—
XLM-R-large	**88.7**	**78.2**	**83.7**	**82.5**	**77.2**	**71.7**	**79.1**	**83.0**	**80.8**	**82.2**	**75.6**	**71.2**	**77.4**	**78.0**	**79.3**	**79.2**
mBART (ours)	77.5	68.0	70.7	68.8	66.7	62.2	68.6	72.1	69.6	70.1	63.4	62.6	66.6	65.0	69.7	68.1
PARADISE (w/o dict.)	**83.3**	72.9	77.2	75.7	64.4	**66.9**	73.4	74.8	75.7	**77.7**	68.5	67.4	71.0	73.3	75.0	73.1
PARADISE	83.0	**74.0**	**79.0**	**76.5**	**68.5**	66.8	**74.3**	**76.0**	**76.4**	**77.7**	**70.2**	**70.5**	**72.3**	**74.2**	**75.4**	**74.3**

Table 8: Accuracy of zero-shot crosslingual classification on the XNLI dataset. Bold numbers highlight the highest scores across languages on the existing models (upper part) and PARADISE variants (bottom part). Results for previous work are sourced from Hu et al. (2020, 2021); Xue et al. (2021).

Language	Data source	Data size (GB)
En	Wiki	14G
De	Wiki	5.9G
Fr	Wiki	4.5G
Es	Wiki	3.7G
Ja	Wiki	3.0G
Ru	Wiki	6.2G
Ar	Wiki	1.7G
Ne	CC100	3.8G
Si	CC100	3.7G
Ro	Wiki+WLM	2.5G
Zh	Wiki+WLM	4.4G
El	Wiki+WLM	2.9G
Eu	Wiki+OSCAR	0.6G
Bg	Wiki+OSCAR	2.5G
Hi	Wiki+OSCAR	2.3G
Sw	Wiki+CC100	1.1G
Th	Wiki+OSCAR	2.4G
Ur	Wiki+OSCAR	1.9G
Vi	Wiki+OSCAR	2.8G
Tr	Wiki+OSCAR	2.4G
Total	—	72G

Table 9: Monolingual Data Statistics. Wiki refers to Wikipedia, and WLM refers to the News Crawl data from CommonCrawl used in WMT.

Language	Data source	Data size (GB)	# Pairs
Ar	UNPC	2.0G	5554595
Bg	ParaCrawl	1.9G	6470710
De	ParaCrawl	2.0G	9685483
El	ParaCrawl	2.0G	6676200
Es	ParaCrawl	2.0G	9138031
Eu	OPUS	0.1G	585210
Fr	ParaCrawl	2.0G	8485669
Hi	IITB	0.4G	1609682
Ja	JParaCrawl	2.0G	6366802
Ne	CCAligned	0.2G	487157
Ro	ParaCrawl	1.3G	6160525
Ru	ParaCrawl	1.6G	5377911
Si	CCAligned	0.2G	619730
Sw	OPUS	0.2G	699719
Th	OpenSubtitles	0.4G	3281533
Tr	OpenSubtitles	2.0G	32077240
Ur	CCAligned	0.3G	1371930
Vi	OpenSubtitles	0.2G	3505276
Zh	UNPC	2.0G	7706183
Total	—	23G	126882448

Table 10: Parallel Data Statistics

When does CLIP generalize better than unimodal models? When judging human-centric concepts

Romain Bielawski
ANITI, UT & CerCo, CNRS, France
romain.bielawski@univ-tlse3.fr

Benjamin Devillers
ANITI, UT & CerCo, CNRS, France
benjamin.devillers@univ-tlse3.fr

Tim Van De Cruys
Université de Louvain, Belgique
tim.vandecruys@kuleven.be

Rufin VanRullen
ANITI, UT & CerCo, CNRS, France
rufin.vanrullen@cnrs.fr

Abstract

CLIP, a vision-language network trained with a multimodal contrastive learning objective on a large dataset of images and captions, has demonstrated impressive zero-shot ability in various tasks. However, recent work showed that in comparison to unimodal (visual) networks, CLIP's multimodal training does not benefit generalization (e.g. few-shot or transfer learning) for standard visual classification tasks such as object, street numbers or animal recognition. Here, we hypothesize that CLIP's improved unimodal generalization abilities may be most prominent in domains that involve human-centric concepts (cultural, social, aesthetic, affective...); this is because CLIP's training dataset is mainly composed of image annotations made by humans for other humans. To evaluate this, we use 3 tasks that require judging human-centric concepts: sentiment analysis on tweets, genre classification on books or movies. We introduce and publicly release a new multimodal dataset for movie genre classification. We compare CLIP's visual stream against two visually trained networks and CLIP's textual stream against two linguistically trained networks, as well as multimodal combinations of these networks. We show that CLIP generally outperforms other networks, whether using one or two modalities. We conclude that CLIP's multimodal training is beneficial for both unimodal and multimodal tasks that require classification of human-centric concepts.

1 Introduction

Vision-language pretraining in neural networks is gaining popularity due to the growing interest in multimodal tasks such a Visual Question Answering or Image Captioning (Anderson et al., 2017; Lu et al., 2019; Li et al., 2019; Singh et al., 2019), but also to the availability of online resources that allow to build large-scale training datasets without manual annotations (Radford et al., 2021; Jia et al., 2021). In theory, training a model on multimodal data should help improve its representation of data from each of the modalities. For an image-text model, for instance, the image features could be enriched by the abstraction of the linguistic data –the semantic grounding property, and inversely, the linguistic features could gain informativeness through visual grounding (Harnad, 1990).

Unfortunately, this does not always happen in practice. Recently, Devillers et al. (2021) evaluated the visual generalization abilities of CLIP (Radford et al., 2021), a popular network trained with a contrastive learning objective on more than 400M image-caption pairs scraped from the web, and other multimodal models (Sariyildiz et al., 2020; Desai and Johnson, 2020). They showed that for standard object classification tasks (e.g. digit, fashion item or natural image classification), multimodal networks like CLIP underperformed compared to other unimodal (vision-only) models like BiT-M (Kolesnikov et al., 2019) in transfer learning, few-shot learning and unsupervised learning settings. Here, we revisit this question using datasets focusing on more "human-centric" concepts.

Human learning generally involves interacting with multimodal data. Thus, one could expect that CLIP's representations of images and text should be somewhat closer to human representations than those learned by unimodal models. Moreover, given that CLIP was trained on image-caption pairs from a variety of sources from the Internet (including social networks), we can assume that an important part of its training captions was written by humans for other humans. This is different from standard vision datasets, in which labels or annotations are sometimes human-generated (e.g. through Amazon's Mechanical Turk), but always produced for machine-learning purposes. Again, this difference should bring CLIP's representations closer to human ones when compared to unimodal models.

Proceedings of the 7th Workshop on Representation Learning for NLP, pages 29 - 38
May 26, 2022

Thus, there should exist at least *some specific tasks* for which CLIP's multimodal training provides advantages over unimodal models. As an example, consider the task of assigning a genre to a movie based on its poster and title. This requires retrieving fine-grained information about, among other things, the artistic, emotional or stylistic aspect of an image or a piece of text (or both). This can only be properly achieved if the model's training offered appropriate exposure to such human-centric concepts. Here, we use the term *human-centric* whenever a concept refers to cultural, social, aesthetic and/or affective components of the world.

We thus make the hypothesis that CLIP should perform better than unimodal models in generalization tasks where human-centric concepts are involved. We evaluate this hypothesis on three tasks involving such human-centric concepts: sentiment analysis on tweets; genre classification of books; genre classification of movies. All tasks can be performed based on visual data (images), text data (tweet, book or movie title, movie plot summary), or both. For the movie genre classification, we introduce a new, large-scale multimodal dataset obtained by a crawling on The Movie Database (TMDb). As detailed below, we find that CLIP outperforms unimodal models in both vision and text-based classification, as well as pairwise combinations of these unimodal models in the case of multimodal (image+text) classification. Consequently, CLIP establishes a new SOTA on these tasks.

We provide our code for reproducibility[1].

2 Models

We compare CLIP (trained contrastively on both images and text) against several unimodal models. For fairer comparisons, all the vision models are ResNet50 (He et al., 2015) based architectures and all the text models are transformer encoders.

CLIP was trained using a contrastive loss on a large (400M) set of image-text pairs. The training of CLIP consists in creating a joint (multimodal) embedding space. For one batch of image-text pairs, the objective of the network is that the embedding of an image (through a ResNet50 backbone, here simply referred to as CLIP) and the embedding of its text description (through a transformer backbone, here referred to as CLIP-T) are as close as possible, while the embedding of an image and the embeddings of text descriptions of other images in the batch are as far as possible. After training, the text encoder and the image encoder can be used as single-modality encoders.

For unimodally trained vision networks, we use two pretrained ResNet50-based models: the standard ResNet50 that was trained for classification on ImageNet-1K (here referred to as RN50), and BiT-M that was trained on ImageNet-22K (Deng et al., 2009).

For unimodal text embeddings, we test two standard text encoders against CLIP's: Bert-large and Bert-base (Devlin et al., 2018). We use the Bert sentence transformer version (Reimers and Gurevych, 2019), based on Bert's [CLS] token and fine-tuned on SNLI (Bowman et al., 2015) and MultiNLI (Williams et al., 2018). Among the transformer encoders provided in the HuggingFace (Hug) repository at the time our experiments were conducted, these were the two best-performing across several text classification tasks, and are now still close to SOTA. These versions of Bert-large and Bert-base are fine-tuned on downstream text classification tasks, but we refer to them in this paper simply as Bert-large and Bert-base.

Although all 3 text encoders are transformer encoders (Vaswani et al., 2017), they do not have the same number of parameters. Bert-large has 300M, Bert-base has 110M, and CLIP-T has 80M parameters. This gives a structural disadvantage to CLIP-T, which only strengthens our conclusions, as we found CLIP-T to be the overall best-performing text model.

We consider both unimodal tasks (classification of images or text), as well as multimodal tasks (classification of image-text pairs). When performing a unimodal task, the encoding of the image (resp. the text) is used directly by the corresponding classifier. When performing a multimodal task (image-text based classification), the encoding of an image by a visual model and the encoding of the corresponding text by a textual model are simply concatenated to create the multimodal vector that is used for the classification.

For BiT-M and RN50, we use the last layer output before the classification head used for their training, which counts 2048 dimensions. For CLIP, we use the latent vector in the multimodal space generated by the visual pipeline, counting 1024 dimensions; for CLIP-T, the one generated by the textual pipeline (1024 dimensions); and for the

[1] Link not displayed here to preserve anonymity

two Bert models, we use the vectors directly provided by the Sentence Transformer pipelines (1024-dimensional for Bert-large and 768-dimensional for Bert-small).

Figure 1: An original cover from the Book Cover dataset (left) and the associated masked cover (right). The title, the name of the author and parts of the text have been blacked out by the EAST algorithm, while the white text was incompletely detected, but subsequently blurred by the second algorithm. This sample belongs to the "Children's books" genre. Its title is: "Frances Audio Collection CD (I Can Read Level 2)". This image is copyright from Amazon.com, Inc. and used here for academic purpose only.

3 Datasets

We evaluate the models on three datasets composed of labelled image and text data, that can be inputted as pairs for multimodal classification tasks, or used as single inputs for unimodal classification tasks. The language part of all these datasets is in English.

3.1 MVSA

MVSA or "Multi-View Sentiment Analysis" (Niu et al., 2016) is a dataset of pairs of images and associated text from Twitter, labelled with three possible sentiments (Positive, Neutral or Negative). Each image and each piece of text has three labels given by three different users, adding up to 6 labels for each image-text pair. We assign a score for each label (Positive: 2, Neutral: 1, Negative: 0) and we compute the rounded average score for each pair. By doing so, we get only one label per image-text pair that we can then use for single-label classification across modalities.

3.2 Book covers

The Book Covers dataset was introduced by Iwana et al. (2017). It consists of 57k images of book covers scraped from the Amazon website, with their title as text information. Each pair of cover+title is labelled with one genre among 30 possibilities. A cleaner version of the dataset, removing one genre and grouping two similar ones, with only 28 classes and 55.1k images, was later introduced by Lucieri et al. (2020). This is the dataset we use for our experiments.

3.3 Plotster and TMDb

We introduce and publicly release the *Plotster* dataset[2], obtained by crawling TMDb (www.themoviedb.org) using their provided API. It consists of 207,902 triplets of {poster, title, plot} (split in 189,185 train samples and 18,717 test samples), with each having several potential labels among 19 genres. A representative sample from this dataset is shown in Figure 2. Typically, each movie has between 1 and 6 genres, with an average of 1.7. Each poster is an RGB image of 900×600 pixels (height$\times$width). Plots have an average length of 310.8 characters, and titles an average length of 18.6 characters. For text input, in unimodal or multimodal settings, we can choose either plot or title. The results of both configurations were computed and are displayed in this paper.

Figure 2: A data sample from *Plotster*. The image displayed here is property of The Walt Disney Company / Marvel Entertainment and under the CC BY-SA 2.0 license.

A previous crawling on TMDb had been made by Mangolin et al. (2020). It contained only 10,594 movies, as the authors aimed to retrieve other pieces of data such as trailer video clips and subtitles. They had not included titles in their dataset. From these movies, 10,554 (i.e., 99.6%) can also be found in *Plotster*. For comparison, we isolated the posters and plots from this dataset, and verified that our results obtained on the full *Plotster* were still valid on this subset.

In another control experiment, we verified that CLIP's improved performance on the *Plotster*

[2]Link not displayed here to preserve anonymity

Vision \ Text	None	Bert-base	Bert-large	CLIP-T
None	∅	63.33 ± 0.18	64.02 ± 0.74	<u>64.60</u> ± 0.30
RN50	55.17 ± 0.37	63.93 ± 0.36	63.92 ± 0.55	64.13 ± 0.37
BiT-M	60.0 ± 1.46	61.93 ± 2.05	63.16 ± 2.82	62.77 ± 0.72
CLIP	**63.07** ± 0.23	**<u>66.03</u>** ± 0.15	**<u>66.03</u>** ± 0.6	65.58 ± 0.38

Table 1: Accuracies for the MVSA dataset. CLIP is the best vision model, CLIP-T the best text model. All text models perform similarly in both unimodal and multimodal setting, except when paired with CLIP (which yields the best performance of each column).

Vision		None	Bert-base	Bert-large	CLIP-T
None		∅	54.70 ± 0.25	54.92 ± 0.43	<u>57.28</u> ± 0.27
Standard	RN50	10.04 ± 4.33	54.85 ± 0.52	55.53 ± 0.39	57.20 ± 0.49
	BiT-M	29.33 ± 0.92	50.11 ± 0.57	50.49 ± 0.59	52.60 ± 0.46
	CLIP	**53.75** ± 0.23	60.38 ± 0.34	60.62 ± 0.27	**<u>60.66</u>** ± 0.26
Masked	RN50	10.41 ± 2.43	54.26 ± 0.25	55.11 ± 0.17	57.26 ± 0.29
	BiT-M	24.87 ± 0.99	48.93 ± 0.77	50.09 ± 0.71	52.08 ± 0.59
	CLIP	**33.04** ± 0.21	57.86 ± 0.45	58.47 ± 0.40	**<u>59.54</u>** ± 0.28

Table 2: Accuracies for the Book Cover dataset (standard images on top, masked images on the bottom). CLIP and CLIP-T are the best performing models of each unimodal test, and together provide the best multimodal combination for both standard and masked images. Masks diminish the performance of all models (and their combinations), but the advantage for CLIP (and CLIP-T) remains.

dataset was not a result of specific movie posters, plots and titles from TMDb having been included in CLIP's training (as the training set is not public, there is no direct way to determine this). For our control experiment, we crawled TMDb again, looking for movies with a release date later than January 5, 2021, date of the OpenAI blog post introducing CLIP. We thus assume that most of this data could not have been included in CLIP's training dataset. The new crawl resulted in 20,280 movies, only 93 of which had been present in the original *Plotster* dataset. We tested on these 20,280 new samples the classifiers trained on *Plotster* (only in unimodal settings), and report the corresponding results.

3.4 Masking

CLIP has been found to have an ability to "read" text inside images (Goh et al., 2021). As most of the images in the Book Cover dataset and in *Plotster* have text on them, and as this text could be informative about the genre of the book or movie, we worried that this ability could give CLIP an unfair advantage over other vision models. To minimize this possibility, we created alternative versions of these two datasets by applying a masking procedure on the images (see Figure 1). We used the EAST algorithm (Zhou et al., 2017) to generate bounding boxes around text; if the score given to a text detection reached a certain threshold, a black rectangle was applied over the corresponding bounding box. On top of that, a second algorithm detects the remaining small white text using a thresholding method, a saturation filter and a size filter, and then does a Telea inpainting (Telea, 2004) to remove it. On 10 randomly selected posters, we verified that this algorithm masked or blurred 84% of the readable characters. It masked or blurred 95% of them on 10 randomly selected book covers as well.

The results on the datasets with masks are reported along with those of the originals.

4 Results

To compare the generalization capabilities of our text, vision, and multimodal models, we focus on transfer learning and few-shot learning settings.

4.1 Transfer learning

Our first experiment is transfer learning. We use the pretrained networks (see Section 2) with frozen weights as encoders, and train a new classification head for each of our datasets in unimodal or multimodal settings.

For transfer learning in single-label classification (sentiment on MVSA, book genre), we plug on top of the frozen feature vector encoder one dense layer (ReLu activations) bringing the dimensions down

Vision \ Text		None	Title			Plot		
			Bert-base	Bert-large	CLIP-T	Bert-base	Bert-large	CLIP-T
None		∅	.314 ± .01	.323 ± .01	.397 ± .00	.582 ± .00	.599 ± .01	.612 ± .00
Standard	RN50	.090 ± .01	.338 ± .01	.363 ± .01	.393 ± .02	.578 ± .01	.599 ± .01	.599 ± .01
	BiT-M	.415 ± .01	.490 ± .01	.499 ± .01	.507 ± .01	.625 ± .01	.637 ± .01	.631 ± .01
	CLIP	**.526** ± .01	.559 ± .01	.558 ± .01	**.593** ± .01	.672 ± .00	.683 ± .00	**.687** ± .00
Masked	RN50	.070 ± .01	.335 ± .02	.352 ± .01	.383 ± .02	.576 ± .01	.597 ± .01	.596 ± .01
	BiT-M	.372 ± .00	.457 ± .02	.480 ± .01	.490 ± .01	.617 ± .01	.631 ± .01	.621 ± .01
	CLIP	**.449** ± .01	.525 ± .01	.534 ± .01	**.564** ± .00	.658 ± .00	.667 ± .00	**.676** ± .00

Table 3: f1-scores for the *Plotster* dataset. CLIP is the best model in vision, CLIP-T the best in text whether titles or plots are given as input, and CLIP+CLIP-T is the best multimodal combination in all cases. The masking doesn't affect the advantage for CLIP.

to 256, and then another dense layer (softmax activation) for the classification. We then train only the weights of these 2 layers on the classification task with a Cross-Entropy Loss; therefore the network learns to output a probability density over the classes.

For multi-label classification (movie genres) the loss is a Binary Cross-Entropy Loss, and therefore the second dense layer outputs a number between 0 and 1 for each class. As the ground-truth label vector for one sample is an 19-dimensional one-hot vector, we round the 19-dimensional prediction of the network to get a binary predicted label vector. A f1-score (Pedregosa et al., 2011) comparing the predicted label vector to the ground-truth vector is reported, as raw accuracy is not a reliable measurement for multi-label classification. The f1-score is computed for each movie, and subsequently averaged over the test set of each dataset. For f1-scores, as for accuracy, the higher the better.

Tables 1 and 2 show the results on the single-label datasets: MVSA and Book Cover. The first column corresponds to the result of the vision-only experiment, the first line to those of the text-only experiments, and the other cells display the results of the multimodal ones. Table 3 shows the results for the multi-label dataset (Plotster). In all tables, the best vision-only performance is highlighted in **bold**, the best text-only is underlined and the best multimodal one is **both underlined and bold**. The standard deviation is calculated over five experiments with different random seeds and random initialization of the weights of the classifiers.

On MVSA (Table 1), CLIP is the best performing vision-only model and CLIP-T the best text-only model. The best multimodal combinations are CLIP+Bert-base and CLIP+Bert-large, with CLIP+CLIP-T near the same level (less than 0.5 percentage point behind). This is not unexpected, as CLIP-T counts much fewer parameters than Bert-base or Bert-large (see section 2).

For the Book Cover dataset (Table 2), CLIP is by far the best performing vision model, both with the standard covers and with the masked covers as input. The difference between CLIP's accuracy (53.8%) and the other two (RN50: 10.0%; BiT-M: 29.3%) remains high in the masked configuration (with CLIP at 33.0% and the other two below 25%), even though CLIP has lost the ability to read the text on the covers. This indicates that CLIP's reading ability is not the sole explanation for its advantage over vision-only models. CLIP-T is again the best text-only model. Here, the best multimodal combination is CLIP+CLIP-T for both standard and masked configurations. Finally, compared to previously established SOTA performance on the Book Cover dataset by Lucieri et al. (2020), CLIP easily beats the previous visual SOTA (27.8 % accuracy), CLIP-T the previous textual SOTA (55.6%), and CLIP+CLIP-T the previous bimodal SOTA (55.7%).

Concerning our new *Plotster* dataset (Table 3), similar conclusions emerge. In vision-only conditions, RN50 performs relatively poorly; in the standard dataset, CLIP largely outperforms BiT, and this difference decreases but remains in the masked dataset. In text-only conditions, CLIP-T is the best model, both with titles and plots as input. Finally, in the multimodal settings, CLIP+CLIP-T is always the best-performing combination, whether using standard or masked images, title or plot as textual inputs. As before, the prevalence of CLIP in all task settings, even when text has been removed from the movie posters, indicates that its superiority in our movie genre transfer learning task is not solely due to its reading ability. We surmise that this advantage reflects a form of semantic grounding resulting from CLIP's multimodal training.

We also tested CLIP, CLIP-T and their combination on a subset of *Plotster* corresponding to the dataset of Mangolin et al. (2020), in order to compare with previous SOTA values. We found that CLIP beats the previously established visual SOTA (f1-score of 0.603 against 0.409), CLIP-T the textual SOTA (f1-score of 0.589 against 0.488) and CLIP+CLIP-T the bimodal SOTA (0.670 against 0.628).

In a separate control experiment, we tested all our models (trained on the entire *Plotster* training set) on a new set of movies, all released after OpenAI's initial blogpost introducing the CLIP model. On this new test set, CLIP's f1-score changes from 0.526 to 0.439, BiT's goes from 0.415 to 0.318 and RN50's from 0.090 to 0.020. CLIP-T's (with title as text input) goes from 0.397 to 0.276, Bert-large from 0.323 to 0.237 and Bert-base from 0.314 to 0.229. The general diminution of the f1-score across all networks is probably due to the fact that features trained to classify older movies do not work equally well when they are applied to more recent movies. Nevertheless, CLIP and CLIP-T remain the top-performing models; as it is unlikely that these recent movie posters and captions had been included in CLIP's training dataset, we conclude that CLIP's high transfer-learning performance on *Plotster* is not a consequence of prior exposure to these stimuli, but a true form of generalization.

In general, we see that in all the unimodal settings, CLIP outperforms the other vision models, and CLIP-T the other text models. This is true, even though CLIP has roughly the same number of parameters than RN50 or BiT-M, and fewer dimensions in its latent space (and thus, less parameters in its classifier head). Similarly, CLIP-T counts much fewer parameters than Bert-base or Bert-large (although it has a higher-dimensional latent space than Bert-small). In most of the multimodal settings, changing from one visual model to CLIP or from one textual model to CLIP-T improves performance (the only exceptions are for CLIP-T on MVSA and on *Plotster* with plots as text inputs). The best multimodal models always involve CLIP, and also involve CLIP-T in all cases except MVSA. This makes the CLIP + CLIP-T combination the best overall multimodal model in our experiments.

4.2 Few-shot learning

The second experiment we conduct is a visual few-shot learning task: we measure test classification accuracy based on exposure to a small number of randomly chosen training samples (or "prototypes") from each class. We can thus compare the results for our datasets with those of Devillers et al. (2021), who also measured visual few-shot learning performance.

In their paper, Devillers et al. (2021) used a single prototype vector for each class, obtained by averaging the latent representation of the N randomly drawn training samples for that class. Here, we prefer to retain all N individual samples as prototypes, and use a 1-nearest-neighbor (1-NN) classifier (Pedregosa et al., 2011) to classify the new vectors. We verified that this method, when applied to the same datasets as in (Devillers et al., 2021), does not alter their conclusion (see the first plot of Figure 3). To select the class prototypes of *Plotster* (which is a multiclass dataset), we randomly choose movies with a given class label. For example, a movie with genres "adventure" and "action" could be randomly chosen as a prototype of either genre. Moreover, when predicting the genres of a movie using the 1-NN classifier, we predict all the genres of the closest prototype.

Figure 3 reports the few-shot accuracy on the Book Covers and MVSA datasets as well as the f1 score for the *Plotster* datasets. Contrary to the conclusion of Devillers et al. (2021) using standard visual datasets (see Figure 3, left), our results show a clear advantage to CLIP in our more "human-centric" visual tasks, even when masks are applied. For MVSA, the networks required more samples (between 20 and 100) to reach above-chance accuracy than for the other datasets (that use 1 to 10 samples). In that specific case, the three models are more difficult to distinguish, but CLIP still appears better than the other two visual models.

4.3 Summary

In the visual domain, CLIP systematically outperforms the unimodal vision models in transfer learning (Tables 1-3) and in visual few-shot learning (Figure 3), despite having a smaller embedding space than the other two ResNet50-based models. Part of CLIP's superiority may be due to its ability to read, but the advantage remains when text is removed from the images. This conclusion goes

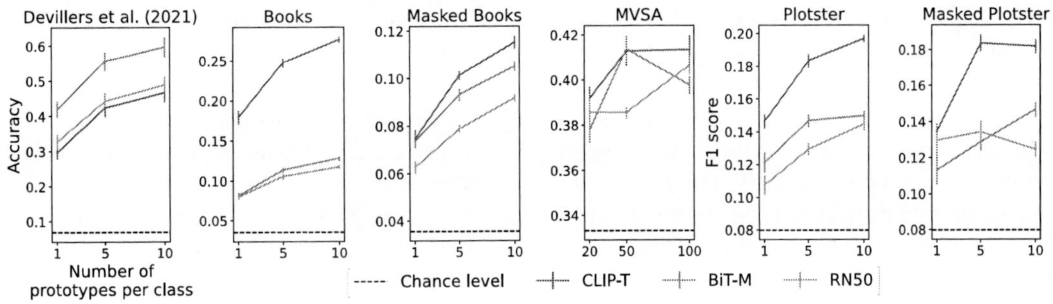

Figure 3: Few-shot learning accuracy (vision-only) over single label datasets (Book Covers, MVSA) and f1-score over the multilabel *Plotster* datasets. The leftmost panel reports average accuracy on 6 standard visual datasets used in Devillers et al. (2021) – namely CIFAR10, CIFAR100, CUB, FashionMNIST, MNIST and SVHN. Accuracy was recomputed using the same method as for our datasets; the conclusions are identical to those of Devillers et al. (2021): CLIP does not perform better than RN50 or BiT in this few-shot learning setting. On the contrary, for our datasets CLIP outperforms the two other vision models. The advantage is reduced but still present when masks are applied.

against the observations of Devillers et al. (2021) using standard visual datasets (including SVHN, a digit reading dataset), where CLIP was never better (and often slightly worse) than other ResNet50 based models, including RN50 and BiT-M. We explain this difference by the nature of the classification performed: our tasks involve human-centric concepts, as defined earlier.

In the text domain, CLIP-T, despite having been trained with fewer parameters than the other two transformers (Bert-small and Bert-large), is systematically the best performing model in transfer learning.

Across seven multimodal settings (MVSA dataset; Book Covers dataset [with / without masks]; *Plotster* with [titles / plots] $\times$ [with / without masks]), CLIP+CLIP-T was the best multimodal combination in six cases. In the remaining case (MVSA), it was a tie between CLIP+Bert-large and CLIP+Bert-small (two language models that count many more parameters than CLIP-T).

We think that the semantic grounding provided by linguistic inputs when training CLIP's visual stream, and respectively, the visual grounding provided by image features when training the CLIP-T language model, shaped their latent space in a way that makes it possible to better grasp the human-centric components of an image or a text.

5 Discussion and conclusion

CLIP's generalization abilities were originally described in the context of zero-shot learning (Radford et al., 2021), but they may also extend to other settings, including transfer learning and few-shot learning. Past work has revealed that this is not always the case (Devillers et al., 2021). Considering the latent representations learned by CLIP may help us better understand when multimodal training does or does not benefit generalization abilities, continuing the work of Hossain et al. (2019). In our case, it appears that one of the domains where the improvement is most significant is when human-centric concepts are being judged.

During their joint contrastive training, CLIP and CLIP-T have learned to extract common information between image and text modalities, so that the two streams would result in similar embedding vectors. This means that the representation of text in CLIP-T has been enriched with visual data, and symmetrically, that the representation of images in CLIP has been improved by semantic or linguistic enrichment. This is what is collectively referred to as the "semantic grounding" property (Harnad, 1990; Bender and Koller, 2020). However, another consequence of this multimodal contrastive training is that when learning a common ground between modalities, some relevant information could be lost. For text, what cannot be directly linked to images (including grammatical or syntactic properties); and for images, what is not directly relevant to the text description (including fine-grained visual details that are rarely mentioned in the corresponding caption). This information loss might be the reason why CLIP was found to perform worse than standard vision-only models in a unimodal setting with standard visual datasets (Devillers et al., 2021). For the same reason, one could actually expect that in a multimodal setting, the combination of CLIP's vision and text streams (CLIP+CLIP-T) could lead to worse performance than other combinations (e.g. RN50+Bert). The unimodal networks are trained to capture the relevant features of their modality, and when combined, could cover the multimodal feature space more fully than CLIP, a network trained to discard information that is not redundant across modalities. Our results show that, at least in our human-centric classification tasks, this limitation was not consequential: CLIP, CLIP-T and their combination often performed optimally. This may be because human-centric information is particularly well captured by features expressed in *both* images and text, rather than in each modality independently. On the other hand, this same reasoning could explain why CLIP+Bert combinations performed slightly better than CLIP+CLIP-T on MVSA: Bert may have provided additional information not captured by CLIP, which was lacking in CLIP-T because of their redundant embeddings (or, this might simply be due to the fact that Bert has many more parameters than CLIP-T).

Our suggestion that CLIP (and CLIP-T) perform particularly well when judging human-centric concepts resonates with recent findings relating CLIP's representations to human brain representations. Goh et al. (2021) reported that some artificial neurons in CLIP's visual stream (but not in standard visual models like Inception or ResNet) are systematically activated by specific "concepts" such as a particular person, emotion, country, religion, etc. Furthermore, these neurons could be equally activated by visual features (e.g., a photograph or drawing of the person's face) or by written text (e.g., the person's name). The authors related this multimodal invariance to properties of specific biological neurons found in the human hippocampus and temporal medial lobe, called "concept cells": these cells would also systematically activate when presented with a picture, drawing or written word representing a specific concept, such as a photograph of the actress Jennifer Aniston or her written name (Quiroga et al., 2005; Reddy and Thorpe, 2014). Indeed, more recently Choksi et al. (2021) compared brain fMRI representations in the human hippocampus with the patterns of representations measured in various vision models. They found that CLIP and other networks trained with multimodal objectives were more similar to human hippocampus representations than standard vision models (including RN50 and BiT-M). This could explain why a multimodal network like CLIP performs better when judging "human-centric concepts".

To conclude, we think that it is crucial to investigate the specific domains in which a multimodal training such as CLIP's can (or cannot) improve generalization. Our work indicates that *multimodality* will be key for developing algorithms designed for human-centric tasks (even for *unimodal* tasks) such as detecting emotions, analyzing personality, conducting a conversation or, more generally, when human-machine interactions are involved.

6 Acknowledgements

All book cover images and book titles are copyright Amazon.com, Inc. The display of the images are transformative and are used as fair use for academic purposes.

All posters displayed here are property of The Walt Disney Company / Marvel Entertainment and under the CC BY-SA 2.0 license.

This research was supported by ANITI ANR grant ANR-19-PI3A-0004 and COCOBOTS ANR-DLR bilateral French-German project ANR-21-FAI2-0005.

References

Huggingface sentence transformer repository. https://huggingface.co/sentence-transformers. Accessed: 2022-02-21.

Peter Anderson, Xiaodong He, Chris Buehler, Damien Teney, Mark Johnson, Stephen Gould, and Lei Zhang. 2017. Bottom-up and top-down attention for image captioning and VQA. *CoRR*, abs/1707.07998.

Emily M. Bender and Alexander Koller. 2020. Climbing towards NLU: On meaning, form, and understanding in the age of data. In *Proceedings of the 58th Annual Meeting of the Association for Computational Linguistics*, pages 5185–5198, Online. Association for Computational Linguistics.

Samuel R. Bowman, Gabor Angeli, Christopher Potts, and Christopher D. Manning. 2015. A large annotated corpus for learning natural language inference. In *Proceedings of the 2015 Conference on Empirical Methods in Natural Language Processing (EMNLP)*. Association for Computational Linguistics.

Bhavin Choksi, Milad Mozafari, Rufin Vanrullen, and Leila Reddy. 2021. Multimodal neural networks better explain multivoxel patterns in the hippocampus. In *Neural Information Processing Systems (NeurIPS) conference: 3rd Workshop on Shared Visual Representations in Human and Machine Intelligence (SVRHM 2021)*.

Jia Deng, Wei Dong, Richard Socher, Li-Jia Li, Kai Li, and Li Fei-Fei. 2009. Imagenet: A large-scale hierarchical image database. In *2009 IEEE conference on computer vision and pattern recognition*, pages 248–255. Ieee.

Karan Desai and Justin Johnson. 2020. Virtex: Learning visual representations from textual annotations. *CoRR*, abs/2006.06666.

Benjamin Devillers, Bhavin Choksi, Romain Bielawski, and Rufin VanRullen. 2021. Does language help generalization in vision models? In *Proceedings of the 25th Conference on Computational Natural Language Learning*, pages 171–182, Online. Association for Computational Linguistics.

Jacob Devlin, Ming-Wei Chang, Kenton Lee, and Kristina Toutanova. 2018. BERT: pre-training of deep bidirectional transformers for language understanding. *CoRR*, abs/1810.04805.

Gabriel Goh, Nick Cammarata †, Chelsea Voss †, Shan Carter, Michael Petrov, Ludwig Schubert, Alec Radford, and Chris Olah. 2021. Multimodal neurons in artificial neural networks. *Distill*. Https://distill.pub/2021/multimodal-neurons.

Stevan Harnad. 1990. The symbol grounding problem. *Physica D: Nonlinear Phenomena*, 42(1):335–346.

Kaiming He, Xiangyu Zhang, Shaoqing Ren, and Jian Sun. 2015. Deep residual learning for image recognition. *CoRR*, abs/1512.03385.

MD. Zakir Hossain, Ferdous Sohel, Mohd Fairuz Shiratuddin, and Hamid Laga. 2019. A comprehensive survey of deep learning for image captioning. *ACM Comput. Surv.*, 51(6).

Brian Kenji Iwana, Syed Tahseen Raza Rizvi, Sheraz Ahmed, Andreas Dengel, and Seiichi Uchida. 2017. Judging a book by its cover.

Chao Jia, Yinfei Yang, Ye Xia, Yi-Ting Chen, Zarana Parekh, Hieu Pham, Quoc V. Le, Yun-Hsuan Sung, Zhen Li, and Tom Duerig. 2021. Scaling up visual and vision-language representation learning with noisy text supervision. *CoRR*, abs/2102.05918.

Alexander Kolesnikov, Lucas Beyer, Xiaohua Zhai, Joan Puigcerver, Jessica Yung, Sylvain Gelly, and Neil Houlsby. 2019. Large scale learning of general visual representations for transfer. *CoRR*, abs/1912.11370.

Liunian Harold Li, Mark Yatskar, Da Yin, Cho-Jui Hsieh, and Kai-Wei Chang. 2019. Visualbert: A simple and performant baseline for vision and language. *CoRR*, abs/1908.03557.

Jiasen Lu, Dhruv Batra, Devi Parikh, and Stefan Lee. 2019. Vilbert: Pretraining task-agnostic visiolinguistic representations for vision-and-language tasks. *CoRR*, abs/1908.02265.

Adriano Lucieri, Huzaifa Sabir, Shoaib Ahmed Siddiqui, Syed Tahseen Raza Rizvi, Brian Kenji Iwana, Seiichi Uchida, Andreas Dengel, and Sheraz Ahmed. 2020. Benchmarking deep learning models for classification of book covers. *SN Computer Science*, 1(3):139.

Rafael B. Mangolin, Rodolfo Miranda Pereira, Alceu S. Britto Jr., Carlos Nascimento Silla Jr., Valéria Delisandra Feltrim, Diego Bertolini, and Yandre M. G. Costa. 2020. A multimodal approach for multi-label movie genre classification. *CoRR*, abs/2006.00654.

Teng Niu, Shiai Zhu, Lei Pang, and Abdulmotaleb El-Saddik. 2016. Sentiment analysis on multi-view social data. In *MultiMedia Modeling*, page 15–27.

Fabian Pedregosa, Gaël Varoquaux, Alexandre Gramfort, Vincent Michel, Bertrand Thirion, Olivier Grisel, Mathieu Blondel, Peter Prettenhofer, Ron Weiss, Vincent Dubourg, Jake Vanderplas, Alexandre Passos, David Cournapeau, Matthieu Brucher, Matthieu Perrot, and Édouard Duchesnay. 2011. Scikit-learn: Machine learning in python. *Journal of Machine Learning Research*, 12(85):2825–2830.

R Quian Quiroga, Leila Reddy, Gabriel Kreiman, Christof Koch, and Itzhak Fried. 2005. Invariant visual representation by single neurons in the human brain. *Nature*, 435(7045):1102–1107.

Alec Radford, Jong Wook Kim, Chris Hallacy, Aditya Ramesh, Gabriel Goh, Sandhini Agarwal, Girish Sastry, Amanda Askell, Pamela Mishkin, Jack Clark, Gretchen Krueger, and Ilya Sutskever. 2021. Learning transferable visual models from natural language supervision. *CoRR*, abs/2103.00020.

Leila Reddy and Simon J Thorpe. 2014. Concept cells through associative learning of high-level representations. *Neuron*, 84(2):248–251.

Nils Reimers and Iryna Gurevych. 2019. Sentence-bert: Sentence embeddings using siamese bert-networks. *CoRR*, abs/1908.10084.

Mert Bülent Sariyildiz, Julien Perez, and Diane Larlus. 2020. Learning visual representations with caption annotations. *CoRR*, abs/2008.01392.

Amanpreet Singh, Vivek Natarajan, Meet Shah, Yu Jiang, Xinlei Chen, Dhruv Batra, Devi Parikh, and Marcus Rohrbach. 2019. Towards VQA models that can read. *CoRR*, abs/1904.08920.

Alexandru Telea. 2004. An image inpainting technique based on the fast marching method. *Journal of Graphics Tools*, 9.

Ashish Vaswani, Noam Shazeer, Niki Parmar, Jakob Uszkoreit, Llion Jones, Aidan N. Gomez, Lukasz Kaiser, and Illia Polosukhin. 2017. Attention is all you need. *CoRR*, abs/1706.03762.

Adina Williams, Nikita Nangia, and Samuel Bowman. 2018. A broad-coverage challenge corpus for sentence understanding through inference. In *Proceedings of the 2018 Conference of the North American Chapter of the Association for Computational Linguistics: Human Language Technologies, Volume 1 (Long Papers)*, pages 1112–1122. Association for Computational Linguistics.

Xinyu Zhou, Cong Yao, He Wen, Yuzhi Wang, Shuchang Zhou, Weiran He, and Jiajun Liang. 2017. EAST: an efficient and accurate scene text detector. *CoRR*, abs/1704.03155.

From Hyperbolic Geometry Back to Word Embeddings

Sultan Nurmukhamedov
Yandex School of Data Analysis
soltustik@gmail.com

Thomas Mach
University of Potsdam
mach@uni-potsdam.de

Arsen Sheverdin
University of Amsterdam
arsen.sheverdin@student.uva.nl

Zhenisbek Assylbekov
Nazarbayev University
zhassylbekov@nu.edu.kz

Abstract

We choose random points in the hyperbolic disc and claim that these points are already word representations. However, it is yet to be uncovered which point corresponds to which word of the human language of interest. This correspondence can be approximately established using a pointwise mutual information between words and recent alignment techniques.

1 Introduction

Vector representations of words are ubiquitous in modern natural language processing (NLP). There are currently two large classes of word embedding models: they build (1) static and (2) contextualized word vectors correspondingly.

Static embeddings map each *word type* into a vector of real numbers, regardless of the context in which the word type is used. The most prominent representatives of this class of models are WORD2VEC (Mikolov et al., 2013b,a) and GLOVE (Pennington et al., 2014). The obvious problem with this approach is the representation of polysemous words, such as *bank*—it becomes unclear whether we are talking about a financial institution, or we are talking about the river bank.

Contextualized word embeddings, such as ELMO (Peters et al., 2018) and BERT (Devlin et al., 2019), solve this problem by mapping each *word token* into a vector space depending on the context in which the given word token is used, i.e. the same word will have different vector representations when used in different contexts. The second approach can nowadays be considered mainstream, despite relatively few papers offering theoretical justifications for contextualized word embeddings.

For static embeddings, on the contrary, there is a number of theoretical works, each of which offers its own version of what is happening when word vectors are trained. An incomplete list of such works includes those of Levy and Goldberg (2014), Arora et al. (2016), Hashimoto et al. (2016), Gittens et al. (2017), Tian et al. (2017), Ethayarajh et al. (2019), Allen et al. (2019), Allen and Hospedales (2019), Assylbekov and Takhanov (2019), Zobnin and Elistratova (2019). Other advantages of static embeddings over contextualized ones include faster training (few hours instead of few days) and lower computing requirements (1 consumer-level GPU instead of 8–16 non-consumer GPUs). Morevoer, static embeddings are still an integral part of deep neural network models that produce contextualized word vectors, because embedding lookup matrices are used at the input and output (softmax) layers of such models. Therefore, we consider it necessary to further study static embeddings.

Several recent works (Nickel and Kiela, 2017; Tifrea et al., 2019) argue that static word embeddings should be better trained in hyperbolic spaces than in Euclidean spaces, and provide empirical evidence that word embeddings trained in hyperbolic spaces need less dimensions to achieve the same quality as state-of-the-art Euclidean vectors.[1] Usually such works motivate the hyperbolicity of word embeddings by the fact that hyperbolic spaces are better suited for embedding hierarchical structures. Words themselves often denote concepts with an underlying hierarchy. An example of such a hierarchy is the WORDNET database, an excerpt of which is shown in Fig. 1.

In the present paper we will investigate where the hyperbolicity originates from. If we take the state-of-the-art Euclidean embeddings, is it possible to establish a direct connection between them and their counterparts from a hyperbolic word embedding? This was answered positively by Assylbekov and Jangeldin (2020) who established a chain of connections: from word embeddings to

[1] The quality of word vectors is usually measured by the performance of downstream tasks, such as similarity, analogies, part-of-speech tagging, etc.

Proceedings of the 7th Workshop on Representation Learning for NLP, pages 39 - 45
May 26, 2022

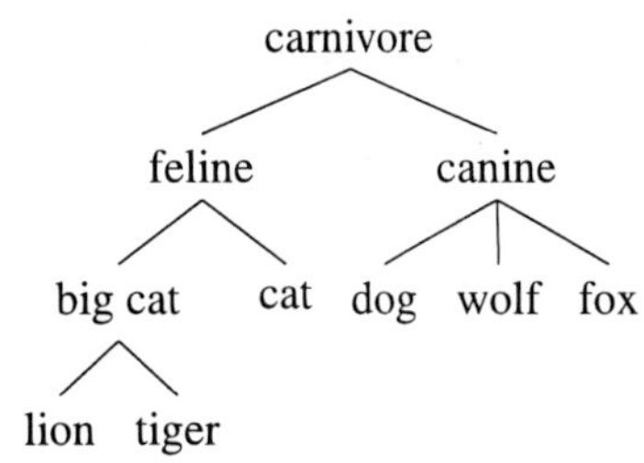

Figure 1: An excerpt from the WORDNET database.

co-occurrence matrices, then to complex networks, and, finally, to hyperbolic spaces. In this paper, to provide an additional justification for the constructed chain, we propose a way to move from the final point, hyperbolic spaces, to the initial one, word embeddings. We show that drawing random points from the hyperbolic plane results in a set of points that reasonably well resembles word embeddings. In fact, we can match these points to word embeddings. Contrary, the same trick does not work with points drawn at random in the Euclidean space. Thus, one can argue that the hyperbolic space provides the underlying structure for word embeddings, while in the Euclidean space this structure has to be superimposed.

Notation

We denote with $\mathbb{R}$ the real numbers. Bold-faced lowercase letters ($\mathbf{x}$) denote vectors, plain-faced lowercase letters (x) denote scalars, bold-faced uppercase letters ($\mathbf{A}$) denote matrices, $\langle\mathbf{x},\mathbf{y}\rangle$ is the Euclidean inner product. We use $\mathbf{A}_{a:b,c:d}$ to denote a submatrix located at the intersection of rows $a, a+1, \ldots, b$ and columns $c, c+1, \ldots, d$ of $\mathbf{A}$. 'i.i.d.' stands for 'independent and identically distributed', 'p.d.f' stands for 'probability distribution function'. We use the sign $\propto$ to abbreviate 'proportional to', and the sign $\sim$ to abbreviate 'distributed as'.

Assuming that words have already been converted into indices, let $\mathcal{W} := \{1, \ldots, n\}$ be a finite vocabulary of words. Following the setup of the widely used WORD2VEC model (Mikolov et al., 2013a,b), we use *two* vectors per each word i: (1) $\mathbf{w}_i \in \mathbb{R}^d$ when $i \in \mathcal{W}$ is a center word, (2) $\mathbf{c}_i \in \mathbb{R}^d$ when $i \in \mathcal{W}$ is a context word; and we assume that $d \ll n$.

In what follows we assume that our dataset consists of co-occurence pairs (i, j). We say that "the words i and j co-occur" when they co-occur in a fixed-size window of words. Let $\#(i,j)$ be the number of times the words i and j co-occur.

2 Background: From Word Embeddings to Hyperbolic Space

Our departure point is the skip-gram with negative sampling (SGNS) word embedding model of Mikolov et al. (2013b) that maximizes the following objective function

$$\sum_{i\in\mathcal{W}}\sum_{j\in\mathcal{W}} \#(i,j)\log\sigma(\langle\mathbf{w}_i,\mathbf{c}_j\rangle) + k\cdot\mathbb{E}_{j'\sim p}[\log\sigma(-\langle\mathbf{w}_i,\mathbf{c}_{j'}\rangle)], \quad (1)$$

where $\sigma(x)=\frac{1}{1+e^{-x}}$ is the logistic sigmoid function, p is a smoothed unigram probability distribution for words,[2] and k is the number of negative samples to be drawn. Interestingly, training SGNS is approximately equivalent to finding a low-rank approximation of a shifted pointwise mutual information (PMI) matrix (Levy and Goldberg, 2014) in the form

$$\log\frac{p(i,j)}{p(i)p(j)} - \log k \approx \langle\mathbf{w}_i,\mathbf{c}_j\rangle, \quad (2)$$

where the left-hand side is the shifted PMI between i and j, and the right-hand side is an ij-th element of a matrix with rank $\le d$ since $\mathbf{w}_i, \mathbf{c}_j \in \mathbb{R}^d$. This approximation was later re-derived by Arora et al. (2016), Zobnin and Elistratova (2019), Assylbekov and Takhanov (2019), and Allen et al. (2019) under different sets of assuptions. In a recent paper, Assylbekov and Jangeldin (2020) showed that the removal of the sigmoid transformation in the SGNS objective (1) gives word embeddings comparable in quality with the original SGNS embeddings. A maximization of such modified objective results in a low-rank approximation of a *squashed shifted* PMI (σSPMI) matrix, defined as

$$\mathbf{A}_{ij} := \sigma\left(\log\frac{p(i,j)}{p(i)p(j)} - \log k\right). \quad (3)$$

Moreover, treating the σSPMI matrix as a connection probabilities matrix of a random graph, the authors show that such graph is a *complex network*, that is it has strong clustering and scale-free degree distribution, and according to Krioukov et al. (2010), such graph possesses an effective hyperbolic geometry underneath. The following chain

[2]The authors of SGNS suggest $p(i) \propto \#(i)^{3/4}$.

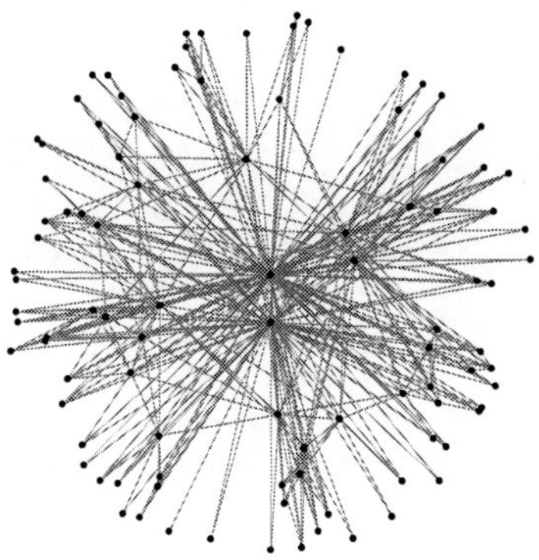

Figure 2: Random hyperbolic graph.

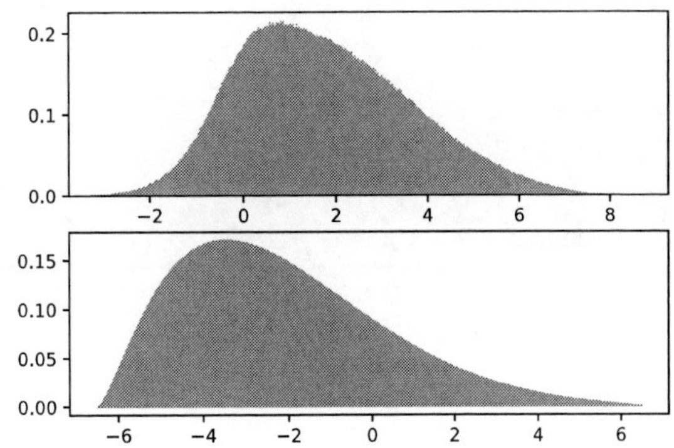

Figure 3: Distribution of PMI values (top) and of $R - X$.

summarizes this argument:

Word Embeddings $\longrightarrow$ σSPMI $\longrightarrow$
Complex Network $\longrightarrow$ Hyperbolic Space

In our work, we go from the final point (hyperbolic space) to the starting one (word embeddings), and the next section provides the details of our method.

3 Method: From Hyperbolic Geometry to Word Embeddings

It is difficult to visualize hyperbolic spaces because they cannot be isometrically embedded into any Euclidean space.[3] However, there exist models of hyperbolic spaces: each model emphasizes different aspects of hyperbolic geometry, but no model simultaneously represents all of its properties. We will consider here the so-called *native* model (Krioukov et al., 2010), in which the hyperbolic plane $\mathbb{H}^2$ is represented by a disk of radius R, and we use polar coordinates (r, θ) to specify the position of any point $v \in \mathbb{H}^2$, where the radial coordinate r equals the hyperbolic distance of v from the origin. Given this notation, the distance x between two points with coordinates (r, θ) and (r', θ') satisfies the hyperbolic law of cosines

$$\cosh x = \cosh r \cosh r' - \sinh r \sinh r' \cos(\theta - \theta'), \quad (4)$$

for the hyperbolic space of constant curvature -1.[4] A key property of hyperbolic spaces is that they expand faster than Euclidean spaces. E.g., a circle with radius r has in the Euclidean plane a length of $2\pi r = \Theta(r)$ and an area of $\pi r^2 = \Theta(r^2)$, while its length and area in the hyperbolic plane are $2\pi \sinh(r) = \Theta(e^r)$ and $2\pi(\cosh r - 1) = \Theta(e^r)$ correspondingly. It is noteworthy that in a balanced tree with branching factor b, the number of nodes that are r edges from the root grows as $\Theta(b^r)$, i.e. exponentially with r, leading to the suggestion that hierarchical complex networks with tree-like structures might be easily embeddable in hyperbolic space.

Based on the above facts, we construct a random hyperbolic (RHG) graph as in the work of Krioukov et al. (2010): we place randomly n points (nodes) into a hyperbolic disk of radius R, and each pair of nodes (i, j) is connected with probability $\sigma(R - x_{ij})$, where x_{ij} is the hyperbolic distance (4) between points i and j. Angular coordinates of the nodes are sampled from the uniform distribution: $\theta \sim \mathcal{U}[0, 2\pi]$, while the radial coordinates are sampled from the exponential p.d.f.

$$\rho(r) = \frac{\alpha \sinh \alpha r}{\cosh \alpha R - 1} = \Theta(e^{\alpha r}).$$

The hyperparameters R and α are chosen based on the total number of nodes n, the desired average degree $\bar{k}$ and the power-law exponent γ according to the equations (22) and (29) of Krioukov et al. (2010). An example of such RHG is shown in Figure 2. Notice, that the connection probabilities matrix of our graph is

$$\mathbf{B}_{ij} := \sigma(R - x_{ij}),$$

[3]This means that we cannot map points of a hyperbolic space into points of a Euclidean space in such way that the distances between points are preserved.

[4]Defining constant curvature is beyond the scope of our paper. We just mention here that there are only three types of isotropic spaces: Euclidean (zero curvature), spherical (positively curved), and hyperbolic (negatively curved).

Method	Word Similarity			POS Tagging	
	WS353	MEN	M. TURK	CoNLL-2000	BROWN
SGNS	.678	.656	.690	90.77	92.60
PMI + SVD	.669	.674	.666	92.25	93.76
σSPMI + SVD	.648	.622	.666	92.76	93.78
RHG + SVD + Align	.406	.399	.509	92.23	93.19
Random + Align	.165	.117	.111	81.89	89.39

Table 1: Evaluation of word embeddings on the similarity and POS tagging tasks. For the similarity tasks the evaluation metric is the Spearman's correlation with human ratings, for the POS tagging tasks it is accuracy. *Random* stands for random vectors that were obtained as i.i.d. draws from $\mathcal{N}(\mathbf{0}, \mathbf{I})$.

Comparing this to (3), we see that if $\mathbf{A}$ and $\mathbf{B}$ induce structurally similar graphs then the distribution of the PMI values $\log \frac{p(i,j)}{p(i)p(j)}$ should be similar to the distribution of $R - x_{ij}$ values (up to a constant shift). To test this empirically, we compute a PMI matrix of a well-known corpus, `text8`, and compare the distribution of the PMI values with the p.d.f. of $R - X$, where X is a distance between two random points of a hyperbolic disk (the exact form of this p.d.f. is given in Proposition A.1). The results are shown in Figure 3. As we can see, the two distributions are similar in the sense that both are unimodal and right-skewed. The main difference is in the shift—distribution of $R - X$ is shifted to the left compared to the distribution of the PMI values.

We hypothesize that the nodes of the RHG treated as points of the hyperbolic space are *already* reasonable word embeddings for the words of our vocabulary $\mathcal{W}$. The only thing that we do not know is the correspondence between words $i \in \mathcal{W}$ and nodes of the RHG. Instead of aligning words with nodes, we can align their vector representations. For this, we take singular value decompositions (SVD) of $\mathbf{A}$ and $\mathbf{B}$:

$$\mathbf{A} = \mathbf{U}_A \boldsymbol{\Sigma}_A \mathbf{V}_A^\top, \quad \mathbf{B} = \mathbf{U}_B \boldsymbol{\Sigma}_B \mathbf{V}_B^\top,$$

and then obtain embedding matrices by

$$\mathbf{W}_A := \mathbf{U}_{A,1:n,1:d} \boldsymbol{\Sigma}_{A,1:d,1:d}^{1/2} \in \mathbb{R}^{n \times d}$$
$$\mathbf{W}_B := \mathbf{U}_{B,1:n,1:d} \boldsymbol{\Sigma}_{B,1:d,1:d}^{1/2} \in \mathbb{R}^{n \times d}$$

as in the work of Levy and Goldberg (2014). An ith row in $\mathbf{W}_A$ is an embedding of the word $i \in \mathcal{W}$, while an ith row in $\mathbf{W}_B$ is an embedding of the RHG's node i. To align these two sets of embeddings we apply a recent stochastic optimization method of Grave et al. (2019) that solves

$$\min_{\mathbf{Q} \in \mathcal{O}_d} \min_{\mathbf{P} \in \mathcal{P}_n} \|\mathbf{W}_A \mathbf{Q} - \mathbf{P} \mathbf{W}_B\|_2^2,$$

where $\mathcal{O}_d$ is the set of $d \times d$ orthogonal matrices and $\mathcal{P}_d$ is the set of $n \times n$ permutation matrices. As one can see, this method assumes that *alignment* between two sets of embeddings is not only a permutation from one set to the other, but also an orthogonal transformation between the two. Once the alignment is done, we treat $\mathbf{P}\mathbf{W}_B$ as an embedding matrix for the words in $\mathcal{W}$.

4 Evaluation

In this section we evaluate the quality of word vectors resulting from a RHG[5] against those from the SGNS, PMI, and σSPMI. We use the `text8` corpus mentioned in the previous section. We were ignoring words that appeared less than 5 times (resulting in a vocabulary of 71,290 tokens). We set window size to 2, subsampling threshold to 10^{-5}, and dimensionality of word vectors to 200. The SGNS embeddings were trained using our custom implementation.[6] The PMI and BPMI matrices were extracted using the HYPERWORDS tool of Levy et al. (2015) and SVD was performed using the PYTORCH library of Paszke et al. (2019).

The embeddings were evaluated on word similarity and POS tagging tasks. For word similarity we used WORDSIM (Finkelstein et al., 2002), MEN (Bruni et al., 2012), and M.TURK (Radinsky et al., 2011) datasets. For POS tagging we trained a simple classifier[7] by feeding in the embedding of a current word and its nearby context to predict its part-of-speech (POS) tag:

$$\widehat{\text{POS}}_t = \text{softmax}(\sigma(\mathbf{A}[\mathbf{w}_{t-2}; \ldots; \mathbf{w}_{t+2}] + \mathbf{b}))$$

[5]Our code is available at `https://github.com/soltustik/RHG`

[6]`https://github.com/zh3nis/SGNS`

[7]feedforward neural network with one hidden layer and softmax output layer

where $[\mathbf{x};\mathbf{y}]$ is concatenation of $\mathbf{x}$ and $\mathbf{y}$. The classifier was trained on CoNLL-2000 (Tjong Kim Sang and Buchholz, 2000) and BROWN (Kucera et al., 1967) datasets.

The results of evaluation are provided in Table 1. As we see, vector representations of words generated from a RHG lag behind in word similarity tasks from word vectors obtained by other standard methods. Note, however, that the similarity task was designed with Euclidean geometry in mind. Even though our RHG-based vectors are also ultimately placed in the Euclidean space (otherwise the alignment step would not have been possible), their nature is inherently non-Euclidean. Therefore, the similarity scores for them may not be indicative. So, for example, when RHG vectors are fed into a nonlinear model for POS tagging, they are comparable with other types of vectors.

We notice that random vectors—generated as i.i.d. draws from $\mathcal{N}(\mathbf{0},\mathbf{I})$ and then aligned to the embeddings from σSPMI—show poor results in the similarity tasks and underperform all other word embedding methods in the POS tagging tasks. This calls into question whether multivariate Gaussian is a reasonable (prior) distribution for word vectors as was suggested by Arora et al. (2016), Assylbekov and Takhanov (2019).

5 Conclusion and Future Work

In this work we show that word vectors can be obtained from hyperbolic geometry without explicit training. We obtain the embeddings by randomly drawing points in the hyperbolic plane and by finding correspondence between these points and the words of the human language. This correspondence is determined by the relation (hyperbolic distance) to other words. This method avoids the, often expensive, training of word vectors in hyperbolic spaces as in Tifrea et al. (2019). A direct comparison is not what this paper attempts—our method is cheaper but produces word vectors of lower quality. Our method simply shows that word vectors do fit better into hyperbolic space than into Euclidean space.

Finally, we want to sketch a possible direction for future work. The hyperbolic space is a special case of a Riemannian manifold. Are Riemannian manifolds better suited for word vectors? In particular which manifolds should one use? At the moment, there is only limited empirical knowledge to address these questions. For instance, Gu et al. (2019) obtained word vectors of better quality, according to the similarity score, in the product of hyperbolic spaces, which is still a Riemannian manifold but not a hyperbolic space anymore. We are hopeful that future work may provide an explanation for this empirical fact.

Acknowledgements

Zhenisbek Assylbekov was supported by the Program of Targeted Funding "Economy of the Future" #0054/ПЦФ-НС-19. The work of Sultan Nurmukhamedov was supported by the Nazarbayev University Faculty-Development Competitive Research Grants Program, grant number 240919FD3921. The authors would like to thank anonymous reviewers for their feedback.

References

Carl Allen, Ivana Balazevic, and Timothy Hospedales. 2019. What the vec? towards probabilistically grounded embeddings. In *Proceedings of NeurIPS*.

Carl Allen and Timothy Hospedales. 2019. Analogies explained: Towards understanding word embeddings. In *Proceedings of ICML*.

Sanjeev Arora, Yuanzhi Li, Yingyu Liang, Tengyu Ma, and Andrej Risteski. 2016. A latent variable model approach to pmi-based word embeddings. *Transactions of the Association for Computational Linguistics*, 4:385–399.

Zhenisbek Assylbekov and Alibi Jangeldin. 2020. Squashed shifted pmi matrix: bridging word embeddings and hyperbolic spaces. In *Proceedings of AJCAI*.

Zhenisbek Assylbekov and Rustem Takhanov. 2019. Context vectors are reflections of word vectors in half the dimensions. *Journal of Artificial Intelligence Research*, 66:225–242.

Elia Bruni, Gemma Boleda, Marco Baroni, and Nam-Khanh Tran. 2012. Distributional semantics in technicolor. In *Proceedings of ACL*.

Jacob Devlin, Ming-Wei Chang, Kenton Lee, and Kristina Toutanova. 2019. Bert: Pre-training of deep bidirectional transformers for language understanding. In *Proceedings of NAACL-HLT*.

Kawin Ethayarajh, David Duvenaud, and Graeme Hirst. 2019. Towards understanding linear word analogies. In *Proceedings of ACL*.

Lev Finkelstein, Evgeniy Gabrilovich, Yossi Matias, Ehud Rivlin, Zach Solan, Gadi Wolfman, and Eytan Ruppin. 2002. Placing search in context: The concept revisited. *ACM Transactions on information systems*, 20(1):116–131.

Alex Gittens, Dimitris Achlioptas, and Michael W Mahoney. 2017. Skip-gram- zipf+ uniform= vector additivity. In *Proceedings of ACL*, pages 69–76.

Edouard Grave, Armand Joulin, and Quentin Berthet. 2019. Unsupervised alignment of embeddings with wasserstein procrustes. In *Proceedings of AISTATS*.

Albert Gu, Frederic Sala, Beliz Gunel, and Christopher Ré. 2019. Learning mixed-curvature representations in product spaces. In *7th International Conference on Learning Representations, ICLR 2019, New Orleans, LA, USA, May 6-9, 2019*. OpenReview.net.

Tatsunori B Hashimoto, David Alvarez-Melis, and Tommi S Jaakkola. 2016. Word embeddings as metric recovery in semantic spaces. *Transactions of the Association for Computational Linguistics*, 4:273–286.

Dmitri Krioukov, Fragkiskos Papadopoulos, Maksim Kitsak, Amin Vahdat, and Marián Boguná. 2010. Hyperbolic geometry of complex networks. *Physical Review E*, 82(3):036106.

Henry Kucera, Henry Kučera, and Winthrop Nelson Francis. 1967. *Computational analysis of present-day American English*. Brown university press.

Omer Levy and Yoav Goldberg. 2014. Neural word embedding as implicit matrix factorization. In *Proceedings of NeurIPS*.

Omer Levy, Yoav Goldberg, and Ido Dagan. 2015. Improving distributional similarity with lessons learned from word embeddings. *Transactions of the Association for Computational Linguistics*, 3:211–225.

Tomas Mikolov, Kai Chen, Greg Corrado, and Jeffrey Dean. 2013a. Efficient estimation of word representations in vector space. *arXiv preprint arXiv:1301.3781*.

Tomas Mikolov, Ilya Sutskever, Kai Chen, Greg S Corrado, and Jeff Dean. 2013b. Distributed representations of words and phrases and their compositionality. In *Proceedings of NeurIPS*.

Maximillian Nickel and Douwe Kiela. 2017. Poincaré embeddings for learning hierarchical representations. In *Advances in neural information processing systems*, pages 6338–6347.

Adam Paszke, Sam Gross, Francisco Massa, Adam Lerer, James Bradbury, Gregory Chanan, Trevor Killeen, Zeming Lin, Natalia Gimelshein, Luca Antiga, et al. 2019. Pytorch: An imperative style, high-performance deep learning library. In *Proceedings of NeurIPS*.

Jeffrey Pennington, Richard Socher, and Christopher Manning. 2014. Glove: Global vectors for word representation. In *Proceedings of EMNLP*.

Matthew E Peters, Mark Neumann, Mohit Iyyer, Matt Gardner, Christopher Clark, Kenton Lee, and Luke Zettlemoyer. 2018. Deep contextualized word representations. In *Proceedings of NAACL-HLT*.

Kira Radinsky, Eugene Agichtein, Evgeniy Gabrilovich, and Shaul Markovitch. 2011. A word at a time: computing word relatedness using temporal semantic analysis. In *Proceedings of the 20th international conference on World wide web*, pages 337–346. ACM.

Ran Tian, Naoaki Okazaki, and Kentaro Inui. 2017. The mechanism of additive composition. *Machine Learning*, 106(7):1083–1130.

Alexandru Tifrea, Gary Bécigneul, and Octavian-Eugen Ganea. 2019. Poincaré glove: Hyperbolic word embeddings. In *Proceedings of ICLR*.

Erik F. Tjong Kim Sang and Sabine Buchholz. 2000. Introduction to the CoNLL-2000 shared task chunking. In *Fourth Conference on Computational Natural Language Learning and the Second Learning Language in Logic Workshop*.

Alexey Zobnin and Evgenia Elistratova. 2019. Learning word embeddings without context vectors. In *Proceedings of the 4th Workshop on Representation Learning for NLP (RepL4NLP-2019)*, pages 244–249.

A Auxiliary Results

Proposition A.1. *Let X be a distance between two points that were randomly uniformly placed in the hyperbolic disk of radius R. The probability distribution function of X is given by*

$$f_X(x) = \int_0^R \int_0^R \frac{\sinh(x)\rho(r_1)\rho(r_2)dr_1dr_2}{\pi\sqrt{1 - A(r_1, r_2, x)}\sinh(r_1)\sinh(r_2)}, \quad (5)$$

where $A(r_1, r_2, x) = \frac{\cosh(r_1)\cosh(r_2) - \cosh(x)}{\sinh(r_1)\sinh(r_2)}$, *and* $\rho(r) = \frac{\alpha \sinh \alpha r}{\cosh \alpha R - 1}$.

Proof. Let us throw randomly and uniformly two points (r_1, θ_1) and (r_2, θ_2) into the hyperbolic disk of radius R, i.e. $r_1, r_2 \overset{\text{i.i.d.}}{\sim} \rho(r)$, $\theta_1, \theta_2 \overset{\text{i.i.d.}}{\sim} \text{Uniform}[0, 2\pi)$. Let X be the distance between these points (X is a random variable). Let γ be the angle between these points, then $\gamma := \pi - |\pi - |\theta_1 - \theta_2|| \sim \text{Uniform}[0, \pi)$ and thus

$$f_{\cos\gamma}(t) = \frac{1}{\pi\sqrt{1 - t^2}}, \quad t \in [-1, 1].$$

Since the distance in our model of hyperbolic plane is given by

$$X = \cosh^{-1}[\cosh r_1 \cosh r_2 - \sinh r_1 \sinh r_2 \cos\gamma]$$

we have

$$\begin{aligned}
&\Pr(X \leq x) \\
&= \Pr\left(\cos\gamma \geq \underbrace{\frac{\cosh r_1 \cosh r_2 - \cosh x}{\sinh r_1 \sinh r_2}}_{A(r_1, r_2, x)}\right) \\
&= \Pr(\cos\gamma \geq A(r_1, r_2, x)) \\
&= \int_{A(r_1,r_2,x)}^{+\infty} \frac{1}{\pi\sqrt{1-t^2}} \\
&= \frac{1}{2} - \frac{\sin^{-1} A(r_1, r_2, x)}{\pi},
\end{aligned}$$

and therefore

$$\begin{aligned}
f_{X|r_1,r_2}(x) &= \frac{d}{dx}\left[\frac{1}{2} - \frac{\sin^{-1} A(r_1, r_2, x)}{\pi}\right] \\
&= \frac{\sinh x}{\pi\sqrt{1 - A(r_1, r_2, x)}\sinh(r_1)\sinh r_2}
\end{aligned}$$

for $x \in (|r_1 - r_2|, r_1 + r_2)$. Integrating $f_{X|r_1,r_2}(x)\rho(r_1)\rho(r_2)$ with respect to r_1 and r_2 we get (5). □

A Comparative Study of Pre-trained Encoders for Low-Resource Named Entity Recognition

Yuxuan Chen[1] **Jonas Mikkelsen**[1]
Arne Binder[1] **Christoph Alt**[2,3] **Leonhard Hennig**[1]
[1]German Research Center for Artificial Intelligence (DFKI)
[2]Humboldt Universität zu Berlin [3]Science of Intelligence
[1]*{yuxuan.chen, jonas.mikkelsen, arne.binder, leonhard.hennig}@dfki.de*
[2]*christoph.alt@posteo.de*

Abstract

Pre-trained language models (PLM) are effective components of few-shot named entity recognition (NER) approaches when augmented with continued pre-training on task-specific out-of-domain data or fine-tuning on in-domain data. However, their performance in low-resource scenarios, where such data is not available, remains an open question. We introduce an encoder evaluation framework, and use it to systematically compare the performance of state-of-the-art pre-trained representations on the task of low-resource NER. We analyze a wide range of encoders pre-trained with different strategies, model architectures, intermediate-task fine-tuning, and contrastive learning. Our experimental results across ten benchmark NER datasets in English and German show that encoder performance varies significantly, suggesting that the choice of encoder for a specific low-resource scenario needs to be carefully evaluated.

1 Introduction

Pre-trained language models (PLM) have been shown to be very effective few-shot learners for a wide range of natural language processing tasks (Brown et al., 2020; Gao et al., 2021), as they capture semantically and syntactically rich representations of text via self-supervised training on large-scale unlabeled datasets (Peters et al., 2018; Devlin et al., 2019). Recent research in few-shot named entity recognition (NER) has leveraged such representations, e.g. for metric learning on task-specific out-of-domain[1] data (Fritzler et al., 2019; Yang and Katiyar, 2020), optionally augmented by continued pre-training with distantly supervised, in-domain data (Huang et al., 2021). However, there has been no systematic comparison of the NER performance of such representations in low-resource scenarios without task-specific out-of-domain data and very limited in-domain data; a prevalent setting in many practical applications.

In this paper we conduct a comparative study to answer the following research questions: How well do representations learnt by different pre-trained models encode information that benefits these low-resource scenarios? What can we observe for different categories of encoders, such as encoders trained with masked language modeling, versus encoders that are additionally fine-tuned on downstream tasks, or optimized with contrastive learning? How do they perform across different datasets and languages? We present an evaluation framework inspired by few-shot learning to evaluate representations obtained via different pre-training strategies, model architectures, pre-training data, and intermediate-task fine-tuning in low-resource NER scenarios of varying difficulty (see Figure 1).

We find that the choice of encoder can have significant effects on low-resource NER performance, with F1 scores differing by up to 25% between encoders, and simply picking an encoder of the BERT family at random will usually not yield the best results for a given scenario. We observe that while BERT in general performs adequately, ALBERT and RoBERTa outperform BERT by a large margin in many cases, with ALBERT being especially strong in very low-resource settings with only one available labeled example per class.

The main contributions of this study are: (1) a systematic performance evaluation of a wide range of encoders pre-trained with different strategies, such as masked language modeling, task-specific fine-tuning, and contrastive learning on the task of low-resource named entity recognition; (2) an evaluation on ten benchmark NER datasets in two languages, English and German; (3) an encoder-readout evaluation framework that can be easily extended with additional scenarios, encoders, datasets, and readout approaches; which we release at `https://github.com/dfki-nlp/fewie`.

[1]Out-of-domain and in-domain refer to NER-specific data with disjoint label spaces, i.e. $\mathcal{Y}_{out} \neq \mathcal{Y}_{in}$.

Proceedings of the 7th Workshop on Representation Learning for NLP, pages 46 - 59
May 26, 2022 ©2022 Association for Computational Linguistics

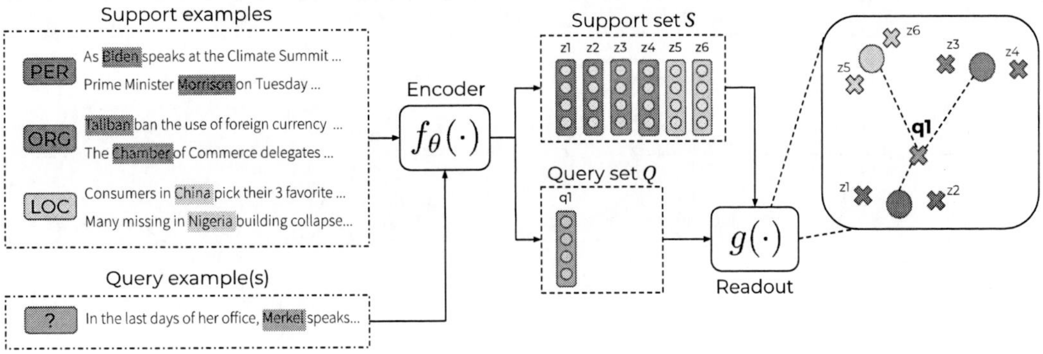

Figure 1: Encoder-readout evaluation framework. For each of the N classes, we randomly sample K support tokens including their sentence context, and an unlabeled query token with sentential context. The encoder $f_{\boldsymbol{\theta}}(\cdot)$ provides an embedding (or representation) for each token, and the readout module $g(\cdot)$ assigns a class to a query token by comparing its representation $\boldsymbol{q}_j$ to the representations $\{\boldsymbol{z}_1, \ldots, \boldsymbol{z}_{N\times K}\}$ of the support tokens. Depending on the readout approach, the c-th class in $\mathcal{S}$ is represented either by its prototype embedding (as shown in the example) or by its set of associated token embeddings, e.g. for nearest neighbor classification. In this example $\boldsymbol{q}_1$ representing *Merkel* would be assigned the class *PER* based on the closest class prototype embedding (red circle).

2 Encoder Evaluation Framework

To simulate low-resource NER scenarios of varying difficulty, we draw inspiration from the evaluation of few-shot learning methods. We first give a formal definition of the few-shot NER task, and then introduce the encoder evaluation framework itself.

2.1 Few-shot NER task definition

NER is typically formulated as a sequence labeling problem, where the input is a sequence of tokens $\mathbf{X} = \{x_1, x_2, \cdots, x_T\}$ and the output is the corresponding T-length sequence of entity type labels $\mathbf{Y} = \{y_1, y_2, \cdots, y_T\}$. In contrast, few-shot learning is cast as an episodic N-way K-shot problem, where in each episode, N classes are sampled with K examples each to construct a support set $\mathcal{S} = \{\mathbf{X}_i, \mathbf{Y}_i\}_{i=1}^{N\times K}$ for learning, and K' examples per class are sampled to create a query set $\mathcal{Q} = \{\mathbf{X}_j, \mathbf{Y}_j\}_{j=1}^{N\times K'}$ for evaluation ($\mathcal{S} \cap \mathcal{Q} = \emptyset$). In a sequence labeling problem like NER, samples are typically sentences, due to the importance of contextual information for token classification, but care has to be taken to ensure that the sampled sentences contain no other entities. In particular, there should be no entity overlap between the support and the query sets (Ding et al., 2021).

2.2 Encoder-Readout Framework

Our framework consists of two modules, an encoder $f(\cdot)$ and a readout module $g(\cdot)$, as shown in Figure 1. The encoder provides an embedding $\boldsymbol{z} = f_{\boldsymbol{\theta}}(x)$ of a token x, where $\boldsymbol{\theta}$ denotes the parameters of the encoder. The readout module is responsible for assigning a class to each token x' in the query set $\mathcal{Q}$ given the support set $\mathcal{S}$. Depending on the readout approach, the c-th class in $\mathcal{S}$ is represented either by its prototype embedding or by its associated set of token embeddings, e.g. for nearest neighbor classification. The decision is made by comparing the embedding $\boldsymbol{q} = f_{\boldsymbol{\theta}}(x')$ with each of the N class prototypes built from the support set $\mathcal{S}$, or with each of the token-level embeddings.

3 Experiments

We illustrate the evaluation framework using a representative set of encoders pre-trained with different strategies. We then give details of the readout approaches, the datasets we used, and all other experimental settings.

3.1 Encoders

We group encoders into four categories, depending on their type of pre-training:

PLM These models are pre-trained on a large general corpus in a self-supervised manner without any task-specific fine-tuning. We consider six representative encoders for English: BERT cased and uncased (Devlin et al., 2019), SpanBERT (Joshi et al., 2020), XLNet (Yang et al., 2019), ALBERT (Lan et al., 2020) and RoBERTa (Liu et al., 2019), and three encoders for German: deepset's BERT, GottBERT (Scheible et al., 2020) and XLM-RoBERTa (Conneau et al., 2020).[2]

[2]HuggingFace model identifiers for these and all other

Language	Dataset	Domain	# Entity types	Entity tag set
English	CoNLL-2003$_{\text{EN}}$	News	4	LOC,MISC,ORG,PER
	OntoNotes 5.0	News, Dialogue	18	CARDINAL,DATE,EVENT,MONEY,...
	Few-NERD$_{\text{coarse}}$	General	8	art,building,event,product,...
	Few-NERD$_{\text{fine}}$	General	66	art-film,product-car,other-law,...
	WNUT-17	Social Media	6	corporation,creative-work,group,...
	WikiAnn	General	3	LOC,ORG,PER
	WikiGold	General	4	LOC,MISC,ORG,PER
	Zhang et al.	e-Commerce	4	ATTRIBUTE,BRAND,COMPONENT,PRODUCT
German	CoNLL-2003$_{\text{DE}}$	News	4	LOC,MISC,ORG,PER
	GermEval 2014	General	12	LOC,LOCderiv,LOCpart,ORG,...
	Smartdata	News, General	16	DISASTER-TYPE,DISTANCE,LOCATION,...

Table 1: Statistics of the evaluated datasets

Fine-tuned PLM Recent research has shown that intermediate-task training can result in significant performance gains on the target task even in low-resource settings (Vu et al., 2020; Poth et al., 2021). We evaluate three BERT encoders that are fine-tuned on token-level, sentence-level, and document-level intermediate tasks, respectively: BERT$_{\text{POS}}$ for part-of-speech tagging, BERT$_{\text{MNLI}}$, fine-tuned on the MultiNLI dataset (Williams et al., 2018), and BERT$_{\text{SQuAD}}$ for extractive question answering (Rajpurkar et al., 2016). Evaluating these encoders may allow us to observe whether the representation granularity induced by the tasks they were fine-tuned on has an effect on NER performance: While token-level part-of-speech tag information is a staple feature of classic NER approaches (Finkel et al., 2005), it is less clear if encoders trained on tasks that require conceptual representations (and possibly understanding) of sentence- and document-length context, learn entity representations useful for NER.

PLM fine-tuned on NER We also experiment with BERT$_{\text{CoNLL}}$, a BERT model fine-tuned on the CoNLL-2003 NER dataset. As this model's hidden representations have been adapted to NER, we expect it to exhibit better performance than the other representations. The most interesting question of using this model is whether its representations transfer to NER datasets with non-CoNLL tagsets.

PLM with contrastive learning For each of the English PLM encoders, we apply contrastive learning to learn representations with better separability. The idea of contrastive learning is to pull positives closer and push negatives away in the representation space during the pre-training phase (Rethmeier and Augenstein, 2021). We use the loss function proposed by Chopra et al. (2005):

$$\mathcal{L}_{CL}(x_i, x_j; \boldsymbol{\theta}) := \mathbb{1}_{y_i=y_j} \cdot \|f_{\boldsymbol{\theta}}(x_i) - f_{\boldsymbol{\theta}}(x_j)\| \\ + \mathbb{1}_{y_i \neq y_j} \cdot \max\left(0, \epsilon - \|f_{\boldsymbol{\theta}}(x_i) - f_{\boldsymbol{\theta}}(x_j)\|\right).$$

To guarantee that this label-aware contrastive learning conforms to the few-shot setting, we construct positive/negative pairs from the support set: Given an N-way K-shot support set, for each of the N classes we construct 1 positive pair and K negative pairs.[3]

3.2 Readout approaches

We analyze three variants for the readout approach:[4] (1) **Logistic Regression (LR)**, a linear classification algorithm that can be extended to multinomial logistic regression to deal with multi-class (N-way) settings, such as the one discussed here. (2) **k-Nearest Neighbor (NN)**, a non-parametric classification method adopted in metric space. As proposed in StructShot (Yang and Katiyar, 2020), we set $k = 1$ to find the exact nearest token in the support set. (3) **Nearest Centroid (NC)** works similar to **NN**, but instead of computing the distance between the query and every instance in the embedding space, we represent each class by the centroid of all token embeddings belonging to this class, and assign the query to the class with the nearest centroid.

3.3 Datasets

In order to provide a comprehensive evaluation, we evaluate all encoders on a range of

models are listed in Appendix A.

[3]One extra example per class is needed for $K = 1$ to build one positive pair for this class. This extra example is involved only in the contrastive learning phase and not introduced to the encoding and readout steps.

[4]Computational details of the readout approaches can be found in Appendix B.

datasets covering different languages and domains, including seven English benchmarks: CoNLL-2003 (Tjong Kim Sang and De Meulder, 2003), Few-NERD (Ding et al., 2021), OntoNotes 5.0 (Weischedel et al., 2013), WikiAnn (Pan et al., 2017), WNUT-17 (Derczynski et al., 2017), WikiGold (Balasuriya et al., 2009), and the dataset of Zhang et al. (2020). For German, we selected the following three datasets: CoNLL-2003 (Tjong Kim Sang and De Meulder, 2003), Smartdata (Schiersch et al., 2018) and GermEval 2014 (Benikova et al., 2014). Table 1 lists the domains and tagset details of each dataset.

3.4 Experimental settings / Hyperparameters

Datasets We use the BIO tagging schema by default and the IO schema only when BIO is not provided by the original dataset (in case of Few-NERD, OntoNotes 5.0 and WikiGold). WikiGold and the dataset of Zhang et al. (2020) do not provide train/test splits, we therefore use the full dataset to sample support and query sets. For all other datasets, test splits are used for sampling.[5]

General settings For each dataset, we evaluate our methods under three few-shot scenarios: 5-way 1-shot, 5-way 5-shot and 5-way 10-shot. To produce accurate performance estimates, we sample 600 episodes for each scenario and report the mean token-level micro-F1 score over all episodes, averaged over all positive classes, and excluding the 'O' class.

Encoders Max-length is fixed at 128. We use randomly initialized, static embeddings as the baseline encoder (*Random*). For contrastive learning, we use the Adam optimizer and set the learning rate to be 5×10^{-5} and the number of epochs to be 1 across all encoders.

Readout approaches We L2-normalize the encoder embeddings before feeding them to the readout model. For NN and NC classification, Euclidean distance serves as the similarity metric between tokens. For LR, an L2-penalty is applied to the coefficients. All reported results use LR as the default readout method, unless specified otherwise, as we found LR to perform best on average (see Section 4.4).

Framework implementation We implement our low-resource NER encoder evaluation framework using the HuggingFace Transformers library (Wolf et al., 2020), Hydra (Yadan, 2019), and PyTorch (Paszke et al., 2019). Additional scenarios, encoders, and datasets can be easily added simply by creating new experiment configurations. Adding new readout methods is also a simple matter of a few lines of code.

[5]For Few-NERD, we use the test data from the "supervised" split.

4 Results and Discussion

4.1 Comparison of PLM encoders

We first analyze PLM encoders which have not been fine-tuned on any task.

English results Table 2 presents the experimental results of English-language encoders for different scenarios and datasets. For all scenarios and datasets, the PLM encoders outperform the randomly initialized baseline by a large margin. As expected, the NER classification performance of the encoders increases with higher K, i.e. with more instances per class in the support set. Overall, the level of performance across various datasets of this encoder-only approach to low-resource NER is surprisingly good: We observe that ALBERT achieves a token-level F1 score of $F1 = 72.8$ on CoNLL-2003, XLNet a score of $F1 = 85.7$ on Few-NERD fine-grained, and RoBERTa a score of $F1 = 83.8$ on OntoNotes 5.0. While these results are not directly comparable to those of state-of-the-art, fully supervised approaches due to the differences in the evaluation setup, they are achieved essentially fine-tuning-free, and with much fewer labeled instances per class.

Encoder analysis The best-performing encoders, on average and across datasets, are ALBERT, RoBERTa, and BERT. ALBERT is by far the best encoder for $K = 1$, but the other encoders achieve comparable performance or outperform ALBERT for $K \geq 5$. Even though ALBERT is an order of magnitude smaller in terms of its number of parameters than either BERT or RoBERTa, it provides very competitive embeddings in our evaluation setup. As can be expected, $\text{BERT}_{\text{cased}}$ consistently outperforms $\text{BERT}_{\text{uncased}}$ for datasets with tag sets where casing provides useful information for NER (e.g. CoNLL, WikiGold), but does not necessarily perform better if the tag set contains entity types whose instances use lower-case spelling. XLNet achieves mixed results, mainly depending on the dataset – on CoNLL-2003, WikiAnn and WNUT-17, its F1 scores are significantly lower for all scenarios than those of the best encoder, while on Few-NERD fine-grained, XLNet achieves the

Dataset	K	Random	BERT↓	BERT↑	ALBERT↓	RoBERTa↑	SpanBERT↑	XLNet↑
$\text{CoNLL-2003}_{\text{EN}}$	1	9.52	21.96	22.04	**33.03**†	21.71	18.39	18.49
	5	12.53	60.94	62.17	**68.33**†	64.49	43.22	44.82
	10	13.71	66.11	68.79	**72.76**	72.09	49.79	52.43
OntoNotes 5.0	1	18.66	42.71	45.09	**50.45**†	42.74	34.30	38.40
	5	19.73	74.68	77.70	77.66	**78.70**	65.64	72.60
	10	18.88	80.92	82.70	82.10	**83.80**†	74.14	78.38
$\text{Few-NERD}_{\text{coarse}}$	1	12.12	25.99	28.52	**35.67**†	28.12	23.34	25.93
	5	15.59	53.85	56.04	**59.14**	58.66	45.50	52.32
	10	16.04	59.44	63.20	63.30	**65.52**†	52.65	61.94
$\text{Few-NERD}_{\text{fine}}$	1	21.14	49.74	48.50	**54.27**†	51.27	39.13	47.02
	5	21.00	80.12	79.26	78.08	81.70	71.93	**82.73**
	10	20.62	84.07	83.21	81.17	84.95	78.39	**85.73**
WNUT-17	1	18.86	25.71	25.67	**28.47**†	25.43	23.14	24.36
	5	19.11	51.56	50.58	**55.12**	54.59	42.29	42.26
	10	18.52	58.77	60.37	60.41	**63.93**†	48.84	49.74
WikiAnn	1	12.07	24.53	25.92	**32.63**†	24.80	22.67	22.06
	5	15.64	48.33	52.29	**53.11**†	51.34	40.60	36.81
	10	16.95	54.84	59.48	59.10	**60.83**	46.44	44.19
WikiGold	1	3.71	18.40	21.30	**32.30**†	20.63	14.90	18.01
	5	10.02	49.19	55.54	55.87	**56.08**	41.07	45.44
	10	11.62	55.85	63.91	61.23	**64.84**	48.09	53.85
Zhang et al.	1	13.49	37.39	36.82	**41.23**†	38.79	25.83	31.25
	5	17.08	63.19	62.17	62.73	**66.44**†	49.08	57.69
	10	16.21	67.45	67.09	66.61	**70.16**†	54.80	63.79

Table 2: Token-level micro-F1 scores of PLM encoders and a random baseline for 5-way K-shot scenarios, with logistic regression readout. † denotes scores with significant difference to the next-best encoder's score ($\alpha = 0.05$). ↑ and ↓ indicate cased and uncased models.

Dataset	K	Random	BERT↑	Gott-BERT↑	XLM-R↑
$\text{CoNLL-2003}_{\text{DE}}$	1	12.53	29.42	26.27	**30.65**
	5	15.38	**65.98**	58.37	65.22
	10	16.00	**71.43**	64.77	71.18
GermEval 2014	1	17.52	25.89	24.08	**27.24**
	5	20.70	**61.79**†	54.06	58.51
	10	18.33	**71.18**†	60.30	65.37
Smartdata	1	26.12	51.12	49.96	**53.17**
	5	23.52	**82.50**†	79.30	80.89
	10	21.55	**86.01**	83.10	85.66

Table 3: Token-level micro-F1 scores of German PLM encoders and a random baseline under 5-way K-shot scenarios, with logistic regression readout. † denotes scores with a significant difference to the next-best encoder's score ($\alpha = 0.05$). ↑ indicates cased models.

best score of all encoders. SpanBERT on average shows the worst performance of all encoders, with F1 scores in most scenarios several percentage points lower than even those of XLNet. This suggests that SpanBERT's span-level masking and training with a span boundary objective produce token-level embeddings that are less well separable by the logistic regression classifier.

Dataset analysis On a per-dataset basis, we can observe the following from Table 2: On CoNLL-2003, ALBERT outperforms the next-best encoder $\text{BERT}_{\text{cased}}$ for $K = 1$ by 11% F1, and achieves a best score of $F1 = 72.8$ for $K = 10$, closely followed by RoBERTa. XLNet's and SpanBERT's F1 scores are more than 20% lower than those of ALBERT for $K = 5$ and $K = 10$. On Few-NERD with coarse labels, ALBERT is again the best encoder at $K = 1$. For $K = 10$, RoBERTa achieves $F1 = 65.5$, but the other encoders except for SpanBERT perform almost as well. Using the fine-grained labels of Few-NERD, all encoders achieve around 80% F1 score. The overall picture is similar for OntoNotes 5.0 and the dataset of Zhang et al., with ALBERT being the best encoder at $K = 1$ and RoBERTa outperforming the other encoders at $K = 10$. BERT and XLNet show competitive performance to ALBERT and RoBERTa, yielding slightly lower F1 scores in all scenarios. This trend is also confirmed for the remaining datasets, WikiAnn, WNUT-17 and WikiGold, with ALBERT and RoBERTa being the strongest contenders, and BERT often catching up

Dataset	K	BERT↓	B_{POS}↓	B_{MNLI}↓	B_{SQuAD}↓
CoNLL-2003$_{EN}$	1	21.96	**43.01**†	22.29	35.05
	5	60.94	65.72	61.34	**65.94**
	10	66.11	68.46	64.71	**68.50**
OntoNotes 5.0	1	42.71	**50.85**†	42.99	47.83
	5	74.68	66.17	75.29	**76.37**
	10	80.92	68.02	**80.94**	79.68
Few-NERD$_{coarse}$	1	25.99	34.70	26.08	**35.07**
	5	53.85	49.88	52.52	**59.77**†
	10	59.44	52.78	58.17	**63.09**†
Few-NERD$_{fine}$	1	49.74	43.97	46.71	**51.17**
	5	**80.12**†	63.08	77.14	78.58
	10	**84.07**†	66.43	81.26	81.58
WNUT-17	1	25.71	**32.04**†	25.12	29.04
	5	**51.56**	44.90	48.50	51.05
	10	**58.77**†	49.11	56.30	54.58
WikiAnn	1	24.53	32.92	23.35	**33.33**
	5	48.33	43.54	46.94	**55.93**†
	10	54.84	45.70	53.47	**63.37**†
WikiGold	1	18.40	**37.46**†	20.33	30.80
	5	49.19	**55.54**†	50.86	53.96
	10	55.85	55.62	55.81	**57.99**†
Zhang et al.	1	37.39	**45.67**†	37.29	40.90
	5	**63.19**	59.58	62.98	61.01
	10	**67.45**	60.61	66.23	61.95

(a) Micro-F1 scores of BERT, and fine-tuned $BERT_{POS}$, $BERT_{MNLI}$ and $BERT_{SQuAD}$.

Dataset	Overlap	K	BERT↓	B_{CoNLL}↓
CoNLL-2003$_{EN}$	1.00	1	21.96	**90.46**†
		5	60.94	**94.73**†
		10	66.11	**94.40**†
WikiGold	1.00	1	18.40	**68.83**†
		5	49.19	**81.40**†
		10	55.85	**84.68**†
WikiAnn	0.75	1	24.53	**55.15**†
		5	48.33	**67.22**†
		10	54.84	**71.34**†
Few-NERD$_{coarse}$	0.50	1	25.99	**53.25**†
		5	53.85	**70.04**†
		10	59.44	**72.66**†
WNUT-17	0.25	1	25.71	**44.96**†
		5	51.56	**63.99**†
		10	58.77	**69.76**†
OntoNotes 5.0	0.16	1	42.71	**58.99**†
		5	74.68	**76.21**†
		10	**80.92**†	77.75
Few-NERD$_{fine}$	0	1	49.74	**59.36**†
		5	**80.12**	79.70
		10	**84.07**†	82.00
Zhang et al.	0	1	37.39	**49.22**†
		5	63.19	**65.40**†
		10	**67.45**	66.13

(b) Micro-F1 scores of BERT and $BERT_{CoNLL}$. The datasets are listed in descending order of tag set overlap with CoNLL-2003, as measured by Jaccard Index.

Table 4: Token-level micro-F1 scores of fine-tuned encoders under 5-way K-shot scenarios, with LR readout. † denotes scores with significant difference to the next-best encoder's score ($\alpha = 0.05$). ↓ indicates uncased models.

in terms of F1 scores with increasing K.

German results Table 3 shows the results of German-language encoders and the random baseline on three evaluation datasets. Similar to the English results, we observe that: (i) BERT, GottBERT and XLM-RoBERTa all benefit from more support instances, i.e. achieve a better performance with a larger training set, and outperform the random baseline by a large margin. (ii) XLM-RoBERTa shows the best performance across datasets in one-shot settings, whereas BERT outperforms the other encoders for $K \geq 5$. (iii) GottBERT's encodings yield features that are less useful for low-resource NER, resulting in worse performance than the other two encoders in all scenarios.

On CoNLL-2003, BERT achieves a micro-F1 score of 71.4 at $K = 10$, XLM-R a competitive score of 71.2, while GottBERT only achieves $F1 = 64.8$. Similar performance differences between the three encoders can be observed for the other two datasets at $K = 5$ and $K = 10$. At $K = 1$, XLM-R consistently outperforms BERT and GottBert, with GottBERT showing the worst performance. The results show that BERT, a model trained with less, but likely quality training data (Wikipedia, OpenLegalData, News) produces representations that are more suited for low-resource NER in most of the evaluated settings, compared to GottBERT (145GB of unfiltered web text), and XLM-RoBERTa (≈100GB filtered CommonCrawl data for German).

4.2 Fine-tuned encoders

Fine-tuned PLM The next group of encoders we analyze are encoders fine-tuned on an intermediate task, in our case POS tagging, NLI, and QA. Results are shown in Table 4a. We can see that using a BERT encoder fine-tuned on POS tagging significantly improves F1 scores at $K = 1$ for all datasets except Few-NERD fine-grained, on average by about 9 points. However, for $K \geq 5$, $BERT_{POS}$'s performance is significantly worse than that of BERT for the majority of datasets, except CoNLL-2003 and WikiGold.

The $BERT_{MNLI}$ model's performance is competitive with the base BERT model's, with no statistically significant differences. Fine-tuning on this sentence-level task, which is rather unrelated to NER, hence seems to have neither negative nor positive effects on the resulting token embeddings.

Embeddings obtained from $\text{BERT}_{\text{SQuAD}}$, fine-tuned on document-level span extraction, outperform BERT in most settings, often with statistical significance. However, on some datasets (e.g. WNUT-17, $\text{Few-NERD}_{\text{fine}}$), $\text{BERT}_{\text{SQuAD}}$'s scores are lower than BERT's for $K \geq 5$. Compared to the other fine-tuned encoders, $\text{BERT}_{\text{SQuAD}}$ performs better in general for $K \geq 5$. Its good performance may be attributed to the fact that approximately 41.5% of the answers in the SQuAD dataset correspond to common entity types, and another 31.8% to common noun phrases (Rajpurkar et al., 2016).

The observations for these three encoders coincide with the intuition, that the more relevant the knowledge encoded by the intermediate task is w.r.t. the target task, the more likely an improvement on the target task becomes.

PLM fine-tuned on NER Table 4b shows the results obtained for $\text{BERT}_{\text{CoNLL}}$, an encoder that was fine-tuned on CoNLL-2003. As can be expected, this encoder performs very well on the CoNLL-2003 test set, with large F1 gains in all scenarios. For most of the other datasets, F1 scores are also significantly improved for all settings of K, especially with a large tagset overlap. These results coincide with the intuition that the higher the tagset overlap, the larger the improvement. However, we note that some of these datasets are constructed from other data sources, e.g. web and social media texts, which indicates some transferability of the CoNLL-2003-tuned representations. Even for datasets where there is little or no overlap (OntoNotes 5.0, Zhang et al.), there are at least some gains at $K = 1$. However, at $K = 10$, the performance of the embeddings obtained from $\text{BERT}_{\text{CoNLL}}$ is significantly worse than that of the base BERT model.

4.3 PLM with contrastive learning

Table 5 compares the results of English encoders before and after contrastive learning. In general, results are mixed: For ALBERT and SpanBERT, using CL improves F1 scores in most cases, often with significant differences, whereas for BERT, RoBERTa and XLNET, the base encoders mostly exhibit (marginally) better performance.

Encoder analysis We observe that ALBERT benefits the most from contrastive learning, with significant F1 gains in 5 out of 12 comparisons, followed by SpanBERT (3), XLNet (1), BERT (1) and RoBERTa (0). Surprisingly, it achieves slightly higher F1-scores on Few-NERD coarse-grained and significantly higher F1-scores on WikiGold in all three scenarios. For 1-shot scenario on CoNLL-2003, ALBERT also gets a large F1 increase by 3.68%, the best improvement among all encoders.

Dataset analysis Few-NERD coarse-grained and WikiGold show better compatibility with contrastive learning, with 11 and 8 F1 improvements out of 15 comparisons after contrastive learning, respectively, compared with CoNLL-2003 (6) and OntoNotes 5.0 (4). Specifically, all five encoders have F1 gains on Few-NERD dataset in the one-shot scenario.

4.4 Readout approaches

Finally, Table 6 compares the different readout approaches on the CoNLL-2003 and OntoNotes 5.0 datasets, using ALBERT. For $K >= 5$, Logistic Regression outperforms Nearest Centroid and Nearest Neighbor classification, while for one-shot scenarios Nearest Neighbor performs best. NC is outperformed by LR and NN in all scenarios but 5-shot on OntoNotes 5.0. This suggests that with very few samples, the raw token embedding information, as used by NN, is a better representation of a class than the averaged embeddings as produced by LR and CN, but with more samples, weighted embeddings obtained with LR are more useful.

5 Related Work

Few-shot NER Recent work on few-shot NER has primarily focused on integrating additional knowledge to support the classification process. Fritzler et al. (2019) are the first to use pre-trained word embeddings for this task. Yang and Katiyar (2020) extend a Nearest Neighbor token-level classifier with a Viterbi decoder for structured prediction over entire sentences. Huang et al (2021) propose to continue pre-training of a PLM encoder with distantly supervised, in-domain data, and to integrate self-training to create additional, soft-labeled training data. Recently, Gao et al. (2021) and Ma et al. (2021) investigate methods for making PLMs better few-shot learners via prompt-based fine-tuning. While these approaches extend standard few-shot learning algorithms in promising di-

Dataset	K	BERT↓		ALBERT↓		RoBERTa↑		SpanBERT↑		XLNet↑	
		w/o CL	CL	w/o CL	CL	w/o CL	CL	w/o CL	CL	w/o CL	CL
CoNLL-2003$_{\text{EN}}$	1	21.96	**23.87**†	33.03	**36.71**†	21.71	**22.57**	**18.39**	17.61	**18.49**	18.25
	5	**60.94**	60.55	**68.33**	66.85	**64.49**	62.45	43.22	**44.23**	44.82	**45.93**
	10	**66.11**	65.03	**72.76**	70.66	**72.09**	70.17	48.79	**49.82**	**52.43**	49.25
OntoNotes 5.0	1	42.71	**42.89**	50.45	**51.38**	**42.74**	41.66	**34.30**	32.95	38.40	**38.64**
	5	**74.68**	74.02	**77.66**	76.65	**78.70**	75.29	**65.64**	64.29	**72.60**	70.66
	10	**80.92**	80.36	**82.10**	81.47	**83.80**	82.51	74.14	**74.72**	**78.38**	75.99
Few-NERD$_{\text{coarse}}$	1	25.99	**27.42**	35.67	**38.16**†	28.12	**29.10**	23.34	**23.40**	25.93	**26.35**
	5	**53.85**	52.97	59.14	**59.71**	**58.66**	55.75	45.50	**46.03**	52.32	**54.91**†
	10	59.44	**59.89**	63.30	**64.53**	**65.52**	62.86	52.65	**55.47**†	**61.94**	61.45
WikiGold	1	**18.40**	16.85	32.30	**34.05**†	**20.63**	19.90	14.90	**15.39**	18.01	**19.13**
	5	49.19	49.19	55.87	**57.67**†	**56.08**	53.91	41.07	**42.92**†	**45.44**	44.21
	10	55.85	**56.87**	61.23	**62.68**†	**64.84**	63.05	48.09	**50.93**†	**53.85**	52.26

Table 5: Token-level micro F1-scores of PLM encoders without and with contrastive learning (CL) for 5-way K-shot scenarios, with logistic regression readout. † denotes scores with a significant ($\alpha = 0.05$) improvement after contrastive learning. ↑ and ↓ indicate cased and uncased models.

Dataset	K	LR	NC	NN
CoNLL-2003$_{\text{EN}}$	1	33.03	35.21	**40.76**†
	5	**68.33**†	61.53	62.24
	10	**72.76**†	62.65	67.79
OntoNotes 5.0	1	50.45	51.52	**52.72**
	5	**77.66**†	72.46	71.04
	10	**82.10**†	73.49	76.11

Table 6: Micro-F1 scores of ALBERT for 5-way K-shot scenarios, comparing Logistic Regression (LR), Nearest Centroid (NC) and Nearest Neighbor (NN) readout approaches.

rections, none of them directly investigate the contribution of different pre-trained representations. As such, our analysis complements these works. Das et al. (2021) present a contrastive pre-training approach for few-shot NER that uses in-domain data to fine-tune token embeddings before few-shot classification. In contrast, we only consider contrastive examples from the sampled few-shot set to conform to the low-resource setting.

Encoder comparisons In parallel to our work, Pearce et al. (2021) compare different Transformer models on extractive question answering and, similar to our results, find RoBERTa to perform best, outperforming BERT. However, they did not reproduce the strong performance we achieved with ALBERT and, unlike our results, found XLNet to be consistently outperforming BERT. Cortiz (2021) compare Transformer models for text-based emotion recognition and also found RoBERTa to perform best with XLNet being (shared) second, again outperforming BERT.

There are several studies that investigate the performance and transferability of PLM representations that have been fine-tuned with task-specific NER data (Pires et al., 2019; Wu and Dredze, 2020; Adelani et al., 2021; Ebrahimi and Kann, 2021; Ács et al., 2021). For example, Wu and Dredze (2020) analyze multilingual mBERT representations, with a focus on low-resource languages, i.e. languages that are not well represented in the original mBERT training data. They observe that mBERT's NER performance is worse for very high- and very low-resource languages, and that performance drops significantly with less pretraining and supervised data. Adelani et al. (2021) find that fine-tuned XLM-R-large representations outperform fine-tuned mBERT representations in 7 of 10 evaluated African languages, which they attribute to the larger pretraining data size of XLM-R. Ebrahimi and Kann (2021) find that continued pretraining with Bible data from over 1600 languages improves zero-shot NER performance of XLM-R representations.

Our work can also be viewed as a kind of probing task (Conneau et al., 2018; Belinkov and Glass, 2019; Tenney et al., 2019; Petroni et al., 2019; Kassner et al., 2021), since we analyze how much information about named entities is preserved in the pre-trained representations, as measured by a linear classifier.

6 Conclusion

We presented a systematic, comparative study of pre-trained encoders on the task of low-resource named entity recognition. We find that encoder performance varies significantly depending on the scenario and the mix of pre-training and fine-tuning strategies. This suggests that the choice of encoders for a particular setting in current state-of-the-art low-resource NER approaches may need to be carefully (re-)evaluated. We also find that PLM encoders achieve reasonably good token classification performance on many English and German NER datasets with as little as 10 examples per class, in a fine-tuning-free setting. In particular, ALBERT turned out to be a very strong contender in one-shot settings, whereas RoBERTa often outperforms other PLMs in settings with more examples. For German, BERT shows the best average performance across scenarios, with XLM-R being more useful in one-shot settings.

One obvious direction for future work is to evaluate additional encoders, in particular models that are pre-trained in an entity-aware manner (Peters et al., 2019; Zhang et al., 2019), and PLMs for low-resource languages that are trained on much smaller corpora or underrepresented in multilingual PLMs. While our analysis is limited to NER, another future direction would be to adapt the encoder-readout framework in order to evaluate other low-resource classification tasks.

Acknowledgments

We would like to thank Nils Feldhus, David Harbecke, and the anonymous reviewers for their valuable comments and feedback on the paper. This work has been supported by the German Federal Ministry for Economic Affairs and Climate Action as part of the project PLASS (01MD19003E), and by the German Federal Ministry of Education and Research as part of the project CORA4NLP (01IW20010). Christoph Alt is supported by the Deutsche Forschungsgemeinschaft (DFG, German Research Foundation) under Germany's Excellence Strategy – EXC 2002/1 "Science of Intelligence" – project number 390523135.

References

Judit Ács, Dániel Lévai, and Andras Kornai. 2021. Evaluating transferability of BERT models on uralic languages. In *Proceedings of the Seventh International Workshop on Computational Linguistics of Uralic Languages*, pages 8–17, Syktyvkar, Russia (Online). Association for Computational Linguistics.

David Ifeoluwa Adelani, Jade Abbott, Graham Neubig, Daniel D'souza, Julia Kreutzer, Constantine Lignos, Chester Palen-Michel, Happy Buzaaba, Shruti Rijhwani, Sebastian Ruder, Stephen Mayhew, Israel Abebe Azime, Shamsuddeen H. Muhammad, Chris Chinenye Emezue, Joyce Nakatumba-Nabende, Perez Ogayo, Aremu Anuoluwapo, Catherine Gitau, Derguene Mbaye, Jesujoba Alabi, Seid Muhie Yimam, Tajuddeen Rabiu Gwadabe, Ignatius Ezeani, Rubungo Andre Niyongabo, Jonathan Mukiibi, Verrah Otiende, Iroro Orife, Davis David, Samba Ngom, Tosin Adewumi, Paul Rayson, Mofetoluwa Adeyemi, Gerald Muriuki, Emmanuel Anebi, Chiamaka Chukwuneke, Nkiruka Odu, Eric Peter Wairagala, Samuel Oyerinde, Clemencia Siro, Tobius Saul Bateesa, Temilola Oloyede, Yvonne Wambui, Victor Akinode, Deborah Nabagereka, Maurice Katusiime, Ayodele Awokoya, Mouhamadane MBOUP, Dibora Gebreyohannes, Henok Tilaye, Kelechi Nwaike, Degaga Wolde, Abdoulaye Faye, Blessing Sibanda, Orevaoghene Ahia, Bonaventure F. P. Dossou, Kelechi Ogueji, Thierno Ibrahima DIOP, Abdoulaye Diallo, Adewale Akinfaderin, Tendai Marengereke, and Salomey Osei. 2021. MasakhaNER: Named entity recognition for African languages. *Transactions of the Association for Computational Linguistics*, 9:1116–1131.

Dominic Balasuriya, Nicky Ringland, Joel Nothman, Tara Murphy, and James R. Curran. 2009. Named entity recognition in Wikipedia. In *Proceedings of the 2009 Workshop on The People's Web Meets NLP: Collaboratively Constructed Semantic Resources (People's Web)*, pages 10–18, Suntec, Singapore. Association for Computational Linguistics.

Yonatan Belinkov and James Glass. 2019. Analysis methods in neural language processing: A survey. *Transactions of the Association for Computational Linguistics*, 7:49–72.

Darina Benikova, Chris Biemann, and Marc Reznicek. 2014. NoSta-D named entity annotation for German: Guidelines and dataset. In *Proceedings of the Ninth International Conference on Language Resources and Evaluation (LREC'14)*, pages 2524–2531, Reykjavik, Iceland. European Language Resources Association (ELRA).

Tom Brown, Benjamin Mann, Nick Ryder, Melanie Subbiah, Jared D Kaplan, Prafulla Dhariwal, Arvind Neelakantan, Pranav Shyam, Girish Sastry, Amanda Askell, Sandhini Agarwal, Ariel Herbert-Voss, Gretchen Krueger, Tom Henighan, Rewon Child, Aditya Ramesh, Daniel Ziegler, Jeffrey Wu, Clemens Winter, Chris Hesse, Mark Chen, Eric Sigler, Mateusz Litwin, Scott Gray, Benjamin Chess, Jack Clark, Christopher Berner, Sam McCandlish, Alec Radford, Ilya Sutskever, and Dario Amodei. 2020. Language models are few-shot learners. In *Advances in Neural Information Processing Systems*, volume 33, pages 1877–1901. Curran Associates, Inc.

Sumit Chopra, Raia Hadsell, and Yann LeCun. 2005. Learning a similarity metric discriminatively, with application to face verification. In *2005 IEEE Computer Society Conference on Computer Vision and Pattern Recognition (CVPR'05)*, volume 1, pages 539–546. IEEE.

Alexis Conneau, Kartikay Khandelwal, Naman Goyal, Vishrav Chaudhary, Guillaume Wenzek, Francisco Guzmán, Edouard Grave, Myle Ott, Luke Zettlemoyer, and Veselin Stoyanov. 2020. Unsupervised cross-lingual representation learning at scale. In *Proceedings of the 58th Annual Meeting of the Association for Computational Linguistics*, pages 8440–8451, Online. Association for Computational Linguistics.

Alexis Conneau, Germán Kruszewski, Guillaume Lample, Loïc Barrault, and Marco Baroni. 2018. What you can cram into a single \backslash$&!#* vector: Probing sentence embeddings for linguistic properties. In *Proceedings of the 56th Annual Meeting of the Association for Computational Linguistics (Volume 1: Long Papers)*, pages 2126–2136, Melbourne, Australia. Association for Computational Linguistics.

Diogo Cortiz. 2021. Exploring transformers in emotion recognition: a comparison of bert, distillbert, roberta, xlnet and electra. *CoRR*, abs/2104.02041.

Sarkar Snigdha Sarathi Das, Arzoo Katiyar, Rebecca J. Passonneau, and Rui Zhang. 2021. Container: Few-shot named entity recognition via contrastive learning. *CoRR*, abs/2109.07589.

Leon Derczynski, Eric Nichols, Marieke van Erp, and Nut Limsopatham. 2017. Results of the WNUT2017 shared task on novel and emerging entity recognition. In *Proceedings of the 3rd Workshop on Noisy User-generated Text*, pages 140–147, Copenhagen, Denmark. Association for Computational Linguistics.

Jacob Devlin, Ming-Wei Chang, Kenton Lee, and Kristina Toutanova. 2019. BERT: Pre-training of deep bidirectional transformers for language understanding. In *Proceedings of the 2019 Conference of the North American Chapter of the Association for Computational Linguistics: Human Language Technologies, Volume 1 (Long and Short Papers)*, pages 4171–4186, Minneapolis, Minnesota. Association for Computational Linguistics.

Ning Ding, Guangwei Xu, Yulin Chen, Xiaobin Wang, Xu Han, Pengjun Xie, Haitao Zheng, and Zhiyuan Liu. 2021. Few-NERD: A few-shot named entity recognition dataset. In *Proceedings of the 59th Annual Meeting of the Association for Computational Linguistics and the 11th International Joint Conference on Natural Language Processing (Volume 1: Long Papers)*, pages 3198–3213, Online. Association for Computational Linguistics.

Abteen Ebrahimi and Katharina Kann. 2021. How to adapt your pretrained multilingual model to 1600 languages. In *Proceedings of the 59th Annual Meeting of the Association for Computational Linguistics and the 11th International Joint Conference on Natural Language Processing (Volume 1: Long Papers)*, pages 4555–4567, Online. Association for Computational Linguistics.

Jenny Rose Finkel, Trond Grenager, and Christopher Manning. 2005. Incorporating Non-local Information into Information Extraction Systems by Gibbs Sampling. In *Proceedings of the 43rd Annual Meeting on Association for Computational Linguistics*, ACL '05, pages 363–370, Stroudsburg, PA, USA. Association for Computational Linguistics.

Alexander Fritzler, Varvara Logacheva, and Maksim Kretov. 2019. Few-shot classification in Named Entity Recognition Task. *Proceedings of the 34th ACM/SIGAPP Symposium on Applied Computing - SAC '19*, pages 993–1000. ArXiv: 1812.06158.

Tianyu Gao, Adam Fisch, and Danqi Chen. 2021. Making pre-trained language models better few-shot learners. In *Proceedings of the 59th Annual Meeting of the Association for Computational Linguistics and the 11th International Joint Conference on Natural Language Processing (Volume 1: Long Papers)*, pages 3816–3830, Online. Association for Computational Linguistics.

Jiaxin Huang, Chunyuan Li, Krishan Subudhi, Damien Jose, Shobana Balakrishnan, Weizhu Chen, Baolin Peng, Jianfeng Gao, and Jiawei Han. 2021. Few-shot named entity recognition: An empirical baseline study. In *Proceedings of the 2021 Conference on Empirical Methods in Natural Language Processing*, pages 10408–10423, Online and Punta Cana, Dominican Republic. Association for Computational Linguistics.

Mandar Joshi, Danqi Chen, Yinhan Liu, Daniel S. Weld, Luke Zettlemoyer, and Omer Levy. 2020. SpanBERT: Improving pre-training by representing and predicting spans. *Transactions of the Association for Computational Linguistics*, 8:64–77.

Nora Kassner, Philipp Dufter, and Hinrich Schütze. 2021. Multilingual LAMA: Investigating knowledge in multilingual pretrained language models. In *Proceedings of the 16th Conference of the European Chapter of the Association for Computational Linguistics: Main Volume*, pages 3250–3258, Online. Association for Computational Linguistics.

Zhenzhong Lan, Mingda Chen, Sebastian Goodman, Kevin Gimpel, Piyush Sharma, and Radu Soricut. 2020. ALBERT: A lite BERT for self-supervised learning of language representations. In *8th International Conference on Learning Representations, ICLR 2020, Addis Ababa, Ethiopia, April 26-30, 2020*. OpenReview.net.

Yinhan Liu, Myle Ott, Naman Goyal, Jingfei Du, Mandar Joshi, Danqi Chen, Omer Levy, Mike Lewis, Luke Zettlemoyer, and Veselin Stoyanov. 2019.

Roberta: A robustly optimized BERT pretraining approach. *CoRR*, abs/1907.11692.

Ruotian Ma, Xin Zhou, Tao Gui, Yiding Tan, Qi Zhang, and Xuanjing Huang. 2021. Template-free prompt tuning for few-shot ner. *CoRR*, abs/2109.13532.

Xiaoman Pan, Boliang Zhang, Jonathan May, Joel Nothman, Kevin Knight, and Heng Ji. 2017. Cross-lingual name tagging and linking for 282 languages. In *Proceedings of the 55th Annual Meeting of the Association for Computational Linguistics (Volume 1: Long Papers)*, pages 1946–1958, Vancouver, Canada. Association for Computational Linguistics.

Adam Paszke, Sam Gross, Francisco Massa, Adam Lerer, James Bradbury, Gregory Chanan, Trevor Killeen, Zeming Lin, Natalia Gimelshein, Luca Antiga, Alban Desmaison, Andreas Kopf, Edward Yang, Zachary DeVito, Martin Raison, Alykhan Tejani, Sasank Chilamkurthy, Benoit Steiner, Lu Fang, Junjie Bai, and Soumith Chintala. 2019. Pytorch: An imperative style, high-performance deep learning library. In H. Wallach, H. Larochelle, A. Beygelzimer, F. d'Alché-Buc, E. Fox, and R. Garnett, editors, *Advances in Neural Information Processing Systems 32*, pages 8024–8035. Curran Associates, Inc.

Kate Pearce, Tiffany Zhan, Aneesh Komanduri, and Justin Zhan. 2021. A comparative study of transformer-based language models on extractive question answering. *CoRR*, abs/2110.03142.

Matthew Peters, Mark Neumann, Mohit Iyyer, Matt Gardner, Christopher Clark, Kenton Lee, and Luke Zettlemoyer. 2018. Deep Contextualized Word Representations. In *Proceedings of the 2018 Conference of the North American Chapter of the Association for Computational Linguistics: Human Language Technologies, Volume 1 (Long Papers)*, pages 2227–2237, New Orleans, Louisiana. Association for Computational Linguistics.

Matthew E. Peters, Mark Neumann, Robert Logan, Roy Schwartz, Vidur Joshi, Sameer Singh, and Noah A. Smith. 2019. Knowledge enhanced contextual word representations. In *Proceedings of the 2019 Conference on Empirical Methods in Natural Language Processing and the 9th International Joint Conference on Natural Language Processing (EMNLP-IJCNLP)*, pages 43–54, Hong Kong, China. Association for Computational Linguistics.

Fabio Petroni, Tim Rocktäschel, Sebastian Riedel, Patrick Lewis, Anton Bakhtin, Yuxiang Wu, and Alexander Miller. 2019. Language models as knowledge bases? In *Proceedings of the 2019 Conference on Empirical Methods in Natural Language Processing and the 9th International Joint Conference on Natural Language Processing (EMNLP-IJCNLP)*, pages 2463–2473, Hong Kong, China. Association for Computational Linguistics.

Telmo Pires, Eva Schlinger, and Dan Garrette. 2019. How multilingual is multilingual BERT? In *Proceedings of the 57th Annual Meeting of the Association for Computational Linguistics*, pages 4996–5001, Florence, Italy. Association for Computational Linguistics.

Clifton Poth, Jonas Pfeiffer, Andreas Rücklé, and Iryna Gurevych. 2021. What to pre-train on? Efficient intermediate task selection. In *Proceedings of the 2021 Conference on Empirical Methods in Natural Language Processing*, pages 10585–10605, Online and Punta Cana, Dominican Republic. Association for Computational Linguistics.

Pranav Rajpurkar, Jian Zhang, Konstantin Lopyrev, and Percy Liang. 2016. SQuAD: 100,000+ questions for machine comprehension of text. In *Proceedings of the 2016 Conference on Empirical Methods in Natural Language Processing*, pages 2383–2392, Austin, Texas. Association for Computational Linguistics.

Nils Rethmeier and Isabelle Augenstein. 2021. A primer on contrastive pretraining in language processing: Methods, lessons learned and perspectives. *CoRR*, abs/2102.12982.

Raphael Scheible, Fabian Thomczyk, Patric Tippmann, Victor Jaravine, and Martin Boeker. 2020. Gottbert: a pure german language model. *CoRR*, abs/2012.02110.

Martin Schiersch, Veselina Mironova, Maximilian Schmitt, Philippe Thomas, Aleksandra Gabryszak, and Leonhard Hennig. 2018. A German Corpus for Fine-Grained Named Entity Recognition and Relation Extraction of Traffic and Industry Events. In *Proceedings of the Eleventh International Conference on Language Resources and Evaluation (LREC 2018)*, Miyazaki, Japan. European Language Resources Association (ELRA).

Ian Tenney, Patrick Xia, Berlin Chen, Alex Wang, Adam Poliak, R. Thomas McCoy, Najoung Kim, Benjamin Van Durme, Sam Bowman, Dipanjan Das, and Ellie Pavlick. 2019. What do you learn from context? Probing for sentence structure in contextualized word representations. In *International Conference on Learning Representations*.

Erik F. Tjong Kim Sang and Fien De Meulder. 2003. Introduction to the CoNLL-2003 shared task: Language-independent named entity recognition. In *Proceedings of the Seventh Conference on Natural Language Learning at HLT-NAACL 2003*, pages 142–147.

Tu Vu, Tong Wang, Tsendsuren Munkhdalai, Alessandro Sordoni, Adam Trischler, Andrew Mattarella-Micke, Subhransu Maji, and Mohit Iyyer. 2020. Exploring and predicting transferability across NLP tasks. In *Proceedings of the 2020 Conference on Empirical Methods in Natural Language Processing (EMNLP)*, pages 7882–7926, Online. Association for Computational Linguistics.

Ralph Weischedel, Martha Palmer, Mitchell Marcus, Eduard Hovy, Sameer Pradhan, Lance Ramshaw, Nianwen Xue, Ann Taylor, Jeff Kaufman, Michelle Franchini, et al. 2013. Ontonotes release 5.0 ldc2013t19. *Linguistic Data Consortium, Philadelphia, PA*, 23.

Adina Williams, Nikita Nangia, and Samuel Bowman. 2018. A broad-coverage challenge corpus for sentence understanding through inference. In *Proceedings of the 2018 Conference of the North American Chapter of the Association for Computational Linguistics: Human Language Technologies, Volume 1 (Long Papers)*, pages 1112–1122. Association for Computational Linguistics.

Thomas Wolf, Lysandre Debut, Victor Sanh, Julien Chaumond, Clement Delangue, Anthony Moi, Pierric Cistac, Tim Rault, Rémi Louf, Morgan Funtowicz, Joe Davison, Sam Shleifer, Patrick von Platen, Clara Ma, Yacine Jernite, Julien Plu, Canwen Xu, Teven Le Scao, Sylvain Gugger, Mariama Drame, Quentin Lhoest, and Alexander M. Rush. 2020. Transformers: State-of-the-art natural language processing. In *Proceedings of the 2020 Conference on Empirical Methods in Natural Language Processing: System Demonstrations*, pages 38–45, Online. Association for Computational Linguistics.

Shijie Wu and Mark Dredze. 2020. Are all languages created equal in multilingual BERT? In *Proceedings of the 5th Workshop on Representation Learning for NLP*, pages 120–130, Online. Association for Computational Linguistics.

Omry Yadan. 2019. Hydra - a framework for elegantly configuring complex applications. Github.

Yi Yang and Arzoo Katiyar. 2020. Simple and effective few-shot named entity recognition with structured nearest neighbor learning. In *Proceedings of the 2020 Conference on Empirical Methods in Natural Language Processing (EMNLP)*, pages 6365–6375, Online. Association for Computational Linguistics.

Zhilin Yang, Zihang Dai, Yiming Yang, Jaime Carbonell, Russ R Salakhutdinov, and Quoc V Le. 2019. Xlnet: Generalized autoregressive pretraining for language understanding. *Advances in neural information processing systems*, 32.

Hanchu Zhang, Leonhard Hennig, Christoph Alt, Changjian Hu, Yao Meng, and Chao Wang. 2020. Bootstrapping named entity recognition in E-commerce with positive unlabeled learning. In *Proceedings of The 3rd Workshop on e-Commerce and NLP*, pages 1–6, Seattle, WA, USA. Association for Computational Linguistics.

Zhengyan Zhang, Xu Han, Zhiyuan Liu, Xin Jiang, Maosong Sun, and Qun Liu. 2019. ERNIE: Enhanced language representation with informative entities. In *Proceedings of the 57th Annual Meeting of the Association for Computational Linguistics*, pages 1441–1451, Florence, Italy. Association for Computational Linguistics.

A Additional Training Details

We used a single RTXA6000-GPU for all experiments. The average runtime per scenario (dataset, encoder) for 600 episodes was approximately 1 minute (1-shot), 3 minutes (5-shot) and 6 minutes (10-shot). Constrastive pre-training was also performed on the same single RTXA6000-GPU, and took approximately 1 hour of GPU-time, including hyperparameter search.

For contrastive pre-training, the following hyperparameters were manually tuned: learning rate in $[2 \times 10^{-5}, 5 \times 10^{-5}]$, the number of epochs in $[1, 2, 5]$. We used the most occurrences of F1-gains across all encoders and scenarios on CoNLL-2003 dataset as criterion for hyperparameter selection.

All pre-trained models evaluated in this study were used as they are available from HuggingFace's model hub, without any modifications. Table 7 lists the model identifiers. We used HuggingFace's dataset hub for all datasets except the dataset by Zhang et al. (2020), which is used here with the permission of the authors.

Model	HuggingFace ID
BERT↓	bert-base-uncased
BERT↑	bert-base-cased
ALBERT	albert-base-v2
RoBERTa	roberta-base
SpanBERT	SpanBERT/spanbert-base-cased
XLNET	xlnet-base-cased
BERT DE	bert-base-german-cased
GottBERT	uklfr/gottbert-base
XLM-R	xlm-roberta-base
BERT_{POS}	vblagoje/bert-english-uncased-finetuned-pos
$\text{BERT}_{\text{MNLI}}$	textattack/bert-base-uncased-MNLI
$\text{BERT}_{\text{SQuAD}}$	csarron/bert-base-uncased-squad-v1
$\text{BERT}_{\text{CoNLL}}$	dslim/bert-base-NER-uncased

Table 7: HuggingFace model identifiers of evaluated encoders

B Readout approaches

Logistic Regression (LR) is a linear classification algorithm that can be extended to multinomial logistic regression to deal with multi-class (N-way) settings, such as the one discussed here. The probability that query token x' belongs to the c-th class is given by:

$$\Pr(y = c) = \frac{\text{score}(x', c)}{\sum_{i=1}^{N} \text{score}(x', i)} \qquad (1)$$
$$\text{score}(x', i) := \exp(W_i \cdot f_{\theta}(x')),$$

where W is a matrix of N rows learned from the support set $\mathcal{S}$, and W_i denotes the i-th row of W. score$(\cdot)$ serves as the metric to measure the affinity between token x' and the prototype of class c, and the prediction is given by

$$y^* = \arg \max_{c \in \{1, \cdots, N\}} \text{score}(x', c).$$

k-Nearest Neighbor (NN) is a non-parametric classification method adopted in metric space. As proposed in STRUCTSHOT (Yang and Katiyar, 2020), we set $k = 1$ to find the exact nearest token in the support set. Given a query token x',

$$\begin{aligned} y^* &= \arg \min_{c \in \{1, \cdots, N\}} d_c(x') \\ d_c(x') &:= \min_{x \in \mathcal{S}_c} d\big(f_{\theta}(x'), f_{\theta}(x)\big), \end{aligned} \qquad (2)$$

where $\mathcal{S}_c$ is the set of support tokens whose tags are c, and d denotes the distance between two embeddings in the representation space.

Nearest Centroid (NC) works similar to **NN**. In contrast, for each query token x', instead of computing the distance between $f_{\theta}(x')$ and every instance in the embedding space, we represent each class by the centroid $\mathbf{c}_c$ of all embeddings belonging to this class, and assign token x' to the class with the nearest centroid:

$$\begin{aligned} y^* &= \arg \min_{c \in \{1, \cdots, N\}} d\big(f_{\theta}(x'), \mathbf{c}_c\big) \\ \mathbf{c}_c &= \frac{1}{|\mathcal{S}_c|} \sum_{x \in \mathcal{S}_c} f_{\theta}(x). \end{aligned} \qquad (3)$$

C Entity tag sets of English datasets

We list the full entity tag sets for all English benchmarks. Overlap entity tags with $\text{CoNLL-2003}_{\text{EN}}$ are highlighted with underline.

C.1 $\text{CoNLL-2003}_{\text{EN}}$

<u>LOC</u>, <u>MISC</u>, <u>ORG</u>, <u>PER</u>.

C.2 OntoNotes 5.0

CARDINAL, DATE, EVENT, FAC, GPE, LANGUAGE, LAW, <u>LOC</u>, MONEY, NORP, ORDINAL, <u>ORG</u>, PERCENT, <u>PERSON</u>, PRODUCT, QUANTITY, TIME, WORK_OF_ART.

C.3 $\text{Few-NERD}_{\text{coarse}}$

art, building, event, <u>location</u>, <u>organization</u>, <u>other</u>[6], <u>person</u>, product.

[6] $\text{Few-NERD}_{\text{coarse}}$ sets non-entity as 'O' and various entity types as 'other'. Therefore, we treat 'other' as 'MISC' in this case.

C.4 Few-NERD$_{\text{fine}}$

art-broadcastprogram, art-film, art-music, art-other, art-painting, art-writtenart, building-airport, building-hospital, building-hotel, building-library, building-other, building-restaurant, building-sportsfacility, building-theater, event-attack/battle/war/militaryconflict, event-disaster, event-election, event-other, event-protest, event-sportsevent, location-GPE, location-bodiesofwater, location-island, location-mountain, location-other, location-park, location-road/railway/highway/transit, organization-company, organization-education, organization-government/governmentagency, organization-media/newspaper, organization-other, organization-politicalparty, organization-religion, organization-showorganization, organization-sportsleague, organization-sportsteam, other-astronomything, other-award, other-biologything, other-chemicalthing, other-currency, other-disease, other-educationaldegree, other-god, other-language, other-law, other-livingthing, other-medical, person-actor, person-artist/author, person-athlete, person-director, person-other, person-politician, person-scholar, person-soldier, product-airplane, product-car, product-food, product-game, product-other, product-ship, product-software, product-train, product-weapon

C.5 WNUT-17

corporation, creative-work, group, location, person, product.

C.6 WikiAnn

LOC, ORG, PER.

C.7 WikiGold

LOC, MISC, ORG, PER.

C.8 Zhang et al.

ATTRIBUTE, BRAND, COMPONENT, PRODUCT.

Clozer: Adaptable Data Augmentation for Cloze-style Reading Comprehension

Holy Lovenia*, Bryan Wilie*, Willy Chung*, Min Zeng*,
Samuel Cahyawijaya, Su Dan, Pascale Fung
Center for Artificial Intelligence Research (CAiRE)
The Hong Kong University of Science and Technology
(hlovenia, bwilie, whcchung, min.zeng)@connect.ust.hk

Abstract

Task-adaptive pre-training (TAPT) alleviates the lack of labelled data and provides performance lift by adapting unlabelled data to downstream task. Unfortunately, existing adaptations mainly involve deterministic rules that cannot generalize well. Here, we propose Clozer, a sequence-tagging based cloze answer extraction method used in TAPT that is extendable for adaptation on any cloze-style machine reading comprehension (MRC) downstream tasks. We experiment on multiple-choice cloze-style MRC tasks, and show that Clozer performs significantly better compared to the oracle and state-of-the-art in escalating TAPT effectiveness in lifting model performance, and prove that Clozer is able to recognize the gold answers independently of any heuristics.

1 Introduction

Endowing machines with the proficiency to read, understand, and reason from unstructured text information is an ongoing aspiration in natural language processing. This aim raises a notable research focus: machine reading comprehension (MRC). Given a question, the goal of MRC is to infer the correct answer based on important cues gathered through understanding relevant context passage. MRC tasks vary in structure, depending on their question construction (e.g., cloze-style) and answer type (e.g., multiple-choice) (Zeng et al., 2020).

Various methods using large pre-trained language models (LMs) have been proposed in MRC tasks. In recent years, adaptation methods such as task adaptive pre-training (TAPT) have been widely adopted for MRC tasks (Xie et al., 2021; Wang et al., 2021; Glass et al., 2020). TAPT uses in-domain unlabelled data of the downstream task to generate a synthetic pre-training dataset adapted to the downstream task through certain data augmentation methods, depending on the downstream task in use. For multiple-choice cloze-style MRC, data augmentation often involves two steps: 1) answer extraction or selection and 2) pseudo-answer

*The authors contributed equally to this work.

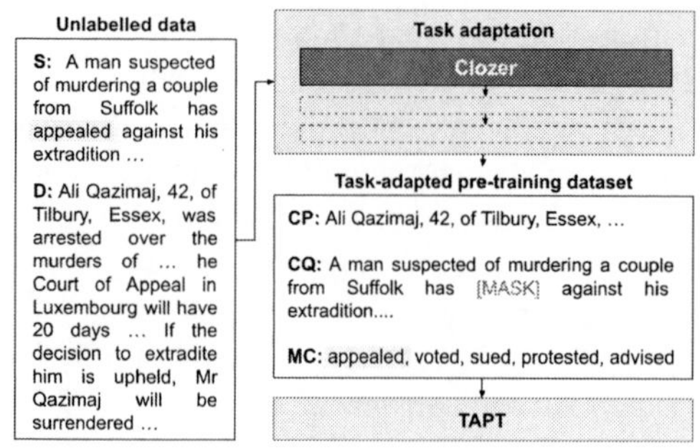

Figure 1: Clozer extracts an answer for TAPT

generation (Figure 1). Both steps have been adopted in several studies with varying implementations (Welbl et al., 2017; Onishi et al., 2016; Yang et al., 2020). One notable work presents TA-MAMC (Gururangan et al., 2020), which achieves state-of-the-art performance by adopting the TAPT framework. However, this method relies heavily on the downstream task's heuristics in the answer selection step, which hinders its applicability to other multiple-choice cloze-style MRC tasks.

In this paper, we take a step towards generalized synthetic pre-training dataset construction, to use TAPT to solve multiple-choice cloze-style MRC. We propose Clozer, a cloze answer extraction based on sequence tagging developed independently of pre-defined rules to improve the generalizability of the TAPT method for the cloze-style MRC tasks. Clozer learns the intrinsic pattern of the downstream task dataset and acts as an answer extractor for the unlabelled data (Figure 1). To adapt to the downstream task, the extractions are grouped with several other options to form a triplet of {*context passage, cloze question, multiple-choice options*}, following the standard multiple-choice cloze-style MRC task format, as a synthetic sample for the second pre-training phase. We conduct our experiments on two downstream tasks. Our experimental results show that employing Clozer in TAPT provides a substantial performance boost, while being generally applicable for both multiple-choice MRC tasks we experiment on.

Proceedings of the 7th Workshop on Representation Learning for NLP, pages 60 - 66
May 26, 2022 ©2022 Association for Computational Linguistics

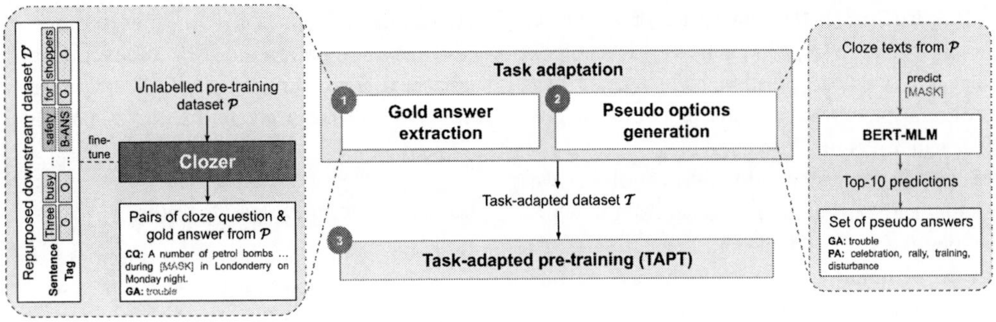

Figure 2: Method pipeline for Clozer-based TAPT

Our contributions are as follows: 1) to the best of our knowledge, we are the first to introduce an automatic generalizable cloze answer extraction method to support a generalized TAPT method for multiple-choice cloze-style MRC tasks; 2) we show that Clozer significantly outperforms all other baselines on two multiple-choice cloze-style MRC tasks without relying on any task-specific heuristics; and 3) we present further analysis to explain the effectiveness and efficiency of our Clozer and provide insight on how to improve its generalizability.

2 Related Work

Task-adaptive pre-training Howard and Ruder (2018) propose Universal Language Model Fine-tuning (ULMFiT), which pre-trains an LM on a large general-domain corpus and fine-tunes it on the target task. Second-phase pre-training has been used to improve the performance of an LM for certain downstream tasks such as text classification (Sun et al., 2019). Studies on TAPT (Gururangan et al., 2020; Pruksachatkun et al., 2020) prove that the performance boost it obtains can be on par with domain-adaptive pre-training, with the benefit of using a much smaller but relevant corpus. TAPT has proved effective in many downstream tasks such as abstractive summarization (Yu et al., 2021) and dialogue systems (Zhang et al., 2021a).

Answer extraction Tan et al. (2018) develop an extraction-then-synthesis framework to synthesize answers from extraction results. Specifically, the answer extraction model is first employed to predict the most important sub-spans from the passage, then the answer synthesis model takes the sub-spans as additional features along with the question and passage to further elaborate the final answers. Xiong et al. (2016) introduce the Dynamic Coattention Network (DCN) for a question-answering task, which learns the co-dependent representations of the question and the passages. Seo et al. (2016) introduce the Bi-Directional Attention Flow (BIDAF) network to match the question and passages. It uses the BIDAF mechanism to get a query-aware context representation without early summarization.

Sequence tagging Sequence tagging is utilized to assign a label for each token (i.e., word) in a sequence. While it's commonly applied for tasks like named entity recognition (NER), part-of-speech (POS) tagging, and text chunking, Yao et al. (2013); Wilie et al. (2020) prove that it is feasible to use this approach to construct cloze questions by extracting an answer span from a complete sentence. Yao et al. (2013) cast answer extraction as an answer sequence-tagging task, utilizing a linear-chain conditional random field (CRF) with tree edit distance (TED) and traditional contextual features.

3 Methodology

Our method follows the pipeline described in Figure 2. We follow TAPT's objective, in which a model learns on a small task-relevant set of data instead of doing another round of masked language modeling (MLM) for pre-training. Utilizing Clozer, we adapt a large unlabelled pre-training dataset based on the downstream task, which could be any multiple-choice cloze-style MRC task.

We define the pre-training dataset $\mathcal{P} = \{(d_i^{\mathcal{P}}, s_i^{\mathcal{P}})\}_{i=1}^{n}$ with $d_i^{\mathcal{P}}$ as a document and $s_i^{\mathcal{P}}$ as a summary or a single sentence related to the passage $d_i^{\mathcal{P}}$. $\mathcal{P}$ could be any unlabelled data of document and sentence pairs, e.g., headline-content of news, title-body of articles, and synopsis-narration of stories. Through the task adaptation, we reconstruct $\mathcal{P}$ into a synthetic cloze-style MRC task, where the resulting task-adapted pre-training dataset is represented by $\mathcal{T} = \{(c_i^{\mathcal{T}}, q_i^{\mathcal{T}}, o_i^{\mathcal{T}}, l_i^{\mathcal{T}})\}_{i=1}^{m}$. It follows the structure of the downstream task dataset $\mathcal{D} = \{(c_i^{\mathcal{D}}, q_i^{\mathcal{D}}, o_i^{\mathcal{D}}, l_i^{\mathcal{D}})\}_{i=1}^{m}$, where $c_i^{\mathcal{D}}$ is a context passage, $q_i^{\mathcal{D}}$ is a cloze question, $o_i^{\mathcal{D}} \in o_1, \ldots, o_k$ is a set of multiple-choice options, and $l_i^{\mathcal{D}}$ is the gold answer's index as the correct label.

We split the task adaptation into 1) gold answer extraction and 2) pseudo options generation, which are explained in §3.1 and §3.2 respectively. Afterwards, we employ TAPT using the task-adapted dataset $\mathcal{T}$, the details of which are provided in §3.3.

3.1 Gold answer extraction

Gold answer extraction (GAE) represents the pre-training dataset's summary as a cloze question by taking out a gold answer, which depends on the downstream task's notion of what is a correct answer. We tackle this problem by utilizing Clozer to learn from the downstream task and identify the appropriate gold answers by sequence tagging. First, we repurpose the cloze questions and gold answers in the downstream task as a token classification dataset. We use the tag `B-ANS` for the gold answer and the tag `O` for other words in the cloze question.

Afterwards, we fine-tune Clozer on this repurposed dataset so it can learn and approximate the downstream task's pattern of determining the gold answers. It is worth mentioning that, due to its independence from any heuristic rules, our Clozer method is not constrained to a single specific interpretation of gold answers. It can be adapted to extract any type of cloze answers (e.g., abstract meaning) depending on the downstream task dataset. We next use Clozer to predict the pre-training dataset's summaries and extract the gold answers. We replace the gold answers in the summaries with the `[MASK]` token to form cloze questions and pass the questions on to the next step. We drop candidates with zero or more than one gold answer.

3.2 Pseudo options generation

Pseudo answer generation (POG) employs a pre-trained masked LM to predict the `[MASK]` token. For each cloze question, we obtain the model's top predictions and filter out the ones that are incomplete or too similar to the gold answer. We randomly pick k predictions as pseudo options. We discard data samples with fewer than k remaining predictions. After this step, each pre-training dataset sample consists of a context paragraph, a cloze question, a gold answer, and four pseudo options. Following the downstream task dataset structure, we recast the gold answer and pseudo options as $\{o_1, o_2, ..., o_k\}$ in random order. The gold answer's option index becomes the label. In cases beyond the scope of this work where multiple-choice is not required by the cloze task, POG is skipped.

3.3 Task-adaptive pre-training

We feed the task-adapted dataset to a pre-trained multiple-choice classification model for TAPT. The final step is to fine-tune the model on the downstream task and evaluate it. To see how Clozer performs against other available methods, we present the results of three baselines, where we employ a directly fine-tuned model, TA-MAMC, and an oracle in place of Clozer in the GAE step. The baselines will be further explained in §4.

4 Experiment

Dataset As explained in §3, the methodology requires the usage of a pre-training dataset and a downstream task. In the experiment, we apply Clozer for the TAPT method on two downstream tasks separately. Both are multiple-choice cloze-style MRC tasks and are obtained from the subtask 1 and subtask 2 of ReCAM (Zheng et al., 2021). Given a context passage and multiple choice options, the appropriate gold answer must be derived to complete a cloze question. The first task defines its gold answers as imperceptible concepts, while the second defines them as hypernyms. For the pre-training dataset $\mathcal{P}$, we use XSUM (Narayan et al., 2018), an abstractive news summarization dataset.

Baseline To see how Clozer-based TAPT performs against other methods, we employ three baselines for the experiment: **1) direct fine-tuning**, where a pre-trained multiple-choice model applies no TAPT and is immediately fine-tuned on the downstream task; **2) TA-MAMC**, which selects gold answers by emulating the POS-tag distribution of the downstream task's training data; and **3) oracle**, whose answer selection is built upon heuristic rules specific to each downstream task.

The oracle utilizes a psycholinguistic database of abstract words (Coltheart, 1981) to select the *imperceptible* concepts as the gold answers in the first task. For the second task, it uses a hypernym hierarchy from WordNet (Changizi, 2008) to determine the gold answers. Both heuristics are chosen because they are used to select the original gold (i.e., correct) answers in the ReCAM dataset creation.

Approach	ReCAM 1		ReCAM 2	
	Acc	F1	Acc	F1
Direct FT	64.16%	64.15%	64.75%	64.65%
TA-MAMC†	64.99%	64.99%	67.69%	67.68%
Oracle	65.83%	65.80%	68.60%	68.50%
Clozer	**65.95%**	**65.96%**	**73.56%**	**73.45%**

Table 1: Performance comparison on the test sets of the downstream tasks. **Bold** marks the best results. †We reproduce this approach based on Zhang et al. (2021b).

Task adapter	ReCAM 1		ReCAM 2	
	Post-GAE	Post-POG	Post-GAE	Post-POG
TA-MAMC	155017	47699	155858	48358
Oracle	94954	29073	75920	23520
Clozer	120073	35073	181476	53368

Table 2: Number of data samples left after the **GAE** and **POG** for different task-adapter methods.

Training and evaluation In the GAE, our Clozer is implemented using a pre-trained ELECTRA-base (Clark et al., 2020), while for the POG and TAPT, we initialize the model using a pre-trained BERT-base model (Devlin et al., 2019). Since only the training set and the development set of both downstream tasks are labelled, we split the original training set with a ratio of 80:20 to form a training set and a validation set. We use the development set as a test set. Accuracy and F1-score are used to assess the methods' performance on the test set.

5 Results and Analysis

5.1 Overall results

We present our experimental results in Table 1. Without additional TAPT, the direct fine-tuning method yields the lowest results. In comparison, TA-MAMC, which relies on POS-tag distribution, performs slightly better, and the oracle, which exploits the downstream tasks' heuristic rules, achieves the best scores among our baselines. Our proposed Clozer method, however, surpasses all baselines in both downstream tasks, by around 2% for task 1 and 9% for task 2. While Clozer provides substantial improvements, there is a considerable discrepancy between both performances due to the way the tasks are defined. We further discuss Clozer's performance discrepancy in §5.3.

5.2 Quality of answer extraction methods

As shown in Table 2, the oracle, which derives its understanding of the answers from the semantics provided by the heuristic rules, has the fewest data after the GAE step (94k out of 200k), because the heuristic rules it is built upon are deterministic and leave no room for randomness. TA-MAMC's POS-tag distribution approach provides some knowledge of the target's syntax but represents no semantic ties to ReCAM's answers (i.e., imperceptible concepts and hypernyms).

However, TA-MAMC has the benefit of excluding fewer examples than the oracle. Our Clozer finds a middle ground by being more generalizable compared to both baselines, while producing a better answer extraction quality (Table 1). Clozer shows superior results with only 5k more data samples in task 2 and with 12k fewer data samples in task 1. This shows that, while the amount of data contributes to the performance lift, the quality of the extracted answers in the synthetic task-adapted dataset is indispensable.

5.3 Clozer's performances on different downstream tasks

While TAPT lifts the model performance by 2% for task 1 and 9% for task 2, the difference between the tasks is glaring. We argue that this is largely due to the amount of synthetic data left after applying the task adaptation, as shown in Table 2, with 35k samples left in task 1 and 53k samples in task 2. This shows that the definition of abstractness chosen by ReCAM for gold answers in task 1 is more complex than the definition used by task 2, which causes the answers in task 1 to be harder to grasp by all of the approaches, including our Clozer.

This is coherent as ReCAM defines *imperceptible* concepts in task 1 using a model-based approach, which in turn introduces an innate bias to the definition. This causes identifying answers in task 1 to be conceptually more complex than in task 2, where the answers are simply nouns and verbs derived from a hypernym hierarchy. This is also in line with Zheng et al. (2021), who show that the cross-task performance drops significantly more for models trained on task 2 trying to make predictions on task 1, rather than the opposite. Examples of this complexity difference are in Appendix A.

6 Conclusion

We have proposed Clozer, an automatic generalizable cloze answer extraction method, to help in synthetic TAPT dataset construction in multiple-choice cloze-style MRC tasks. Performing TAPT with gold answers extracted by our ELECTRA-based Clozer produces stronger models than the baselines in terms of effectiveness (i.e., performance) and efficiency (i.e., the amount of data used in TAPT). Moreover, we also show that the quality of Clozer's extracted answers is higher, despite its independence from the downstream task's heuristics

Acknowledgement

This work has been supported by the China NSFC Project (No. NSFC21EG14), School of Engineering PhD Fellowship Award, the Hong Kong University of Science and Technology and PF20-43679 Hong Kong PhD Fellowship Scheme, Research Grant Council, Hong Kong.

References

Mark A. Changizi. 2008. Economically organized hierarchies in wordnet and the oxford english dictionary. *Cognitive Systems Research*, 9(3):214–228.

Kevin Clark, Minh-Thang Luong, Quoc V. Le, and Christopher D. Manning. 2020. Electra: Pre-training text encoders as discriminators rather than generators. In *International Conference on Learning Representations*.

Max Coltheart. 1981. The mrc psycholinguistic database. *The Quarterly Journal of Experimental Psychology Section A*, 33(4):497–505.

Jacob Devlin, Ming-Wei Chang, Kenton Lee, and Kristina Toutanova. 2019. Bert: Pre-training of deep bidirectional transformers for language understanding. In *Proceedings of the 2019 Conference of the North American Chapter of the Association for Computational Linguistics: Human Language Technologies, Volume 1 (Long and Short Papers)*, pages 4171–4186.

Michael Glass, Alfio Gliozzo, Rishav Chakravarti, Anthony Ferritto, Lin Pan, G P Shrivatsa Bhargav, Dinesh Garg, and Avi Sil. 2020. Span selection pre-training for question answering. In *Proceedings of the 58th Annual Meeting of the Association for Computational Linguistics*, pages 2773–2782, Online. Association for Computational Linguistics.

Suchin Gururangan, Ana Marasović, Swabha Swayamdipta, Kyle Lo, Iz Beltagy, Doug Downey, and Noah A. Smith. 2020. Don't stop pretraining: Adapt language models to domains and tasks. In *Proceedings of the 58th Annual Meeting of the Association for Computational Linguistics*, pages 8342–8360, Online. Association for Computational Linguistics.

Jeremy Howard and Sebastian Ruder. 2018. Universal language model fine-tuning for text classification. *arXiv preprint arXiv:1801.06146*.

Shashi Narayan, Shay B. Cohen, and Mirella Lapata. 2018. Don't give me the details, just the summary! topic-aware convolutional neural networks for extreme summarization. In *Proceedings of the 2018 Conference on Empirical Methods in Natural Language Processing*, pages 1797–1807, Brussels, Belgium. Association for Computational Linguistics.

Takashi Onishi, Hai Wang, Mohit Bansal, Kevin Gimpel, and David McAllester. 2016. Who did what: A large-scale person-centered cloze dataset. In *Proceedings of the 2016 Conference on Empirical Methods in Natural Language Processing*, pages 2230–2235.

Yada Pruksachatkun, Jason Phang, Haokun Liu, Phu Mon Htut, Xiaoyi Zhang, Richard Yuanzhe Pang, Clara Vania, Katharina Kann, and Samuel Bowman. 2020. Intermediate-task transfer learning with pre-trained language models: When and why does it work? In *Proceedings of the 58th Annual Meeting of the Association for Computational Linguistics*, pages 5231–5247.

Minjoon Seo, Aniruddha Kembhavi, Ali Farhadi, and Hannaneh Hajishirzi. 2016. Bidirectional attention flow for machine comprehension. *arXiv preprint arXiv:1611.01603*.

Chi Sun, Xipeng Qiu, Yige Xu, and Xuanjing Huang. 2019. How to fine-tune BERT for text classification? *CoRR*, abs/1905.05583.

Chuanqi Tan, Furu Wei, Nan Yang, Bowen Du, Weifeng Lv, and Ming Zhou. 2018. S-net: From answer extraction to answer synthesis for machine reading comprehension. In *Proceedings of the AAAI Conference on Artificial Intelligence*, volume 32.

Ye Wang, Yanmeng Wang, Haijun Zhu, Bo Zeng, Zhenghong Hao, Shaojun Wang, and Jing Xiao. 2021. PINGAN omini-sinitic at SemEval-2021 task 4:reading comprehension of abstract meaning. In *Proceedings of the 15th International Workshop on Semantic Evaluation (SemEval-2021)*, pages 820–826, Online. Association for Computational Linguistics.

Johannes Welbl, Nelson F Liu, and Matt Gardner. 2017. Crowdsourcing multiple choice science questions. In *Proceedings of the 3rd Workshop on Noisy User-generated Text*, pages 94–106.

Bryan Wilie, Karissa Vincentio, Genta Indra Winata, Samuel Cahyawijaya, Xiaohong Li, Zhi Yuan Lim, Sidik Soleman, Rahmad Mahendra, Pascale Fung, Syafri Bahar, and Ayu Purwarianti. 2020. IndoNLU: Benchmark and resources for evaluating Indonesian natural language understanding. In *Proceedings of the 1st Conference of the Asia-Pacific Chapter of the Association for Computational Linguistics and the 10th International Joint Conference on Natural Language Processing*, pages 843–857, Suzhou, China. Association for Computational Linguistics.

Xin Xie, Xiangnan Chen, Xiang Chen, Yong Wang, Ningyu Zhang, Shumin Deng, and Huajun Chen. 2021. ZJUKLAB at SemEval-2021 task 4: Negative augmentation with language model for reading comprehension of abstract meaning. In *Proceedings of the 15th International Workshop on Semantic Evaluation (SemEval-2021)*, pages 810–819, Online. Association for Computational Linguistics.

Caiming Xiong, Victor Zhong, and Richard Socher. 2016. Dynamic coattention networks for question answering. *arXiv preprint arXiv:1611.01604*.

Yiben Yang, Chaitanya Malaviya, Jared Fernandez, Swabha Swayamdipta, Ronan Le Bras, Ji-Ping Wang, Chandra Bhagavatula, Yejin Choi, and Doug Downey. 2020. Generative data augmentation for commonsense reasoning. In *Findings of the Association for Computational Linguistics: EMNLP 2020*, pages 1008–1025.

Xuchen Yao, Benjamin Van Durme, Chris Callison-Burch, and Peter Clark. 2013. Answer extraction as sequence tagging with tree edit distance. In *Proceedings of the 2013 conference of the North American chapter of the association for computational linguistics: human language technologies*, pages 858–867.

Tiezheng Yu, Zihan Liu, and Pascale Fung. 2021. Adaptsum: Towards low-resource domain adaptation for abstractive summarization. *arXiv preprint arXiv:2103.11332*.

Changchang Zeng, Shaobo Li, Qin Li, Jie Hu, and Jianjun Hu. 2020. A survey on machine reading comprehension—tasks, evaluation metrics and benchmark datasets. *Applied Sciences*, 10(21):7640.

Boliang Zhang, Ying Lyu, Ning Ding, Tianhao Shen, Zhaoyang Jia, Kun Han, and Kevin Knight. 2021a. A hybrid task-oriented dialog system with domain and task adaptive pretraining. *arXiv preprint arXiv:2102.04506*.

Jing Zhang, Yimeng Zhuang, and Yinpei Su. 2021b. TA-MAMC at SemEval-2021 task 4: Task-adaptive pretraining and multi-head attention for abstract meaning reading comprehension. In *Proceedings of the 15th International Workshop on Semantic Evaluation (SemEval-2021)*, pages 51–58, Online. Association for Computational Linguistics.

Boyuan Zheng, Xiaoyu Yang, Yu-Ping Ruan, Zhenhua Ling, Quan Liu, Si Wei, and Xiaodan Zhu. 2021. SemEval-2021 task 4: Reading comprehension of abstract meaning. In *Proceedings of the 15th International Workshop on Semantic Evaluation (SemEval-2021)*, pages 37–50, Online. Association for Computational Linguistics.

A Examples of Gold Selection with Clozer

David Beckham has expressed his pride at helping London win their 2012 olympics bid despite not being picked in great britains football squad.
A 22 year old man arrested on suspicion of murder following the death of Lewis Siddall has been released on bail.
A cow which got into the water at Aberdeen harbour has been shot after a rescue effort failed to coax it ashore.
Streets in Wales are blighted by discarded cigarette butts with 86 of roads strewn with smoking related litter a charity survey shows.
It is officially a regeneration area and dyke house in Hartlepool has newly built smart houses but they are in the minority.
Wales flyhalf Dan Biggar says he is learning to cope with the pressure of wearing the famous number 10 jersey.

Table A1: Examples of gold selections in summaries taken from both dowstream tasks with Clozer. Highlighted in yellow is the gold answer chosen according to the first definition of abstractness, *imperceptibility*, and in blue the answer according to the second definition, *non-specificity* (for hypernyms), in each example.

For task 1 (ReCAM 1), abstractness follows the definition of imperceptibility, meaning any concept that can't be perceived directly in the physical world according to a psycholinguistic database (Coltheart, 1981). Task 2 (ReCAM 2) defines abstractness as non-specificity, representing nouns and verbs relatively high in a hypernym hierarchy (Changizi, 2008). Examples of the difference between both are illustrated in Table A1.

As discussed in §5.3, the abstract concepts chosen for ReCAM 1 are intuitively harder to define compared to the concepts for ReCAM 2, even for humans (**pride, suspicion** vs **picked, following**). However, this also shows that without being given any rules, our Clozer still manages to grasp the underlying mechanics originally chosen to extract the abstract words in both tasks.

We refer to the original work (Zheng et al., 2021) on building the ReCAM dataset for more details on the reason why those two definitions of abstractness have been chosen.

Analyzing Gender Representation in Multilingual Models

Hila Gonen[1] **Shauli Ravfogel**[2,3] **Yoav Goldberg**[2,3]
[1]Paul G. Allen School of Computer Science & Engineering, University of Washington
[2]Computer Science Department, Bar Ilan University
[3]Allen Institute for Artificial Intelligence
{hilagnn, shauli.ravfogel, yoav.goldberg}@gmail.com

Abstract

Multilingual language models were shown to allow for nontrivial transfer across scripts and languages. In this work, we study the structure of the internal representations that enable this transfer. We focus on the representation of gender distinctions as a practical case study, and examine the extent to which the gender concept is encoded in *shared subspaces* across different languages. Our analysis shows that gender representations consist of several prominent components that are shared across languages, alongside language-specific components. The existence of language-independent and language-specific components provides an explanation for an intriguing empirical observation we make: while gender classification transfers well across languages, interventions for gender removal, trained on a single language, do not transfer easily to others.

1 Introduction

Pretrained models of contextualized representations (Peters et al., 2018; Devlin et al., 2019; Liu et al., 2020) are known in their ability to capture both explicit and implicit information during training. A special case of these models are multilingual models (Devlin et al., 2019; Conneau et al., 2020), which are pretrained with texts in multiple languages. These models were shown to induce the emergence of similar representations in different languages, a phenomenon that was put to use for transfer between languages in end-tasks (Pires et al., 2019; Muller et al., 2020; Gonen et al., 2020). However, the underlying mechanism is still not clear, and we do not know yet the full extent to which the representations of these models share information across languages.

The rise of pretrained models has been accompanied with growing concern regarding sensitive information they might encode, e.g. gender or ethnic distinctions. Pretrained language models were shown to be sensitive to gender information, both when it is explicitly stated in texts, as well as when it can be inferred from implicit information (Zhao et al., 2019; May et al., 2019). We still lack a complete understanding of what the model captures, and the ways to control and change the information in this context as well.

In this work, we aim to shed light on the way gender, a popular use case of a human-interpretable concept, is represented in multilingual models, and whether it is encoded in a language-dependant way. In a series of experiments, we uncover a surprising finding: gender-identification ability is highly transferable across languages (section 4.1) but neutralizing gender identification is not (section 4.2). While these two findings may seem contradictory at first glance, this is explained by several levels of gender marking: both cross-lingual and language-specific (section 5).

We start our analysis by training gender classifiers and examining their ability to transfer across languages. We then proceed to identifying "gender subspaces" — subspaces that encode gender — in each language, with the goal of understanding which information is language-specific, and which is shared across languages. Following recent work on linear interventions (Ravfogel et al., 2020; Elazar et al., 2021; Ravfogel et al., 2021, 2022), we take an "amnesic" approach: we study the extent to which **neutralizing** the gender subspace in one language interferes with gender prediction in another language. Finally, we analyze the similarity in the gender-encoding components across languages.

We find that while linear probes for gender transfer well between languages — that is, a gender classifier that is trained on one language predicts gender well in another language, the method we employ for neutralizing gender fails to transfer across languages. A deeper analysis reveals a fine-grained organization of the gender-encoding subspaces across languages: they are spanned by a few main directions, which are largely similar across

Proceedings of the 7th Workshop on Representation Learning for NLP, pages 67 - 77
May 26, 2022

languages; but in addition to these directions, there are other directions that are language-specific. The existence of several similar directions explains the high degree of transferability of linear gender classifiers across languages, while the existence of a large amount of language-specific information explains the inability to efficiently remove gender information in one language based on another language's representation.

We summarize our findings and contributions as follows: (a) we show that gender-identification is highly transferable across languages (Section 4.1); (b) we find that neutralizing gender identification does not transfer well across languages (Section 4.2); (c) we demonstrate that gender subspaces are spanned by a few directions that are largely similar across languages; and also by other directions that are language-specific (Section 5.1); (d) we find that the directions that are shared across languages are the most dominant ones (Section 5.2).

The code for our experiments is available at `https://github.com/gonenhila/multilingual_gender`.

2 Related Work

Multilingual Representation Analysis Pires et al. (2019) begin a line of work that studies mBERT's representations and capabilities. They inspect the model's zero-shot transfer abilities using different probing experiments, and propose a way to map sentence representations in different languages, with some success. Karthikeyan et al. (2020) further analyze the properties that affect zero shot transfer of bilingual BERTs. Wu and Dredze (2019) perform transfer learning from English to 38 languages, on 5 different downstream tasks and report good results. Wang et al. (2019) learn alignment between contextualized representations, and use it for zero shot transfer. Dufter and Schütze (2020) make an attempt to control different aspects of mBERT and identify those that contribute the most to its transfer ability.

Beyond focusing on zero-shot transfer abilities, an additional line of work studies the representations of mBERT and the information it stores. Using hierarchical clustering based on the CCA similarity scores between languages, Singh et al. (2019) are able to construct a tree structure that faithfully describes relations between languages. Chi et al. (2020) learn a linear syntax-subspace in mBERT, and point out to syntactic regularities in the representations that transfer across languages. In Cao et al. (2019), the authors define the notion of *contextual* word alignment and show improvement in zero-shot transfer after fine-tuning accordingly. In Libovický et al. (2020), the authors assume that mBERT's representations have a language-neutral component, and a language-specific component and provide an experimental setting to partially support this assumption. Finally, in Gonen et al. (2020), the authors propose an explicit *decomposition* of the representations to language-encoding and language-neutral components, and also demonstrate that implicit word-level translations can be easily distilled from the model when exposed to the proper stimuli.

Unlike previous works, we pay attention specifically to how gender is manifested in the representations, as a case study for the analysis of a concrete societal property. We do that by focusing on the information included in the representations themselves, rather than on downstream tasks.

Gender Representation in Multilingual Models To the best of our knowledge, no previous work focuses on the way gender is represented in multilingual models and the extent to which such representations are shared across languages.

Some work has been done on identifying and mitigating gender bias in languages other than English (Zhou et al., 2019; Bartl et al., 2020). Gonen et al. (2019) identify and debias a new type of gender bias, unique to gender-marking languages. Williams et al. (2021) look at the relationships between the grammatical genders of inanimate nouns and their co-occurring adjectives and verbs. In Zmigrod et al. (2019), the authors suggest a method for converting between masculine-inflected and feminine-inflected sentences in morphologically rich languages, and use them for counterfactual data augmentation in order to reduce gender stereotyping.

Zhao et al. (2020) analyze gender bias in multilingual word embeddings, and evaluate it intrinsically and extrinsically. They point to several factors that influence the gender bias in multilingual embeddings, among which are the pretrained monolingual word embeddings, and the alignment method used. Additionally, Liang et al. (2020) focus on contextualized embeddings, analyze the gender representation in BERT, and also put efforts into English-Chinese cross lingual debiasing. Finally, Bansal et al. (2021) focus on Indian languages when debiasing multilingual embeddings.

3 Datasets and Multilingual Representations

For our experiments we use the BiosBias Dataset (De-Arteaga et al., 2019), the Multilingual BiosBias Dataset (Zhao et al., 2020) and the multilingual BERT model (mBERT, (Devlin et al., 2019)) as detailed below.

Multilingual Gender Data. De-Arteaga et al. (2019) collected the English BiosBias dataset, a set of short-biographies written in third person, and annotated by perceived gender. To do so they identified online biographies, written in English, from Common Crawl, by filtering for lines that match a pattern of a name and an occupation.[1] Gender is labeled using heuristics, based on names and pronouns. In their work, they have demonstrated that profession classifiers trained on this dataset condition on the gender concept, resulting in fairness issues. Zhao et al. (2020) evaluate the bias in cross-lingual transfer settings, for which they have created the Multilingual BiosBias (MLBs) Dataset which contains a similar set of biographies in three additional languages: French, Spanish and German. Note that these are not translations of the English portion, but are crawled independently with a similar method.

For our experiments we use both datasets, so that we have biographies in English, Spanish and French.[2] To decrease noise, we filter out examples of professions with less than 500 occurrences. Table 1 describes the statistics of the dataset in all languages. Note that the dataset is not balanced with respect to gender, especially for French and Spanish (same as before our filtering), and that the English portion is significantly larger. Following (De-Arteaga et al., 2019), we split randomly into Train/Dev/Test sets with ratio of 65%/10%/25%, while ensuring that the main class (professions) is balanced across them. Unfortunately, biographies data for more languages is not available at this point, so we opt to use English, French and Spanish only.

[1]A sequence of two capitalized words followed by "is a(n) (xxx) *title*," where *title* is a profession from BLS Standard Occupation Classification system.

[2]Since the datasets are not available online, we used the scripts the authors provide for crawling them ourselves. The German portion we were able to extract was too small, so we decided to avoid experimenting with it.

	examples	female	male	majority	# prof
En	255682	118344	137338	53.71	28
Fr	42773	12196	30577	71.49	19
Es	46931	12867	34064	72.58	27

Table 1: Statistics of the MLBs dataset.

Multilingual Representations. To study the representation of the gender concept in a multilingual setting, we use multilingual BERT (mBERT,[3] 110M parameters) (Devlin et al., 2019). For each example in the dataset, we extract its representation from mBERT by averaging the last-layer representations in context of all the tokens in the paragraph.

4 Gender Representation across Languages

4.1 Transfer of Gender Probes

As a first step in understanding gender representation in multilingual models, we start with a basic experiment that aims to evaluate the extent to which gender is represented similarly across languages. The goal of this experiment is to check whether features that help predict the gender of a contextualized representation in one language are also predictive of gender in another language.

To this end, we train a linear classifier (logistic Regression classifier, trained in SKlearn[4] with default parameters) for gender classification in a SOURCE language, and use it as is to predict the gender in a TARGET language. The training is done over the mBERT representations of the training examples (see Section 3).

The results, presented in Table 2, indicate that gender classifiers transfer very well across languages, with only a slight degradation in performance when applied in a different language. For example, the accuracy of the English gender classifier in-language is 99.27%, and when the French or Spanish classifiers are used to predict gender in the English data, the accuracy is 98.10% and 97.29%, respectively. The same trend is observed for the French and Spanish datasets. These results suggest that gender information is linearly accessible in mBERT representations and is shared between languages.

[3]Implemented with HuggingFace (Wolf et al., 2020).

[4]https://scikit-learn.org/stable/

	En train	Fr train	Es train
En test	**99.27**	98.10	97.29
Fr test	95.97	**97.50**	94.61
Es test	84.04	84.10	**85.97**

Table 2: Accuracy of gender classification across languages with linear classifiers. Rows represent the language of the prediction data, columns represent the language in which the classifier was trained.

4.2 Cross-lingual Linear Gender Removal

The experiment described above suggests that some gender components are shared between languages. As bias mitigation techniques focus on the *removal* of gender information, a natural question that arises is whether mitigation efforts trained on one language would transfer to another. This question is important for two reasons. First, if possible, this has a potential practical utility – e.g., enabling bias mitigation in low-resource languages, for which training data is scarce. Second, the degree of success in transfer of bias mitigation efforts is a complementary way to assess whether the representation of gender is indeed multilingual.

Previous experiments on removing the gender concept from neural representations show encouraging results in-language for English. These are done using INLP (Ravfogel et al., 2020), an existing approach for the identification and neutralization of "concept subspaces", e.g. the gender concept. In these experiments, Ravfogel et al. (2020) show they manage to neutralize the ability of linear probes to recover gender information from the representations. In light of the above results that show high quality *transfer* of gender classifiers **across** languages, we leverage the INLP method, and attempt to *remove* gender information from the representations **across** languages.

Note that the goal of the following experiment is not *debiasing* gender but rather *analyzing* gender directions across langauges – INLP is used in this experiment as an analysis tool, rather than a debiasing tool. In what follows, we give an overview of INLP, and then describe the experiment and its results.

Iterative Nullspace Projection (INLP) INLP (Ravfogel et al., 2020) aims to remove linearly-decodable information from vector representations.

INLP constructs a concept subspace iteratively, by finding directions of the relevant concept (e.g. gender) and neutralizing them by projecting the representations onto their nullspace. On each iteration, a classifier is trained on the representations, which were projected onto the nullspace of the previous classifiers, i.e., the classifier is optimized to identify *residual* information which was not captured by previous directions. This iterative procedure relies on the intuition that in order to find a subspace whose neutralization *hinders* the ability to predict some concept, one first needs to identify the directions that *encode* that concept, and only then neutralize them.

Formally, given a dataset of representations X (in our case, mBERT representations) and annotations Z for the information to be removed (gender) the method renders Z linearly unpredictable from X. It does so by iteratively training linear predictors $w_1, \ldots, w_n$ of Z, calculating the projection matrix onto their nullspace $P_N := P_N(w_1), \ldots, P_N(w_n)$, and transforming $X \leftarrow P_N X$. By the nullspace definition, this guarantees $w_i P_N X = 0, \forall w_i$, i.e., the features that w_i uses for gender prediction are neutralized. Note that the guarantee is only with respect to linear separation.

While the nullspace $N(w_1, \ldots, w_n)$ is a subspace in which Z is not linearly predictable, the complement rowspace $R(w_1, \ldots, w_n)$ is a subspace of the representation space X that corresponds to the property Z. In our case, the nullspace is the *gender neutral subspace* and the rowspace is the *gender subspace*. As part of the analysis in this work, we utilize INLP in two complementary ways: (1) we use the *nullspace* projection matrix P_N to zero out the gender subspace, in order to render the representations gender-neutral,[5] this projection is onto the **gender-neutral subspace**; and (2) we use the *rowspace* projection matrix $P_R = I - P_N$ to project mBERT representations onto the **gender subspace**, keeping only the parts that are useful for gender prediction.

Method We start by training INLP in one language (En, Fr or Es) and identifying the complementing subspaces: the gender-neutral subspace – *nullspace*, and the gender subspace – *rowspace* (the latter is used in Section 5). We then neutralize the gender subspace in *another* language. Finally, we examine the influence of this intervention and asses the effect of gender information reduction.

[5] to the extent that gender is indeed encoded in a linear subspace, and that INLP finds this subspace.

Importantly, the directions are **learned** by INLP and are not predefined according to a word list or in any other manual manner.

We run INLP with the objective of identifying the gender, with SVM classifiers (using SKlearn) for 100 iterations.[6] We use the average representations of the training paragraphs (averaging over the final-layer in-context representations of all tokens).

Results Tables 3 and 4 depict the results of gender and profession predictions (with Logistic Regression) in each language (rows) before and after applying INLP (each column stands for a different language for training INLP). In-language, the accuracy of gender prediction drops to majority after applying INLP, while profession classification is only slightly hurt. For example, for English we get gender prediction accuracy of 53.7 compared to 99.3 before applying INLP, and profession prediction accuracy of 78.1 compared to 79.9 before applying INLP. Note that this is the **expected** behaviour as a result of applying INLP, since INLP is designed to remove as much information as possible for the *guarded attribute*, namely gender, with minimal effect on the main task. Indeed (Ravfogel et al., 2020) show the same result for English in the original paper. However, across languages, there is virtually no effect, both for gender prediction and profession prediction. For example, English gender and profession predictions drop from 99.3 to 98.1 and from 79.9 to 79.5, respectively, after applying Spanish INLP. This result is surprising in light of the high quality transfer of gender identification across languages shown in the previous experiment (Section 4.1, Table 2).

Interestingly, the largest drops in performance of profession classification due to application of INLP are in-language. This can be explained by the inherent correlations between gender and profession signals – removing gender information hurts the ability to predict the profession in the same language. This is not the case across languages since, as seen by the gender prediction results, gender information is not removed from the representations when applying INLP across languages.

	before	En INLP	Fr INLP	Es INLP
En	99.3	53.7	97.6	98.1
Fr	97.8	95.1	71.4	94.9
Es	85.7	82.8	82.6	72.5

Table 3: Gender prediction before and after applying INLP. Rows stand for the language in which we predict, columns stand for the language in which we train INLP. We use 100 iterations of INLP in each language.

	before	En INLP	Fr INLP	Es INLP
En	79.9	78.1	79.2	79.5
Fr	73.0	72.4	68.2	72.4
Es	57.8	57.1	57.3	51.8

Table 4: Profession prediction before and after applying INLP. Rows stand for the language in which we predict, columns stand for the language in which we train INLP. We use 100 iterations of INLP in each language.

5 Analyzing the Cross-linguality of Gender Representation

At first glance, the two results presented in the previous section look contradicting: linear gender classification transfers well across languages while gender removal using INLP does not. In this section we provide a detailed analysis that accounts for this discrepancy and sheds light on the arrangement of gender in multilingual representations – this is essentially the main result of this work. Under this more fine-grained view we present, we see that gender representation is neither shared between languages nor unique per language, but is actually only partially shared between languages. This allows for some transferability (as seen in Section 4.1), but prevents gender removal across languages (as seen in Section 4.2).

To define the term "partial sharing" formally, we represent gender in each language as a collection of linear directions that together span the gender subspace of that language. This collection of directions can be identified using INLP: when training INLP in a specific language, we get a sequence of orthogonal linear classifiers that are able to predict gender with a decreasing level of accuracy, with the first classifier being the most accurate one. Together, these directions define the gender subspace of the language. This formulation allows us to more easily analyze the extent to which gender is similarly encoded across languages.

We hypothesize that the two aforementioned results are compatible because **some of these gender directions are shared between languages, while others are language-specific**. The shared directions allow high quality transfer of gender

[6]as we have noticed that 100 iterations are enough to remove gender information in-language for all three languages.

classification across languages, while the language-specific directions allow gender prediction even after applying INLP cross-lingually since they are not identified in the source language. In what follows, we devise two experiments to verify this hypothesis and quantify this phenomenon.

5.1 Shared Gender Directions across Languages

High Level Description and Intuition In the following experiment we analyze the relation between gender representations in the different languages. For that we leverage the formulation of gender representation as a collection of many different directions in the space. We aim to answer the following question: *are gender directions fully shared across languages, fully disjoint, or split (i.e. some are shared across languages and some are disjoint)*?

Concretely, in order to derive a measure of overlap between two given subspaces, we measure the effect of neutralizing the gender subspace of one language, on the total variance in the gender subspace of *another* languages; intuitively, the larger the overlap is between the gender subspaces in both languages, the larger the drop in variance is expected to be.

Method Given two languages A and B we propose the following pipeline: (i) project the representations of language A *onto its gender subspace* in order to discard information that is not predictive of gender in that language; (ii) project the already-projected representations *onto the gender-neutral subspace* of language B in order to remove the gender-information captured in the subspace of language B; (iii) measure the drop in the total variance of the representations of language A between steps i and ii.

To draw a more fine-grained view of the transfer of gender-neutralization, in step iii we perform Principle Component Analysis (PCA), and record the total variance explained by the first n principle components. Thus, we ask not only how does the gender-neutralizing in language B affect the gender subspace of language A, but also *which* PCA directions are affected. Concretely, we plot the total explained variance by the first n principle components. If the intervention does not change the plot at all, this means that the two gender subspaces are completely orthogonal, and if the variance drops to zero at once, this means that the two gender subspaces are completely aligned.

Compared Representations We start by training INLP and obtaining a collection of 100[7] gender directions in each language (En, Fr and Es), from the most prominent to the least prominent one. We compare different sets of representations as detailed below, for English vs. French, English vs. Spanish and French vs. Spanish (the explanation below is assuming English vs. French):

- ORIG: Original representations (in English).
- ENGENDER: ORIG projected on the English gender subspace (rowspace).
- ENRAND: ORIG projected with a random matrix with the same dimensions as the EnGender matrix (for comparison).
- ENGENDER+FRNEUTRAL: ENGENDER projected on the French gender-neutral subspace (nullspace).
- ENGENDER+FRRAND: ENGENDER projected on a random matrix with the same dimensions as the French gender-neutral matrix (for comparison).
- ENGENDER+ENNEUTRAL: ENGENDER projected on English gender-neutral subspace (nullspace, as a sanity check).

Result Analysis The results are shown in Figure 1. The plots support our initial hypothesis: indeed, we find that gender directions are shared between languages, but only partially. Focusing on English vs. French, we can see that as expected, the curve of ENGENDER+FRNEUTRAL (cyan) is lower than that of ENGENDER (blue), implying that there are shared gender directions between English and French. Recall that projecting the representations on the English gender subspace (ENGENDER) keeps mainly English gender directions, and then projecting on the French gender-neutral subspace (ENGENDER+FRNEUTRAL) removes French gender directions. If no directions are shared, this should result with similar values for both ENGENDER and ENGENDER+FRNEUTRAL. However, the sharing is only partial: if all directions are shared, we expect ENGENDER+FRNEUTRAL to be zero (similar to ENGENDER+ENNEUTRAL), which is not the case.

[7]We use 100 for each language even when INLP required less iterations to converge, so as to be consistent across languages and avoid artifacts due to the number of dimensions.

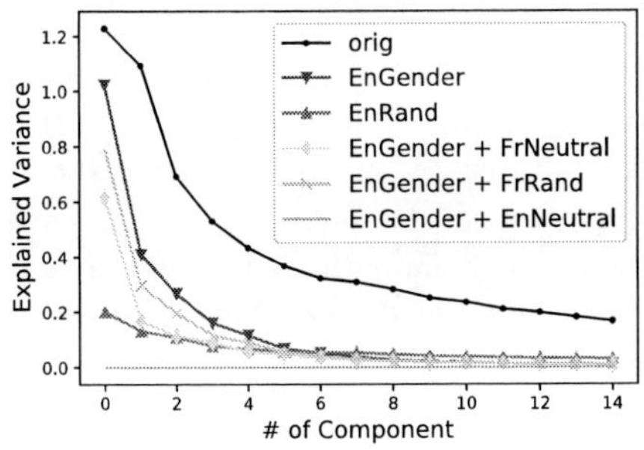

(a) English and French.

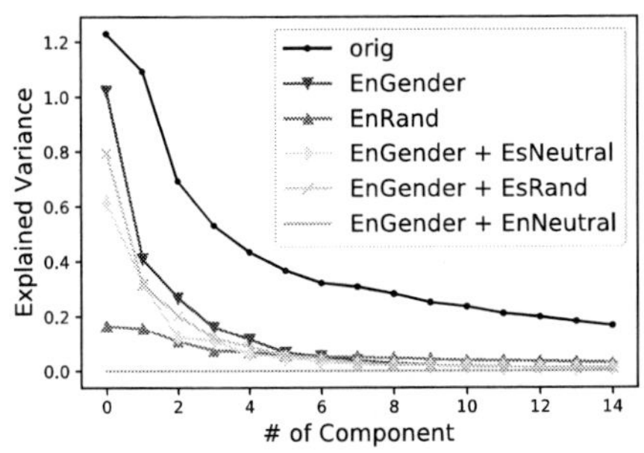

(b) English and Spanish.

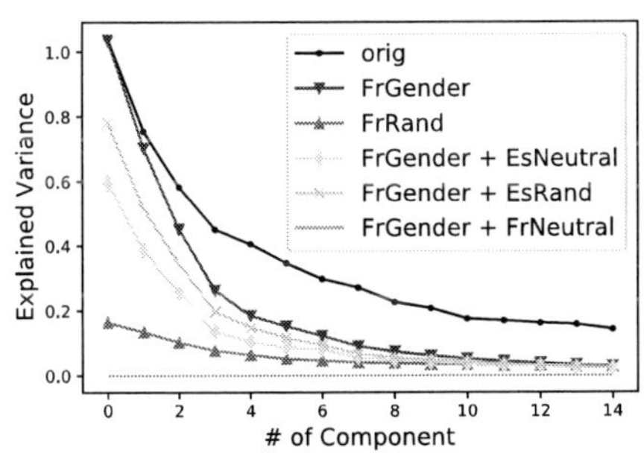

(c) French and Spanish.

Figure 1: Explained variance of PCA of different representations, for all three language pairs.

Controls The EnGender+FrRand projections are intended as reference for EnGender+FrNeutral. If there are shared gender directions between English and French, we expect the curve of EnGender+FrNeutral to be lower than that of EnGender+FrRand, since by projecting on the French gender-neutral subspace we are expected to lose more information than with a random projection with the same dimensions. In Figure 1a we see that the curve of EnGender+FrNeutral (cyan) is indeed lower than that of EnGender+FrRand (pink), indicating that the loss of information is not due to random shared directions.

Note also that the curve of EnGender (blue) is significantly higher than that of EnRand (red). We hypothesize that this is due to the fact that gender is usually dominant in natural texts, especially in a dataset that includes information about individuals, as this one. Thus, keeping only gender information by projecting on the English gender subspace keeps a large portion of the information, compared to projecting on arbitrary directions of the same dimension.

Another sanity check is obtained by projecting EnGender on the English gender-neutral subspace (EnGender+EnNeutral), this should, by definition, result in a 0 line, which is indeed the case (orange).

5.2 Similarities of Dominant Directions

In the previous section we established the hypothesis that some gender directions are shared between languages while others are language-specific. Now, we turn to perform a more fine-grained analysis where we look at the specific directions in the different languages.

We look at the first 100 classifiers (trained during INLP) in two languages, and compute all pairwise cosine similarities between them (across languages). This leads us to a surprising result – only the **first** classifiers in both languages are similar to each other, while the rest are not: we get that the 3 highest similarities are between the first English classifier and the first French classifier, between the second English classifier and the second French classifier, and between the third English classifier and the third French classifier, with values of 0.777, 0.597 and 0.453, respectively. For comparison, the average absolute cosine similarity among all pairwise similarities of the first 100 classifiers in English and French is 0.037. This result means that not only are some directions shared cross-lingually while others are not, but also that the most dominant directions are those that are shared, while the less predictive directions are those that are language specific.

Figure 2 depicts the similarities of the ith classifiers for the two languages (English-French, English-Spanish and French-Spanish). We also plot the gender classification accuracy in-language for reference. This result completes the picture and serves as an explanation for the extremely high quality transfer of gender classification across languages – the most dominant directions that represent gender in each languages are cross-lingual, which enables high accuracy in zero-shot transfer of linear gender classifiers across languages. However, less dominant gender directions are language specific, but are predictive enough so as to prevent gender neutralization across languages using INLP.

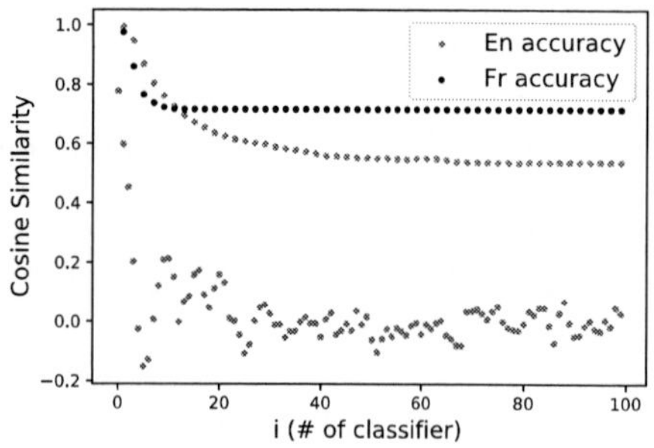

(a) Similarity between the ith classifiers in En and Fr.

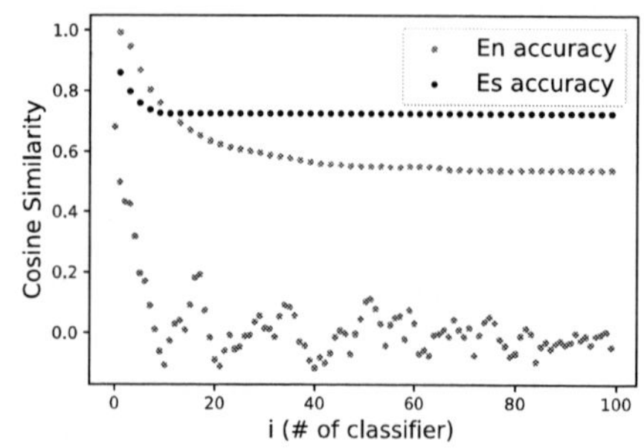

(b) Similarity between the ith classifiers in En and Es.

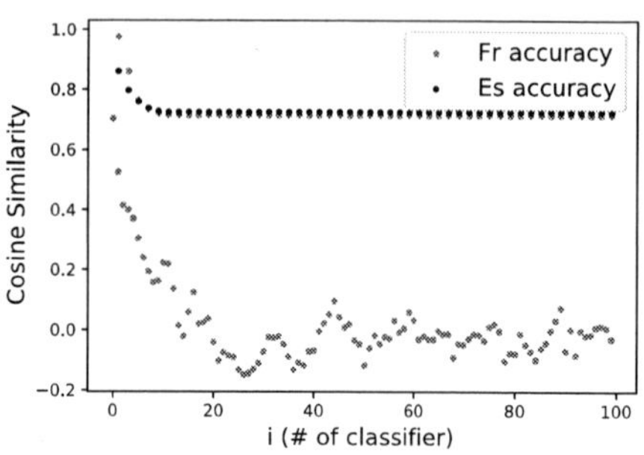

(c) Similarity between the ith classifiers in Fr and Es.

Figure 2: Similarity between the ith classifiers (blue) in all three language pairs. The gender classification accuracy in-language (black and red) is added for reference.

5.3 Accuracy across Languages

Finally, we also look at the performance of each classifier (trained during INLP) across languages. In Figure 3, we depict the gender prediction accuracy in-language and across languages. We consistently get that the performance of the first 2-3 classifiers trained in-language and also across languages is relatively similar, with a significant divergence between in-language and across languages training for the subsequent classifiers. This matches the observation of high similarity only between the first classifiers across the different languages.

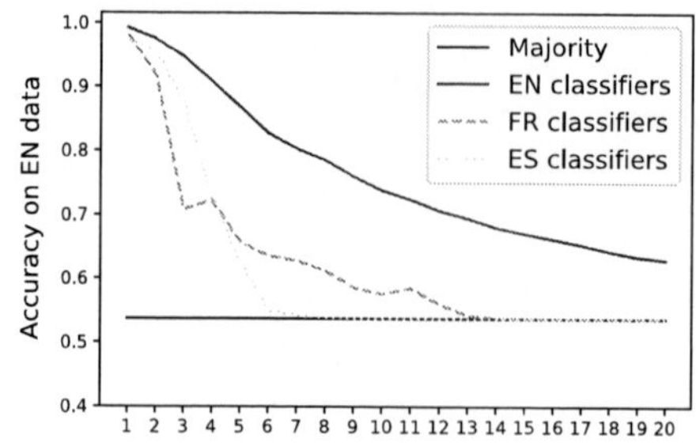

(a) Gender prediction accuracy in English.

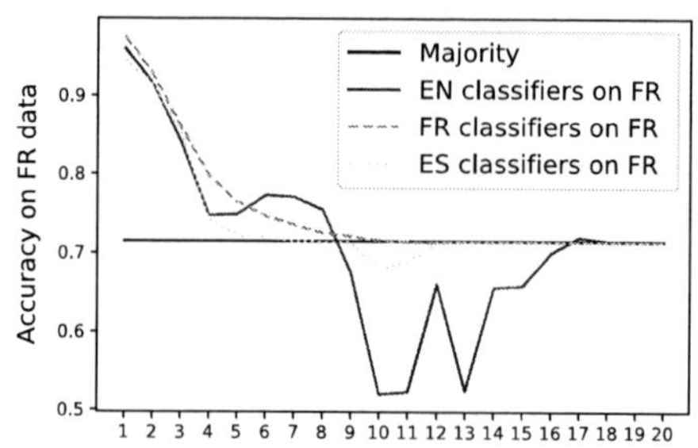

(b) Gender prediction accuracy in French.

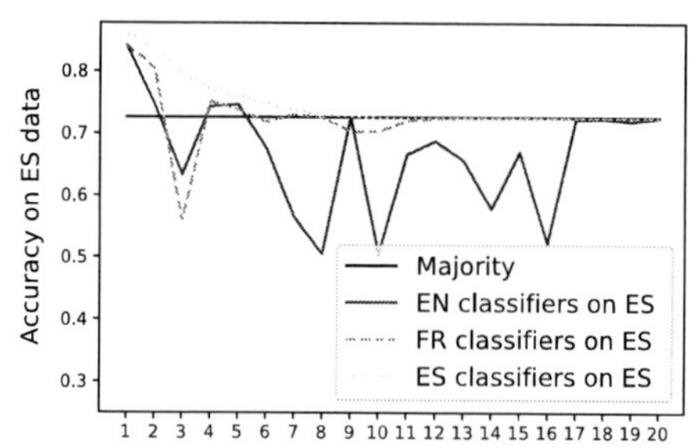

(c) Gender prediction accuracy in Spanish.

Figure 3: Gender prediction accuracy with the different classifiers in- and across-languages.

6 Conclusion

Towards better understanding of the underlying mechanism of multilingual modeling, in this work we focus on the way gender is represented across languages. We analyze and quantify the extent to which gender information is shared in multilingual representations in English, French and Spanish.

We find that on the one hand, gender prediction transfers very well across languages: training a linear classifier on English data yields a high quality classifier for French and Spanish as well (true for all three languages in both directions). On the other hand, our attempt to transfer gender removal in cross-lingual manner was unsuccessful.

We show that these two results are compatible, and together they shed light on the structure of the representation space: we provide experimental evidence that the most salient directions are shared between languages (enabling good transfer of the classifiers), while others are unique per language (interfering with gender removal across languages). The key observation is that a *single* "good" direction of the gender subspace in one language is enough for cross-lingual gender prediction transfer, while transfer of gender neutralization requires *all* directions to be shared, otherwise, the remaining ones can be used to recover gender information after the removal of the shared ones.

7 Ethical Considerations

Gender bias mitigation has attracted a lot of attention as a practical and socially important field of study. This paper contributes to this effort by studying the internal organization of gender representations. We note that gender and bias are complicated and multi-faceted constructs. When studying gender bias in neural models, we unavoidably rely on a narrow notion of binary gender, as reflected in several annotated datasets. As such, we see this study as a preliminary attempt that is based on a relatively narrow concept of gender, that does not reflect the subtle ways by which gender bias is manifested. We advise for caution when applying the conclusions of this study to other notions of gender or different definitions of bias.

We acknowledge that gender is not a binary property. Due to lack of existing resources, we use binary gender as a rough approximation of reality. We hope to account for this in future work.

Acknowledgements

We would like to thank Ran Levy for valuable ideas and feedback. This project received funding from the Europoean Research Council (ERC) under the Europoean Union's Horizon 2020 research and innovation programme, grant agreement No. 802774 (iEXTRACT).

References

Srijan Bansal, Vishal Garimella, Ayush Suhane, and Animesh Mukherjee. 2021. Debiasing multilingual word embeddings: A case study of three indian languages. In *Proceedings of the 32nd ACM Conference on Hypertext and Social Media*, pages 27–34.

Marion Bartl, Malvina Nissim, and Albert Gatt. 2020. Unmasking contextual stereotypes: Measuring and mitigating BERT's gender bias. In *Proceedings of the Second Workshop on Gender Bias in Natural Language Processing*, pages 1–16, Barcelona, Spain (Online). Association for Computational Linguistics.

Steven Cao, Nikita Kitaev, and Dan Klein. 2019. Multilingual alignment of contextual word representations. In *International Conference on Learning Representations*.

Ethan A. Chi, John Hewitt, and Christopher D. Manning. 2020. Finding universal grammatical relations in multilingual BERT. *CoRR*, abs/2005.04511.

Alexis Conneau, Kartikay Khandelwal, Naman Goyal, Vishrav Chaudhary, Guillaume Wenzek, Francisco Guzmán, Edouard Grave, Myle Ott, Luke Zettlemoyer, and Veselin Stoyanov. 2020. Unsupervised cross-lingual representation learning at scale. In *Proceedings of the 58th Annual Meeting of the Association for Computational Linguistics*.

Maria De-Arteaga, Alexey Romanov, Hanna Wallach, Jennifer Chayes, Christian Borgs, Alexandra Chouldechova, Sahin Geyik, Krishnaram Kenthapadi, and Adam Tauman Kalai. 2019. Bias in bios: A case study of semantic representation bias in a high-stakes setting. In *Proceedings of the Conference on Fairness, Accountability, and Transparency*.

Jacob Devlin, Ming-Wei Chang, Kenton Lee, and Kristina Toutanova. 2019. BERT: Pre-training of deep bidirectional transformers for language understanding. In *Proceedings of the 2019 Conference of the North American Chapter of the Association for Computational Linguistics: Human Language Technologies, Volume 1 (Long and Short Papers)*, pages 4171–4186, Minneapolis, Minnesota. Association for Computational Linguistics.

Philipp Dufter and Hinrich Schütze. 2020. Identifying elements essential for BERT's multilinguality. In *Proceedings of the 2020 Conference on Empirical Methods in Natural Language Processing (EMNLP)*, pages 4423–4437, Online. Association for Computational Linguistics.

Yanai Elazar, Shauli Ravfogel, Alon Jacovi, and Yoav Goldberg. 2021. Amnesic probing: Behavioral explanation with amnesic counterfactuals. *Transactions of the Association for Computational Linguistics*, 9:160–175.

Hila Gonen, Yova Kementchedjhieva, and Yoav Goldberg. 2019. How does grammatical gender affect noun representations in gender-marking languages? In *Proceedings of the 23rd Conference on Computational Natural Language Learning (CoNLL)*, Hong Kong, China.

Hila Gonen, Shauli Ravfogel, Yanai Elazar, and Yoav Goldberg. 2020. It's not Greek to mBERT: Inducing word-level translations from multilingual BERT. In *Proceedings of the Third BlackboxNLP Workshop on Analyzing and Interpreting Neural Networks for NLP*, Online.

K Karthikeyan, Zihan Wang, Stephen Mayhew, and Dan Roth. 2020. Cross-lingual ability of multilingual bert: An empirical study. In *International Conference on Learning Representations*.

Sheng Liang, Philipp Dufter, and Hinrich Schütze. 2020. Monolingual and multilingual reduction of gender bias in contextualized representations. In *Proceedings of the 28th International Conference on Computational Linguistics*, pages 5082–5093, Barcelona, Spain (Online). International Committee on Computational Linguistics.

Jindřich Libovický, Rudolf Rosa, and Alexander Fraser. 2020. On the language neutrality of pre-trained multilingual representations. In *Findings of the Association for Computational Linguistics: EMNLP 2020*, pages 1663–1674, Online. Association for Computational Linguistics.

Yinhan Liu, Myle Ott, Naman Goyal, Jingfei Du, Mandar Joshi, Danqi Chen, Omer Levy, Mike Lewis, Luke Zettlemoyer, and Veselin Stoyanov. 2020. Roberta: A robustly optimized bert pretraining approach. In *ICLR*.

Chandler May, Alex Wang, Shikha Bordia, Samuel R. Bowman, and Rachel Rudinger. 2019. On measuring social biases in sentence encoders. In *Proceedings of the 2019 Conference of the North American Chapter of the Association for Computational Linguistics: Human Language Technologies, Volume 1 (Long and Short Papers)*, Minneapolis, Minnesota. Association for Computational Linguistics.

Benjamin Muller, Beno^ıt Sagot, and Djame Seddah. 2020. Can multilingual language models transfer to an unseen dialect? a case study on north african arabizi. *arXiv:2005.00318*.

Matthew E. Peters, Mark Neumann, Mohit Iyyer, Matt Gardner, Christopher Clark, Kenton Lee, and Luke Zettlemoyer. 2018. Deep contextualized word representations. In *Proceedings of the 2018 Conference of the North American Chapter of the Association for Computational Linguistics: Human Language Technologies, Volume 1 (Long Papers)*, pages 2227–2237, New Orleans, Louisiana. Association for Computational Linguistics.

Telmo Pires, Eva Schlinger, and Dan Garrette. 2019. How multilingual is multilingual BERT? In *Proceedings of the 57th Annual Meeting of the Association for Computational Linguistics*, pages 4996–5001, Florence, Italy. Association for Computational Linguistics.

Shauli Ravfogel, Yanai Elazar, Hila Gonen, Michael Twiton, and Yoav Goldberg. 2020. Null it out: Guarding protected attributes by iterative nullspace projection. In *Proceedings of the 58th Annual Meeting of the Association for Computational Linguistics*, pages 7237–7256, Online. Association for Computational Linguistics.

Shauli Ravfogel, Grusha Prasad, Tal Linzen, and Yoav Goldberg. 2021. Counterfactual interventions reveal the causal effect of relative clause representations on agreement prediction. In *Proceedings of the 25th Conference on Computational Natural Language Learning*, pages 194–209, Online. Association for Computational Linguistics.

Shauli Ravfogel, Michael Twiton, Yoav Goldberg, and Ryan Cotterell. 2022. Linear adversarial concept erasure. *arXiv preprint arXiv:2201.12091*.

Jasdeep Singh, Bryan McCann, Richard Socher, and Caiming Xiong. 2019. BERT is not an interlingua and the bias of tokenization. In *Proceedings of the 2nd Workshop on Deep Learning Approaches for Low-Resource NLP (DeepLo 2019)*, pages 47–55, Hong Kong, China. Association for Computational Linguistics.

Yuxuan Wang, Wanxiang Che, Jiang Guo, Yijia Liu, and Ting Liu. 2019. Cross-lingual BERT transformation for zero-shot dependency parsing. In *Proceedings of the 2019 Conference on Empirical Methods in Natural Language Processing and the 9th International Joint Conference on Natural Language Processing (EMNLP-IJCNLP)*, pages 5721–5727, Hong Kong, China. Association for Computational Linguistics.

Adina Williams, Ryan Cotterell, Lawrence Wolf-Sonkin, Damián Blasi, and Hanna Wallach. 2021. On the relationships between the grammatical genders of inanimate nouns and their co-occurring adjectives and verbs. *Transactions of the Association for Computational Linguistics*, 9:139–159.

Thomas Wolf, Lysandre Debut, Victor Sanh, Julien Chaumond, Clement Delangue, Anthony Moi, Pierric Cistac, Tim Rault, Remi Louf, Morgan Funtowicz, Joe Davison, Sam Shleifer, Patrick von Platen, Clara Ma, Yacine Jernite, Julien Plu, Canwen Xu, Teven Le Scao, Sylvain Gugger, Mariama Drame, Quentin Lhoest, and Alexander Rush. 2020. Transformers: State-of-the-art natural language processing. In *Proceedings of the 2020 Conference on Empirical Methods in Natural Language Processing: System Demonstrations*, pages 38–45, Online. Association for Computational Linguistics.

Shijie Wu and Mark Dredze. 2019. Beto, bentz, becas: The surprising cross-lingual effectiveness of BERT.

In *Proceedings of the 2019 Conference on Empirical Methods in Natural Language Processing and the 9th International Joint Conference on Natural Language Processing (EMNLP-IJCNLP)*, pages 833–844.

Jieyu Zhao, Subhabrata Mukherjee, Saghar Hosseini, Kai-Wei Chang, and Ahmed Hassan Awadallah. 2020. Gender bias in multilingual embeddings and cross-lingual transfer. In *Proceedings of the 58th Annual Meeting of the Association for Computational Linguistics*, Online. Association for Computational Linguistics.

Jieyu Zhao, Tianlu Wang, Mark Yatskar, Ryan Cotterell, Vicente Ordonez, and Kai-Wei Chang. 2019. Gender bias in contextualized word embeddings. In *Proceedings of the 2019 Conference of the North American Chapter of the Association for Computational Linguistics: Human Language Technologies, Volume 1 (Long and Short Papers)*, Minneapolis, Minnesota.

Pei Zhou, Weijia Shi, Jieyu Zhao, Kuan-Hao Huang, Muhao Chen, Ryan Cotterell, and Kai-Wei Chang. 2019. Examining gender bias in languages with grammatical gender. In *Proceedings of the 2019 Conference on Empirical Methods in Natural Language Processing and the 9th International Joint Conference on Natural Language Processing (EMNLP-IJCNLP)*, pages 5276–5284, Hong Kong, China. Association for Computational Linguistics.

Ran Zmigrod, Sabrina J. Mielke, Hanna Wallach, and Ryan Cotterell. 2019. Counterfactual data augmentation for mitigating gender stereotypes in languages with rich morphology. In *Proceedings of the 57th Annual Meeting of the Association for Computational Linguistics*, Florence, Italy. Association for Computational Linguistics.

Detecting Textual Adversarial Examples Based on Distributional Characteristics of Data Representations

Na Liu[1] Mark Dras[1] Wei Emma Zhang[2]
[1] School of Computing, Macquarie University
[2] School of Computer Science, The University of Adelaide
na.liu8@students.mq.edu.au, mark.dras@mq.edu.au
wei.e.zhang@adelaide.edu.au

Abstract

Although deep neural networks have achieved state-of-the-art performance in various machine learning tasks, adversarial examples, constructed by adding small non-random perturbations to correctly classified inputs, successfully fool highly expressive deep classifiers into incorrect predictions. Approaches to adversarial attacks in natural language tasks have boomed in the last five years using character-level, word-level, phrase-level, or sentence-level textual perturbations. While there is some work in NLP on defending against such attacks through proactive methods, like adversarial training, there is to our knowledge no effective general reactive approaches to defence via detection of textual adversarial examples such as is found in the image processing literature. In this paper, we propose two new reactive methods for NLP to fill this gap, which unlike the few limited application baselines from NLP are based entirely on distribution characteristics of learned representations: we adapt one from the image processing literature (Local Intrinsic Dimensionality (LID)), and propose a novel one (MultiDistance Representation Ensemble Method (MDRE)). Adapted LID and MDRE obtain state-of-the-art results on character-level, word-level, and phrase-level attacks on the IMDB dataset as well as on the later two with respect to the MultiNLI dataset. For future research, we publish our code [1].

1 Introduction

Highly expressive deep neural networks are fragile against adversarial examples, constructed by carefully designed small perturbations of normal examples, that can fool deep classifiers to make wrong predictions (Szegedy et al., 2013). Crafting adversarial examples in images involves adding small non-random perturbations to many pixels in inputs that should be correctly classified by a target model. These perturbations can force high-efficacy models into incorrect classifications and are often imperceptible to humans (Szegedy et al., 2013; Goodfellow et al., 2014; Moosavi-Dezfooli et al., 2016; Papernot et al., 2016b; Carlini and Wagner, 2017b; Chen et al., 2018). However, when adversarial examples have been studied in the context of text, to our knowledge, only Miyato et al. (2016) aligns closely with the original intuition of adversarial examples in applying perturbations to word embeddings, which are inputs of deep neural nets. Rather, most adversarial attack techniques use more practical semantics-preserving textual changes other than embedding perturbations, at character-level, word-level, phrase-level, or sentence-level (Pruthi et al., 2019; Jia and Liang, 2017; Alzantot et al., 2018; Ribeiro et al., 2018; Ren et al., 2019; Iyyer et al., 2018; Yoo and Qi, 2021; Li et al., 2020, 2021; Jin et al., 2020); see Table 1. This variety increases the difficulty of detecting textual adversarial examples.

Generating adversarial examples to attack deep neural nets and protecting deep neural nets from adversarial examples have been extensively studied in image classification tasks (Szegedy et al., 2013; Goodfellow et al., 2014; Moosavi-Dezfooli et al., 2016; Papernot et al., 2016b; Carlini and Wagner, 2017b; Chen et al., 2018; Papernot et al., 2016a; Feinman et al., 2017; Ma et al., 2018; Lee et al., 2018). However, in the natural language domain, only crafting of adversarial examples has been comprehensively considered (Jia and Liang, 2017; Alzantot et al., 2018; Ribeiro et al., 2018; Ren et al., 2019; Iyyer et al., 2018). Defence against textual adversaries, primarily through increasing the robustness of deep neural networks, is much less studied (Jia et al., 2019; Pruthi et al., 2019). In the image processing space, Cohen et al. (2020) refers to these as *proactive* defence methods, and Carlini and Wagner (2017a) notes that they can be evaded by optimization-based attacks, such as constructing new loss functions; in the NLP space,

[1]Code available at https://github.com/NaLiuAnna/MDRE

Proceedings of the 7th Workshop on Representation Learning for NLP, pages 78 - 90
May 26, 2022 ©2022 Association for Computational Linguistics

	Example	Prediction
Original	This is a story of two misfits who don't stand a chance alone, but together they are magnificent.	Positive
Character-level (Pruthi et al., 2019)	TZyTis is a sotry of two misifts who don't stad a ccange alUone, but tpgthr they are mgnificent.	Negative
Word-level (Alzantot et al., 2018)	This is a conte of two who don't stands a opportunities alone, but together they are opulent.	Negative
Phrase-level (Iyyer et al., 2018)	Why don't you have two misfits who don't stand a chance alone, but together they're beautiful.	Negative
Sentence-level (Jia and Liang, 2017)	This is a story of two misfits who don't stand a chance alone, but together they are magnificent. ready south hundred at size expected worked whose turn poor.	Negative

Table 1: Examples of textual adversarial instances on a sentiment analysis task

Yoo and Qi (2021) observes that generating word-level textual adversaries for proactive adversarial training are computationally expensive because of necessary search and constraints based on sentence encoding. Consequently, Feinman et al. (2017); Ma et al. (2018); Lee et al. (2018); Papernot and McDaniel (2018) explore *reactive* defence methods (Cohen et al., 2020) in the image processing space: these focus on distinguishing real from adversarial examples, in order to detect them before they are passed to neural networks. These reactive defences have been explored in only a limited way in the NLP space (Mozes et al., 2021). Importantly, these few methods rely on procedures like testing word substitutions, quite unlike those in the image processing space, which are functions of the learned representations.

The contributions of this paper are two textual adversarial reactive detectors as follows:

- Adapting the Local Intrinsic Dimensionality (LID) method from image processing to the text domain.
- Proposing a MultiDistance Representation Ensemble Method (MDRE).

Both of them are based on distribution differences of semantic representations between normal examples and adversarial examples. They achieve state-of-the-art results across a range of attack methods and domains.

2 Related Work

In this section, we briefly review state-of-the-art work on defending neural networks against both image and textual adversarial examples.

Image Adversarial Defences: Adversarial training (Goodfellow et al., 2014) using adversarial examples to augment training data or adding an adversarial objective to a loss function, and defensive distillation framework (Papernot et al., 2016a) which transfers knowledge between same structured teacher and student models, are two effective proactive defence methods. For reactive defences, Feinman et al. (2017); Ma et al. (2018); Papernot and McDaniel (2018); Lee et al. (2018) have all proposed approaches that use the learned representations of the classifier that the attacker is trying to fool, and then with a variety of techniques to identify characteristics of the adversarial examples' learned representations that permit the detection of whether a data point is adversarial or original; these techniques involve kernel density estimations in a feature space of a last hidden layer and Bayesian uncertainty estimates, Local Intrinsic Dimensionality, Deep k-Nearest Neighbors, and Mahalanobis distance-based confidence scores respectively.

Textual Adversarial Defences: Adversarial training (Goodfellow et al., 2014) is a commonly used defence method to augment training data with adversarial examples and their correct labels, which has been effective in Li et al. (2016), Li et al. (2017), Ribeiro et al. (2018), and Ebrahimi et al. (2018), but has limited utility in Pruthi et al. (2019) and Jia and Liang (2017). Jia et al. (2019) applies interval bound propagation (IBP) to minimize an upper bound of possible candidate sentences' losses when facing word substitution adversaries. Jones et al. (2020) introduced robust encodings (RobEn) to cluster words and typos, and produced one encoding for each cluster to harness adversarial typos. Zhou et al. (2019) proposed the learning to discriminate perturbations (DISP) framework to block character-level and word-level adversarial perturbations by recognising and replacing perturbed words. Mozes et al. (2021) noticed and verified a characteristic of word-level adversaries that replacement words are less likely to occur than their substitutions, therefore, they constructed a rule-based, model-agnostic frequency-guided word substitutions (FGWS) algorithm, which is the only existing textual reactive defence method as far as we know.

3 Methods

3.1 Adapted Local Intrinsic Dimensionality (LID)

From among the reactive image processing methods, we selected the Local Intrinsic Dimensionality (LID) approach of Ma et al. (2018) as one that can be directly adapted to textual representations. The approach of Ma et al. (2018) uses LID to reveal the local distance distribution for a reference point representation to its neighbours, and uses outputs of each layer from the target deep neural network as an input point representations. LID was initially presented for dimension reduction (Houle et al., 2012). Ma et al. (2018) introduced LID to characterize the local data submanifolds in the vicinity of reference points and detect adversarial samples from their originals. The LID definition is as follows.

Definition 3.1 (Local Intrinsic Dimensionality (Ma et al., 2018)). Given a data sample $x \in X$, let $R > 0$ be a random variable denoting the distance from x to other data samples. If the cumulative distibution function $F(r)$ of R is positive and continuously differentiable at distance $r > 0$, the LID of x at distance r is given by:

$$LID_F(r) \triangleq \lim_{\epsilon \to 0} \frac{ln(F((1+\epsilon)\cdot r)/F(r))}{ln(1+\epsilon)} = \frac{r \cdot F'(r)}{F(r)} \tag{1}$$

whenever the limit exists.

To simplify computation, given a reference sample $x \sim \mathcal{P}$, where $\mathcal{P}$ represents the data distribution, the Maximum Likelihood Estimator of the LID at x is defined as follows (Ma et al., 2018):

$$\widehat{LID}(x) = -\left(\frac{1}{k}\sum_{i=1}^{k}\log\frac{r_i(x)}{r_k(x)}\right)^{-1} \tag{2}$$

where $r_i(x)$ is the distance between x and its ith nearest neighbor within a sample of points drawn from $\mathcal{P}$, k is the number of nearest neighbors. Since the logarithmic function $f(x) = \log_a(x)$ for any base a and the negative reciprocal function $f(x) = -x^{-1}$ are monotonically increasing functions when their independent variables are positive, if neighbors of a reference sample x are compact, its estimated LID from Equation (2) is smaller, otherwise, its estimated LID is bigger.

When building a binary classifier to detect adversarial examples using LID in Ma et al. (2018), the inputs are lists of estimated LID from the Equation (2) of different layers' outputs from the target deep neural net, and adversarial and normal examples are two categories of the classifier.

To adapt this to textual representations, we implement same technique — a detection classifier based on LID characterizations derived from different layers' outputs of a deep neural net — but apply this to a Transformer. Here we use $\text{BERT}_{\text{BASE}}$ model (Devlin et al., 2019), although in principle any would be suitable. The x in the Equation (2) is a representation of an input text from a layer's hidden state of the first token of the target ($\text{BERT}_{\text{BASE}}$) model, since self-attention layers are essential modules of a transformer, and the last layer hidden state of the first token is typically used as a component to build a pooled output, a text representation for a classifier. Therefore, an input of a detection classifier for an example is a 12-dimensional vector, where each element illustrates the corresponding layer's estimated LID from the $\text{BERT}_{\text{BASE}}$ model.

3.2 MultiDistance Representation Ensemble Method (MDRE)

Adversarial examples are constructed by adding imperceptible non-random perturbations to inputs of correctly classified test examples to fool highly expressive deep neural nets into incorrect classifications (Szegedy et al., 2013). Motivated by the reasoning behind LID expressed in Equation (2), by Feinman et al. (2017)'s intuition that adversarial samples lie off the true data manifold, and by (Lee et al., 2018)'s recognition that they are out-of-distribution samples by a class-conditional distribution, we assume that samples with a same predicted label from a deep neural net lie on a data submanifold; an adversarial example is generated because perturbations cause a correctly predicted example to transfer from one data submanifold to another, making it an out-of-distribution sample relative to training examples from its data submanifold. Consequently, we posit that it is likely that the Euclidean distance between an adversarial example x' and the nearest neighbor of x' among training examples with the same predicted label as x' is bigger than the Euclidean distance between its corresponding original normal test example x and x's nearest neighbor among training examples with the same predicted label as x.

In natural language processing, most inputs of deep neural networks are learned representations by representation learning models nowadays. Even though current methods of representation learn-

Algorithm 1 MultiDistance Representation Ensemble Method (MDRE)

Input:

$\mathbb{D} = \{\boldsymbol{X}^{(train)}, \boldsymbol{X}^{(norm)}, \boldsymbol{X}^{(adv)}\}$: a dataset; there are k examples in $\boldsymbol{X}^{(norm)}$ and $\boldsymbol{X}^{(adv)}$

H: an array containing m representation learning models

$g : \mathbb{R}^m \to \{0, 1\}$: a binary classification model (MDRE)

$f : \mathbb{R}^n \to \mathbb{R}^l$: a deep neural net that is the target model for an adversarial attack

Output:

Detection accuracy of MDRE: acc

Initializing inputs and labels of g: $\boldsymbol{X} = zeros[2k, m]$, $\boldsymbol{y} = zeros[2k]$
Computing examples' predictions from f of $\mathbb{D}$: $\{\hat{\boldsymbol{y}}^{(train)}, \hat{\boldsymbol{y}}^{(norm)}, \hat{\boldsymbol{y}}^{(adv)}\}$
for $j \in \{0, \cdots, m-1\}$ **do**
  Computing examples' representations from $H[j]$ of $\mathbb{D}$: $\{\boldsymbol{V}_j^{(train)}, \boldsymbol{V}_j^{(norm)}, \boldsymbol{V}_j^{(adv)}\}$
  for $i \in \{0, \cdots, k-1\}$ **do**
    Calculating $d_j^{(norm)}, d_j^{(adv)}$ for examples $\boldsymbol{X}_i^{(norm)}, \boldsymbol{X}_i^{(adv)}$
    $\boldsymbol{X}[i, j] = d_j^{(norm)}$, $\boldsymbol{y}[i] = 0$
    $\boldsymbol{X}[k+i, j] = d_j^{(adv)}$, $\boldsymbol{y}[k+i] = 1$
  end for
end for
Training g by randomly choosing 80% of $\{(\boldsymbol{X}_{i,:}, \boldsymbol{y}_i)\}_{i=0}^{2k-1}$
acc = test accuracy of g using the rest 20% of $\{(\boldsymbol{X}_{i,:}, \boldsymbol{y}_i)\}_{i=0}^{2k-1}$

ing are effective in various tasks (Devlin et al., 2019; Liu et al., 2019; Yang et al., 2019; Lewis et al., 2020), semantic meanings and semantic differences between texts from humans' perspective are not perfectly captured by textual representation vectors (Liu et al., 2020). In addition, as mentioned in Section 1, most textual adversarial generation algorithms do not modify representations, which are input feature vectors of deep neural networks, but modify original texts. Therefore, the assumed characteristic of adversaries in the last paragraph that the Euclidean distances between adversarial examples and their nearest neighbors among training examples in the same submanifolds are bigger than normal examples, may lose efficiency in textual adversarial detection scenarios. To build a stronger reactive classifier, we use ensemble learning to combine distances between representations learned from multiple representation learning models. We construct a more effective MultiDistance Representation Ensemble Method (MDRE), as illustrated in Algorithm 1.

The MDRE is a supervised binary classification model $g : \mathbb{R}^m \to \{0, 1\}$. m is the number of representation learning models; g can be any binary classification model, such as logistic regressions or deep neural nets; $\{0, 1\}$ is the output label set, with 1 corresponding to adversarial examples, 0 to normal examples.

The input of MDRE is a matrix $\boldsymbol{X}$ and each row vector of $\boldsymbol{X}$ is $\boldsymbol{X}_{i,:} = (d_0, d_1 \cdots, d_{m-1}) \in \mathbb{R}^m$. The element of this vector $d_j, 0 \le j \le m-1$ is a Euclidean distance between a semantic representation of a normal or adversarial example $\boldsymbol{v}$ and a representation of its nearest neighbour among training examples with the same predicted label as $\boldsymbol{v}$ through the j-th representation learning model $H[j]$, as $d_j^{(norm)}$ or $d_j^{(adv)}$ in Algorithm 1. To find a nearest neighbour, we compare Euclidean distances between $\boldsymbol{v}$ and all representations among training examples with the same predicted label as $\boldsymbol{v}$ through $H[j]$. In Algorithm 1, $\boldsymbol{X}^{(norm)}$ consists of normal test examples corresponding to the elements of $\boldsymbol{X}^{(adv)}$, where the elements of $\boldsymbol{X}^{(norm)}$ have correct predictions from the target model f, but $\boldsymbol{X}^{(adv)}$ elements have incorrect predictions from f. The training and testing process of MDRE is same as the process of the selected model g.

4 Evaluation

In this section, we evaluate the utilities of the adapted LID and MDRE by using character-level, word-level, and phrase-level upstream attacks on sentiment analysis and natural language inference tasks, and comparing against several baselines: a language model, DISP (Zhou et al., 2019), and

FGWS (Mozes et al., 2021). The experimental results demonstrate that the adapted LID and MDRE outperforms these methods on sentiment analysis and natural language inference tasks for word-level and phrase-level attacks.

4.1 Experimental Setup

4.1.1 Tasks

We apply our approaches and baselines to sentiment analysis and natural language inference tasks, since they are two most commonly used datasets in textual adversarial example generation. The sentiment analysis task has been the most widely used testbed for generating textual adversarial examples (Pruthi et al., 2019; Alzantot et al., 2018; Ribeiro et al., 2018; Ren et al., 2019; Iyyer et al., 2018; Yoo and Qi, 2021; Li et al., 2020), making this the natural domain for these experiments; they have also been popularly applied to the natural language inference task (Alzantot et al., 2018; Iyyer et al., 2018; Yoo and Qi, 2021; Li et al., 2020, 2021; Jin et al., 2020), so we choose this to explore the generality of our methods.

We use the IMDB dataset (Maas et al., 2011) in the sentiment analysis task, which contains 50,000 movie reviews, divided into 25,000 training examples and 25,000 test examples, labelled for positive or negative sentiment. The average number of words per review in the IMDB dataset is 262 when using the Natural Language Toolkit (NLTK) (Bird et al., 2009) to tokenize examples. We set a maximum sequence length of the IMDB dataset to 512 for all following models.

To test the robustness of our methods, the Multi-Genre NLI (MultiNLI) corpus (Williams et al., 2018) and its mismatched test examples, which are derived from sources that differ from the training examples, are used in the natural language inference task. The MultiNLI dataset includes 392,702 training examples and 9,832 mismatched testing examples in which global_label fields are not "-", with three classes: entailment, neutral, and contradiction. The average and maximum word numbers of the MultiNLI dataset are 34 and 416 respectively, using NLTK word tokenizer. We set the maximum sequence length for this dataset to 256.

4.1.2 Attack Methods

We implement three widely used attack methods using character-level, word-level, and phrase-level perturbations to construct adversarial examples. For all types of attacks, we take the $\text{BERT}_{\text{BASE}}$ model as the target model, indicating that adversaries have different predictions with their originals by the $\text{BERT}_{\text{BASE}}$ model.

Character-level. The character-level attack is from Pruthi et al. (2019), which applies swapping, dropping, adding, and keyboard mistakes to a randomly selected word of an original example.

- Swapping: swapping two adjacent internal characters.
- Dropping: removing an internal character.
- Adding: internally inserting a new character.
- Keyboard mistakes: substituting an internal character with one of its adjacent characters in keyboards.

Here, we set maximum numbers of perturbations to half of the maximum sequence lengths of datasets; consequently, for the IMDB dataset, the maximum number of attacks is 256, and for the MultiNLI dataset is 128. If after achieving this number, the prediction of the perturbed text is still consistent with the original example, these attacks fail, and no character-level adversarial example constructed for this original example.

Word-level. We use a method from Alzantot et al. (2018), which is an effective and widely cited word-level threat method. Their approach randomly selects a word in a sentence, replaces it with its synonymous and context fitted word according to the GloVe word vectors (Pennington et al., 2014), counter-fitting word vectors (Mrkšić et al., 2016), and the Google 1 billion words language model (Chelba et al., 2013), and applies population-based genetic algorithms from the natural selection using a combination of crossover and mutation to generate next adversarial generations.

While effective, the initial algorithm is somewhat inefficient and computationally expensive. In implementing this method, Jia et al. (2019) found that computing scores from the Google 1 billion words language model (Chelba et al., 2013) for each iteration in this approach causes its inefficiency; to improve this, they used a faster language model and prevented semantic drift, which is synonyms picked from previous iterations also apply the language model to select words from their neighbour lists. In our experiments, we adapt these modifications by using a faster Transformer-XL architecture (Dai et al., 2019) pretrained on the WikiText-103 dataset (Merity et al., 2016), and not allowing the semantic drift, so that we compute all test examples words' neighbours before attacks.

Dataset	Training.	Validation.	Testing.	Correctly Predicted Test Examples	Adversarial/Original Examples		
					character-level	word-level	phrase-level
IMDB	20,000	5,000	25,000	23,226	12,299	9,627	6,315
MultiNLI	314,162	78,540	9,832	8,062	7,028	3,240	4,340

Table 2: The number of examples used in experiments

In this attack, we also set maximum numbers of perturbations, which are one fifth of the maximum sequence lengths; therefore, for the IMDB dataset is 102, and for the MultiNLI dataset is 51. For an original test example, if the number of attacks reaches this threshold but predictions do not change, no corresponding adversarial example is constructed for this original example.

Phrase-level. The phrase-level attack is from Ribeiro et al. (2018), which uses translators and back translators to generate adversarial examples. As far as we know, this is the only phrase-level perturbation technique that can be used for paragraph-length text. Their approach — termed semantically equivalent adversaries (SEAs) — translates an original sentences into multiple pivot languages, then translates them back to the source language. If there is a back translated sentences that is semantically equivalent to the original sentences, measured by a semantic score greater than a threshold, and it has a different prediction with the original sentences, then it is an adversarial example. Otherwise, this original example has no relevant adversaries.

4.1.3 Target Model

The $\text{BERT}_{\text{BASE}}$ model is implemented as a target model for these three attacks, by which adversarial examples are misclassified. We apportion training sets on both datasets into training subsets and validation subsets, with an 80-20 split. After training, the models achieve 92.90% test accuracy on the IMDB dataset, and for the MultiNLI mismatched test set is 82.01%. The correctly predicted test examples are preserved for subsequent attack processes. After attacks, adversarial examples and their corresponding normal test examples maintain for following detectors as negative and positive examples; in this, we follow the experimental setup used for evaluating reactive defences in the image processing literature (Ma et al., 2018) with an 80/20 training/test split. The number of examples used on the IMDB and MultiNLI datasets and number of originals and adversaries after attacks are shown in Table 2.

4.1.4 Detection Methods

We evaluate three baselines in addition to the adapted LID and MDRE in these experiments.

A language model. The first baseline is built from a language model since even though most attack algorithms intend to construct semantically and syntactically similar adversaries, many textual adversaries are abnormal and ungrammatical, as shown in Table 1. We use the Transformer-XL model pretrained on the WikiText-103 dataset from Hugging Face transformers (Wolf et al., 2020), and obtain language model scores for texts as the product of words prediction proportion scores. We construct a detection classifier by using a logistic regression model with language model scores as inputs; the model acts to learn a threshold on scores to distinguish adversarial examples.

Learning to Discriminate Perturbations (DISP) (Zhou et al., 2019). Our second baseline is the DISP framework, which is the only comparable technique for detecting textual adversarial examples across character-level and word-level attacks to our knowledge. DISP consists of three components: perturbation discriminator, embedding estimator, and hierarchical navigable small word graphs. The perturbation discriminator identifies a set of character-level or word-level perturbed tokens; the embedding estimator predicts embeddings for each perturbed token; then, hierarchical navigable small word graphs map these embeddings to actual words to correct adversarial perturbations. DISP is not itself designed as a adversarial example detector, but we adapt it for that task: if an adversarial example rectified by DISP predicts the same class as the target model predicts for the corresponding initial original example, or the prediction of a normal (non-adversarial) example rectified by DISP isn't changed, we consider DISP to have been successful in its detection. Otherwise, it is not. Since DISP is designed for character-level and word-level attacks, we do not apply it to phrase-level attacks.

Frequency-guided word substitutions (FGWS) (Mozes et al., 2021). Our third baseline is FGWS. Mozes et al. (2021) noticed, and

Dataset	Attack Method	$\text{BERT}_{\text{BASE}}$	$\text{RoBERTa}_{\text{BASE}}$	$\text{XLNet}_{\text{BASE}}$	$\text{BART}_{\text{BASE}}$
IMDB	Character-level	0.3656	0.8613	0.5770	0.8286
	Word-level	0.6999	0.8714	0.7918	0.8425
	Phrase-level	0.1827	0.3224	0.3289	0.3010
MultiNLI	Character-level	0.4848	0.7104	0.6670	0.6457
	Word-level	0.6864	0.7068	0.6870	0.6296
	Phrase-level	0.2795	0.3899	0.3698	0.3325

Table 3: The accuracy of adversarial examples

verified using hypothesis testing, that a characteristic of word-level adversaries was that replacement words are less likely to occur than their substitutions. They use this feature to construct a rule-based, model-agnostic frequency-guided word substitutions (FGWS) algorithm which distinguishes adversarial examples by replacing infrequent words with their higher frequency synonyms. If the replacements cause prediction confidence changes exceeding a threshold, these examples are deemed adversarial examples. FGWS is only designed to be applied to word-level attacks. They use WordNet (Fellbaum, 2005) and GloVe vectors (Pennington et al., 2014) to find neighbors of a word. A word frequency is its number of occurrences in the corresponding dataset's training examples; infrequent words are defined as those words whose frequencies are lower than a threshold. They set this threshold to be the frequency of the word at the {*0*-th, *10*-th, $\cdots$, *100*-th} percentile of word frequencies in training set. If the prediction confidence differences between sequences with replaced words and their corresponding original sequences are higher than a threshold, the original sequences are assumed to be adversarial examples. They set this threshold to the 90%-th confidence difference between words substituted validation set and original validation set in their experiment.

Adapted Local Intrinsic Dimensionality (LID) Following the characterization of our adapted LID from Section 3.1, we use the $\text{BERT}_{\text{BASE}}$ model as in the above baselines. We implement a logistic regression model as the detection classifier as Ma et al. (2018), and the neighborhood size k is tuned using a grid search over 100, 1000, and the range [10, 42) with a step size 2.

MultiDistance Representation Ensemble Method (MDRE). In MDRE, we set $m = 4$, H = [$\text{BERT}_{\text{BASE}}$, $\text{RoBERTa}_{\text{BASE}}$, $\text{XLNet}_{\text{BASE}}$, $\text{BART}_{\text{BASE}}$], and g is a logistic regression model. See Algorithm 1 for more information of notations.

4.2 Experimental Results

Before discussing the effectiveness of the detection classifiers, Table 4 and Table 3 show the accuracy of the sentiment analysis and natural language inference classifiers on normal and adversarial examples from four models with three types of attacks. The $\text{BERT}_{\text{BASE}}$ model is the target model in terms of generating all kinds of adversaries — that is, the adversarial examples are specifically designed to defeat the $\text{BERT}_{\text{BASE}}$ model — so all adversarial instance predictions are incorrect, therefore, the accuracy is 0. However, when we use a different random seed which also modify the order of training examples to fine-tune another $\text{BERT}_{\text{BASE}}$ model used for prediction, its parameters is different from the parameters of the $\text{BERT}_{\text{BASE}}$ model used before. The accuracy of adversaries slightly increases, indicating that BERT model parameters do not converge but fluctuate when using stochastic or mini-batch gradient descent.

Results for detection method accuracy are in Table 5. Adapted LID and MDRE work better than the baselines, except for DISP against character-level attacks on MultiNLI dataset, where the adapted LID is a close second. The detection accuracy on the MultiNLI dataset is lower than the IMDB dataset, although this is not a surprise. It uses the mismatched test set of the MultiNLI dataset which makes the task more challenging. The results show that the adapted LID and MDRE are sensitive to sample distributions, so if some normal test examples representations are from a different distribution of training samples representations, such as noise examples, they will influence their performance.

Adapted LID is often close to MDRE. It is higher

Dataset	$\text{BERT}_{\text{BASE}}$	$\text{RoBERTa}_{\text{BASE}}$	$\text{XLNet}_{\text{BASE}}$	$\text{BART}_{\text{BASE}}$
IMDB	0.9290	0.9532	0.9336	0.9429
MultiNLI	0.8201	0.8671	0.8630	0.8455

Table 4: The accuracy of normal test examples

Dataset	Detecting Method	Character-level Attack	Word-level Attack	Phrase-level Attack
IMDB	Language Model	0.4996	0.4966	0.4838
	DISP	0.8936	0.7714	—
	FGWS	—	0.7958	—
	LID	0.9142	**0.8406**	0.9093
	MDRE	**0.9193**	0.7562	**0.9505**
MultiNLI	Language Model	0.4932	0.4707	0.4997
	DISP	**0.7496**	0.6137	—
	FGWS	—	0.6128	—
	LID	0.7328	0.5849	0.6146
	MDRE	0.7016	**0.6319**	**0.6809**

Table 5: The accuracy for detection classifiers

in word-level attack on the IMDB dataset and character-level attack on the MultiNLI dataset, but it is lower on phrase-level attacks. Relative to its initial application on image classification tasks, the performance of the adapted LID approach is worse. Most accuracy of LID on image adversarial attacks on CIFAR-10, CIFAR-100, and SVHN datasets are over or near 90% (Cohen et al., 2020). However, in our experiments, the average accuracy of the adapted LID is about 77% (against majority class baseline of 50%). This reveals the difficulty of detecting textual adversarial examples.

The performance of the language model is similar to random guess, since the ratio between positive (normal) and negative (adversarial) examples is 1:1. We observed that language model prediction proportion scores are sensitive to the number of words in examples because each word scores is between 0 to 1 and more words leads to lower scores. In addition, in some contexts, scores for synonyms or typos which are out-of-dictionary words, are lower but close to scores of original words, which do not have the large differences that might be expected.

DISP effectively applies the bidirectional language model feature of the $\text{BERT}_{\text{BASE}}$ model and builds a powerful perturbation discriminator, which labels character-level or word-level perturbed tokens to 1, and unperturbed tokens to 0. The perturbation discriminator achieves F_1 scores of 95.06% on the IMDB dataset and 97.67% on the MultiNLI dataset, using their own adversaral attack methods. However, the embedding estimator predicts embeddings through inputting 5-grams with masked middle tokens to a $\text{BERT}_{\text{BASE}}$ model with one layer feed-forward head on top and outputting embeddings of these masked tokens from 300-dimensional pretrained FastText English word vectors (Mikolov et al., 2018). This is challenging and restricts the overall performance of DISP.

Intuitively, adversaries' predictions are different from their original counterparts, which are ordinary language; therefore, adversaries may contain rare and infrequent words. According to an English word frequency dataset,[2] some words frequencies in examples of Alzantot et al. (2018) are shown in Table 6. We can find that the intuition is correct

org.	org. freq.	sub.	sub. freq.
terrible	8,610,277	horrific	1,017,211
		horrifying	491,916
considered	57,378,298	regarded	6,892,622
kids	96,602,880	youngstars	—
runner	7,381,022	racer	3,625,077
battling	1,340,424	—	—
strives	1,415,683	—	—

Table 6: Original and modified sample words frequencies in examples of Alzantot et al. (2018)

that replacement words frequencies drop compared with substitutions; however, they may be higher than other normal words. Therefore, using one threshold makes it difficult to separate adversarially substituted words from all normal words. Alternative approaches to applying the characteristic of adversarial words frequencies may work better. We note that it is perhaps surprising, then, that our representation-based detection methods outperform FGWS that do incorporate frequency information from the raw text input. This underscores the usefulness of the distributional information available in the learned representations.

We show detection methods applied to examples from the MultiNLI dataset in the Appendix A supplement.

4.3 Ablation Analysis of MDRE

The key ideas behind MDRE is that (1) adversarial examples are out-of-distribution samples rela-

[2]The english word frequency: `https://www.kaggle.com/rtatman/english-word-frequency`

Dataset	Detecting Method	Character-level Attack	Word-level Attack	Phrase-level Attack
IMDB	$\text{MDRE}_{\text{BERT}}$	0.8941	0.7541	0.9129
	$\text{MDRE}_{\text{RoBERTa}}$	0.8606	0.6645	0.9287
	$\text{MDRE}_{\text{XLNet}}$	0.7226	0.5962	0.7819
	$\text{MDRE}_{\text{BART}}$	0.8951	0.6858	0.9327
MultiNLI	$\text{MDRE}_{\text{BERT}}$	0.6102	0.5903	0.6382
	$\text{MDRE}_{\text{RoBERTa}}$	0.6853	0.5903	0.6526
	$\text{MDRE}_{\text{XLNet}}$	0.6323	0.6227	0.6452
	$\text{MDRE}_{\text{BART}}$	0.6824	0.6366	0.6740

Table 7: The accuracy of detection classifiers for ablation analysis of MDRE

tive to training examples from their data submanifolds and (2) ensemble learning can help identify this. Therefore, we combine four representation learning models: $\text{BERT}_{\text{BASE}}$, $\text{RoBERTa}_{\text{BASE}}$, $\text{XLNet}_{\text{BASE}}$, and $\text{BART}_{\text{BASE}}$ to produce MDRE as described in Section 4.1.4. In order to explore the effects of these two components and each representation learning model, we apply $\text{MDRE}_{\text{BERT}}$, $\text{MDRE}_{\text{RoBERTa}}$, $\text{MDRE}_{\text{XLNet}}$, $\text{MDRE}_{\text{BART}}$ models, where $m = 1$, $H =$ [$\text{BERT}_{\text{BASE}}$], [$\text{RoBERTa}_{\text{BASE}}$], [$\text{XLNet}_{\text{BASE}}$], and [$\text{BART}_{\text{BASE}}$] respectively.

The results are shown in Table 7 which reveals all models work in detecting textual adversarial examples: the detection accuracy on both the IMDB and MultiNLI datasets, and all upstream adversarial attacks is substantially higher than random guess (50%). Comparing with the results of MDRE on the IMDB and MultiNLI datasets from Table 5, ensemble learning helps to build a stronger detector except word-level attack on the MultiNLI dataset.

5 Conclusion and Future work

In this paper, we adapted Local Intrinsic Dimensionality (LID) method (Ma et al., 2018) from image processing and proposed a simple and general textual adversarial reactive detector, MultiDistance Representation Ensemble Method (MDRE), based on the distribution characteristics of adversarial examples representations, that they are out-of-distribution samples and lie off the true data manifold. The experimental results show adapted LID and MDRE achieve state-of-the-art results on detecting character-level, word-level, and phrase-level adversaries on the IMDB dataset as well as on the later two with respect to the MultiNLI dataset. The results show that it is possible to construct adversarial example detectors using only the learned representations, and not relying on various textual substitution processes as in the baselines.

As discussed in Section 3, adapted LID uses estimated Local Intrinsic Dimensionality on text representations form different layers outputs of a target model, and MDRE is implemented on Euclidean distances between samples' representations and representations of their nearest neighbors among the training examples with the same predicted labels from different representation learning models, to characterise representation distribution differences between adversarial examples and normal examples. In terms of future work and the LID approach, Athalye et al. (2018) found that in the image processing space, LID is vulnerable to their Backward Pass Differentiable Approximiation (BPDA) attack; it would be useful to investigate whether this is the case in the text space, and if so, other detection methods from image processing may be worth looking into. With respect to MDRE, as it is a kind of nearest-neighbour ensembling approach, looking into other possibilities falling within that space could be productive. More generally, exploring more effective distribution characteristics of data semantic representations among adversarial and normal examples, may help to build better detectors.

References

Moustafa Alzantot, Yash Sharma, Ahmed Elgohary, Bo-Jhang Ho, Mani Srivastava, and Kai-Wei Chang. 2018. Generating natural language adversarial examples. In *Proceedings of the 2018 Conference on Empirical Methods in Natural Language Processing*, pages 2890–2896, Brussels, Belgium. Association for Computational Linguistics.

Anish Athalye, Nicholas Carlini, and David Wagner. 2018. Obfuscated gradients give a false sense of security: Circumventing defenses to adversarial examples. In *Proceedings of the 35th International Conference on Machine Learning*, volume 80 of *Proceedings of Machine Learning Research*, pages 274–283. PMLR.

Steven Bird et al. 2009. *Natural language processing with Python: analyzing text with the natural language toolkit.* " O'Reilly Media, Inc.".

Nicholas Carlini and David Wagner. 2017a. Adversarial examples are not easily detected: Bypassing ten detection methods. In *Proc. 10th AISec workshop*, pages 3–14.

Nicholas Carlini and David Wagner. 2017b. Towards evaluating the robustness of neural networks. In *Proc. IEEE S&P*, pages 39–57.

Ciprian Chelba et al. 2013. One billion word benchmark for measuring progress in statistical language modeling. *arXiv preprint arXiv:1312.3005*.

Pin-Yu Chen et al. 2018. Ead: elastic-net attacks to deep neural networks via adversarial examples. In *Proc. AAAI*.

Gilad Cohen et al. 2020. Detecting adversarial samples using influence functions and nearest neighbors. In *Proc. IEEE/CVF CVPR*, pages 14453–14462.

Zihang Dai, Zhilin Yang, Yiming Yang, Jaime Carbonell, Quoc Le, and Ruslan Salakhutdinov. 2019. Transformer-XL: Attentive language models beyond a fixed-length context. In *Proceedings of the 57th Annual Meeting of the Association for Computational Linguistics*, pages 2978–2988, Florence, Italy. Association for Computational Linguistics.

Jacob Devlin, Ming-Wei Chang, Kenton Lee, and Kristina Toutanova. 2019. BERT: Pre-training of deep bidirectional transformers for language understanding. In *Proceedings of the 2019 Conference of the North American Chapter of the Association for Computational Linguistics: Human Language Technologies, Volume 1 (Long and Short Papers)*, pages 4171–4186, Minneapolis, Minnesota. Association for Computational Linguistics.

Javid Ebrahimi, Anyi Rao, Daniel Lowd, and Dejing Dou. 2018. HotFlip: White-box adversarial examples for text classification. In *Proceedings of the 56th Annual Meeting of the Association for Computational Linguistics (Volume 2: Short Papers)*, pages 31–36, Melbourne, Australia. Association for Computational Linguistics.

Reuben Feinman et al. 2017. Detecting adversarial samples from artifacts. *arXiv preprint arXiv:1703.00410*.

Christiane Fellbaum. 2005. Wordnet and wordnets. In Alex Barber, editor, *ELL*, pages 2–665. Elsevier.

Ian J Goodfellow et al. 2014. Explaining and harnessing adversarial examples. *arXiv preprint arXiv:1412.6572*.

M. E. Houle et al. 2012. Generalized expansion dimension. In *2012 IEEE 12th ICDM Workshops*, pages 587–594.

Mohit Iyyer, John Wieting, Kevin Gimpel, and Luke Zettlemoyer. 2018. Adversarial example generation with syntactically controlled paraphrase networks. In *Proceedings of the 2018 Conference of the North American Chapter of the Association for Computational Linguistics: Human Language Technologies, Volume 1 (Long Papers)*, pages 1875–1885, New Orleans, Louisiana. Association for Computational Linguistics.

Robin Jia and Percy Liang. 2017. Adversarial examples for evaluating reading comprehension systems. In *Proceedings of the 2017 Conference on Empirical Methods in Natural Language Processing*, pages 2021–2031, Copenhagen, Denmark. Association for Computational Linguistics.

Robin Jia, Aditi Raghunathan, Kerem Göksel, and Percy Liang. 2019. Certified robustness to adversarial word substitutions. In *Proceedings of the 2019 Conference on Empirical Methods in Natural Language Processing and the 9th International Joint Conference on Natural Language Processing (EMNLP-IJCNLP)*, pages 4129–4142, Hong Kong, China. Association for Computational Linguistics.

Di Jin et al. 2020. Is bert really robust? a strong baseline for natural language attack on text classification and entailment.

Erik Jones, Robin Jia, Aditi Raghunathan, and Percy Liang. 2020. Robust encodings: A framework for combating adversarial typos. In *Proceedings of the 58th Annual Meeting of the Association for Computational Linguistics*, pages 2752–2765, Online. Association for Computational Linguistics.

Kimin Lee et al. 2018. A simple unified framework for detecting out-of-distribution samples and adversarial attacks. *arXiv preprint arXiv:1807.03888*.

Mike Lewis, Yinhan Liu, Naman Goyal, Marjan Ghazvininejad, Abdelrahman Mohamed, Omer Levy, Veselin Stoyanov, and Luke Zettlemoyer. 2020. BART: Denoising sequence-to-sequence pre-training for natural language generation, translation, and comprehension. In *Proceedings of the 58th Annual Meeting of the Association for Computational Linguistics*, pages 7871–7880, Online. Association for Computational Linguistics.

Dianqi Li, Yizhe Zhang, Hao Peng, Liqun Chen, Chris Brockett, Ming-Ting Sun, and Bill Dolan. 2021. Contextualized perturbation for textual adversarial attack. In *Proceedings of the 2021 Conference of the North American Chapter of the Association for Computational Linguistics: Human Language Technologies*, pages 5053–5069, Online. Association for Computational Linguistics.

Linyang Li, Ruotian Ma, Qipeng Guo, Xiangyang Xue, and Xipeng Qiu. 2020. BERT-ATTACK: Adversarial attack against BERT using BERT. In *Proceedings of the 2020 Conference on Empirical Methods in Natural Language Processing (EMNLP)*, pages 6193–6202, Online. Association for Computational Linguistics.

Yitong Li, Trevor Cohn, and Timothy Baldwin. 2016. Learning robust representations of text. In *Proceedings of the 2016 Conference on Empirical Methods in Natural Language Processing*, pages 1979–1985, Austin, Texas. Association for Computational Linguistics.

Yitong Li, Trevor Cohn, and Timothy Baldwin. 2017. Robust training under linguistic adversity. In *Proceedings of the 15th Conference of the European Chapter of the Association for Computational Linguistics: Volume 2, Short Papers*, pages 21–27, Valencia, Spain. Association for Computational Linguistics.

Yinhan Liu et al. 2019. Roberta: A robustly optimized bert pretraining approach. *arXiv preprint arXiv:1907.11692*.

Zhiyuan Liu et al. 2020. *Representation learning for natural language processing*. Springer Nature.

Xingjun Ma et al. 2018. Characterizing adversarial subspaces using local intrinsic dimensionality. *arXiv preprint arXiv:1801.02613*.

Andrew L. Maas, Raymond E. Daly, Peter T. Pham, Dan Huang, Andrew Y. Ng, and Christopher Potts. 2011. Learning word vectors for sentiment analysis. In *Proceedings of the 49th Annual Meeting of the Association for Computational Linguistics: Human Language Technologies*, pages 142–150, Portland, Oregon, USA. Association for Computational Linguistics.

Stephen Merity et al. 2016. Pointer sentinel mixture models.

Tomas Mikolov, Edouard Grave, Piotr Bojanowski, Christian Puhrsch, and Armand Joulin. 2018. Advances in pre-training distributed word representations. In *Proceedings of the Eleventh International Conference on Language Resources and Evaluation (LREC 2018)*, Miyazaki, Japan. European Language Resources Association (ELRA).

Takeru Miyato et al. 2016. Adversarial training methods for semi-supervised text classification. *arXiv preprint arXiv:1605.07725*.

Seyed-Mohsen Moosavi-Dezfooli et al. 2016. Deepfool: a simple and accurate method to fool deep neural networks. In *Proc. CVPR*, pages 2574–2582.

Maximilian Mozes, Pontus Stenetorp, Bennett Kleinberg, and Lewis Griffin. 2021. Frequency-guided word substitutions for detecting textual adversarial examples. In *Proceedings of the 16th Conference of the European Chapter of the Association for Computational Linguistics: Main Volume*, pages 171–186, Online. Association for Computational Linguistics.

Nikola Mrkšić, Diarmuid Ó Séaghdha, Blaise Thomson, Milica Gašić, Lina M. Rojas-Barahona, Pei-Hao Su, David Vandyke, Tsung-Hsien Wen, and Steve Young. 2016. Counter-fitting word vectors to linguistic constraints. In *Proceedings of the 2016 Conference of the North American Chapter of the Association for Computational Linguistics: Human Language Technologies*, pages 142–148, San Diego, California. Association for Computational Linguistics.

Nicolas Papernot and Patrick McDaniel. 2018. Deep k-nearest neighbors: Towards confident, interpretable and robust deep learning. *arXiv preprint arXiv:1803.04765*.

Nicolas Papernot et al. 2016a. Distillation as a defense to adversarial perturbations against deep neural networks. In *Proc. IEEE S&P*, pages 582–597. IEEE.

Nicolas Papernot et al. 2016b. The limitations of deep learning in adversarial settings. In *2016 IEEE EuroS&P*, pages 372–387.

Jeffrey Pennington, Richard Socher, and Christopher Manning. 2014. GloVe: Global vectors for word representation. In *Proceedings of the 2014 Conference on Empirical Methods in Natural Language Processing (EMNLP)*, pages 1532–1543, Doha, Qatar. Association for Computational Linguistics.

Danish Pruthi, Bhuwan Dhingra, and Zachary C. Lipton. 2019. Combating adversarial misspellings with robust word recognition. In *Proceedings of the 57th Annual Meeting of the Association for Computational Linguistics*, pages 5582–5591, Florence, Italy. Association for Computational Linguistics.

Shuhuai Ren, Yihe Deng, Kun He, and Wanxiang Che. 2019. Generating natural language adversarial examples through probability weighted word saliency. In *Proceedings of the 57th Annual Meeting of the Association for Computational Linguistics*, pages 1085–1097, Florence, Italy. Association for Computational Linguistics.

Marco Tulio Ribeiro, Sameer Singh, and Carlos Guestrin. 2018. Semantically equivalent adversarial rules for debugging NLP models. In *Proceedings of the 56th Annual Meeting of the Association for Computational Linguistics (Volume 1: Long Papers)*, pages 856–865, Melbourne, Australia. Association for Computational Linguistics.

Christian Szegedy et al. 2013. Intriguing properties of neural networks. *arXiv preprint arXiv:1312.6199*.

Adina Williams, Nikita Nangia, and Samuel Bowman. 2018. A broad-coverage challenge corpus for sentence understanding through inference. In *Proceedings of the 2018 Conference of the North American Chapter of the Association for Computational Linguistics: Human Language Technologies, Volume 1 (Long Papers)*, pages 1112–1122, New Orleans, Louisiana. Association for Computational Linguistics.

Thomas Wolf, Lysandre Debut, Victor Sanh, Julien Chaumond, Clement Delangue, Anthony Moi, Pierric Cistac, Tim Rault, Remi Louf, Morgan Funtowicz, Joe Davison, Sam Shleifer, Patrick von Platen, Clara Ma, Yacine Jernite, Julien Plu, Canwen Xu, Teven Le Scao, Sylvain Gugger, Mariama Drame, Quentin Lhoest, and Alexander Rush. 2020. Transformers: State-of-the-art natural language processing. In *Proceedings of the 2020 Conference on Empirical Methods in Natural Language Processing: System Demonstrations*, pages 38–45, Online. Association for Computational Linguistics.

Zhilin Yang et al. 2019. Xlnet: Generalized autoregressive pretraining for language understanding. *arXiv preprint arXiv:1906.08237*.

Jin Yong Yoo and Yanjun Qi. 2021. Towards improving adversarial training of NLP models. In *Findings of the Association for Computational Linguistics: EMNLP 2021*, pages 945–956, Punta Cana, Dominican Republic. Association for Computational Linguistics.

Yichao Zhou, Jyun-Yu Jiang, Kai-Wei Chang, and Wei Wang. 2019. Learning to discriminate perturbations for blocking adversarial attacks in text classification. In *Proceedings of the 2019 Conference on Empirical Methods in Natural Language Processing and the 9th International Joint Conference on Natural Language Processing (EMNLP-IJCNLP)*, pages 4904–4913, Hong Kong, China. Association for Computational Linguistics.

A Experimental Results Samples

Samples of outputs produced by the word-level attack and four detection classifiers on the MultiNLI dataset are shown in Table 8, to illustrate where some detection methods work while others do not. The DISP and FGWS baselines both also produce 'corrected' text; their outputs are included here.

In our experiments, the best accuracy of FGWS is when the frequency threshold is 92 and the threshold for the difference in prediction confidence is about 0.1916, therefore, if a word appears in the MultiNLI dataset training set and its occurrence frequency in the training corpus is lower than 92, it will be replaced by another word that is semantically similar and has higher occurrence frequency in the training set. If after transformations, the difference in prediction confidence before and after exceeds 0.1916, this example is considered as an adversarial example.

In example (a), MDRE, adapted LID, and DISP are successful, but FGWS does not detect this word-level adversarial example, because the occurrence frequency of the substituted word *shopping* for *store* is 1153 which is higher than the threshold 92, but original words *mentioning* and *buffer* are replaced by *name* and *pilot* respectively, since their occurrence frequencies are 67 and 30 in the MultiNLI training set which are lower than the threshold 92. From the DISP output, we can see that it detects *shopping* as a problem word and it is substituted by *do*.

In example (b), only adapted LID is successful. This is an odd (but not atypical) example in that the premise is not grammatical in written English, which might cause its representation differ from normal examples and lead MDRE to predict wrong. However, the prediction confidence about the premise and the hypothesis are unrelated from $\text{BERT}_{\text{BASE}}$ model is 90.49%, therefore, the word-level adversarial method have to make many changes to both premise and hypothesis to fool the target classifier. All words occurrence frequencies are above the threshold 92. FGWS and DISP fail in detecting most substitution words in this adversarial example.

In example (c), only MDRE and FGWS are successful. As with example (a), there is only a single word change. Even though *dipped* is not an infrequent word, there are only 45 occurrences in the MultiNLI training corpus, which is lower than the threshold 92, so FGWS detects it. The language model detector doesn't detect these three adversarial examples, since it fails to learn a threshold on the language model scores to separate normal and adversarial examples, and predict nearly all examples as normal examples.

Original example prediction: Entailment
Premise: Finally, it might be worth mentioning that the program has the capacity to store in a temporary memory buffer about 100 words (proper names, for instance) that it has identified as not stored in its dictionary. **Hypothesis**: It's possible to store words in a temporary dictionary, if they don't appear in a regular dictionary.
Word-level adversarial example prediction: Neutral
Premise: Finally, it might be worth mentioning that the program has the capacity to store in a temporary memory buffer about 100 words (proper names, for instance) that it has identified as not stored in its dictionary. **Hypothesis**: It's possible to shopping words in a temporary dictionary, if they don't appear in a regular dictionary.
DISP output of this word-level adversarial example
Premise: Finally, it might be worth that that the program has the capacity to store in a temporary memory buffer about 100 words (proper names, for instance) that it has identified as not stored in its dictionary. **Hypothesis**: It's possible to do words in a temporary dictionary, if they don't appear in a regular dictionary.
FGWS output of this word-level adversarial example
Premise: Finally, it might be worth name that the program has the capacity to store in a temporary memory pilot about 100 words (proper names, for instance) that it has identified as not stored in its dictionary. **Hypothesis**: It's possible to shopping words in a temporary dictionary, if they don't appear in a regular dictionary.

(a) An example with MDRE, adapted LID, and DISP correct predictions;
FGWS and the language model incorrect predictions on the adversarial example

Original example prediction: Neutral
Premise: I've been going up as a progress in school, so I, it will be a good change for me. **Hypothesis**: I think further change can help me improve even more.
Word-level Adversarial Example prediction: Entailment
Premise: I've been going up as a progress in teaching, so I, it will be a good amendment for me . **Hypothesis**: I thought further alter can support me improvement even more.
DISP output of this word-level adversarial example
Premise: I've been going up as a progress in teaching, so I think it will be a good amendment for me. **Hypothesis**: I thought further that can support and improvement even more.
FGWS output of this word-level adversarial example
Premise: I've been going up as a progress in teaching, so I, it will be a good amendment for me. **Hypothesis**: I thought further alter can support me improvement even more.

(b) An example with adapted LID correct prediction;
MDRE, DISP, FGWS, and the language model incorrect predictions on the adversarial example

Original example prediction: Contradiction
Premise: Increased profit came from missing fewer sales by being in stock a higher percentage of the time. **Hypothesis**: Profits declined because less sales were missed.
Word-level adversarial example prediction: Entailment
Premise: Increased profit came from missing fewer sales by being in stock a higher percentage of the time . **Hypothesis**: Profits dipped because less sales were missed .
DISP output of this word-level adversarial example
Premise: Increased profit came from missing fewer sales by being in stock a higher percentage of the time . **Hypothesis**: Profits dipped because less sales were missed .
FGWS output of this word-level adversarial example
Premise: Increased profit came from missing fewer sales by being in stock a higher percentage of the time . **Hypothesis**: Profits duck because less sales were missed .

(c) An example with MDRE, FGWS correct predictions;
adapted LID, DISP, and the language model incorrect predictions on the adversarial example

Table 8: Examples of detection results on the MultiNLI dataset

A Vocabulary-Free Multilingual Neural Tokenizer for End-to-End Task Learning

Md Mofijul Islam[†,*], **Gustavo Aguilar**[‡], **Pragaash Ponnusamy**[‡]
Clint Solomon Mathialagan[‡], **Chengyuan Ma**[‡], **Chenlei Guo**[‡]
University of Virginia [†], Amazon.com [‡]
mi8uu@virginia.edu, {gustalas, ponnup, matclint, mchengyu, guochenl}@amazon.com

Abstract

Subword tokenization is a commonly used input pre-processing step in most recent NLP models. However, it limits the models' ability to leverage end-to-end task learning. Its frequency-based vocabulary creation compromises tokenization in low-resource languages, leading models to produce suboptimal representations. Additionally, the dependency on a fixed vocabulary limits the subword models' adaptability across languages and domains. In this work, we propose a vocabulary-free neural tokenizer by distilling segmentation information from heuristic-based subword tokenization. We pre-train our character-based tokenizer by processing unique words from multilingual corpus, thereby extensively increasing word diversity across languages. Unlike the predefined and fixed vocabularies in subword methods, our tokenizer allows end-to-end task learning, resulting in optimal task-specific tokenization. The experimental results show that replacing the subword tokenizer with our neural tokenizer consistently improves performance on multilingual (NLI) and code-switching (sentiment analysis) tasks, with larger gains in low-resource languages. Additionally, our neural tokenizer exhibits a robust performance on downstream tasks when adversarial noise is present (typos and misspelling), further increasing the initial improvements over statistical subword tokenizers.

1 Introduction

Subword tokenization methods, such as BPE (Sennrich et al., 2016), Word-Piece (Schuster and Nakajima, 2012), and Unigram (Kudo, 2018), rely on a predefined vocabulary to tokenize text. This vocabulary is built based on frequencies of word fragments. As a result, rare words are highly fragmented into many subpieces, whereas the integrity of the most frequent words is substantially preserved (Bostrom and Durrett, 2020). This vocabulary bias is magnified in

Table 1: Segmentation of *Workshop* in different languages. Subword tokenizers over-segment low-resources languages (Arabic and Thai) and create junk tokens, whereas our neural tokenizer reduces the junk tokens.

Tokenizers	Word Languages		
	Arabic	Thai	English
BPE	ور / شة / عمل	การ/ประชุม/เชิง/ปฏิบัติ/การ	workshop
Unigram	ورش / ة / عمل	การประชุม/เชิง/ปฏิบัติการ	work/shop
Word-piece	ور / شة / عمل	การ/ประช/ุม/เชิ/ง/ปฏิ/บัติ/การ	workshop
Neural	ورشة / عمل	การประชุมเชิงปฏิบัติการ	workshop

multilingual settings, where low-resource languages are heavily discriminated in favor of high-resource ones (Tay et al., 2021; Chung et al., 2020; Wang et al., 2021) (see Table 1). Additionally, a subword vocabulary is often defined while processing a (large) pre-training corpus, thereafter remaining fixed. Consequently, when the data samples are drawn from a different distribution (e.g., multilingual text vs. linguistic code-switching, formal writing vs. arbitrary spellings, or simply by adversarial manipulation), the subword tokenizers struggle to adapt and poorly segment the input, in some cases defaulting to character pieces. These issues usually get reflected in downstream tasks when using pre-trained models that rely on subword tokenization (Devlin et al., 2019). The models cannot adapt their predefined static vocabulary, thereby employing suboptimal tokenization for downstream tasks (Clark et al., 2021). We argue that this represents an important bottleneck in the NLP pipeline, where models could become truly end-to-end, but they lag behind due to the only not-learnable component.

To address the aforementioned issues, we design a vocabulary-free neural tokenizer, which we train in two phases. First, in the pre-training phase, we train our neural tokenizer by distilling the segmentation information from a subword tokenizer. In the multilingual setting, our neural tokenizer learns from the language-specific subword tokenizers so that it is not biased towards high-resource languages. After the pre-training phase, the neural tokenizer segments the character sequence without requiring a predefined

* Work performed as summer intern at Amazon Alexa AI.

Proceedings of the 7th Workshop on Representation Learning for NLP, pages 91 - 99
May 26, 2022 ©2022 Association for Computational Linguistics

vocabulary. In the second phase, we employ an end-to-end learning approach, which allows our neural tokenizer to adapt the tokenization behavior to the downstream task. Such an end-to-end approach is not feasible for models with subword tokenizers due to the predefined vocabulary and their strong ties to the models' embedding layer. Additionally, unlike the subword tokenizers, our neural tokenizer does not require a vocabulary, and its versatile alphabet reduces the bias towards high-resource languages (i.e., there is not unbalanced word coverage favoring specific languages).

We compare the impact of our approach with respect to the subword tokenizers in downstream monolingual, multilingual, and code-switching tasks. For multilingual NLI, the results show that our neural tokenizer generally improves the model performance, with substantially larger gains for low-resource languages (+11 absolute points of accuracy for Thai, +8 for Arabic, and +4 for Swahili). For code-switched Spanish-English sentiment analysis, our neural tokenizer also outperforms the baseline tokenizers, demonstrating better language generalization capabilities. We inspect the robustness of our neural tokenizer in the presence of noisy text through adversarial manipulation (e.g., typos and spelling variations), and we find that the tokenization result is much more resilient to generate *junk tokens* (i.e., excessive fragmentation of subword pieces) than the subword tokenizers. Finally, we provide extensive experimental analyses that consistently suggest to adopt our approach for more robust and versatile representations of text.

2 Related Work

2.1 Subword Tokenization

Several subword tokenization approaches have been proposed to segment the input text in the NLP pipeline, such as BPE (Sennrich et al., 2016), Word-Piece (Schuster and Nakajima, 2012), Unigram (Kudo, 2018), and SentencePiece (Kudo and Richardson, 2018). These tokenizers use a frequency-based approach to determine the vocabulary from a corpus. Although these subword tokenization approaches improve upon previous rule-based methods, recent studies show that subword tokenization leads the model to produce suboptimal representations (Bostrom and Durrett, 2020; Wang et al., 2021; Chung et al., 2020; Kudo, 2018). For instance, Bostrom and Durrett (2020) evaluate the impact of Byte Pair Encoding (BPE) tokenization on language model pretraining, and the results suggest that BPE leads to suboptimal representations. Due to the data imbalance among the languages, the impact of multilingual tokenization on the representations is profound (Tay et al., 2021; Wang et al., 2021)—i.e., the tokenizers are prone to excessive fragmentation of subwords due to the lack of word coverage leading to meaningless tokens.

To reduce the undermining effects of subword tokenization, several approaches have been proposed. For example, Kudo (2018) introduced a subword regularization approach to probabilistically sample multiple segmentations to improve neural machine translation models. Along this line, Wang et al. (2021) shows that multilingual representations can be improved by utilizing multiple input segmentations. Although these approaches improve the model's representations by using multiple subword segmentation, they ultimately rely on heuristic-based subword tokenization with a fixed vocabulary. Thus, the limitations of the heuristic-based tokenization still persist, such as restricting the model's ability to leverage end-to-end task learning while adapting to an optimal downstream tokenization.

2.2 Character-level Models

Although subword tokenization alleviates the out-of-vocabulary problem, it relies on a static vocabulary, which prevents end-to-end learning. A natural alternative to that deficiency is to replace the subword tokenization with a character-level approach and learn the representations directly from the character sequence (Graves, 2013; Sutskever et al., 2011; Radford et al., 2017). These character-based approaches can adapt more easily to noisy text, code-switched languages, and adversarial manipulation to extract the representation (Clark et al., 2021; Tay et al., 2021; Hwang and Sung, 2017; Pinter et al., 2019; Akbik et al., 2018; Xie et al., 2018; Aguilar et al., 2020b). However, the character-based approaches may not capture the token-level representation, which degrades downstream task performance. Moreover, these method have to process longer sequences at the character level, thus increasing quadratically the complexity of the models (Clark et al., 2021; Aguilar et al., 2020b; Costa-jussà and Fonollosa, 2016).

Several approaches have been proposed to downsample the character sequence to sub-token sequence (Tay et al., 2021; Clark et al., 2021). For example, Clark et al. (2021) deterministically combined a fixed number of characters' representations to reduce the model complexity. Along this line, Tay et al. (2021) downsampled the sequence of character vectors by a fixed factor to produce latent subwords representations. Furthermore, Zhang et al. (2019) produced character n-grams, which are hashed and summed to obtain word embeddings for downstream tasks. Since these approaches deterministically reduce the sequence length in the downsampling operation, they may not capture the morphological information, potentially struggling to learn representations on noisy text.

3 Method

We propose a learnable tokenizer that is trained to convert sequence of characters into meaningful subword-level tokens. Consider the multilingual alphabet Ψ (i.e., a closed set of letters) and the character sequence $c = [c_1, \ldots, c_n]$ that represents a word of length n and $c_i \in \Psi$. We aim at learning the corresponding IOB[1] sequence of tags $t = [t_1, \ldots, t_n]$ that groups characters into the desired tokenization:

$$p_\theta(t \mid c, \ell) = f_\theta(c, \ell) \quad (1)$$

Here ℓ denotes the language of the word. The model f_θ can be any neural architecture that allows a one-to-one mapping from the input to the output.[2] We condition the model on ℓ in the multilingual setting, while the monolingual variant does not require it.

A trained neural tokenizer, f_θ, is capable of providing tokenization as a stand-alone tool, which can be compared directly to the standard subword tokenizers (e.g., controlling by the task-specific model in a downstream setting). Additionally, a trained neural tokenizer can expose the internal representations of a segmentation so that it enables end-to-end task learning by optimizing the tokenization towards the task particularities. We describe both scenarios in more detail in the following subsections.

3.1 Pre-training

We rely on the assumption that statistical subword tokenizers learn reasonable tokenization until they start over-segmenting the text due to the target vocabulary size and the infrequent subword occurrences. To stick to a data-driven approach (hence, avoiding language specific heuristics), we choose a subword tokenizer, i.e. Unigram (Kudo, 2018), to generate our ground-truth segmentation while also discarding over fragmented sequences. For example, if the subword tokenizer segments **tricycles** as **tri/cycle/s**, then the ground-truth label is `BIIBIIIIB`. We train our neural tokenizer using the negative log-likelihood objective over the subword tokenizer segments:

$$\mathcal{L} = -\sum_i t_i \log p_\theta(t_i \mid c, \ell) \quad (2)$$

Our neural tokenizer not only mimics the more prominent (and insightful) patterns from the subword tokenizer, but it also generalizes such behaviors to unseen words.

Pre-training Dataset: We generate a pre-training corpus by curating space-separated tokens from the Wikipedia articles (e.g., removing hyperlinks, HTML tags, and tokens whose lengths are beyond 30 characters). Additionally, we use two heuristics to improve the ground-truth label from the subword tokenizer. First, if the input sequence is less than four, we do not segment into subwords. Second, if the subword tokenizer creates more than 50% subwords with a single character, we discard the ground-truth label and do not tokenize. These heuristics discard the junk tokenization of the subword tokenizer, especially when the input comes from low-resource languages and noisy text.

3.2 End-to-End Task Learning

While the pre-training provides a stand-alone neural tokenizer tool, we can also leverage the model's hidden representations for end-to-end task learning. Recall that the neural tokenizer provides a tagging sequence for the segmented tokens based on its internal character-level vectors. Such tags can be used to group and reduce the dimensionality of the internal representations (e.g., via max-pooling). Our neural tokenizer is based on the LSTM architecture, so we use the LSTM output vectors and max-pool them according to the tokenization tags (although this approach is invariant to LSTM).

$$\begin{aligned} [h_1, \ldots, h_n] &= \text{LSTM}([c_1, \ldots, c_n]) \\ r_i &= \text{maxpool}([h_i, \ldots, h_j]) \end{aligned} \quad (3)$$

where the interval $[i, j]$ denotes the characters of a single subword (i.e., an IOB segment), $h_i \in \mathbb{R}^{1\times d}$ and $r_i \in \mathbb{R}^{1\times d}$ are vectors of dimensionality d. We use the resulting vectors r as the subword representations, which we can feed to any task-specific model on a downstream scenario. Note that we effectively

[1]The beginning (B), inside (I), and outside (O) tagging schema denoting the word boundaries at the character level.

[2]We stick to the LSTM architecture for all our experiments since this simplifies iterations over pre-training and fine-tuning.

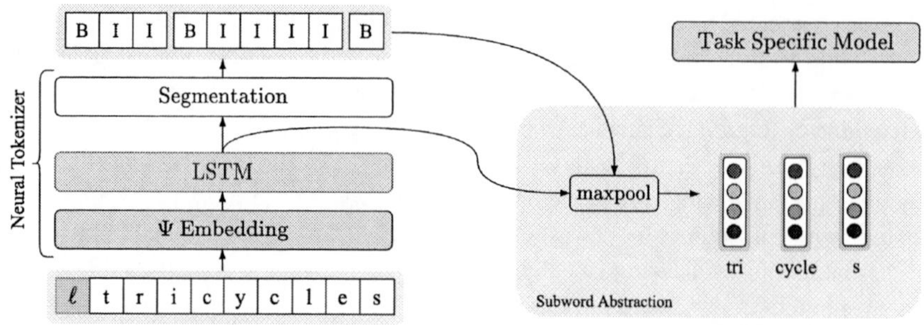

(a) Pretraining (b) Fine-tuning

Figure 1: The neural tokenizer architecture and its two settings: (a) Pre-training and (b) Fine-tuning. (a) In the pre-training setting, the model is trained to segment the sequence of characters by outputting the correct IOB tags according to the statistical subword tokenizer. (b) In the fine-tuning setting, the model uses the trained segmentation layer to predict the tags and max-pool the corresponding vectors (e.g., tri/cycle/s). These vectors are passed directly to the task-specific model, bypassing the need for vocabulary and embedding layers. In the backpropagation step of the fine-tuning setting, all the parameters in the shadow boxes are updated (i.e., the alphabet embedding, LSTM, and the task-specific parameters).

bypass the need of a vocabulary, while also enabling the task-specific model to adjust the pre-trained tokenization parameters towards the task domain in an end-to-end manner.

3.3 Neural Tokenizer Variants

The neural tokenizer model can be used to segment the input for a task model in a general-purpose setting, such as a task with monolingual input (i.e., ℓ is constant). However, we need to slightly change the neural tokenizer model for multilingual and mixed-lingual (code-switched) settings to improve the tokenization and internal representations. We describe two variants of our neural tokenizer: *multilingual* and *mixed-lingual* neural tokenizers.

Multilingual Neural Tokenizer: Multilingual subword tokenizers are designed to segment the text with an fixed multilingual vocabulary, irrespective of the input language. While this may be practical, it has severe effects on the tokenization behavior, disregarding dissimilar linguistic properties across languages (e.g., morphology). Thus, if a language identifier ℓ is available with the input, the neural tokenizer can condition the tokenization on ℓ. We achieve such behavior by simply including the identifier ℓ at the beginning of the sequence, which extends the alphabet Ψ with the same number of languages ℓ we are including in the pre-training data.

Additionally, since multilingual subword tokenizers cannot tokenize low-resource languages appropriately due to the dominance of the high-resource languages in their vocabulary, we use monolingual subword tokenizers to generate the ground-truth segmentation labels for pre-training. Using monolingual subword tokenizers helps our neural tokenizer avoid bias towards any languages, especially the high-resource languages. Thus, we distill the tokenization knowledge from the multiple monolingual subword tokenizers into our neural tokenizer.

Mixed-Lingual Neural Tokenizer: In mixed-lingual settings, such as in code-switching, we may not have access to the language identifiers ℓ of the input words or sentences. Thus, we need to train a neural tokenizer to segment text with mixed languages without relying on language identifiers of the input tokens. To do so, we change the pre-training dataset to train the neural tokenizer with and without language tags, hence forcing our model to generalize when the language tags are provided as well as when they are missing. We replicate the dataset for training the model with and without language tags.

4 Experimental Setup

4.1 Neural Tokenizer Model

We design the neural tokenizer character encoder with a character embedding layer of 64 dimensions followed by a two-layer bidirectional LSTM (Bi-LSTM) that generates 128-dimensional vectors. We use a fully connected layer of shape 128×2 followed by a softmax operation to predict the character-level segmentation label. The predicted labels represent whether a character is the beginning or part of a subword.[3]

4.2 Pre-training Neural Tokenizer

In the pre-training phase of the monolingual neural tokenizer, we have developed a monolingual Unigram subword tokenizer with a vocabulary size

[3]Note that the O tag of the IOB schema is not used here.

of $30,000$ to generate the ground-truth segmentation labels. To train multilingual and mixed-lingual (code-switched) neural tokenizers, we have developed monolingual Unigram tokenizers with a vocabulary of $30,000$ for each language. We fixed the vocabulary size by following monolingual vocabulary size of BERT (Devlin et al., 2019).

We have utilized Adam optimizer with weight decay regularization and cosine annealing warm restarts with an initial learning rate set to $3e^{-4}$ to train the neural tokenizer. In the cosine annealing warm restarts learning scheduler, we set the cycle length (T_0) and cycle multiplier (T_{mult}) to 3 and 2, respectively. We have trained the models for 6 epochs and selected the best model based on the minimum validation loss.

4.3 Baseline Tokenizers

We have developed subword tokenizers, such as BPE, Unigram, and Word-Piece, for the experimental evaluations. We developed two versions of these subword tokenizers: monolingual and multilingual. Following state-of-the-art model with subword tokenizer (Devlin et al., 2019), we have fixed the vocabulary size of monolingual and multilingual tokenizers to 30000 and 120000, respectively. We have used the Wikipedia dataset to develop the vocabulary of these tokenizers.

4.4 Downstream Task Model

We have evaluated the impact of our neural and heuristic-based subword tokenizers on the two downstream tasks: natural language inference (NLI) in monolingual and multilingual settings and sentiment analysis with code-switched languages. For the baselines models with subword tokenization, the segmented subwords are projected to create feature embeddings of size 256. For the model with our neural tokenizer, we max-pool the character embeddings to create the subword-level representations of size 128. We project these pooled representations to the embeddings of size 256 to match the subword representations' dimension of the baseline tokenizers. We have used a two-layers Bidirectional LSTM with the hidden feature embeddings of size 256 for extracting the task representations. In the experimental evaluations, we have used the same task model architecture with the subword tokenizer and our neural tokenizer. All the models are trained from scratch for fair experimental evaluations.

5 Experimental Results and Discussion

We have evaluated the impact of our neural and subword tokenizers on multilingual and monolingual natural language inference (NLI) tasks and on a sentiment analysis task with code-switched language. We also evaluated the impact of tokenizers in the presence of noisy data (typos and misspelling).

5.1 Evaluations on Multilingual NLI Tasks

We have conducted the experimental analysis to evaluate the impact of neural and baseline tokenizers on multilingual NLI tasks with five languages: Arabic (ar), English (en), Russian (ru), Swahili (sw), and Thai (th). We have used XNLI dataset (Conneau et al., 2018) for this experimentation. We have developed three multilingual tokenizers (BPE, Unigram, and Word-piece) with a vocabulary size of $120,000$. Moreover, we have developed another baseline, called Character-based Model, which segments input based on space without using any vocabulary and pools character embedding to create word-level representations. These representations are used for downstream task. Finally, we have used the same downstream learning architecture (Described in Section 4.4) with all the above-mentioned tokenizers and multilingual neural tokenizers.

Results and Discussion: The experimental results in Table 2 suggest that the neural tokenizer outperforms the evaluated baseline tokenizers across all languages for the NLI task. Especially, neural tokenizer achieves substantially larger gains for the low-resource languages over the baseline tokenizers, such as +11 absolute points of accuracy for Thai (th), +8 for Arabic (ar), and +4 for Swahili (sw). For the English, neural tokenizer slightly improves the performance compared to the baseline tokenizers.

The reasoning behind the performance improvement of neural tokenizer is that it segments the input based on lexical similarity and thus create better segmentations, especially for the low-resource languages. As the subword tokenizers use a vocabulary with the most frequent subwords in a corpus, these tokenizers over-segment the input of low-resource languages and create junk tokens, which lead to the performance degradation.

We have also noticed similar phenomena in our qualitative analysis, presented in Figure 2 and 3. Subword tokenizers over-segment the words from the low-resources languages compared to the high-resources languages (Figure 2). For example, the subword tokenizers create at least 10 subwords for

Table 2: Multilingual NLI task performance comparison of various tokenization approaches.

Tokenizers	Vocab Size	Model Params (Millions)	Languages (Accuracy %)				
			ar	sw	th	ru	en
BPE	120,000	67.8 M	51.81	50.66	51.32	54.77	57.57
Unigram	120,000	67.8 M	53.78	51.32	56.09	53.13	57.24
Word-Piece	120,000	67.8 M	50.66	50.00	43.26	54.61	57.57
Character-based Model	-	33.4 M	53.29	46.88	44.41	52.80	50.99
Neural	-	**33.4 M**	**61.51**	**53.95**	**68.42**	**60.69**	**58.22**

more than 20% words in the multilingual NLI corpus. On the other hand, the neural tokenizer creates fewer subwords than the baseline tokenizers, including the Unigram, which is used to pre-train our neural tokenizer. Specifically, the neural tokenizer reduces the number of subwords for the low-resource languages, such as Thai (th) and Swahili (sw). As the neural tokenizer distills the segmentations knowledge from the language-specific tokenizer, it does not bias towards the high-resource languages. Additionally, we have observed that subword tokenizer over-segment the hypothesis and premise from low-resource languages, such as Arabic (ar), Swahili (sw), and Thai (th), compared to the neural tokenizer (Figure 3). This over-segmentation leads to performance degradation for the NLI task with low-resource languages.

Additionally, one can argue that instead of using the neural tokenizer, we can use a Character-based Model to extract characters embedding for downstream task learning. To validate this argument, we have developed a baseline, called Character-based Model, which segments input based on space without using any vocabulary and pools character embedding to create word-level representations for downstream task learning. This Character-based Model is trained end-to-end to learn characters embedding from input character sequence and generate task representation to produce task output. The results in Table 2 suggest that although it achieves comparable performance to the baseline subword tokenizers, there is a considerable performance gap between the Character-based Model and the neural tokenizer across all the languages.

Moreover, our neural tokenizer achieved these performance improvements with half the model size compared to the model with baseline tokenizers. Because the model with baseline subword tokenizer has to allocate most of the model parameters to learn the subword embeddings. On the other hand, neural tokenizer creates the subword embeddings by pooling the character-level representations, which reduces the model size.

Table 3: Monolingual (English) NLI task performance comparison with various tokenization approaches

Tokenizer	Vocab Size	Model Params (Millions)	Accuracy (%)
BPE	30,000	44.8 M	57.85
BPE	70,000	65.3 M	59.94
Unigram	30,000	44.8 M	58.65
Unigram	70,000	65.3 M	58.01
Word-Piece	30,000	44.8 M	58.65
Word-Piece	70,000	65.3 M	58.33
Neural	69,480	65.0 M	59.94
Neural	-	**33.3 M**	**60.58**

5.2 Experimental Evaluations on Monolingual NLI Tasks

We have investigated whether the neural tokenizer can outperform the baseline subword tokenizers on monolingual NLI tasks. We have developed three baseline subword tokenizers (BPE, Unigram, and Word-Piece) with the vocabulary of sizes 30,000 and 70,000. To ensure a fair comparison, we have also trained our neural tokenizer in the monolingual setting. Moreover, we have applied our neural tokenizer on the same corpus as the baseline tokenizers and produced a vocabulary for the neural tokenizer. In this vocabulary-based setting, we tokenize the input based on the fixed vocabulary, similar to baseline subword tokenizers. In this experimental evaluation, we have selected the English language.

Results and Discussion: The experimental results in Table 3 suggest that our neural tokenizer shows comparable performance to the subword tokenizers on the monolingual NLI task. Moreover, the model with our neural tokenizer achieves a similar performance to the model with the subword tokenizers. However, the neural tokenizer helps to achieve similar performance with a smaller model. This performance improvement of neural tokenizers with reduced model size attributes that we can utilize our neural tokenizer to extract representations for downstream tasks instead of employing a resource-intensive model with subword tokenizers.

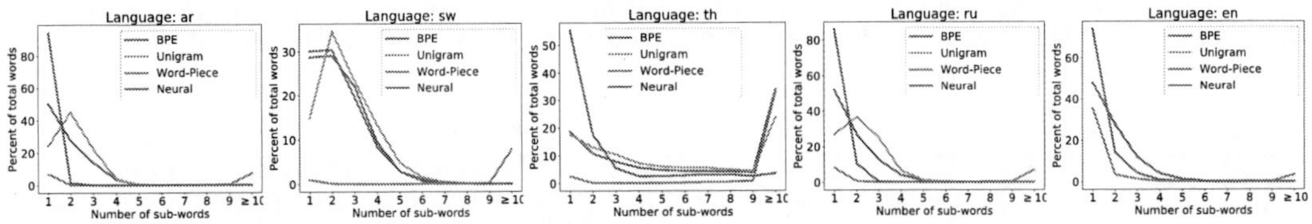

Figure 2: Impact of tokenizer to segment words into different number of subwords in low and high resource languages.

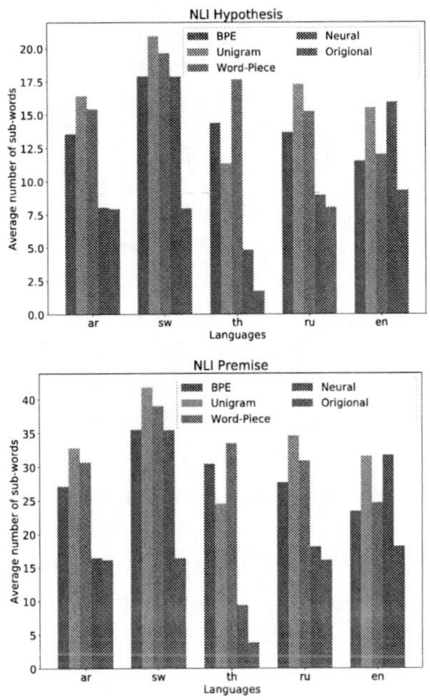

Figure 3: Average number of subwords of hypothesis and premise from low and high resource languages, which are tokenized by different tokenizers.

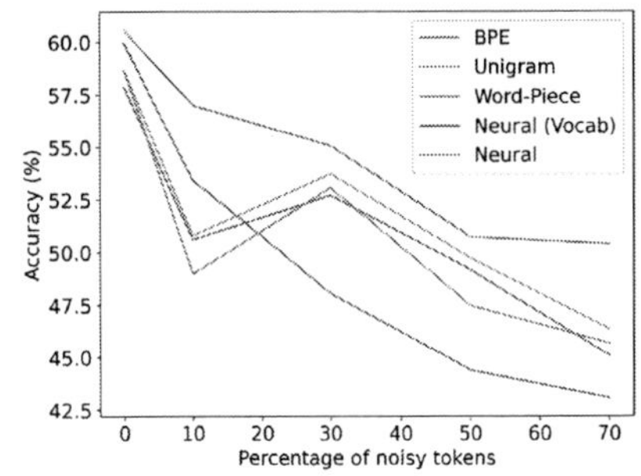

(a) Accuracy of NLI (English) Task

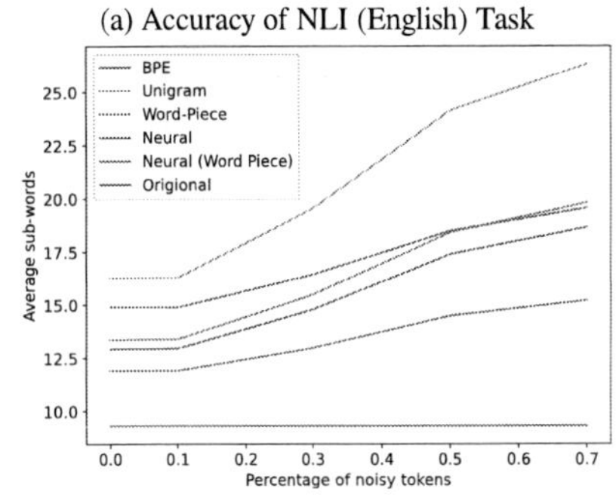

(b) Average number of segmented subwords

Figure 4: Performance comparison of tokenizers on monolingual (English) NLI task with noisy text (typos and misspelling).

5.3 Experimental Evaluations on Noisy Text

We have evaluated the impact of tokenizer on monolingual (English) NLI task in the presence of noisy text (typos and misspelling). For this experimental evaluation, we have developed baseline monolingual (English) tokenizers (BPE, Unigram, and WordPiece) with a vocabulary size of 30,000. We have developed a monolingual neural tokenizer trained, which is trained using a Unigram subword tokenizer with a vocabulary size of $30,000$. Moreover, we have developed a vocabulary-based neural tokenizer, where we used our neural tokenizer to segment the Wikipedia corpus with the English language and create a vocabulary with the most frequent subwords. We have used this vocabulary to tokenize the hypothesis and premise of the NLI task. We adversarially introduce noise to the $0\% - 70\%$ input words, such as typos and misspelling, using TextAttack Library (Morris et al., 2020).

Results and Discussion: The experimental results in Fig 4 suggest that the performance of the models with vocabulary-based subword tokenizers degrade with the increased amount of noisy words in the input. Although the performance of the model with our vocabulary-free neural tokenizer degrades with the increased amount of noisy words, it outperforms all the evaluated tokenization approaches. Especially, our neural tokenizer outperforms the Unigram subword tokenizer, which is used to train our neural tokenizer.

As the subword tokenizers use a fixed vocabulary, they can not appropriately segment the text from the out-of-distribution and introduce junk tokens. These junk tokens lead the model to create suboptimal representations and thus degrade the downstream task's performance. On the other hand, neural tokenizer segments the input based on lexical similarity, and thus it creates better segmentation in the presence of

Table 4: Segmentation of words using Unigram and Neural Tokenizer, which is trained using Unigram subword tokenizer. Red colored words are with noise (typos and misspelling).

Input	Unigram	Neural
tricycles	t/ r/ i/ cycle/ s	tricycle/ s
trycycles	t/ r/ y/ cycle/ s	trycycle/ s
improving	improv/ ing	improv/ ing
improbing	imp/ robin/ g	improbing
timeline	timeline	time/ line
timlline	t/ i/ m/ l/ line	timlline
swimming	s/ w/ imming	s/ w/ imming
swiming	swim/ ing	swiming
workshop	workshop	workshop
worksops	works/ o/ p/ s	worksops
biotechnology	biotechnolog/ y	biotechnolog/ y
bitechnology	b/ i/ t/ echnology	bitechnolog/ y

noise, such as typos and misspelling. However, the vocabulary-based neural tokenizer's performance degrades with the increased percentage of noisy words. Because, in the vocabulary-based neural tokenization, if a subword does not present in the vocabulary, then we replace that subword with an *<UNK>* (unknown) token. As a result, vocabulary-based neural tokenizers create many *<UNK>* junk subwords in the presence of noise and thus hurting the task performance.

Additionally, the tokenizations present in Table. 4 suggest that our neural tokenizer helps to improve the segmentations quality of the Unigram subword tokenizer in the presence of noise (e.g., typos and spelling variations). For example, Unigram creates junk tokens in segmenting *tricycles*. Our neural tokenizer, trained using Unigram, reduces the junk tokens and creates morphologically aligned segmentation. However, in some cases, such as segmenting swiming, the Unigram tokenizer creates better segmentation than our neural tokenizer.

5.4 Experimental Evaluations on Code-Switched Language

We have evaluated the impact of the tokenizers on the sentiment analysis task with the Spanish-English code-switched languages. We have used the Lince dataset and the evaluation benchmark (Aguilar et al., 2020a). We have developed three baseline tokenizers (BPE, Unigram, Word-Piece) with a vocabulary size of 60,000. We have also trained a neural tokenizer in the mixed-lingual settings (Section 3.3), where the training dataset is developed from the Spanish and English Wikipedia articles.

Results and Discussion: The experimental results in Table 5 suggest that our neural tokenizer outperforms the subword tokenizers, including the Unigram subword tokenizer, on the sentiment analysis task with code-switched languages. Unlike the heuristic-based subword tokenization, neural tokenizer allows end-to-end task learning, which helps to improve the task's performance.

Table 5: Performance comparison of tokenizers on sentiment analysis task with code-switched languages (Spanish-English).

Tokenizer	Vocab Size	Accuracy (%)
BPE	60,000	49.39
Unigram	60,000	49.18
Word-Piece	60,000	48.43
Character-based Model	-	45.63
Neural	-	**51.41**

Our neural tokenizer and the heuristic-based tokenizers segment the input into subwords, and the task models use the subword embeddings. These models, which use the subword embeddings, outperform the Character-based Model, where character representations are used for downstream task learning. Because in the code-switched language settings, extracting subword embeddings can be beneficial to create aligned multilingual representations, which help to improve the sentiment analysis task performance. Thus, appropriately segmenting input with code-switched languages is crucial to improve performance in the code-switched language settings.

6 Conclusion

We propose a neural tokenizer to segment text without a vocabulary, which allows end-to-end task learning. The experimental evaluations on multilingual NLI task suggest that our neural tokenizer reduces the model size and improves the task's performance for low-resources languages, such as Arabic, Swahili, and Thai. Moreover, the neural tokenizer outperforms subword tokenizers on the NLI task with noisy text (typos and misspelling). The qualitative analysis also suggests that our neural tokenizer improves the tokenizations of the subword tokenizers, which is used to train our neural tokenizer. Additionally, the neural tokenizer shows comparable performance on sentiment analysis task with code-switched languages. The experimental results suggest that our neural tokenizer can distill the segmentations knowledge from multiple subword tokenizers to improve the tokenization. This finding opens future research avenues to design a learnable tokenizer for improving the state-of-the-art subword tokenization and the downstream task's performance.

References

Gustavo Aguilar, Sudipta Kar, and Thamar Solorio. 2020a. LinCE: A centralized benchmark for linguistic code-switching evaluation. In *Proceedings of the 12th Language Resources and Evaluation Conference*, pages 1803–1813, Marseille, France. European Language Resources Association.

Gustavo Aguilar, Bryan McCann, Tong Niu, Nazneen Rajani, Nitish Keskar, and Thamar Solorio. 2020b. Char2subword: Extending the subword embedding space using robust character compositionality. *arXiv preprint arXiv:2010.12730*.

Alan Akbik, Duncan Blythe, and Roland Vollgraf. 2018. Contextual string embeddings for sequence labeling. In *Proceedings of the 27th international conference on computational linguistics*, pages 1638–1649.

Kaj Bostrom and Greg Durrett. 2020. Byte pair encoding is suboptimal for language model pretraining. In *EMNLP*, pages 4617–4624.

Hyung Won Chung, Dan Garrette, Kiat Chuan Tan, and Jason Riesa. 2020. Improving multilingual models with language-clustered vocabularies. In *Proceedings of the 2020 Conference on Empirical Methods in Natural Language Processing (EMNLP)*, pages 4536–4546.

Jonathan H Clark, Dan Garrette, Iulia Turc, and John Wieting. 2021. Canine: Pre-training an efficient tokenization-free encoder for language representation. *arXiv preprint arXiv:2103.06874*.

Alexis Conneau, Ruty Rinott, Guillaume Lample, Adina Williams, Samuel R. Bowman, Holger Schwenk, and Veselin Stoyanov. 2018. Xnli: Evaluating cross-lingual sentence representations. In *Proceedings of the 2018 Conference on Empirical Methods in Natural Language Processing*. Association for Computational Linguistics.

Marta R. Costa-jussà and José A. R. Fonollosa. 2016. Character-based neural machine translation. In *Proceedings of the 54th Annual Meeting of the Association for Computational Linguistics (Volume 2: Short Papers)*, pages 357–361, Berlin, Germany. Association for Computational Linguistics.

Jacob Devlin, Ming-Wei Chang, Kenton Lee, and Kristina Toutanova. 2019. BERT: Pre-training of deep bidirectional transformers for language understanding. In *Proceedings of the 2019 Conference of the North American Chapter of the Association for Computational Linguistics: Human Language Technologies, Volume 1 (Long and Short Papers)*, pages 4171–4186, Minneapolis, Minnesota. Association for Computational Linguistics.

Alex Graves. 2013. Generating sequences with recurrent neural networks. *arXiv preprint arXiv:1308.0850*.

Kyuyeon Hwang and Wonyong Sung. 2017. Character-level language modeling with hierarchical recurrent neural networks. In *2017 IEEE International Conference on Acoustics, Speech and Signal Processing (ICASSP)*, pages 5720–5724. IEEE.

Taku Kudo. 2018. Subword regularization: Improving neural network translation models with multiple subword candidates. In *Proceedings of the 56th Annual Meeting of the Association for Computational Linguistics (Volume 1: Long Papers)*, pages 66–75.

Taku Kudo and John Richardson. 2018. Sentencepiece: A simple and language independent subword tokenizer and detokenizer for neural text processing. *arXiv preprint arXiv:1808.06226*.

John Morris, Eli Lifland, Jin Yong Yoo, Jake Grigsby, Di Jin, and Yanjun Qi. 2020. Textattack: A framework for adversarial attacks, data augmentation, and adversarial training in nlp. In *EMNLP: System Demonstrations*, pages 119–126.

Yuval Pinter, Marc Marone, and Jacob Eisenstein. 2019. Character eyes: Seeing language through character-level taggers.

Alec Radford, Rafal Jozefowicz, and Ilya Sutskever. 2017. Learning to generate reviews and discovering sentiment.

Mike Schuster and Kaisuke Nakajima. 2012. Japanese and korean voice search.

Rico Sennrich, Barry Haddow, and Alexandra Birch. 2016. Neural machine translation of rare words with subword units. In *Proceedings of the 54th Annual Meeting of the Association for Computational Linguistics (Volume 1: Long Papers)*, pages 1715–1725.

Ilya Sutskever, James Martens, and Geoffrey Hinton. 2011. Generating text with recurrent neural networks. In *Proceedings of the 28th International Conference on International Conference on Machine Learning*, pages 1017–1024.

Yi Tay, Vinh Q. Tran, Sebastian Ruder, Jai Gupta, Hyung Won Chung, Dara Bahri, Zhen Qin, Simon Baumgartner, Cong Yu, and Donald Metzler. 2021. Charformer: Fast character transformers via gradient-based subword tokenization.

Xinyi Wang, Sebastian Ruder, and Graham Neubig. 2021. Multi-view subword regularization. In *Proceedings of the 2021 Conference of the North American Chapter of the Association for Computational Linguistics: Human Language Technologies*, pages 473–482.

Jiateng Xie, Zhilin Yang, Graham Neubig, Noah A Smith, and Jaime G Carbonell. 2018. Neural cross-lingual named entity recognition with minimal resources. In *Proceedings of the 2018 Conference on Empirical Methods in Natural Language Processing*, pages 369–379.

Hao Zhang, Richard Sproat, Axel H. Ng, Felix Stahlberg, Xiaochang Peng, Kyle Gorman, and Brian Roark. 2019. Neural models of text normalization for speech applications. *Comput. Linguistics*, 45(2):293–337.

Identifying the Limits of Cross-Domain Knowledge Transfer for Pretrained Models

Zhengxuan Wu
Stanford University
wuzhengx@stanford.edu

Nelson F. Liu
Stanford University
nfliu@cs.stanford.edu

Christopher Potts
Stanford University
cgpotts@stanford.edu

Abstract

There is growing evidence that pretrained language models improve task-specific fine-tuning even where the task examples are radically different from those seen in training. We study an extreme case of transfer learning by providing a systematic exploration of how much transfer occurs when models are denied any information about word identity via random scrambling. In four classification tasks and two sequence labeling tasks, we evaluate LSTMs using GloVe embeddings, BERT, and baseline models. Among these models, we find that only BERT shows high rates of transfer into our scrambled domains, and for classification but not sequence labeling tasks. Our analyses seek to explain why transfer succeeds for some tasks but not others, to isolate the separate contributions of pretraining versus fine-tuning, to show that the fine-tuning process is not merely learning to unscramble the scrambled inputs, and to quantify the role of word frequency. Furthermore, our results suggest that current benchmarks may overestimate the degree to which current models actually understand language.

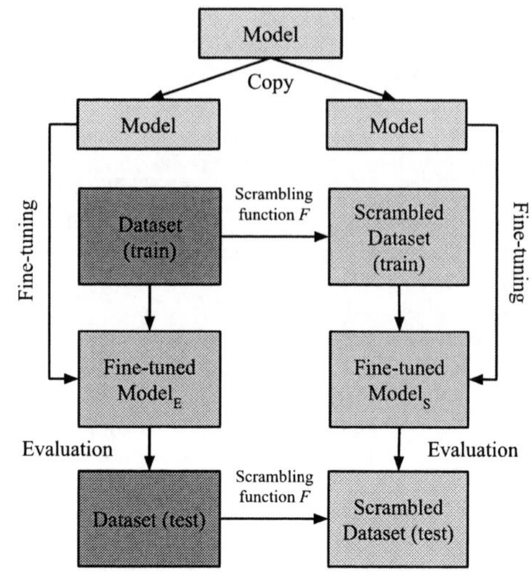

Figure 1: An overview of our experiment paradigm. Starting with a model (e.g., pretrained BERT, GloVe-initialized LSTM, etc.), we copy it and fine-tune it on the regular and scrambled train set using a scrambling function F. The model is then evaluated on regular and scrambled test sets. Our paper explores different options for F and a number of variants of our models to try to quantity the amount of transfer and identify its sources.

1 Introduction

Fine-tuning pretrained language models has proven to be highly effective across a wide range of NLP tasks; the leaderboards for standard benchmarks are currently dominated by models that adopt this general strategy (Rajpurkar et al., 2016, 2018; Wang et al., 2018; Yang et al., 2018; Wang et al., 2019). Recent work has extended these findings in even more surprising ways: Artetxe et al. (2020), Karthikeyan et al. (2019), and Tran (2020) find evidence of transfer between natural languages, and Papadimitriou and Jurafsky (2020) show that pretraining language models on non-linguistic data such as music and computer code can improve test performance on natural language.

Recently, Tamkin et al. (2020) show that BERT's performance on downstream GLUE tasks suffers only marginally even if some layers are reinitialized before fine-tuning, and Gauthier and Levy (2019), Zanzotto et al. (2020), Pham et al. (2020), and Sinha et al. (2021) show that BERT-like models are largely insensitive to word order changes. In this work, we extend this line of research by providing a systematic exploration of how much cross-domain transfer we see when the model is denied any information about word identity.

Figure 1 gives an overview of our core experimental paradigm: starting with two identical copies of a single pretrained model for English, we finetune one on English examples and the other on scrambled English sentences, using a scrambling function F (Section 3), and then we evaluate the resulting models. We apply this paradigm to four

Proceedings of the 7th Workshop on Representation Learning for NLP, pages 100 - 110
May 26, 2022

classification tasks and two sequence modeling tasks, and we evaluate bag-of-words baselines, LSTMs with GloVe initialization and rich attention mechanisms, and BERT. Our central finding is that, for BERT, high rates of transfer occur on classification tasks, but not sequence labeling tasks

To better understand why such transfer is successful for some tasks but not others, we pursue a number of hypotheses. First, we assess whether the transfer occurs if only word identities are scrambled among words with similar frequencies. Second, we assess whether our matching methods might actually be inserting semantic consistency into the scrambling process by matching synonyms. Third, we analyze the learning dynamics behind such transfer by studying the effects of model pretraining.

Our findings suggest that performance on existing tasks may be less informative than previously thought about the degree to which a model understands language. Our pretrained models transfer knowledge in our tasks even when they are denied any information about word identity. Thus, a large percentage of their success might trace to factors that have nothing to do with communication or understanding. After all, our scrambled data do not have the semantics of English, or indeed of any language.

2 Related work

2.1 Studies of Why Transfer Happens

There are diverse efforts underway to more deeply understand why transfer occurs. Probing tests often involve fitting supervised models on internal representations in an effort to determine what they encode. Such work suggests that BERT representations encode non-trivial information about morphosyntax and semantics (Tenney et al., 2019; Liu et al., 2019; Hewitt and Manning, 2019; Manning et al., 2020) and perhaps weakly encode world knowledge such as relations between entities (Da and Kasai, 2019; Petroni et al., 2019), but that they contain relatively little information about pragmatics or role-based event knowledge (Ettinger, 2020). Newer feature attribution methods (Sundararajan et al., 2017) and intervention methods (McCoy et al., 2019; Vig et al., 2020; Geiger et al., 2020) are corroborating these findings while also yielding a picture of the internal causal dynamics of these models.

Another set of strategies for understanding transfer involves modifying network inputs or internal representations and studying the effects of such changes on task performance, as in the above-cited work by Tamkin et al. (2020), Gauthier and Levy (2019), Zanzotto et al. (2020), Pham et al. (2020), and Sinha et al. (2021).

Scrambling Method	Sentence
Original English (No Scrambling)	“the worst titles in recent cinematic **history**”
Similar Frequency	“a engaging semi is everyone dull **dark**”
Random	“kitsch theatrically tranquil andys loaf shorty **lauper**”

Table 1: An example from the SST-3 dataset and its two scrambled variants.

2.2 Extreme Cross-Domain Transfer

Cross-domain transfer is not limited to monolingual cases (Karthikeyan et al., 2019). With modifications to its tokenizer, English-pretrained BERT improves performance on downstream multilingual NLU tasks (Artetxe et al., 2020; Tran, 2020). Papadimitriou and Jurafsky (2020) show that pretraining language models on structured non-linguistic data (e.g., MIDI music or Java code) improves test performance on natural language. Our work complements and advances these efforts along two dimensions. First, we challenge models with extremely ambitious cross-domain settings and find that BERT shows a high degree of transfer, and we conduct a large set of follow-up experiments to help identify the sources and limitations of such transfer.

3 Experimental Paradigm

We now describe the evaluation paradigm summarized in Figure 1 (Section 3.1), with special attention to the scrambling functions F that we consider (Sections 3.2–3.3).

3.1 Evaluation Pipeline

Figure 1 shows our main evaluation paradigm for testing the transfer abilities of a model without word identity information. On the left side, we show the classic fine-tuning pipeline (i.e., we fine-tune on the original English training set and evaluate on the original English test set). On the right side, we show our new evaluation pipeline: starting from a single model, we (1) fine-tune it with a corrupted training split where regular English word identities are removed and then (2) evaluate the model on a version of the evaluation set that is corrupted in the same manner. The paradigm applies equally to models without any pretraining and with varying degrees of pretraining for their model parameters.

3.2 Scrambling with Similar Frequency

To remove word identities, we scrambled each sentence in each dataset by substituting each word w with a new word w' in the vocabulary of the dataset. For Scrambling with Similar Frequency, we use the following rules:

1. w and w' must have the same sub-token length according to the BERT tokenizer; and
2. w and w' must have similar frequency.

The first rule is motivated by the concern that sub-token length may correlate with word frequency, given that rarer and longer words may be tokenized into more sub-tokens. The second rule is the core of the procedure. The guiding idea is that word frequency is often reflected in learned embeddings (Gong et al., 2018), so this scrambling procedure might preserve useful information and thus help to identify the source of transfer. Table 1 shows an example, and our supplementary materials provide details on the matching algorithm and additional examples of scrambled sentences.

3.3 Random Scrambling

To better understand the role of frequency in domain transfer, we also consider a word scrambling method that does not seek to match word frequencies. For this, we simply shuffle the vocabulary and match each word with another random word in the vocabulary without replacement.[1] We include the distributions of the difference in frequency for every matched word pair in our supplementary materials, to show that each word is paired with a new word with drastically different frequency in the dataset.

4 Models

In this section, we describe the models we evaluated within our paradigm. Our supplementary materials provide additional details about how the models were designed, optimized, and evaluated.

BERT For our BERT model (Devlin et al., 2019), we import weights from the pretrained BERT-base model through the HuggingFace `transformers` library (Wolf et al., 2020). For sequence classification tasks, we append a classification head after the `[CLS]` token embedding in the last layer of the BERT model. If an input example contains a pair of sentences, we concatenate them using a `[SEP]` token in between. For sequence labeling tasks, we append a shared classification head to each token embedding in the last layer of the BERT model.

Our supplementary materials provide results for `DeBERTa` models (He et al., 2021) as well.

LSTM We contextualize our results by comparing them against a strong LSTM-based model (Hochreiter and Schmidhuber, 1997). We lowercase each input sentence and tokenize it by separating on spaces and punctuation. We then use 300-dimensional GloVe embeddings (Pennington et al., 2014)[2] as inputs to a single-layer recurrent neural network with LSTM cells, with a hidden size of 64. We use dot-product attention (Luong et al., 2015) to formulate a context vector for each sentence. Finally, we pass the context vector through a multilayer perceptron (MLP) layer with a hidden size of 64 to get the final prediction. For an input example with a pair of sentences, we concatenate two sentences together with a separator token before feeding them into our LSTM encoder. For sequence labeling tasks, we directly feed the hidden state at each position to the MLP layer to get the final prediction.

Bag-of-Words (BoW) Model We compare against a BoW classifier, which provides an estimate of model performance when only word co-occurrence information is available. For each sentence in a dataset, we first formulate a BoW vector that uses unigram representations. Then, we feed the BoW vector through a softmax classifier. For examples with a pair of sentences, we create two BoW vectors for each sentence, and concatenate them together before feeding them into the linear layer for predicting labels. For sequence labeling tasks, we use conditional random fields (Lafferty et al., 2001) with character-level unigram BoW features.

Dummy Model We include a random classifier that generates predictions randomly proportional to the

[1]We also tried to pair words by the reverse order of frequencies, which yielded similar results, so we report only random scrambling results here.

[2]We use the Common Crawl cased version: `http://nlp.stanford.edu/data/glove.840B.300d.zip`

Dataset	Standard Models (Train and Test on English)				Scrambled Models (Train and Test on Scrambled English)			
	BERT	LSTM	BoW	Dummy	BERT-Scrambled		LSTM-Scrambled	
					Similar Frequency	Random	Similar Frequency	Random
SST-3	.71 (.02)	.62 (.01)	.59 (.00)	.33 (.02)	.65 (.01)	.64 (.02)	.57 (.02)	.56 (.02)
SNLI	.91 (.02)	.78 (.02)	66 (.02)	.33 (.01)	.84 (.01)	.82 (.02)	.72 (.00)	.71 (.01)
QNLI	.91 (.02)	.68 (.02)	.62 (.01)	.50 (.01)	.82 (.01)	.79 (.02)	.62 (.01)	.61 (.01)
MRPC	.86 (.01)	.72 (.02)	.70 (.02)	.50 (.02)	.82 (.02)	.78 (.02)	.69 (.00)	.68 (.00)
EN-EWT	.97 (.01)	.85 (.02)	.65 (.01)	.09 (.01)	.86 (.01)	.81 (.02)	.80 (.01)	.72 (.01)
CoNLL-2003	.95 (.01)	.75 (.01)	.28 (.02)	.02 (.01)	.74 (.01)	.72 (.02)	.61 (.02)	.56 (.01)

Table 2: Model performance results for models trained on original English and on scrambled English. Standard deviations are reported for all entries.

class distribution of the training set. We use this model to further contextualize our results.

5 Tasks

Sequence Classification We select four NLU datasets for sequence classification. We consider sentiment analysis (SST-3; Socher et al., 2013), where SST-3 is a variant of the Stanford Sentiment Treebank with positive/negative/neutral labels; we train on the phrase- and sentence-level sequences in the dataset and evaluate only on its sentence-level labels. Additionally, we include natural language inference (QNLI; Demszky et al., 2018 and SNLI; Bowman et al., 2015) and paraphrase (MRPC; Dolan and Brockett, 2005). QNLI is derived from a version of the Stanford Question Answering Dataset (SQuAD; Rajpurkar et al. 2016). For sequence classification tasks, we use Macro-F1 scores for SST-3, and accuracy scores for the other NLU tasks.

Our supplementary materials provide results for the full GLUE benchmark (Wang et al., 2018).

Sequence Labeling In contrast to sequence classification, where the classifier only considers the [CLS] token of the last layer and predicts a single label for a sentence, sequence labeling requires the model to classify all tokens using their contextualized representations. We select two datasets covering distinct tasks: part-of-speech detection (POS) and named entity recognition (NER). We used the Universal Dependencies English Web Treebank (EN-EWT; Silveira et al. 2014) for POS and CoNLL-2003 (Tjong Kim Sang and De Meulder, 2003) for NER. For sequence labeling tasks, we used Micro-F1 (i.e., accuracy with full labels) for POS and F1 scores for NER.

6 Results

In this section, we analyze the fine-tuning performance of BERT on scrambled datasets. Table 2 shows performance results. We focus for now on the results for Scrambling with Similar Frequency. Additionally, we also include baseline models trained with original sentences for comparison purposes. When training models on each task, we select models based on performance on the dev split during fine-tuning. We report average performance results across runs with three different random seeds.

6.1 Sequence Classification

Comparing the second column (BERT models trained and tested on English) with the sixth column (BERT models trained and tested on Scrambled English with Similar Frequency Scrambling) in Table 2, we see that BERT maintains strong performance for all sequence classification tasks even when the datasets are scrambled. More importantly, we find that BERT fine-tuned with a scrambled dataset performs significantly better than the LSTM model (with GloVe embeddings) trained and evaluated on standard English data

For example, on the MRPC task, BERT evaluated with scrambled data experiences a less than 5% performance drop, and shows significantly better performance than the best LSTM model (a 13.9% improvement). BERT evaluated with scrambled QNLI experiences the biggest drop (a 9.89% decrease). However, this still surpasses the best LSTM performance by a large margin (a 20.6% improvement).

Table 2 also presents performance results for other baseline models, which can be used to assess the intrinsic difficulty of each task. Our results suggest that BERT models fine-tuned with scrambled tasks remain very strong across the board, and they remain stronger than the best LSTM baseline models (those trained and tested on regular English) in all the classification tasks.

The overall performance of the LSTM models is worth further attention. The LSTMs are far less successful at our tasks than the BERT models. However, it seems noteworthy that scrambling does not lead to catastrophic failure for these models. Rather, they maintain approximately the same performance in the scrambled and unscrambled conditions. This might seem at first like evidence of some degree of transfer. However, as we discuss in Section 7.3, the more likely explanation is that the LSTM is simply being retrained more or less from scratch in the two conditions.

6.2 Sequence Labeling

For a more complex setting, we fine-tuned BERT on sequence labeling tasks, and evaluated its transfer abilities without word identities (i.e., using datasets that are scrambled in the same way as in our sequence classification tasks). The bottom two rows of Table 2 show performance results for these tasks, where the goal of the BERT model is to classify every token correctly. As shown in Table 2, BERT experiences a significant drop when evaluated with a scrambled dataset for a sequence labeling task. For LSTMs trained with scrambled sequence labeling tasks, we also observe bigger drops compared with sequence classification tasks. For CoNLL-2003, the LSTM with GloVe embeddings drops from its baseline counterpart (a 18.7% decrease). Our results suggest that transfer learning without word identities is much harder for sequence labeling tasks. One intuition is that sequence labeling tasks are more likely to rely on word identities given the fact that classification (i.e., labeling) is at the token-level.

7 Analysis

7.1 Frequency Effects

Preserving word frequencies during scrambling may lead to higher performance when training and evaluating on scrambled datasets. To assess how much of the observed transfer relates to this factor, we can compare Scrambling with Similar Frequency (SSF) with Random Scrambling (RS), as described in Section 3. As shown in Table 2, performance drops slightly if we use RS. For sequence classification tasks, RS experiences 1–5% drops in performance compared with SSF. For sequence labeling tasks, the difference is slightly larger: about 2–6%. This suggests that word frequency is indeed one of the factors that affects transfer, though the differences are relatively small, indicating that this is not the only contributing factor. This is consistent with similar findings due to Karthikeyan et al. 2019 for multilingual BERT.

7.2 Does Scrambling Preserve Meaning?

Another potential explanation is that our scrambling methods tend to swap words that are predictive of the same labels. For example, when we are substituting words with similar frequencies in SST-3, "good" may be swapped with "great" since they may have similar frequencies in a sentiment analysis dataset. To rule this out, we conducted zero-shot evaluation experiments with our BoW model on sequence classification tasks. The rationale here is that, to the extent that our swapping preserved the underlying connection between features and class labels, this should show up directly in the performance of the BoW model. For example, just swapping of "good" for "great" would hardly affect the final scores for each class. If there are a great many such invariances, then it would explain the apparent transfer.

Figure 2 shows the zero-shot evaluation results of our BoW model on all sequence classification datasets. Our results show that both scrambling methods result in significant performance drops, which suggests that word identities are indeed destroyed by our procedure, which again shines the spotlight on BERT as the only model in our experiments to find and take advantage of transferable information.

7.3 Transfer or Simple Retraining?

Our results on classification tasks show that English-pretrained BERT can achieve high performance when fine-tuned and evaluated on scrambled data. Is this high performance uniquely enabled by transfer from BERT's pretrained representations, or is BERT simply re-learning the token identities from its scrambled fine-tuning data?

To distinguish between these two hypotheses, we first examine whether randomly-initialized BERT models can also achieve high performance when fine-tuned and evaluated on scrambled data. We study models of varying capacity by modulating the number of BERT Transformer blocks. We use datasets scrambled with SSF.

Dataset	LSTM-Baseline	LSTM-Scrambled Similar Frequency GloVe	LSTM-Scrambled Similar Frequency No GloVe
SST-3	.62 (.01)	.57 (.02)	.58 (.01)
SNLI	.78 (.02)	.72 (.00)	.71 (.00)
QNLI	.68 (.02)	.62 (.01)	.61 (.01)
MRPC	.72 (.02)	.69 (.00)	.69 (.00)
EN-EWT	.85 (.02)	.80 (.01)	.79 (.01)
CoNLL-2003	.75 (.01)	.61 (.02)	.60 (.01)

Table 3: Performance results for LSTM models trained on regular English and on English with Scrambling with Similar Frequency, with GloVe embeddings and with randomly initialized embeddings.

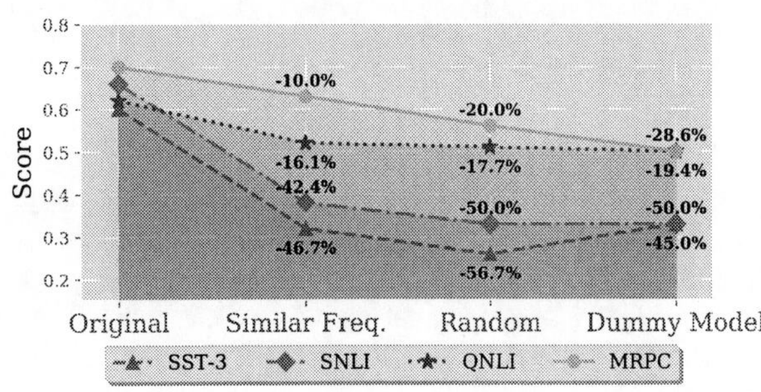

Figure 2: Zero-shot evaluation with the Bag-of-Word (BoW) model on scrambled datasets and the dummy model. Numbers are the differences between the current points and the first points in percentages.

We compare these varying-depth randomly-initialized models against BERT models pretrained on English. To modulate the capacity of these pretrained models, we progressively discard the later Transformer layers (i.e., we make predictions from intermediate layers). Comparing these models is a step toward disentangling the performance gains of pretraining from the performance gains relating to model capacity.

Figure 3 summarizes these experiments. The red line represents our fine-tuning results, across different model sizes. The shaded area represents the performance gain from pretraining when training and testing on scrambled data. Pretraining yields consistent gains across models of differing depths, with deeper models seeing greater gains.

For sequence labeling tasks, the patterns are drastically different: the areas between the two lines are small. Since the randomly-initialized and pretrained models achieve similar performance when fine-tuned and tested on scrambled data, pretraining is not beneficial. This suggests that BERT hardly transfers knowledge when fine-tuned for sequence labeling with scrambled data.

Table 3 shows our results when training LSTMs without any pretrained embeddings. Unlike with BERT, GloVe initialization (a pretraining step) hardly impacts model performance across all tasks. Our leading hypothesis here is that the LSTMs may actually relearn all weights without taking advantage of pretraining. All of our LSTM models have parameter sizes around 1M, whereas the smallest BERT model (i.e., with a single Transformer layer) is around 3.2M parameters. Larger models may be able to rely more on pretraining.

Overall, these results show that we do see transfer of knowledge, at least for classification tasks, but that there is variation between tasks in how much transfer actually happens.

7.4 Assessing Transfer with Frozen BERT Parameters

We can further distinguish the contributions of pretraining versus fine-tuning by freezing the BERT parameters and seeing what effect this has on cross-domain transfer. Ethayarajh (2019) provides evidence that early layers are better than later ones for classifier fine-tuning, so we explore the effects of this freezing for all the layers in our BERT model. We use datasets scrambled with SSF.

As shown in Figure 4, performance scores drop significantly if we only fine-tune the classifier head and freeze the rest of the layers in BERT, across three of our tasks. However, we find that performance scores change significantly depending on which layer we append the classifier head to. Consistent with Ethayarajh's findings, contextualized embeddings in lower layers tend to be more predictive. For example, if we freeze BERT weights and use the contextualized embeddings from the second layer for SST-3, the model reaches peak performance compared with contextualized embeddings from other layers. More importantly, the trend of the green line follows the red line in Figure 4, especially for SST-3 and QNLI. The only exception is MRPC, where the red line plateaus but the green line keeps increasing. This could be an artifact of the size of the dataset, since MRPC only contains around 3.7K training examples. Our results suggest that pretrained weights in successive self-attention layers provide a good initial point for the fine-tuning process.

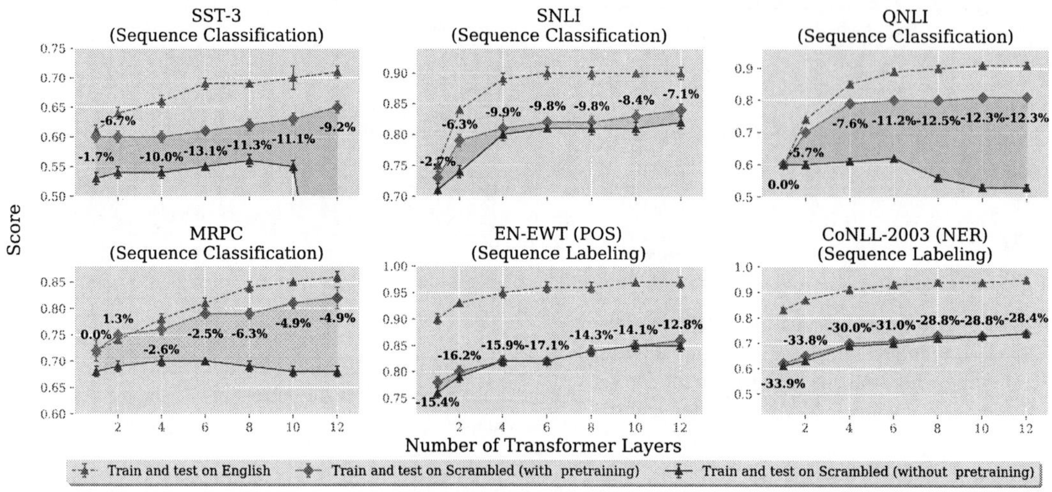

Figure 3: Performance results when fine-tuning end-to-end for different number of Transformer layers. Annotated numbers are the differences between the red lines and the green lines in percentages. Scoring for each task is defined in Section 5.

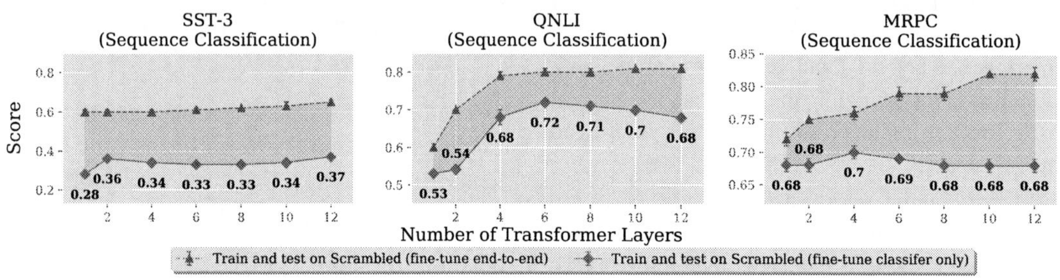

Figure 4: Performance results when fine-tuning only the classifier head by freezing all preceeding layers in BERT (red line) vs. fine-tuning end-to-end, which includes the classifier head and BERT with different numbers of layers (green line). Numbers are scores for the red lines. Scoring for each task is defined in Section 5.

7.5 Probing for Word Identity Reassociations

We further investigate the learning dynamics of our fine-tuned models. Specifically, we study whether our fine-tuned models reassociate word identities with tokens for our sequence classification tasks. To do this, we measure the cosine similarities between words and their scrambled counterparts before and after the fine-tuning process.[3] To the extent that these similarities are increased after fine-tuning, we have evidence that fine-tuning has learned to ressociate words with their scrambled counterparts. We use datasets scrambled with SSF.

We find essentially no evidence for such reassociations. As shown in Figure 5, the correlation distributions before fine-tuning and after are extremely similar. This suggests that our fine-tuned models rarely reassociate word identities in the embedding layer.

To push this analysis a step further, we probe whether word identities are recovered through Transformer layers by adapting the probing method with control task from Hewitt and Liang (2019). Formally, we use an MLP classifier to predict the word identity for w using the contextualized hidden representations of its scrambled counterpart w'. For our control task, we ask the probe to predict random word identities. The difference in performance between these two conditions is know as *selectivity*, and it estimates the degree to which the word identities are recoverable, taking the power of the probe model into account. As shown in Figure 5, our results suggest that relatively little information about the scrambling map is latent in these representations, across tasks and model layers.

[3]We only consider shared words in the model vocabulary and our scrambling maps, which includes 30% of words in the model vocabulary.

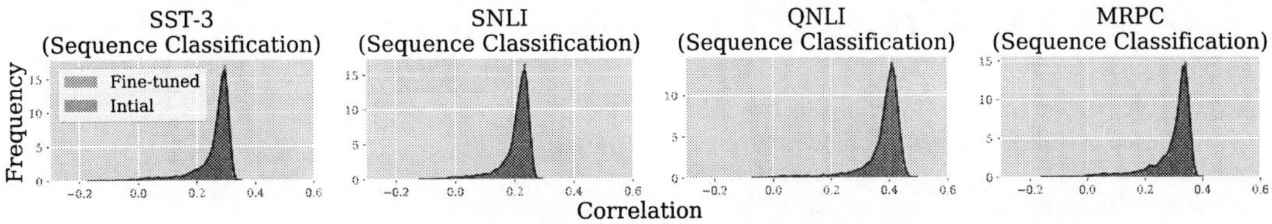

Figure 5: Correlations between cosine similarities of word embeddings before fine-tuning v.s. fine-tuning with scrambled datasets. Measurements of correlations are defined in Section 7.5.

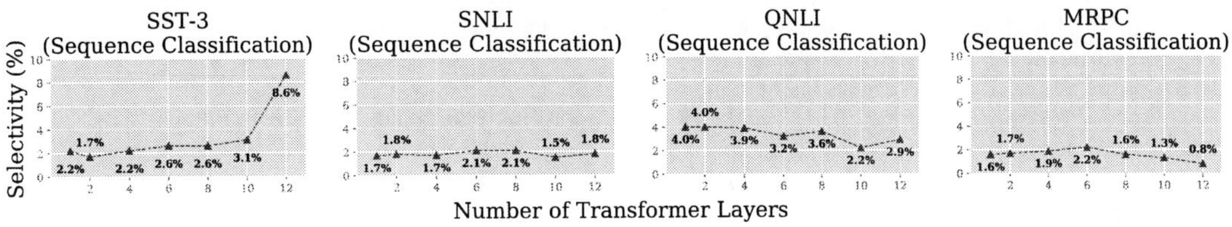

Figure 6: Accuracy of word identity probes when applied to hidden states of each layer comparing to the control task introduced by Hewitt and Liang (2019). Measurements of accuracies are defined in Section 7.5.

8 Conclusion

In this paper, we propose an evaluation pipeline for pretrained models by testing their transfer abilities when they are denied all information about word identity. Specifically, we take an English pretrained BERT off-the-shelf and fine-tune it with a scrambled English dataset. We conduct analyses across six tasks covering both classification and sequence labeling. By evaluating performance against multiple baselines, we aim to assess where BERT can transfer knowledge even without word identities. We find considerable transfer for BERT as compared to even powerful baselines, but only for classification tasks.

What is the source of successful cross-domain transfer with BERT? We find that word frequency contributes, but only to a limited extent: scrambling with matched word frequencies consistently outperforms scrambling with unmatched word frequencies, but transfer still occurs robustly even with random scrambling. We are also able to determine that both pretraining and fine-tuning are important and interacting factors in this transfer; freezing BERT weights during task-specific training leads to much less transfer, but too much task-specific training erodes the benefits of pretraining and in turn reduces the amount of transfer observed.

These analyses begin to piece together a full account of these surprising transfer results for BERT, but they do not fully explain our experimental results. Recent literature suggests at least two new promising avenues to explore. First, Sinha et al. (2021) seek to help characterize the rich distributional prior that models like BERT may be learning, which suggests that higher-order notions of frequency play a significant role in transfer. Second, the findings of Ethayarajh (2019) may be instructive: through successful layers, BERT seems to perform specific kinds of dimensionality reduction that help with low-dimensional classification tasks. Our results concerning layer-wise variation are consistent with this.

Our results are also highly relevant to questions of benchmarking in NLP. It is widely assumed that the benchmark tasks we considered here can help illuminate the capacity of modern NLP systems to process and understand language. However, in our experiments, fine-tuned BERT models are successful at these tasks even in scrambled conditions that render all the examples meaningless, which should lead us to think critically about whether success in the usual unscrambled conditions is reliable evidence of understanding.

References

Mikel Artetxe, Sebastian Ruder, and Dani Yogatama. 2020. On the cross-lingual transferability of monolingual representations. In *Proceedings of the 58th Annual Meeting of the Association for Computational Linguistics*, pages 4623–4637.

Samuel Bowman, Gabor Angeli, Christopher Potts, and Christopher D Manning. 2015. A large annotated corpus for learning natural language inference. In *Proceedings of the 2015 Conference on Empirical*

Methods in Natural Language Processing, pages 632–642.

Jeff Da and Jungo Kasai. 2019. Cracking the contextual commonsense code: Understanding commonsense reasoning aptitude of deep contextual representations. *EMNLP 2019*, page 1.

Dorottya Demszky, Kelvin Guu, and Percy Liang. 2018. Transforming question answering datasets into natural language inference datasets.

Jacob Devlin, Ming-Wei Chang, Kenton Lee, and Kristina Toutanova. 2019. BERT: Pre-training of deep bidirectional transformers for language understanding. In *Proceedings of the 2019 Conference of the North American Chapter of the Association for Computational Linguistics: Human Language Technologies, Volume 1 (Long and Short Papers)*, pages 4171–4186, Minneapolis, Minnesota. Association for Computational Linguistics.

William B Dolan and Chris Brockett. 2005. Automatically constructing a corpus of sentential paraphrases. In *Proceedings of the Third International Workshop on Paraphrasing (IWP2005)*.

Kawin Ethayarajh. 2019. How contextual are contextualized word representations? comparing the geometry of bert, elmo, and gpt-2 embeddings. In *Proceedings of the 2019 Conference on Empirical Methods in Natural Language Processing and the 9th International Joint Conference on Natural Language Processing (EMNLP-IJCNLP)*, pages 55–65.

Allyson Ettinger. 2020. What bert is not: Lessons from a new suite of psycholinguistic diagnostics for language models. *Transactions of the Association for Computational Linguistics*, 8:34–48.

Jon Gauthier and Roger Levy. 2019. Linking artificial and human neural representations of language. In *Proceedings of the 2019 Conference on Empirical Methods in Natural Language Processing and the 9th International Joint Conference on Natural Language Processing (EMNLP-IJCNLP)*, pages 529–539, Hong Kong, China. Association for Computational Linguistics.

Atticus Geiger, Kyle Richardson, and Christopher Potts. 2020. Neural natural language inference models partially embed theories of lexical entailment and negation. In *Proceedings of the Third BlackboxNLP Workshop on Analyzing and Interpreting Neural Networks for NLP*, pages 163–173, Online. Association for Computational Linguistics.

Chengyue Gong, Di He, Xu Tan, Tao Qin, Liwei Wang, and Tie-Yan Liu. 2018. Frage: Frequency-agnostic word representation. In *Advances in Neural Information Processing Systems*, volume 31. Curran Associates, Inc.

Pengcheng He, Xiaodong Liu, Jianfeng Gao, and Wei Chen. 2021. DeBERTa: Decoding-enhanced BERT with disentangled attention. In *2021 International Conference on Learning Representations*.

John Hewitt and Percy Liang. 2019. Designing and interpreting probes with control tasks. In *Proceedings of the 2019 Conference on Empirical Methods in Natural Language Processing and the 9th International Joint Conference on Natural Language Processing (EMNLP-IJCNLP)*, pages 2733–2743.

John Hewitt and Christopher D Manning. 2019. A structural probe for finding syntax in word representations. In *Proceedings of the 2019 Conference of the North American Chapter of the Association for Computational Linguistics: Human Language Technologies, Volume 1 (Long and Short Papers)*, pages 4129–4138.

Sepp Hochreiter and Jürgen Schmidhuber. 1997. Long short-term memory. *Neural Computation*, 9(8):1735–1780.

K Karthikeyan, Zihan Wang, Stephen Mayhew, and Dan Roth. 2019. Cross-lingual ability of multilingual bert: An empirical study. In *International Conference on Learning Representations*.

John D. Lafferty, Andrew McCallum, and Fernando C. N. Pereira. 2001. Conditional random fields: Probabilistic models for segmenting and labeling sequence data. In *Proceedings of the Eighteenth International Conference on Machine Learning*, ICML '01, page 282–289, San Francisco, CA, USA. Morgan Kaufmann Publishers Inc.

Nelson F Liu, Matt Gardner, Yonatan Belinkov, Matthew E Peters, and Noah A Smith. 2019. Linguistic knowledge and transferability of contextual representations. In *Proceedings of the 2019 Conference of the North American Chapter of the Association for Computational Linguistics: Human Language Technologies, Volume 1 (Long and Short Papers)*, pages 1073–1094.

Minh-Thang Luong, Hieu Pham, and Christopher D Manning. 2015. Effective approaches to attention-based neural machine translation. In *Proceedings of the 2015 Conference on Empirical Methods in Natural Language Processing*, pages 1412–1421.

Christopher D Manning, Kevin Clark, John Hewitt, Urvashi Khandelwal, and Omer Levy. 2020. Emergent linguistic structure in artificial neural networks trained by self-supervision. *Proceedings of the National Academy of Sciences*, 117(48):30046–30054.

R. Thomas McCoy, Tal Linzen, Ewan Dunbar, and Paul Smolensky. 2019. RNNs implicitly implement tensor product representations. In *In Proceedings of the 7th International Conference on Learning Representations*, New Orleans, USA.

Isabel Papadimitriou and Dan Jurafsky. 2020. Learning music helps you read: Using transfer to study linguistic structure in language models. In *Proceedings of the 2020 Conference on Empirical Methods in Natural Language Processing (EMNLP)*, pages 6829–6839.

Jeffrey Pennington, Richard Socher, and Christopher D Manning. 2014. GloVe: Global vectors for word representation. In *Proceedings of the 2014 Conference on Empirical Methods in Natural Language Processing*, pages 1532–1543.

Fabio Petroni, Tim Rocktäschel, Sebastian Riedel, Patrick Lewis, Anton Bakhtin, Yuxiang Wu, and Alexander Miller. 2019. Language models as knowledge bases? In *Proceedings of the 2019 Conference on Empirical Methods in Natural Language Processing and the 9th International Joint Conference on Natural Language Processing (EMNLP-IJCNLP)*, pages 2463–2473.

Thang M Pham, Trung Bui, Long Mai, and Anh Nguyen. 2020. Out of order: How important is the sequential order of words in a sentence in natural language understanding tasks? *arXiv preprint arXiv:2012.15180*.

Pranav Rajpurkar, Robin Jia, and Percy Liang. 2018. Know what you don't know: Unanswerable questions for SQuAD. In *Proceedings of the 56th Annual Meeting of the Association for Computational Linguistics (Volume 2: Short Papers)*, pages 784–789, Melbourne, Australia. Association for Computational Linguistics.

Pranav Rajpurkar, Jian Zhang, Konstantin Lopyrev, and Percy Liang. 2016. SQuAD: 100,000+ questions for machine comprehension of text. In *Proceedings of the 2016 Conference on Empirical Methods in Natural Language Processing*, pages 2383–2392, Austin, Texas. Association for Computational Linguistics.

Natalia Silveira, Timothy Dozat, Marie-Catherine de Marneffe, Samuel Bowman, Miriam Connor, John Bauer, and Christopher D. Manning. 2014. A gold standard dependency corpus for English. In *Proceedings of the Ninth International Conference on Language Resources and Evaluation (LREC-2014)*.

Koustuv Sinha, Robin Jia, Dieuwke Hupkes, Joelle Pineau, Adina Williams, and Douwe Kiela. 2021. Masked language modeling and the distributional hypothesis: Order word matters pre-training for little. ArXiv:2104.06644.

Richard Socher, Alex Perelygin, Jean Wu, Jason Chuang, Christopher D Manning, Andrew Y Ng, and Christopher Potts. 2013. Recursive deep models for semantic compositionality over a sentiment treebank. In *Proceedings of the 2013 Conference on Empirical Methods in Natural Language Processing*, pages 1631–1642.

Mukund Sundararajan, Ankur Taly, and Qiqi Yan. 2017. Axiomatic attribution for deep networks. In *Proceedings of the 34th International Conference on Machine Learning*, volume 70 of *Proceedings of Machine Learning Research*, pages 3319–3328, International Convention Centre, Sydney, Australia. PMLR.

Alex Tamkin, Trisha Singh, Davide Giovanardi, and Noah Goodman. 2020. Investigating transferability in pretrained language models. In *Findings of the Association for Computational Linguistics: EMNLP 2020*, pages 1393–1401, Online. Association for Computational Linguistics.

Ian Tenney, Dipanjan Das, and Ellie Pavlick. 2019. Bert rediscovers the classical nlp pipeline. In *Proceedings of the 57th Annual Meeting of the Association for Computational Linguistics*, pages 4593–4601.

Erik F. Tjong Kim Sang and Fien De Meulder. 2003. Introduction to the CoNLL-2003 shared task: Language-independent named entity recognition. In *Proceedings of the Seventh Conference on Natural Language Learning at HLT-NAACL 2003*, pages 142–147.

Ke Tran. 2020. From english to foreign languages: Transferring pre-trained language models. *arXiv preprint arXiv:2002.07306*.

Jesse Vig, Sebastian Gehrmann, Yonatan Belinkov, Sharon Qian, Daniel Nevo, Yaron Singer, and Stuart Shieber. 2020. Causal mediation analysis for interpreting neural nlp: The case of gender bias.

Alex Wang, Yada Pruksachatkun, Nikita Nangia, Amanpreet Singh, Julian Michael, Felix Hill, Omer Levy, and Samuel Bowman. 2019. Superglue: A stickier benchmark for general-purpose language understanding systems. In *Advances in Neural Information Processing Systems*, volume 32. Curran Associates, Inc.

Alex Wang, Amanpreet Singh, Julian Michael, Felix Hill, Omer Levy, and Samuel Bowman. 2018. Glue: A multi-task benchmark and analysis platform for natural language understanding. In *Proceedings of the 2018 EMNLP Workshop BlackboxNLP: Analyzing and Interpreting Neural Networks for NLP*, pages 353–355.

Thomas Wolf, Lysandre Debut, Victor Sanh, Julien Chaumond, Clement Delangue, Anthony Moi, Pierric Cistac, Tim Rault, Remi Louf, Morgan Funtowicz, Joe Davison, Sam Shleifer, Patrick von Platen, Clara Ma, Yacine Jernite, Julien Plu, Canwen Xu, Teven Le Scao, Sylvain Gugger, Mariama Drame, Quentin Lhoest, and Alexander Rush. 2020. Transformers: State-of-the-art natural language processing. In *Proceedings of the 2020 Conference on Empirical Methods in Natural Language Processing: System Demonstrations*, pages 38–45, Online. Association for Computational Linguistics.

Zhilin Yang, Peng Qi, Saizheng Zhang, Yoshua Bengio, William Cohen, Ruslan Salakhutdinov, and Christopher D. Manning. 2018. HotpotQA: A dataset for diverse, explainable multi-hop question answering. In *Proceedings of the 2018 Conference on Empirical Methods in Natural Language Processing*, pages 2369–2380, Brussels, Belgium. Association for Computational Linguistics.

Fabio Massimo Zanzotto, Andrea Santilli, Leonardo Ranaldi, Dario Onorati, Pierfrancesco Tommasino, and Francesca Fallucchi. 2020. Kermit: Complementing transformer architectures with encoders of explicit syntactic interpretations. In *Proceedings of the 2020 Conference on Empirical Methods in Natural Language Processing (EMNLP)*, pages 256–267.

Temporal Knowledge Graph Reasoning with Low-rank and Model-agnostic Representations

Ioannis Dikeoulias[1], Saadullah Amin[2], Günter Neumann[1,2]

[1]Department of Computer Science [2]Department of Language Science and Technology
Saarland Informatics Campus, D3.2, Saarland University, Saarbrücken, Germany
German Research Center for Artificial Intelligence (DFKI), Saarbrücken, Germany
{ioannis.dikeoulias,saadullah.amin,guenter.neumann}@dfki.de

Abstract

Temporal knowledge graph completion (TKGC) has become a popular approach for reasoning over the event and temporal knowledge graphs, targeting the completion of knowledge with accurate but missing information. In this context, tensor decomposition has successfully modeled interactions between entities and relations. Their effectiveness in static knowledge graph completion motivates us to introduce Time-LowFER, a family of parameter-efficient and time-aware extensions of the low-rank tensor factorization model LowFER. Noting several limitations in current approaches to represent time, we propose a cycle-aware time-encoding scheme for time features, which is model-agnostic and offers a more generalized representation of time. We implement our methods in a unified temporal knowledge graph embedding framework, focusing on time-sensitive data processing. The experiments show that our proposed methods perform on par or better than the state-of-the-art semantic matching models on two benchmarks.

1 Introduction

Knowledge graphs offer promising technologies to structure and organize common-sense and domain-specific knowledge and form the information basis for many anticipated technological foundations. Their importance is signified by downstream applications, including speech recognition, sentiment analysis, and knowledge base question answering (Dai et al., 2020). In this context, event and temporal knowledge graphs prove worthy successors of static knowledge graphs, targeting the augmentation of static relational data with temporal meta information. Fig. 1 presents a temporal sub-graph from Wikidata (Vrandečić, 2012), where we are interested in answering the question:

Who was the president of the U.S. in 1961?

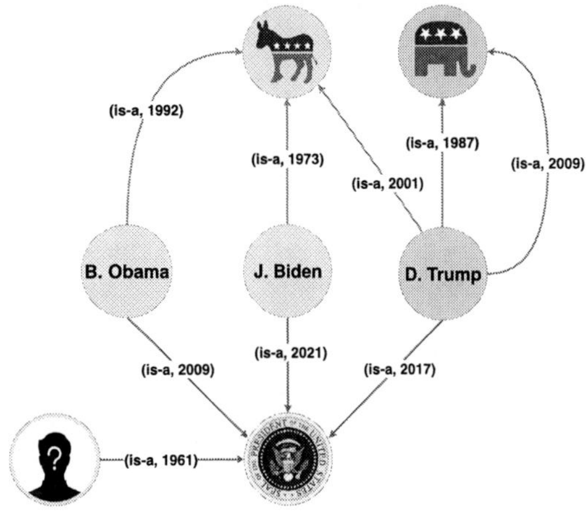

Figure 1: Time-sensitive relationships of U.S. presidents with the democratic and republican parties along with their timestamps. Temporal knowledge graph completion (TKGC) aim to perform time-aware reasoning over the KG to answer questions of type *(?, is-a, US_president, 1961)* with an answer *J. F. Kennedy*.

Temporal information opens new opportunities for many time-sensitive domains, including time-series forecasting, biomedical event extraction, and time-sensitive crime reconstruction. However, temporal knowledge graphs show many inconsistencies and lack data quality across different dimensions, including the accuracy, completeness, and timeliness of facts. The quality of evolving knowledge constitutes a challenging task due to the volatile nature of knowledge. To approach the problem of both completeness and correctness in temporal knowledge graphs, this work addresses the task of temporal link prediction and introduces time-aware extensions of the parameter efficient and expressive static embedding model LowFER (Amin et al., 2020). More precisely, we formulate the main contributions of this paper as follows:

- We identify characteristic time-extension themes for extending static knowledge graph embedding models.

Proceedings of the 7th Workshop on Representation Learning for NLP, pages 111 - 120
May 26, 2022

- We propose Time-LowFER, a family of time-aware and parameter efficient extensions of LowFER to temporal knowledge graphs.

- We identify limitations in temporal representation learning and propose a time-sensitive encoding scheme based on multi-recurrent cycle-aware time decomposition.

- We introduce a unified time-aware knowledge graph embedding framework focusing on time-sensitive data processing.

2 Related Work

TKGC is a prevalent task in temporal knowledge graph reasoning and targets the incompleteness and timeliness of entailed facts. Formally, the task of TKGC is formulated as: given a temporal knowledge graph $\mathcal{G} \subseteq \mathcal{E} \times \mathcal{R} \times \mathcal{E} \times \mathcal{T}$ of quadruples (s, p, o, t) where $s, o \in \mathcal{E}$ represent entities, $p \in \mathcal{P}$ represent predicates and $t \in \mathcal{T}$ represent timestamps, the task is to answer either the query $(s, p, ?, t)$ or $(?, p, o, t)$. For the sake of completeness, we refer to s and o also as subject (head) and object (tail) entities, and to p as relation (predicate), also commonly denoted by r.

TKGC approaches are divided into (a) *geometric embedding models* using distance-based scoring functions, (b) *semantic matching models* using similarity-based scoring functions, and (c) *deep learning models*. In this work, we focus on the group of semantic matching models, commonly referred to as factorization-based models. The most prominent static models in this area are DistMult (Yang et al., 2015), SimplE (Kazemi and Poole, 2018), ComplEx (Trouillon et al., 2016) and TuckER (Balazevic et al., 2019). Further, noting characteristic patterns throughout several time-aware extensions of static embedding models, we identified four distinct temporal extension themes Fig. 2(b): (1) inclusion-based, (2) feature-based, (3) regularization-based, and (4) aggregation-based extensions.

2.1 Inclusion-based extensions

Inclusion-based approaches represent extensions, where time features are exposed directly to the underlying embedding model. Time features are considered individual input signals, favoring a more expressive inclusion of time information within the model.

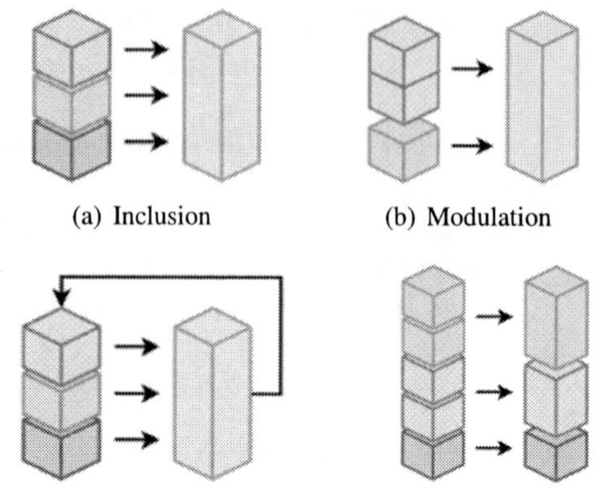

(a) Inclusion (b) Modulation

(c) Regularization (d) Aggregation

Figure 2: Schematic illustration of time extension types: (a) inclusion-based; (b) modulation-based; (c) regularisation-based; and (d) aggregation-based.

A prominent example for inclusion-based time extension is TTransE (Leblay and Chekol, 2018), representing time as temporal translation of entity-relation features. Similarly, TeRo (Xu et al., 2020a) considers individual time features via temporal rotation of entity features. Both models incorporate time as a separate feature and can learn more expressive interactions between input features.

2.2 Modulation-based extensions

Modulation-based extensions are the most commonly used approaches for the time-aware extension of static embedding models. In this context, modulation describes regulating a base signal using a separate modulation signal, i.e., time-based relation modulation allows for a time-sensitive parametrization of relation embeddings.

Most common approaches are TNTComplEx (Lacroix et al., 2020) and TuckERTNT (Shao et al., 2021), which extend their static base models ComplEx (Trouillon et al., 2016) and TuckER (Balazevic et al., 2019) via a temporal modulation of either entity or relation features. Similarly, diachronic embeddings (Goel et al., 2020) represent a model-agnostic and time-aware extension of static embedding models via modulation of entity-specific parameters. In contrast to inclusion-based extensions, modulation-based extensions do not expose time directly to the underlying embedding model. Therefore, modulation is model-agnostic and similarly allows for a parameter-efficient extension of static embedding models.

2.3 Regularization-based extensions

Regularization-based extensions include techniques that impose consistency constraints on learnable feature representations. A commonly used scheme for time-aware regularization is temporal smoothness regularizers, which leverage the semantic nearness of the nearby timestamps.

Both TuckERTNT (Shao et al., 2021), and TNT-ComplEx (Lacroix et al., 2020) implement this type of smoothness regularization scheme. The authors minimize the nuclear p-norm (N3, 3-norm) of the discrete derivative of two nearby time embeddings, effectively penalizing sharp time gradients. Likewise, for TransE-TAE (Jiang et al., 2016) the authors introduce time-wise regularization schemes that enforce constraints for the temporal ordering or disjointness of facts. This way, embedding models are less prone to overfitting and allow for improved generalization to underlying data.

2.4 Aggregation-based extensions

Aggregation-based extensions leverage the compositionality of features such as clustering, grouping, averaging, and sampling.

An application of this idea has been implemented by TeMP (Wu et al., 2020), which introduces time-based subgraph clusters that group information together that occurs within a specific time range. Similarly, ATiSE (Xu et al., 2020b) and TeRo (Xu et al., 2020a) introduce a temporal granularity parameter that varies the temporal sampling rate at which facts are discretized over time.

3 Low-rank Representation

Tensor factorization models decompose the order-3 and order-4 binary tensor into a compressed tensor and a set of factor matrices, respectively, for static and temporal KGs. TuckER (Balazevic et al., 2019) proposed a Tucker decomposition model for static KGs and showed that existing semantic matching models could be subsumed in their formulation. Noting the cubic growth of core tensor in TuckER, LowFER (Amin et al., 2020) proposed an efficient parameter initialization of the core tensor using low-rank factorized bilinear pooling. Due to its ability to handle arbitrary relations (*fully expressive*), parameter efficiency, generalization abilities, and state-of-the-art performance in embedding-based models for static KGs (Zhu et al., 2021), we extend it to the temporal KGs.

3.1 LowFER

LowFER (Amin et al., 2020) introduces a low-rank decomposition of the core tensor in TuckER, reducing the parameter growth from $\mathcal{O}(d^3)$ to $\mathcal{O}(kd^2)$, with d and k being the embedding dimension and factorization rank, respectively. Given subject entity and relation embeddings $\mathbf{e}_s$ and $\mathbf{e}_p$, LowFER approximates the interaction tensor using two low-rank projection matrices $\mathbf{U} \in \mathbb{R}^{d_e \times kd_e}$ and $\mathbf{V} \in \mathbb{R}^{d_r \times kd_e}$. More specifically, both entity and relation features are projected to high-dimensional spaces $\mathbf{U}^T\mathbf{e}_s$ and $\mathbf{V}^T\mathbf{e}_p$, followed by Hadamard product (denoted by $\circ$) and k-sized non-overlapping summation pooling:

$$f(e_s, e_p, e_o) = \langle \mathbf{g}(e_s, e_p), \mathbf{e}_o \rangle$$

where $\langle ., . \rangle$ defines dot product and $\mathbf{g}$ represents a vector-valued function, performing factorized bilinear pooling:

$$g(e_s, e_p) := \text{SumPool}(\mathbf{U}^T\mathbf{e}_s \circ \mathbf{V}^T\mathbf{e}_p, k),$$

and $\mathbf{e}_o$ represents the target entity. LowFER can generalize the TuckER model. Moreover, for $k \leq \min(d_e, d_r)$ with d_e, d_r as entity and relation dimensions, respectively, LowFER is able to accurately represent TuckER's core tensor $\mathcal{W}_{\text{tucker}}$. In addition, given the subsumption of TuckER, LowFER is equally fully expressive and thus able to represent arbitrary relations, e.g., symmetric, reflexive, and transitive, among others.

3.2 Time-LowFER

This section introduces Time-LowFER, a family of time-aware extensions of the bilinear embedding model LowFER. These include (i) LowFER-TNT: a modulation-based extension following time-relation modulation (Lacroix et al., 2020), (ii) LowFER-CFB: an inclusion-based extension using chained bilinear pooling, and (iii) LowFER-FTP: a reduced variant of the latter, with factorized trilinear pooling.

3.3 Factorized Bilinear Pooling

Following existing works of Lacroix et al. (2020); Shao et al. (2021), we propose two variants of time modulation also referred to as time modulation (T) and time-no-time modulation (TNT), which extends the factorized bilinear pooling of LowFER. The first variant (T) performs a simple temporal modulation of relation features e_r using time features e_t. We refer to this extension as LowFER-T and formulate its scoring function as follows:

$$f(e_s, e_p, e_o, e_t) = \langle \mathbf{g}(e_s, e_p, e_t), \mathbf{e}_o \rangle$$

where e_t is time embedding and $\mathbf{g}$ is defined as:

$$g(e_s, e_p, e_t) = \mathbf{U}^T \mathbf{e}_s \circ \mathbf{V}^T (\mathbf{e}_p \odot \mathbf{e}_t)$$

Time modulation (T), denoted by $\odot$, enables LowFER-T to learn joint time-aware representations of entity and relation features such that learned feature-to-feature interactions now incorporate the dynamics of the overlying knowledge graph with more precise predictions.

However, not all predicates are similarly affected by time or show reduced sensitivity to temporal changes in related facts. For instance, the predicate *born_in* is not changing over time, however the predicate *works_at* (most probably) will. To capture both dynamic and static characteristics of temporal relations, we follow Lacroix et al. (2020) and propose a time-no-time (TNT) variant of LowFER, which calculates a combined representation of static and dynamic relations. We refer to this extension as LowFER-TNT and formulate the function $\mathbf{g}$ as:

$$g(e_s, e_p, e_t) = \mathbf{U}^T \mathbf{e}_s \circ \mathbf{V}^T (\mathbf{e}_p^t \odot \mathbf{e}_t + \mathbf{e}_p)$$

$\mathbf{e}_p^t$ denotes the time-aware relation embedding and e_p the static relation feature. Both T and TNT variants of LowFER do not modify the assumptions of the underlying methods, i.e., the approximation of TuckER's core interaction tensor. Therefore, both modulation-based extensions are fully expressive and can be seen as (time-aware) generalizations of LowFER, while equally, TNT subsumes T.

3.4 Chained Factorized Bilinear Pooling

Time features encode latent dynamics of evolving knowledge graphs and allow for a time-aware classification of relational links, i.e., time features set crucial constraints on feature interactions, similarly disqualifying the existence of specific graph structures for a given time range. For instance, after *(U.S.) presidential elections*, the link *is_president* will remain static for at least four years. Similarly, the *signing* of international climate agreements would imply a change of *demands* for government and industry. However, bilinear models (Section 3.3) are solely defined over two variables, making them less suitable for multivariate analysis, e.g., entity, relation, and time features. We propose a multilinear method based on bilinear chaining for use in multivariate learning to overcome these limitations.

More precisely, we define a k-fold chaining of bilinear models through the nesting of bilinear transformations:

$$\begin{aligned} &B_k^C(x_1, \ldots, x_{k+1}) \\ &= (B_1 \circ \cdots \circ B_k)(x_1, \ldots, x_{k+1}) \\ &= B_k(B_{k-1}(\ldots, x_k), x_{k+1}), \end{aligned}$$

where $B_1, \ldots, B_k$ denote bilinear transformations, $(x_1, \ldots, x_{k+1})$ denote the input features and the $\circ$ here represents the function composition operator. Following LowFER, we introduce a time-aware extension of LowFER based on two-fold chaining of factorized bilinear methods.

$$g(e_s, e_p, e_t) := \text{SumPool}((B_1 \circ B_2)(e_s, e_p, e_t), k)$$

where B_1 and B_2 denote two nested bilinear transformations. Similarly, the above equation can be rewritten in terms of three low-rank projection matrices, $\mathbf{U}, \mathbf{V}$ as similar to LowFER and $\mathbf{Q} \in \mathbb{R}^{dr \times kd_e}$ as:

$$\begin{aligned} &g(e_s, e_p, e_t) \\ &= \text{SumPool}(\mathbf{U}^T \mathbf{e}_s \circ \mathbf{R}^T (\mathbf{V}^T \mathbf{e}_p \circ \mathbf{Q}^T \mathbf{e}_t), k) \end{aligned}$$

We refer to this method as chained factorized bilinear (CFB) pooling. CFB learns two joint representations between relation and time features and once between entities and the joint representation of time-relation features. However, we note that the intermediate projection matrix $\mathbf{R} \in \mathbb{R}^{kd_e \times kd_e}$ is likely to share redundant parameters with both relation and time projection matrices $\mathbf{V}$ and $\mathbf{Q}$.

3.5 Factorized Trilinear Pooling

CFB enables the computation of fine-grained interactions between different feature spaces. However, CFB introduces redundant parameters via the intermediate projection of joint time-relation features. To retain the efficiency of the original low-rank bilinear method, we introduce a (reduced) specialization of the CFB, which omits the intermediate feature projection. Replacing $\mathbf{R}$ by an identity matrix $\mathbf{I}$, we formulate the respective method via a three-way Hadamard product or entity, relation, and time features, followed by summation pooling:

$$g(e_s, e_p, e_t) \\ = \text{SumPool}(\mathbf{U}^T\mathbf{e}_s \circ \mathbf{V}^T\mathbf{e}_p \circ \mathbf{Q}^T\mathbf{e}_t, 1),$$

Where $\mathbf{U}$, $\mathbf{V}$, and $\mathbf{Q}$ are the low-rank projection matrices, note the factorization rank, k is set to 1.

4 Cycle-aware Time Embedding

In this section, we propose a novel extension technique for embedding time features ($\mathbf{e}_t$), which relies on multi-recurrent cycle-aware (MRCA) time decomposition and is model-agnostic. We first explain the concept of *multi-recurrence* and then show its application for *cycle-aware encoding* of time features.

Temporal recurrence denotes the concept of expressing time as recurrent component within a certain time frame e.g., a *week* occurs approximately four times per *month* or equally a *year* contains four *seasons*. In this context, we speak of *multi-recurrence*, if a time frame is expressed in terms of multiple cycles, e.g., a *year* entails four *seasons*, 12 *months*, *52* weeks and *365* days. Multi-recurrence is expressible for all time concepts with one or more underlying recurrent cycles. Even more, (long-term) cycles themselves are also expressible in terms of more fine-grained (short-term) cycles.

Our multi-recurrent cycle-aware (MRCA) encoding uses a mapping ψ^{cyc} of timestamps T to a set of recurrence encodings $C^{m \times l}$:

$$\psi^{cyc} : T \to C^{m \times l} \\ t_i \mapsto (\phi^{rec}_{W_1}(t_i), \ldots, \phi^{rec}_{W_m}(t_i)),\ 1 \le i \le n,$$

where each recurrence encoding $\phi^{rec}_{W_k}$ defined upon cycle window W_k, uses a mapping of timestamps T to a set of cycle indices C^l:

$$\phi^{rec}_{W_k} : T \to C^l \\ t_i \mapsto (c^k_1, \ldots, c^k_l),\ 1 \le k \le m,$$

and each time component c^k_p with $1 \le p \le l$ is defined as:

$$c^k_p = \begin{cases} v & \text{if } p\text{-}th \text{ subcycle exists in } W_k \\ 0 & \text{else} \end{cases}.$$

Here, n denotes the number of timestamps, m is the number of time windows, and l is the number of recurrent subcycles. Now, to generate the cycle-aware multi-recurrent time embedding, we consider

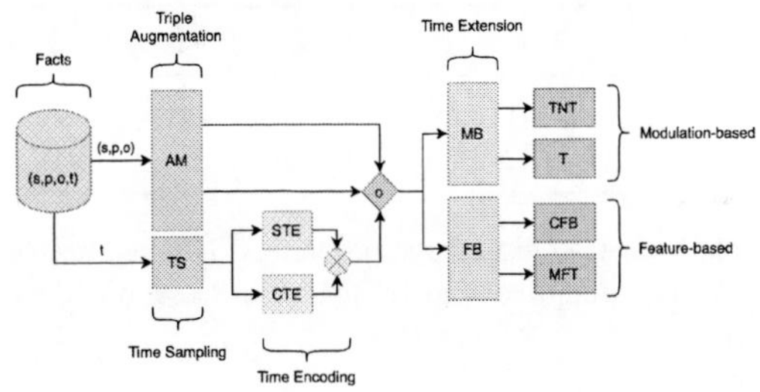

Figure 3: Overview of data processing and modeling pipeline in the CHRONOKGE framework. A quadruple fact is processed using triple augmentation and time sampling (*green*), and afterward, timestamps are decomposed into subcomponents (*yellow*). Then, the processed quadruple is passed to the respective temporal extension (*orange*) and model variation (*violet*).

the following five components and their respective cycle decompositions[1]:

$$\begin{aligned} \phi^{rec}_W(t_i) &\quad \to (c^W_d) \\ \phi^{rec}_M(t_i) &\quad \to (c^M_d, c^M_w) \\ \phi^{rec}_S(t_i) &\quad \to (c^S_d, c^S_w, c^S_m) \\ \phi^{rec}_Y(t_i) &\quad \to (c^Y_d, c^Y_w, c^Y_m, c^Y_s) \\ \phi^{rec}_G(t_i) &\quad \to (c^G_1, c^G_{10}, c^G_{100}, c^G_{1000}) \end{aligned}$$

Where W, M, S, Y, G denote the weekly, monthly, seasonal, yearly, and global components, respectively, and d, w, m, s, y denote the daily, weekly, monthly, seasonal, and yearly subcycles. The components $c_1, c_{10}, c_{100}, c_{1000}$ denote the positional year component for single years, decades, centuries and milleniums, respectively. The final cycle-aware time encoding ψ^{MRCA} is then generated by summing over all cycle decompositions of each separate recurrence mapping $\phi^{rec}_{W_k}$:

$$\begin{aligned} \mathbf{e}_t = \psi^{MRCA}(t) &= \sum_{i=1}^{l_1}(\phi^{rec}_G(t))_i + \sum_{i=1}^{l_2}(\phi^{rec}_Y(t))_i \\ &+ \sum_{i=1}^{l_3}(\phi^{rec}_S(t))_i + \sum_{i=1}^{l_4}(\phi^{rec}_M(t))_i \\ &+ \sum_{i=1}^{l_5}(\phi^{rec}_W(t))_i \end{aligned}$$

[1]The generation of recurrent time cycles rely on prior knowledge of empirically defined periods, e.g., a week has seven days, a month has 30 days, a year consists of approximately 365 days, e.t.c.

	#E	#R	#T	time span	gran.	MD.	TQ.	MC.
ICEWS14	7,129	230	365	2014	daily	✗	✗	✗
ICEWS05-15	10,488	251	4,017	2005-2015	daily	✗	✗	✗

Table 1: Data statistics and properties: No. entities (E), no. relations (R), no. timestamps (T), time span, time granularity, multiple domains (MD), temporal qualifier (TQ), and manual curation (MC).

5 Experiments and Results

5.1 Data

ICEWS (Integrated Crisis Early Warning System) was founded in 2008 as a DARPA program and is currently maintained by Lockheed Martin. The conflict warning system collects news about political events from different digital and social media platforms and stores the extracted information in the associated ICEWS database.

ICEWS14 is a subset of the ICEWS database, including facts from the year 2014. It consists of 7,129 distinct entities, 230 relations, and 365 timestamps with 24 hours (daily) temporal granularity.

ICEWS05-15 is another subset of the ICEWS database, including facts between the start of 2005 and the end of 2015. It consists of 10,488 distinct entities, 251 relations, and 4,017 timestamps with a temporal granularity of 24 hours (daily). In Table 1 we provide an overview of the datasets.

5.2 Implementation

For implementation, we developed an extensible temporal knowledge representation learning framework CHRONOKGE[2]. Fig. 3 shows the data and modeling pipeline in the framework. We present more details in Appendix A.1.

For training, we use the Adam (Kingma and Ba, 2015) optimizer with a learning rate of 0.01 and a decay rate of 0.99. We perform 1-N scoring with binary cross-entropy loss and choose a batch size of 1000. We further apply a label smoothing of 0.01 to the target labels. The embedding dimension of entities, relations, and time is set to 300. We use $k = 32$ in LowFER-TNT and LowFER-CFB, and use dropout following Amin et al. (2020).

5.3 Baselines

We choose the static LowFER model for our experiments to apply to our proposed temporal extensions. Since LowFER is a semantic matching linear model, we only compare our results with the extensions of such linear models. In particular, we use as baselines the time-aware extension of both ComplEx (TComplEx, TNTComplEx) (Lacroix et al., 2020), TuckER (TuckERT, TuckERTNT) (Shao et al., 2021) as well as SimplE (DE-SimplE) and DistMult (DE-DistMult) (Goel et al., 2020).

[2]`https://github.com/iodike/ChronoKGE`

5.4 Time and No-Time Modulation

Following the findings of Shao et al. (2021) and Lacroix et al. (2020), we only modulate relations with time information (instead of entities). For both ICEWS datasets, as depicted in Table 2, we see persistent improvements in the TNT-extension over the T-extension. It shall be noted that both TuckERTNT and TNTComplEx use time and embedding regularization schemes, where Time-LowFER extensions are reported without any regularization that can further improve the results.

While the T-extension learns a time-aware relation that primarily relies on temporal information, the TNT extends it by learning an additional (static) relation embedding as shown in Fig. 4. This effect is beneficial for highly frequent relations (light areas), which should not rely too strictly on time. In contrast, temporal information is much more valuable for relations that occur less frequently (dark areas) and should be incorporated with a higher weighting.

5.5 Chained and Factorized Bilinear Pooling

Now we evaluate Chained Factorized Bilinear (CFB) pooling and Factorized Trilinear (FTP) pooling. As shown in Table 2, the LowFER-CFB outperforms all baselines, including the T and TNT extensions of LowFER. This can be attributed to the additional expressive modeling capacity of LowFER-CFB with multi-layered bilinear interactions. CFB learns more accurate feature fusion between all three input modalities. However, the inclusion of intermediate feature projections favors the redundancy of captured feature interactions. Therefore, while the CFB offers improved results (w.r.t. MRR) over the FTP, it is more vulnerable to overfitting.

	ICEWS14				ICEWS05-15			
	MRR	H@10	H@3	H@1	MRR	H@10	H@3	H@1
DE-DistMult◇	0.501	0.708	0.569	0.392	0.484	0.718	0.546	0.366
DE-SimplE◇	0.526	0.725	0.592	0.418	0.513	0.748	0.578	0.392
TComplEx†	0.560	0.730	0.610	0.470	0.580	0.760	0.640	0.490
TNTComplEx†	0.560	0.740	0.610	0.460	0.600	0.780	0.650	0.500
TuckERT‡	0.594	0.731	0.640	0.518	0.627	0.769	0.674	0.550
TuckERTNT‡	0.604	0.753	0.655	0.521	**0.638**	0.783	0.686	**0.559**
LowFER-T	0.584	0.734	0.630	0.505	0.559	0.714	0.605	0.476
LowFER-TNT	0.586	0.735	0.632	0.507	0.562	0.717	0.608	0.480
LowFER-CFB	**0.623**	0.757	**0.671**	**0.549**	**0.638**	0.791	**0.690**	0.555
LowFER-FTP	0.617	**0.765**	0.665	0.537	0.625	**0.792**	0.681	0.534

Table 2: Time-LowFER performance on ICEWS datasets. ◇ Results taken from (Goel et al., 2020). † Results taken from (Lacroix et al., 2020). ‡ Results taken from (Shao et al., 2021).

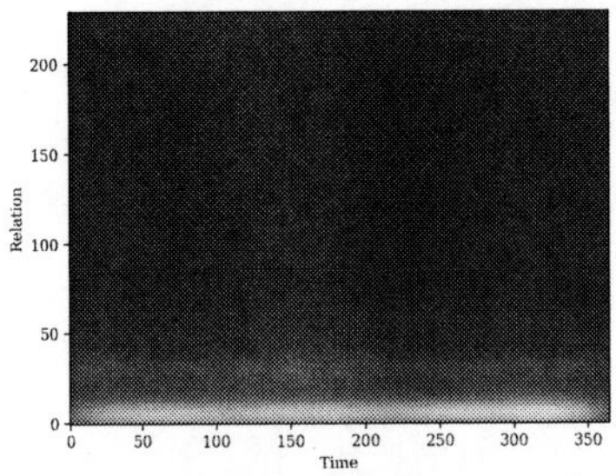

(a) ICEWS14

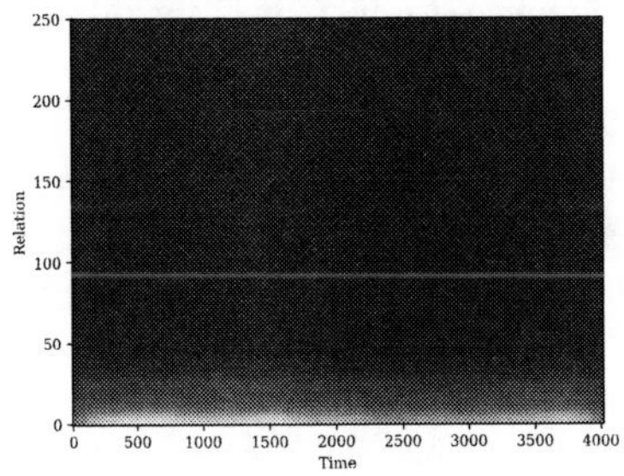

(b) ICEWS05-15

Figure 4: Time-relation heatmap: (a) for ICEWS14; and (b) for ICEWS05-15.

5.6 Simple and Cycle-aware Time Encoding

In this experiment, we evaluate two approaches for timestamp encoding, Simple Time Encoding (STE), which performs a bijective projection of timestamps to natural numbers, and Cyclical Time Encoding (CTE), which relies on multi-recurrent cycle-aware time decomposition (MRCA). CTE targets specific limitations in representation learning of absolute timestamps, such as its inability to learn shared representations across different timestamps. By introducing cyclical time components, time features to benefit from an improved sharing of parameters within individual embedding subspaces and allow for an increased generalization of short-term events. Technically, CTE reduces the multi-collinearity of low-latent time features and allows for an improved semantic separability across individual representations.

In CTE, we focus on high recall and therefore concentrate primarily on the Hits@10 metric in our evaluation. Detailed results are provided in Table 3. The MRCA-algorithm uses predefined time cycles, which are divided into 10 short-term (in-year) cycles and four long-term (multi-year) cycles, particularly favouring the dense distribution of time information for ICEWS datasets (see Figure 4(a), 4(b)). As a consequence, both ICEWS datasets show increased results (w.r.t Hits@10) with an increase of 3.4% (ICEWS14) and 5.7% (ICEWS05-15) for modulation-based extensions as well as 1.4% (ICEWS14) for feature-based extensions.

5.7 Time Sampling Rate

In this section, we investigate the effect of time sampling in TKGC. Following the approach of Xu et al. (2020a) and Xu et al. (2020b), we include a time granularity parameter, allowing to sample timestamps from a given dataset at different sampling rates. In particular, we investigate sampling rates in the power of two $\{1.0, 2.0, \ldots, 1024.0\}$,

		ICEWS14				ICEWS05-15			
		MRR	H@10	H@3	H@1	MRR	H@10	H@3	H@1
STE	LowFER-T	0.584	0.734	0.630	0.505	0.559	0.714	0.605	0.476
	LowFER-TNT	0.586	0.735	0.632	0.507	**0.562**	0.717	0.608	**0.480**
CTE	LowFER-T	**0.600**	0.764	**0.654**	**0.511**	0.556	**0.771**	**0.621**	0.442
	LowFER-TNT	0.583	**0.769**	0.640	0.485	0.549	0.767	0.614	0.434

Table 3: STE and CTE results for T/TNT-extensions on ICEWS datasets.

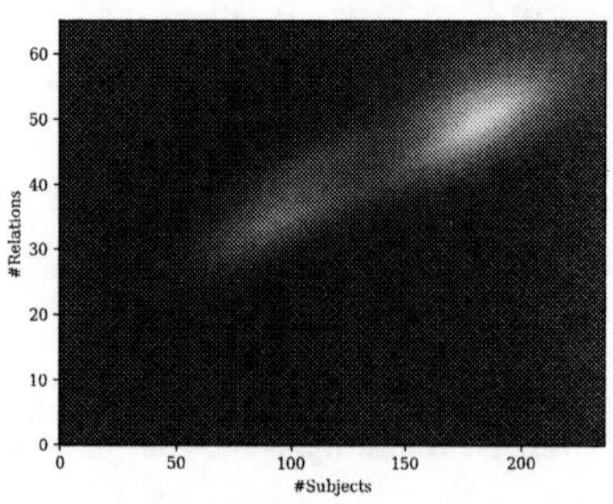

(a) ICEWS14

(b) ICEWS05-15

Figure 5: Time concentration heatmap: (a) for ICEWS14; and (b) for ICEWS05-15.

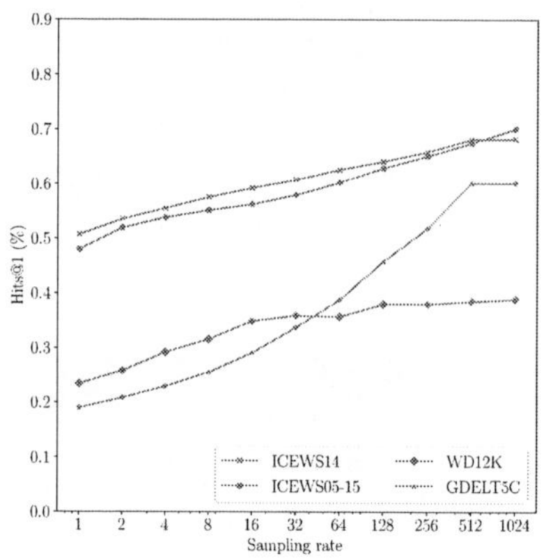

Figure 6: Influence of increasing time sampling rates.

where 1.0 represents the initial sampling rate, in which timestamps are discretized w.r.t to time granularity.

Sampling timestamps at lower rates cause the underlying temporal KG to aggregate facts into smaller time clusters, up to the extreme case where all facts are linked only to one timestamp. In other words, with increasing time sampling rates, a temporal knowledge graph is synthetically transformed into a static KG. While time sampling does not represent a viable extension for evaluating time-sensitive embedding models, it allows examining the significance of temporal facts for individual benchmark datasets.

6 Conclusion

In this work, we introduced Time-LowFER, a family of time-aware extensions of the bilinear factorization model LowFER. Following existing work in temporal link prediction, we extended LowFER using time-modulated relations (TNT). Further, noting several limitations of modulation-based extensions, we proposed two feature-based extensions of LowFER, which are based on bilinear chaining (CFB) and trilinear fusion (FTP). In particular, we showed that the FTP represents a parameter-efficient specialization of the CFB, while CFB offers state-of-the-art results among semantic matching models for temporal link prediction.

In addition, we investigated four different approaches for time-aware extension of static embedding models and outlined, despite the increased popularity of time modulation techniques, the superiority of feature-based KGE extensions. Furthermore, we investigated the process of time encoding in representation learning and proposed a model-agnostic method (CTE) for encoding timestamps based on multi-recurrent cycle-aware (MRCA) time decomposition.

Acknowledgments

The authors would like to thank the anonymous reviewers for their helpful feedback. The work was partially funded by the European Union (EU) Horizon 2020 research and innovation programme through the project Precise4Q (777107) and the German Federal Ministry of Education and Research (BMBF) through the project CoRA4NLP (01IW20010). The authors also acknowledge the cluster compute resources provided by the DFKI.

References

Saadullah Amin, Stalin Varanasi, Katherine Ann Dunfield, and Günter Neumann. 2020. Lowfer: Low-rank bilinear pooling for link prediction. In *Proceedings of the 37th International Conference on Machine Learning, ICML 2020, 13-18 July 2020, Virtual Event*, volume 119 of *Proceedings of Machine Learning Research*, pages 257–268. PMLR.

Ivana Balazevic, Carl Allen, and Timothy Hospedales. 2019. TuckER: Tensor factorization for knowledge graph completion. In *Proceedings of the 2019 Conference on Empirical Methods in Natural Language Processing and the 9th International Joint Conference on Natural Language Processing (EMNLP-IJCNLP)*, pages 5185–5194, Hong Kong, China. Association for Computational Linguistics.

Yuanfei Dai, Shiping Wang, Neal N Xiong, and Wenzhong Guo. 2020. A survey on knowledge graph embedding: Approaches, applications and benchmarks. *Electronics*, 9(5):750.

Rishab Goel, Seyed Mehran Kazemi, Marcus Brubaker, and Pascal Poupart. 2020. Diachronic embedding for temporal knowledge graph completion. In *The Thirty-Fourth AAAI Conference on Artificial Intelligence, AAAI 2020, The Thirty-Second Innovative Applications of Artificial Intelligence Conference, IAAI 2020, The Tenth AAAI Symposium on Educational Advances in Artificial Intelligence, EAAI 2020, New York, NY, USA, February 7-12, 2020*, pages 3988–3995. AAAI Press.

Tingsong Jiang, Tianyu Liu, Tao Ge, Lei Sha, Baobao Chang, Sujian Li, and Zhifang Sui. 2016. Towards time-aware knowledge graph completion. In *Proceedings of COLING 2016, the 26th International Conference on Computational Linguistics: Technical Papers*, pages 1715–1724, Osaka, Japan. The COLING 2016 Organizing Committee.

Seyed Mehran Kazemi and David Poole. 2018. Simple embedding for link prediction in knowledge graphs. In *Advances in Neural Information Processing Systems 31: Annual Conference on Neural Information Processing Systems 2018, NeurIPS 2018, December 3-8, 2018, Montréal, Canada*, pages 4289–4300.

Diederik P. Kingma and Jimmy Ba. 2015. Adam: A method for stochastic optimization. In *3rd International Conference on Learning Representations, ICLR 2015, San Diego, CA, USA, May 7-9, 2015, Conference Track Proceedings*.

Timothée Lacroix, Guillaume Obozinski, and Nicolas Usunier. 2020. Tensor decompositions for temporal knowledge base completion. In *8th International Conference on Learning Representations, ICLR 2020, Addis Ababa, Ethiopia, April 26-30, 2020*. OpenReview.net.

Julien Leblay and Melisachew Wudage Chekol. 2018. Deriving validity time in knowledge graph. In *Companion Proceedings of the The Web Conference 2018*, pages 1771–1776.

Adam Paszke, Sam Gross, Francisco Massa, Adam Lerer, James Bradbury, Gregory Chanan, Trevor Killeen, Zeming Lin, Natalia Gimelshein, Luca Antiga, et al. 2019. Pytorch: An imperative style, high-performance deep learning library. *Advances in neural information processing systems*, 32.

Pengpeng Shao, Dawei Zhang, Guohua Yang, Jianhua Tao, Feihu Che, and Tong Liu. 2021. Tucker decomposition-based temporal knowledge graph completion. *Knowledge-Based Systems*, page 107841.

Théo Trouillon, Johannes Welbl, Sebastian Riedel, Éric Gaussier, and Guillaume Bouchard. 2016. Complex embeddings for simple link prediction. In *Proceedings of the 33nd International Conference on Machine Learning, ICML 2016, New York City, NY, USA, June 19-24, 2016*, volume 48 of *JMLR Workshop and Conference Proceedings*, pages 2071–2080. JMLR.org.

Denny Vrandečić. 2012. Wikidata: A new platform for collaborative data collection. In *Proceedings of the 21st international conference on world wide web*, pages 1063–1064.

Jiapeng Wu, Meng Cao, Jackie Chi Kit Cheung, and William L. Hamilton. 2020. TeMP: Temporal message passing for temporal knowledge graph completion. In *Proceedings of the 2020 Conference on Empirical Methods in Natural Language Processing (EMNLP)*, pages 5730–5746, Online. Association for Computational Linguistics.

Chengjin Xu, Mojtaba Nayyeri, Fouad Alkhoury, Hamed Shariat Yazdi, and Jens Lehmann. 2020a. TeRo: A time-aware knowledge graph embedding via temporal rotation. In *Proceedings of the 28th International Conference on Computational Linguistics*, pages 1583–1593, Barcelona, Spain (Online). International Committee on Computational Linguistics.

Chenjin Xu, Mojtaba Nayyeri, Fouad Alkhoury, Hamed Yazdi, and Jens Lehmann. 2020b. Temporal knowledge graph completion based on time series gaussian embedding. In *International Semantic Web Conference*, pages 654–671. Springer.

Bishan Yang, Wen-tau Yih, Xiaodong He, Jianfeng Gao, and Li Deng. 2015. Embedding entities and relations for learning and inference in knowledge bases. In *3rd International Conference on Learning Representations, ICLR 2015, San Diego, CA, USA, May 7-9, 2015, Conference Track Proceedings*.

Zhaocheng Zhu, Zuobai Zhang, Louis-Pascal Xhonneux, and Jian Tang. 2021. Neural bellman-ford networks: A general graph neural network framework for link prediction. *Advances in Neural Information Processing Systems*, 34.

A Experimental Setup and Hyperparameters

The experiments of our work are conducted on a *SLURM* computing cluster. The virtual environments are initiated over a Unix-based system running *Ubuntu* 18.04.5 (Bionic Beaver) with kernel version 5.4.0-80-generic. Each job uses a single RTX3090 GPU (Ampere) with 24GB of shared memory and 8 CPUs. All experiments are built using the machine learning framework *PyTorch* at version 1.9.0 and NVIDIA's graphics programming interface *CUDA* with toolkit version 11.1.

In addition, we performed HPT using Optuna's hyper-parameter optimization framework. We configured the tuner to perform combined (relative/independent) sampling and used a median pruner with a warm-up threshold of 10% and set startup trials to 10. Further, we activated early stopping and set a maximum timeout of 24h. For fine-tuning, we set learning rate $\in \{0.1, 0.01, 0.001, 0.0001\}$, decay rate $\in \{0.1, 0.01, 0.001, 0.0001\}$, batch size $\in \{128, 256, 512, 1024\}$ and label smoothing $\in \{0.1, 0.01, 0.001\}$. We selected the best parameters for the final experiments and set the batch size to 1024.

B ChronoKGE Framework

CHRONOKGE is a unified graph embedding framework for the development of time-aware knowledge graph completion models. It is implemented in Python and builds upon PyTorch's (Paszke et al., 2019). Our framework focuses on time-sensitive representation learning tasks for temporal and event knowledge graphs and offers an easy-to-use and flexible library with various time-focused functionalities, including time-specific sampling and encoding routines.

CHRONOKGE supports multiple temporal knowledge graphs with diverse graph schemas and offers a dynamic interface for adding new knowledge graphs. Similarly, our framework provides an easy interface to add new or extend existing learning models. Therefore, several generic embedding models are already available within the `model.kge` package, which extend PyTorch's default `nn.Module` by integrating commonly required methods in knowledge representation learning. In addition, it provides a customizable and flexible package for defining experimental jobs as well as additional modules for training. To support hyper-parameter optimization, we integrated a parameter tuning system which is based on the *Optuna*[3] framework. The tuning system is part of the integrated `chrono_kge.tuner` package and allows for an automatic search of optimal hyper-parameters.

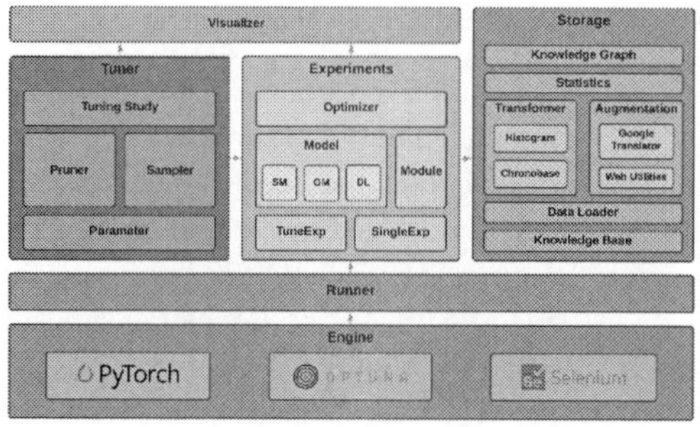

Figure 7: Overview of the ChronoKGE framework.

C Limitations

In its current form, our proposed methods can overfit since they lack commonly used regularization schemes, such as time-smoothness and nuclear 3-norm (Lacroix et al., 2020; Shao et al., 2021). However, extending our work with regularization schemes is straightforward. In terms of the design choices, LowFER-CFB offers a more expressive representation. However, it is computationally more expensive (7.85 sec/epoch for LowFER-CFB compared to 4.19 sec/epoch for LowFER-TNT on ICEWS-14) and MRCA, despite offering a generalized time representation, has limited performance gains and further adds a computational footprint (2.19 additional seconds per epoch on ICEWS-14 for LowFER-TNT).

[3] https://optuna.org

ANNA: Enhanced Language Representation for Question Answering

Changwook Jun, Hansol Jang, Myoseop Sim, Hyun Kim, Jooyoung Choi,
Kyungkoo Min and **Kyunghoon Bae**
LG AI Research
{cwjun, hansol.jang, myoseop.sim, hyun101.kim, jooyoung.choi, mingk24, k.bae}@lgresearch.ai

Abstract

Pre-trained language models have brought significant improvements in performance in a variety of natural language processing tasks. Most existing models performing state-of-the-art results have shown their approaches in the separate perspectives of data processing, pre-training tasks, neural network modeling, or fine-tuning. In this paper, we demonstrate how the approaches affect performance individually, and that the language model performs the best results on a specific question answering task when those approaches are jointly considered in pre-training models. In particular, we propose an extended pre-training task, and a new neighbor-aware mechanism that attends neighboring tokens more to capture the richness of context for pre-training language modeling. Our best model achieves new state-of-the-art results of 95.7% F1 and 90.6% EM on SQuAD 1.1 and also outperforms existing pre-trained language models such as RoBERTa, ALBERT, ELECTRA, and XLNet on the SQuAD 2.0 benchmark.

PASSAGE Architecturally, the school has a Catholic character. Atop the Main Building's gold dome is a golden statue of the Virgin Mary. Immediately in front of the Main Building and facing it, is a copper statue of Christ with arms upraised with the legend "Venite Ad Me Omnes". Next to the Main Building is the Basilica of the Sacred Heart. Immediately behind the basilica is the Grotto, a Marian place of prayer and reflection. It is a replica of the grotto at Lourdes, France where the Virgin Mary reputedly appeared to Saint Bernadette Soubirous in 1858. At the end of the main drive (and in a direct line that connects through 3 statues and the Gold Dome), is a simple, modern stone statue of Mary."

QUESTION: What sits on top of the Main Building at Notre Dame?

ANSWER: a golden statue of the Virgin Mary

Figure 1: Example of a passage with a pair of question and answer sampled from the SQuAD 1.1 dataset.

1 Introduction

Question answering (QA) is the task of answering given questions, which demands a high level of language understanding and machine reading comprehension abilities. As pre-trained language models based on a transformer encoder (Vaswani et al., 2017) have brought a huge improvement in performance on a broad range of natural language processing (NLP) tasks including QA tasks, methodologies for QA tasks are widely used to develop applications such as dialog systems (Bansal et al., 2021) and chat-bots (Hemant et al., 2022; Duggirala et al., 2021) in a variety of domains.

Pre-trained language models like BERT (Devlin et al., 2018) are designed to represent individual words for contextualization. However, recent extractive QA tasks such as Stanford Question Answering Dataset (SQuAD) benchmarks (Rajpurkar et al., 2016, 2018) involve reasoning relationships between spans of texts that include a group of two or more words in the evidence document (Lee et al., 2016). In the example, as shown in Figure 1, "a golden statue of the Virgin Mar", the correct answer for the question "What sits on top of the Main Building at Notre Dame?", is a group of words consisting of nouns and other words and is called as a noun phrase, which performs as a noun in a sentence. Since predicting a span of answer texts including a start and end positions may be challenging for self-supervised training rather than predicting an individual word, we introduce a novel pre-training approach that extends a standard masking scheme to wider spans of texts such as a noun-phrase rather than an entity level and prove that this approach is more effective for an extractive QA task by outperforming existing models.

In this paper, we present a new pre-training approach, **ANNA** (**A**pproach of **N**oun-phrase based language representation with **N**eighbor-aware **A**ttention), which is designed to better under-

Proceedings of the 7th Workshop on Representation Learning for NLP, pages 121 - 132
May 26, 2022 ©2022 Association for Computational Linguistics

stand syntactic and contextual information based on comprehensive experimental evaluation of data processing, pre-training tasks, attention mechanisms. First, we extend the conventional pre-training tasks. Our models are trained to predict not only individual tokens but also an entire span of noun phrases during the pre-training procedure. This noun-phrase span masking scheme lets models learn contextualized representations in the whole span level, which benefits predicting answer texts for the specific extractive QA tasks. Second, we enhance the self-attention approach by incorporating a novel neighbor-aware mechanism in the transformer architecture (Vaswani et al., 2017). We find that more consideration of relationships between neighboring tokens by masking diagonality in attention matrix is helpful for contextualized representations. Additionally, we use a larger volume of corpora for pre-training language models and find that using a lot of additional datasets does not guarantee the best performance.

We evaluate our proposed models on the SQuAD datasets which is a major extractive QA benchmarks for pre-trained language models. For SQuAD 1.1 task, ANNA achieves new state-of-the-art results of 90.6% Exact Match (EM) and 95.7% F1-score (F1). When evaluated on the SQuAD 2.0 development dataset, the results show that our proposed approaches obtain competitive performance outperforming self-supervised pre-training models such as BERT, ALBERT, RoBERTa, and XLNet models.

We summarize our main contributions as follows:

- We propose a new pre-trained language model, ANNA that is designed to address extractive QA tasks. ANNA is trained to predict the masked group of words that is an entire noun phrase, in order to better learn syntactic and contextual information by taking advantage of span-level representations.
- We introduce a novel transformer encoding mechanism stacking new neighbor-aware self-attention on an original self-attention in the transformer encoder block. The proposed method takes into account neighbor tokens more importantly than identical tokens during the computation of attention scores.
- ANNA establishes new state-of-the-art results on the SQuAD 1.1 leaderboard and outperforms existing pre-trained language models for the SQuAD 2.0 dataset.

2 Related works

Pre-trained contextualized word representations There have been many recent efforts on pre-training language representation models aiming for capturing linguistic and contextual information, and the models have brought a significant improvement of performance in a variety of NLP tasks. ELMo (Peters et al., 2018) is a deep contextualized word representation to learn complex characteristics of word use across linguistic contexts, and pre-trained models with these representations have shown noticeable improvements in many NLP challenges. BERT (Devlin et al., 2018) is a pre-trained language model with a deep bidirectional long short-term memory, which learns context in text using the masked language modeling (MLM) and the next sentence prediction (NSP) objectives for self-supervised pre-training. The latest language models (Liu et al., 2019; Lan et al., 2019; Yang et al., 2019b; Radford et al., 2018; Raffel et al., 2019a; Lewis et al., 2019) influenced by BERT mainly employ the transformer architecture (Vaswani et al., 2017) for pre-training but are trained with similar or extended to the pre-training objectives used in BERT implementation for enhancement of performance. There also exist many attempts to improve the capabilities of the standard transformer mechanism in contextualized word representations.

Extension of MLM Many recent studies have attempted to use different pre-training objectives by extending the MLM task in language modeling including BART (Lewis et al., 2019) and T5 (Raffel et al., 2019b). ELECTRA (Clark et al., 2020) introduces a new pre-training method of replaced token detection that replaces input tokens with alternative samples and detects whether the tokens are replaced or not. MASS (Song et al., 2019) is pre-trained on the sequence to sequence framework where fragments of input sentences are masked, and the masked fragment is predicted in its decoder part. XLNet (Yang et al., 2019b) adopts a span-based masking approach that predicts a masked subsequent span of tokens in a context of tokens autoregressively. SpanBERT (Joshi et al., 2020) and REALM (Guu et al., 2020) employ a span masking scheme that masks spans of tokens rather than random individual tokens, and the model is designed to learn span representations during pre-training. Similarly, LUKE (Yamada et al., 2020), ERNIE (Zhang et al., 2019), and KnowBERT (Peters et al., 2019) learn joint representations of words and entities by incorporating knowledge of entity embeddings.

Improvement of Attention Mechanism Since the standard transformer architecture has flexibility, many studies have shown the implementation of Transformer-based variants for improving further performance on language modeling and NLP tasks such as machine translation. (Shaw et al., 2018) extends self-attention mechanism by incorporating embeddings of relative positions or distances between sequence elements, which is beneficial for performance improvement in machine translation tasks. (Yang et al., 2019a) introduces a context-aware self-attention approach that improves the self-attention with additional contextual information. (Sukhbaatar et al., 2019) presents a novel attention method extending the self-attention layer with persistent vectors storing information which plays a similar role as the feed-forward layer. (Fan et al., 2021) proposes a mask attention network that is a sequential layered structure incorporated a new dynamic mask attention layer with the self-attention and feed-forward networks.

3 Methodology

We introduce a novel transformer encoder architecture integrating a new neighbor-aware mechanism for pre-training a language model. Figure 2 demonstrates the architecture of ANNA model. ANNA extends the original transformer encoder blocks by including a neighbor-aware self-attention layer stacked on a multi-head self-attention layer.

3.1 Neighbor-aware Self-Attention

In this study, we propose a neighbor-aware attention mechanism. In an attention matrix, there is a pattern of diagonal line that illustrates a token more attends to itself, but less influences to other tokens. To give more attention to related tokens, we implement a new neighbor-aware attention mechanism that is designed to mitigate influences of identical tokens by ignoring the diagonality in an attention matrix when attention scores are computed. Instead, other tokens are more attended, so that the neighbor-aware mechanism enhances better understanding for relationships between tokens in inputs. Here, we integrate a neighbor-aware self-attention layer between the self-attention and the feed-forward network. The original attention information of a token, passed through the self-attention and the residual connection, is passed through the neighbor-aware self-attention again, so the token can more reflect a context to understand the sentence.

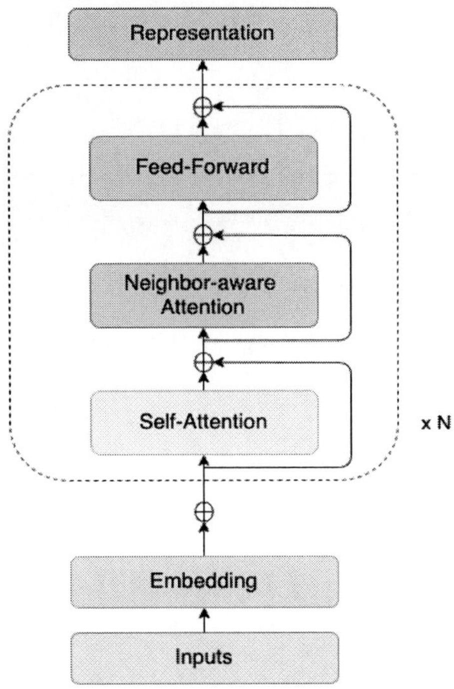

Figure 2: Architecture of ANNA.

As the self-attention layer shown in Figure 2 is adopted from the standard transformer architecture (Vaswani et al., 2017), we denote the self-attention as A_S that is calculated using query (Q), key (K) and value (V) projections as follows:

$$A_S(Q, K, V) = S_S(Q, K)V \tag{1}$$

$$S_S(Q, K) = \left[\frac{exp(Q_i K_j^T / \sqrt{d_k})}{\sum_k exp(Q_i K_k^T / \sqrt{d_k})} \right] \tag{2}$$

where Q, K and V represent HW_q, HW_k and HW_v, respectively. $H \in R^{L \times d}$ denoted as the input hidden vectors, L is the length of the input sequence, and d is the hidden size. $W_q, W_k, W_v \in R^{d \times d}$ are the projection matrices, and d_k is the query/key dimension. $A_S, A_N \in R^{L \times L}$ represents the attention matrices.

We define the Neighbor-aware Attention layer presented with A_N as follows:

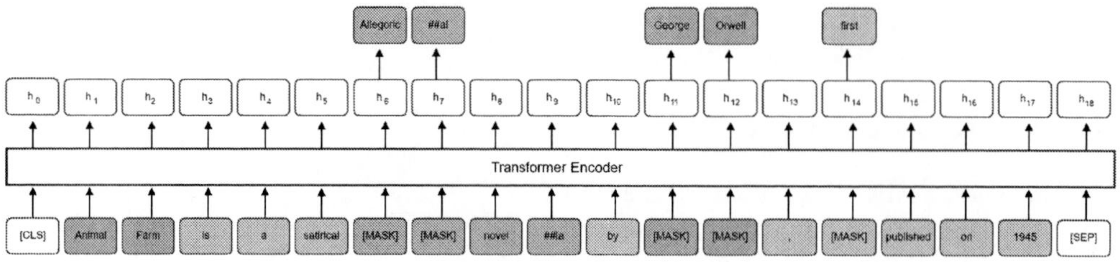

Figure 3: Example of the input sequence "*Animal Farm is a satirical allegorical novella by George Orwell, first published on 1945*" for pre-training ANNA. Different types of masking schemes are illustrated with such colors: masking a noun or noun phrase span (Orange), a whole word masking (Blue), and a wordpiece token masking (Green).

$$A_N(Q, K, V) = S_N(Q, K)V$$

$$S_N(Q, K) = \frac{M(i, j)exp(Q_i K_j^T / \sqrt{d_k})}{\sum_k M(i, j)exp(Q_i K_k^T / \sqrt{d_k})}$$

$$M(i, j) = \begin{cases} 0, & \text{if i = j} \\ 1, & \text{others} \end{cases}$$

where M denotes a mask that functions to omit capturing interactions of identical tokens. The interactions between each pair of input tokens x_i and x_j at positions *i* and *j* for $0 \leq i, j \leq L$ are calculated except for $i = j$.

3.2 Pre-training Task

We present a new pre-training task for training ANNA model. We follow the conventional MLM pre-training objective similar to BERT (Devlin et al., 2018). BERT is more sensible and effective to deeply represent context fusing the left and the right text with the MLM objective rather than unidirectional language models (Radford et al., 2018, 2019; Brown et al., 2020) or shallow Bi-LSTM models (Clark et al., 2018; Huang et al., 2015). In addition, a new masking scheme is applied for focusing on noun phrases in order to train our language model for better understanding syntactic and lexical information considering the specific downstream tasks. Here, we define three different masking schemes as illustrated in Figure 3. First, we use a span masking scheme that masks a group of texts in a span-level adopted by SpanBERT (Joshi et al., 2020). In this study, nouns or noun phrases identified by spaCy's parser (Honnibal and Montani, 2017) are randomly masked for span masking selection. Then we apply a whole word masking approach that masks all of the sub-tokens correspondings to a word at once, while we randomly mask tokens not included in the above two cases.

Following BERT, we randomly select 15% of the tokens in input sequences, and 80% of the selected tokens are replaced with the special token [MASK]. We keep 10% of the tokens in the rest of them unchanged, and the other 10% are replaced with randomly selected tokens. Our language model is also designed to train for the prediction of each token in the masked span by computing the cross-entropy loss function. However, the next sentence prediction (NSP) objective used in the BERT implementation is not used in this study, as RoBERTa (Liu et al., 2019) removes the NSP task due to performance decreases on downstream tasks.

3.3 Vocabulary and Tokenizer

In this study, we build a new vocabulary of 127,490 wordpieces that are extracted from the English Common Crawl corpus (Raffel et al., 2019a) and English Wikipedia dump datasets. The vocabulary consists of sub-words (30%) tokenized by the WordPiece algorithm (Wu et al., 2016), and 70% of the rest include noun-phrase words in their original form. We aim to prevent words from being out of vocabulary words and also keep noun phrases as the original forms so that our model is able to take many words in order to better learn human linguistic understanding during training.

In addition, we propose a new approach of word tokenization to suit our vocabulary used to pre-train ANNA model. This approach avoids separating words by special symbols since our vocabulary contains words including special characters by tokenizing noun-phrase words with white space only. Many studies use a subword-based word representation method for efficiency in vocabulary. A

Words	BERT tokens	ANNA tokens
Sant'Egidio	Sant , ' , E , ##gi , ##dio	Sant'Egidio
COVID-19	CO , ##VI , ##D , - , '19'	COVID-19
U.S.	U , . , S , .	U.S.
Ph.D.	Ph , . , D , .	Ph.D.
l'amour	l , ' , am , ##our	l'amour
non-profit	non , - , profit	non-profit
X-Files	X , - , Files	X-Files
UTF-16	U , ##TF , - , 16	UTF-16
C++	C , + , +	C++

Table 1: Comparison of tokenization results between BERT and ANNA.

word is represented with several subword units tokenized by BERT tokenizer as exampled in Table 1. However, we do not follow this conventional tokenization method (Wu et al., 2016), since we use a span masking scheme that masks an entire noun phrase randomly selected during a pre-training procedure. It is not suitable to train models as the length of masking tokens gets longer if subword units are used for the span masking scheme. We also aim to represent a whole-word token rather than subword units when attention scores are calculated. We implement an ANNA tokenizer in order to enhance a better understanding of contexts by not separating words as much as possible. Table 1 compares word tokenization results between BERT and ANNA tokenizers.

3.4 Pre-training Datasets

We use an English Wikipedia dataset like BERT (Devlin et al., 2018), and add publicly available English-language corpora such as a Colossal-Cleaned version of Common Crawl (C4) corpus (Raffel et al., 2019a), Books3 (Gao et al., 2020), and OpenWebText2 (OWT2) extended from WebText (Radford et al., 2019) and OpenWebTextCorpus (Gokaslan and Cohen) for pre-training our models. Details of datasets and pre-processing techniques are described in Appendix B.

With the extensive data pre-processing procedure, we gain the size of 12GB, 580GB, 51GB, and 22GB for Wikipedia, C4, Books3, and OWT2, respectively. The pre-processed texts are tokenized into 410B word-piece tokens in total for pre-training our models.

In this study, we conduct an experiment in order to investigate whether the use of different sources of data for pre-training language models affects model performance on downstream tasks. We compare the performance of models pre-trained with different datasets in Table 2. We observe that C4 improves performance on the SQuAD 1.1 task when it is added to the Wikipedia dataset, but that models pre-trained over Books3 and OWT2 datasets are not beneficial for performance increases. We also find that the use of the larger volume of data including all of these four corpora is not helpful to improve performance. Thus we use both the C4 data and the Wikipedia corpus for pre-training ANNA models. Pre-training details for ANNA models can be found in Appendix A.

Corpora	EM	F1
Wikipedia	85.51	90.99
Wikipedia + C4	**85.90**	**91.02**
Wikipedia + Books3	85.40	90.79
Wikipedia + OWT2	84.79	90.27
ALL	85.14	90.22

Table 2: Comparison of model performance pre-trained with the different data sources. Models pre-trained with different pre-training corpora are evaluated on the SQuAD1.1 dataset. ALL includes the four datasets of Wikipedia, C4, Books3, and OWT2. Due to the limitation of computing resources, $\text{ANNA}_{\text{Base}}$ model is used for this experiment.

4 Experiments

In this section, we present the fine-tuning results of ANNA transferred to specific extractive question answering tasks.

We evaluate ANNA on SQuAD 1.1 and 2.0 tasks that are well-known machine reading comprehension benchmarks in the NLP area, and some NLU tasks. The dataset of SQuAD 1.1 consists of around 100k pairs of a question and an answer along with Wikipedia passages where the answers are included. This task is to predict a correct span of an answer text for a given question from the corresponding Wikipedia passage (Rajpurkar et al., 2016). For SQuAD 2.0, the dataset is extended to the SQuAD 1.1 dataset by combining over 50,000 unanswerable questions, so that systems are required to predict answers to both answerable and unanswerable questions (Rajpurkar et al., 2018). We follow the fine-tuning procedure of BERT (Devlin et al., 2018), but the provided SQuAD training dataset only is used for fine-tuning, while BERT augments its training dataset with other QA datasets available in public.

SQuAD 1.1 Table 3 indicates the results of our best performing system compared with top results on the SQuAD 1.1 leaderboard. We also compare ours with BERT baselines. ANNA establishes a new state-of-the-art result on this task outperforming LUKE (Yamada et al., 2020) by EM 0.4 points and F1 0.3 points on the test dataset. LUKE is the latest best performing system in the leaderboard, and it is designed for contextualized representations of words and entities. As for a comparison with SpanBERT (Joshi et al., 2020) that masks contiguous sequences of token for span representations, ANNA also achieves better performance by both EM 1.8 points and F1 1.1 points.

SQuAD 2.0 ANNA is evaluated on SQuAD 2.0 development dataset, and the results are compared with the published pre-trained language models (Devlin et al., 2018; Liu et al., 2019; Lan et al., 2019; Yang et al., 2019b; Clark et al., 2020) in Table 4, which demonstrates that ANNA outperforms all of those language models and in particular, produces performance increases than ELECTRA by 0.4 points of EM and 0.2 points of F1.

GLUE The General Language Understanding Evaluation (GLUE) benchmark is a collection of datasets used for training and evaluation diverse natural language understanding tasks (Wang et al., 2018). Since fine-tuning on GLUE is currently in progress, we show the results of the tasks that we complete in Appendix A.

5 Model Analysis

We conduct additional experiments in terms of perspectives such as data processing, pre-training task, and attention mechanisms. We report a detailed analysis of how those approaches affect the performance of ANNA on a specific downstream task individually. In this study, $\text{ANNA}_{\text{Base}}$ model is used for these additional experiments due to the limitation of computing resources.

5.1 Effect of ANNA Tokenization

As mentioned in Section 3.3, we build a new vocabulary containing noun-phrase words in their original format. For this, we introduce a new word tokenization strategy that keeps words in the original formats for noun phrases, which suits for our vocabulary. We compare our tokenization approach with the standard word-piece split approach, and find that ANNA tokenization performs better as shown in table 5.

5.2 Effect of Data Processing

We describe several data pre-processing techniques we conduct to build a high-quality dataset for pre-training ANNA in Section 3.4. Here we demonstrate how the use of the data processing techniques affects the performance on the extractive question answering task. There exist documents with a variety of ranges of word length in the pre-training corpora. For a generation of an input sequence, documents containing less than 100 words are filtered out, while the others are split into multiple sentence chunks. Due to the maximum sequence length of 512, we limit the size of the chunks to not exceeding approximately 300 words. We observe that the data processing procedure making a suitable word length for the max sequence length is helpful to improve performance slightly as shown in Table 6. However, the input sequences overlapped with 128 tokens at the back and front between successive sentence chunks rather hurt system performance.

5.3 Effect of Pre-training Mechanism

We investigate how different MLM objectives affect the performance of models on a specific downstream task. During a pre-training procedure, a model is trained with a deep bidirectional representation of input sequences. First, we concatenate part-of-speech (POS) tags to each word, then we apply a whole word masking approach to explore whether a masking method employing syntactic information is helpful to understand the context. We also mask tokens identified as named entities and noun phrases instead of masking single tokens randomly. In all of the experiments, we use the same percentage of 15% for the masking tasks. Table 7 compares results on the SQuAD 1.1 task for models using those MLM schemes. Comparing with the standard MLM approach that simply masks

System	Dev EM	Dev F1	Test EM	Test F1
$\text{BERT}_{\text{Large}}$ (Devlin et al., 2018)	84.2	91.1	85.1	91.8
$\text{BERT}_{\text{Large}}$ (ensemble)	-	-	87.4	93.1
SpanBERT (Joshi et al., 2020)	-	-	88.8	94.6
$\text{XLNet}_{\text{Large}}$ (Yang et al., 2019b)	89.0	94.5	89.9	95.1
LUKE (Yamada et al., 2020)	89.8	95.0	90.2	95.4
$\text{ANNA}_{\text{Base}}$	87.0	92.8	-	-
$\text{ANNA}_{\text{Large}}$	**90.0**	**95.4**	**90.6**	**95.7**

Table 3: Performance of systems evaluated on the SQuAD 1.1 datasets.

System	SQuAD 2.0 Dev EM	SQuAD 2.0 Dev F1
$\text{BERT}_{\text{Large}}$ (Devlin et al., 2018)	79.0	81.8
$\text{ALBERT}_{\text{Large}}$ (Lan et al., 2019)	85.1	88.1
RoBERTa (Liu et al., 2019)	86.5	89.4
$\text{XLNet}_{\text{Large}}$ (Yang et al., 2019b)	87.9	90.6
$\text{ELECTRA}_{\text{Large}}$ (Clark et al., 2020)	88.0	90.6
$\text{ANNA}_{\text{Large}}$	**88.4**	**90.8**

Table 4: Performance of systems evaluated on the SQuAD 2.0 development dataset.

	SQuAD1.1 Dev EM	SQuAD1.1 Dev F1
WordPiece tokenizer	85.3	90.8
ANNA tokenizer	**86.3**	**91.2**

Table 5: Ablation study of our tokenizer comparing to BERT tokenizer

15% of tokens, the pre-trained models using Entity and Noun-phrase MLM schemes improve performance, but the approach masking words including POS tags decreases performance than the standard MLM. Thus we use the Noun-phrase MLM approach to pre-train ANNA models for final results.

5.4 Effect of Neighbor-aware Self-Attention

We attempt to implement a new transformer encoder focusing on relatives, entities, or neighbors in input tokens in order to enhance capturing syntactic and contextual information. Firstly, we extend the original self-attention based on the transformer in order to consider relationships between input tokens. The relation matrix of input tokens is simply added when attention scores are computed. For an entity-self-attention that focuses on named entities, we identify named entities in text and then compute additional attention scores to those entities for learning effective representations. We describe the mechanism of a neighbor-aware self-attention in detail in Section 3.1. We report that the neighbor-aware self-attention approach performs better than the original self-attention and other transformer modifications on the extractive question-answering task in Table 8. We consider that the neighbor-aware mechanism is effective to capture relation information of neighboring tokens in an input sequence.

5.5 Effect of Layer-stacking Approach

We examine how approaches to stack sub-layers in a transformer encoder architecture impact performance. We compose a transformer encoder block by collaborating three sub-layers such as a self-attention, a neighbor-aware self-attention, and a feed-forward network in different combinations. We evaluate the models using different combination methods of stacking layers and report the results on the SQuAD 1.1 dataset in Table 9.

We observe that a self-attention substituted with a neighbor-aware attention in an original transformer architecture decreases performance by F1 0.5 points. When a neighbor-aware attention is stacked between a self-attention and a feed-forward network, the model slightly performs better than the original transformer. The sequential layered structure of a self-attention, a neighbor-aware attention, and a feed-forward network achieve the best performance on the exact matching criteria,

Data Processing	SQuAD1.1 Dev EM	SQuAD1.1 Dev F1
Wiki+C4 (Without sentence chunking)	85.9	91.0
Wiki+C4 (Sentence chunking with 128 token-overlap)	85.0	90.5
Wiki+C4 (Sentence chunking)	**86.3**	**91.2**

Table 6: Comparison of model performance pre-trained with the use of different data processing techniques.

Model	SQuAD1.1 Dev EM	SQuAD1.1 Dev F1
Standard MLM	83.7	89.1
w/POS	80.7	87.1
Entity	85.3	90.8
Noun phrase	**86.3**	**91.2**

Table 7: Results of different masking schemes during the pre-training task.

Model	SQuAD1.1 Dev EM	SQuAD1.1 Dev F1
Self-Att.	85.9	91.1
Relative-QK-Att.	86.0	91.1
Relative-QV-Att.	85.2	90.7
Entity-Self-Att.	85.7	90.9
Neighbor-Aware-Att.	**86.4**	**91.4**

Table 8: Comparison of model performance pre-trained with different transformer variants. Att is an abbreviation for Attention. The Self-Att. scores are the mean of multiple runs.

which demonstrates that our proposed approach has an effect on the extractive question answering task. We consider that attention scores computed in a self-attention layer are re-weighted to actually related tokens by ignoring identical tokens during the computation of attention scores in the neighbor-aware attention so that the neighbor-aware mechanism is helpful to capture relationships between input tokens.

6 Conclusion

In this paper, we present a novel pre-trained language representation model, ANNA which improves the original transformer encoder architecture by collaborating a neighbor-aware mechanism, and is pre-trained for contextualized representations of words and noun phrases in a span level. The experimental results show that ANNA achieves a new state-of-the-art on the specific extractive question answering task by outperforming published language model systems including BERT baselines, as well as the latest top system on the corresponding leaderboard. There are two main directions for future research: (1) validating the competitiveness of ANNA to a variety of NLP tasks; and (2) enhancing the robustness of ANNA in order to apply for real-world question answering tasks in business.

Model	SQuAD1.1 Dev EM	SQuAD1.1 Dev F1
SA → FFN	85.9	91.1
NAA → FFN	85.5	90.6
SA → SA → FFN	85.5	91.0
NAA → NAA → FFN	86.1	91.5
NAA → SA → FFN	86.1	91.4
SA → NAA → FFN	**86.4**	**91.4**

Table 9: Performance of different stacking approaches of Self-attention (SA), Neighbor-aware-attention (NAA) and Feed-forward-network (FNN) layers in transformer encoder blocks. The SA-FNN scores are the mean of multiple runs.

References

Aakash Bansal, Zachary Eberhart, Lingfei Wu, and Collin McMillan. 2021. A neural question answering system for basic questions about subroutines. In *2021 IEEE International Conference on Software Analysis, Evolution and Reengineering (SANER)*, pages 60–71. IEEE.

Tom B Brown, Benjamin Mann, Nick Ryder, Melanie Subbiah, Jared Kaplan, Prafulla Dhariwal, Arvind Neelakantan, Pranav Shyam, Girish Sastry, Amanda Askell, et al. 2020. Language models are few-shot learners. *arXiv preprint arXiv:2005.14165*.

Kevin Clark, Minh-Thang Luong, Quoc V Le, and Christopher D Manning. 2020. Electra: Pre-training text encoders as discriminators rather than generators. *arXiv preprint arXiv:2003.10555*.

Kevin Clark, Minh-Thang Luong, Christopher D Manning, and Quoc V Le. 2018. Semi-supervised sequence modeling with cross-view training. *arXiv preprint arXiv:1809.08370*.

Jacob Devlin, Ming-Wei Chang, Kenton Lee, and Kristina Toutanova. 2018. Bert: Pre-training of deep bidirectional transformers for language understanding. *arXiv preprint arXiv:1810.04805*.

Vishnu Dutt Duggirala, Rhys Sean Butler, and Farnoush Banaei Kashani. 2021. ita: A digital teaching assistant. In *CSEDU (2)*, pages 274–281.

Zhihao Fan, Yeyun Gong, Dayiheng Liu, Zhongyu Wei, Siyuan Wang, Jian Jiao, Nan Duan, Ruofei Zhang, and Xuanjing Huang. 2021. Mask attention networks: Rethinking and strengthen transformer. *arXiv preprint arXiv:2103.13597*.

Leo Gao, Stella Biderman, Sid Black, Laurence Golding, Travis Hoppe, Charles Foster, Jason Phang, Horace He, Anish Thite, Noa Nabeshima, et al. 2020. The pile: An 800gb dataset of diverse text for language modeling. *arXiv preprint arXiv:2101.00027*.

Aaron Gokaslan and Vanya Cohen. Openwebtext corpus.

Kelvin Guu, Kenton Lee, Zora Tung, Panupong Pasupat, and Ming-Wei Chang. 2020. Realm: Retrieval-augmented language model pre-training. *arXiv preprint arXiv:2002.08909*.

P Hemant, Pramod Kumar, and CR Nirmala. 2022. Effect of loss functions on language models in question answering-based generative chat-bots. In *Machine Learning, Advances in Computing, Renewable Energy and Communication*, pages 271–279. Springer.

Matthew Honnibal and Ines Montani. 2017. spaCy 2: Natural language understanding with Bloom embeddings, convolutional neural networks and incremental parsing. To appear.

Zhiheng Huang, Wei Xu, and Kai Yu. 2015. Bidirectional lstm-crf models for sequence tagging. *arXiv preprint arXiv:1508.01991*.

Mandar Joshi, Danqi Chen, Yinhan Liu, Daniel S Weld, Luke Zettlemoyer, and Omer Levy. 2020. Spanbert: Improving pre-training by representing and predicting spans. *Transactions of the Association for Computational Linguistics*, 8:64–77.

Diederik P Kingma and Jimmy Ba. 2014. Adam: A method for stochastic optimization. *arXiv preprint arXiv:1412.6980*.

Zhenzhong Lan, Mingda Chen, Sebastian Goodman, Kevin Gimpel, Piyush Sharma, and Radu Soricut. 2019. Albert: A lite bert for self-supervised learning of language representations. *arXiv preprint arXiv:1909.11942*.

Kenton Lee, Shimi Salant, Tom Kwiatkowski, Ankur Parikh, Dipanjan Das, and Jonathan Berant. 2016. Learning recurrent span representations for extractive question answering. *arXiv preprint arXiv:1611.01436*.

Mike Lewis, Yinhan Liu, Naman Goyal, Marjan Ghazvininejad, Abdelrahman Mohamed, Omer Levy, Ves Stoyanov, and Luke Zettlemoyer. 2019. Bart: Denoising sequence-to-sequence pre-training for natural language generation, translation, and comprehension. *arXiv preprint arXiv:1910.13461*.

Yinhan Liu, Myle Ott, Naman Goyal, Jingfei Du, Mandar Joshi, Danqi Chen, Omer Levy, Mike Lewis, Luke Zettlemoyer, and Veselin Stoyanov. 2019. Roberta: A robustly optimized bert pretraining approach. *arXiv preprint arXiv:1907.11692*.

Matthew E Peters, Mark Neumann, Mohit Iyyer, Matt Gardner, Christopher Clark, Kenton Lee, and Luke Zettlemoyer. 2018. Deep contextualized word representations. *arXiv preprint arXiv:1802.05365*.

Matthew E Peters, Mark Neumann, Robert L Logan IV, Roy Schwartz, Vidur Joshi, Sameer Singh, and Noah A Smith. 2019. Knowledge enhanced contextual word representations. *arXiv preprint arXiv:1909.04164*.

Alec Radford, Karthik Narasimhan, Tim Salimans, and Ilya Sutskever. 2018. Improving language understanding by generative pre-training.

Alec Radford, Jeffrey Wu, Rewon Child, David Luan, Dario Amodei, Ilya Sutskever, et al. 2019. Language models are unsupervised multitask learners. *OpenAI blog*, 1(8):9.

Colin Raffel, Noam Shazeer, Adam Roberts, Katherine Lee, Sharan Narang, Michael Matena, Yanqi Zhou, Wei Li, and Peter J. Liu. 2019a. Exploring the limits of transfer learning with a unified text-to-text transformer. *arXiv e-prints*.

Colin Raffel, Noam Shazeer, Adam Roberts, Katherine Lee, Sharan Narang, Michael Matena, Yanqi Zhou, Wei Li, and Peter J Liu. 2019b. Exploring the limits of transfer learning with a unified text-to-text transformer. *arXiv preprint arXiv:1910.10683*.

Pranav Rajpurkar, Robin Jia, and Percy Liang. 2018. Know what you don't know: Unanswerable questions for squad. *arXiv preprint arXiv:1806.03822*.

Pranav Rajpurkar, Jian Zhang, Konstantin Lopyrev, and Percy Liang. 2016. Squad: 100,000+ questions for machine comprehension of text. *arXiv preprint arXiv:1606.05250*.

Peter Shaw, Jakob Uszkoreit, and Ashish Vaswani. 2018. Self-attention with relative position representations. *arXiv preprint arXiv:1803.02155*.

Nakatani Shuyo. 2010. Language detection library for java. *Retrieved Jul*, 7:2016.

Kaitao Song, Xu Tan, Tao Qin, Jianfeng Lu, and Tie-Yan Liu. 2019. Mass: Masked sequence to sequence pre-training for language generation. *arXiv preprint arXiv:1905.02450.*

Sainbayar Sukhbaatar, Edouard Grave, Guillaume Lample, Herve Jegou, and Armand Joulin. 2019. Augmenting self-attention with persistent memory. *arXiv preprint arXiv:1907.01470.*

Ashish Vaswani, Noam Shazeer, Niki Parmar, Jakob Uszkoreit, Llion Jones, Aidan N Gomez, Łukasz Kaiser, and Illia Polosukhin. 2017. Attention is all you need. *Advances in neural information processing systems*, 30.

Alex Wang, Amanpreet Singh, Julian Michael, Felix Hill, Omer Levy, and Samuel R Bowman. 2018. Glue: A multi-task benchmark and analysis platform for natural language understanding. *arXiv preprint arXiv:1804.07461.*

Yonghui Wu, Mike Schuster, Zhifeng Chen, Quoc V Le, Mohammad Norouzi, Wolfgang Macherey, Maxim Krikun, Yuan Cao, Qin Gao, Klaus Macherey, et al. 2016. Google's neural machine translation system: Bridging the gap between human and machine translation. *arXiv preprint arXiv:1609.08144.*

Ikuya Yamada, Akari Asai, Hiroyuki Shindo, Hideaki Takeda, and Yuji Matsumoto. 2020. Luke: deep contextualized entity representations with entity-aware self-attention. *arXiv preprint arXiv:2010.01057.*

Baosong Yang, Jian Li, Derek F Wong, Lidia S Chao, Xing Wang, and Zhaopeng Tu. 2019a. Context-aware self-attention networks. In *Proceedings of the AAAI Conference on Artificial Intelligence*, volume 33, pages 387–394.

Zhilin Yang, Zihang Dai, Yiming Yang, Jaime Carbonell, Russ R Salakhutdinov, and Quoc V Le. 2019b. Xlnet: Generalized autoregressive pretraining for language understanding. *Advances in neural information processing systems*, 32.

Zhengyan Zhang, Xu Han, Zhiyuan Liu, Xin Jiang, Maosong Sun, and Qun Liu. 2019. Ernie: Enhanced language representation with informative entities. *arXiv preprint arXiv:1905.07129.*

Appendices

A Performance on GLUE

At this stage, we have not submitted our results to the official GLUE leaderboard [1], since we currently work on fine-tuning for the GLUE benchmark. Instead, we report our results on the tasks that we have completed the evaluation so far as shown in Table 10. We compare performance with two baseline models, BERT and SpanBERT, as the former is a pre-trained language model using a standard encoder architecture, and the later is pre-trained to predicts spans of texts, and motivated our noun-phrase masking approach. Comparing to the baselines, ANNA outperforms those baselines on every task, and gains the improvement of 1.7% accuracy over SpanBERT in average. For further improvement of performance on GLUE, we continue to work on fine-tuning.

B Pre-training Datasets and Pre-processing

In this study, we use several large corpora for pre-training language models. As shown in Table 11, the total size of data is about 900GB for the four corpora.

For pre-training language models with a large volume of corpora, it is crucial to generate high-quality data for inputs. We use heuristic pre-processing techniques to improve the data quality for the generation of input sequences as follows:

- Each document is split into sentences, and we filter the sentences including less than 10 words out due to their incompleteness. Also, documents with less than 100 words are ignored for input sequences.
- Text noises such as paragraph separators, special characters, URL addresses, and directory paths are heuristically filtered by regular expressions.
- For Books3 data, non-English documents are deleted by a language-detection module (Shuyo, 2010) which is utilized for the deletion of documents written in non-English words in the Common Crawl dataset.
- Since the maximum sequence length is 512 tokens, we split the pre-processed documents into multiple sentence chunks that do not exceed the predefined maximum length for the input of pre-training.

C Pre-training Details

Table 12 summarizes hyperparameters that we use for pre-training our two models: $\text{ANNA}_{\text{Base}}$ (L=12, H=768, A=12, Total Parameters=160M) and $\text{ANNA}_{\text{Large}}$ (L=24, H=1024, A=16, Total Parameters=550M). We use the maximum sequence length of 512, the Adam optimization (Kingma and Ba, 2014) with learning rates of 2e-4 and 1e-4 is used for the large and base models, respectively.

[1] https://gluebenchmark.com/leaderboard

	CoLA	SST-2	MRPC	STS-B	QQP	MNLI	QNLI	RTE	Avg.
$\text{BERT}_{\text{Large}}$	60.5	94.9	89.3/85.4	87.6/86.5	72.1/89.3	86.7/85.9	92.7	70.1	82.5
SpanBERT	64.3	94.8	90.9/87.9	89.9/89.1	71.9/89.5	88.1/87.7	94.3	79.0	85.0
RoBERTa	67.8	96.7	92.3/89.8	92.2/91.9	74.3/90.2	90.8/90.2	95.4	88.2	87.6
ANNA	**65.8**	**96.4**	**91.4/88.4**	**91.5/90.9**	**73.5/89.5**	**90.1/89.7**	**95.0**	**83.7**	**86.7**

Table 10: Comparison results on the GLUE development set. The "Avg." column is slightly different than the official GLUE scores, since the scores of WNLI and AX tasks are excluded in the average.

	Wikipedia	C4	*Books3*	*OWT2*
Size of text	16GB	730GB	100GB	62GB
Token counts for text	3.3B	160B	22B	13B
Size of pre-processed text	12GB	580GB	51GB	22GB
Token counts for pre-processed text	2.6B	126B	12B	5B

Table 11: Statistics of four corpora for pre-training including before and after the pre-processing procedure.

Our large model $\text{ANNA}_{\text{Large}}$ is trained on 256 TPU v3 for 1M steps with the batch size of 2048, and it takes about 10 days.

Hyper-parameter	$\text{ANNA}_{\text{Large}}$	$\text{ANNA}_{\text{Base}}$
Number of layers	24	12
Hidden size	1024	768
FFN inner hidden size	4096	3072
Attention heads	16	12
Attention head size	64	64
Dropout	0.1	0.1
Warmup steps	10k	10k
Learning rates	2e-4	1e-4
Batch size	2048	1024
Weight decay	0.01	0.01
Max steps	1M	1M
Learning rate decay	Linear	Linear
Adam ε	1e-6	1e-6
Adam β_1	0.9	0.9
Adam β_2	0.999	0.999
Number of TPU	266	64
Training time	10 days	5 days

Table 12: Hyperparameters for pre-training ANNA models.

Response to reviewers' comments

We would like to thank all reviewers for their comments, and address the comments in this page. R and A refer to reviewers' comments and their answers to the comments, respectively.

R1: Some parts of the Model Analysis lack insights on the experimental results: the impact of tokenization is still understandable, but many other experiments raise further questions: for instance, why does one layer stacking approach work better than the other? It will be much more impactful to understand the deeper details here.
A1: Some research on attention stacking such as (Mask Attention Networks: Rethinking and Strengthen Transformer) show that sequential attention layers stacked with an additional attention layer that used a different masking approach improve performance. Our experiments present that capturing the global semantics followed by capturing interactions with neighbors is beneficial for performance improvement.

R2: The authors do not say if they will release their code (in spite of providing the details on hyperparams etc.). This will hurt future works that try to replicate or improve on the results, especially since the work claims to achieve SOTA results.
A2: We are planning to release our source codes via GitHub. As we are a commercial company, however, it is taking a while since there are some processes to get approval for code release. We hope to release source codes of the ANNA model shortly.

R3: L67: Not the first paper to perform span masking (eg. SpanBERT).
A3: In line 67, the "First" means the order of what we are presenting in our paper, not meaning that this work is the first paper to perform span masking. To make it clear, we changed "First" with "Firstly".

R4: (Minor) The paper is sprinkled with writing errors and could use another round of proofreading and surface-level revision.
A4: Sorry for the writing errors. We tried to proofread thoroughly for revision.

R5: The claim "We assume that a single self-attention layer in Transformer encoder may be insufficient to learn context" is not very convincing. Why do you assume that, based on what? Do you have a proof of that assumption?
A5: We meant that there's something to supplement for the standard attention mechanism, and thus tried to implement the neighbor-aware attention. To avoid ambiguity, we deleted the sentence in revision.

R6: I am not sure why the proposed neighbor-aware attention is specifically good for QA. Why did you pick that task, and why was this particular improvement proposed for this task specifically? is there some intuition or something special about that?
A6: Our team is interested in the question-answering task. We found that many of the answers have long sequences including phrases illustrated in Figure 1, as well as short answers. Thus we hypothesized word span might be more beneficial for the QA task rather than a single word. For future work, we plan to upgrade our model and extend it to other tasks.

R7: The Self-Att. scores in Table 8 and SA-FNN scores in Table 9 are "the mean of multiple runs.". Why only these, why not all numbers in the table? Is this a fair comparison? How are the numbers in the other rows obtained?
A7: The difference between the experimental results in Tables 8 and 9 was not noticeable on the first try. Thus we tried multiple runs to get fair results.

R8: can you elaborate more in terms of the pre-training objectives, i.e., the noun-phrase prediction, e.g., an equation that can describe the overall loss function?
A8: At the last paragraph in Section 3.2, we describe how we train our pre-trained language model mentioning that 'Following BERT, ... Our language model is also designed to train for the prediction of each token in the masked span by computing the cross-entropy loss function.'

R9: on SQUAD 2.0, is the result SOTA?
A9: Not achieved the SOTA on SQuAD2.0 yet.

R10: have you evaluated on other downstream tasks except the QA?
A10: In Appendix A, Table 10 shows results on the GLUE benchmark.

Isomorphic Cross-lingual Embeddings for Low-Resource Languages

Sonal Sannigrahi[1,2] **Jesse Read**[2]
[1]Saarland University
[2]École Polytechnique
sosa00001@stud.uni-saarland.de jesse.read@polytechnique.edu

Abstract

Cross-Lingual Word Embeddings (CLWEs) are a key component to transfer linguistic information learnt from higher-resource settings into lower-resource ones. Recent research in cross-lingual representation learning has focused on offline mapping approaches due to their simplicity, computational efficacy, and ability to work with minimal parallel resources. However, they crucially depend on the assumption of embedding spaces being approximately isomorphic i.e. sharing similar geometric structure, which does not hold in practice, leading to poorer performance on low-resource and distant language pairs. In this paper, we introduce a framework to learn CLWEs, without assuming isometry, for low-resource pairs via joint exploitation of a related higher-resource language. In our work, we first pre-align the low-resource and related language embedding spaces using offline methods to mitigate the assumption of isometry. Following this, we use joint training methods to develops CLWEs for the related language and the target embedding space. Finally, we remap the pre-aligned low-resource space and the target space to generate the final CLWEs. We show consistent gains over current methods in both quality and degree of isomorphism, as measured by bilingual lexicon induction (BLI) and eigenvalue similarity respectively, across several language pairs: {Nepali, Finnish, Romanian, Gujarati, Hungarian}-English. Lastly, our analysis also points to the relatedness as well as the amount of related language data available as being key factors in determining the quality of embeddings achieved.

1 Introduction

In a world with over 7000 spoken languages, out of which nearly 43% are endangered, there is an acute need for accurate language technology systems that ensure equal access of resources in a predominantly digital world[1]. Early successes in neural natural language tasks were primarily data-driven and English focused (Belinkov and Glass, 2019), however as we move on to low-resource, multi-lingual scenarios it becomes imperative to develop meaningful representations.

Taking machine translation (MT) as an example, we have observed remarkable progress over the last few years propelled by advances in neural language modelling. This success has been mainly confined to major world languages (Hassan et al., 2018; Liu et al., 2020), however, a significant proportion of languages are endangered or otherwise have a very scarce amount of digital resources which presents serious challenges for training MT systems. Rather than traditional expert-guided feature engineering, neural MT (NMT), like deep neural architectures more generally, require notoriously large data sets from which to extract features automatically in the context of hidden layers; for example with recurrent (Cho et al., 2014; Schmidhuber and Hochreiter, 1997), and attention mechanisms (Bahdanau et al., 2014). It is for this reason that the most impressive results (e.g., (Liu et al., 2020; Barrault et al., 2019)) come from languages with large scale digital resources such as parallel corpora with which to train them. This is, however, not the case for most minority languages.

Current research in expanding natural language tools for low-resource settings has focused on transferring information from languages for which we have sufficient data to model correctly (Chen et al., 2019; Lample et al., 2018, 2017). In order to achieve this, cross-lingual word embeddings (CLWEs) are important which is what we focus on in this work. As CLWEs represent words from multiple languages in a shared vector space, they are key in promoting language sharing across low and high-resource languages. The two primary ap-

[1] http://www.unesco.org/languages-atlas/en/statistics.html

Proceedings of the 7th Workshop on Representation Learning for NLP, pages 133 - 142
May 26, 2022

proaches in learning CLWEs are: 1) *mapping methods* which independently map monolingual word embeddings by learning a linear transformation matrix to project them into another monolingual space with very little supervision i.e requiring a *weak cross-lingual signal* (Artetxe et al., 2018a; Mikolov et al., 2013) or 2) *joint methods* which jointly optimise monolingual as well as cross-lingual learning objectives using parallel corpora thus requiring a *strong cross-lingual signal.* (Gouws et al., 2016; Luong et al., 2015; Lample et al., 2018)

As mapping methods use transformation matrices to align embedding spaces they make the crucial assumption that, regardless of domain or linguistic differences, these spaces are *approximately isomorphic* i.e. they share a similar structure (Vulić et al., 2020)[2]. It has been shown that this assumption does not hold in general and therefore the benefit of mapping methods requiring little to no cross-lingual signal can no longer be taken advantage of directly in low-resource scenarios (Søgaard et al., 2018; Vulić et al., 2020). At the same time, while joint methods do not make the isomorphism assumption they are inapplicable in low-resource settings due to their high data requirements (Ormazabal et al., 2019). While most recent work in low-resource CLWEs have focused on reducing the supervision signal as much as possible (Artetxe et al., 2018c), further study points to this not being the best approach (Vulić et al., 2019). We claim that in addition to utilising monolingual resources, related language parallel data can be crucial in artificially generating isomorphic embedding spaces between the source and target.

In this paper, we address the limitations outlined above by proposing an alternative method to learn CLWEs for low-resource and distant language pairs. Contrary to previous approaches, we combine the benefits from both mapping and joint-training methods to develop high-quality, isomorphic embeddings. In our proposed framework, we maintain the low level of supervision as obtained by mapping methods while still guarding the isomorphic embeddings achieved by joint-training by independently aligning source and target embeddings to a related higher-resource language. We apply our method in several low-resource settings and conduct evaluations on bilingual lexicon induction and eigenvalue similarity. Our experiments show that, despite no additional source-target parallel data, our approach outperforms conventional mapping and joint-training methods on both evaluation metrics.

The main contributions of this work can be outlined as the following:

- We introduce a framework combining mapping and joint methods to learn isomorphic cross-lingual embeddings for low-resource language pairs.
- We successfully employ CLWEs in challenging, low-resource scenarios without the use of explicit source-target parallel data.
- We achieve significant gains over state-of-the-art methods in both bilingual word induction as well as eigenvalue similarity.

2 Related Work

Cross-Lingual Word Embeddings CLWEs aim to represent words from several languages into a shared embedding space which allows for several applications in low-resource areas such as transfer learning (Peng et al., 2021), NMT (Artetxe et al., 2018c), and Bilingual Lexicon Induction (BLI) (Patra et al., 2019). Largely, there are two classes of approaches to learn CLWEs: **mapping** and **joint** methods. While the former aims to map monolingually learnt embeddings together, the latter simultaneously learns both embedding spaces using some cross-lingual supervision (i.e. a cross-lingual signal). Common approaches to achieve this cross-lingual signal come from parallel corpora aligned at the word (Luong et al., 2015) or sentence level (Gouws et al., 2015). In addition to this, later methods proposed the use of comparable corpora (Vulić and Moens, 2016) or large bilingual dictionaries (Duong et al., 2016) as a form of supervision. For a more detailed survey of methods and limitations of CLWEs, the reader is referred to (Ruder et al., 2019).

Offline Mapping As mapping methods map monolingual embedding spaces together, instead of relying on a cross-lingual signal (such as in joint methods) they work by finding a transformation matrix that can be applied to the individual embedding spaces. In the case of supervised learning, a large bilingual dictionary would have been used as supervision however Artetxe et al. (2018b)

[2]Two vector spaces are said to be isomorphic if there is an invertible linear transformation from one to the other.

get rid of this requirement via a self-learning strategy. Their approach is based on a robust iterative method combined with initialisation heuristics to get state-of-the-art performance using offline mapping. Most of these methods align spaces using a linear transformation- usually imposing orthogonality constraints- in turn assuming that the underlying structure of these embeddings are largely similar. Several works (Søgaard et al., 2018; Vulić et al., 2020) have shown that this assumption does not hold when working with non-ideal scenarios such as low-resource or typologically different language pairs. In order to mitigate this assumption, Mohiuddin et al. (2020) learn a non-linear map in a latent space, Nakashole (2018) uses maps that are only locally linear, and Glavaš and Vulić (2020) propose to learn a separate map for each word. However these are supervised methods, meaning they suffer from limitations of hubbness and isomorphism as outlined in Ormazabal et al. (2019). To address these limitations, Ormazabal et al. (2021) proposes a method in which they fix the target language embeddings, and learn a new set of embeddings for the source language that are aligned with them using self-learning. Their method outperforms current mapping, joint, as well hybrid methods on the MUSE dataset (Conneau et al., 2018).

Joint-Training The fundamental limitations of offline methods are not faced by joint-training methods if there is a strong cross-lingual signal available (Ormazabal et al., 2019). In practice, however, we don't always have access to such forms of supervision therefore recent works have attempted to reduce the supervision level so as to preserve the isomorphism achieved by joint methods while still being as widely applicable as mapping methods. Lample et al. (2018) use concatenated monolingual corpora in different languages and learn word embeddings over this constructed corpus, using identical words as anchor points. Devlin et al. (2019) use a bidirectional transformer to learn a multilingual embedding space which showed significant progress in the zero-shot cross-lingual transfer task. Further extending upon these works, Wang et al. (2020) effectively combined joint and mapping based methods in their framework "joint-align" however their method was not tested on distant language low-resource pairs. In their work, they use fully unsupervised joint initialisation as the first step, vocabulary reallocation where they "unshare" some vocabulary to better align them, and lastly they perform a refinement step using off-the-shelf alignment methods. Furthermore, for low-resource setups Kementchedjhieva et al. (2018) propose Multi-support Generalized Procrustes Analysis (MGPA) which learns a three-way alignment between English, a low-resource language, and a supporting related language. In addition to Wang et al. (2020), Woller et al. (2021) show the benefit of using related languages in the context of CLWEs. In their work, they use a two step approach where they first use joint-align to learn a CLWE between the low-resource and related language and as a next step they map it to the target language to build the final multilingual embedding space. Although they focus on the use case of Occitan via French, Spanish, and Catalan, we show that this type of approach is well motivated across several language pairs.

3 Methodology

Given two embedding spaces, X and Y, for languages x and y respectively, our goal is to align them together without any direct parallel data between them and without assuming orthogonality/structural similarity. In order to do this, let us consider a third embedding space, Z, of a language z related to the source x. Furthermore, let there also be sufficient parallel data between y and z to jointly learn their aligned embedding spaces (Ormazabal et al., 2019). Our approach first aligns the spaces X and Z using an unsupervised offline mapping method (Artetxe et al., 2018b). Vulić et al. (2020) find that for typologically similar languages that have in-domain monolingual corpora, isomorphism in their learnt vector spaces is preserved. To that end, due to the linguistic similarities between x and z we may perform offline mapping. Figure 1 shows a visualisation of how these two embedding spaces are aligned using an induced seed dictionary as per Artetxe et al. (2018b). For further details about the offline alignment, the reader is referred to read the original paper.

Once the space X is aligned to the monolingual space Z, we wish to also align Y to Z as well. Due to the typological differences between the two languages, we can no longer assume isometry of their embedding spaces therefore can no longer use offline mapping methods. However, due to higher-resource nature of z, we have access to parallel

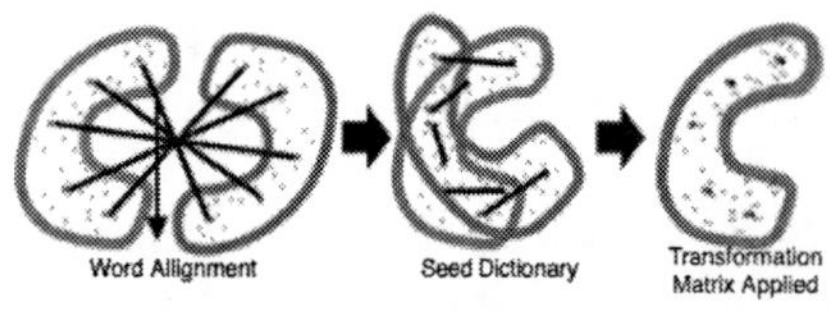

Figure 1: Toy visualisation of mapped cross lingual embedding spaces with red representing one language and blue the other

corpora between y and z. This allows us to apply joint-training approaches (Luong et al., 2015) to simultaneously learn their embeddings. As found in Ormazabal et al. (2019), under ideal conditions of having parallel data, joint-training approaches produce isomorphic embeddings that perform better than their offline counterparts in bilingual lexicon induction despite the non-relatedness of the languages considered. As shown in Figure 2, we can now produce two embedding spaces, Source aligned to Related and Target aligned to Related while preserving isomorphism. As a final step in our alignment framework, we use the $z-$aligned embedding spaces, $\tilde{X}$ and $\tilde{Y}$, to induce the final cross-lingual word embedding spaces. Now that both X and Y are projected onto Z, they share structural similarity which permits the use of offline mapping on $\tilde{X}$ and $\tilde{Y}$. Figure 2 shows the complete alignment framework to produced the resultant isomorphic embedding spaces.

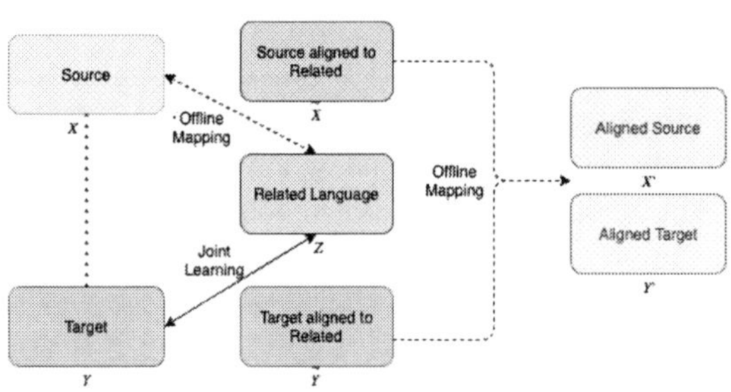

Figure 2: Visualisation of our proposed alignment method in context; dotted lines represent lack of parallel data between language pairs

Our proposed framework can be summarised in the following steps:

1. For a source-target pair, choose a related higher-resource language to the low-resource target such that there is **sufficient** source-related parallel data to perform joint mapping. (Ormazabal et al., 2019)
2. Use offline mapping (Artetxe et al., 2018b) to align related and source language into a shared embedding space. Due to their relatedness, these resultant embeddings remain isomorphic as the assumption in mapping methods hold true.
3. Use joint training (Luong et al., 2015) to map related and target language into a shared embedding space using the higher-resource parallel data between them. As this is the highest level of supervision possible, we ensure that the embedding spaces remain isomorphic.
4. Lastly, map the aligned-source and aligned-target embeddings using unsupervised mapping methods as they are now isometric in nature following the alignment to the related language for both the source and target.

This framework uses the low cross-lingual signal utilised by mapping techniques while still maintaining the isomorphism of the resultant embedding spaces as in joint approaches. This is achieved by exploiting the existing isomorphism between embeddings as much as possible by pre-aligning the spaces via a pivot-language. However, unlike pivot-based MT we do not compound errors across embedding spaces due to the final refinement step done by mapping the aligned embeddings into their shared cross-lingual space (Dabre et al., 2020). The first step of cross-lingual mapping, allows us to internalise the structure of the low-resource embedding space by pre-aligning with the related language. In the second step, we re-learn a joint embedding space for the related language and the target. In the last stage, the offline mapping makes use of the internalised structure by associating the modified source embedding space with the modified target embedding space which have both independently been aligned to the same related language.

With this pipeline, we are able to target a large group of low-resource languages which belong to higher-resource language families for instance, English-Nepali via Hindi. Linguistically, Nepali and Hindi are quite similar as they share the same script and also have 80% of subword tokens in common when using a shared BPE vocabulary of 100k subword units (Lample and Conneau, 2019). In this work, we perform experiments on several low-resource language pairs to show the effectiveness of our approach in various language families- specifically we look at Uralic, Indo-European, and Romance languages.

Our goal is not to fully replace current methods of learning cross-lingual word representations but to aid them in the area of low-resource languages. As shown by Ormazabal et al. (2019), depending on the type of resources available as well as the languages considered, different methods can be preferred. While current approaches perform well for several languages and resource levels (Ormazabal et al., 2021), their performance still leaves room for improvement in the low-resource, typologically diverse area. Despite the simplicity of our method, our experiments show that we perform competitively on quality as well as degree of isomorphism across all low-resource pairs considered. Due to the reliance on a sufficiently resourced related language, our method is not applicable to every low-resource pair however referring to the task of related-language NMT we see that there is indeed a large group of languages that could benefit from this approach (Dabre et al., 2020).

4 Experimental Design

In this section we discuss the datasets used, training settings for different configurations used in our experiments, and lastly the evaluation metrics used to assess the embedding spaces produced by our framework.

4.1 Datasets

In our work, we train CLWEs between English and five other low-resource languages: Nepali (ne), Finnish (fi), Romanian (ro), Gujarati (gu), and Hungarian (hu). We use pre-trained fasttext word embeddings (Grave et al., 2018) which uses Wikipedia dumps and Common Crawl for all languages. In addition to this, we use available parallel data between the following related language pairs respectively: English-Hindi (hi) for Nepali, English-Estonian (et) for Finnish, English-Italian (it) for Romanian, English-Hindi (hi) for Gujarati, and English-Finnish (fi) for Hungarian. We obtain the data from IIT Bombay[3] for En-Hi and from the WMT workshops[4]. We preprocess all the data using Moses scripts and tokenise using BPE. For the Indic languages, we use IndicNLP[5] for word segmentation. Table 1 details the statistics of the approximate corpus sizes used for learning monolingual embeddings. For evaluation, we use the gold-standard bilingual dictionary from the MUSE dataset (Conneau et al., 2018) for Finnish and for the remaining language pairs, we use bilingual dictionaries published by Pavlick et al. (2014). To show the relatedness of the languages chosen, we report genetic proximities[6] of the pairs with their related languages in Table 3.

Languages	Sentences	Tokens
Ne	92.3K	2.8M
Fi	6M	91M
Ro	88.6K	2.28M
Gu	382K	6M
Hu	1M	15M
En	67.8M	2.0B

Table 1: Monolingual Training Corpora sizes

Language Pairs	Segments
Hi-En	1.5M
Et-En	1.7M
It-En	151M
Fi-En	6.2M

Table 2: Parallel Training Corpora sizes

x	z	y	Gen. Proximity (↓)
Nepali	Hindi	En	19.4
Finnish	Estonian	En	16.7
Gujarati	Hindi	En	31.8
Romanian	Italian	En	29.4
Hungarian	Finnish	En	62.2

Table 3: Language Set-Ups with Genetic Proximity of Source and Related language where lower is better

4.2 Training Settings

Mapping: Using fasttext (Grave et al., 2018) with the default parameters[7], we first gather

[3]http://www.cfilt.iitb.ac.in/iitb_parallel/

[4]http://www.statmt.org

[5]https://github.com/anoopkunchukuttan/indic_nlp_library

[6]https://www.elinguistics.net/Compare_Languages.aspx

[7]These are 300-dimensional vectors with 10 negative samples, a sub-sampling threshold of 1e-5 and 5 training iterations

monolingual word embeddings for each of the respective languages. After this, we map the embeddings to a cross-lingual space using VecMap (Artetxe et al., 2018b) in the **unsupervised mode** as we do not have any bilingual dictionaries. In this mode an initial solution is found using heuristics and iteratively refined.

Joint Training: To train the embeddings jointly, we use the BiVec tool proposed by Luong et al. (2015) which is an extension of skip-gram algorithm aiming to predict the context around both the source and target word aligned to a given parallel corpus at the word level. We use the same hyperparameters as in the mapping methods.

In addition to the mapping and joint-training methods trained as described earlier, we also train Joint Align (Wang et al., 2020). We use the official implementation[8] on preprocessed tokenised data to train a non-contextual model in specific as we are working on non-contextual word embeddings. Furthermore, we replace the default RCLS retrieval step with unsupervised VecMap to have more consistency across the baselines. We also train other baseline models, namely Multi-support GPA (Kementchedjhieva et al., 2018) where we incorporate pre-trained monolingual embeddings of the respective related language. Lastly, we train the model proposed from Woller et al. (2021) which used Joint Align for the first alignment step and supervised MUSE (using identical character strings as the supervision signal) for the second.

4.3 Evaluation Metrics

We evaluate our embeddings on two aspects: the quality and degree of isomorphism achieved between the source and target. As in Ormazabal et al. (2019), we measure this by bilingual lexicon induction (BLI) and eigenvalue similarity respectively. Firstly, we induce the word-level translations by linking neighbouring source-target word translations in the resultant embeddings spaces using CSLS retrieval and finally evaluate the induced dictionary against the English-Target bilingual dictionary released by Pavlick et al. (2014)[9] to compute precision scores for the BLI task using the MUSE evaluation scripts (Conneau et al., 2018).

Next, we measure eigenvalue similarity for the embeddings following the procedure in Søgaard et al. (2018) on centralised and normalised embeddings. We perform the same evaluations across different cross-lingual alignment methods on all the considered language pairs.

5 Results and Discussion

In this section, we discuss our main experimental results on BLI and eigenvalue similarity across the chosen language pairs. Furthermore, we also conduct ablation tests on our learnt embeddings to further verify the sources of improvements.

5.1 BLI

Results in Table 4 report the BLI scores for the different baselines and our proposed method. We use the Low-Resource to English language direction however MGPA can only be trained with the related and low-resource language at the target. As per Woller et al. (2021), we evaluate the resultant Low-Resource-English embeddings afterwards. Across all language pairs, we see substantial gains from our method as compared to mapping, joint, and other hybrid baselines. Woller et al. (2021) outperform our approach on two language pairs (Ne-En, Gu-En) which we suspect is due to Joint-Align's performance in comparison to regular Joint training. However, these improvements are not consistent. As Joint-Align uses a vocabulary re-sharing step, we can hypothesise that for language pairs with significant vocabulary overlap this step might be useful in learning better alignments. In particular, Joint Align on average performs poorly on most language pairs, suggesting that it is inapplicable in a truly low-resource scenario. VecMap performs well overall, however, our approach outperforms VecMap by a significant margin. Despite using VecMap and a purely joint-training based approach without any additional source-target supervision, the gains in the scores are substantial. Interestingly, our method performs well even in the case of fi $\rightarrow$ en where we use Estonian as the related language; Estonian is in fact lower-resource than Finnish, however our performance suggests that "pivoting" via Estonian was still helpful in learning Finnish-English word embeddings. Therefore, even if the embeddings learnt in the intermediate stages are not ideal, the structural alignments earned are ultimately helpful in obtaining better source-target embeddings.

[8] https://github.com/thespectrewithin/joint_align

[9] https://cs.brown.edu/people/epavlick/data.html

	ne → en	fi → en	ro → en	gu → en	hu → en	**avg**
VecMap (Artetxe et al., 2018b)	52.3	61.9	61.6	45.4	53.2	54.8
Joint (Luong et al., 2015)	21.3	30.5	31.4	33.4	25.5	28.4
JointAlign (Wang et al., 2020)	24.5	31.3	28.2	35.4	26.5	25.2
MGPA (Kementchedjhieva et al., 2018)	41.6	55.7	57.3	39.6	45.7	47.9
JointAlign+MUSE (Woller et al., 2021)	**59.4**	62.5	62.6	**49.1**	55.8	57.8
Ours	58.4	**65.2**	**64.5**	48.4	**56.3**	**58.6**

Table 4: Precision at 1 scores of proposed method and previous works on BLI (higher is better)

5.2 Eigenvalue Similarity

In eigenvalue similarity, mapping methods perform much worse than joint training (Table 5). This finding is in line with the literature (Ormazabal et al., 2019), and is explained by the high linguistic divergence between English and source languages, resulting in embeddings that are far less isomorphic. Our hybrid approach performs even better than joint methods and achieved the best eigenvalue similarity score across all language pairs, showing that we do indeed obtain isometric embeddings while still not requiring the higher level of supervision in joint learning approaches. Although our proposed framework does not make any significant changes to the mapping and joint components, the combination of the two cross-lingual approaches leads to better embeddings both in terms of quality, shown by the performance in BLI, as well as structure, shown by the eigenvalue similarity scores. In addition to this, MGPA as well as Woller et al. (2021)'s method attains good eigenvalue similarity scores suggesting that the incorporation of a related language is indeed helpful

5.3 Ablation Tests

To study where the improvements of the cross-lingual encoding method come from, we conduct several ablation tests (results in Table 7), assessing the contribution of different embedding schemes to the final quality of the embeddings: firstly, we look at the initial unaligned monolingual embeddings, next we look at the embeddings that are independently aligned to the related language, and lastly we look at the embeddings after the final offline map has been constructed. These embedding schemes allows us to verify the importance of the intermediate structural alignments via the related language. As expected the unaligned embeddings have a near 0 BLI score, suggesting that the initial embeddings do not have any linking however as the score is still non-zero we can attribute this to identical words across some language pairs. However, the intermediate embeddings obtained (Related-Aligned in Table 7) have a significant jump in performance even though there is no explicit alignment between the source and target at this stage. This intermediate performance is surprisingly close to the final performance obtained by Joint Align as well, which suggests that the related-language strategy allows for a better understanding of word associations even before performing the final step of offline mapping.

Next, we studied the relevance of the relatedness as well as amount of parallel language of the related language. For this ablation test, we took three languages of different degrees of relatedness to each source language and then we measured the improvements between the intermediate embedding space aligned to the related language and the final embedding space between the source and the target. Doing so allowed us to further isolate intermediate improvements as obtained by the related languages and their final contribution in the quality of the learnt embeddings. We report results in Table 6. Consistently, across all the language pairs considered the BLI scores take a sharp drop as we reduce the relatedness (as measured by lexical similarity) of the intermediate language. The scores here point to relatedness of the chosen language as being one of the key factors in improving downstream performance. These results are in line with findings from Woller et al. (2021) where the relatedness of Catalan to Occitan was the driving force in their performance even though the resource levels of French and Spanish were significantly higher than Catalan.

6 Conclusion and Future Work

In this work, we developed a framework to learn cross-lingual word embeddings in low-resource scenarios. We addressed limitations of both offline as well as joint training methods to develop high

	ne → en	fi → en	ro → en	gu → en	hu → en	**avg**
VecMap (Artetxe et al., 2018b)	205.8	118.2	176.4	189.3	94.5	156.8
Joint (Luong et al., 2015)	48.6	30.3	41.2	42.5	35.6	39.7
JointAlign (Wang et al., 2020)	56.2	45.5	50.1	48.2	38.6	47.7
MGPA (Kementchedjhieva et al., 2018)	58.4	48.1	48.3	52.5	35.1	48.8
JointAlign+MUSE (Woller et al., 2021)	38.3	28.1	35.6	37.1	28.1	33.4
Ours	**37.5**	**23.4**	**32.7**	**33.2**	**26.6**	**30.7**

Table 5: Eigenvalue Similarity Scores (lower is better)

ne → en			**fi → en**			**ro → en**			**gu → en**			**hu → en**		
hi	gu	et	et	hu	hi	it	fr	de	hi	ta	fr	fi	et	fr
24.7	21.3	15.8	33.4	27.1	19.6	33.8	30.7	21.3	24.6	16.8	14.6	23.9	22.8	13.6
58.4	42.3	30.5	65.2	54.3	38.1	64.5	61.3	42.6	48.4	32.3	29.6	56.3	55.3	36.7

Table 6: BLI Scores P@1 for different related languages. Top row provides scores from intermediate cross-lingual embeddings achieved after prior alignment to the related language, the second row provides scores after the full alignment scheme.

Embeddings	BLI Score
Our Method	
Unaligned	0.4
Related-Aligned	24.6
Full Alignment	58.6
Offline Mapping	
Unaligned	0.4
Mapped	54.8
Joint Align	
Unaligned	0.4
Aligned	25.2

Table 7: Ablation Tests on Different Embeddings, reporting average Precision @ 1 score

quality, isomorphic embeddings for several low-resource language pairs. In particular, we maintain the low cross-lingual signal as required by offline methods while still obtaining structurally sound/isomorphic embeddings as in joint-training based approaches. Our method works by exploiting a higher-resource related-language to jointly learn a cross-lingual space between the related-language and target while also learning a cross-lingual space between the source and the related language using offline mapping. Due to the pre-alignment with a related-language, the resultant cross-lingual spaces are now structurally similar and can be mapped to each other without breaking any orthogonality assumption. Whilst our approach does not change the individual components at all, we obtain far superior results in both BLI as well as eigenvalue similarity across all languages. On a high-level, the gains in our method can be attributed to incorporating more linguistic information in the low-resource language via the related language. This would in turn allow for better modelling of the structure of the embedding spaces without explicitly requiring additional source-target parallel data. As our ablation tests show, indeed the intermediate embeddings themselves have some performance gains even though the source and target embeddings are not aligned to each other yet.

Future work in this direction would include verifying how high-resource the related language needs to be to still see performance gains. In addition to this, we would like to explore how the relatedness of the pivot language affects the performance of the learnt embeddings. Specifically, we would like to discover to what extent isomorphism is preserved in related language pairs- permitting the use of offline methods in more distant languages. Studying this would allows us to suggest further generalisations of our approach to cover a wider range of language families.

References

Mikel Artetxe, Gorka Labaka, and Eneko Agirre. 2018a. Generalizing and improving bilingual word embedding mappings with a multi-step framework of linear transformations. In *Proceedings of the Thirty-Second AAAI Conference on Artificial Intelligence*, pages 5012–5019.

Mikel Artetxe, Gorka Labaka, and Eneko Agirre. 2018b. A robust self-learning method for fully unsupervised cross-lingual mappings of word embeddings. In *Proceedings of the 56th Annual Meeting of the Association for Computational Linguistics (Volume 1: Long Papers)*, pages 789–798.

Mikel Artetxe, Gorka Labaka, Eneko Agirre, and Kyunghyun Cho. 2018c. Unsupervised neural machine translation.

Dzmitry Bahdanau, Kyunghyun Cho, and Yoshua Bengio. 2014. Neural machine translation by jointly learning to align and translate. *arXiv preprint arXiv:1409.0473*.

Loïc Barrault, Ondřej Bojar, Marta R. Costa-jussà, Christian Federmann, Mark Fishel, Yvette Graham, Barry Haddow, Matthias Huck, Philipp Koehn, Shervin Malmasi, Christof Monz, Mathias Müller, Santanu Pal, Matt Post, and Marcos Zampieri. 2019. Findings of the 2019 conference on machine translation (WMT19). In *Proceedings of the Fourth Conference on Machine Translation (Volume 2: Shared Task Papers, Day 1)*, pages 1–61, Florence, Italy. Association for Computational Linguistics.

Yonatan Belinkov and James Glass. 2019. Analysis methods in neural language processing: A survey.

Xilun Chen, Ahmed Hassan Awadallah, Hany Hassan, Wei Wang, and Claire Cardie. 2019. Multi-source cross-lingual model transfer: Learning what to share. In *Proceedings of the 57th Annual Meeting of the Association for Computational Linguistics*, pages 3098–3112, Florence, Italy. Association for Computational Linguistics.

Kyunghyun Cho, Bart Van Merriënboer, Dzmitry Bahdanau, and Yoshua Bengio. 2014. On the properties of neural machine translation: Encoder-decoder approaches. *arXiv preprint arXiv:1409.1259*.

Alexis Conneau, Guillaume Lample, Marc'Aurelio Ranzato, Ludovic Denoyer, and Hervé Jégou. 2018. Word translation without parallel data.

Raj Dabre, Chenhui Chu, and Anoop Kunchukuttan. 2020. A survey of multilingual neural machine translation. *ACM Comput. Surv.*, 53(5).

Jacob Devlin, Ming-Wei Chang, Kenton Lee, and Kristina Toutanova. 2019. Bert: Pre-training of deep bidirectional transformers for language understanding.

Long Duong, Hiroshi Kanayama, Tengfei Ma, Steven Bird, and Trevor Cohn. 2016. Learning crosslingual word embeddings without bilingual corpora. In *Proceedings of the 2016 Conference on Empirical Methods in Natural Language Processing*, pages 1285–1295, Austin, Texas. Association for Computational Linguistics.

Goran Glavaš and Ivan Vulić. 2020. Non-linear instance-based cross-lingual mapping for non-isomorphic embedding spaces. In *Proceedings of the 58th Annual Meeting of the Association for Computational Linguistics*, pages 7548–7555, Online. Association for Computational Linguistics.

Stephan Gouws, Yoshua Bengio, and Greg Corrado. 2015. Bilbowa: Fast bilingual distributed representations without word alignments. In *Proceedings of the 32nd International Conference on Machine Learning*, volume 37 of *Proceedings of Machine Learning Research*, pages 748–756, Lille, France. PMLR.

Stephan Gouws, Yoshua Bengio, and Greg Corrado. 2016. Bilbowa: Fast bilingual distributed representations without word alignments.

Edouard Grave, Piotr Bojanowski, Prakhar Gupta, Armand Joulin, and Tomas Mikolov. 2018. Learning word vectors for 157 languages. In *Proceedings of the International Conference on Language Resources and Evaluation (LREC 2018)*.

Hany Hassan, Anthony Aue, Chang Chen, Vishal Chowdhary, Jonathan Clark, Christian Federmann, Xuedong Huang, Marcin Junczys-Dowmunt, William Lewis, Mu Li, Shujie Liu, Tie-Yan Liu, Renqian Luo, Arul Menezes, Tao Qin, Frank Seide, Xu Tan, Fei Tian, Lijun Wu, Shuangzhi Wu, Yingce Xia, Dongdong Zhang, Zhirui Zhang, and Ming Zhou. 2018. Achieving human parity on automatic chinese to english news translation.

Yova Kementchedjhieva, Sebastian Ruder, Ryan Cotterell, and Anders Søgaard. 2018. Generalizing Procrustes analysis for better bilingual dictionary induction. In *Proceedings of the 22nd Conference on Computational Natural Language Learning*, pages 211–220, Brussels, Belgium. Association for Computational Linguistics.

Guillaume Lample and Alexis Conneau. 2019. Cross-lingual language model pretraining.

Guillaume Lample, Alexis Conneau, Ludovic Denoyer, and Marc'Aurelio Ranzato. 2017. Unsupervised machine translation using monolingual corpora only. *arXiv preprint arXiv:1711.00043*.

Guillaume Lample, Myle Ott, Alexis Conneau, Ludovic Denoyer, and Marc'Aurelio Ranzato. 2018. Phrase-based and neural unsupervised machine translation.

Xiaodong Liu, Kevin Duh, Liyuan Liu, and Jianfeng Gao. 2020. Very deep transformers for neural machine translation. *arXiv preprint arXiv:2008.07772*.

Minh-Thang Luong, Hieu Pham, and Christopher D Manning. 2015. Bilingual word representations with monolingual quality in mind. In *Proceedings of the 1st Workshop on Vector Space Modeling for Natural Language Processing*, pages 151–159.

Tomas Mikolov, Quoc V Le, and Ilya Sutskever. 2013. Exploiting similarities among languages for machine translation. *arXiv preprint arXiv:1309.4168*.

Tasnim Mohiuddin, M Saiful Bari, and Shafiq Joty. 2020. LNMap: Departures from isomorphic assumption in bilingual lexicon induction through non-linear mapping in latent space. In *Proceedings of the 2020 Conference on Empirical Methods in Natural Language Processing (EMNLP)*, pages 2712–2723, Online. Association for Computational Linguistics.

Ndapa Nakashole. 2018. NORMA: Neighborhood sensitive maps for multilingual word embeddings. In *Proceedings of the 2018 Conference on Empirical Methods in Natural Language Processing*, pages 512–522, Brussels, Belgium. Association for Computational Linguistics.

Aitor Ormazabal, Mikel Artetxe, Gorka Labaka, Aitor Soroa, and Eneko Agirre. 2019. Analyzing the limitations of cross-lingual word embedding mappings. In *Proceedings of the 57th Annual Meeting of the Association for Computational Linguistics*, pages 4990–4995, Florence, Italy. Association for Computational Linguistics.

Aitor Ormazabal, Mikel Artetxe, Aitor Soroa, Gorka Labaka, and Eneko Agirre. 2021. Beyond offline mapping: Learning cross lingual word embeddings through context anchoring.

Barun Patra, Joel Ruben Antony Moniz, Sarthak Garg, Matthew R. Gormley, and Graham Neubig. 2019. Bilingual lexicon induction with semi-supervision in non-isometric embedding spaces. In *Proceedings of the 57th Annual Meeting of the Association for Computational Linguistics*, pages 184–193, Florence, Italy. Association for Computational Linguistics.

Ellie Pavlick, Matt Post, Ann Irvine, Dmitry Kachaev, and Chris Callison-Burch. 2014. The language demographics of Amazon Mechanical Turk. *Transactions of the Association for Computational Linguistics*, 2:79–92.

Xutan Peng, Yi Zheng, Chenghua Lin, and Advaith Siddharthan. 2021. Summarising historical text in modern languages.

Sebastian Ruder, Ivan Vulić, and Anders Søgaard. 2019. A survey of cross-lingual word embedding models. *Journal of Artificial Intelligence Research*, 65:569–631.

Jürgen Schmidhuber and Sepp Hochreiter. 1997. Long short-term memory. *Neural Comput*, 9(8):1735–1780.

Anders Søgaard, Sebastian Ruder, and Ivan Vulić. 2018. On the limitations of unsupervised bilingual dictionary induction. *arXiv preprint arXiv:1805.03620*.

Ivan Vulić, Goran Glavaš, Roi Reichart, and Anna Korhonen. 2019. Do we really need fully unsupervised cross-lingual embeddings?

Ivan Vulić and Marie-Francine Moens. 2016. Bilingual distributed word representations from document-aligned comparable data.

Ivan Vulić, Sebastian Ruder, and Anders Søgaard. 2020. Are all good word vector spaces isomorphic?

Zirui Wang, Jiateng Xie, Ruochen Xu, Yiming Yang, Graham Neubig, and Jaime Carbonell. 2020. Cross-lingual alignment vs joint training: A comparative study and a simple unified framework.

Lisa Woller, Viktor Hangya, and Alexander Fraser. 2021. Do not neglect related languages: The case of low-resource Occitan cross-lingual word embeddings. In *Proceedings of the 1st Workshop on Multilingual Representation Learning*, pages 41–50, Punta Cana, Dominican Republic. Association for Computational Linguistics.

Video Language Co-Attention with Multimodal Fast-Learning Feature Fusion for VideoQA

Adnen Abdessaied*, Ekta Sood*, Andreas Bulling
Institute for Visualization and Interactive Systems (VIS)
University of Stuttgart, Germany
{adnen.abdessaied,ekta.sood,andreas.bulling}@vis.uni-stuttgart.de

Abstract

We propose the Video Language Co-Attention Network (VLCN) – a novel memory-enhanced model for Video Question Answering (VideoQA). Our model combines two original contributions: A multimodal fast-learning feature fusion (FLF) block and a mechanism that uses self-attended language features to *separately* guide neural attention on both static and dynamic visual features extracted from individual video frames and short video clips. When trained from scratch, VLCN achieves competitive results with the state of the art on both MSVD-QA and MSRVTT-QA with 38.06% and 36.01% test accuracies, respectively. Through an ablation study, we further show that FLF improves generalization across different VideoQA datasets and performance for question types that are notoriously challenging in current datasets, such as long questions that require deeper reasoning as well as questions with rare answers[1].

1 Introduction

Video Question Answering (VideoQA) has emerged as a challenging task at the intersection of natural language processing and computer vision. In contrast to image-based visual question answering (Lu et al., 2016; Anderson et al., 2018; Yu et al., 2019), VideoQA takes dynamic visual content (a video) as input (Xu et al., 2017; Gao et al., 2018; Li et al., 2019). This poses new challenges given that generating correct answers requires models to analyze spatial, appearance-based features of individual video frames *jointly* with the temporal, motion-based dynamics across multiple frames (Zhu et al., 2017).

However, there still is a semantic gap between the visual and language channels (Lei et al., 2018; Sun et al., 2021; Song et al., 2018) that prior work has tried to close by leveraging external memory (Kim et al., 2018, 2019; Fan et al., 2019). While external memory allows models to cache sequential information and retrieve relevant multimodal content (Patel et al., 2021), latest models still suffer from decreased performance, for example on ambiguous questions that require deeper reasoning abilities.

Moreover, current deep neural models for VideoQA are limited in that they only gradually learn during training. In contrast, human cognition leverages two different learning systems: a gradual and a fast-learning system (McClelland et al., 1995).The interplay between the fast and gradual duel learning systems is essential for humans to learn new representations, hence to generalizing (McClelland et al., 2020b). Current networks lack a similar fast-learning mechanism, which impedes their ability to efficiently reason and generalize to unseen data since the fast learning system acts as an encoder of new information which is then transferred to the gradual learning system for referencing and consolidating (Arani et al., 2021).

To address these limitations, we propose the Video Language Co-Attention Network (VLCN) – a novel memory-enhanced model for VideoQA. VLCN implements a video language co-attention module that uses self- and guided-attention to align language features of the question with static and dynamic visual features extracted from videos. As such, the module offers complementary information that our network attends to, independently of each other, when visually grounding a question. Furthermore, VLCN features a novel multimodal fast-learning fusion (FLF) block that helps the model to deal with challenging questions that need deeper reasoning and understanding. Inspired by the cognitive fast-learning system (McClelland et al., 2019), we leverage the differentiable neural computer (DNC) to incorporate an external memory which the network learns how to use by freeing and reusing its memory slots.

We seamlessly integrate our novel video language co-attention module as well as the fast-learning feature fusion approach in the recent transformer-based MCAN network (Yu et al., 2019). We show

*Equal contribution.

[1]Our code is publicly available at the project website `https://www.perceptualui.org/publications/abdessaied22_repl4NLP/`

Proceedings of the 7th Workshop on Representation Learning for NLP, pages 143 - 155
May 26, 2022 ©2022 Association for Computational Linguistics

that our model achieves competitive results with the state of the art on two challenging datasets – MSVD-QA and MSRVTT-QA. Our results further show that our model performs better on ambiguous questions and can better reason not only about questions with rare answers but also longer questions that require a deeper understanding of both the question and the visual input. In addition, we show that FLF facilitates generalization across different VideoQA datasets via transfer learning.

2 Related Work

Our work is related to previous works on 1) attention mechanisms in VideoQA, and 2) memory-enhanced networks.

Attention Mechanisms in VideoQA. Neural attention mechanisms have become the de-facto standard in machine comprehension tasks (Sood et al., 2020; Yu et al., 2019; Li et al., 2019). In VideoQA, attention mechanisms are particularly important given that the information necessary to generate correct answers is scattered across frames – many of which are redundant or even irrelevant to the question at hand (Patel et al., 2021).

Ye et al. (2017) introduced the attribute-augmented attention network that learned temporally attended video representations according to semantic attributes. Xu et al. (2017) reported new state-of-the-art performance by applying question-guided attention over both the appearance and motion features of individual as well as multiple video frames. Motivated by the challenge to capture long-range dependencies, Li et al. (2019) used a transformer-based co-attention network to exploit the global dependencies of the text and the temporal dynamics of the videos. Yang et al. (2020) leveraged BERT (Devlin et al., 2018) to obtain richer contextual feature representations over the question. More recently, Seo et al. (2021) proposed a two-stream multimodal video transformer based architecture (CoMVT) that jointly attends over words in text and visual objects and scenes to learn visual-dialogue context. Although CoMVT achieves state-of-the-art results on multiple downstream VideoQA datasets, it requires a computationally-demanding pretraning stage on 1.2M instructional videos.

These previous methods have used question features to guide attention over either frame or clip-level visual features, and some applied self and co-attention to individual frames. Our work, however, is the first to use self-attention on the question which then *separately* guides the attention over both individual video frames and clips.

Memory-enhanced Networks. In parallel, other works have focused on augmenting models with external memory components to improve their reasoning capabilities particularly over long-range data that are common in many visiolinguistic tasks, e.g. images with many objects or videos with a large number of frames. One of the first methods introduced a memory component over simple facts for question answering (Weston and Bordes, 2015).

The introduction of end-to-end trainable models popularized the use of external memory components (Sukhbaatar et al., 2015). Driven by the insight that memory access is similar to neural attention (Collier and Beel, 2019), other works integrated attention mechanisms to allow networks to better interact with their external memory through read and write operations, such as the Neural Turing Machine (NTM) (Graves et al., 2014) or the Differential Neural Computer (DNC) (Graves et al., 2016). The latter includes a dynamic memory allocation scheme that enables it to learn how to effectively free and reuse memory slots.

Several works aimed to leverage the potential of memory-enhanced networks for VideoQA. Na et al. (2017) applied memory over the video frames using multi-layered CNNs read and write networks to capture richer temporal dynamics of frame-level sequence information. Xue et al. (2018) obtained syntax parse trees over questions and then stored these into memory, allowing their model to perform better on more complex questions. Fan et al. (2019) used one memory component to effectively learn global context information from appearance and motion features in combination with another question-memory to help understand the complex semantics of questions and highlight queried subjects. Gao et al. (2018) used a co-memory attention mechanism to generate attention from motion and appearance cues. More recently, Yin et al. (2020) achieved new state-of-the-art results on MSVD-QA (Xu et al., 2017) by using a DNC (Graves et al., 2016) to encode the textual information of the question and the visual information of the video.

While previous works used memory-enhanced networks to *extract* linguistic and visual features, we propose a memory-augmented block adapted from the DNC to potentially emulate the human-like fast-learning capabilites (McClelland et al., 2020a) and use it to *fuse* multimodal features previously attended by an encoder-decoder transformer-based co-attention module instead.

3 Method

We propose the Video Language Co-Attention Network (VLCN) that integrates two original contributions (see Figure 1): First, we propose to use self- and guided-attention to *separately* align the language features with the static and dynamic visual features extracted from single video frames and frame sequences (clips). Second, we introduce Fast-Learning Fusion (FLF) – a novel memory-enhanced multimodal block that learns a single fused repre-

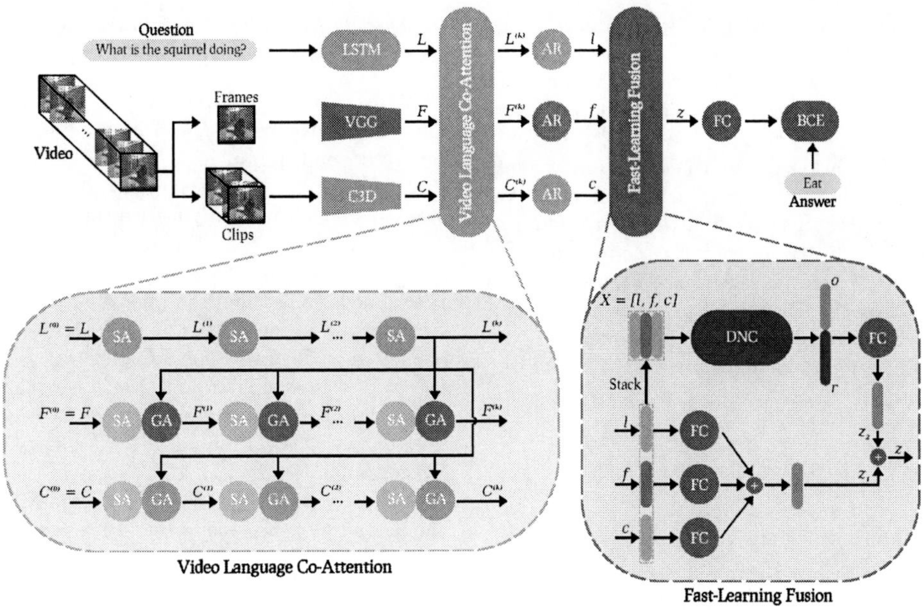

Figure 1: Architecture of the proposed Video Language Co-attention Network (VLCN). Our model aligns three different types of input (language features L, static visual features F and dynamic visual features C) using self- and guided-attention. Then, it fuses the attended reduced features (l, f and c) with the help of Fast-Learning Fusion (Fast-Learning Fusion (FLF)) – a novel memory-augmented multimodal fusion block. AR = Attention Reduction.

sentation of all features (i.e. language, static and dynamic visual features).

3.1 Feature Representation

In contrast to images, videos consist of multiple frames that capture temporal object dynamics and motion features. Combinations of static and dynamic visual features have therefore become the de-facto standard for video representations (Xu et al., 2017; Le et al., 2020a) in VideoQA. We adopt the same approach in our Video Language Co-Attention Network (VLCN).

Visual Features. For each video, we first sample n_v evenly-distributed frames and clips where a clip is a sequence of 16 consecutive video frames. Then, we apply a VGG network (Simonyan and Zisserman, 2014) pre-trained on ImageNet (Russakovsky et al., 2015) and a C3D network[2] (Ji et al., 2012) pre-trained on Sports1M (Karpathy et al., 2014) on these sampled frames and clips, respectively. The activations of their last d_v-dimensional fully-connected layers are our static and dynamic visual features.

This results in a set of static frame features $F = [f_1, \dots, f_{n_v}] \in \mathbb{R}^{n_v \times d_v}$ and a set of dynamic clip features $C = [c_1, \dots, c_{n_v}] \in \mathbb{R}^{n_v \times d_v}$.

Language Features. Question tokens are represented using 300-D GloVe embeddings (Pennington et al., 2014) and encoded with a Long Short-Term Memory (LSTM) network (Hochreiter and Schmidhuber, 1997) with d_l hidden dimensions. Thus, each question is represented as a matrix $L \in \mathbb{R}^{n_l \times d_l}$, where n_l is the number of question tokens.

[2]`https://github.com/DavideA/c3d-pytorch`

3.2 Video Language Co-Attention

The intuition behind our overall approach is the way humans typically answer questions about videos: first, we read the question. Then, we consider the visual input, i.e. its static (colours, objects and shapes) and dynamic (movements and actions) visual features, to answer it. VLCN uses stacked video language co-attention layers in an encoder-decoder fashion (see Figure 1). Given a set of features, each layer simultaneously computes the self-attention of the question, frames and clips features. Then, the self-attended question features of the last layer, i.e. $L^{(K)}$, are used to *separately* guide the attention over the frames and clip features in a bottom up manner (Anderson et al., 2018). At the core of self- and guided-attention sits a multi-head attention block (Vaswani et al., 2017) that computes a scaled dot-product of a query $q \in \mathbb{R}^{1 \times d}$ and a set of n keys $K \in \mathbb{R}^{n \times d}$, where d is a common hidden dimension. A softmax function is then applied to obtain the attention weights A on the values $V \in \mathbb{R}^{n \times d}$ following:

$$A = \text{softmax}(\frac{qK^T}{\sqrt{d}})V. \quad (1)$$

Similar to (Vaswani et al., 2017), attention weights A are computed for multiple queries $Q \in \mathbb{Q}^{n \times d}$ at the same time using Equation (1). The outputs of the final video language co-attention layers $L^{(K)} \in \mathbb{R}^{n_l \times d}$, $F^{(K)} \in \mathbb{R}^{n_v \times d}$ and $C^{(K)} \in \mathbb{R}^{n_v \times d}$ encode information about the attention weights over the question tokens and visual semantics. We reduce them to get the final attended features $l, f, v \in \mathbb{R}^d$ by linearly combining the rows of $L^{(K)}$, $F^{(K)}$ and $C^{(K)}$, respectively (see Figure 1). Taking the language features as an example, we first process $L^{(K)}$ by a multi-layer Feed-Forward Network (FFN) followed by a softmax to obtain the attention weights that we use to linearly combine the rows of $L^{(K)}$ as:

$$a = \text{softmax}(\text{FFN}(L^{(K)})) \in [0, 1]^{n_l}, \quad (2)$$

$$l = \sum_{i=1}^{n_l} a_i L^{(K)}[i, :] \in \mathbb{R}^d. \quad (3)$$

3.3 Fast-Learning Feature Fusion

We opted to use the DNC as a basis for this approach given that it is, to our knowledge, the most capable memory-augmented model to date that can be trained in an end-to-end fashion (Graves et al., 2016). In previous works (Graves et al., 2016; Yin et al., 2020), the DNC was heavily used to process long input sequences. However, its capability to treat shorter input sequences remains unexplored even though it has been argued for by cognitive science to be capable of emulating the human fast-learning system proposed in the complementary learning systems theory (McClelland et al., 1986, 2019). In our work, we leverage it —for the first time —to fuse our three multi-modal inputs (i.e. language, static, and dynamic visual features) within the VideoQA task.

Differential Neural Computer (DNC). The DNC consists of two major components: A neural network controller and an external memory. At each time-step t, the controller receives an input vector x_t and emits an output vector y_t. In addition, it receives a set of R read vectors $\{r_{t-1}^i\}_{i=1}^R$ from the $N \times W$ memory matrix M_{t-1} of the previous time-step $t-1$. Both controller inputs and the read vectors are concatenated to form the final input vector $\chi_t = [x_t; r_{t-1}^1; \ldots; r_{t-1}^R]$. Theoretically, the controller can be a network of any type. However, it is common to use an LSTM network with L hidden layers. The output vector y_t is computed via

$$y_t = W_h[h_t^1; \ldots; h_t^L] + W_r[r_t^1; \ldots; r_t^R], \quad (4)$$

where W_h and W_r are learnable weights and $\mathbf{h_t} = \{h_t^i\}_{i=1}^L$ are the hidden states of the LSTM controller. These hidden states are used to parameterize one write and R read heads to interact with the $N \times W$ external memory matrix through the so-called *fast-learning* connections. Further details on the DNC can be found in (Graves et al., 2016).

Feature Fusion. First, the reduced language and visual features l, f and c (see Figure 1) are projected and summed to get the first intermediate output z_1. Then, they are duplicated and stacked one after another to form the input sequence $X = [l, f, c] = [x_1, x_2, x_3] \in \mathbb{R}^{3 \times d}$ to the DNC. The output sequence $Y = [y_1, y_2, y_3] \in \mathbb{R}^{3 \times d}$ is summed along the first dimension to obtain the final output o and the last R read vectors are concatenated to form the global read vector r. Finally, the second intermediate output z_2 is obtained by projecting $[o; r]$ onto the same space as z_1 and the final output z is computed by summing z_1 and z_2. We concatenated the last read vectors to the DNC's output to preserve the memory information from the last step of processing the input sequences.

Answer Prediction. Given that VideoQA is formulated as a classification task, the fused features z are projected onto the answer space using a fully-connected layer. A sigmoid function is applied to train the network with binary cross-entropy (BCE) loss (see Figure 1).

4 Experiments

Datasets. We conducted experiments on two open-ended VideoQA datasets: MSVD-QA and MSRVTT-QA (Xu et al., 2017). They are, in turn, based on the Microsoft Research Video Description Corpus (MSVD) (Chen and Dolan, 2011) and the Microsoft Research Video to Text (MSRVTT) (Xu et al., 2016) datasets, respectively. Both datasets contain automatically generated questions that fall into five different categories: *what, who, how, when* and *where*. MSVD-QA has a total number of 1200 videos and 50 505 question-answer pairs and comes with three splits based on the videos: The training, validation, and test sets account for 61%, 13%, and 26% of the total number of videos, respectively. Similarly, MSRVTT-QA has three splits with 10 000 videos and 243 680 question-answer pairs in total. The training, validation, and test sets account for 65%, 5%, and 30% of the total number of videos, respectively. Further details on the datasets can be found in Appendix A.1.

Implementation Details. For each video, we sampled $n_v = 20$ frames and clips and used them to generate the static and dynamic visual features. We set the dimensionality of the input question features d_l and input visual features d_v (static and dynamic) to 512 and 4,096, respectively. The fused features z_1, z_2 and z had a dimension $d_z = 1,024$. Following (Vaswani et al., 2017), we set the latent dimension d of the multi-head attention block to 512 and the number of heads to eight, i.e. each had a dimensionality of 64. Since VideoQA is formulated as a classification task, similar to (Xu et al., 2017), we used the most frequent 1,000 ground-truth answers of the training and validation splits as our answer candidates. The number of video language co-attention layers K was fixed to six. Finally, for the DNC[3] in the FLF block we used a two-layer bidirectional LSTM network (Hochreiter and Schmidhuber, 1997) with 512 hidden dimensions as a controller as well as four read and one write heads to interact with the 512×64 external memory matrix. We used Adam (Kingma and Ba, 2014) with $\beta_1 = 0.9, \beta_2 = 0.98$ to optimize the weights of our model over a maximum of 30 epochs. We set the base learning rate to 10^{-4}. The batch-size was fixed to 64 and 32 during training and evaluation, respectively. We implemented our model in PyTorch (Paszke et al., 2019). It is based on a Visual Question Answering (VQA) open-source implementation[4] and will be made publicly available together with our pre-trained models. All experiments were conducted on one Nvidia Tesla V100 GPU with 32GB VRAM.

Ablated Models. In all experiments that follow we denote with *VLCN* our full model that uses a DNC inside the FLF block and whose architecture is illustrated in Figure 1. Although we experimented with training the DNC with different permutations of its inputs, we did not obtain any improvements in terms of performance when we changed the order of the input features. Therefore, we kept the same order that we used to encode the features (i.e. $[l, f, c]$). We additionally implemented different ablated versions of our model to study the impact of the proposed video language co-attention and fast-learning fusion:

- *MCAN*: This is the original MCAN model as proposed in (Yu et al., 2019) but adapted for VideoQA. We trained it using the concatenated static and dynamic visual features as they share the same dimensionality d_v. This model was not equipped with our novel video-language co-attention and fast-learning feature fusion.

- *VLCN−FLF*: For this model we used a simple multimodal fusion by summing the reduced features l, f and c, i.e. only the first intermediate output z_1 was passed through to the subsequent parts of the network (see Figure 1).

- *VLCN+LSTM*: For this model we only used the controller of the DNC, i.e. a two-layer bidirectional LSTM with 512 hidden dimensions, to compute the second intermediate output z_2 by summing the outputs of the LSTM and projecting them onto the same space as z_1. This model did not have the external long-term memory matrix and the fast-learning connections.

Model Training. We evaluated the robustness of our model and its ablated versions by training each five times with five different seeds. We report the performance as $\mu \pm \sigma$, where μ and σ are the average and standard deviation of the ensemble-accuracy on MSVD-QA and MSRVTT-QA *test*.

Question Length and Answer Frequency. Complementing analyses according to common question type categories (*what, who, how, when* and *where*), we propose two other question-binning strategies: In the first strategy, questions are put into three bins based on question length. The first bin contains questions with up to three words, the second bin between four and eight, and the last bin with more than nine words. The longer the question, the harder it should be for the model to answer as it requires deeper reasoning and understanding. In the second strategy, questions are binned according to the frequency rank of their ground-truth answers in the training and validation splits. The first bin contains questions whose ground-truths are the 100 most frequent answers. The second contains questions whose ground-truths are the next 200 most frequent answers. The last bin contains the rest of the questions, i.e. questions with the scarcest 700 answers. The rarer answers to a question are, the more difficult it should be for the model to answer correctly.

Transfer Learning of the FLF Weights. MSRVTT-QA includes more questions and longer videos compared to MSVD-QA: The average video lengths of MSRVTT-QA and MSVD-QA are 20 and 10 seconds, respectively (Aafaq et al., 2019). Performance on MSRVTT-QA should thus benefit from the knowledge acquired while training on MSVD-QA (Pan and Yang, 2010). Through transfer-learning of the *fast-learning connections* and *the DNC controller weights* learned from MSVD-QA, FLF should be able to better interact with its external memory when dealing with questions from MSRVTT-QA. To study this hypothesis, we conducted the following experiment: We trained an ensemble of five VLCNs using five different seeds on MSVD-QA. Then, we trained two further ensembles of five VLCNs on MSRVTT-QA using the same seeds: For one ensemble, we initialised the FLF weights of each model with those learned from MSVD-QA and fine-tuned them on MSRVTT-QA. We call these models *VLCN+FT*. For models in the second ensemble we trained these weights from scratch. Additionally, we experimented with fine-tuning the entire architecture of the FLF block instead. These experiments did not yield any performance improvements and we decided not to include them in this work.

[3] `https://github.com/ixaxaar/pytorch-dnc`

[4] `https://github.com/MILVLG/mcan-vqa`

5 Results

Comparison with the State of the Art. VLCN achieves competitive performance with the state of the art on both MSVD-QA and MSRVTT-QA. On MSVD-QA, our best model reaches an overall accuracy of 38.06% compared to 35.70%, 36.10%, and 36.20% achieved by CoMVT (scratch) (Seo et al., 2021), HCRN (Le et al., 2020b), and MA-DRNN (Yin et al., 2020), respectively. This corresponds to a relative improvement of 1.86% over the state of the art when the latter is trained from scratch (see Table 1). Although CoMVT can reach an overall accuracy of 42.60%, this was only possible after a computationally-demanding pretraining stage on HowToFUP (Miech et al., 2019) —a dataset consisting of 1.2M instructional videos for the task of Future Utterance Prediction (FUP). On the most diverse question types our model achieves a higher accuracy on *what* ($\sim$ 4% increase) and performs slightly worse on *who* compared to MA-DRNN. On the other types *how*, *when* and *where*, our model performs on par with the state of the art methods. As depicted in Table 2, our best VLCN model achieves an overall accuracy of 36.01% on MSRVTT-QA – the second best performance after CoMVT which achieves 37.30% accuracy when trained from scratch and 39.50% after pretaining on HowToFUP.

Ablation Study. Our analysis of the question length shows that VLCN achieves the best performance across all question length bins on MSVD-QA and on long questions, i.e. questions with length bigger than three, on MSRVTT-QA (see Tables 3 and 4). By comparing the first two rows of Table 3 and Table 4, we can see that VLCN−FLF outperforms MCAN across all of the question length bins of MSVD-QA and on very long questions (≥ 9) of MSRVTT-QA. This suggests that our co-attention approach helps the model make reliable predictions when the question becomes more complex compared to the simple question-guided attention over the *stacked* visual features. We hypothesize that the static and dynamic visual features offer complementary information that our network needs to attend to, independently of each other, while trying to visually ground the question. By removing the external memory of the FLF block and using a plain LSTM network, VLCN+LSTM falls behind on all question length bins resulting in an overall accuracy decrease of 0.84% and 0.8% on MSVD-QA and MSRVTT-QA, respectively, compared to VLCN (see Tables 3 and 4). We hypothesize that the proposed external memory is indispensable when answering questions that exceed the working memory capacity of the model, i.e. in this case of the LSTM network.

We then analyzed the performance of our ablated versions with respect to the answer frequency bins (see Table 5). On MSVD-QA, VLCN achieves the best results on the most challenging questions, i.e. questions whose answers are not amongst the 100 most frequent, and performs on par with VLCN−FLF on questions with the 100 most frequent answers. Although VLCN+LSTM performs on par with VLCN and improves on the performance of MCAN and VLCN−FLF on the most challenging questions, it falls behind VLCN when it comes to the easier questions with the most frequent answers. This results in an overall accuracy decrease of 0.5% compared to VLCN.

Similarly, VLCN outperforms all of its ablated versions on the most challenging questions of MSRVTT-QA (see Table 6). In contrast to MSVD-QA, VLCN+LSTM does not reach superior results on the most challenging questions compared to MCAN and VLCN−FLF. Performance on such questions only improves when using the external memory. In fact, VLCN achieves 20.97% and 5.84% on questions with the second 100 most frequent answers and questions with the scarcest 700 answers, respectively. This translates into a relative improvement of 2.49% and 3.89% compared to the second best models on such answer frequency bins, i.e. MCAN and VLCN+LSTM, respectively (see Table 6). It is interesting to see the difficulty of answering questions with rare ground truth answers as highlighted by the severe drop in performance for the last answer frequency bin of Table 5 and Table 6. We do not think that this is related to a language understanding problem as suggested by the error analysis we conducted on the ablated versions. Please refer to Appendix A.2 for more details.

Transfer Learning. The last two rows of Tables 4 and 6 show the importance of curriculum learning (Bengio et al., 2009). By fine-tuning the converged weights of FLF from MSVD-QA on MSRVTT-QA, VLCN+FT reaches new state of the art result on MSRVTT-QA by improving the accuracy on all question length and answer frequency bins compared to VLCN. This indicates that transfer learning of the fast-learning connections of FLF is possible and improves performance across different datasets. Further details about the effect of fine-tuning on the performance on individual question types can be found in Appendix A.3.

Qualitative Analysis. Figure 2 shows sample attention maps learned by the last video language co-attention layer together with the predictions of our model and its ablated versions. These predictions are depicted in the orange box, where *other* denotes the ablated versions of our full VLCN model. Further examples can be found in Appendix A.4. The language self-attention $SA(L)$ and the guided-attention over the clips $G(C, L)$ show that VLCN

Model	Question Type					
	What	Who	How	When	Where	All
ST-VQA (Jang et al., 2017)	18.10	50.00	**83.80**	72.40	28.60	31.30
Co-Mem (Gao et al., 2018)	19.60	48.70	81.60	74.10	31.70	31.70
HMEMA (Fan et al., 2019)	22.40	50.10	73.00	70.70	42.90	33.70
SSML (Amrani et al., 2020)	–	–	–	–	–	35.13
QueST (Jiang et al., 2020)	24.50	**52.90**	79.10	72.40	**50.00**	36.10
HCRN (Le et al., 2020b)	–	–	–	–	–	36.10
MA-DRNN (Yin et al., 2020)	24.30	51.60	82.00	**86.30**	26.30	36.20
CoMVT (Seo et al., 2021)						
Scratch	–	–	–	–	–	35.70
Pretrained	–	–	–	–	–	**42.60**
VLCN (Ours)	**28.42**	51.29	81.08	74.13	46.43	38.06

Table 1: Performance comparison of VLCN with the state of the art on MSVD-QA *test*. The table shows the overall accuracy as well as the accuracy with respect to individual question types in %.

Model	Question Type					
	What	Who	How	When	Where	All
ST-VQA(Jang et al., 2017)	24.50	41.20	78.00	76.50	34.90	30.90
Co-Mem (Gao et al., 2018)	23.90	42.50	74.10	69.00	**42.90**	32.00
HMEMA(Fan et al., 2019)	26.50	43.60	82.40	76.00	28.60	33.00
QueST (Jiang et al., 2020)	27.90	**45.60**	**83.00**	75.70	31.60	34.60
SSML (Amrani et al., 2020)	–	–	–	–	–	35.00
HCRN (Le et al., 2020b)	–	–	–	–	–	35.60
CoMVT (Seo et al., 2021)						
Scratch	–	–	–	–	–	37.30
Pretrained	–	–	–	–	–	**39.50**
VLCN (Ours)	**30.69**	44.09	79.82	**78.29**	36.80	36.01

Table 2: Performance comparison of VLCN with the state of the art on MSRVTT-QA *test*. The table shows the overall accuracy as well as the accuracy with respect to individual question types in %.

Model	Question Length (number of words)			
	1-3	4-8	≥ 9	All
MCAN_{avg}	35.83 ± 1.30	36.37 ± 0.33	38.13 ± 0.98	36.64 ± 0.44
$\text{VLCN}-\text{FLF}_{\text{avg}}$	37.85 ± 1.63	36.89 ± 0.28	38.32 ± 0.53	37.16 ± 0.27
$\text{VLCN+LSTM}_{\text{avg}}$	39.40 ± 1.64	36.38 ± 0.29	38.33 ± 0.61	36.82 ± 0.31
VLCN_{avg}	$\mathbf{39.48 \pm 0.73}$	$\mathbf{37.37 \pm 0.21}$	$\mathbf{38.65 \pm 0.52}$	$\mathbf{37.66 \pm 0.21}$

Table 3: Performance comparison of different ablated versions of our model on MSVD-QA *test*. The table shows the average accuracy and standard deviation $\mu \pm \sigma$ for each length bin in %.

Model	Question Length (number of words)			
	1-3	4-8	≥ 9	All
MCAN_{avg}	$\mathbf{38.94 \pm 0.46}$	36.15 ± 0.16	33.35 ± 0.18	35.49 ± 0.16
$\text{VLCN}-\text{FLF}_{\text{avg}}$	38.49 ± 0.46	35.85 ± 0.17	33.42 ± 0.27	35.29 ± 0.16
$\text{VLCN+LSTM}_{\text{avg}}$	38.45 ± 0.35	35.82 ± 0.12	33.15 ± 0.19	35.20 ± 0.12
VLCN_{avg}	38.31 ± 0.41	36.57 ± 0.18	33.45 ± 0.15	35.77 ± 0.15
$\text{VLCN+FT}_{\text{avg}}$	38.92 ± 0.27	$\mathbf{36.78 \pm 0.02}$	$\mathbf{33.65 \pm 0.08}$	$\mathbf{36.00 \pm 0.01}$

Table 4: Performance comparison of different ablated versions of our model on MSRVTT-QA *test*. The table shows the average accuracy and standard deviation $\mu \pm \sigma$ for each length bin in %.

attends to the word *doing* the most. The high values of the last column of $G(L, C)$ indicate that the model is searching for possible clips that align well with the action *doing*. This highlights the importance of the independent language guided-attention over the clips. However, the guided-attention map over the frames $G(L, F)$ is flat indicating that the model is not sure which frames are important to answer the question. This uncertainty is alleviated by the efficient fast-learning feature fusion of FLF that

Model	Answer Frequency Bin			
	1-100	101-300	$\geq$ 301	All
MCAN_{avg}	50.40 ± 0.55	16.09 ± 0.47	2.76 ± 0.18	36.64 ± 0.44
$\text{VLCN-FLF}_{\text{avg}}$	$\mathbf{51.37 \pm 0.19}$	15.72 ± 0.90	2.49 ± 0.73	37.16 ± 0.27
$\text{VLCN+LSTM}_{\text{avg}}$	50.57 ± 0.86	16.57 ± 1.01	3.25 ± 0.72	36.82 ± 0.31
VLCN_{avg}	51.35 ± 0.36	$\mathbf{17.80 \pm 0.42}$	$\mathbf{3.35 \pm 0.17}$	$\mathbf{37.66 \pm 0.21}$

Table 5: Performance comparison of different ablated versions of our model on MSVD-QA *test*. The table shows the average accuracy and standard deviation $\mu \pm \sigma$ for each frequency bin in %.

Model	Answer Frequency Bin			
	1-100	101-300	$\geq$ 301	All
MCAN_{avg}	$\mathbf{48.90 \pm 0.34}$	17.08 ± 0.74	3.26 ± 0.29	35.49 ± 0.16
$\text{VLCN-FLF}_{\text{avg}}$	48.64 ± 0.11	16.90 ± 0.59	3.28 ± 0.35	35.29 ± 0.16
$\text{VLCN+LSTM}_{\text{avg}}$	48.53 ± 0.21	16.62 ± 0.44	3.39 ± 0.29	35.20 ± 0.12
VLCN_{avg}	47.70 ± 0.24	20.97 ± 0.25	5.84 ± 0.18	35.77 ± 0.15
$\text{VLCN+FT}_{\text{avg}}$	48.03 ± 0.11	$\mathbf{20.98 \pm 0.33}$	$\mathbf{5.88 \pm 0.12}$	$\mathbf{36.00 \pm 0.01}$

Table 6: Performance comparison of different ablated versions of our model on MSRVTT-QA *test*. The table shows the average accuracy and standard deviation $\mu \pm \sigma$ for each frequency bin in %.

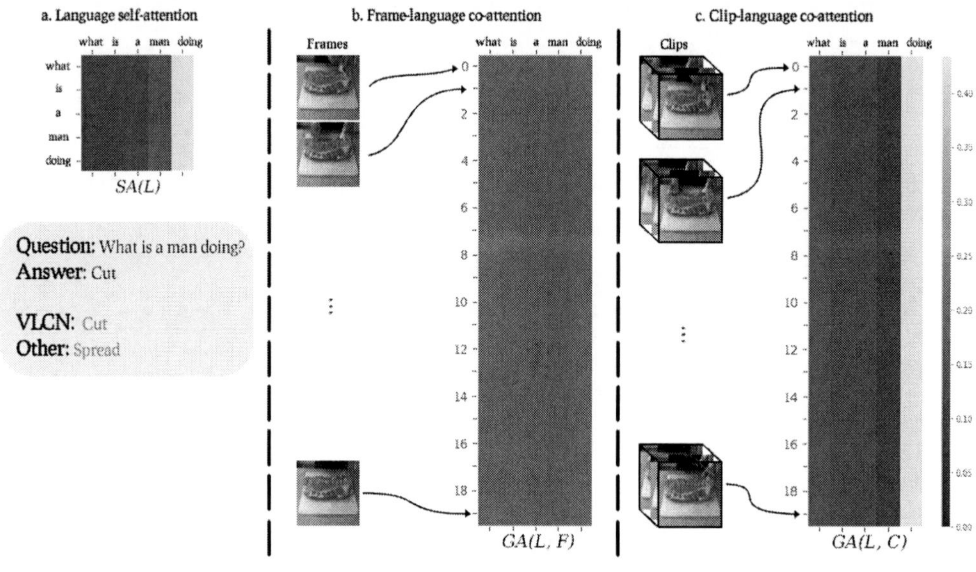

Figure 2: Visualization of the attention maps learned by the last video language co-attention layer. The indices [0, 19] indicate the individual 20 frames and clips of the video (some of which are shown).

leads our full VLCN model to predict the correct answer. While all of the ablated versions predict the wrong answer *spread*, our VLCN model answers the question correctly by predicting *cut*.

6 Conclusion

In this work, we proposed the Video Language Co-Attention Network (VLCN) for VideoQA. At its core are two distinct novel contributions: Stacked co-attention layers in an encoder-decoder framework to *separately* guide self-attended language features over both static video frame and dynamic clip features; and Fast-Learning Fusion (FLF) – a memory-enhanced multimodal block to efficiently fuse the reduced features. We demonstrated that the combination of both results in significant improvements and competitive performance with state-of-the-art models on the challenging MSVD-QA and MSRVTT-QA datasets. We also demonstrated the particular advantage of our model in dealing with long questions that require deeper reasoning or questions with rare answers. Finally, further experiments showed that our FLF block allows our model to generalize better across different datasets via transfer learning.

Acknowledgments

A. Bulling was funded by the European Research Council (ERC; grant agreement 801708). E. Sood was funded by the Deutsche Forschungsgemeinschaft (DFG, German Research Foundation) under Germany's Excellence Strategy - EXC 2075 - 390740016.

References

Nayyer Aafaq, Ajmal Mian, Wei Liu, Syed Zulqarnain Gilani, and Mubarak Shah. 2019. Video Description: A Survey of Methods, Datasets, and Evaluation Metrics. *Association for Computing Machinery*, 52(6).

Elad Amrani, Rami Ben-Ari, Daniel Rotman, and Alex Bronstein. 2020. Noise estimation using density estimation for self-supervised multimodal learning. *arXiv preprint arXiv:2003.03186*.

Peter Anderson, Xiaodong He, Chris Buehler, Damien Teney, Mark Johnson, Stephen Gould, and Lei Zhang. 2018. Bottom-up and top-down attention for image captioning and visual question answering. In *Proc. IEEE Conference on Computer Vision and Pattern Recognition (CVPR)*, pages 6077–6086.

Elahe Arani, Fahad Sarfraz, and Bahram Zonooz. 2021. Learning fast, learning slow: A general continual learning method based on complementary learning system. In *International Conference on Learning Representations*.

Yoshua Bengio, Jérôme Louradour, Ronan Collobert, and Jason Weston. 2009. Curriculum learning. In *Proc. International Conference on Machine Learning (ICML)*, page 41–48.

David Chen and William B Dolan. 2011. Collecting highly parallel data for paraphrase evaluation. In *Proc. Annual Meeting of the Association for Computational Linguistics (ACL)*, pages 190–200.

Mark Collier and Joeran Beel. 2019. Memory-augmented neural networks for machine translation. *arXiv preprint arXiv:1909.08314*.

Jacob Devlin, Ming-Wei Chang, Kenton Lee, and Kristina Toutanova. 2018. Bert: Pre-training of deep bidirectional transformers for language understanding. *arXiv preprint arXiv:1810.04805*.

Chenyou Fan, Xiaofan Zhang, Shu Zhang, Wensheng Wang, Chi Zhang, and Heng Huang. 2019. Heterogeneous memory enhanced multimodal attention model for video question answering. In *Proc. IEEE Conference on Computer Vision and Pattern Recognition (CVPR)*, pages 1999–2007.

Jiyang Gao, Runzhou Ge, Kan Chen, and Ram Nevatia. 2018. Motion-appearance co-memory networks for video question answering. In *Proc. IEEE Conference on Computer Vision and Pattern Recognition (CVPR)*, pages 6576–6585.

Alex Graves, Greg Wayne, and Ivo Danihelka. 2014. Neural turing machines. *arXiv preprint arXiv:1410.5401*.

Alex Graves, Greg Wayne, Malcolm Reynolds, Tim Harley, Ivo Danihelka, Agnieszka Grabska-Barwińska, Sergio Gómez Colmenarejo, Edward Grefenstette, Tiago Ramalho, John Agapiou, et al. 2016. Hybrid computing using a neural network with dynamic external memory. *Nature*, 538:471–476.

Sepp Hochreiter and Jürgen Schmidhuber. 1997. Long short-term memory. *Neural computation*, 9:1735–1780.

Yunseok Jang, Yale Song, Youngjae Yu, Youngjin Kim, and Gunhee Kim. 2017. Tgif-qa: Toward spatio-temporal reasoning in visual question answering. In *Proc. IEEE Conference on Computer Vision and Pattern Recognition (CVPR)*, pages 2758–2766.

Shuiwang Ji, Wei Xu, Ming Yang, and Kai Yu. 2012. 3D convolutional neural networks for human action recognition. *IEEE transactions on pattern analysis and machine intelligence*, 35:221–231.

Jianwen Jiang, Ziqiang Chen, Haojie Lin, Xibin Zhao, and Yue Gao. 2020. Divide and Conquer: Question-Guided Spatio-Temporal Contextual Attention for Video Question Answering. *Proc. Conference on Artificial Intelligence (AAAI)*, 34:11101–11108.

Andrej Karpathy, George Toderici, Sanketh Shetty, Thomas Leung, Rahul Sukthankar, and Li Fei-Fei. 2014. Large-scale Video Classification with Convolutional Neural Networks. In *Proc. IEEE Conference on Computer Vision and Pattern Recognition (CVPR)*.

Junyeong Kim, Minuk Ma, Kyungsu Kim, Sungjin Kim, and Chang D. Yoo. 2019. Progressive attention memory network for movie story question answering. In *Proc. IEEE Conference on Computer Vision and Pattern Recognition (CVPR)*.

Kyung-Min Kim, Seong-Ho Choi, Jin-Hwa Kim, and Byoung-Tak Zhang. 2018. Multimodal dual attention memory for video story question answering. In *Proc. European Conference on Computer Vision (ECCV)*, pages 673–688.

Diederik P Kingma and Jimmy Ba. 2014. Adam: A method for stochastic optimization. *arXiv preprint arXiv:1412.6980*.

Thao Minh Le, Vuong Le, Svetha Venkatesh, and Truyen Tran. 2020a. Hierarchical Conditional Relation Networks for Video Question Answering. In *Proc. IEEE Conference on Computer Vision and Pattern Recognition (CVPR)*.

Thao Minh Le, Vuong Le, Svetha Venkatesh, and Truyen Tran. 2020b. Hierarchical conditional relation networks for video question answering.

In *Proc. IEEE Conference on Computer Vision and Pattern Recognition (CVPR)*, pages 9972–9981.

Jie Lei, Licheng Yu, Mohit Bansal, and Tamara L Berg. 2018. Tvqa: Localized, compositional video question answering. *arXiv preprint arXiv:1809.01696*.

Xiangpeng Li, Jingkuan Song, Lianli Gao, Xianglong Liu, Wenbing Huang, Xiangnan He, and Chuang Gan. 2019. Beyond rnns: Positional self-attention with co-attention for video question answering. In *Proc. Conference on Artificial Intelligence (AAAI)*, volume 33, pages 8658–8665.

Jiasen Lu, Jianwei Yang, Dhruv Batra, and Devi Parikh. 2016. Hierarchical Question-Image Co-Attention for Visual Question Answering. In *Proc. Advances in Neural Information Processing Systems (NeurIPS)*, pages 1–9.

James L McClelland, Felix Hill, Maja Rudolph, Jason Baldridge, and Hinrich Schütze. 2020a. Placing language in an integrated understanding system: Next steps toward human-level performance in neural language models. *National Academy of Sciences*, 117:25966–25974.

James L McClelland, Felix Hill Maja, Rudolph, Jason Baldridge, and Hinrich Schütze. 2019. Extending machine language models toward human-level language understanding. *arXiv preprint arXiv:1912.05877*.

James L McClelland, Bruce L McNaughton, and Andrew K Lampinen. 2020b. Integration of new information in memory: new insights from a complementary learning systems perspective. *Philosophical Transactions of the Royal Society B*, 375(1799):20190637.

James L McClelland, Bruce L McNaughton, and Randall C O'Reilly. 1995. Why there are complementary learning systems in the hippocampus and neocortex: insights from the successes and failures of connectionist models of learning and memory. *Psychological review*, 102(3):419.

James L McClelland, David E Rumelhart, PDP Research Group, et al. 1986. *Parallel distributed processing*, volume 2. MIT press Cambridge, MA.

Antoine Miech, Dimitri Zhukov, Jean-Baptiste Alayrac, Makarand Tapaswi, Ivan Laptev, and Josef Sivic. 2019. HowTo100M: Learning a Text-Video Embedding by Watching Hundred Million Narrated Video Clips. In *ICCV*.

Seil Na, Sangho Lee, Jisung Kim, and Gunhee Kim. 2017. A read-write memory network for movie story understanding. In *Proc. International Conference on Computer Vision (ICCV)*, pages 677–685.

Sinno Jialin Pan and Qiang Yang. 2010. A survey on transfer learning. *IEEE Transactions on Knowledge and Data Engineering*, 22:1345–1359.

Adam Paszke, Sam Gross, Francisco Massa, Adam Lerer, James Bradbury, Gregory Chanan, Trevor Killeen, Zeming Lin, Natalia Gimelshein, Luca Antiga, Alban Desmaison, Andreas Kopf, Edward Yang, Zachary DeVito, Martin Raison, Alykhan Tejani, Sasank Chilamkurthy, Benoit Steiner, Lu Fang, Junjie Bai, and Soumith Chintala. 2019. Pytorch: An imperative style, high-performance deep learning library. In *Proc. Advances in Neural Information Processing Systems (NeurIPS)*, pages 8024–8035.

Devshree Patel, Ratnam Parikh, and Yesha Shastri. 2021. Recent advances in video question answering: A review of datasets and methods. *arXiv preprint arXiv:2101.05954*.

Jeffrey Pennington, Richard Socher, and Christopher Manning. 2014. GloVe: Global vectors for word representation. In *Proc. Conference on Empirical Methods in Natural Language Processing (EMNLP)*, pages 1532–1543.

Olga Russakovsky, Jia Deng, Hao Su, Jonathan Krause, Sanjeev Satheesh, Sean Ma, Zhiheng Huang, Andrej Karpathy, Aditya Khosla, Michael Bernstein, et al. 2015. Imagenet large scale visual recognition challenge. *International journal of computer vision*, 115:211–252.

Paul Hongsuck Seo, Arsha Nagrani, and Cordelia Schmid. 2021. Look Before you Speak: Visually Contextualized Utterances. In *Proc. IEEE Conference on Computer Vision and Pattern Recognition (CVPR)*.

Karen Simonyan and Andrew Zisserman. 2014. Very deep convolutional networks for large-scale image recognition. *arXiv preprint arXiv:1409.1556*.

Xiaomeng Song, Yucheng Shi, Xin Chen, and Yahong Han. 2018. Explore multi-step reasoning in video question answering. In *Proc. International Conference on Multimedia (ACM-MM)*, pages 239–247.

Ekta Sood, Simon Tannert, Philipp Müller, and Andreas Bulling. 2020. Improving Natural Language Processing Tasks with Human Gaze-Guided Neural Attention. In *Proc. Advances in Neural Information Processing Systems (NeurIPS)*, pages 1–15.

Sainbayar Sukhbaatar, Arthur Szlam, Jason Weston, and Rob Fergus. 2015. End-to-end memory networks. *arXiv preprint arXiv:1503.08895*.

Guanglu Sun, Lili Liang, Tianlin Li, Bo Yu, Meng Wu, and Bolun Zhang. 2021. Video question answering: a survey of models and datasets. *Mobile Networks and Applications*, pages 1–34.

Ashish Vaswani, Noam Shazeer, Niki Parmar, Jakob Uszkoreit, Llion Jones, Aidan N Gomez, Ł ukasz Kaiser, and Illia Polosukhin. 2017. Attention is all you need. In *Proc. Advances in Neural*

Information Processing Systems (NeurIPS), volume 30.

Sumit Chopra Jason Weston and Antoine Bordes. 2015. Memory networks. *arXiv preprint arXiv:1410.3916*.

Dejing Xu, Zhou Zhao, Jun Xiao, Fei Wu, Hanwang Zhang, Xiangnan He, and Yueting Zhuang. 2017. Video Question Answering via Gradually Refined Attention over Appearance and Motion. In *Proc. International Conference on Multimedia (ACM-MM)*, page 1645–1653.

Jun Xu, Tao Mei, Ting Yao, and Yong Rui. 2016. MSR-VTT: A large video description dataset for bridging video and language. In *Proc. IEEE Conference on Computer Vision and Pattern Recognition (CVPR)*, pages 5288–5296.

Hongyang Xue, Wenqing Chu, Zhou Zhao, and Deng Cai. 2018. A better way to attend: Attention with trees for video question answering. *IEEE Transactions on Image Processing*, 27(11):5563–5574.

Zekun Yang, Noa Garcia, Chenhui Chu, Mayu Otani, Yuta Nakashima, and Haruo Takemura. 2020. Bert representations for video question answering. In *Proc. IEEE Conference on Computer Vision and Pattern Recognition (CVPR)*, pages 1556–1565.

Yunan Ye, Zhou Zhao, Yimeng Li, Long Chen, Jun Xiao, and Yueting Zhuang. 2017. Video question answering via attribute-augmented attention network learning. In *Proc. Conference on Research and Development in Information Retrieval (ACM-SIGIR)*, pages 829–832.

Chengxiang Yin, Jian Tang, Zhiyuan Xu, and Yanzhi Wang. 2020. Memory Augmented Deep Recurrent Neural Network for Video Question Answering. *IEEE Transactions on Neural Networks and Learning Systems*, 31:3159–3167.

Zhou Yu, Jun Yu, Yuhao Cui, Dacheng Tao, and Qi Tian. 2019. Deep modular co-attention networks for visual question answering. In *Proc. IEEE Conference on Computer Vision and Pattern Recognition (CVPR)*, pages 6281–6290.

Linchao Zhu, Zhongwen Xu, Yi Yang, and Alexander G Hauptmann. 2017. Uncovering the temporal context for video question answering. *International Journal of Computer Vision*, 124(3):409–421.

A Appendix

A.1 Datasets

From Tables 7 and 8 we can see how the questions are not equally-distributed across all of the types. Question type *what* is the most diverse and accounts for 62.63% and 68.53% of the total number of questions in MSVD-QA and MSRVTT-QA, respectively. Our best VLCN model achieves new state-of-the-art performance on this question type across both datasets, i.e. 28.42% and 30.69% on MSVD-QA and MSRVTT-QA, respectively – a relative improvement of 4.12% and 2.79% over MA-DRNN (Yin et al., 2020) and QueST (Jiang et al., 2020).

	Videos	QA pairs	Question Type				
			What	Who	How	When	Where
Train	1200	30 933	19 485	10 479	736	161	72
Val	250	6 415	3995	2168	185	51	16
Test	520	13 157	8149	4552	370	58	28
All	1970	50 505	31 629	17 199	1291	270	116

Table 7: Statistics of MSVD-QA. The table shows the number of videos and question-answer pairs in the *train*, *validation*, and *test* splits as well as the number of questions per question type.

	Videos	QA pairs	Question Type				
			What	Who	How	When	Where
Train	6513	158 581	108 792	43 592	4067	1626	504
Val	497	12 278	8337	3439	344	106	52
Test	2990	72 821	49 869	20 385	1640	677	250
All	10 000	243 680	166 998	67 416	6051	2409	806

Table 8: Statistics of MSRVTT-QA. The table shows the number of videos and question-answer pairs in the *train*, *validation*, and *test* splits as well as the number of questions per question type.

A.2 Ablation Study

Tables 9 and 10 show the ensemble performance of our VLCN model and its ablated versions with respect to individual question types. On MSVD-QA, our full model achieves the best accuracy on the most diverse question type *what* and performs on par with its ablated versions on the remaining question types, i.e. *who*, *how*, *when*, and *where*. Similar results can be observed on MSRVTT-QA: Our full VLCN model achieves the best accuracy on the most diverse question type *what* as well as question type *when* and performs on par with the rest of its ablated versions on the remaining question types *who*, *how*, and *where*.

A.3 Transfer Learning

By observing the last two rows of Table 10, we can see the effect of transfer learning on the performance of our full VLCN model with respect to individual question types. In fact, by fine-tuning the fast-learning connections and the DNC weights inside the FLF block on MSRVTT-QA, we improved the performance on three different questions types, i.e. the most and second most diverse types *what* and *who* as well as question type *when*. This results in a new state-of-the-art overall accuracy of 36.01%.

Model	Question Type				
	What	Who	How	When	Where
MCAN_{avg}	26.94 ± 0.43	49.89 ± 0.43	$\mathbf{82.48 \pm 0.94}$	72.76 ± 0.69	45.71 ± 1.43
$\text{VLCN–FLF}_{\text{avg}}$	27.23 ± 0.58	50.77 ± 0.68	82.00 ± 1.00	$\mathbf{73.79 \pm 1.29}$	45.71 ± 5.72
$\text{VLCN+LSTM}_{\text{avg}}$	26.44 ± 0.69	$\mathbf{51.33 \pm 1.12}$	80.65 ± 3.41	72.06 ± 0.69	$\mathbf{47.14 \pm 5.25}$
VLCN_{avg}	$\mathbf{27.89 \pm 0.30}$	51.14 ± 0.18	81.08 ± 1.30	73.45 ± 0.85	46.43 ± 5.05

Table 9: Performance comparison of different ablated versions of our model on MSVD-QA *test*. The table shows the average accuracy and standard deviation $\mu \pm \sigma$ for each question type in %.

Model	Question Type				
	What	Who	How	When	Where
MCAN_{avg}	29.33 ± 0.03	$\mathbf{45.38 \pm 0.55}$	$\mathbf{83.33 \pm 0.61}$	75.07 ± 0.47	36.48 ± 1.35
$\text{VLCN–FLF}_{\text{avg}}$	29.15 ± 0.18	45.13 ± 0.24	83.01 ± 0.12	75.83 ± 0.76	37.28 ± 1.32
$\text{VLCN+LSTM}_{\text{avg}}$	28.92 ± 0.12	45.36 ± 0.32	83.06 ± 0.26	74.89 ± 1.57	$\mathbf{37.76 \pm 1.55}$
VLCN_{avg}	30.39 ± 0.07	43.92 ± 0.40	80.93 ± 0.90	76.87 ± 0.60	37.58 ± 1.48
$\text{VLCN+FT}_{\text{avg}}$	$\mathbf{30.59 \pm 0.10}$	44.27 ± 0.22	80.44 ± 1.14	$\mathbf{77.75 \pm 0.54}$	36.80 ± 0.44

Table 10: Performance comparison of different ablated versions of our model on MSRVTT-QA *test*. The table shows the average accuracy and standard deviation $\mu \pm \sigma$ for each question type in %.

A.4 Qualitative Analysis

We further show a qualitative example to highlight the supremacy of our full VLCN model over its ablated versions. In Figure 3, we can see how both the language self-attention $SA(L)$ and the guided-attention over the frames $GA(L, F)$ are both flat indicating that the model is having difficulties aligning the multi-modal features. However, the guided-attention over the clips $GA(L, C)$ shows high attention values to the word *who* which is, in this case, the keyword to answer the question *who sat in his chair?* depicted in the orange box. While all of the ablated versions predict the wrong answer *lady*, our VLCN model answers the question correctly by predicting *man*.

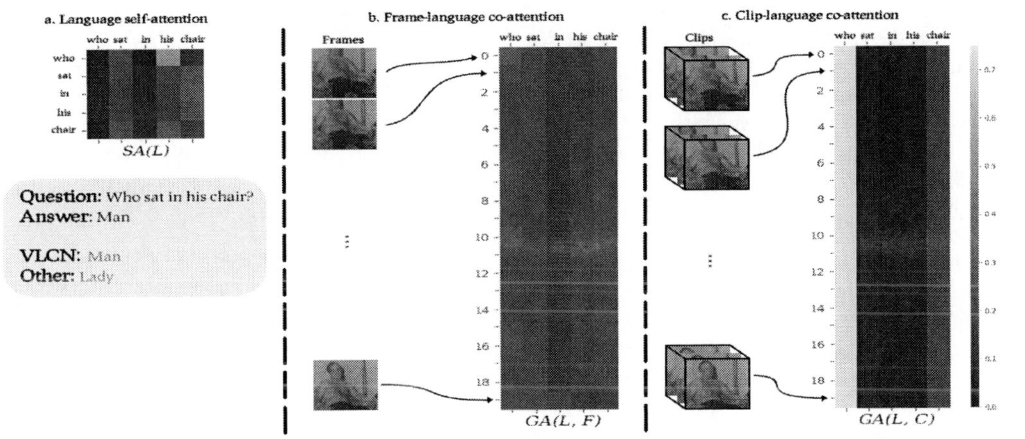

Figure 3: Visualization of the attention maps learned by the last video language co-attention layer. The indices [0, 19] indicate the individual 20 frames and clips of the video (some of which are shown).

Detecting Word-Level Adversarial Text Attacks via SHapley Additive exPlanations

Lukas Huber*
TU Munich,
Department of Informatics,
Germany
lukas1.huber@tum.de

Marc Alexander Kühn*
TU Munich,
Department of Informatics,
Germany
marcalexander.kuehn@tum.de

Edoardo Mosca*
TU Munich,
Department of Informatics,
Germany
edoardo.mosca@tum.de

Georg Groh
TU Munich,
Department of Informatics,
Germany
grohg@in.tum.de

Abstract

State-of-the-art machine learning models are prone to adversarial attacks: Maliciously crafted inputs to fool the model into making a wrong prediction, often with high confidence. While defense strategies have been extensively explored in the computer vision domain, research in natural language processing still lacks techniques to make models resilient to adversarial text inputs. We adapt a technique from computer vision to detect word-level attacks targeting text classifiers. This method relies on training an adversarial detector leveraging Shapley additive explanations and outperforms the current state-of-the-art on two benchmarks. Furthermore, we prove the detector requires only a low amount of training samples and, in some cases, generalizes to different datasets without needing to retrain.

1 Introduction

Adversarial examples are slightly perturbed input samples purposely crafted to fool a target model (Szegedy et al., 2014). Despite being similar to the original samples, they are often misclassified with high confidence (Goodfellow et al., 2015). Without effective defense techniques, machine learning models become unusable in high-stakes situations and safety-critical tasks (Sharma et al., 2019).

Research in computer vision has extensively worked on better understanding adversarial image attacks and developing more robust models (Madry et al., 2018; Ozdag, 2018). However, the literature in *Natural Language Processing (NLP)* has witnessed fewer advances concerning this issue (Mozes et al., 2021; Zhou et al., 2019; Wang et al., 2019).

Text data needs to fulfill several properties such as lexical, grammatical, and semantic constraints. Thus, many efficient adversarial image attacks—e.g. gradient-based ones—are not transferable as they would lead to incorrect characters and non-existing terms (Zhang et al., 2020). However, word-level attacks that can preserve semantical information without introducing noticeable inconsistencies are particularly effective and not detectable via spell checkers (Garg and Ramakrishnan, 2020; Ren et al., 2019).

The lack of defense strategies against word-level text attacks motivates our research as this is a major obstacle to the safe deployment of NLP models. This work's contribution can be summarized as follows:

(1) Based on an analogous idea from computer vision (Fidel et al., 2020), we propose an adversarial attack detector leveraging *SHapley Additive exPlanations* (SHAP) to accurately recognize input manipulations (Lundberg and Lee, 2017). Results show that it outperforms the previous state of the art in adversarial detection on multiple datasets (Mozes et al., 2021).

(2) We analyze our method in terms of data efficiency and generalization. The proposed approach still offers competitive performance when trained on very little data and can even be transferred to unseen datasets while almost matching the previous state of the art.

*These authors contributed equally

Proceedings of the 7th Workshop on Representation Learning for NLP, pages 156 - 166
May 26, 2022 ©2022 Association for Computational Linguistics

(3) Alongside the quantitative analysis and its results, we visualize the space of generated Shapley-value-based explanations. This qualitative analysis sheds light on the reasons behind our method's high performance and desirable properties.

2 Related Work

2.1 Adversarial Text Attacks

An adversarial text attack is an artificial input obtained by modifying a sample from the available data. Normally, the altered text is similar—syntactically, semantically, or both—to the original one. However, their corresponding classification output substantially differs. Attacks can be either *targeted* or *untargeted* (Tao et al., 2018). Attacks of the first type aim to create misclassification results w.r.t. a specific class whereas the latter type wants to generate a misclassification regardless of the exact class.

Methods like DeepWordBug (Gao et al., 2018) or Hotflip (Ebrahimi et al., 2018) introduce character-level noise to create typos and grammatical inconsistencies in the sentence. These adversarial examples appear very similar to the original samples, but do not perfectly preserve their meaning and can be recognized due to their lexical incorrectness.

Other types of attacks instead alter the text at the word level and produce semantically equivalent and grammatically correct sentences to the initial input. Examples of techniques using this strategy are PWWS (Ren et al., 2019), TextFooler (Jin et al., 2020), and BAE (Garg and Ramakrishnan, 2020).

2.2 Defense Strategies for Computer Vision

Robustness against adversarial attacks—and especially their automatic detection—has been more exhaustively researched for computer vision applications rather than for text inputs. Hence, we briefly present a selection of the most promising approaches.

Xu et al. (2018) propose *Feature Squeezing*, based on the assumption that feature spaces are often unnecessarily large and leave extensive possibilities for an attacker to generate adversarial examples. Their approach leverages this fact by comparing the prediction of the original input image with a simplified one. When this difference surpasses a specific threshold, the input is classified as adversarial.

Roth et al. (2019) detect adversarial examples by measuring statistical differences between original and perturbed logits. According to their results, output logits corresponding to adversarial examples exhibit a much larger variation than normal samples when the input is perturbed.

Integrating explainability to detect adversarial examples has already been shown to be beneficial. Fidel et al. (2020) detect patterns in the SHAP signatures of input images (Lundberg and Lee, 2017). For normal samples, the inter-class SHAP signatures share common characteristics. For adversarial examples, however, the SHAP signatures show a mixture between two classes which can easily be detected using an additional classification model.

2.3 Defense Strategies for Natural Language Processing

Character-level attacks can be countered with defenses based on spell checkers (Pruthi et al., 2019; Huang et al., 2019). Nonetheless, those same defenses are extremely vulnerable to word-level attacks capable of preserving language coherence (Wang et al., 2019). Effective methods against syntactically correct attacks are *Adversarial Training* (AT) (Goodfellow et al., 2015), *Dirichlet Neighborhood Ensemble* (DNE) (Zhou et al., 2020), *Adversarial Sparse Convex Combination* (ASCC) (Dong et al., 2021) and *Synonym Encoding Method* (SEM) (Wang et al., 2019). The first three leverage some form of data augmentation to train the model on perturbed samples as well. The last, instead, introduces an encoder step before the target model's input layer and trains it to eliminate potential perturbations.

Particularly relevant for this work are *adversarial detection* methods. In contrast to other defenses, they can explicitly recognize manipulated inputs and send an alert signal. For natural language data, the available methods are *Frequency-Guided Word Substitution* (FGWS) (Mozes et al., 2021) and *learning to DIScriminate Perturbation* (DISP) (Zhou et al., 2019). The first—exploiting frequency properties of adversarial words—is the most recent and accurate method. Its authors showed medium to high F1 detection scores in a range from 62.2-91.4%, varying on the type of attack and target model.

2.4 Feature Relevance Explainability Methods

Among explainability techniques, *feature relevance* methods are often used to explain predictions pro-

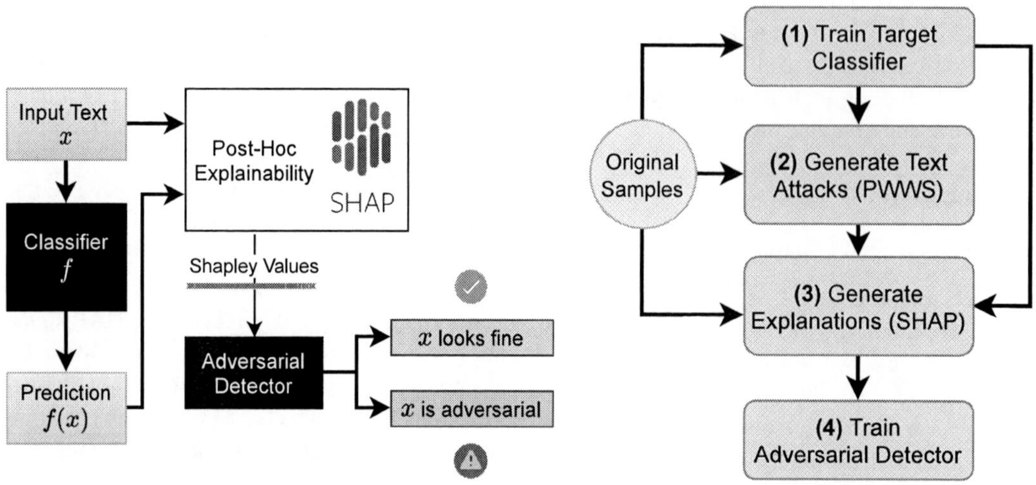

(a) Goal Pipeline

(b) Construction Steps

Figure 1: Our detector for recognizing adversarial examples: the overall pipeline once the detector is trained (a) and the necessary steps in order to train it (b). While generating many adversarial attacks and explanations is required for training, the detector can then be simply "plugged in" and deployed together with the classifier f.

duced by black-box models (Arrieta et al., 2020; Mosca et al., 2021). Their goal is to attribute a relevance score to each input feature. Such value should quantify the effect that the feature has on the output, i.e. their contribution to the model's prediction (Wich et al., 2021).

Some of these methods rely on computing the gradient of the output w.r.t. the input features (Simonyan et al., 2014; Sundararajan et al., 2017). Others, such as LRP (Bach et al., 2015) and DeepLIFT (Shrikumar et al., 2017), are specifically designed for neural networks and follow the information flow in a backward fashion through the model's architecture. The procedure continues one layer at a time until the input features are reached. LIME (Ribeiro et al., 2016) explains black-box models via a local surrogate that approximates their behavior around a single instance. The surrogate can be then interpreted directly to estimate each feature's relevance.

Lundberg and Lee (2017) prove that several popular feature relevance methods—including LIME, LRP, and DeepLIFT—belong to a broader class of approaches: *additive feature relevance methods*. The authors propose a unified view of such methods that, combined with the game-theoretic concept of Shapley values (Shapley, 1952), constitutes the SHAP framework. SHAP-based explanations are covered more in detail in Section 3.2 as they represent a fundamental component of our proposed method.

3 Methodology

Our defense belongs to the adversarial detection category and is strongly inspired by the work of Fidel et al. (2020), which detects image-based adversarial attacks for computer vision models by using SHAP signatures. This work, instead, studies the application of this idea to text attacks for NLP classifiers. As sketched in Figure 1a, our goal pipeline consists of multiple stages. First, the input is fed to a classifier trained on the task-at-hand, which outputs a prediction. Shapley values are then computed w.r.t. the outcome and passed onto a machine-learning detector that predicts whether the sample is an adversarial attack. Note that our detector does not make any assumption on the classifier and is hence model-agnostic.

The classifier targeted by the attacks becomes considerably more robust when used in combination with the adversarial detector. To achieve our goal, we have to take several steps in order to train our detector. These steps—also summarized in Figure 1b for the reader—are described in detail in the next sections.

3.1 Crafting Adversarial Text Attacks

To train and test our detector, we choose to craft attacks semantically similar to the original input. This choice preserves lexical and grammatical co-

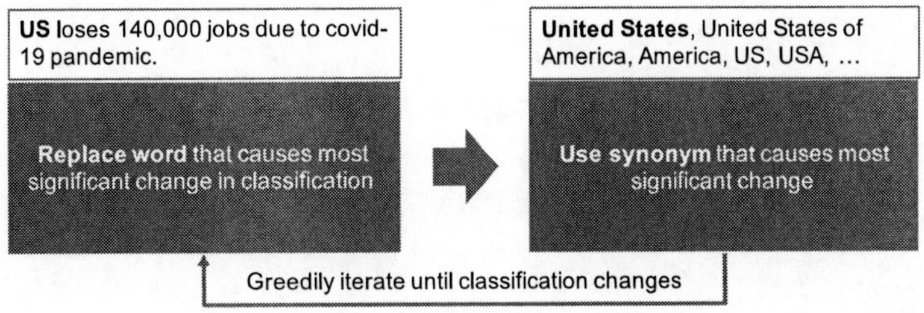

Figure 2: A simplified view of the generation of adversarial examples using PWWS (Ren et al., 2019)

herence also in adversarial sentences. We believe that such attacks are more subtle as they cannot be detected by spell checkers. In practice, for each sample x in the dataset, we generate

$$x^* = x + \Delta x, \|\Delta x\| < \epsilon \tag{1}$$

where Δx is a semantic perturbation and the classes predicted for x and x^* are different. To this end, we utilize the untargeted *Probability Weighted Word Saliency* (PWWS) method by Ren et al. (2019). This approach shows high effectiveness with good transferability. According to human evaluation, PWWS provides realistic examples with lexical correctness and only sporadic grammatical errors or semantic shifting (Ren et al., 2019).

The technique selects the word to be replaced based on two factors. The first is the change in the classification probability after substitution. The second, called *word saliency*, measures the variation in the output probability of the classifier if the word is set to unknown (out of vocabulary). The chosen word is then replaced by a word from a synonym set which causes the most significant change of classification probability. The algorithm greedily iterates until enough words have been replaced to change the final classification label. Figure 2 sketches the core idea behind the method.

3.2 Generating Model Explanations

Whenever classifying an input sentence as either regular or adversarial, our detector needs access to its corresponding feature relevance explanation. In other words, the detector takes its decision based on *how strong* each feature—in our case each word—influences the final model prediction. The assumption is that the model's reaction to original and adversarial samples is different even if the inputs look similar for a human. Thus, the model explanations for the two samples should also substantially differ from each other (Fidel et al., 2020).

We pick SHAP (Lundberg and Lee, 2017) to produce instance-level explanations to train the adversarial detector. This choice is motivated by the empirical superiority proven by its developers (Lundberg and Lee, 2017) and its previous successful applications in detecting attacks in computer vision. However, while Fidel et al. (2020) generate SHAP signatures w.r.t. the penultimate layer of the target model, we produce explanations directly w.r.t. the input sentence as text perturbations are introduced at the word level.

SHAP is based on a game theory concept—called Shapley values (Shapley, 1952)—originally used to fairly distribute a reward to a set of players that contributed to a certain outcome. In our case, the outcome is the model's prediction whereas the input features, i.e. the input words, are the players involved. Since the players most likely contributed differently to the turnout, their payout should differ based on their impact. Given a text classifier f and the set of all available features M, the Shapley value corresponding to each feature i is computed independently. More precisely, it is a weighted average of the relative outcome differences

$$f(S \cup \{i\}) - f(S) \tag{2}$$

across all feature subsets $S \subseteq M \setminus \{i\}$.

As there are $2^{|M|}$ possible choices for S, exact Shapley values are exponentially complex to compute. However, the SHAP framework offers several methods to approximate them accurately and efficiently (Lundberg and Lee, 2017). In our work, we utilize DeepSHAP as it is tailored to deep learning models, which we utilize as targets for the text attacks (Lundberg and Lee, 2017). An official implementation has been made publicly available by the SHAP authors. [1]

Figure 3 shows two examples of explanations generated for *IMDb*, a movie review dataset (Maas

[1] https://github.com/slundberg/shap

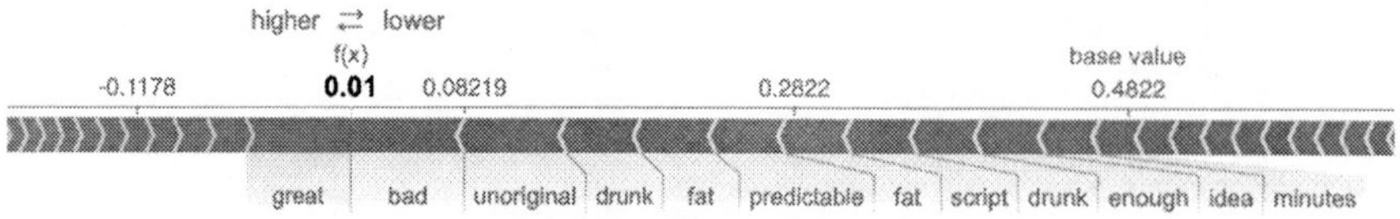

(a) Original SHAP signature

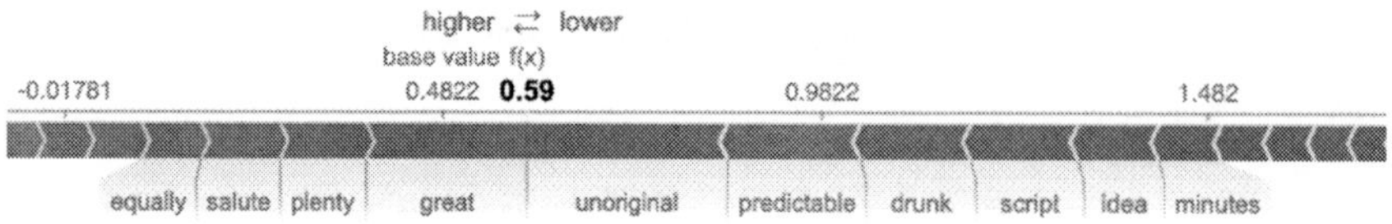

(b) Adversarial SHAP signature

Figure 3: Force plots generated for a sample of the *IMDb* dataset and its corresponding adversarial attack. The *base value* indicates the average model's prediction across the whole dataset and $f(x)$ represents the model output probability for the selected instance. Red attributes drive the predictions towards class 1 (i.e. a positive review) and blue ones towards class 0 (i.e. a negative review). Starting from the base value (~ 0.48) and adding up all word contributions we reach the final prediction of 0.01. Hence, the original sample is classified as negative with high confidence. In the adversarial SHAP signature, most negative words were replaced by synonyms such that the prediction is now positive.

et al., 2011), with DeepSHAP. The first (Figure 3a) was generated from an original sample while the second (Figure 3b) from its corresponding adversarial attack generated with PWWS. As we can see, the attack changes substantially the effect that words have on the prediction. Hence, word-level contributions are a major indicator for detecting parts of a sentence that have a suspiciously high impact on the model decision. This supports our initial hypothesis that SHAP explanations do not rely on image-only properties and therefore can also serve as features for an adversarial detector in the NLP domain.

3.3 Target Model and Detector Architectures

Our pipeline includes two machine learning models: the text classifier trained for the task-at-hand and the adversarial detector.

For consistency with Mozes et al. (2021), used later for performance comparison, we chose a Bidirectional LSTM (Bi-LSTM) (Schuster and Paliwal, 1997) as architecture to be targeted by the adversarial attacks. However, other NLP models can also be utilized as the detector does not make any assumption on the classifier. The text inputs are first trimmed and padded to an equal length of 100. Increasing the input length drastically increases complexity along the pipeline while only yielding minor accuracy gains. Tokens are transformed into GloVe embeddings (Pennington et al., 2014) before being fed to the Bi-LSTM core layer. We attach a fully connected head layer to compute output probabilities. We adjust the number of output neurons based on the dataset currently in use.

SHAP values are extracted from the model for all output classes. Therefore, the SHAP signatures passed to the detector are numerical vectors of dimensionality [#classes $\times$ 100]. Here, each numerical value corresponds to the impact of a single word w.r.t. the model's output. We do not pick any particular architecture for our adversarial detector. Instead, we experiment with a variety of relatively simple machine learning models to test their performance. We include a *random forest* (Breiman, 2001), a *Support Vector Machine* (SVM) (Boser et al., 1992), and a simple two-layer-feed-forward neural network (Rumelhart et al., 1985).

3.4 Overall Pipeline and Experimental Setup

With the methodology for the main steps outlined in the previous sections, we now describe in greater detail how those steps are combined, following what we initially presented in Figure 1b. We repeat the procedure for each text dataset utilized for testing. These will be presented later in our evaluation section (4).

To begin with, we train the Bi-LSTM model on the given dataset. We consider this step concluded once the model converges to a satisfactory accuracy. This is usually around 90% accuracy, depending on the dataset. After that, we utilize PWWS as proposed by Ren et al. (2019)—implemented

	Method	AG_News	IMDb	SST-2	Yelp Polarity	Metric
Our	Neural Network	0.90 / 0.90	**0.96 / 0.96**	0.75 / 0.75	**0.94 / 0.94**	F1 score / Accuracy
	Random Forest	**0.91 / 0.91**	0.87 / 0.87	**0.77 / 0.77**	0.84 / 0.84	F1 score / Accuracy
	SVM	0.90 / 0.90	0.90 / 0.90	0.74 / 0.74	0.89 / 0.89	F1 score / Accuracy
SotA Detector	FGWS (Mozes et al., 2021)	-	0.77	0.63	-	F1 score
Other Defenses	DNE (Zhou et al., 2020)	**0.91**	0.82	-	-	Accuracy
	SEM (Wang et al., 2019)	0.76	0.85	-	-	Accuracy
	ASCC (Dong et al., 2021)	-	0.77	-	-	Accuracy

Table 1: Performance of different detector architectures on the *AG_News, IMDb, SST-2* and *Yelp Polarity* datasets. For comparison, we report also the defense performance of *Frequency-Guided Word Substitutions* (FGWS), *Dirichlet Neighbourhood Ensemble* (DNE), *Synonym Encoding Method* (SEM) and *Adversarial Sparse Convex Combinations* (ASCC).

in the TextAttack library [2]—to produce adversarial attacks targeting our trained NLP model. We generate one attack for each sample in the dataset. Instance-level explanations—i.e. Shapley value approximations—are then created via SHAP, both for normal and adversarial samples (Lundberg and Lee, 2017).

We combine all explanations to compose a balanced dataset for our adversarial detector. The data is split into training and test sets following an 80/20-ratio. We further used the default hyperparameters for all models in the framework. To allow for optimal reproducibility, we seeded all of our experiments. For the neural network-based detector, we pick layers of size 400 using a ReLU activation and an L1 weight regularizer to avoid overfitting. To further increase regularization, Dropout is used (Srivastava et al., 2014). The model is then trained for 10 epochs using the Adam optimizer with a learning rate of 0.001 and β_1, β_2 set to their default values of 0.9 and 0.99 respectively (Kingma and Ba, 2015).

4 Evaluation

4.1 Performance Results

We evaluate our approach on four major datasets often used in research, namely *IMDb* (Maas et al., 2011), *SST-2* (Socher et al., 2013), *Yelp Polarity* and *AG_News* (Zhang et al., 2015). While the last one classifies news articles into four distinct categories, the other three are binary sentiment analysis tasks on movie review data. The reviews are not fed into the detector directly but their corresponding SHAP signatures are instead. The number of samples in the datasets used for the experiment is reported in Table 2. Every dataset consists of a 50:50 split between original and adversarial samples and the sizes are varying between 940 (*Yelp Polarity*) and 100,000 (*AG_News*) samples.

Dataset	Size	#Normal	#Adversarial
AG_News	100,000	50,000	50,000
IMDb	3,580	1,790	1,790
SST-2	3,162	1,581	1,581
Yelp Polarity	940	470	470

Table 2: Sizes of the individual SHAP signature datasets used for training the adversarial detector. All datasets consist of 50% normal and 50% adversarial signatures.

Table 1 shows the performance of various detector architectures on the four datasets together alongside results achieved by previously proposed methods. To the best of our knowledge, the FGWS method proposed by Mozes et al. (2021) is the best detector currently available. With our SHAP-based classifiers, we significantly outperform their method on the *IMDb* dataset by 19% with an F1-score of 96% and on the *SST-2* dataset by 14% with an F1-score of 77%. Relatively simple machine learning models like a random forest or a support vector machine are able to classify the data very accurately. Both Mozes et al. (2021) and our work evaluate their defenses against PWWS targeting a Bi-LSTM model.

Besides adversarial detectors, we also outperform all other existing defenses to the best of our knowledge. On *IMDb*, our approach improves by 11% accuracy compared to the best method (Wang et al., 2019). On *AG_News*, it is matched only by the DNE method from Zhou et al. (2020). For each approach considered, we report the result w.r.t. the configuration achieving the best performance against PWWS from their corresponding original work. For completeness, we mention that Zhou et al. (2019) reports great results but their performance is not comparable as they do not test their method against any well-established attack.

[2] https://github.com/QData/TextAttack

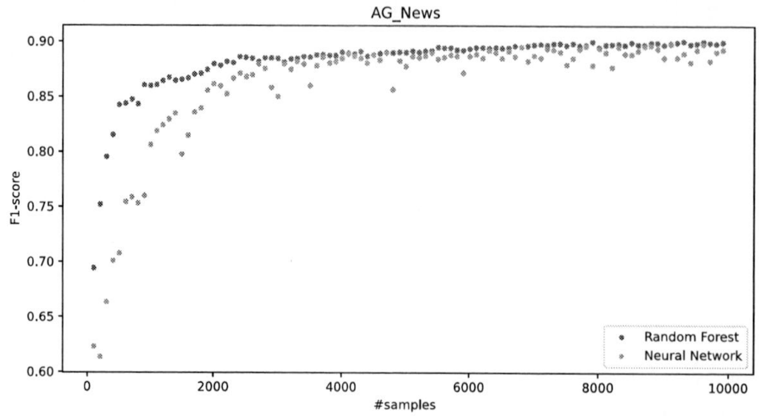

Figure 4: F1-scores for independent runs on the *AG_News* dataset using differently sized subsets of the training data. The F1-score starts to plateau after a few thousand samples for all detectors which shows data efficiency.

Classifier	Unnormalized SHAP	Unnorm. SHAP + Predicted Class	Normalized SHAP
Neural Network	0.90	0.90	0.90
Random Forest	0.91	0.91	0.92
SVM	0.90	0.90	0.90
Linear SVM	0.67	0.67	0.65

Table 3: F1-scores of input modifications for the detectors on the *AG_News* dataset.

To further improve the predictive performance of the model, we also included the predicted class coming from the base model as an input feature for the detector. As shown in Table 3, this had neither a positive nor a negative influence on the performance of the model. Normalizing the SHAP signatures only led to minor improvements for random forests and neural networks. This can be explained by the fact that all input features are Shapley values and are therefore in the same range.

4.2 Transferability

Base-Model	IMDb (Test)	SST-2 (Test)
IMDb	-	0.56
SST-2	0.42	-
Yelp Polarity	**0.71**	**0.66**

Table 4: F1-scores of the inference step with *IMDb* and *SST-2* datasets on neural network base-models which were trained on *IMDb, SST-2* and *Yelp Polarity*.

During our research the question arose whether the detectors are agnostic to the dataset or highly specialized. To evaluate this property, we trained three base-models with a neural network backbone on the *IMDb*, *SST-2* and *Yelp Polarity* datasets. Then, we performed the inference step with the *IMDb* and *SST-2* test sets on all three detectors and observed how the performance varies with different dataset combinations.

The results can be seen in Table 4. We report the strongest results when the detector was tested on the same dataset that was also used during training. This resulted in our competitive F1-scores of 94% on *IMDb* and 77% on *SST-2*. Interestingly, there existed other combinations which also produced results comparable to the state of the art, although the performance dropped compared to our strongest detectors. To be precise, the base-model which was trained on *Yelp Polarity* achieved good F1-scores on test sets of *IMDb* with 71.5% and of *SST-2* with 66%. In comparison, the state-of-the-art detector tested with similarly generated adversarial samples on a LSTM with PWWS by Mozes et al. (2021) achieved F1-scores of 77.4% on *IMDb* and of 63.4% on *SST-2*.

Such results are yet not strong enough to prove full generalization capabilities. However, we find them promising as they indicate that our detectors are in some cases actually transferable to other datasets once trained. Future research is crucial as in practice it allows to reuse models for different tasks.

4.3 Data efficiency

While our approach offers state-of-the-art detection performance of adversarial attacks, the corresponding detector model can be trained with a surprisingly low amount of data. To evaluate this property, we trained a neural network and a random forest on incremental subsets of the *IMDb* dataset where all runs were conducted independently from each other. We started with a dataset size of 100 and incrementally increased the number of samples up to 10,000. From Figure 4 one can directly observe the limited amount of data needed for the model to converge. For a neural network about 4,000 samples are needed before the F1-score starts to plateau. For a random forest classifier even less data is sufficient with around 3,000 samples.

4.4 Qualitative Results

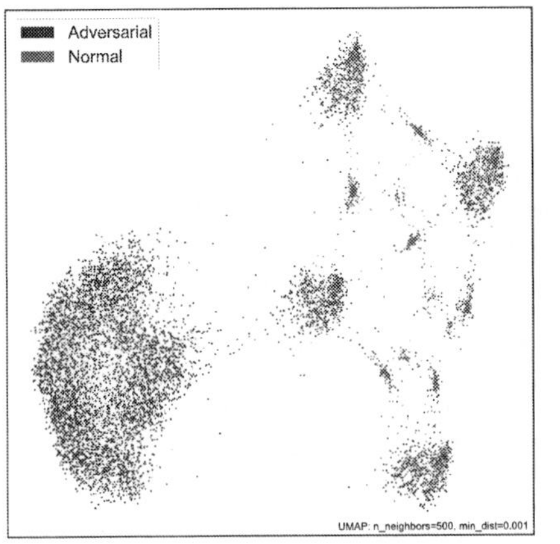

Figure 5: Visualization of the SHAP signatures of the *AG_News* dataset using UMAP. We randomly selected 10% of the samples to avoid overplotting.

In order to understand how the detector is able to distinguish between normal and adversarial inputs, we visualized the SHAP signatures in a two-dimensional space. To project the samples we rely on the UMAP dimensionality reduction algorithm proposed by McInnes et al. (2020). It is based on the fact that most high-dimensional data actually lies on a much lower-dimensional manifold and can be explained by a reduced number of variables. Figure 5 clearly shows four distinct red clusters corresponding to the four classes of the *AG_News* dataset. Regardless of their original class, most of the adversarial samples collapse into a single cluster which is clearly separable from the others. This explains why rather simple detector models are sufficient to accurately differentiate between normal and adversarial inputs. Our result is consistent with the experiments done by Fidel et al. (2020) which performed a similar analysis on SHAP signatures for images from the CIFAR-10 dataset (Krizhevsky et al., 2009).

4.5 Limitations

After the success in computer vision (Fidel et al., 2020), this work shows that SHAP values are also a valuable asset for discriminating between original and adversarial text samples. However, while word-level explanations are particularly effective at detecting word-level attacks, it is unclear how they would transfer to more sophisticated text manipulations. We believe this is a vulnerability as future attacks could involve using negations or paraphrasing whole sentences instead of unigrams.

While the approach's pipeline is intuitive and the results look promising, further research needs to study transferability to more complex target models such as transformers architectures. At the same time, we hope that future research also focuses on creating standard benchmarks to facilitate performance comparisons with previous defense methods.

5 Conclusion

Adversarial text examples are a major challenge for current research and represent an obstacle for safely deploying NLP models in high-stakes applications. While attacks are hard to be distinguished from their corresponding originals, patterns in the model's reaction can be recognized and leveraged using SHAP signatures for detecting manipulated input samples.

Our work trains a machine learning detector using SHAP explanations of normal and adversarial samples generated with PWWS. The proposed method is both intuitive and effective since it allows to detect parts of a sentence that have a suspiciously high impact on the model prediction and therefore distinguishes between regular and manipulated samples. Furthermore, our detector is model-agnostic as it does not make any assumption on the classifier targeted by the attacks.

Our approach achieves high accuracy and considerably outperforms the previous state of the art. In terms of data efficiency, we prove that the method can achieve nearly optimal performance also when using a small portion of the available data for training. A qualitative analysis of the SHAP signature landscape shows most adversarial samples contained in a single cluster, suggesting that model explanations explicitly encode information to separate attacks from their counterpart. We believe this result explains why relatively simple detector architectures suffice to achieve good performance results.

In terms of transferability to multiple datasets, our results are promising but yet not sufficient to prove full generalization capabilities. Although in some cases we match state-of-the-art performance even when training on one dataset and testing on another, our results are highly dependent on the dataset pair.

We encourage future research to continue working on generalization across multiple data sources and to evaluate performance against multiple types of attacks and models. We believe our contribution can help researchers to develop better defense strategies against attacks and thus promoting the safe deployment of NLP models in practice. We release our code to the public to facilitate further research and development [3].

References

Alejandro Barredo Arrieta, Natalia Díaz-Rodríguez, Javier Del Ser, Adrien Bennetot, Siham Tabik, Alberto Barbado, Salvador García, Sergio Gil-López, Daniel Molina, Richard Benjamins, et al. 2020. Explainable artificial intelligence (xai): Concepts, taxonomies, opportunities and challenges toward responsible ai. *Information Fusion*, 58:82–115.

Sebastian Bach, Alexander Binder, Grégoire Montavon, Frederick Klauschen, Klaus-Robert Müller, and Wojciech Samek. 2015. On pixel-wise explanations for non-linear classifier decisions by layer-wise relevance propagation. *PloS one*, 10(7):130–140.

Bernhard E Boser, Isabelle M Guyon, and Vladimir N Vapnik. 1992. A training algorithm for optimal margin classifiers. In *Proceedings of the 5th Annual ACM Workshop on Computational Learning Theory*, pages 144–152.

Leo Breiman. 2001. Random forests. *Machine learning*, 45(1):5–32.

Xinshuai Dong, Anh Tuan Luu, Rongrong Ji, and Hong Liu. 2021. Towards robustness against natural language word substitutions. In *9th International Conference on Learning Representations (ICLR)*.

Javid Ebrahimi, Anyi Rao, Daniel Lowd, and Dejing Dou. 2018. HotFlip: White-box adversarial examples for text classification. In *Proceedings of the 56th Annual Meeting of the Association for Computational Linguistics (Volume 2: Short Papers)*, pages 31–36, Melbourne, Australia. Association for Computational Linguistics.

[3] https://github.com/huberl/adversarial_shap_detect_Repl4NLP

Gil Fidel, Ron Bitton, and Asaf Shabtai. 2020. When explainability meets adversarial learning: Detecting adversarial examples using SHAP signatures. In *2020 International Joint Conference on Neural Networks (IJCNN)*. IEEE.

Ji Gao, Jack Lanchantin, Mary Lou Soffa, and Yanjun Qi. 2018. Black-box generation of adversarial text sequences to evade deep learning classifiers. In *2018 IEEE Security and Privacy Workshops (SPW)*, pages 50–56. IEEE.

Siddhant Garg and Goutham Ramakrishnan. 2020. Bae: Bert-based adversarial examples for text classification. In *Proceedings of the 2020 Conference on Empirical Methods in Natural Language Processing (EMNLP)*, pages 6174–6181.

Ian J. Goodfellow, Jonathon Shlens, and Christian Szegedy. 2015. Explaining and harnessing adversarial examples.

Po-Sen Huang, Robert Stanforth, Johannes Welbl, Chris Dyer, Dani Yogatama, Sven Gowal, Krishnamurthy Dvijotham, and Pushmeet Kohli. 2019. Achieving verified robustness to symbol substitutions via interval bound propagation. In *Proceedings of the 2019 Conference on Empirical Methods in Natural Language Processing and the 9th International Joint Conference on Natural Language Processing (EMNLP-IJCNLP)*, pages 4083–4093.

Di Jin, Zhijing Jin, Joey Tianyi Zhou, and Peter Szolovits. 2020. Is bert really robust? a strong baseline for natural language attack on text classification and entailment. In *Proceedings of the AAAI conference on artificial intelligence*, volume 34, pages 8018–8025.

Diederik P. Kingma and Jimmy Ba. 2015. Adam: A method for stochastic optimization. In *3rd International Conference on Learning Representations, ICLR 2015, San Diego, CA, USA, May 7-9, 2015, Conference Track Proceedings*.

Alex Krizhevsky et al. 2009. Learning multiple layers of features from tiny images.

Scott M. Lundberg and Su-In Lee. 2017. A unified approach to interpreting model predictions. In *Proceedings of the 31st International Conference on Neural Information Processing Systems*, NIPS'17, page 4768–4777, Red Hook, NY, USA. Curran Associates Inc.

Andrew L. Maas, Raymond E. Daly, Peter T. Pham, Dan Huang, Andrew Y. Ng, and Christopher Potts. 2011. Learning word vectors for sentiment analysis. In *Proceedings of the 49th Annual Meeting of the Association for Computational Linguistics: Human Language Technologies*, pages 142–150, Portland, Oregon, USA. Association for Computational Linguistics.

Aleksander Madry, Aleksandar Makelov, Ludwig Schmidt, Dimitris Tsipras, and Adrian Vladu. 2018. Towards deep learning models resistant to adversarial attacks. In *International Conference on Learning Representations*.

Leland McInnes, John Healy, and James Melville. 2020. Umap: Uniform manifold approximation and projection for dimension reduction.

Edoardo Mosca, Maximilian Wich, and Georg Groh. 2021. Understanding and interpreting the impact of user context in hate speech detection. In *Proceedings of the Ninth International Workshop on Natural Language Processing for Social Media*, pages 91–102.

Maximilian Mozes, Pontus Stenetorp, Bennett Kleinberg, and Lewis Griffin. 2021. Frequency-guided word substitutions for detecting textual adversarial examples. In *Proceedings of the 16th Conference of the European Chapter of the Association for Computational Linguistics: Main Volume*, pages 171–186, Online. Association for Computational Linguistics.

Mesut Ozdag. 2018. Adversarial attacks and defenses against deep neural networks: A survey. *Procedia Computer Science*, 140:152–161. Cyber Physical Systems and Deep Learning Chicago, Illinois November 5-7, 2018.

Jeffrey Pennington, Richard Socher, and Christopher Manning. 2014. GloVe: Global vectors for word representation. In *Proceedings of the 2014 Conference on Empirical Methods in Natural Language Processing (EMNLP)*, pages 1532–1543, Doha, Qatar. Association for Computational Linguistics.

Danish Pruthi, Bhuwan Dhingra, and Zachary C. Lipton. 2019. Combating adversarial misspellings with robust word recognition. In *Proceedings of the 57th Annual Meeting of the Association for Computational Linguistics*, pages 5582–5591. Association for Computational Linguistics.

Shuhuai Ren, Yihe Deng, Kun He, and Wanxiang Che. 2019. Generating natural language adversarial examples through probability weighted word saliency. In *Proceedings of the 57th Annual Meeting of the Association for Computational Linguistics*. Association for Computational Linguistics.

Marco Tulio Ribeiro, Sameer Singh, and Carlos Guestrin. 2016. Why should i trust you?: Explaining the predictions of any classifier. In *Proceedings of the 22nd ACM SIGKDD international conference on knowledge discovery and data mining*, pages 1135–1144.

Kevin Roth, Yannic Kilcher, and Thomas Hofmann. 2019. The odds are odd: A statistical test for detecting adversarial examples. In *Proceedings of the 36th International Conference on Machine Learning*, volume 97 of *Proceedings of Machine Learning Research*, pages 5498–5507. PMLR.

David E Rumelhart, Geoffrey E Hinton, and Ronald J Williams. 1985. Learning internal representations by error propagation. Technical report, California Univ San Diego La Jolla Inst for Cognitive Science.

M. Schuster and K. K. Paliwal. 1997. Bidirectional recurrent neural networks. *IEEE Transactions on Signal Processing*, 45(11):2673–2681.

Lloyd S. Shapley. 1952. *A Value for n-Person Games*. RAND Corporation, Santa Monica, CA.

P. Sharma, D. Austin, and H. Liu. 2019. Attacks on machine learning: Adversarial examples in connected and autonomous vehicles. In *2019 IEEE International Symposium on Technologies for Homeland Security (HST)*, pages 1–7.

Avanti Shrikumar, Peyton Greenside, and Anshul Kundaje. 2017. Learning important features through propagating activation differences. In *Proceedings of the 34th International Conference on Machine Learning, ICML 2017, Sydney, NSW, Australia, 6-11 August 2017*, volume 70 of *Proceedings of Machine Learning Research*, pages 3145–3153. PMLR.

Karen Simonyan, Andrea Vedaldi, and Andrew Zisserman. 2014. Deep inside convolutional networks: Visualising image classification models and saliency maps. In *2nd International Conference on Learning Representations, ICLR 2014*.

Richard Socher, Alex Perelygin, Jean Wu, Jason Chuang, Christopher D. Manning, Andrew Ng, and Christopher Potts. 2013. Recursive deep models for semantic compositionality over a sentiment treebank. In *Proceedings of the 2013 Conference on Empirical Methods in Natural Language Processing*, pages 1631–1642, Seattle, Washington, USA. Association for Computational Linguistics.

Nitish Srivastava, Geoffrey E. Hinton, Alex Krizhevsky, Ilya Sutskever, and Ruslan Salakhutdinov. 2014. Dropout: a simple way to prevent neural networks from overfitting. *J. Mach. Learn. Res.*, 15(1):1929–1958.

Mukund Sundararajan, Ankur Taly, and Qiqi Yan. 2017. Axiomatic attribution for deep networks. In *Proceedings of the 34th International Conference on Machine Learning-Volume 70*, pages 3319–3328. JMLR. org.

Christian Szegedy, Wojciech Zaremba, Ilya Sutskever, Joan Bruna, Dumitru Erhan, Ian Goodfellow, and Rob Fergus. 2014. Intriguing properties of neural networks. In *International Conference on Learning Representations*.

Guanhong Tao, Shiqing Ma, Yingqi Liu, and Xiangyu Zhang. 2018. Attacks meet interpretability: Attribute-steered detection of adversarial samples. In *Advances in Neural Information Processing Systems*, volume 31. Curran Associates, Inc.

Xiaosen Wang, Hao Jin, and Kun He. 2019. Natural language adversarial attacks and defenses in word level. *arXiv preprint arXiv:1909.06723*.

Maximilian Wich, Edoardo Mosca, Adrian Gorniak, Johannes Hingerl, and Georg Groh. 2021. Explainable abusive language classification leveraging user and network data. In *Joint European Conference on Machine Learning and Knowledge Discovery in Databases*, pages 481–496. Springer.

Weilin Xu, David Evans, and Yanjun Qi. 2018. Feature squeezing: Detecting adversarial examples in deep neural networks. In *Proceedings 2018 Network and Distributed System Security Symposium*. Internet Society.

Wei Emma Zhang, Quan Z. Sheng, Ahoud Alhazmi, and Chenliang Li. 2020. Adversarial attacks on deep-learning models in natural language processing. *ACM Transactions on Intelligent Systems and Technology*, 11(3):1–41.

Xiang Zhang, Junbo Zhao, and Yann LeCun. 2015. Character-level convolutional networks for text classification. In *Proceedings of the 28th International Conference on Neural Information Processing Systems - Volume 1*, NIPS'15, page 649–657, Cambridge, MA, USA. MIT Press.

Yi Zhou, Xiaoqing Zheng, Cho-Jui Hsieh, Kai-wei Chang, and Xuanjing Huang. 2020. Defense against adversarial attacks in nlp via dirichlet neighborhood ensemble. *arXiv preprint arXiv:2006.11627*.

Yichao Zhou, Jyun-Yu Jiang, Kai-Wei Chang, and Wei Wang. 2019. Learning to discriminate perturbations for blocking adversarial attacks in text classification. In *Proceedings of the 2019 Conference on Empirical Methods in Natural Language Processing and the 9th International Joint Conference on Natural Language Processing (EMNLP-IJCNLP)*, pages 4904–4913, Hong Kong, China. Association for Computational Linguistics.

Binary Encoded Word Mover's Distance

Christian Johnson
Universität Osnabrück, Institut für Kognitionswissenschaft
Wachsbleiche 27, 49074 Osnabrück, Germany
cjohnson@uni-osnabrueck.de

Abstract

Word Mover's Distance is a textual distance metric which calculates the minimum transport cost between two sets of word embeddings. This metric achieves impressive results on semantic similarity tasks, but is slow and difficult to scale due to the large number of floating point calculations. This paper demonstrates that by combining pre-existing lower bounds with binary encoded word vectors, the metric can be rendered highly efficient in terms of computation time and memory while maintaining competitive accuracy on several textual similarity benchmarks.

1 Introduction

A textual distance metric which can be used to accurately and quickly quantify the semantic dissimilarity between documents is useful for many natural language processing (NLP) tasks including text classification, document clustering, and document retrieval.

Word Mover's Distance (WMD) proposed by (Kusner et al., 2015) is a variant of the Earth Mover's Distance which measures the semantic distance between texts. Earth Mover's Distance is a well-studied transportation problem for measuring the distance between two probability distributions and was originally proposed for image retrieval applications (Rubner et al., 1998).

WMD leverages semantic distance information from pre-trained neural word embeddings to calculate a minimum transportation cost needed to 'move' the words from one text to those of another (Kusner et al., 2015). Let $c(i, j)$ represent the Euclidean distance transport cost between word embeddings i and j in documents d and d', respectively. The minimum cumulative (weighted) transport cost differentiating the two documents can then be summarized as,

$$\begin{aligned} &\min_{T\geq 0} \sum_{i,j=1}^{n} T_{ij}\, c(i,j) \\ \text{subject to:}\quad &\sum_{j=1}^{n} T_{ij} = d_i \quad \forall i \in \{1, ..., n\} \qquad (1) \\ &\sum_{i=1}^{n} T_{ij} = d'_j \quad \forall j \in \{1, ..., n\} \end{aligned}$$

where T_{ij} represents *how much* of word embedding i travels to word embedding j. Solving this linear program given the above constraints provides the WMD. When evaluated via a *k* Nearest Neighbors (*k*NN) classification task on eight document classification datasets, WMD is demonstrated to outperform a variety of text similarity metrics such as the Okapi BM25, TF-IDF vector distance, and Latent Dirichlet Allocation (Kusner et al., 2015; Blei et al., 2003).

Per Equation 1, embedding distances must be computed for all pairs of unique tokens in the evaluated documents, scaling the time complexity for solving the underlying optimization problem by $O(p^3 \log p)$, where p denotes the number of unique words in a set of query documents. Given these demands, the memory and online computation time requirements for calculating WMD quickly diminish the potential to scale this metric in a production environment, especially as vocabulary size grows.

Kusner et al. and others have introduced several lower bounds to the WMD which reduce computations by relaxing constraints on the original transport problem, albeit with accompanying performance trade-offs. The *Relaxed Word Mover's Distance* (RWMD) is obtained by removing the second or third constraints from Equation 1, reducing the number of distance calculations given that all probability mass for each word in document d is moved to its most similar word in d'. On the aforementioned *k*NN classification task, the

Proceedings of the 7th Workshop on Representation Learning for NLP, pages 167 - 172
May 26, 2022

RWMD produces an average error of 0.56, compared to 0.42 for the original WMD (Kusner et al., 2015).

Werner et al. (Werner and Laber, 2019) propose another lower bound which involves a preprocessing phase for computing real-value distances between vocabulary items. During this phase, distances are computed between each word's r nearest neighbors and stored in a distance matrix M (Werner and Laber, 2019). These precomputed vector distances are retrieved when calculating transport costs $c(i, j)$ between words; if $c(i, j)$ cannot be found in M, a default maximum value c_{max} is used instead. The *Related Relaxed Word Mover's Distance* (Rel-RWMD), which combines the preprocessing phase with the relaxed conditions of the RWMD, is significantly faster to compute while suffering a modest drop in accuracy compared to the WMD on text similarity tasks.

Of final note is the Word Centroid Distance (WCD), which is computed as the distance between the unweighted average of each text's word embedding vectors (Kusner et al., 2015). Although not an alignment-based distance metric, WCD is a competitive metric which likewise leverages neural word embedding vectors.

One pain-point of the original WMD which motivates the use of lookup tables by Werner et al. is the large amount of floating point calculations needed to resolve the underlying transport problem. Floating point arithmetic CPU instructions are generally slower than integer or bit operations. Tissier et al. (Tissier et al., 2019) have proposed an autoencoding methodology for computing binary embeddings as encoded representations of an original, real-valued embedding space. With normalized XOR Hamming distance calculations, these binary vectors allow one to circumvent CPU-intensive floating point arithmetic while also reducing the working memory footprint of the word vectors by up to 97% (Tissier et al., 2019).

This paper contributes a methodology for integrating the binary vectors of Tissier et al. with the existing Rel-RWMD lower bound as the *Binary Encoded Word Mover's Distance* (BEWMD). It is hypothesized that by replacing the default c_{max} value of the Rel-RWMD with normalized binary vector Hamming distances, the proposed metric will produce a more accurate lower-bound to the original WMD while maintaining competitive computation times and, importantly, low memory requirements.

2 Methodology

The proposed lower bound is realized via neural network encoding of real-valued word vectors and manipulation of the Rel-RWMD calculation. An autoencoder network is trained with resort to a novel regularization parameter, while the Rel-RWMD calculation is modified to accommodate the binary-encoded vectors and render it bidirectional.

2.1 Autoencoder Architecture

An autoencoder is a neural network composed of an encoder and a decoder. The encoder forces an input into a representation which is then decoded into a reconstruction of the original input. By comparing the original and reconstructed inputs via a loss function which minimizes their difference, the autoencoder learns an encoded representation of the input data which is assumed to preserve the structure of the original embedding space. Per the methodology of (Tissier et al., 2019), a neural autoencoder with a specialized loss function is employed to produce the binary word vectors which support the proposed lower bound.

The autoencoder is implemented in Python 3.x via Tensorflow 2.x, consisting of an encoder with two hidden layers and a decoder with a single hidden layer. The encoder's input layer is the same size as a single real-valued vector (300 dimensions), while the subsequent hidden layers and the input to the decoder are adaptable to a desired encoded vector size.

2.2 Correlation Based Regularization

This paper's approach deviates from that of (Tissier et al., 2019) in that the loss function used to minimize the difference between inputs and reconstructed vectors contains an additional correlation based regularization term. A standard mean squared error loss function is insufficient to preserve the original vector space's semantic relationships in the encoded vectors, as the network will learn to discard 'too much similarity information from the original space in favor of the reconstruction' (Tissier et al., 2019). Tissier et al. exploit the encoder's weight matrix W, along with its transposition W^T and corresponding identity matrix I to derive an additional differentiable regularization term l_{reg} which is added to the mean square error loss function, as demonstrated in Equation 2.

$$l_{reg} = \frac{1}{2}||W^T W - I||^2 \quad (2)$$

where the loss function, including the mean squared error as l_{rec}, amounts to

$$L = l_{rec} + \lambda_{reg}\ l_{reg} \quad (3)$$

where λ_{reg} is a regularization hyperparameter between 1 and 4. Implementing this regularization parameter per the methodology of (Tissier et al., 2019), it was found that the adjusted loss function indeed improves training, but still results in compressed vectors which discard much of the semantic information contained in the original vector space. Thus, the loss function used in this paper includes an additional regularization parameter determined via correlation analysis of batch-pairwise distance matrices.

Let B denote a single training batch of size m. In all experiments, a batch size of $m = 75$ is used. Considering an $m \times n$ input batch matrix, where n denotes the original vector size of 300 dimensions, the corresponding, binarized code batch matrix will be an $m \times k$ matrix, where k denotes the size of the reduced vectors.

Computing the pairwise $m \times m$ Euclidean distance matrices B_X and B_Y for both the input and encoded vector spaces, respectively, one converts the matrices into ranks rB_X and rB_Y to compute the Spearman rank correlation coefficient r_s as

$$r_s = \frac{cov(rB_X, rB_Y)}{\sigma_{rB_X}\ \sigma_{rB_Y}} \quad (4)$$

where $cov(rB_X, rB_Y)$ denotes the covariance of the rank variables, while σ_{rB_X} and σ_{rB_Y} are the standard deviations of the rank variables. This calculation of the Spearman correlation coefficient is used because it allows for tie rank values, which is conceivable given the limited range of Hamming distances possible with the binary vectors. This coefficient is then integrated into the loss function as

$$L = l_{rec} + \lambda_{reg}(l_{reg} + r_s) \quad (5)$$

The additional regularizer r_s is summed with l_{reg} such that its contribution to the loss is also modulated by the hyperparameter λ_{reg}. Given that both regularization terms serve the same purpose with respect to the reconstruction loss (preserving distance information from the original vector space), it is sensible to combine them in this way and avoid the need for an additional regularization hyperparameter. With this new parameter, the adjusted objective function results in faster convergence and improves the binary embeddings' performance on downstream tasks, presumably by preserving more distance information from the original vector space. This improved loss function suggests that localized distance correlations are a valuable training objective.

2.3 Proposed Lower Bound Calculation

The resultant binary encoded word embeddings are integrated into a modified version of the Rel-RWMD, where they are used to compute a normalized Hamming distance in cases where the cosine distance between two word embeddings cannot be found in a precomputed lookup table (cache) C, defining the transport cost $c(i, j)$ between two words as:

$$c(i,j) = \begin{cases} 0, & \text{if } i = j \\ cosine(i,j) & \text{if } cosine(i,j) \in C \\ Hamming(i,j) & \text{otherwise} \end{cases} \quad (6)$$

As mentioned, the RWMD removes either the second or third constraint from Equation 1 to create the two relaxed solutions $\ell_1(d, d')$ and $\ell_2(d', d)$. These solutions require only the identification of each word's nearest neighbor from the other document in either of the two directions, given that each word's mass will be transferred entirely to its most similar word in the other document. Rather than opting for one of the two lower bounds (Rel-RWMD uses the maximum of the two), the solution presented in this paper computes both lower bounds and combines them via summation to render the distance calculation bidirectional. This summation approach is supported by the fusion methodology evaluated by (Hamann, 2018). Thus, the Binary Encoded Word Mover's Distance (BEWMD) is defined as

$$\begin{aligned} BEWMD &= \frac{\alpha + \beta}{2} \\ \text{where:} \quad \alpha &= \frac{1}{n} \cdot \min \sum_{i,j=1}^{n} c(i,j) \\ \beta &= \frac{1}{n} \cdot \min \sum_{j,i=1}^{n} c(j,i) \end{aligned} \quad (7)$$

Note that the summed costs are divided by the document length n, in order to constrain the metric to a value between 0 and 1; the sum of the pendant unidirectional transport costs α and β is likewise divided by 2. Cosine distance is employed rather than Euclidean given that angular distance is theoretically more-resilient to variations in vector magnitude which are semantically-irrelevant artifacts of the vector-training process, as in the methodologies of (Mikolov et al., 2013; Zhang et al., 2018).

3 Results

Per the methodology of (Werner and Laber, 2019; Dai et al., 2015), BEWMD performance on a downstream semantic-similarity task is evaluated via the Stanford Triplets Wikipedia benchmark[1]. Metrics are assessed according to their ability to distinguish for a triplet of documents D^1, D^2, D^3, which pair of documents is most-related. Success for a single triplet is achieved if a metric computes the lowest distance score for the most-related document pair, namely D^1 and D^2. Triplet documents are Wikipedia articles which were preprocessed to remove non-alphanumeric characters and tokens which are not embedded under the attested models, in order to maintain computation time comparability across all tested metrics.

The autoencoder model used to produce the encoded vectors was fitted to pretrained word vectors from *FastText* (Bojanowski et al., 2016) (Common Crawl, 600B tokens)[2]. Consequently, all other distance metrics which rely on pretrained word embeddings used the same vectors. The autoencoder is fitted to the first 300,000 word vectors, which, given that the vectors are sorted by frequency, are assumed to be highly-representative of the full vector space. Training lasted for ten epochs with $\lambda_{reg} = 4$. Original real-valued vectors of 300 floating-point dimensions are encoded to 512-bit representations, per the register sizes of AVX-512 CPUs. Although the WMD was originally defined with Euclidean distances, cosine rather than Euclidean distance is used to compute the cost $c(i, j)$ for all metrics, so as to avoid spurious comparisons with BEWMD.

Tables 1, 2, and 3 demonstrate metric performance in terms of test error, offline, and online computation time, respectively. Table 4 documents the memory requirements of any vector models or lookup tables used during online computations. Online computation time is recorded as average time per evaluation iteration, or seconds required to evaluate a single triplet during online distance calculation. Offline computation time is defined as the amount of computation time in minutes to perform any one-time preprocessing such as the fitting of neural network models or calculation of lookup tables. Results are reported from Python implementations of the relevant metrics, where identical vector models or cache lookup tables are, where possible, used to maintain comparability across the metrics. The RWMD and Rel-RWMD lower bounds are interpreted as the maximum of the two possible relaxed solutions $\ell_1(d, d')$ and $\ell_2(d', d)$ (Kusner et al., 2015). The c_{max} value used when calculating Rel-RWMD is set to 0.8. All metrics are evaluated against the same 300 triplets. Calculations were performed on a machine with an Intel i7-8565U CPU and 8GB RAM.

BEWMD	*WCD*	*WMD*	*RWMD*	*Rel-RWMD*
0.393	0.436	**0.389**	0.594	0.641

Table 1: Triplets test error as a value between 0 and 1

BEWMD	*WCD*	*WMD*	*RWMD*	*Rel-RWMD*
283.50	0.00	0.00	0.00	88.85

Table 2: Offline computation time (min)

BEWMD	*WCD*	*WMD*	*RWMD*	*Rel-RWMD*
1.68	**0.006**	23.18	19.39	0.52

Table 3: Online computation time (sec/iter)

BEWMD	*WCD*	*WMD*	*RWMD*	*Rel-RWMD*
836	4409	4409	4409	**790**

Table 4: Online memory requirements (MB)

Additionally, this paper compares metric performance on three of the *k*NN benchmarks from (Kusner et al., 2015): *BBC Sport* contains sports articles between 2004-2005, *Classic* contains sets of sentences from academic papers, and *Ohsumed* is a collection of medical abstracts categorized by disease groups. Datasets are retrieved from the repository associated with the original paper[3]. Each dataset is subsampled to 100 randomly-selected samples (80 train, 20 test) across 5 sampling iterations. Table 5 shows the evaluated datasets and mean *k*NN

[1] http://cs.stanford.edu/ quocle/triplets-data.tar.gz

[2] https://fasttext.cc/docs/en/english-vectors.html

[3] https://github.com/mkusner/wmd

test classification error across all 5 random subsamplings for each metric. In all cases, a value of $k = 5$ is used. The same preprocessing techniques employed during the aforementioned Triplets evaluation were also used when performing the distance calculations which support the *k*NN evaluation. Although the reported results cannot address those from the original paper, they provide an additional indication of the proposed metric's performance relative to its peers.

	BEWMD	*WCD*	*WMD*	*RWMD*	*Rel-RWMD*
BBC Sport	0.12	**0.07**	0.16	0.23	0.45
Classic	**0.11**	0.25	0.14	0.21	0.42
Ohsumed	**0.58**	0.6	0.6	0.65	0.7

Table 5: Mean test error on kNN classification task

4 Discussion

Results on these limited tasks demonstrate that the proposed metric is competitive with the original WMD in terms of test error while offering respectable online computation time improvements and a lower memory footprint.

Comparing BEWMD Triplets performance to that of the other metrics, it can be ascertained that for this task it is the most accurate lower bound to the original WMD. Notably, the BEWMD offers a clear improvement upon the Rel-RWMD, assumedly by utilizing normalized binary vector Hamming distances as opposed to a default c_{max} value (Werner and Laber, 2019). Furthermore, BEWMD test error is highly-competitive with the original WMD, confirming the accuracy of the encoded vectors as compared to their real-valued counterparts.

Results for the three *k*NN benchmark tasks further substantiate BEWMD as a consistently-effective lower bound. BEWMD consistenly outperforms RWMD, Rel-RWMD, and even the original WMD. These results pose the hypothesis that the encoded vectors can offer a more-effective word representation for certain tasks. However, rigorous evaluation of the potential representation advantages offered by the encoded vectors is outside the scope of this paper.

Regarding computation and memory demands, BEWMD compares favorably with RWMD and Rel-RWMD, offering a reasonable computation time trade-off against the Rel-RWMD when BEWMD's improved test error is considered. All metrics which employ the real-valued vectors demand some 4GB of memory, while BEWMD and Rel-RWMD benefit from the reduced memory footprint of precomputed lookup tables and binary encoded vectors. Optimization of the BEWMD calculation so as to remove the need for precomputed lookup tables altogether remains a promising next step for further reducing the memory demands of the proposed metric.

It is worth noting the efficacy of WCD given that, in terms of Triplets test error alone, this metric outperforms all WMD lower bounds except the BEWMD. Furthermore, *k*NN benchmark evaluations place WCD consistently ahead of RWMD and Rel-RWMD, even surpassing WMD on the *BBC Sport* dataset. Although WCD requires more memory than either BEWMD or Rel-RWMD, its low computation time coupled with a relatively low test error on several evaluations pose this metric as a pragmatic alternative to WMD and the proposed metric for many use-cases.

These evaluations suggest that the BEWMD offers a balanced alternative to the original WMD, improving speed up to 14x while achieving competitive test error on several tasks. Furthermore, BEWMD's reduced memory footprint makes it suitable for low-resource compute environments. The demonstrated benefits of the BEWMD are, however, offset by its considerable offline computations, which demand, under the experimental parameters used in this paper, some 4 hours to compute both the encoded vectors and the nearest neighbor lookup table. For applications under constrained hardware where an upfront computation investment is tolerable, the BEWMD offers a consistently optimal lower bound to the original WMD.

As an ethical aside, it must be mentioned that optimized libraries for several of the lower bounds presented here outperform the evaluated BEWMD Python implementation in terms of online computation time, and it is not this paper's intent to evade these performance discrepencies. The evaluations presented here aim only to compare lower bound performance using comparable software implementations.

This paper suggests that binary encoded word vectors are valuable towards improving the scalability of WMD-derived distance metrics. The presented lower bound may be enhanced by optimizing the distance calculation in order to circumvent WMD approximation or the need for precomputed lookup tables.

References

David Blei, Andrew Ng, and Michael Jordan. 2003. Latent dirichlet allocation. *Journal of Machine Learning Research*, 3:993–1022.

Piotr Bojanowski, Edouard Grave, Armand Joulin, and Tomas Mikolov. 2016. Enriching word vectors with subword information. *Transactions of the Association for Computational Linguistics*, 5.

Andrew Dai, Christopher Olah, and Quoc Le. 2015. Document embedding with paragraph vectors.

Felix Hamann. 2018. A neural embedding compressor for scalable document search. page 0.

Matt Kusner, Y. Sun, N.I. Kolkin, and Kilian Weinberger. 2015. From word embeddings to document distances. *Proceedings of the 32nd International Conference on Machine Learning (ICML 2015)*, pages 957–966.

Tomas Mikolov, G.s Corrado, Kai Chen, and Jeffrey Dean. 2013. Efficient estimation of word representations in vector space. pages 1–12.

Yossi Rubner, Carlo Tomasi, and Leonidas Guibas. 1998. Metric for distributions with applications to image databases. pages 59–66.

Julien Tissier, Amaury Habrard, and Christophe Gravier. 2019. Near-lossless binarization of word embeddings. In *AAAI*.

Matheus Werner and Eduardo Laber. 2019. Speeding up word mover's distance and its variants via properties of distances between embeddings.

Ruqing Zhang, Jiafeng Guo, Yanyan Lan, Jun Xu, and Xueqi Cheng. 2018. *Aggregating Neural Word Embeddings for Document Representation*, pages 303–315.

Unsupervised Geometric and Topological Approaches for Cross-Lingual Sentence Representation and Comparison

Shaked Haim Meirom[1] and **Omer Bobrowski**[1,2]
[1] Viterbi Faculty of Electrical & Computer Engineering, Technion - Israel Institute of Technology
[2] School of Mathematical Sciences, Queen Mary University of London
{shakedmeirom@campus, omer@ee}.technion.ac.il

Abstract

We propose novel structural-based approaches for the generation and comparison of cross lingual sentence representations. We do so by applying geometric and topological methods to analyze the structure of sentences, as captured by their word embeddings. The key properties of our methods are: (a) They are designed to be *isometric invariant*, in order to provide language-agnostic representations. (b) They are fully unsupervised, and use no cross-lingual signal. The quality of our representations, and their preservation across languages, are evaluated in similarity comparison tasks, achieving competitive results. Furthermore, we show that our structural-based representations can be combined with existing methods for improved results.

1 Introduction

Word embeddings are driven by distributional concepts, i.e. words can be described by their surrounding words. For example, the words "dog" and "cat" often occur in similar contexts, and therefore their embeddings are expected to be nearby, and to have similar distances to other words. Such similarities are inherent to the real world (e.g., a dog is similar to a cat), and therefore should be language-agnostic. For that reason, the embedding spaces of different languages are expected to be near-isomorphic (Miceli Barone, 2016). Notably, Vulić et al. (2020) demonstrated that high degree of isomorphism can be reached with sufficient monolingual resources. This assumption has enabled various applications at the word level, e.g. generating cross-lingual word embeddings by mapping monolingual vector spaces (Artetxe et al., 2018; Conneau et al., 2018).

In this paper, we take a step further, leveraging the approximate isomorphism between monolingual spaces at the *sentence* level. Considering each sentence as a point cloud (made by its word embeddings), our key argument is that these point clouds retain geometric and topological structures that should be preserved across languages. Therefore, they have the potential to enable language-agnostic sentence representations.

We investigate different approaches for extracting and utilizing such structures. Firstly, we devise a geometric approach, based on the intra-distances of the word embeddings in a sentence. Secondly, we explore a topological approach, borrowing methods from Topological Data Analysis (TDA). Briefly, TDA provides algebraic-topological methods to extract global structural information from shapes. These methods are coordinate free and invariant to isometries (Carlsson, 2009; Zomorodian, 2012), which is highly desired in our setting. Our main goal is to employ these structure-based features to generate novel cross-lingual sentence representations, in a *fully unsupervised* manner.

In order to evaluate the cross-lingual nature of our representations, we experiment with similarity comparison tasks, including bilingual sentence retrieval (Guo et al., 2018) and machine translation quality estimation (Specia et al., 2020).

Our contributions can be summarized as follows. (1) Proposing the novel concept of exploiting the isomorphism of word embedding spaces at the sentence level. (2) Devising fully unsupervised methods for cross-lingual sentence representation, based on geometric and topological approaches. (3) Providing measures of similarity for the new representations. (4) Evaluating the extent to which these representations are preserved across languages, via downstream similarity comparison tasks.

2 Isometry of Word Embedding Spaces

Measuring and utilizing the similarities between word embedding spaces, is a well-studied topic in NLP. In this context, a standard assumption is that monolingual word embedding spaces are approximately isomorphic. A common use for such near-isomorphism is to search for a linear trans-

Proceedings of the 7th Workshop on Representation Learning for NLP, pages 173 - 183
May 26, 2022

formation between the embedding spaces of different languages (Artetxe et al., 2018; Mikolov et al., 2013a; Glavaš et al., 2019). Other studies argue that a better practice is to consider orthogonal transformations (Xing et al., 2015; Smith et al., 2017). These transformations have been used to induce bilingual dictionaries (Xing et al., 2015; Artetxe et al., 2018), as well as cross-lingual transfer learning (Ruder et al., 2019). In fact, mapping-based approaches have become a prevalent way to learn cross-lingual embedding spaces.

The isomorphism assumption is also used in fully unsupervised settings, including unsupervised bilingual lexicon induction (Artetxe et al., 2018; Conneau et al., 2018) and unsupervised machine translation (Lample et al., 2018; Artetxe et al., 2019). Here, the alignment between the monolingual embedding spaces cannot be achieved by mapping pre-existing bilingual dictionaries. Instead, it is achieved either by using adversarial training (Conneau et al., 2018) or by comparing the distribution of similarities or distances of the word embeddings across languages (Artetxe et al., 2018; Alvarez-Melis and Jaakkola, 2018).

As explained by Xu and Koehn (2021), the isomorphism of embedding spaces can be extended to isometry, using normalization techniques. As the isometry of word embedding spaces becomes the premise for a large variety of methods, the following question arises: **can we leverage the isometry of word embeddings at the *sentence* level?**

Our approach is to take the embedding of a sentence to be the word-by-word embedding, resulting in a point-cloud (finite collection of points). Assuming nearly-isometric word embeddings, one would expect that the geometric and topological structures of these point clouds are preserved across languages to some extent. For this reason, we devised methods to extract such structural information from sentences and provide means to compare the structures of different sentences.

3 Related Work

Various studies of unsupervised cross-lingual sentence representations rely on aggregation of either mapped word embeddings or contextualized word embeddings from pre-trained multilingual models (Smith et al., 2017; Conneau et al., 2018; Xu and Koehn, 2021; Kvapilíková et al., 2020). These studies often rely (implicitly or explicitly) on the isometry assumption between word vector spaces, for constructing cross lingual mappings. However, they do not utilize the isometry for generating sentence representations.

Closer to our work are studies using structural similarities between languages. Both Aldarmaki et al. (2018) and Alvarez-Melis and Jaakkola (2018) exploit the preservation of geometric structures between monolingual vector spaces for cross lingual mapping of word embeddings. However, neither refer to geometric structures of sentences.

Finally, several studies have used topological approaches in NLP related tasks, such as word sense disambiguation (Jakubowski et al., 2020) and text visualization (Sami and Farrahi, 2017). TDA methods were also used to generate sentence and document representations. Zhu (2013) was the first to introduce the concept of topological text representation. Built on this idea, recent studies designed various methods for document representations by computing persistent homology (see Section 6.2) over their word embeddings. These methods were evaluated on tasks such as document classification and discourse analysis (Tymochko et al., 2020; Gholizadeh et al., 2020; Savle et al., 2019). Most related to our work is Michel et al. (2017), where persistence diagrams were used to represent documents and sentences. Their final representation and comparison of sentences are quite different than ours, and achieved negative results in classification and clustering tasks. To the best of our knowledge, no previous study used topological-based approaches in cross-lingual tasks.

4 Sentence Distance Matrix

In this section we present the fundamental element of our pipeline – the *Sentence Distance Matrix* (SDM). Representing sentences by point clouds, the geometric information about the sentence can be encoded by the pairwise distances between the words. Formally, let $X = (x_1, ..., x_n)$ be a collection of word embeddings. We define SDM_X to be the $n \times n$ matrix whose entries are given by $(\mathrm{SDM}_X)_{i,j} = \mathrm{dist}(x_i, x_j)$, where dist can be any metric in the embedding space.

The motivation for using SDMs, is that in the hypothetical case where X and Y represent equal-length sentences[1], with parallel words, and in languages with perfectly-isometric word embeddings, we have $\mathrm{SDM}_X = \mathrm{SDM}_Y$. Realistically, while translated words are not always parallel, they are ex-

[1]We will treat non-equal sentence lengths in Section 6.1.

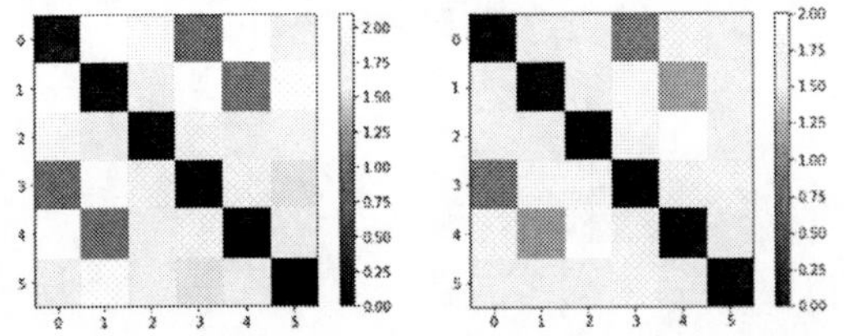

(a) 'dog', 'stood', 'floor', 'cat', 'sat', 'mat'

(b) 'perro', 'paró', 'suelo', 'gato' , 'sentó', 'alfombra'

Figure 1: SDMs for an English sentence (a) and its Spanish translation (b), stopwords removed. Note the pairs dog-cat and stood-sat are close in both languages.

pected to be semantically related. In addition, while perfect-isometry does not exist, we do expect to have near-isometric embeddings. Thus, we expect translated sentences to have $\text{SDM}_X \approx \text{SDM}_Y$, implying that the SDM is a good candidate to represent and compare the structure of sentences.

We demonstrate the resemblance between the SDMs of sentences in different languages in the following example. The Spanish sentence:

> *El perro se paró en el suelo y el gato se sentó en la alfombra,*

is a translation of the following English sentence:

> *The dog stood on the floor and the cat sat on the mat.*

The SDMs of these sentences are presented in Figure 1. The resemblance between the English sentence and its Spanish translation is apparent through their SDMs.

Defining suitable metrics to compare between SDMs (see Sections 5 and 6), will enable us measure similarity between sentences in different languages, *without any supervised or bilingual signal*. This measurement can be useful in many NLP tasks, such as Machine Translation Quality Estimation (Specia et al., 2020), Parallel Corpus Filtering (Koehn et al., 2020), Parallel Corpus mining (Guo et al., 2018) and Cross-Lingual Plagiarism Detection (Danilova, 2013). In addition, such multilingual representations can be useful in cross lingual transfer learning (Ruder et al., 2019).

5 Toy Example

To demonstrate the potential of SDMs, we start with a simple experiment. As we argued earlier, the SDMs of sentences and their translations should be similar, especially if the translation uses parallel words (word-by-word translation). This suggests that SDMs can achieve high performance in a suitable bilingual sentence retrieval setting, which measures the accuracy on retrieving the translation of a sentence from a given bilingual corpus.

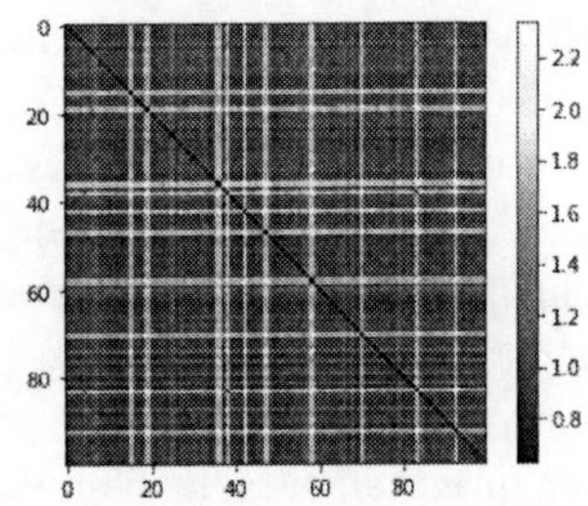

Figure 2: Distances between SDMs of English sentences and SDMs of parallel Italian sentences.

Accuracy	En-It	It-En
P@1	0.939 ± 0.008	0.902 ± 0.006
P@5	0.979 ± 0.003	0.957 ± 0.006
P@10	0.987 ± 0.003	0.969 ± 0.05

Table 1: Results of bilingual sentence retrieval, based on word-by-word translations, using SDMs as the distance measure between sentences.

The experiment settings are as follows. We use the English-Italian dataset provided by Dinu et al. (2014) and Artetxe et al. (2016). The dataset contains monolingual word embeddings trained with word2vec using the CBOW method with negative sampling (Mikolov et al., 2013a)[2]. We apply length normalization and mean centering to all embeddings. In addition to the embeddings, the dataset also contains a bilingual dictionary, split into a training set of 5,000 word pairs and a test set of 1,500 word pairs, both are uniformly distributed in frequency bins. We use the training bilingual dictionary, and removed repetitions[3], which resulted in a dictionary of 3,281 word pairs. We generate a bilingual corpus of 1,000 artificial sentence pairs using random sampling from the bilingual dictionary, such that each sentence is made of a sequence of 20 random words, and its parallel sentence is made of the translations of these words.

Next, we calculate the SDM of each sentence (a 20×20 distance matrix), using the Euclidean distance. In order to measure the distance between the English and Italian sentences, we use the Frobenius norm of the difference between their respective SDMs. This results in a 1000×1000 distance matrix, the first 100×100 block of which is presented

[2]The hyper-parameters and corpora used to create the dataset are described in Artetxe et al. (2016).

[3]Words which appear more than once in the dictionary.

in Figure 2. The sentences have the same order in both languages. Therefore, the distance between each sentence and its translation appears in the diagonal. One can easily notice that the diagonal tends to contain the lowest values, supporting our intuition that translations should have the closest SDM to their source sentences.

To provide quantitative evaluation we used the mean accuracy measure. We count how many times the correct translation of a source sentence is retrieved, and report mean precision@k for $k = 1, 5, 10$, by repeating the experiment 10 times. The results are provided in Table 1. Note that even though the SDMs do not rely on any supervised or bilingual signal, the results are near-perfect. This demonstrates the potential of SDMs in cross-lingual settings, and the preservation of the geometric structure of sentences across languages.

6 Methods

In this section, we describe how to utilize SDMs for sentence representation in the realistic case, where parallel sentences in different languages may differ in length and word ordering. Section 6.1 describes a direct approach – interpolating the SDMs of parallel sentences to have the same size, enabling a direct matrix comparison. Section 6.2 describes a vastly different approach – extracting topological structure information from the SDMs using TDA.

6.1 A Geometric Approach

In Section 5 we showed that the Frobenius norm is an effective method to measure similarity between SDMs of sentences in different languages. However, this procedure requires that the compared sentences share the same length and order. In reality however, this is often not the case. In this section we propose a framework that generalizes this procedure to the most generic setting.

The first challenge to address is different sentence lengths. To this end, we propose to rescale the SDM matrices. Matrix rescaling is a fundamental challenge in the field of image processing, e.g. when zooming in (upscaling) or zooming out (downscaling). We use the well-known B-spline interpolation method introduced by Hou and Andrews (1978), and refined by Unser et al. (1991). Briefly, in order to upscale an SDM we find the piecewise polynomial function that best approximates the original matrix values, and then sample this function at the desired resolution. The resulting pipeline is presented in Figure 3, and is referred to as *interpolated SDM* (ISDM).

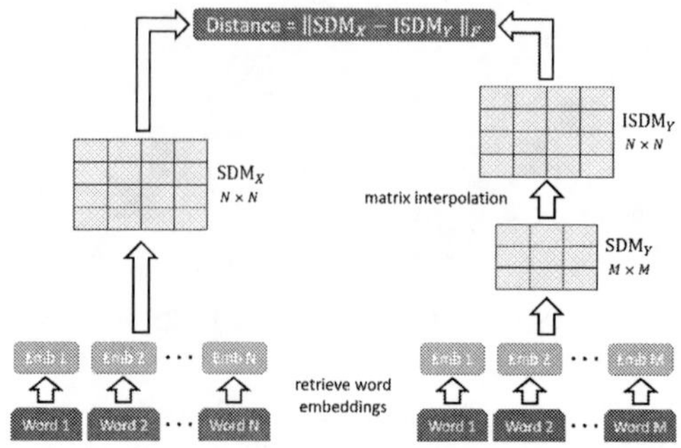

Figure 3: Interpolated SDMs pipeline. The word embeddings of each sentence are used to generate an SDM. The smaller SDM is then interpolated to match the size of the larger one. Using Frobenius norm we can now measure the distance between the sentences.

The next challenge we need to address is the different word ordering between parallel sentences. Intuitively, we propose to match words based on their geometric representation (encoded by the SDM) rather than their position within the sentence, without any bilingual signal. Given two sentences, we take the columns of their interpolated SDMs (vaguely representing words) and search for the optimal matching that minimizes the Frobenius norm. This variation of the pipeline is referred to as *order-aware interpolated SDM* (OSDM).

6.2 A Topological Approach

In this section, we propose a vastly different method to represent and compare sentences, by extracting robust information from the SDMs, describing the topological structure of sentences.

6.2.1 Topological Data Analysis

Topological Data Analysis (TDA) promotes the use of mathematical topology in analyzing data and networks (Carlsson, 2009; Zomorodian, 2012; Zhu, 2013). The key idea is that topology can be used to study the shape of data in a qualitative way that is isometric invariant and robust to continuous deformations. In this section we briefly introduce the relevant concepts and tools of TDA, and discuss how to adapt them for sentence analysis.

The Vietoris-Rips complex. A *simplicial complex* is a high-dimensional generalization of a graph, consisting of vertices, edges, triangles, tetrahedra, and higher dimensional faces. In order to extract structural information from point clouds (word embeddings in our setting), a common practice in TDA

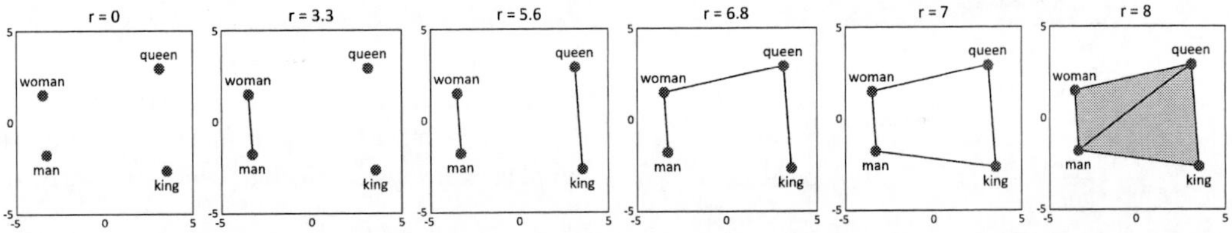

Figure 4: VR complexes of word embeddings, for an increasing diameter r (using the Euclidean distance). For instance, $\text{VR}_{(r=5.6)}$ includes two 1-dimensional faces (edges), since there are two subsets of size 2, whose diameter is less than 5.6. The embeddings were extracted using GloVe (Pennington et al., 2014), and transformed to $\mathbb{R}^2$ using PCA, for visualization purposes. Note that the last step introduces two 2-dimensional faces (triangles).

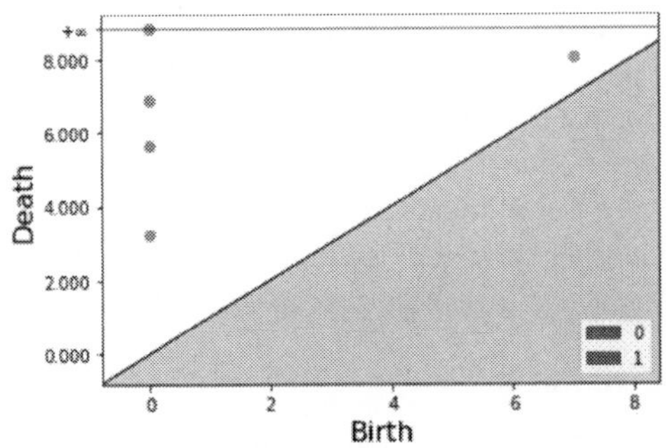

Figure 5: Persistence diagram for the sequence of VR complexes in Figure 4. The red points mark connected components (0-cycles), and their deaths occur when two components merge. For example, at $r \approx 3.3$ a 0-dimensional cycle dies, as the components of "man" and "woman" merge. The blue point marks a hole (1-cycle), appearing at $r \approx 7$ and later filled in at $r \approx 8$.

is to first construct a simplicial complex known as the Vietoris-Rips (VR) complex. Given a point cloud P, the vertex set of $\text{VR}_r(P)$ is just P, and its k-dimensional faces are all subsets $S \subset P$ of size $k+1$, whose diameter is less than r. In Figure 4 we present a sequence of VR complexes, for a point cloud P made by the word embeddings of the well-known word set "king", "queen", "man", and "woman".

Homology is an algebraic topological structure that characterizes the shape of topological spaces. If X is a topological space (e.g., the VR complex), we attach to it a sequence of vector spaces (or groups) denoted $H_0(X)$, $H_1(X)$, $H_2(X)$, etc. The basis elements of $H_0(X)$ correspond to the connected components (referred to as 0-cycles) of X, $H_1(X)$ – to loops surrounding holes in X (1-cycles), $H_2(X)$ – to closed surfaces enclosing "bubbles" in X (2-cycles). Generally, $H_k(X)$ represents information about "k-dimensional cycles", which can be thought of as k-dimensional surfaces that are empty from within. For more details, see (Hatcher, 2002).

Persistent Homology (PH) is the core method used in TDA, whose goal is to extract robust multi-scale topological information from data. Consider the $\text{VR}_r(P)$ complex described above. Increasing the value of r, k-cycles may form at various times (r), and later terminate (merge with another component or fill in). The k-th persistent homology, denoted PH_k, tracks this birth-death process. The information provided by PH_k is often summarized by a *persistence diagram*, which is a collection of points in the plane, where the x and y coordinates represent the birth and death times of a cycle, respectively. In Figure 5 we present the persistence diagram extracted from the sequence of VR complexes in Figure 4. This example demonstrates the unique information captured by PH, which in this example highlights the circular relationship between the words king→queen→woman→man→king.

Wasserstein Distance is the most commonly used metric to compare between persistence diagrams, based on an optimal matchings of their points. For every two diagrams D_1, D_2 we denote by $\hat{D}_1, \hat{D}_2$ their augmented versions that include the diagonal line (death=birth). This allow for matchings that add or remove points from each diagram, by assigning them with the nearest point on the diagonal. The p-Wasserstein distance is then

$$W_p(D_1, D_2) := \inf_{\phi:\hat{D}_1 \to \hat{D}_2} \Big(\sum_{x \in \hat{D}_1} \|x - \phi(x)\|^p \Big)^{1/p},$$

where ϕ goes over all possible bijections.

6.2.2 Order-Aware Persistence Diagrams

We wish to use persistent homology to extract and compare the structural information of sentences. In order to do so, we take our point clouds to be the word embeddings of a sentence, and compute the persistent homology for the VR complex, using the distances calculated by the SDM. To measure similaity between two sentences, we use the Wasser-

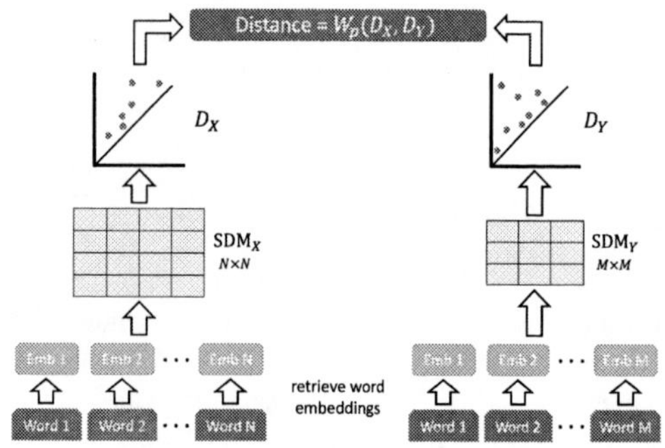

Figure 6: Topological distance pipeline. The word embeddings of each sentence are used to generate an SDM. The SDMs are used to generate the persistence diagrams for the VR complex. The Wasserstein distance is used to measure the similarity between the diagrams.

stein distance of their corresponding persistence diagrams. See Figure 6 for the complete pipeline.

Note that each step of the pipeline is isometric invariant, and therefore allows for cross-lingual representation and similarity measurement. In addition, while the proposed method compares structural information of sentences, it does *not* require them to have the same length (as opposed to the comparison of raw SDMs). One drawback of this pipeline is that it is oblivious to the word ordering within sentences. Next, we wish to present two possible solutions to address this issue.

The first solution is to enrich the diagrams with the positions of the words within a given sentence. Note that in the case of the VR complex, each death event in PH corresponds to an edge e^* entering the complex, as the parameter value r increases. Denote by pos_1, pos_2 the positions of the words that are the end-points of e^*. We create an augmented diagram, where each cycle is represented by four coordinates $(\mathrm{birth}, \mathrm{death}, \mathrm{pos}_1, \mathrm{pos}_2)$. We refer to the result as the *order-aware persistence diagram* (OPD). To compare between two such diagrams, D_1 and D_2, we devised an adaptation of the Wasserstein distance, where the diagonal of D_1 is augmented by taking the pos_1, pos_2 values to be the average word positions of all cycles in D_2, and vice verse.

The second method is inspired by the "time skeleton" concept suggested by Zhu (2013). The key idea is to encode the flow of the sentence into the VR complex, by placing an edge between every two words at adjacent positions in the sentence (at $r = 0$), independently of the distance between their embeddings. We refer to these edges as *sequence edges*. This method increases the expressiveness of H_1 (i.e., holes), since all adjacent words are connected immediately, enabling early appearances of holes. On the other hand, note that the resulting VR complex is always connected, hence H_0 is trivial.

7 Experiments and Results

In this section we want to examine the preservation of our new representations across languages, by evaluating their performance in real-world tasks. In particular, we will focus on tasks that are based on similarity between parallel sentences. Note that the proposed methods are *fully unsupervised*, in the sense that they do not use any task-specific training or cross-lingual data. We will evaluate the effectiveness of our methods as well as their combination with other unsupervised methods (i.e. without increasing the level of supervision).

7.1 Bilingual Sentence Retrieval

The objective of bilingual sentence retrieval is to find the translation of sentences in a source language from a list of candidates in the target language. In this section we want to show that our methods can be used to enhance the performance of existing semantic-based methods for the fully unsupervised version of this task.

We evaluate on the English-Spanish and English-Russian language pairs of the UN parallel corpus (Ziemski et al., 2016). We consider 2,000 source sentences queries and 20,000 possible target sentences for each direction[4]. For the monolingual word representations, we use pre-trained fasttext word embeddings (Grave et al., 2018).

For the baseline, we use the fully unsupervised version of Vecmap (Artetxe et al., 2018) to map monolingual word embeddings into a cross-lingual space. We aggregate the word embeddings by mean-pooling, in order to represent sentences. The pipeline we examine has two steps: (1) use the baseline to list the top 10 nearest neighbours of each source sentence. (2) Re-rank this list using our novel representations.

For the first step, we score all possible sentence pairs using the cosine distance between their embeddings. We mitigate the hubness problem of embedding spaces using the margin-based approach of Artetxe and Schwenk (2019)[5]. We then create

[4]We considered sentences with at least 5 words, and stripped punctuation as a pre-processing step.

[5]We used the Ratio variant with parameter $k = 10$.

	English-Spanish						English-Russian					
	En→Es			Es→En			En→Ru			Ru→En		
	P@1	P@5	MAP	P@1	P@5	MAP	P@1	P@5	MAP	P@1	P@5	MAP
Vecmap	45.4	64.0	.535	56.2	73.3	.634	36.3	55.9	.448	45.1	65.0	.535
ISDM	39.4	58.0	.480	56.6	71.7	.634	37.1	55.6	.449	42.5	61.1	.511
OSDM	40.3	60.1	.490	4.93	70.9	.586	**42.7**	**58.7**	**.494**	35.2	57.7	.452
OPD$_0$	52.7	68.5	.593	60.5	76.1	.671	40.5	58.2	.480	51.1	69.7	.589
OPD$_1$	51.5	67.3	.583	59.7	76.1	.665	39.2	58.0	.469	50.8	68.4	.583
OPD$_{0+1}$	**53.6**	**68.5**	**.599**	**60.7**	**76.4**	**.672**	40.6	58.4	.480	**51.5**	**69.7**	**.592**
OPD$_2$	46.7	64.8	.545	57.0	74.1	.641	38.1	56.6	.461	46.1	66.6	.546
OPD$_{0+1+2}$	51.7	67.2	.584	58.9	74.8	.657	40.3	59.1	.479	49.7	68.7	.578

Table 2: Results for the fully unsupervised bilingual sentence retrieval, as described in Section 7.1. OPD$_{a+b}$ stands for a linear combination between the baseline, OPD$_a$ and OPD$_b$. We highlight the best result for each direction.

an ordered list of the top 10 nearest neighbours of each source sentence.

In the second step, we wish to enhance the baseline ranking by applying our new geometric and topological methods. The methods we examine are: (1) interpolated SDM (ISDM), (2) order-aware interpolated SDM (OSDM), and (3) order-aware k-cycles persistence diagrams (OPD$_k$)[6]. We use each of these methods to compute the distance between every source sentence and its 10 nearest neighbors, found in step 1. We note that the calculations in this step are applied directly to the monolingual word embeddings (rather than the Vecmap embeddings). Next, we create new scores for each sentence pair by a linear combination of the baseline distance (from step 1) and the structure-based distances[7]. Finally, we re-rank the top nearest neighbours lists according to the new scores. As this is a retrieval task, we follow Glavaš et al. (2019) and use the Mean Average Precision (MAP), in addition to precision@k (with $k \in \{1, 5\}$) for the evaluation.

We report the average results (across all sentence queries) in Table 2. As can be seen, using our structure-based methods improves the results of the baseline on all fronts. Remarkably, the improvement (15% on average for P@1, and 10% on average for MAP), does not rely on any additional data or training. In most cases, the combination between OPD$_0$ and OPD$_1$ yields the best results, except for one case in which the OSDM triumphs. It is also interesting to note that the distance provided by OPD$_2$ improves the results as well. While the structural information provided by 2-cycles is less intuitive (and consequently is uncommonly used in applications), our results indicate that such high-dimensional topological structures do carry significant information in language processing.

7.2 Machine Translation Quality Estimation

The goal here is to predict quality scores for translated sentences, in a way that is consistent with human perceived scores, referred to as *direct assessment*. Since the objective is to compare parallel sentences, this is a suitable scenario to test our novel representations across languages.

The implementation details are as follows. We generate monolingual word representations, based on pre-trained BPEmb subword embeddings (Heinzerling and Strube, 2018). These embeddings were chosen in order to properly deal with out-of-vocabulary words. For words that consist of multiple subwords, we take average of the subword vectors. This common practice outperforms other aggregation methods (Bommasani et al., 2020).

We use the monolingual embeddings to calculate the structural-based distances between every source sentence and its translation[8], using the methods proposed in Section 6. We take the inverse of the distance as the predicted quality score. We tested our methods separately as well as combined (taking linear combinations of the respective scores[9]). We note that for the topological approach, we always used OPD$_0$ and OPD$_1$ together, as this method demonstrated superior results.

We tested this pipeline on the language pairs English-German (en-de) and Sinhala-English (si-en), of the WMT2020 Quality Estimation shared task (Specia et al., 2020). Each language pair includes 1,000 source sentences and their translations, produced by state-of-the-art NMT models.

[6] For the OPD$_1$ we utilize the sequence edges method.

[7] The weights of the linear combination were chosen according to preliminary experiments, and were usually balanced, slightly favoring our methods.

[8] As a pre-processing step, we remove stopwords and stripped punctuation.

[9] The coefficients were optimized manually in preliminary experiments.

We compare the results of our methods to the supervised baseline of the shared task, which uses LSTM-based Predictor-Estimator approach (Kim et al., 2017), and to the following competitors.

TransQuest (Ranasinghe et al., 2020) is the winner method of the shared task. The method uses an ensemble of two architectures, which rely on pre-trained XLM-R large transformer models, and are fine-tuned on quality estimation datasets.

FVCRC (Zhou et al., 2020) is an unsupervised method based on a BERTScore (Zhang et al., 2020). The method relies on pre-trained transformer-based models (mBert, XLM) to extract word (or subword) embeddings. It aligns the embeddings using cosine similarity based greedy matching, and predicts the quality score as the sum of the respective similarities. It enhances the alignments using explicit cross-lingual knowledge from external models.

Bergamot-LATTE, glass-box (Fomicheva et al., 2020) is an unsupervised method that assumes access to the machine translation model. It extracts features from the model output and uses uncertainty quantification to predict the translation quality.

As most of the competing methods rely on pre-trained transformer-based models, we also wish to evaluate the merge between these models and our framework. We do so in a way that keeps the combined pipeline fully unsupervised (avoiding fine-tuning and bilingual knowledge). To this end, we adapted the FVCRC approach to be fully unsupervised, replacing their alignment procedure with optimal transportation matching[10]. We refer to this fully unsupervised transformer-based method as *cross lingual matching* (CLM)[11].

Following the shared task guidelines, we present the Pearson correlation between the predicted and the manually annotated scores in Table 3. Note that both of our approaches (geometric and topological) provide meaningful and competitive results, even though they are *fully unsupervised* and do not rely on any cross-lingual signal or external model. Interestingly, the combinations between our geometric and topological approaches has yielded superior results. More specifically, the results reveal that our methods outperform the *supervised* baseline as well as the unsupervised methods in the en-de direction. In addition, in the si-en direction, the combination between CLM and our methods performs better than its competitor – the unsupervised FVCRC, and better than the supervised baseline.

Method	Supervision	en→de	si→en
TransQuest	Sup.	0.55	0.68
Baseline	Sup.	0.15	0.37
FVCRC	Unsup.*	0.11	**0.39**
Bergamot-LATTE	Unsup.**	**0.26**	**0.51**
ISDM	Fully Unsup.	0.12	0.26
OSDM	Fully Unsup.	**0.27**	0.16
OPD	Fully Unsup.	**0.20**	0.19
ISDM + OPD	Fully Unsup.	**0.19**	0.29
OSDM + OPD	Fully Unsup.	**0.27**	0.18
CLM + OPD	Fully Unsup.	0.13	**0.45**
CLM + OSDM	Fully Unsup.	0.14	**0.45**

Table 3: Pearson correlation with direct assessment scores for the WMT2020 Machine Translation Quality Estimation shared task. The '+' sign stands for a linear combination between methods. Unsupervised results improving the supervised baseline are highlighted. *FVCRC uses explicit bilingual signal. **Bergamot-LATTE relies on the MT model scores.

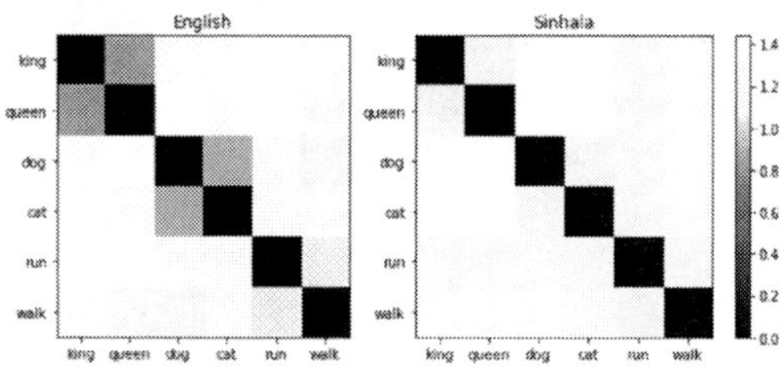

Figure 7: Comparing word embeddings of English and Sinhala. To demonstrate the inferior quality of the Sinhala word embeddings, we present the distance matrices for six words in English and their translations in Sinhala. We observe that similar meaning corresponds to short distances between the word embeddings in English. However, the same is not true for Sinhala.

We attribute the relative lower performance of our methods in the si-en direction to the poor representation of the monolingual word embeddings for Sinhala, as a low resource language. The representation capability and the expressiveness of the distances between the pre-trained word embeddings are demonstrated at Figure 7. Generally, the performance of our methods will be improved if the degree of isomorphism between the relevant word vector spaces is increased. This can be achieved, for example, by training the word embeddings with additional monolingual data, as suggested by Vulić et al. (2020). This is left as future work.

8 Conclusion and Future Work

We introduced the concept of leveraging the isometry of word embedding spaces at the sentence

[10]Specifically we use the Sinkhorn distance (Cuturi, 2013).

[11]As FVCRC, our implementation also uses BERTScore.

level. This enabled us to propose geometric and topological approaches that facilitate fully unsupervised generation of cross-lingual sentence representations, together with suitable similarity measures.

We conducted cross-lingual experiments, where our standalone methods have achieved competitive results on different tasks. Moreover, we observed that combining our methods with traditional ones has led to notable enhanced performance. We should emphasize that this was achieved *without any additional data or training*. We conclude that geometric and topological structures of sentences are preserved to a significant level across languages. Interestingly, our experiments show that the shapes we extract have complex structures. For example, in many cases we found meaningful homological cycles in various degrees. We note that these representations are weaker on scenarios with low degree of isomorphism, e.g. due to lack of monolingual data (Vulić et al., 2020).

A promising direction for future work is to utilize the proposed representations in cross-lingual transfer learning (training a model on one language and using it on another language).

Finally, we note that the main motivation for this work was to promote the use of geometric and topological approaches in core NLP tasks, and especially cross-lingual tasks. We believe that the ideas and methods we presented here will contribute to the future development of this line of research.

Acknowledgements

The authors are grateful to Roi Reichart for helpful comments and feedback, especially regarding the relevant NLP tasks. OB was supported in part by the Israel Science Foundation, Grant 1965/19.

References

Hanan Aldarmaki, Mahesh Mohan, and Mona Diab. 2018. Unsupervised word mapping using structural similarities in monolingual embeddings. *Transactions of the Association for Computational Linguistics*, 6:185–196.

David Alvarez-Melis and Tommi Jaakkola. 2018. Gromov-Wasserstein alignment of word embedding spaces. In *Proceedings of the 2018 Conference on Empirical Methods in Natural Language Processing*, pages 1881–1890.

Mikel Artetxe, Gorka Labaka, and Eneko Agirre. 2016. Learning principled bilingual mappings of word embeddings while preserving monolingual invariance. In *Proceedings of the 2016 Conference on Empirical Methods in Natural Language Processing*, pages 2289–2294.

Mikel Artetxe, Gorka Labaka, and Eneko Agirre. 2018. A robust self-learning method for fully unsupervised cross-lingual mappings of word embeddings. In *Proceedings of the 56th Annual Meeting of the Association for Computational Linguistics*, pages 789–798.

Mikel Artetxe, Gorka Labaka, and Eneko Agirre. 2019. An effective approach to unsupervised machine translation. In *Proceedings of the 57th Annual Meeting of the Association for Computational Linguistics*, pages 194–203.

Mikel Artetxe and Holger Schwenk. 2019. Margin-based parallel corpus mining with multilingual sentence embeddings. In *Proceedings of the 57th Annual Meeting of the Association for Computational Linguistics*, pages 3197–3203.

Rishi Bommasani, Kelly Davis, and Claire Cardie. 2020. Interpreting Pretrained Contextualized Representations via Reductions to Static Embeddings. In *Proceedings of the 58th Annual Meeting of the Association for Computational Linguistics*, pages 4758–4781.

Gunnar Carlsson. 2009. Topology and data. *Bulletin of the American Mathematical Society*, 46(2):255–308.

Alexis Conneau, Guillaume Lample, Marc'Aurelio Ranzato, Ludovic Denoyer, and Hervé Jégou. 2018. Word translation without parallel data. *Proceedings of ICLR 2018.*

Marco Cuturi. 2013. Sinkhorn distances: Lightspeed computation of optimal transport. In *Advances in Neural Information Processing Systems*, volume 26, pages 2292–2300. Curran Associates, Inc.

Vera Danilova. 2013. Cross-language plagiarism detection methods. In *Proceedings of the Student Research Workshop associated with RANLP 2013*, pages 51–57.

Georgiana Dinu, Angeliki Lazaridou, and Marco Baroni. 2014. Improving zero-shot learning by mitigating the hubness problem. *Proceedings of the 3rd International Conference on Learning Representations (ICLR2015), workshop track.*

Marina Fomicheva, Shuo Sun, Lisa Yankovskaya, Frédéric Blain, Vishrav Chaudhary, Mark Fishel, Francisco Guzmán, and Lucia Specia. 2020. BERGAMOT-LATTE submissions for the WMT20 quality estimation shared task. In *Proceedings of the Fifth Conference on Machine Translation*, pages 1010–1017.

Shafie Gholizadeh, Armin Seyeditabari, and Wlodek Zadrozny. 2020. A novel method of extracting topological features from word embeddings. *arXiv preprint arXiv:2003.13074.*

Goran Glavaš, Robert Litschko, Sebastian Ruder, and Ivan Vulić. 2019. How to (properly) evaluate cross-lingual word embeddings: On strong baselines, comparative analyses, and some misconceptions. In *Proceedings of the 57th Annual Meeting of the Association for Computational Linguistics*, pages 710–721.

Edouard Grave, Piotr Bojanowski, Prakhar Gupta, Armand Joulin, and Tomas Mikolov. 2018. Learning word vectors for 157 languages. In *Proceedings of the Eleventh International Conference on Language Resources and Evaluation*, Miyazaki, Japan.

Mandy Guo, Qinlan Shen, Yinfei Yang, Heming Ge, Daniel Cer, Gustavo Hernandez Abrego, Keith Stevens, Noah Constant, Yun-Hsuan Sung, Brian Strope, and Ray Kurzweil. 2018. "effective parallel corpus mining using bilingual sentence embeddings". In *"Proceedings of the Third Conference on Machine Translation: Research Papers"*, pages "165–176".

Allen Hatcher. 2002. *Algebraic topology*. Cambridge University Press.

Benjamin Heinzerling and Michael Strube. 2018. BPEmb: Tokenization-free pre-trained subword embeddings in 275 languages. In *Proceedings of the Eleventh International Conference on Language Resources and Evaluation (LREC 2018)*.

Hsieh Hou and H Andrews. 1978. Cubic splines for image interpolation and digital filtering. *IEEE Transactions on acoustics, speech, and signal processing*, 26(6):508–517.

Alexander Jakubowski, Milica Gasic, and Marcus Zibrowius. 2020. Topology of word embeddings: Singularities reflect polysemy. In *Proceedings of the Ninth Joint Conference on Lexical and Computational Semantics*, pages 103–113.

Hyun Kim, Jong-Hyeok Lee, and Seung-Hoon Na. 2017. Predictor-estimator using multilevel task learning with stack propagation for neural quality estimation. In *Proceedings of the Second Conference on Machine Translation*, pages 562–568.

Philipp Koehn, Vishrav Chaudhary, Ahmed El-Kishky, Naman Goyal, Peng-Jen Chen, and Francisco Guzmán. 2020. Findings of the wmt 2020 shared task on parallel corpus filtering and alignment. In *Proceedings of the Fifth Conference on Machine Translation*, pages 726–742.

Ivana Kvapilíková, Mikel Artetxe, Gorka Labaka, Eneko Agirre, and Ondřej Bojar. 2020. Unsupervised multilingual sentence embeddings for parallel corpus mining. *Proceedings of the 58th Annual Meeting of the Association for Computational Linguistics: Student Research Workshop*, pages 255–262.

Guillaume Lample, Alexis Conneau, Ludovic Denoyer, and Marc'Aurelio Ranzato. 2018. Unsupervised machine translation using monolingual corpora only. In *International Conference on Learning Representations*.

Antonio Valerio Miceli Barone. 2016. Towards cross-lingual distributed representations without parallel text trained with adversarial autoencoders. In *Proceedings of the 1st Workshop on Representation Learning for NLP*, pages 121–126.

Paul Michel, Abhilasha Ravichander, and Shruti Rijhwani. 2017. Does the geometry of word embeddings help document classification? a case study on persistent homology-based representations. In *Proceedings of the 2nd Workshop on Representation Learning for NLP*, pages 235–240.

Tomas Mikolov, Ilya Sutskever, Kai Chen, Greg S Corrado, and Jeff Dean. 2013a. Distributed representations of words and phrases and their compositionality. In *Advances in Neural Information Processing Systems*, volume 26, page "3111–3119".

Jeffrey Pennington, Richard Socher, and Christopher D. Manning. 2014. Glove: Global vectors for word representation. In *Empirical Methods in Natural Language Processing (EMNLP)*, pages 1532–1543.

Tharindu Ranasinghe, Constantin Orasan, and Ruslan Mitkov. 2020. TransQuest: Translation quality estimation with cross-lingual transformers. In *Proceedings of the 28th International Conference on Computational Linguistics*, pages 5070–5081.

Sebastian Ruder, Ivan Vulić, and Anders Søgaard. 2019. A survey of cross-lingual word embedding models. *Journal of Artificial Intelligence Research*, page 569–630.

Ishrat Rahman Sami and Katayoun Farrahi. 2017. A simplified topological representation of text for local and global context. In *Proceedings of the 25th ACM international conference on Multimedia*, pages 1451–1456.

Ketki Savle, Wlodek Zadrozny, and Minwoo Lee. 2019. Topological data analysis for discourse semantics? In *Proceedings of the 13th International Conference on Computational Semantics - Student Papers*, pages 34–43.

Samuel L Smith, David HP Turban, Steven Hamblin, and Nils Y Hammerla. 2017. Offline bilingual word vectors, orthogonal transformations and the inverted softmax. *International Conference on Learning Representations*.

Lucia Specia, Frédéric Blain, Marina Fomicheva, Erick Fonseca, Vishrav Chaudhary, Francisco Guzmán, and André F. T. Martins. 2020. Findings of the WMT 2020 shared task on quality estimation. In *Proceedings of the Fifth Conference on Machine Translation*, pages 743–764, Online. Association for Computational Linguistics.

Sarah Tymochko, Zachary New, Lucius Bynum, Emilie Purvine, Timothy Doster, Julien Chaput, and Tegan Emerson. 2020. Argumentative topology: Finding loop(holes) in logic. *arXiv preprint arXiv:2011.08952*.

Michael Unser, Akram Aldroubi, Murray Eden, et al. 1991. Fast b-spline transforms for continuous image representation and interpolation. *IEEE Transactions on pattern analysis and machine intelligence*, 13(3):277–285.

Ivan Vulić, Sebastian Ruder, and Anders Søgaard. 2020. Are all good word vector spaces isomorphic? *Proceedings of the 2020 Conference on Empirical Methods in Natural Language Processing (EMNLP)*, pages 3178–3192.

Chao Xing, Dong Wang, Chao Liu, and Yiye Lin. 2015. Normalized word embedding and orthogonal transform for bilingual word translation. In *Proceedings of the 2015 Conference of the North American Chapter of the Association for Computational Linguistics: Human Language Technologies*, pages 1006–1011.

Haoran Xu and Philipp Koehn. 2021. Cross-lingual bert contextual embedding space mapping with isotropic and isometric conditions. *arXiv preprint arXiv:2107.09186*.

Tianyi Zhang, Varsha Kishore, Felix Wu, Kilian Q. Weinberger, and Yoav Artzi. 2020. Bertscore: Evaluating text generation with bert. In *International Conference on Learning Representations*.

Lei Zhou, Liang Ding, and Koichi Takeda. 2020. Zero-shot translation quality estimation with explicit cross-lingual patterns. *Proceedings of the 5th Conference on Machine Translation (WMT)*, page 1068–1074.

Xiaojin Zhu. 2013. Persistent homology: An introduction and a new text representation for natural language processing. In *IJCAI*, pages 1953–1959.

Michał Ziemski, Marcin Junczys-Dowmunt, and Bruno Pouliquen. 2016. The United Nations parallel corpus v1.0. In *Proceedings of the Tenth International Conference on Language Resources and Evaluation (LREC'16)*, pages 3530–3534.

Afra Zomorodian. 2012. Topological data analysis. *Advances in applied and computational topology*, 70:1–39.

A Study on Entity Linking Across Domains: Which Data is Best for Fine-Tuning?

Hassan Soliman[1,2] **Heike Adel**[1]
Mohamed Gad-Elrab[1] **Dragan Milchevski**[1] **Jannik Strötgen**[1]

[1]Bosch Center for Artificial Intelligence, Renningen, Germany
[2]Saarland University, Saarbrücken, Germany
[1]`firstname.lastname@de.bosch.com`
[2]`s8hasoli@stud.uni-saarland.de`

Abstract

Entity linking disambiguates mentions by mapping them to entities in a knowledge graph (KG). One important question in today's research is how to extend neural entity linking systems to new domains. In this paper, we aim at a system that enables linking mentions to entities from a general-domain KG and a domain-specific KG at the same time. In particular, we represent the entities of different KGs in a joint vector space and address the questions of which data is best suited for creating and fine-tuning that space, and whether fine-tuning harms performance on the general domain. We find that a combination of data from both the general and the special domain is most helpful. The first is especially necessary for avoiding performance loss on the general domain. While additional supervision on entities that appear in both KGs performs best in an intrinsic evaluation of the vector space, it has less impact on the downstream task of entity linking.

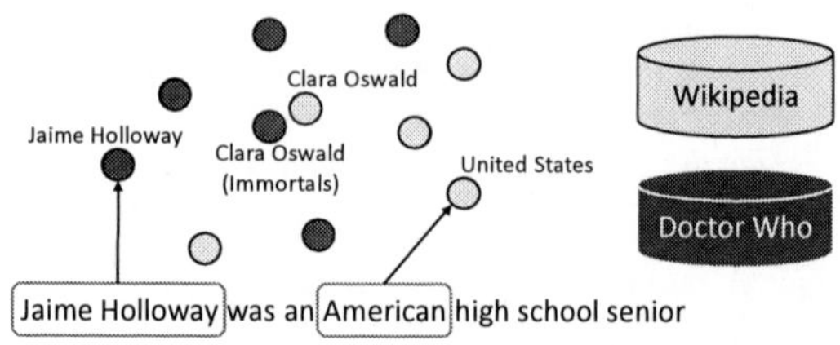

Figure 1: Illustration of entity linking to two KGs (Wikipedia and Doctor Who) at the same time by representing the entities of both graphs in a joint vector space. Colors indicate the KG to which the entities belong.

1 Introduction

Entity linking, i.e., the task of disambiguating mentions in text by linking them to entities of a knowledge graph (KG), is key to many semantic applications, such as KG population, question answering or information retrieval (Sevgili et al., 2021). In the context of KGs, a domain is characterized, i.a., by the set and distribution of entities (Onoe and Durrett, 2020). For KGs from special domains, the availability of annotated data for training entity linking is limited. Thus, there is a need for methods that work across domains in low-resource settings, such as transfer or few-shot learning techniques (Hedderich et al., 2021).

Given a KG from a special domain, it is useful for many applications to not treat this KG in isolation but still be able to link mentions to the general domain as well. Figure 1 illustrates this. Without combining the KGs *Wikipedia* and *Doctor Who*, it would not be possible to link all mentions of the example sentence to their respective entities. Early works prior to neural entity linking (Hoffart et al., 2011) allow linking to multiple KGs by combining the KGs before applying the methods. In the context of neural networks, a more elegant way is to combine different KGs via a *joint vector space* (Gupta et al., 2017). This also enables us to learn similar embeddings for overlapping entities, i.e., entities that appear in more than one KG, which would arguably be more difficult when only uniting triple sets. In Figure 1, the entities "Clara Oswald" and "Clara Oswald (Immortals)" are an example of overlapping entities.

In this paper, we aim at methods for adding a KG from a specific target domain into an existing vector space from a source-domain KG and fine-tuning the joint vector space to improve the entity linking results. While some recent work has considered zero-shot entity linking (Logeswaran et al., 2019; Wu et al., 2020), a systematic investigation on which data sources are most useful for fine-tuning entity linking systems, is still missing. Thus, the first research question we address is: *Which data is best suited for fine-tuning joint vector spaces of KGs?*

Furthermore, it is unclear how fine-tuning on the target domain affects the vector space of the source-domain KG. Thus, the second research question we pose is: *Does fine-tuning harm performance of entity linking on the general domain?*

Proceedings of the 7th Workshop on Representation Learning for NLP, pages 184 - 190
May 26, 2022 ©2022 Association for Computational Linguistics

To answer these research questions, we present a systematic investigation of the impact of different information sources on the vector space (intrinsic evaluation) as well as on the entity linking performance (extrinsic evaluation). Further, we will publish the list of overlapping entities that we created along with this paper to ensure reproducibility.

2 Related Work

As in other fields of natural language processing, deep learning became the predominant approach in entity linking (He et al., 2013; Sun et al., 2015; Francis-Landau et al., 2016; Yamada et al., 2016; Gupta et al., 2017; Kolitsas et al., 2018). In today's research, the usage of pre-trained language models, such as BERT (Devlin et al., 2019), is particularly popular (Peters et al., 2019; Logeswaran et al., 2019; Humeau et al., 2020; Wu et al., 2020).

In this paper, we aim at a neural entity linking system which allows linking mentions to more than one KG by creating a joint vector space for entity representations from different KGs. Related to this, Gupta et al. (2017) propose a method to create a joint vector space for entities from different sources that are represented by different means, such as descriptions, contexts or fine-grained types. In the context of entity linking across domains, Onoe and Durrett (2020) build a domain-independent system that relies on fine-grained entity types. In contrast, Logeswaran et al. (2019) and Wu et al. (2020) utilize descriptions of entities from KGs to obtain entity representations. In particular, Logeswaran et al. (2019) propose domain-adaptive pre-training to apply entity linking to unseen entities from a KG of a new domain. Wu et al. (2020) build on that work but train their model only on labeled data from a general domain (Wikipedia). Vyas and Ballesteros (2021) generalize those models and allow them to handle arbitrary KGs with entities represented by an arbitrary set of attribute-value pairs.

In contrast to those works, we also take into account overlapping entities between the two KGs and study which impact fine-tuning on different data sources has on the joint vector space as well as on entity linking performance.

3 Linking Model and Extension Method

In this section, we detail the entity linking model and describe how the model can be extended to a new domain.

3.1 Entity Linking Model

To be able to directly compare with state-of-the-art related work, we build upon the entity linking model proposed by Wu et al. (2020). It consists of three parts (context encoder, candidate encoder and cross-encoder) which are used in two phases (candidate generation and candidate ranking). Note that our extension approach is independent of the underlying system though.

Candidate generation. In this step, the context encoder creates a vector representation for a mention given a textual context. Similarly, the candidate encoder embeds a candidate entity from the knowledge graph given its textual description. For both model parts, a BERT encoder is used and the CLS token serves as the output embedding. For candidate generation, the k most similar entities to a given mention are retrieved where similarity is measured by cosine similarity between the entity and the mention embeddings.

Candidate ranking. For candidate ranking, the cross-encoder estimates how likely a mention represents a candidate entity. For this, a third BERT model is used that receives as input the concatenation of the textual context of the mention and the title and description of the candidate entity. Its CLS token is then fed into a feed-forward layer to compute a score that is trained to be higher for the correct candidate entity than for wrong candidate entities.

3.2 Extension to New Domains

To extend the model to a new domain, we fine-tune the weights θ of the context and candidate encoders.

Information Sources for Fine-Tuning. In our experiments, we investigate which data or which set of data is most promising for fine-tuning. For this, we use the following information sources: (i) data annotated with entities from the KG of the *target domain* (T), (ii) additional data that is annotated with entities from the KG of the *source domain* (S), and (iii) a list of *overlapping entities* between the KG from the source domain and the KG of the target domain (O). The following paragraphs describe how the data sources are used for fine-tuning.

Fine-Tuning Loss Functions. For fine-tuning on data annotated with entity information from a KG

	Domain	Entities	Mentions			Overlapping (O)	
			Train*	Dev*	Test	Candidates	Filtered
T	American Football	31,929	3,000	320	578	24,074	22,928
	Doctor Who	40,281	6,360	640	1,334	10,458	3,611
	Fallout	16,992	2,500	320	466	2,876	752
	Final Fantasy	14,044	4,360	640	1,041	1,495	413
S	Wikipedia (Reddit)	5,903,538	7,711	409	1,328	-	-

Table 1: Statistics for the datasets used in our experiment (* corresponds to the fine-tuning phase).

(i.e., settings S and T), we use the following loss function:

$$s(a, b) := a^{\top} b$$

$$L_\theta = \sum_{m,e \in D} \big(- s(v_m, v_e) + \log \sum_{c \in C_e} \exp(s(v_m, v_c)) \big) \quad (1)$$

where D is a dataset, annotated with mentions m and their corresponding entities e, v_m is the representation of the context encoder of mention m in a textual context, v_e is the representation of the candidate encoder of the textual description of entity e from the KG and C_e is a randomly sampled batch of negative entities from the KG.

For fine-tuning on the list of overlapping entities (i.e., setting O), we use the following loss function:

$$\begin{aligned} L_\theta = \sum_{e_{KG1}, e_{KG2} \in D} & \big(- 2 \cdot s(v_{e_{KG1}}, v_{e_{KG2}}) \\ & + \log \sum_{c \in C_{e_{KG2}}} \exp(s(v_{e_{KG1}}, v_c)) \\ & + \log \sum_{c \in C_{e_{KG1}}} \exp(s(v_{e_{KG2}}, v_c)) \big) \end{aligned} \quad (2)$$

where D is the list of overlapping entities, e_{KG1} is an entity that appears in KG 1, e_{KG2} is its counter entity from KG 2 and $v_{e_{KG1}}$ and $v_{e_{KG2}}$ are the representations of their textual descriptions from the two KGs, and s is defined as in Equation 1. $C_{e_{KG2}}$ and $C_{e_{KG1}}$ are randomly sampled batches of negative entities from the list of overlapping entities (that are from KG 2 and KG 1, respectively, and do not overlap with $v_{e_{KG1}}$ and $v_{e_{KG2}}$, respectively). This loss function encourages overlapping entities from KG 1 and KG 2 to have similar vector representations in the joint vector space while it pushes representations of other entity pairs further apart.

Combination of Information Sources. We also experiment with combinations of the different information sources described above. In particular when combining settings S and T, in each epoch, we first present batches from S to the model followed by batches from T. When adding O to a combination, we first fine-tune the model on S and/or T (using loss function 1) and then continue fine-tuning on O (using loss function 2).

4 Experiments and Results

In this section, we present our study and report the effects of fine-tuning on the latent representation as well as on the downstream task of entity linking.

Baseline. We use the neural entity linking model BLINK (Wu et al., 2020) as our baseline model.[1]

Fine-tuning Configurations. We experiment with the following combinations of the information sources presented in Section 3.2: S, T, TO, TS, TOS.[2] Hyperparameters are provided in Section A of the appendix.

4.1 Data

Data from target domain (T). The experimental setup requires *domain-specific* entity linking data which is split into fine-tuning and test set. To the best of our knowledge, there is no benchmark available for this. Therefore, we adopt the Wikia dataset for zero-shot entity linking across domains (Logeswaran et al., 2019). We select four domains (*American Football, Doctor Who, Fallout, Final Fantasy*) and randomly split each domain into fine-tuning (train and dev) and test sets (see top part of Table 1). Throughout the experiments, we consider Wikipedia as the *source-domain KG* and one of the domains from Wikia as the *target-domain KG*.

Data from source domain (S). As additional contextual data for source-domain entities, we adopt the Reddit dataset (Botzer et al., 2021) that contains Reddit blog posts with mentions linked to

[1]It has been trained on an English Wikipedia dump from May 2019, using over 5.9M pages as entities (page titles are used as entity names and summary paragraphs as descriptions) and around 9M Wikipedia interlinks as mention-entity annotations. For further details, please see Wu et al. (2020).

[2]We focus on combinations with T since combinations without T did not perform well in preliminary experiments.

Target KG →	American Football		Doctor Who		Fallout		Final Fantasy	
Model	MRR	ACS	MRR	ACS	MRR	ACS	MRR	ACS
BLINK	0.4991	0.9938	0.4607	0.9650	0.4071	0.9603	0.3623	0.9532
T	0.4982	0.9892	0.3926	0.9095	0.3533	0.9317	0.4136*	0.9515
TO	0.4990	0.9919	**0.4932***	0.9784*	**0.4558***	0.9680*	**0.4400***	0.9628
TS	**0.4999**	**0.9958***	0.4323	0.9605	0.4223*	0.9676*	0.4072*	0.9746*
TOS	0.4995	0.9896	0.4619	**0.9830***	0.4534*	**0.9820***	0.4209*	**0.9791***

Table 2: Intrinsic evaluation of overlapping entities between each domain-specific KG and Wikipedia KG. * shows statistically different results in comparison to BLINK (randomization test, $\alpha = 0.005$ with Bonferroni correction).

	Target KG →	American Football		Doctor Who		Fallout		Final Fantasy	
	Model	AP@1	MAP@10	AP@1	MAP@10	AP@1	MAP@10	AP@1	MAP@10
Eval on target KG	BLINK	0.1747	0.4104	0.4108	0.4810	0.3412	0.4444	0.3833	0.5179
	S	0.1713	0.3732	0.5337*	0.6191*	0.4249*	0.5295*	0.3881	0.5433
	T	**0.2093***	**0.4606***	**0.6169***	0.6925*	0.4313*	0.5510*	0.3871	0.5405
	TO	0.1938	0.4103	0.5697*	0.6558*	0.4485*	0.5590*	0.3439	0.4881
	TS	0.2076	0.4583*	0.6124*	**0.7124***	**0.4657***	**0.5915***	**0.4121**	**0.5710***
	TOS	0.1540	0.3292	0.5345*	0.6149*	0.4227*	0.5405*	0.3910	0.5486*
Eval on source KG	BLINK	0.8479	0.8973	0.8509	0.8985	0.8509	0.8987	0.8494	0.8987
	S	**0.8727**	**0.9051**	0.8750*	**0.9063**	**0.8788***	**0.9089**	0.8758*	0.9070
	T	0.8539	0.8994	0.8209	0.8556	0.8057	0.8464	0.8599	0.8991
	TO	0.8524	0.8953	0.8532	0.8865	0.8381	0.8714	0.8630	0.8956
	TS	0.8607	0.8957	0.8582	0.8976	0.8599	0.8965	0.8788*	**0.9085**
	TOS	0.8170	0.8386	**0.8773***	0.9062	0.8637	0.8858	**0.8795***	0.9038

Table 3: Extrinsic evaluation: entity linking. Source KG is Wikipedia in all cases. For the evaluation on the target KG, the domain-specific test set is used. For the evaluation on the source KG, the Reddit test set is used. * shows statistically different results in comparison to BLINK (randomization test, $\alpha = 0.005$ with Bonferroni correction).

Wikipedia entities. We choose the mentions with gold annotations as test set and the mentions with bronze and silver annotations as fine-tuning set.[3] The bottom part of Table 1 shows statistics on the data from the source domain.

Overlapping entities (O). To obtain overlapping entities between the source KG and each of the domain-specific KGs, we first create a candidate list with strict string matching of the entity name aliases (titles of Wikipedia/Wikia pages) from the source and target KGs. Second, we filter this list based on the semantic similarity of the textual descriptions of the entities. In particular, we embed the descriptions with the Roberta-large sentence transformer model by Reimers and Gurevych (2019) and filter the list of candidate entity pairs based on the cosine similarity between their vectors. We set the matching threshold for the cosine similarity to 0.5. Statistics of the overlapping entities are shown on the right side of Table 1.

To ensure the quality of the extracted lists of overlapping entities, we sample 100 entity pairs per domain and manually check their correctness.

[3]The annotation quality bronze/silver/gold was determined based on inter-annotator agreement by Botzer et al. (2021).

Table 4 shows results. Especially for the domains with the largest number of overlapping entities (*American Football* and *Doctor Who*), the number of correct entity pairs is quite high, indicating the usefulness of that information source for our experiments.

Target KG	Correct	Wrong	Unclear
American Football	100	0	0
Doctor Who	84	10	6
Fallout	79	15	6
Final Fantasy	65	17	18

Table 4: Manual analysis of 100 randomly sampled overlapping entities per target domain. The table shows the number of correctly and wrongly identified overlapping entity pairs. The column Unclear shows the number of pairs for which we did not have enough information to assess their correctness.

4.2 Intrinsic Evaluation of Vector Space

We first investigate the effect of fine-tuning on the latent representations of the entities. Intuitively, the better the fine-tuning, the closer the overlapping entities should be in the space. To assess that, we compute the cosine similarity between the vector of the target-domain entity and the vector of its counter entity from the source KG for each pair in the list of overlapping entities and aggregate the results to the *Average Cosine Similarity (ACS)*. Thus, ACS reflects the average of cosine similarities between overlapping entities.

In addition, we assess the rank of the counter entity in the list of nearest neighbors in the vector space for each entity of the list of overlapping entities. Ideally, the counter entity should have a high rank. We evaluate this with the *Mean Reciprocal Rank (MRR)*, a measure from information retrieval.

Table 2 compares the embeddings generated by our models to the embeddings generated by the baseline model (BLINK) in the four domains. Most fine-tuning configurations outperform the baseline model. This shows the value of fine-tuning for the joint vector space in general. For all domains except for *American Football*, MRR and ACS are enhanced up to 7.77% and 2.59%, respectively, with fine-tuning on overlapping entities (O) providing most performance gains. For *American Football*, the results are closer to the baseline and fine-tuning on overlapping entities (O) does not enhance performance compared to fine-tuning on source and target data (TS). This could be explained by the larger number of overlapping entities in this domain (see Table 1). In general, the results show that fine-tuning on target data only (T) is not sufficient and especially fine-tuning on overlapping entities (O) helps improving the vector space.[4]

4.3 Entity Linking Results

To evaluate entity linking, we use the standard measures of *average precision for the top-1* entity (*AP@1*) and the *mean average precision for the top-10* entities (*MAP@10*).

In the upper part of Table 3, we report the results of applying the fine-tuned models to a set of unseen documents with entities from the different target domains. As shown in the table, fine-tuning outperforms BLINK. Interestingly, even fine-tuning on source entities (S) helps in three out of four domains when evaluating on the target KG. Training on both target and source KG entities (TS) achieves the best performance for all domains with an increase of up to 20% in both MAP and AP measures. Including overlapping entities does not further enhance the performance. An explanation for this could be that the entity linking system does not rely on the candidate generation step alone (which requires a good joint vector space) but in addition uses a cross-encoder in the candidate ranking step that re-evaluates each pair of mention and candidate entity, taking the combination of their contexts into account.

In order to ensure that the fine-tuned model still performs well on mentions of entities from the source KG, we also evaluate it on the test data from Reddit. The results can be found in the bottom part of Table 3. Fine-tuning on the source KG only (S) improves the baseline system BLINK as expected. In contrast, fine-tuning on the target KG only (T) harms the performance on the source KG test set a bit. When the model is trained on a combination of entities from both target and source KGs (TS/TOS), performance on the source-KG test set is enhanced in most cases.

With respect to our research questions, we can conclude that *a combination of data with mentions linked to entities from both the source and the target KG* is most suited for fine-tuning and that *especially adding training data from the source-domain KG* avoids performance loss on the source domain. With this fine-tuning setup, we obtain a robust system that can link mentions to both source and target-domain KGs at the same time.

5 Conclusion

In this paper, we presented a systematic investigation of extending an entity linking system to a new domain by creating a joint vector space. Our results showed that it is helpful to add data from both the source domain and the target domain. While an additional supervision on entities that appear in both knowledge graphs improves the quality of the vector space, it has less impact on the downstream task of entity linking. Additional data linked to the source-domain KG avoids performance loss on the general domain and is, thus, especially useful to achieve a system that can link mentions to both source and target-domain KGs at the same time.

Acknowledgments

We would like to thank Dietrich Klakow, the members of the BCAI NLP&KRR research group and the anonymous reviewers for their helpful comments.

[4]Note that the dataset used for fine-tuning on O is the same that we use for the intrinsic evaluation. The reason is that we only aim at analyzing the effects of fine-tuning on the overlapping entities in the joint vector space without the necessity for generalization to an unseen dataset. The effects on the unseen test sets for entity linking are described in Section 4.3.

References

Nicholas Botzer, Yifan Ding, and Tim Weninger. 2021. Reddit entity linking dataset. *Information Processing & Management*, 58(3).

Jacob Devlin, Ming-Wei Chang, Kenton Lee, and Kristina Toutanova. 2019. BERT: Pre-training of deep bidirectional transformers for language understanding. In *Proceedings of the 2019 Conference of the North American Chapter of the Association for Computational Linguistics: Human Language Technologies, Volume 1 (Long and Short Papers)*, pages 4171–4186, Minneapolis, Minnesota. Association for Computational Linguistics.

Matthew Francis-Landau, Greg Durrett, and Dan Klein. 2016. Capturing semantic similarity for entity linking with convolutional neural networks. In *Proceedings of the 2016 Conference of the North American Chapter of the Association for Computational Linguistics: Human Language Technologies*, pages 1256–1261, San Diego, California. Association for Computational Linguistics.

Nitish Gupta, Sameer Singh, and Dan Roth. 2017. Entity linking via joint encoding of types, descriptions, and context. In *Proceedings of the 2017 Conference on Empirical Methods in Natural Language Processing, EMNLP 2017, Copenhagen, Denmark, September 9-11, 2017*, pages 2681–2690. Association for Computational Linguistics.

Zhengyan He, Shujie Liu, Mu Li, Ming Zhou, Longkai Zhang, and Houfeng Wang. 2013. Learning entity representation for entity disambiguation. In *Proceedings of the 51st Annual Meeting of the Association for Computational Linguistics (Volume 2: Short Papers)*, pages 30–34, Sofia, Bulgaria. Association for Computational Linguistics.

Michael A. Hedderich, Lukas Lange, Heike Adel, Jannik Strötgen, and Dietrich Klakow. 2021. A survey on recent approaches for natural language processing in low-resource scenarios. In *Proceedings of the 2021 Conference of the North American Chapter of the Association for Computational Linguistics: Human Language Technologies*, pages 2545–2568, Online. Association for Computational Linguistics.

Johannes Hoffart, Mohamed Amir Yosef, Ilaria Bordino, Hagen Fürstenau, Manfred Pinkal, Marc Spaniol, Bilyana Taneva, Stefan Thater, and Gerhard Weikum. 2011. Robust disambiguation of named entities in text. In *Proceedings of the 2011 Conference on Empirical Methods in Natural Language Processing*, pages 782–792, Edinburgh, Scotland, UK. Association for Computational Linguistics.

Samuel Humeau, Kurt Shuster, Marie-Anne Lachaux, and Jason Weston. 2020. Polyencoders: Architectures and pre-training strategies for fast and accurate multisentence scoring. In *8th International Conference on Learning Representations, ICLR 2020*, Addis Ababa, Ethiopia.

Nikolaos Kolitsas, Octavian-Eugen Ganea, and Thomas Hofmann. 2018. End-to-end neural entity linking. In *Proceedings of the 22nd Conference on Computational Natural Language Learning*, pages 519–529, Brussels, Belgium. Association for Computational Linguistics.

Lajanugen Logeswaran, Ming-Wei Chang, Kenton Lee, Kristina Toutanova, Jacob Devlin, and Honglak Lee. 2019. Zero-shot entity linking by reading entity descriptions. In *Proceedings of the 57th Annual Meeting of the Association for Computational Linguistics*, pages 3449–3460, Florence, Italy. Association for Computational Linguistics.

Yasumasa Onoe and Greg Durrett. 2020. Fine-grained entity typing for domain independent entity linking. In *Proceedings of the AAAI Conference on Artificial Intelligence*, pages 8576–8583, New York, NY, USA. AAAI Press.

Matthew E. Peters, Mark Neumann, Robert Logan, Roy Schwartz, Vidur Joshi, Sameer Singh, and Noah A. Smith. 2019. Knowledge enhanced contextual word representations. In *Proceedings of the 2019 Conference on Empirical Methods in Natural Language Processing and the 9th International Joint Conference on Natural Language Processing (EMNLP-IJCNLP)*, pages 43–54, Hong Kong, China. Association for Computational Linguistics.

Nils Reimers and Iryna Gurevych. 2019. Sentence-BERT: Sentence embeddings using Siamese BERT-networks. In *Proceedings of the 2019 Conference on Empirical Methods in Natural Language Processing and the 9th International Joint Conference on Natural Language Processing (EMNLP-IJCNLP)*, pages 3982–3992, Hong Kong, China. Association for Computational Linguistics.

Özge Sevgili, Artem Shelmanov, Mikhail Arkhipov, Alexander Panchenko, and Chris Biemann. 2021. Neural entity linking: A survey of models based on deep learning. *arXiv:2006.00575*.

Yaming Sun, Lei Lin, Duyu Tang, Nan Yang, Zhenzhou Ji, and Xiaolong Wang. 2015. Modeling mention, context and entity with neural networks for entity disambiguation. In *Proceedings of the 24th International Conference on Artificial Intelligence, IJCAI 2015)*, page 1333–1339, Buenos Aires, Argentina. AAAI Press.

Yogarshi Vyas and Miguel Ballesteros. 2021. Linking entities to unseen knowledge bases with arbitrary schemas. In *Proceedings of the 2021 Conference of the North American Chapter of the Association for Computational Linguistics: Human Language Technologies, NAACL-HLT 2021, Online, June 6-11, 2021*, pages 834–844. Association for Computational Linguistics.

Ledell Wu, Fabio Petroni, Martin Josifoski, Sebastian Riedel, and Luke Zettlemoyer. 2020. Scalable zero-shot entity linking with dense entity retrieval. In

Proceedings of the 2020 Conference on Empirical Methods in Natural Language Processing (EMNLP), pages 6397–6407, Online. Association for Computational Linguistics.

Ikuya Yamada, Hiroyuki Shindo, Hideaki Takeda, and Yoshiyasu Takefuji. 2016. Joint learning of the embedding of words and entities for named entity disambiguation. In *Proceedings of The 20th SIGNLL Conference on Computational Natural Language Learning*, pages 250–259, Berlin, Germany. Association for Computational Linguistics.

A Hyperparameters

Hyperparameters	Values
Fine-tuning Batch Size	16
Learning Rate	3e-5
Number of Epochs	5
Candidate Generation: Top K	10
Mention with Context: Max Context Length	128
Entity with Description: Max Description Length	128

Table 5: Hyperparameters for fine-tuning.

All settings, i.e., all combinations of information sources (S, T, TS, TO and TOS) share the same hyperparameters for fine-tuning. They are provided in Table 5.

For learning rate and number of epochs, we followed the proposed values by Wu et al. (2020). In addition, we applied early stopping to store the best model checkpoint based on the model performance on the validation set.

We set the number of candidate entities k to 10 and the maximum number of tokens in the context of mention and entity to 128 in order to save computation costs. Note that we applied the same k and context lengths when evaluating the baseline BLINK model.

Fine-tuning and evaluation was performed on a Tesla V100 GPU. All our experiments were run on a carbon-neutral GPU cluster.[5]

B Ethical Considerations

We acknowledge the ACL Code of Ethics. In particular, we only use well-known benchmark datasets for our evaluation. Both the Wikia and the Reddit dataset do not include personal data, such as information about the authors of the posts (Logeswaran et al., 2019; Botzer et al., 2021). The list of overlapping entities that we will publish does not contain any privacy-related or IP-related content either.

[5]The Bosch Group is carbon neutral. Administration, manufacturing and research activities do no longer leave a carbon footprint. This also includes GPU clusters on which the experiments have been performed.

TRAttack: Text Rewriting Attack Against Text Retrieval

Junshuai Song, Jiangshan Zhang, Jifeng Zhu, Mengyun Tang, Yong Yang
Tencent, China
{jasonjssong,jiangszhang,jifengzhu,mengyuntang, coolcyang}@tencent.com

Abstract

Text retrieval has been widely-used in many online applications to help users find relevant information from a text collection. In this paper, we study a new attack scenario against text retrieval to evaluate its robustness to adversarial attacks under the black-box setting, in which attackers want their own texts to always get high relevance scores with different users' input queries and thus be retrieved frequently and can receive large amounts of impressions for profits. Considering that most current attack methods only simply follow certain fixed optimization rules, we propose a novel text rewriting attack (TRAttack) method with learning ability from the multi-armed bandit mechanism. Extensive experiments conducted on simulated victim environments demonstrate that TRAttack can yield texts that have higher relevance scores with different given users' queries than those generated by current state-of-the-art attack methods. We also evaluate TRAttack on Tencent Cloud's and Baidu Cloud's commercially-available text retrieval APIs, and the rewritten adversarial texts successfully get high relevance scores with different user queries, which shows the practical potential of our method and the risk of text retrieval systems.

User Input Queries	Ori.	Adv.
怎么锻炼逻辑思维能力? How to exercise logical thinking skills?	✓	✓
想提升理解能力和逻辑能力? Want to enhance comprehension and logical skills?	×	✓
填字游戏能提高逻辑思维吗? Can crosswords enhance logical thinking?	×	✓
Ori.: 怎么锻炼逻辑思维能力, 让自己更加有效率的学习和工作? How to exercise logical thinking skills to study and work more efficiently? Adv.: 怎么锻炼逻辑思维能力, 让自己方为有智用的自课和工作?		

Table 1: The retrieval results of three different user input queries on an original text (Org. for short) and the adversarial rewritten text (Adv. for short), in which the green words in Org. are replaced with the red words for adversarial goals. '✓' represents that the text is retrieved by the corresponding query.

1 Introduction

Text retrieval is a popular and important technology for solving information explosion. In many commercial systems, such as Baidu Knows[1], Answer[2] and StackExchange[3], text retrieval is the key to find relevant content and help search engines to return the information that users want (Trotman et al., 2014). With the development of deep neural networks, many deep learning-based models (Kalchbrenner et al., 2014; Devlin et al., 2018; Sun et al., 2019) are proposed for measuring text relevance. Though the quality of retrieval results is greatly improved, these deep learning-based models (Li et al., 2019a; Song et al., 2020) also bring unexpected serious risks to the text retrieval systems due to their vulnerability.

In this paper, we study a new attack problem in the text retrieval area, in which texts are ranked based on their relevance scores with different user queries. Previous researchers have studied adversarial attacks on retrieval systems (Li et al., 2019a, 2021a). However, the attack goal is to completely subvert the top-k retrieval results of a given single query, with which attackers can deceive the target information retrieval system into retrieving irrelevant content for evading the censorship of professional monitors. Different from the above attack problem, here we focus on a new attack goal

[1] https://zhidao.baidu.com/
[2] https://www.answers.com/
[3] https://stackexchange.com/

Proceedings of the 7th Workshop on Representation Learning for NLP, pages 191 - 203
May 26, 2022

where attackers aim to find adversarial texts that can get high relevance scores with many different user queries at the same, and thus there is a high probability for their texts to be retrieved and receive large amounts of impressions (Li et al., 2019b).

This new text retrieval attack problem is realistic as attackers always want more impressions and get more profits than normal users. Table 1 illustrates an attack example, in which the adversarial text is successfully retrieved by all three queries while the original text can be retrieved by one of them only. Attackers can obtain much more impressions and thus get more profits from the text retrieval platform. To verify how serious this form of attack is and facilitate the development of the corresponding countermeasures, we emphasize that it is crucial to develop practical attack methods that can find adversarial texts against existing text retrieval systems.

Query-based adversarial example generation frameworks (Morris et al., 2020; Zeng et al., 2021) could be a good solution for solving the above attack problem under the black-box setting. These methods continuously interact with the victim environment and then iteratively update the generated adversarial examples by received reward signals. However, most of them only simply follow certain fixed optimization rules (Li et al., 2018; Alzantot et al., 2018; Zang et al., 2019) to generate adversarial examples. In other words, they only optimize the adversarial results instead of the attack policies, which greatly limits their attack performance.

For launching attacks more effectively, we propose a novel text rewriting attack (TRAttack) method that can optimize attack policies and examples at the same time by learning from the historical attack knowledge. TRAttack follows the word replacement framework so that it can preserve semantic consistency and language fluency of adversarial examples well. For learning from attack knowledge, we choose reinforcement learning (Sutton and Barto, 2018) to carefully balance the exploration and exploitation in the learning process due to the small number of training samples and expensive interactive costs with the victim environments. Specifically, we choose the well-known multi-armed bandit (MAB) (Kuleshov and Precup, 2014; Lattimore and Szepesvári, 2020; Li et al., 2021b) method. With MAB, the substitutes of each word are viewed as arms to be selected and TRAttack iteratively updates their sampling weights by evaluating the expected adversarial rewards in following iterations for better attack performance. Our main contributions are summarized as follows:

- We discuss a new possible attack threat in text retrieval and formulate the corresponding attack problem to study its robustness to adversarial attacks.
- We develop a novel reinforcement learning-based query-efficient text rewriting attack (TRAttack) method that can achieve high attack performance against text retrieval under the black-box setting.
- We compare TRAttack with existing popular query-based methods and TRAttack achieves much better attack performance. We also successfully attack commercial APIs provided by Tencent Cloud[4] and Baidu Cloud[5], which shows the potential risks of text retrieval systems as APIs could be used in real online applications.

2 Related Work

Language Modeling With the development of deep learning-based natural language processing (Devlin et al., 2018; Cui et al., 2020; Xiao et al., 2020), the quality of text retrieval has been greatly improved in recent years. RNN (Chung et al., 2014; Lipton et al., 2015) is a typical way to encode sequential text information, while convolutional neural networks (CNN) (Liu et al., 2018) and attention-based modeling methods (Vaswani et al., 2017; Zhou et al., 2018) are also used to extract high-dimensional representations for texts. BERT (Devlin et al., 2018; Cui et al., 2020) is a transformer-based method that is bidirectionally trained and has a deeper sense of language context, presenting state-of-the-art results in a wide variety of NLP tasks. Further, many variants based on BERT are proposed and achieve better performance, such as SpanBERT (Joshi et al., 2020), ERNIE (Sun et al., 2019; Xiao et al., 2020), etc. These language modeling methods can be adopted in text retrieval and have boosted the quality of retrieval results (Sakata et al., 2019).

[4] https://cloud.tencent.com/
[5] https://ai.baidu.com/

Adversarial Methods in NLP We consider the most realistic and challenging black-box attack scenario, where attackers have no prior knowledge of the victim model. They can only interact with the victim model to get useful information and optimize their attacks (Zang et al., 2020; Zeng et al., 2021; Morris et al., 2020). Li et al. (2018) follow the idea of greedy word replacement and propose TextBugger. TextFooler (Jin et al., 2020) and PWWS (Ren et al., 2019) are similar to TextBugger, but both of them make stricter restrictions on every single modification for generating plausible and semantically similar adversarial examples. Alzantot et al. (2018) develop Genetic via genetic algorithms. Zang et al. (2019) further propose PSO based on a particle swarm optimization-based search algorithm to generate adversarial examples. BERT-Attack (Li et al., 2020) and BAE (Garg and Ramakrishnan, 2020) use pre-trained masked language models exemplified by BERT to achieve adversarial goals while the generated examples are fluent and semantically preserved.

3 Text Rewriting Attack

In this section, we first formally define the new attack problem against text retrieval under the black-box setting and then introduce the details of our proposed text rewriting attack method.

3.1 Problem Definition

For a query input q, retrieval systems return a list of texts: $X_q = \{x_1, x_2, ..., x_k \mid f(q, x_i) \leq f(q, x_j), s.t.\ i \leq j\}$ ordered by their relevance scores (or similarities) with q where $f(\cdot)$ is the relevance function and k is the size of X_q. As shown in Table 1, attackers' goal is to generate adversarial texts that have 'abnormally' high relevance to many given user queries meanwhile, so that there is a high probability for their texts to be retrieved and thus they can receive large amounts of impressions.

For a text x, we use n_x to represent the number of impressions that it receives in a period of time. Formally, it can be calculated as:

$$n_x = \sum_q s(q, x) \qquad (1)$$

where $s(q, x)$ represents whether the text x is retrieved by the query q. Then, the attackers' goal is to find a text x_{adv} that can get $n_{x_{adv}}$ as high as possible.

To make n_x computable in our experiments, we set $s(q, x) > 0$ when x belongs to the top-k relevance texts of the query q, otherwise we have $s(q, x) = 0$. Considering that higher ranking orders usually represent larger probabilities to be exposed to users, we further specifically define $s(q, x) = (k - r + 1)/k$ to assign higher values for texts that have higher ranking orders $r \in [1, k]$ under a query q. We have $s(q, x) \in [0, 1]$. Besides, we define Q_x as the query set that a retrieval system receives in a period of time where the queries and x are on the same topic. Then the objective function can be approximately written as:

$$\arg\max_{x_{adv}} \sum_q^{Q_t} s(q, x_{adv}) \qquad (2)$$

where the adversarial goal is to find the text x_{adv} that can always receive high ranking orders under given relevant queries in Q_x and thus maximize $n_{x_{adv}} = \sum_q^{Q_t} s(q, x_{adv})$. Note, retrieval systems calculate relevance scores for ranking different query-text pairs, but these scores are not available to attackers. They can only optimize their attack goals with statistical signals. In our experiments, we adopt the above approximated $n_{x_{adv}}$ in Equation 2 as the adversarial goal under the black-box setting, and also use it to guide the optimization of adversarial attacks.

3.2 Text Rewriting Algorithm

Text rewriting can be implemented by directly generating adversarial texts from scratch (Lipton et al., 2015; Zang et al., 2020) or replacing partial words in the original text only (Li et al., 2020). Since the perturbation budget in the second word replacement framework can be easily bounded to preserve the fluencies and semantics of adversarial texts (Li et al., 2020; Garg and Ramakrishnan, 2020), we also adopt it in TRAttack. The key difference is that there is a particularly-designed memory in TRAttack for caching historical' attack knowledge. Specifically, the memory learns effective word replacement policies that can greatly boost the attack performance. We carefully launch the solution based on MAB, which achieves a good balance between exploration and exploitation as the attack goes on. How to sample from and update the memory are two important questions. In the following, we first introduce the core idea and structure of the memory H in TRAttack, and then give the details of the solutions for the above two questions.

Memory Design with MAB With the MAB mechanism, we need to store some specific information for balancing the exploration and exploitation in the learning process. Specifically, we choose the upper confidence bound (UCB) bandit method in TRAttack. Equation 3 illustrate that how UCB chooses actions (arms) based on existing knowledge:

$$a^* = \arg\max_a r(a) + c\sqrt{\frac{\ln m}{N(a)}} \tag{3}$$

where $r(a)$ is the estimated reward of choosing the arm a, $N(a)$ is the number of times that arm a has been selected before and m is the overall number of players done on the current bandit problem. $r(a)$ and $c\sqrt{\frac{\ln m}{N(a)}}$ represent the exploitation part and the exploration part in UCB, respectively. c is a hyper-parameter to control the level of exploration. At the beginning, UCB encourages exploration as $c\sqrt{\frac{\ln m}{N(a)}}$ is relatively large with a small $N(a)$ for each arm. With the learning process, UCB will concentrate on exploitation, selecting the arm with the highest estimated reward.

Memory in TRAttack TRAttack follows the word replacement framework for generating adversarial examples, and we equip TRAttack with MAB in the word replacement process. Specifically, for a word w, the substitutes of it are viewed as arms to be selected in MAB. We design the memory $H_w = [(s_1, r(s_1), N(s_1)), ..., (s_j, r(s_j), N(s_j))]$ for each word w to store specific information about its substitutes (arms), where s_j represents the j-th potential substitute. $r(s_j)$ and $N(s_j)$ are the estimated reward of replacing w with s_j and the number of times that w has been replaced by s_j before. With H_w on every word w, we can conduct the word replacement policy similar to Equation 3. However, it is costly to fully explore the search space as the standard UCB does because there is a large number of potential substitutes for each word in TRAttack.

To optimize the efficiency of convergence, we further make two updates in TRAttack. First, we manually set the maximum number of substitutes for each word to $L = 200$ to reduce the search space and thus speed up the model convergence. Secondly, we use a function $g(m)$ negatively correlated with m to replace the original hyper-parameter c in Equation 3, with which we can actively reduce exploration in the learning process and further accelerate the model convergence. Though the above two updates may lead to suboptimal results, it is necessary for TRAttack because of the high learning costs against text retrieval systems in practice. Then, we have Equation 4 in TRAttack for selecting word substitutes:

$$\arg\max_s r(s) + g(m)\sqrt{\frac{\ln m}{N(s)}} \quad s.t.\ s \in H_w \text{ and } |H_w| \leq L \tag{4}$$

To make sure that TRAttack will concentrate on exploitation after a few iterations in practice, we generally require that $g(m)\sqrt{\frac{\ln m}{N(s)}}$ tends to 0 with the increase of m even that $N(s)$ of a substitute s is small. In other words, the word substitute selection in TRAttack can gradually totally depend on the substitute reward so that TRAttack can achieve high performance within the expected time frame.

Overall, for each word w, we use a list H_w to store its substitutes with corresponding rewards and accumulated numbers of times that they have been selected. We have $H = \{H_w; w \in W\}$ where W represents the whole word set in a retrieval system. Besides, TRAttack adopts masked language models to generate word substitutes as (Li et al., 2020) for ensuring that the adversarial text is fluent and semantically preserved. As a result, we have an empty H_w for each word w at the beginning. All word substitutes are gradually collected and merged into H with the learning process. More details about the substitute generation and the maintenance of H will be introduced in the following parts.

TRAttack with Memory Algorithm 1 shows the complete text rewriting process of TRAttack for a given text x and it mainly contains 3 steps.

Step 1: Text Expanding (Optional) Considering that there are usually some short texts consisting of a few words only, word replacement may easily result in adversarial examples with obviously different semantics. To overcome the above problem, we propose to expand texts first and then replace the words that are newly added only for well-preserving the text semantic. To achieve this goal, we choose existing famous pre-trained language models (Radford et al., 2019; Zhang et al.,

2020) to expand the original text directly. As language models may generate long texts, we manually stop the text expanding process when meeting the first question mark or full stop.

In such a way, x_{adv} could be viewed as the concatenation of x and an additional expanded trigger text x_t and we have $x_{adv} = \text{concat}(x, x_t)$. Then, our attack goal can be formulated as replacing the words in x_t to improve the relevance scores between x_{adv} and different users' queries. In practice, attackers can even manually expand x instead of adopting language models and thus this step is optional in TRAttack. TRAttack can also directly conduct attacks base on x as most existing methods (Zeng et al., 2021) without text expanding.

Step 2: Word Replacement with Memory For an initialized adversarial text $x_{adv} = \text{concat}(x, x_t)$, we first decide the word replacement order in x_t, and then choose specific word substitutes with the help of the memory H for generating effective adversarial examples.

For the word importance, there have been many solutions for estimating it (Li et al., 2020; Garg and Ramakrishnan, 2020). Here we calculate the word importance of each w in a text x_t by deleting it from x_{adv} and computing the average decrease in the probability of predicting the correct relevance label y with the corresponding queries in Q_x. Then we sort the words in x_t by their importance and get $I = [w_1, w_2, ..., w_{|x_t|}]$ for further word replacement.

For a selected word w to be replaced, we then need to decide the word substitute set S_w for it and conduct the word replacement operation for better attack performance. Following the idea in (Li et al., 2020), we generate word substitutes for a word w by masking it in x_{adv} and feeding the masked x_{adv} into a well-trained masked language model, in which the genuine nature of the masked language model makes sure that the texts with the generated substitutes are relatively fluent and also preserve most semantic information. Each time, we use the top-M predictions from a masked language model to initialize S_w first, and then update S_w with learned H_w for better word replacement choices. On the one hand, for the substitutes that are new and do not appear in H_w before, we use S^*_w to represent them and make sure all the substitutes in S^*_w are selected by default, which helps us to continuously enrich the candidate substitutes of different words. On the other hand, we select the other $M - |S^*_w|$ substitutes from the learned memory H_w for the current word w and get S^{**}_w. Finally, we reconstruct $S_w \leftarrow S^*_w \cup S^{**}_w$.

Algorithm 1 Text Rewriting Attack

Input: Text x, query set Q_x, memory $H = \{H_w; w \in W\}$, number of substitutes M, number of memory size L
Output: Adversarial text x_{adv}
Expand x and get the initialized $x_{adv} \leftarrow \text{concat}(x, x_t)$
Sort the words in x_t by their estimated importance and get $I \leftarrow [w_1, w_2, ..., w_{|x_t|}]$
for $i \leftarrow 1$ to $|x_t|$ **do**
  Generate the top-M substitutes for w_i using masked language models and use them to initialize S_{w_i}
  $S^*_{w_i} \leftarrow S_{w_i} \setminus (S_{w_i} \cap H_{w_i})$
  Select $M - |S^*_w|$ words from H_{w_i} as $S^{**}_{w_i}$ according to Equation 4
  $S_{w_i} \leftarrow S^*_{w_i} \cup S^{**}_{w_i}$
  for $j \leftarrow 1$ to $|S_{w_i}|$ **do**
    Get x'_{adv} by replacing w_i with s_j
    Calculate the reward $r'(s_j)$
    if $r'(s_j) > 0$ **then**
      $x_{adv} \leftarrow x'_{adv}$
  Update H_{w_i}
return Adversarial text x_{adv}

The selection of substitutes from H_w is based on Equation 4. For $r(s)$, we define it based on the attack performance improvement between x'_{adv} and x_{adv} where x'_{adv} is obtained by replacing w with s in x_{adv}. Specifically, we set $r(s) = (n_{x'_{adv}} - n_{x_{adv}})/|Q_x|$, where $1/|Q_x|$ is used for normalization, and we have $r(s) \in [-1, 1]$. With the learning process, a word substitute s with better historical attack performance will have a larger $r(s)$ and thus have a larger chance to be selected in the future, which can boost the attack performance of TRAttack. For $g(m)$, we define $g(m) = \frac{c}{m}$ and $c = 50$ is a constant. In this setting, $g(m)\sqrt{\frac{\ln m}{N(w)}}$ tends to 0 with the increase of m and thus we can successfully actively reduce exploration for achieving high attack performance within limited attack attempts and costs.

Step 3: Memory Update For each substitute $s \in S_w$ with the newly calculated reward $r'(s)$ in the current iteration, we update H_w following the below rules. If s is new to H_w, we directly merge it into H_w. If s already appears in H_w, we use the following Equation 5 to update $r(s)$ of s in H_w:

$$r(s) = \frac{r(s) * N(s) + r'(s)}{N(s) + 1} \quad (5)$$

And then we set $N(s) \leftarrow N(s) + 1$. Besides, if the size of H_w exceeds L, we additionally remove the substitutes with relatively low $r(\cdot)$ in H_w and make sure that $|H_w|$ does not exceed L.

4 Experiments

4.1 Experimental Settings

Dataset LCQMC (Liu et al., 2018) is a large-scale Chinese question matching corpus collected from Baidu Knows. BQ-Corpus (Chen et al., 2018) contains question pairs from online bank custom service logs. We use these 2 publicly-available datasets for text retrieval in our experiments. Overall, there are 256433 and 35395 different texts in LCQMC and BQ-Corpus, respectively.

Evaluation Metric We adopt 4 metrics for evaluating different attack methods comprehensively. For the attack performance, we define $R(x_{adv}) = n_{x_{adv}}/|Q_x|$ to represent the attack performance of a generated adversarial text x_{adv} where $1/|Q_x|$ is used for normalization. For the quality of adversarial examples, we adopt the common metric perplexity (PPL) (Li et al., 2020) as (Zang et al., 2019), and use the cosine similarity between text embeddings as an approximation for the semantic consistency (Jin et al., 2020). As only x_t in x_{adv} is modified, we test PPL and semantic consistency on it by default. Besides, we report the number of interactions of each method, which is another important metric for evaluating the attack costs.

Text Retrieval Systems Given a user query q, the text retrieval system computes relevance between q and existing texts in the system and then returns the most relevant texts to the user. Due to a large number of the corpus in real-world systems, there are usually two stages for text retrieval: candidate generation and ranking (Yang et al., 2019). In our experiments, we simulate different retrieval systems. Specifically, we adopt the popular BM25 (Trotman et al., 2014) for selecting 100 texts as candidates each time and then use different ranking models to rank them by calculating their relevance scores with different given queries. We choose 4 different representative language models as the ranking model, including LSTM, CNN, BERT (Cui et al., 2020) and ERNIE-Gram (Xiao et al., 2020). Most of the above ranking models have been introduced in Section 2 and their implementation details can be found in Appendix A.

Overall, we use the 4 text retrieval models and the 2 datasets to construct 8 different simulated text retrieval environments as the testbeds for experimental evaluation. If a generated adversarial text x_{adv} frequently receives large relevance scores with different user queries, it will have high ranking orders in users' retrieval results most of the time, leading to a high $R(x_{adv})$. In order to fully demonstrate the changes of the ranking results of generated adversarial examples, we set $k = 100$ that is the number of candidates by default when calculating $R(\cdot)$.

4.2 Comparison with Query-based Attack Baselines

We compare TRAttack with 4 popular query-based adversarial methods that work well under the black-box setting, including TextBugger (Li et al., 2018), PWWS (Ren et al., 2019), Genetic (Alzantot et al., 2018), PSO (Zang et al., 2019) and BERT-Attack (Li et al., 2020). TextBugger and PWWS are greedy methods, in which they first sort words in given texts by importance and then replace them with carefully selected substitutes for achieving adversarial goals. Genetic and PSO are representative population-based search algorithms. For generating effective adversarial examples, both of them first initialize a text set (the size is set to 20 in our experiments) and then iteratively update them with different evolutionary algorithms. For BERT-Attack, it is also a greedy word replacement method and we replace the masked language model in it with Chinese-BERT-wwm (Cui et al., 2019) for conducting adversarial attacks in Chinese. As for our method TRAttack, we adopt Chinese-BERT-wwm as the masked language model for generating word substitutes as well. For the parameters, we set $M = 36$ and $L = 200$ by default. Besides, for a fair comparison, we adopt the optional text expanding process with CPM (Zhang et al., 2020) in all attack methods.

The comparison results[6] are illustrated in Table 2. In each testbed, we randomly choose 500 texts to generate adversarial examples and calculate the average results. As we can see, TRAt-

[6]We discuss the experimental results on the LCQMC dataset in Section 4.2 and the results on the BQ-Corpus dataset are reported in Appendix due to the page limitation.

Method	Num.	Per.	PPL	Sem.
TextBugger	151	0.8126	1106	0.5117
PWWS	197	0.7115	565	0.6625
Genetic	807	0.5599	432	0.8233
PSO	306	0.4705	432	0.8781
BERT-Attack	137	0.7533	995	0.9129
TRAttack	141	0.8341	1159	0.9015

(a) The simulated text retrieval system with LSTM

Method	Num.	Per.	PPL	Sem.
TextBugger	151	0.6519	917	0.4868
PWWS	197	0.5581	532	0.7162
Genetic	807	0.4423	404	0.8252
PSO	306	0.4089	403	0.8852
BERT-Attack	137	0.6514	795	0.9177
TRAttack	141	0.6772	1104	0.9079

(b) The simulated text retrieval system with CNN

Method	Num.	Per.	PPL	Sem.
TextBugger	151	0.6891	841	0.7062
PWWS	197	0.6369	722	0.7059
Genetic	807	0.5436	512	0.8178
PSO	310	0.5028	362	0.8229
BERT-Attack	137	0.6492	971	0.9078
TRAttack	141	0.6636	1355	0.9014

(c) The simulated text retrieval system with BERT

Method	Num.	Per.	PPL	Sem.
TextBugger	151	0.7506	797	0.6819
PWWS	197	0.7107	475	0.7216
Genetic	807	0.6290	335	0.8414
PSO	307	0.5891	321	0.8361
BERT-Attack	137	0.6831	914	0.9126
TRAttack	141	0.7037	1375	0.9086

(d) The simulated text retrieval system with ERNIE-Gram

Table 2: Attack results on different simulated text retrieval systems on the LCQMC dataset. Num., Per. and Sem. represent the number of interactions, the attack performance $R(\cdot)$ and the semantic consistency, respectively.

tack achieves the best results on the whole. In TextBugger, it defines some 'bug' generation ways for adversarial attacks. Though it achieves high attack performance, most of its generated adversarial texts are less fluent and semantically consistent compared with other methods. PWWS follows the greedy word replacement framework. As the synonym-based word substitute generation method with thesauri like WordNet (Miller, 1995) always provides very limited synonyms for many words, we use the embedding-based word substitute generation method as TextBugger in it for better attack performance. In our experiments, PWWS receives lower Per. than TextBugger while PPL and Sem. are usually better.

Genetic and PSO are population-based methods. For PSO, as the sememe-based word substitute generation method (Zang et al., 2019) also greatly reduces the number of potential word substitutes, we adopt the embedding-based word substitute generation method in it as well. In our experiments, both of these two methods receives relatively low attack performance compared with other methods, which may be due to the fact that they usually need a long period of evolution (large Num.) to achieve satisfying results.

BERT-Attack adopts masked language models to generate adversarial examples and receives relatively high Per. and Sem. in our tests at a low attack cost. TRAttack follows the similar framework with it and can further get an obvious improvement on Per., while PPL and Sem. are slightly worse than BERT-Attack. This is due to that we always choose words that can achieve high attack performance from the learned memory in TRAttack, but these newly selected words may slightly damage the fluency and semantic consistence sometimes. Here, to illustrate the advantages of our method more comprehensively, we conduct additional experiments for TRAttack. Specifically, We test TRAttack by reducing different numbers of words that can be replaced by substitutes in it. The results conducted on the simulated text retrieval system based on LSTM and the LCQMC dataset are reported in Table 3.

Value	Num.	Per.	PPL	Sem.
1	127	0.7923	836	0.9153
2	114	0.7478	691	0.9250
3	101	0.7139	557	0.9281
4	88	0.6674	496	0.9395

Table 3: Attack results with different reduced numbers of words that can be replaced.

As we can see, with a larger reduced number of words that can be replaced, TRAttack gradually receives better PPL and Sem. while Per. becomes smaller. An important experimental result is that TRAttack achieves better performance on all the 4 metrics than BERT-Attack when the reduced number is set to 1, which clearly shows the advantages of TRAttack. Overall, we can say that TRAttack achieves the best performance among all compared methods by optimizing the attack policies (memory) and examples meanwhile. Besides, it is worth mentioning that the learned knowledge in TRAttack is general and can be continuously updated with new attack results, which is the key advantage and foundation for TRAttack to further achieve better attack performance in the future. We also illustrate an adversarial example generated by TRAttack in Table 9 in Appendix, which can successfully receive high relevance scores with 10 different queries.

4.3 Parameter Analysis

Tables 4 and 5 show the test results of TRAttack regarding two different hyper-parameters on the simulated text retrieval system based on LSTM and the LCQMC dataset: the number of substitutes M and the memory size L.

Value	Num.	Per.	PPL	Sem.
6	42	0.7206	868	0.9040
12	74	0.7710	966	0.9080
24	113	0.8117	1053	0.9065
36	141	0.8341	1159	0.9015
48	171	0.8429	1233	0.9038

Table 4: Attack results with different M.

Value	Num.	Per.	PPL	Sem.
50	141	0.8175	1138	0.9110
200	141	0.8341	1159	0.9015
500	141	0.8369	1190	0.9067
2000	141	0.8329	1193	0.9033

Table 5: Attack results with different L.

Intuitively, TRAttack can receive better attack performance with a larger M. As we can see in Table 4, the performance improvement gradually becomes insignificant. For balancing the attack performance and other metrics, $M = 36$ could be a good choice for conducting adversarial attacks in practice. As for L, the attack performance can generally be increased along with it increasing. However, as we actively speed up the convergence of TRAttack by $g(m)$ for achieving good performance within limited attack costs, the word replacement policy with a large memory may not be learned well, thus leading to a worse result. As we can see in Table 5, TRAttack receives a relatively good result with $L = 200$.

4.4 Attack Commercial APIs

We have shown that TRAttack can effectively attack simulated text retrieval systems in Section 4.2. Here, we show that TRAttack can also successfully create adversarial texts on commercial text retrieval APIs provided by Tencent Cloud and Baidu Cloud. Due to the QPS limitation, we randomly test 10 samples for both APIs in our experiments.

API	Num.	Per.	PPL	Sem.
Tencent	1761	0.5570	1014	0.8878
Baidu	1712	0.6619	556	0.8951

Table 6: Attack results of TRAttack on the Tencent Cloud's and Baidu Cloud's APIs.

The results are reported in Table 6, in which we iteratively optimize the generated adversarial texts by 10 iterations in TRAttack for better attack performance. As a result, TRAttack successfully generates effective adversarial examples that can increase Per. from 0.3686 to 0.5570 and from 0.4085 to 0.6619 on the Tencent Cloud's and Baidu Cloud's commercial APIs with only about 2000 times of interactions, respectively. Tables 10 and 11 in Appendix show specific attack cases of TRAttack on the commercial APIs. The experiments in this part are conducted as of November 2021.

5 Conclusion

In this paper, we discuss a new realistic attack problem against text retrieval. We follow the word replacement framework and propose TRAttack. Extensive experiments show that benefiting from the the learning ability of MAB, TRAttack achieves better performance than existing methods. The generated adversarial texts by TRAttack can successfully mislead both offline text retrieval models and online commercial APIs, which demonstrates the potential risks of real-world text retrieval systems.

6 Broader Ethical Impact

We explore the potential security issues of text retrieval systems in this paper and propose TRAttack that is experimentally verified to be effective to many text retrieval models. Hope that our approach and discussions could inspire more explorations and designs of advanced defense methods and security policies.

References

Moustafa Alzantot, Yash Sharma, Ahmed Elgohary, Bo-Jhang Ho, Mani Srivastava, and Kai-Wei Chang. 2018. Generating natural language adversarial examples. *arXiv preprint arXiv:1804.07998*.

Jing Chen, Qingcai Chen, Xin Liu, Haijun Yang, Daohe Lu, and Buzhou Tang. 2018. The bq corpus: A large-scale domain-specific chinese corpus for sentence semantic equivalence identification. In *Proceedings of the 2018 conference on empirical methods in natural language processing*, pages 4946–4951.

Junyoung Chung, Caglar Gulcehre, KyungHyun Cho, and Yoshua Bengio. 2014. Empirical evaluation of gated recurrent neural networks on sequence modeling. *arXiv preprint arXiv:1412.3555*.

Yiming Cui, Wanxiang Che, Ting Liu, Bing Qin, Shijin Wang, and Guoping Hu. 2020. Revisiting pretrained models for Chinese natural language processing. In *Proceedings of the 2020 Conference on Empirical Methods in Natural Language Processing: Findings*, pages 657–668, Online. Association for Computational Linguistics.

Yiming Cui, Wanxiang Che, Ting Liu, Bing Qin, Ziqing Yang, Shijin Wang, and Guoping Hu. 2019. Pre-training with whole word masking for chinese bert. *arXiv preprint arXiv:1906.08101*.

Jacob Devlin, Ming-Wei Chang, Kenton Lee, and Kristina Toutanova. 2018. Bert: Pre-training of deep bidirectional transformers for language understanding. *arXiv preprint arXiv:1810.04805*.

Siddhant Garg and Goutham Ramakrishnan. 2020. Bae: Bert-based adversarial examples for text classification. *arXiv preprint arXiv:2004.01970*.

Di Jin, Zhijing Jin, Joey Tianyi Zhou, and Peter Szolovits. 2020. Is bert really robust? a strong baseline for natural language attack on text classification and entailment. In *Proceedings of the AAAI conference on artificial intelligence*, volume 34, pages 8018–8025.

Mandar Joshi, Danqi Chen, Yinhan Liu, Daniel S Weld, Luke Zettlemoyer, and Omer Levy. 2020. Spanbert: Improving pre-training by representing and predicting spans. *Transactions of the Association for Computational Linguistics*, 8:64–77.

Nal Kalchbrenner, Edward Grefenstette, and Phil Blunsom. 2014. A convolutional neural network for modelling sentences. *arXiv preprint arXiv:1404.2188*.

Volodymyr Kuleshov and Doina Precup. 2014. Algorithms for multi-armed bandit problems. *arXiv preprint arXiv:1402.6028*.

Tor Lattimore and Csaba Szepesvári. 2020. *Bandit algorithms*. Cambridge University Press.

Jie Li, Rongrong Ji, Hong Liu, Xiaopeng Hong, Yue Gao, and Qi Tian. 2019a. Universal perturbation attack against image retrieval. In *Proceedings of the IEEE/CVF International Conference on Computer Vision*, pages 4899–4908.

Jinfeng Li, Shouling Ji, Tianyu Du, Bo Li, and Ting Wang. 2018. Textbugger: Generating adversarial text against real-world applications. *arXiv preprint arXiv:1812.05271*.

Linyang Li, Ruotian Ma, Qipeng Guo, Xiangyang Xue, and Xipeng Qiu. 2020. Bert-attack: Adversarial attack against bert using bert. *arXiv preprint arXiv:2004.09984*.

Xiaodan Li, Jinfeng Li, Yuefeng Chen, Shaokai Ye, Yuan He, Shuhui Wang, Hang Su, and Hui Xue. 2021a. Qair: Practical query-efficient black-box attacks for image retrieval. In *Proceedings of the IEEE/CVF Conference on Computer Vision and Pattern Recognition*, pages 3330–3339.

Zhao Li, Junshuai Song, Shichang Hu, Shasha Ruan, Long Zhang, Zehong Hu, and Jun Gao. 2019b. Fair: Fraud aware impression regulation system in large-scale real-time e-commerce search platform. In *2019 IEEE 35th International Conference on Data Engineering (ICDE)*, pages 1898–1903. IEEE.

Zhao Li, Junshuai Song, Zehong Hu, Zhen Wang, and Jun Gao. 2021b. Constrained dual-level bandit for personalized impression regulation in online ranking systems. *ACM Transactions on Knowledge Discovery from Data (TKDD)*, 16(2):1–23.

Zachary C Lipton, John Berkowitz, and Charles Elkan. 2015. A critical review of recurrent neural networks for sequence learning. *arXiv preprint arXiv:1506.00019*.

Xin Liu, Qingcai Chen, Chong Deng, Huajun Zeng, Jing Chen, Dongfang Li, and Buzhou Tang. 2018. Lcqmc: A large-scale chinese question matching corpus. In *Proceedings of the 27th International Conference on Computational Linguistics*, pages 1952–1962.

George A Miller. 1995. Wordnet: a lexical database for english. *Communications of the ACM*, 38(11):39–41.

John Morris, Eli Lifland, Jin Yong Yoo, Jake Grigsby, Di Jin, and Yanjun Qi. 2020. Textattack: A framework for adversarial attacks, data augmentation, and adversarial training in nlp. In *Proceedings of the 2020 Conference on Empirical Methods in Natural Language Processing: System Demonstrations*, pages 119–126.

Alec Radford, Jeffrey Wu, Rewon Child, David Luan, Dario Amodei, Ilya Sutskever, et al. 2019. Language models are unsupervised multitask learners. *OpenAI blog*, 1(8):9.

Shuhuai Ren, Yihe Deng, Kun He, and Wanxiang Che. 2019. Generating natural language adversarial examples through probability weighted word saliency. In *Proceedings of the 57th annual meeting of the association for computational linguistics*, pages 1085–1097.

Wataru Sakata, Tomohide Shibata, Ribeka Tanaka, and Sadao Kurohashi. 2019. Faq retrieval using query-question similarity and bert-based query-answer relevance. In *Proceedings of the 42nd International ACM SIGIR Conference on Research and Development in Information Retrieval*, pages 1113–1116.

Junshuai Song, Zhao Li, Zehong Hu, Yucheng Wu, Zhenpeng Li, Jian Li, and Jun Gao. 2020. Poisonrec: an adaptive data poisoning framework for attacking black-box recommender systems. In *2020 IEEE 36th International Conference on Data Engineering (ICDE)*, pages 157–168. IEEE.

Yu Sun, Shuohuan Wang, Yukun Li, Shikun Feng, Xuyi Chen, Han Zhang, Xin Tian, Danxiang Zhu, Hao Tian, and Hua Wu. 2019. Ernie: Enhanced representation through knowledge integration. *arXiv preprint arXiv:1904.09223*.

Richard S Sutton and Andrew G Barto. 2018. *Reinforcement learning: An introduction*. MIT press.

Andrew Trotman, Antti Puurula, and Blake Burgess. 2014. Improvements to bm25 and language models examined. In *Proceedings of the 2014 Australasian Document Computing Symposium*, pages 58–65.

Ashish Vaswani, Noam Shazeer, Niki Parmar, Jakob Uszkoreit, Llion Jones, Aidan N Gomez, Łukasz Kaiser, and Illia Polosukhin. 2017. Attention is all you need. In *Advances in neural information processing systems*, pages 5998–6008.

Dongling Xiao, Yu-Kun Li, Han Zhang, Yu Sun, Hao Tian, Hua Wu, and Haifeng Wang. 2020. Ernie-gram: Pre-training with explicitly n-gram masked language modeling for natural language understanding. *arXiv preprint arXiv:2010.12148*.

Wei Yang, Haotian Zhang, and Jimmy Lin. 2019. Simple applications of bert for ad hoc document retrieval. *arXiv preprint arXiv:1903.10972*.

Yuan Zang, Bairu Hou, Fanchao Qi, Zhiyuan Liu, Xiaojun Meng, and Maosong Sun. 2020. Learning to attack: Towards textual adversarial attacking in real-world situations. *arXiv preprint arXiv:2009.09192*.

Yuan Zang, Fanchao Qi, Chenghao Yang, Zhiyuan Liu, Meng Zhang, Qun Liu, and Maosong Sun. 2019. Word-level textual adversarial attacking as combinatorial optimization. *arXiv preprint arXiv:1910.12196*.

Guoyang Zeng, Fanchao Qi, Qianrui Zhou, Tingji Zhang, Bairu Hou, Yuan Zang, Zhiyuan Liu, and Maosong Sun. 2021. Openattack: An open-source textual adversarial attack toolkit. In *Proceedings of the 59th Annual Meeting of the Association for Computational Linguistics and the 11th International Joint Conference on Natural Language Processing: System Demonstrations*, pages 363–371.

Zhengyan Zhang, Xu Han, Hao Zhou, Pei Ke, Yuxian Gu, Deming Ye, Yujia Qin, Yusheng Su, Haozhe Ji, Jian Guan, Fanchao Qi, Xiaozhi Wang, Yanan Zheng, Jiannan Cao, Guoyang Zeng, Huanqi Cao, Shengqi Chen, Daixuan Li, Zhenbo Sun, Zhiyuan Liu, Minlie Huang, Wentao Han, Jie Tang, Juanzi Li, and Maosong Sun. 2020. Cpm: A large-scale generative chinese pre-trained language model.

Chang Zhou, Jinze Bai, Junshuai Song, Xiaofei Liu, Zhengchao Zhao, Xiusi Chen, and Jun Gao. 2018. Atrank: An attention-based user behavior modeling framework for recommendation. In *Proceedings of the AAAI Conference on Artificial Intelligence*, volume 32.

A Accuracy of Text Retrieval Models

In both LSTM and CNN, We use an embedding layer to encode words firstly. And then we directly use one LSTM layer to extract the text representation in LSTM while using the CNN structure for CNN. With the representations of a given query and a candidate text, the relevance is predicted by feeding concatenated features of both texts into a 2-layer deep neural network (DNN) with Softmax for calculating probabilities. In BERT and ERNIE-Gram, we directly concatenate the two texts inputs, and use BERT and ERNIE-Gram to get the final representation. The results are also predicted by feeding the representation into a 2-layer DNN with Softmax. The size of word embeddings and the DNN in each model is set to be 128. We adopt CrossEntropy as the loss function and use Adam as the optimizer. For the learning rate, we use $\alpha = 2e-3$ in LSTM and CNN, and $\alpha = 2e-5$ in BERT and ERNIE-Gram.

Models	**LCQMC**	**BQ-Corpus**
LSTM	0.7864	0.6780
CNN	0.7597	0.6671
BERT	0.8888	0.8529
ERNIE-Gram	0.9054	0.8610

Table 7: Accuracy of different models on 2 datasets.

For the model training, we adopt the popular early stopping mechanism for better performance, and Table 7 reports the accuracy of different models on the 2 datasets.

Method	Num.	Per.	PPL	Sem.
TextBugger	145	0.9374	993	0.5286
PWWS	191	0.9296	822	0.5576
Genetic	808	0.7316	681	0.7749
PSO	297	0.6374	353	0.8642
BERT-Attack	127	0.9008	1027	0.9281
TRAttack	132	0.9299	1200	0.9234

(a) The simulated text retrieval system with LSTM

Method	Num.	Per.	PPL	Sem.
TextBugger	145	0.7863	1229	0.5212
PWWS	191	0.7485	749	0.6981
Genetic	808	0.6352	524	0.8233
PSO	298	0.5881	481	0.8842
BERT-Attack	127	0.7969	1110	0.9215
TRAttack	132	0.8383	1452	0.9106

(b) The simulated text retrieval system with CNN

Method	Num.	Per.	PPL	Sem.
TextBugger	145	0.6160	1026	0.5817
PWWS	191	0.5800	921	0.6826
Genetic	808	0.5247	643	0.7900
PSO	298	0.5042	353	0.8591
BERT-Attack	127	0.5916	1703	0.9079
TRAttack	132	0.6004	2294	0.9075

(c) The simulated text retrieval system with BERT

Method	Num.	Per.	PPL	Sem.
TextBugger	145	0.6616	885	0.5553
PWWS	191	0.6271	900	0.6932
Genetic	808	0.5643	641	0.8115
PSO	296	0.5473	554	0.8687
BERT-Attack	127	0.6448	1546	0.9029
TRAttack	132	0.6539	2184	0.9057

(d) The simulated text retrieval system with ERNIE-Gram

Table 8: Attack results on different simulated text retrieval systems on the BQ-Corpus dataset. Num., Per. and Sem. represent the number of interactions, the attack performance $R(\cdot)$ and the semantic consistency, respectively.

User Input Queries	Ori.	Adv.
怎样自己制作文字图片? How to make text pictures?	0.5930 / 0.69	0.9972 / 0.97
谁会自己制作文字图片? Who can make text pictures by yourself?	0.9506 / 0.93	0.9996 / 1.00
哪个网站可以自己制作图片? Which website can we use to make pictures?	0.8650 / 0.35	0.9957 / 0.96
怎样在手机上制作自己的文字图片? How to make my own text pictures on the mobile phone?	0.7229 / 0.26	0.9993 / 0.99
怎么制作自己的网页? How to create my own webpage?	0.1236 / 0.54	0.9962 / 0.94
如何自己制作带音乐、多张图片和文字的电子贺卡? How to make an e-card with music, multiple pictures, and text by myself?	0.9658 / 0.26	0.9996 / 0.99
怎么可以制作自己的网页? How can I make my own webpage?	0.2927 / 0.49	0.9982 / 1.00
火车票图片制作 Train ticket picture making	0.5336 / 0.44	0.9895 / 0.94
自己怎么制作冰淇淋? How to make ice cream by myself?	0.9889 / 0.22	0.9997 / 0.98
读书卡怎样制作? How to make a reading card?	0.9242 / 0.32	0.9999 / 0.98
Ori. : 怎样自己制作文字图片? 有 哪些 软件 可以 帮助我们制 作 文 字 图 片 ? How to make text pictures? Which software can help us make text pictures? Adv.: 怎样自己制作文字图片? 有 那种 软件 支帮 帮助我们制 做 文 本 图 图 ?		

Table 9: A generated adversarial example by TRAttack that successfully receives high $f(\cdot)$ / $s(\cdot)$ under 10 different queries meanwhile on the simulated text retrieval system based on LSTM and the LCQMC dataset.

User Input Queries	Ori.	Adv.
守护甜心第四季什么时候播? When will the fourth season of "Shugo Chara!" be broadcast?	0.5592 / 0.62	0.6417 / 0.64
破产姐妹什么时候播第四季 When will the "Broke Girls" broadcast the fourth season	0.5519 / 0.48	0.6151 / 0.78
活佛济公第四部到底什么时候播 When will the fourth season of "The Legend of Crazy Monk" be broadcast	0.5665 / 0.54	0.6194 / 0.67
爱情回来了什么时候播 When will "Love is Back" be broadcast	0.4966 / 0.07	0.6612 / 0.59
美人制造什么时候播 When will "Cosmetology High" be broadcast	0.4986 / 0.15	0.6627 / 0.69
叶罗丽精灵梦第三季什么时候播? When will the third season of "Yeloli" be broadcast?	0.5067 / 0.28	0.5099 / 0.28
世界上另一个我什么时候播 When will "Another Me in the World" be broadcast	0.5375 / 0.42	0.6524 / 0.72
终极宿舍什么时候播 When will "THE X-DORMITORY" be broadcast	0.4980 / 0.21	0.7200 / 0.78
新少年四大名捕电视剧什么时候播 When will "The Four" be broadcast	0.5294 / 0.44	0.5477 / 0.51
不一样的美男子什么时候播? When will "Special Different Man" be broadcast?	0.4825 / 0.04	0.6579 / 0.76
Ori. : 守护甜心第四季什么时候播? “老友记” 里有 哪些 经 典 台 词 ? When will the fourth season of "Shugo Chara!" be broadcast? What are the classic lines in "Friends"? Adv.: 守护甜心第四季什么时候播? (小友記秀 里有 谁多 经 经 台 辞 ?		

Table 10: A generated adversarial example by TRAttack that successfully receives high $f(\cdot)$ / $s(\cdot)$ under 10 different queries meanwhile on the Tencent Cloud's commercial API.

User Input Queries	Ori.	Adv.
在家可以做的兼职有什么? What are the part-time jobs that can be done at home?	0.8460 / 0.60	0.9553 / 0.95
在家电脑兼职可以做什么 What are the part-time jobs that can be done on the computer at home	0.7734 / 0.61	0.8474 / 0.88
有没有什么在家就可以做的兼职? Are there any part-time jobs that can be done at home?	0.7795 / 0.51	0.9009 / 0.92
可在家做的兼职? Part-time jobs can be done at home?	0.8129 / 0.55	0.9304 / 0.92
在家兼职的工作有哪些 What are the part-time jobs that can be done at home	0.8449 / 0.65	0.8706 / 0.75
有没有在家能做的兼职? Are there any part-time jobs that can be done at home?	0.7280 / 0.32	0.8558 / 0.83
如何在家做淘宝客服兼职 How to be a part-time Taobao customer service at home	0.6210 / 0.24	0.6793 / 0.51
有什么可以在家做的工作 What work can be done at home	0.7704 / 0.39	0.7848 / 0.46
有没有在家做兼职的工作? Are there any part-time jobs that can be done at home?	0.7321 / 0.46	0.7558 / 0.57
有什么工作在家就可以做 What work can be done at home	0.7736 / 0.25	0.7973 / 0.44
Ori. : 在家可以做的兼职有什么? 有什么 工 作是 必须 要 做 的? What are the part-time jobs that can be done at home? What work must be done? Adv.: 在家可以做的兼职有什么? 有什么 职 作是 固必 要 ? 的?		

Table 11: A generated adversarial example by TRAttack that successfully receives high $f(\cdot)$ / $s(\cdot)$ under 10 different queries meanwhil on the Baidu Cloud's commercial API.

On the Geometry of Concreteness

Christian Wartena
Hochschule Hannover
Expo Plaza 12
30539 Hannover, Germany
christian.wartena@hs-hannover.de

Abstract

In this paper we investigate how concreteness and abstractness are represented in word embedding spaces. We use data for English and German, and show that concreteness and abstractness can be determined independently and turn out to be completely opposite directions in the embedding space. Various methods can be used to determine the direction of concreteness, always resulting in roughly the same vector. Though concreteness is a central aspect of the meaning of words and can be detected clearly in embedding spaces, it seems not as easy to subtract or add concreteness to words to obtain other words or word senses like e.g. can be done with a semantic property like gender.

1 Introduction

In the current paper we aim to shed some light on the way concreteness and abstractness are represented in word embeddings. This might help to better understand the concept of concreteness that seems to be an important semantic property used to explain various phenomena in language and language understanding. Ultimately, it might also contribute a little bit to the understanding of the semantic spaces in which we embed words for many tasks.

1.1 Research Questions

The first question we want to address is to what degree concreteness can be represented as a vector in the embedding space. Such a vector v_{concr} should have the property that either the cosine between a vector v_w for a word w and v_{concr} or the length of the projection of v_w on v_{concr} corresponds to the concreteness value w.

The second question concerns the relation between concreteness and abstractness. Is abstractness characterized by a direction in the embeddings space in a similar way as concreteness is, or is abstractness just the absence of concreteness? The studies of Hill and Korhonen (2014) and Naumann et al. (2018) suggest that abstractness could go into many different directions and is quite different from concreteness since abstract words occur in more diverse contexts. On the other hand side, in all psycholinguistic studies concreteness and abstractness are treated as the two extremes on one scale.

Finally, we want to know, whether concreteness is a property that can be added to or removed from words, like e.g. gender can be separated and used to explicitly relate words like *king* to *queen*. There seem to be many cases of regular polysemy in which one reading of the word is more concrete than the other one. Examples are the polysemy between buildings and institutions for words like *school*, *church*, *parliament*, *theater*, etc. or between process and the result of the process (like e.g. *creation*, that can either denote the process of creating something or the thing that is created) or between a function and the person holding that function. In all cases it is clear that one reading is more concrete than the other one. What we want to know is to which extend the difference between the two meanings is determined by concreteness.

1.2 Concreteness

Concreteness is a core semantic property of words that has received a lot of attention in psycholinguistic research. Friendly et al. (1982) define concrete words as words that "refer to tangible objects, materials or persons which can be easily perceived with the senses". Brysbaert et al. (2014) define concreteness as the degree to which the concept denoted by a word refers to a perceptible entity. Theijssen et al. (2011) point out that in general two concepts of concreteness are used that do not completely overlap, namely *sensory perceivability* and *specificity*. However, they also note that most subjects in tests interpret concreteness as *sensory perceivability*. Also in a corpus study they could show that in cases where concreteness plays a role

Proceedings of the 7th Workshop on Representation Learning for NLP, pages 204 - 212

in the choice of a syntactic construction, *sensory perceivability* is the best predictor.

Various studies suggest that concrete and abstract words are represented and processed differently by the human brain (see a.o. Binder et al. (2005); Kousta et al. (2011); Borghi et al. (2017)). E.g. it is assumed that concreteness influences learning, recognition memory and the speed of visual recognition, reading and spelling (Spreen and Schulz, 1966; Hargis and Gickling, 1978; Sadoski et al., 2004; Palmer et al., 2013; Neath and Surprenant, 2020). Moreover, studies conducted on abstract and concrete words also found that the participants remembered concrete words better than the abstract words (for an overview of various studies see e.g. Yui et al., 2017). This difference is explained by the Dual Coding Theory (Paivio, 1970) according to which concrete concepts are stored verbally and visually in mind while abstract concepts are only stored verbally. A difference in recognition ease and speed is explained by the Context Availability Hypothesis (Schwanenflugel and Shoben, 1983; Schwanenflugel, 2013). This hypothesis states that it is crucial to evoke the context of a word to access its meaning and that it is easier to construct the appropriate context for concrete than for abstract words.

Among others Hill et al. (2014) and Naumann et al. (2018) have shown that abstract words occur in more broad and diverse contexts than concrete words. Furthermore, it was noted in several studies (see e.g. (Tanaka et al., 2013)) and investigated in detail by Frassinelli et al. (2017) and Naumann et al. (2018) that concrete words tend to occur in the context of other concrete words and abstract words in the context of other abstract words.

Most studies that collected or predicted concreteness values for words either ignored the fact that many words have several senses or excluded ambiguous words. The statement of Gilhooly and Logie (1980) still seems to be valid: "The problem of word ambiguity has generally been overlooked in compiling lists of words measured on various attributes." Only a few mostly smaller studies collected concreteness judgments for different word senses. These are, as far as we know, (Gilhooly and Logie, 1980) for English, (Hager, 1994) for German, and more recently (Đurđević et al., 2017) for Serbian and both (Reijnierse et al., 2019) and (Scott et al., 2019) for English words.

1.3 Organization of this paper

The remainder of the paper is organized as follows. In section 2 start with an overview of the few studies that try to identify concreteness in embedding spaces. In section 3 we describe the data we have used. In the following sections we present a series of experiments to get a better understanding of the representation of concreteness in embedding spaces: in section 4 we compare several possibilities to determine the direction of concreteness and abstractness in an embedding space, in section 5 we compare the mutual similarity between concrete and abstract words and finally in section 6 we have a short look at the possibilities to represent the meaning of ambiguous words with a concrete and an abstract sense.

2 Related Work

Word embeddings are widely used as a proxy for the meaning of words but in fact word embeddings are chiefly compact representations of the contexts in which they occur. Since concrete words occur preferably in the context of other concrete words and since concrete words are used as object to sensory verbs we expect that concreteness can be found in word embeddings. Indeed a number studies have shown the presence of concreteness in word embeddings: Rothe et al. (2016) try to find low-dimensional feature representations of words in which at least some dimensions correspond to interpretable properties of words. One of these dimensions is concreteness. For training and testing they use Google News embeddings and two subsets of frequent words from the norms of Brysbaert et al. (2014). For their test set of 8,694 frequent words they found a moderate correlation with the human judgments (Kendall's $\tau = 0.623$). Similarly, Hollis and Westbury (2016) investigated which dimensions of word embeddings correlate to one of the classical word norms. They found no direct correlations, but after reducing the number of dimensions for a set of words by applying Singular Value Decomposition, they found a strong correlation between one of the dimensions and concreteness. Charbonnier and Wartena (2019, 2020) train regression models on word embeddings to predict concreteness values, thus showing that concreteness information is present in the embeddings.

3 Materials

The answers to the research questions might depend on the embeddings we use. Nevertheless, we will restrict the experiments to just two embeddings, one for English and one for German, and for the moment being assume that results for other embeddings will be similar.

For English we use the 300 dimensional fastText embeddings without subword information trained on the Common Crawl with 600 billion tokens. For German we also use 300 dimensional fastText embeddings trained on the Common Crawl and Wikipedia. Both embeddings are available at the fastText site (`https://fasttext.cc/`).

The concreteness values are taken from Brysbaert et al. (2014) for English and from the merged dataset from Charbonnier and Wartena (2020) for German. Since concreteness is most clearly defined for nouns, from both datasets we use only nouns for which we also have embeddings. In the data from Brysbaert et al. (2014) the words are rated between 1.0 and 5.0. The ratings for the German data range from 1.0 to 7.0. As examples of concrete nouns we take for the English data all nouns rated above 4.0 and for German all nouns rated above 6.0. As clearly abstract nouns we use nouns rated below 2.7 for English and rated below 4 for German. This results in the numbers given in Table 1.

Table 1: Number of abstract and concrete nouns used.

	English	German
nouns	18,307	3,281
concrete nouns	6,345	753
abstract nouns	5,713	1,072

4 Concreteness vectors

In this section we will compare different methods to build prototypical vectors for concreteness and abstractness.

4.1 Methods

A straightforward method to obtain a vector for concreteness is to take the average embedding of all concrete words and subtract the average embedding of all words. As a second method we can take embeddings of concrete and abstract words, apply principal component analysis (PCA) and hope that the most important component represents concreteness. Finally, we can use use linear regression to find a vector that fits best to the concreteness values in the data set.

Since concreteness is most clearly defined for nouns, we take the average of all embeddings of concrete nouns and subtract the average of all noun vectors. The same can be done for abstract nouns and if, hopefully, the vectors for concreteness and abstractness roughly point in opposite directions, we can compute the average of the concrete and the opposite of the abstract vector, to get one vector representing concreteness and abstractness. Formally, let v_n be the average of the word embeddings of all nouns, v_{cn} the average of all embeddings of all concrete nouns and v_{an} the average of all embeddings of all abstract nouns, for the sets of abstract and concrete nouns as defined in section 3. Now let

$$v_{concr} = v_{cn} - v_n, \qquad (1)$$

$$v_{abstr} = v_{an} - v_n. \qquad (2)$$

For convenience we will use unit vectors defined as usual by setting $\hat{v}_{concr} = \frac{v_{concr}}{|v_{concr}|}$ and $\hat{v}_{abstr} = \frac{v_{abstr}}{|v_{abstr}|}$.

A vector based both on concrete and on abstract words can be defined as

$$v_{ca} = \frac{\hat{v}_{concr} - \hat{v}_{abstr}}{2}, \qquad (3)$$

$$\hat{v}_{ca} = \frac{v_{ca}}{|v_{ca}|}. \qquad (4)$$

For the principal component analysis we take the same sets of concrete and abstract words and put their embeddings in one matrix on which we perform PCA with 12 components. We take the first component as concreteness vector that we will call v_{pca} in the following.

For the regression we use all nouns, not just the most concrete and abstract ones. For all words we use their length normalized embeddings. As first option we use standard multiple linear regression, minimizing the sum of squared errors between real and predicted concreteness value. We let v^2_{regr} be the vector of the regression coefficients. Since we use the squared errors, the linear regression is quite sensitive to outliers. As an alternative we use linear regression with Huber loss function that is defined as:

$$L_H(\alpha) = \begin{cases} \frac{1}{2}(\alpha)^2 & \text{for } |\alpha| \leq \delta, \\ \delta\left(|\alpha| - \frac{1}{2}\delta\right), & \text{otherwise,} \end{cases} \qquad (5)$$

where $\alpha = y - f(x)$ is the residual or prediction error. For both the German and the English data we set $\delta = 0.25$. Finally, we add $\gamma\, ||w||_1$ as a regularization term, where w is the vector of regression coefficients. We set $\gamma = 1 \cdot 10^{-4}$. We call the resulting vector of coefficients v^1_{regr}.

4.2 Results

We do not have any method to access the quality of the vectors obtained by the different methods, but we can at least compare them. Furthermore, we can compute the correlation between real concreteness values of a word and the length of the projections of word embeddings on the concreteness vectors. The later value cannot be seen as a real concreteness prediction, but gives some indication how well the concreteness vector fits to the actual data.

For the English data we find $|v_{concr}| = 0.152$ and $|v_{abstr}| = 0.156$, for German $|v_{concr}| = 0.222$ and $|v_{abstr}| = 0.160$. Here we do not see a noticeable difference between concrete and abstract words.

Tables 2 and 3 give the cosine similarities between the various concreteness vectors for English and German respectively.

The first remarkable observation is that, both for the English and German data, the angle between v_{concr} and v_{abstr} is almost 180 degrees. This is maybe the most remarkable result of the present study: the vectors computed independently for distinct sets of concrete and abstract words are almost perfectly diametrically opposed! This suggests that abstractness and concreteness are indeed to extremes on the scale of the same property.

Furthermore, we see that all vectors are very much alike, except v^2_{regr}, the vector of coefficients of a classical linear regression model. Here indeed extreme values seem to dominate and specify a direction different from those obtained by all other methods.

A second indication for the quality of the concreteness vectors is the degree to which they can be used to predict the concreteness of individual words. Ideally, the length of the projection of a embedding vector on the concreteness vector would correspond to the empirically determined concreteness values. As it is not clear whether the length of an embedding value has any meaning or just the direction is important, we also could assume that the cosine between a word vector and the concreteness vector should be used. In Table 4 we therefore give the correlation (Pearsons's r and Kendalls's τ) for cosine and projection length. We should not interpret these numbers as an attempt to predict the concreteness. In the first place it would be easy to design a better (non linear) prediction model and in the second place we did not split into training and test data to make a sound prediction experiment (However, the vectors were, dependent on the method, computed using only a small part of the data, e.g. only nouns and the results might moreover not change, when one or a few words would be left out from the data).

Again we see that the values for English and German are almost the same. In both cases we see that v^2_{regr} gives the best correlation, which is not very surprising since this vector was optimized for Pearson correlation. More remarkable is the fact that, especially for the English data, the correlation of v^1_{regr} with the concreteness judgements is not much worse. Furthermore, we see that the cosine is a much better predictor for the concreteness values than the projection length. Given that the cosine is just the projection length of the unit vector of the word embedding, this suggests that vector length in word embeddings is not relevant and only the direction matters. Finally, the correlation is in the same order of magnitude as the correlation found by Rothe et al. (2016) but much behind the results from from Charbonnier and Wartena (2019), who use a non-linear classifier and additional morphological information.

5 Diversity of concrete and abstract words

As discussed above it has been observed that abstract words occur in more diverse contexts than concrete words. Does this also mean that abstract words are more diverse? I.e., can words be concrete just in one way but abstract in many different ways? To answer this question we selected randomly 100 words from our set of concrete and 100 from the set of abstract words. We compute the average cosine similarity for all pairs of words within each set and within the union of both sets. The results are given in Table 5. We see here no large differences between the abstract and concrete nouns. The abstract nouns even seem to be slightly more similar to each other than the concrete nouns. This again suggests that abstractness and concreteness are quite symmetric properties. The average similarity within each set (4,950 pairs for each set) is clearly larger that within the entire set of 200 nouns (i.e. 19,900 pairs), showing the importance of concreteness for

Table 2: Cosine similarities between concreteness vectors computed using different methods for English data.

	v_{concr}	v_{abstr}	v_{ca}	v_{pca}	v^1_{regr}	v^2_{regr}
v_{concr}	1.000	-	-	-	-	-
v_{abstr}	-0.945	1.000	-	-	-	-
v_{ca}	0.986	-0.986	1.000	-	-	-
v_{pca}	0.916	-0.882	0.912	1.000	-	-
v^1_{regr}	0.955	-0.960	0.971	0.812	1.000	-
v^2_{regr}	0.630	-0.589	0.618	0.447	0.695	1.000

Table 3: Cosine similarities between concreteness vectors computed using different methods for German data.

	v_{concr}	v_{abstr}	v_{ca}	v_{pca}	v^1_{regr}	v^2_{regr}
v_{concr}	1.000	-	-	-	-	-
v_{abstr}	-0.917	1.000	-	-	-	-
v_{ca}	0.979	-0.979	1.000	-	-	-
v_{pca}	0.937	-0.888	0.932	1.000	-	-
v^1_{regr}	0.945	-0.990	0.988	0.914	1.000	-
v^2_{regr}	0.572	-0.585	0.591	0.457	0.593	1.000

Table 4: Correlation (Pearsons's r) and rank correlation (Kendalls's τ) of concreteness values with the lengths of the projection of each word vector on a concreteness vector and the correlation with the cosines between each word vectors and a concreteness vector for different concreteness vectors.

		projection		cosine	
		P's r	K's τ	P's r	K's τ
English	v_{ca}	0.74	0.61	0.85	0.65
	v_{pca}	0.63	0.55	0.78	0.59
	v^1_{regr}	0.78	0.64	0.86	0.67
	v^2_{regr}	0.81	0.67	0.89	0.71
German	v_{ca}	0.71	0.56	0.80	0.59
	v_{pca}	0.64	0.49	0.74	0.54
	v^1_{regr}	0.72	0.56	0.80	0.60
	v^2_{regr}	0.78	0.62	0.84	0.65

Table 5: Average cosine similarity between 100 abstract and 100 concrete nouns

	English	German
concr	0.13	0.22
abstr	0.15	0.23
concr ∪ abstr	0.11	0.18

similarity in the embedding space.

6 Concreteness and regular polysemy

A word like *school* can refer to the schoolhouse or to the educational institution. In our sets of word embeddings there is only one embedding for all meanings of the word school, even including the sense of a group (as in a school of fish), a group of artists or thinkers and even the verb *to school*. We would hope that if we add a little bit of concreteness to the embedding of school, we get an embedding that is a bit closer to the embedding of schoolhouse and if we add some abstractness, the embedding becomes more similar to other abstract concepts from education. As a first indication to see whether this is indeed the case, we visualize the distances between a few ambiguous words (*school*, *university* and *hospital* for English and *Schule* (school), *Universität* (university) and *Fabrik* (factory) for German) along with some related concrete and abstract words. For each ambiguous word w we use the original embedding v_w as well as $v_w + 0.2\hat{v}_{ca}$ and $v_w - 0.2\hat{v}_{ca}$. We add 0.2 $\hat{v}_{ca}$ since 0.2 is roughly the length of the projection of the most abstract and the most concrete words on $\hat{v}_{ca}$. In the visualization the variants are labeled with the original word and either an a or c. The projection in a two-dimensional space is done with tSNE (Van der Maaten and Hinton, 2008). The results are shown in Figure 1 [1].

[1]The translation of all German words used in this figure and the subsequent tables is given in the appendix.

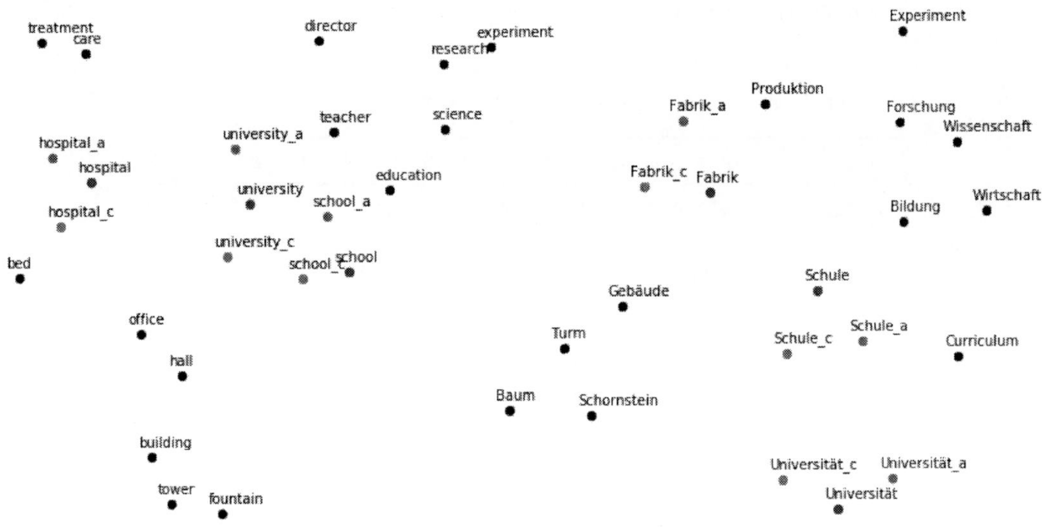

(a) English (b) German

Figure 1: Three ambiguous English (left) and German (right) words with concrete and abstract variants and some related words in a two dimensional projection of the embedding space.

Since we added clearly abstract and concrete words concreteness becomes a clear dimension in the visualization. For all words we see that the concrete variants indeed moved into the direction of the related concrete words and similar for the abstract variants.

In order to know whether the concrete and abstract variants of the embeddings really become more similar to synonyms of the respective senses we selected 10 ambiguous words for English and German along with a closely related word for the abstract and for the concrete sense. For German we selected 10 words that are ambiguous between a building (or location) and an institution. For English we selected words that either denote a process or an actor involved in that process. Here we tried to select words that do not have too many senses, are predominantly used as noun and for the related words we tried to find synonyms that do not have the same ambiguity. Most of the related words were taken from the synsets in WordNet (Miller, 1995) to make the choices somewhat more objective. Now for each word we add (subtract) $0.2\ \hat{v}_{ca}$ and determine how much the resulting vector is closer to the embedding of the related concrete (abstract) word than the original vector. The results for are give in Tables 6 and 7.

In all cases we see that the improvement is very small or even negative. For some of the word pairs, like *Parlament – Parlamentsgebäude* (Parliament - Parliament's house) or *Schule – Schulgebäude*, it seems that the second word is a real synonym of the building sense of the first word and we would expect that the cosine similarity would be much larger when adding the concreteness to the general vector. Thus we have to conclude that though the senses of these ambiguous German words clearly have different degrees of concreteness, the difference between the senses is much more than just the concreteness.

For the English words that are ambiguous between a process and an entity, adding concreteness in two cases even makes the pairs more dissimilar and adding abstractness only in one case makes the word more similar to a synonym of the process reading.

7 Conclusion

We have seen that concreteness can be identified as a direction in the word embedding space. Various methods, based on many words with concreteness values or just on a view highly concrete words give almost the same vector for concreteness. Moreover, the cosine of these vectors with the embeddings of words correlates strongly with the concreteness judgments of human subjects of these words. Thus our first research question can be answered positively.

Furthermore, we see that concreteness and abstractness are quite symmetric properties. We can

Table 6: Ten ambiguous English words with each time one word related to the concrete sense (person or artifact) and one word related to the abstract sense (process). The column after the related word gives the cosine between the embeddings of the word and the related word; the column labeled δ gives the improvement if cosine similarity when adding (resp. subtracting) $0.2\ \hat{v}_{ca}$ to the embedding of the original word.

word	concr. related	cos	δ	abstr. related	cos	δ
passage	passageway	0.52	0.05	transition	0.30	0.00
entry	entranceway	0.32	0.03	debut	0.16	-0.01
creation	world	0.25	-0.00	founding	0.31	-0.02
shot	scene	0.37	0.00	stroke	0.23	-0.02
opposition	opponent	0.51	0.01	resistance	0.38	-0.03
help	assistant	0.19	0.03	assistance	0.58	-0.00
opening	gap	0.36	-0.02	initiative	0.24	0.02
replacement	successor	0.38	-0.07	replacing	0.60	-0.04
storage	storehouse	0.39	0.01	warehousing	0.50	-0.01
shipment	freight	0.50	0.02	dispatch	0.48	-0.02

Table 7: Ten ambiguous German words with each time one word related to the concrete sense (building or location) and one word related to the abstract sense (institution). The column after the related word gives the cosine between the embeddings of the word and the related word; the column labeled δ gives the improvement if cosine similarity when adding (resp. subtracting) $0.2\ \hat{v}_{ca}$ to the embedding of the original word.

word	concr. related	cos	δ	abstr. related	cos	δ
Parlament	Parlamentsgebäude	0.70	0.01	Politik	0.47	0.01
Laden	Schuppen	0.28	0.06	Einzelhandel	0.45	-0.01
Gericht	Gerichtsgebäude	0.57	0.03	Urteil	0.55	0.01
Schule	Schulgebäude	0.64	0.02	Lernen	0.45	0.01
Büro	Bürohaus	0.55	0.01	Arbeit	0.43	0.02
Polizei	Polizeiwache	0.65	0.03	Ordnung	0.27	0.01
Kirche	Kirchturm	0.60	0.05	Religion	0.51	0.01
Universität	Hörsaal	0.42	0.04	Forschung	0.39	0.01
Theater	Schauspielhaus	0.72	-0.00	Kultur	0.46	0.01
Fabrik	Schornstein	0.31	0.07	Produktion	0.57	0.01

compute vectors for concreteness and abstractness independently and found both for English and German that the angle between these vectors is almost 180 degrees. Moreover, we do not see any indication that all concrete form one cluster while abstract words are distributed more uniformly through the embedding space or the other way around. Thus, we also can give a positive answer to the second research question.

Finally, we hoped that we would find pairs of words that just differ w.r.t. the concreteness dimension, like the words king and queen only differ w.r.t. the gender dimension. At least we would like to find words with different senses, where the degree of concreteness is the main difference between the senses. Though there are many polysemous words, that seem to be good candidates and though we can make suggestive visualizations for selected examples, our last experiment is not very encouraging in this respect. In the first place it has to be noted that the evaluation is quite problematic since we do not know what the embedding of the specific senses of a word should be. Nevertheless, at least in the case of the building/institution ambiguity the senses the senses are clearly distinguished by concreteness, but there are many more differences between the senses than just this aspect. The last result does not mean that it is not possible to learn the relation between vectors for different senses of a word in the case of regular polysemy, but the relation is more complex than just linearly adding concreteness to the embedding.

References

Jeffrey R Binder, Chris F Westbury, Kristen A McKiernan, Edward T Possing, and David A Medler. 2005. Distinct brain systems for processing concrete and abstract concepts. *Journal of cognitive neuroscience*, 17(6):905–917.

Anna M Borghi, Ferdinand Binkofski, Cristiano Castelfranchi, Felice Cimatti, Claudia Scorolli, and Luca Tummolini. 2017. The challenge of abstract concepts. *Psychological Bulletin*, 143(3):263.

Marc Brysbaert, Amy Beth Warriner, and Victor Kuperman. 2014. Concreteness ratings for 40 thousand generally known English word lemmas. *Behavior Research Methods*, 46(3):904–911.

Jean Charbonnier and Christian Wartena. 2019. Predicting word concreteness and imagery. In *Proceedings of the 13th International Conference on Computational Semantics-Long Papers*, pages 176–187.

Jean Charbonnier and Christian Wartena. 2020. Predicting the Concreteness of German Words. In *Proceedings of Konvens / SwissText*.

Diego Frassinelli, Daniela Naumann, Jason Utt, and Sabine Schulte m Walde. 2017. Contextual characteristics of concrete and abstract words. In *IWCS 2017 — 12th International Conference on Computational Semantics — Short papers*.

Michael Friendly, Patricia E. Franklin, David Hoffman, and David C. Rubin. 1982. The Toronto Word Pool: Norms for imagery, concreteness, orthographic variables, and grammatical usage for 1,080 words. *Behavior Research Methods & Instrumentation*, 14(4):375–399.

K. J. Gilhooly and R. H. Logie. 1980. Meaning-dependent ratings of imagery, age of acquisition, familiarity, and concreteness for 387 ambiguous words. *Behavior Research Methods & Instrumentation*, 12(4):428–450.

Willy Hager. 1994. Bildhaftigkeit, Konkretheit-Abstraktheit und Bedeutungshaltigkeit von 63 mehrdeutigen Substantiven. In Willi Hager and Marcus Hasselhorn, editors, *Handbuch deutschsprachiger Wortnormen*, chapter 3.6, pages 212–217. Hogrefe Verlag für Psychologie, Göttingen.

Charles H Hargis and Edward E Gickling. 1978. The function of imagery in word recognition development. *The Reading Teacher*, 31(8):870–874.

Felix Hill and Anna Korhonen. 2014. Concreteness and subjectivity as dimensions of lexical meaning. In *Proceedings of the 52nd Annual Meeting of the Association for Computational Linguistics (Volume 2: Short Papers)*, pages 725–731.

Felix Hill, Anna Korhonen, and Christian Bentz. 2014. A quantitative empirical analysis of the abstract/concrete distinction. *Cognitive science*, 38(1):162–177.

Geoff Hollis and Chris Westbury. 2016. The principals of meaning: Extracting semantic dimensions from co-occurrence models of semantics. *Psychonomic bulletin & review*, 23(6):1744–1756.

Stavroula-Thaleia Kousta, Gabriella Vigliocco, David P Vinson, Mark Andrews, and Elena Del Campo. 2011. The representation of abstract words: why emotion matters. *Journal of Experimental Psychology: General*, 140(1):14.

George A Miller. 1995. Wordnet: a lexical database for english. *Communications of the ACM*, 38(11):39–41.

Daniela Naumann, Diego Frassinelli, and Sabine Schulte im Walde. 2018. Quantitative Semantic Variation in the Contexts of Concrete and Abstract Words. In *Proceedings of the 7th Joint Conference on Lexical and Computational Semantics*, pages 76–85, New Orleans, LA, USA.

Ian Neath and Aimée M Surprenant. 2020. Concreteness and disagreement: Comment on Pollock (2018). *Memory & cognition*, 48(4):683–690.

Allan Paivio. 1970. On the functional significance of imagery. *Psychological Bulletin*, 73(6):385.

Shekeila D Palmer, Lucy J MacGregor, and Jelena Havelka. 2013. Concreteness effects in single-meaning, multi-meaning and newly acquired words. *Brain research*, 1538:135–150.

W. Gudrun Reijnierse, Christian Burgers, Marianna Bolognesi, and Tina Krennmayr. 2019. How polysemy affects concreteness ratings: The case of metaphor. *Cognitive Science*, 43(8):e12779.

Sascha Rothe, Sebastian Ebert, and Hinrich Schütze. 2016. Ultradense word embeddings by orthogonal transformation. In *Proceedings of the 2016 Conference of the North American Chapter of the Association for Computational Linguistics: Human Language Technologies*, pages 767–777. Association for Computational Linguistics.

Mark Sadoski, Victor L Willson, Angelia Holcomb, and Regina Boulware-Gooden. 2004. Verbal and nonverbal predictors of spelling performance. *Journal of Literacy Research*, 36(4):461–478.

Paula J Schwanenflugel. 2013. Why are abstract concepts hard to understand? In *The psychology of word meanings*, pages 235–262. Psychology Press.

Paula J Schwanenflugel and Edward J Shoben. 1983. Differential context effects in the comprehension of abstract and concrete verbal materials. *Journal of Experimental Psychology: Learning, Memory, and Cognition*, 9(1):82.

Graham G. Scott, Anne Keitel, Marc Becirspahic, Bo Yao, and Sara C. Sereno. 2019. The glasgow norms: Ratings of 5,500 words on nine scales. *Behavior Research Methods*, 51(3):1258–1270.

Otfried Spreen and Rudolph W. Schulz. 1966. Parameters of abstraction, meaningfulness, and pronunciability for 329 nouns. *Journal of Verbal Learning & Verbal Behavior*, 5(5):459–468.

Shinya Tanaka, Adam Jatowt, Makoto P. Kato, and Katsumi Tanaka. 2013. Estimating content concreteness for finding comprehensible documents. In *Proceedings of the Sixth ACM International Conference on Web Search and Data Mining*, WSDM '13, pages 475–484, New York, NY, USA. ACM.

Daphne Theijssen, Hans van Halteren, Lou Boves, and Nelleke Oostdijk. 2011. On the difficulty of making concreteness concrete. *Computational Linguistics in the Netherlands Journal*, 1:61–77.

Dušica Filipović Đurđević, Aleksandar Kostić, and Zorana Đinđića. 2017. Number, relative frequency, entropy, redundancy, familiarity, and concreteness of word senses: Ratings for 150 serbian polysemous nouns. In *Selected Papers From the 4th and 5th Workshop on Psycholinguistic, Neurolinguistic and Clinical Linguistic Research*, volume 2 of *Studies in Language and Mind*, pages 13–50. Filozofski fakultet u Novom Sadu.

Laurens Van der Maaten and Geoffrey Hinton. 2008. Visualizing data using t-SNE. *Journal of machine learning research*, 9(11).

Lin Yui, Roslin Ng, and Hiran Perera-WA. 2017. Concrete vs abstract words–what do you recall better? a study on dual coding theory. Technical report, PeerJ Preprints.

Appendix: Translation of German words used in the figures and tables.

Word	Translation
Arbeit	work, labor
Baum	tree
Bildung	education
Büro	office
Bürohaus	office building
Curriculum	curriculum
Einzelhandel	retail
Experiment	experiment
Fabrik	factory
Forschung	research
Gebäude	building
Gericht	court
Gerichtsgebäude	court building
Hörsaal	lecture hall
Kirche	church
Kirchturm	church tower
Kultur	culture
Laden	shop
Lernen	to learn
Ordnung	order
Parlament	parliament
Parlamentsgebäude	parliament's house
Politik	politics
Polizei	police
Polizeiwache	Police station
Produktion	production
Religion	religion
Schauspielhaus	playhouse, theater
Schornstein	chimney
Schule	school
Schulgebäude	school building
Schuppen	shed
Theater	theater
Turm	tower
Universität	university
Urteil	verdict, judgment
Wirtschaft	economy
Wissenschaft	science

PALBERT: Teaching ALBERT to Ponder.

Nikita Balagansky, Daniil Gavrilov
Tinkoff
n.n.balaganskiy@tinkoff.ai, d.gavrilov@tinkoff.ai

Abstract

Currently, pre-trained models can be considered the default choice for a wide range of NLP tasks. Despite their SoTA results, there is practical evidence that these models may require a different number of computing layers for different input sequences, since evaluating all layers leads to overconfidence on wrong predictions (namely overthinking). This problem can potentially be solved by implementing adaptive computation time approaches, which were first designed to improve inference speed.

Recently proposed PonderNet may be a promising solution for performing an early exit by treating the exit layer's index as a latent variable. However, the originally proposed exit criterion, relying on sampling from trained posterior distribution on the probability of exiting from i-th layer, introduces major variance in model outputs, significantly reducing the resulting model's performance.

In this paper, we propose Ponder ALBERT (PALBERT) – an improvement to PonderNet with a novel deterministic Q-exit criterion and a revisited model architecture. We compared PALBERT with recent methods for performing an early exit. We observed that the proposed changes can be considered significant improvements on the original PonderNet architecture and outperform PABEE on a wide range of GLUE tasks. In addition, we also performed an in-depth ablation study of the proposed architecture to further understand Lambda layers and their performance.

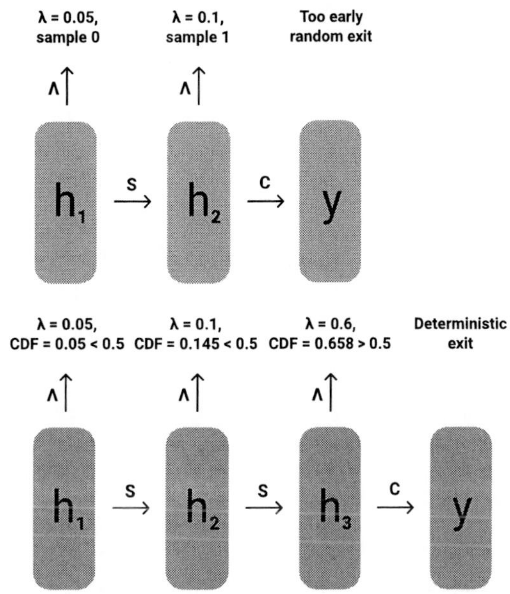

Figure 1: A comparison of the original sampling exit criterion of PonderNet (on the top) and the proposed Q-exit criterion (on the bottom). PonderNet performs sampling from the Bernoulli distribution obtained from the Lambda layer at each step, possibly exiting a model too early or too late. For Q-exit, we evaluate the Cumulative distribution function (CDF) of the probability of exiting at layer i. Once CDF becomes greater than the threshold value (0.5 in this example), we perform an early exit. With such a deterministic criterion, we can perform an early exit from a model more robustly without introducing variance in the exit layer's index during inference.

1 Introduction

These days, fine-tuning pre-trained models on downstream tasks became a de facto standard technique for training NLP models. One model that is widely used in real-world applications is ALBERT (Lan et al., 2020), which is based on the Transformer architecture (Vaswani et al., 2017) with shared layers (i.e., the same layer is evaluated several times to provide an output).

While ALBERT-Base evaluates the Transformer block 12 times, layer sharing makes it possible to evaluate it an arbitrary number of times. Zhou et al. (2020) showed that running ALBERT-Base block for a fixed number of times (10) could increase the accuracy of the fine-tuned model on specific tasks (e.g., MRPC). This phenomenon is called overthinking. Because of this fact, **making models perform an early exit is not only done to in-**

Proceedings of the 7th Workshop on Representation Learning for NLP, pages 213 - 220
May 26, 2022 ©2022 Association for Computational Linguistics

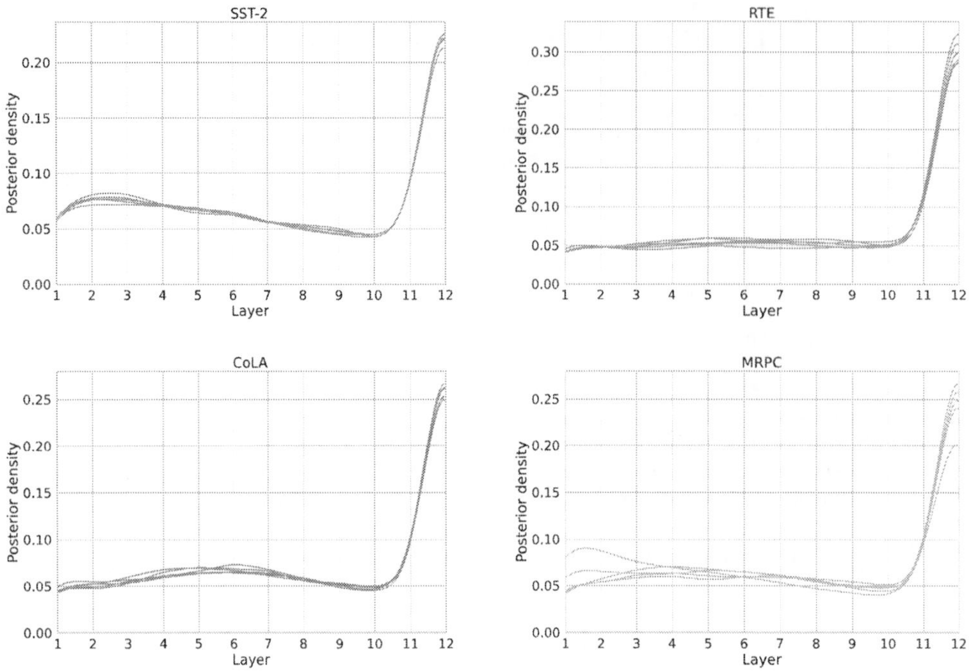

Figure 2: An estimation of $E_{x\sim D}\Big[p(i|x)\Big]$, where $p(i|x)$ is a trained posterior probability of exiting from layer i of PALBERT models across different tasks, and D is the distribution of the training dataset. We took 5 models trained on these tasks and sampled exit layer indices for the training dataset's inputs. We smoothed the obtained probabilities for visibility.

crease inference speed but also to make them more accurate. A recent PABEE (Zhou et al., 2020) solution was designed to overcome this issue by performing an early exit based on the consensus between different classifier heads from different layers. The model stops evaluating when several classifiers in a row produce the same result.

An orthogonal way to perform an early exit from a model is PonderNet (Banino et al., 2021) – a variational approach that treats the exit layer's index as a latent variable. By maximizing the lower bound of the likelihood of the training data, PonderNet trains a model which can predict whether it is necessary to exit from a specific layer during evaluation. However, Banino et al. (2021) proposed to sample from the trained posterior distribution of exiting from each layer during inference, which leads to major variance in model outputs.

This paper proposes **Ponder ALBERT (PALBERT)** – an improvement to PonderNet adapted for ALBERT fine-tuning. Instead of performing an early exit by sampling from the trained posterior distribution during evaluation, we used a novel zero-variance exit criterion, namely **Q-exit**, which evaluates the CDF of the exit layer's probability distribution and perform a deterministic early exit. We also revisited the architectural choices of Lambda layers used to predict the probability of exiting from the current layer in order to make them aware of dynamics in hidden states across previous layers and the number of currently running layers.

We experimented with PALBERT on the GLUE Benchmark datasets (Wang et al., 2018). The ablation study showed that PALBERT produced significantly better results than the original PonderNet architecture adapted for ALBERT fine-tuning. Furthermore, PALBERT outperformed PABEE and is comparable to plain ALBERT fine-tuning, while also exceeding it in speeds. We also analyzed the trained model and provided insights on further improvement of the variational approach for early exiting.

2 Related Work

Most of the approaches used to perform an early exit from a model are based on the probability distribution of predictions: BranchyNet (Teerapittayanon et al., 2016), FastBERT (Liu et al., 2020),

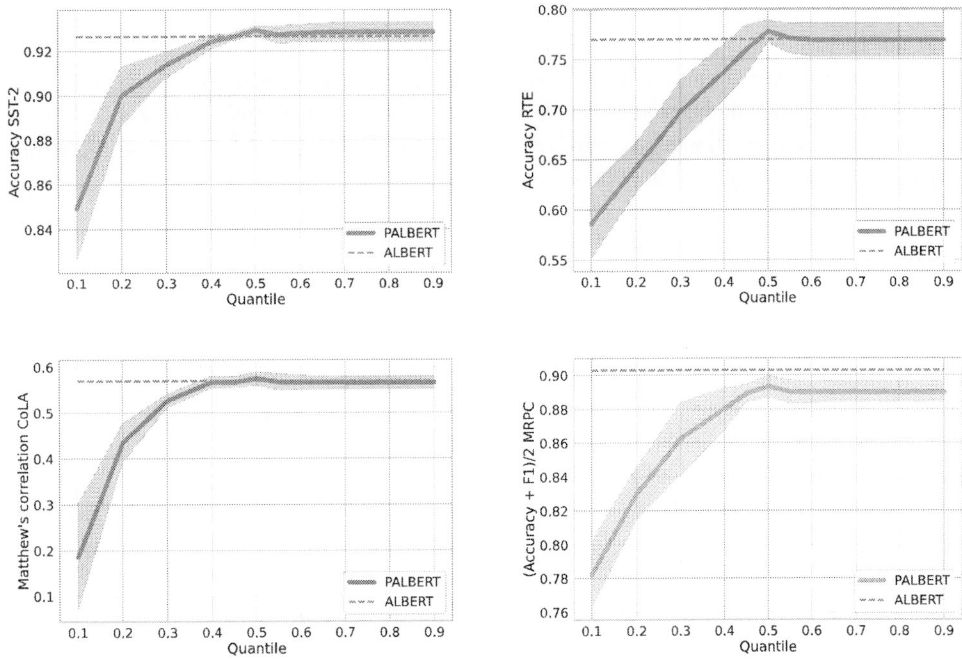

Figure 3: PALBERT score dependency on the Q-exit threshold. We report the mean and std values of task metrics across 5 trained models. See section 4.2 for more details

DeeBERT (Xin et al., 2020), which can be seen as an entropy criterion. However, there is strong practical evidence that classification models' overthinking causes a reduction in predictions' entropy, making these methods difficult to use (Zhou et al., 2020). Furthermore, it is unclear how to adapt entropy methods for regression tasks (Zhou et al., 2020).

Zhou et al. (2020) proposed PABEE – a method to perform an early exit based on several classifiers from the different levels of a model. Once several classifiers in a row (the number of these classifiers is determined by the patience hyperparameter t) produce the same result, we can perform an early exit. LeeBERT (Zhu, 2021) also uses the idea of a consensus-based exiting strategy augmenting the training algorithm with the self-distillation technique and cross-level optimization. Self-distillation is orthogonal to the early exit approach and can be combined with PALBERT. Because of this, we did not include LeeBERT in our experiments and only used PABEE as a consensus-based method.

An alternative way to perform an early exit is the Ponder architecture (Banino et al., 2021), which uses auxiliary Lambda layers to predict whether a model should exit from a specific layer during the runtime. Inputs to Lambda layers used in PonderNet are hidden states from the current layer of a model. PonderNet can be seen as a model with the latent variable that corresponds to the exit layer index, which is trained by maximizing the lower bound of the marginalized likelihood of the data.

During inference, PonderNet authors proposed to sample from the trained posterior distribution of exit layer probabilities. However, this exit criterion can lead to uncertainty in outputs for the same input. Even if the Lambda layer produced probability equal to 0.1 of exiting from the first layer, we could still exit a model too early in one of ten, cases even though the probability was small. We also hypothesize that predicting exiting from a layer based entirely on a single hidden state could be sub-optimal since performing early exit could also depend on the dynamics in hidden states across layers (i.e., Lambda layer should know how hidden states change during the evaluation).

3 Ponder ALBERT

The usual ALBERT evaluation can be defined as a computation of n hidden states $h_i = S(h_{i-1})$ from the input embeddings h_0 of an input sequence x, where $i \in [1; n]$. Once h_n is obtained, it is passed to a classifier block $C(h_n)$ to get the parameters of an output distribution $p(y|x)$. A common way to fine-tune this architecture on downstream tasks is to initialize the embeddings and the S layer by using ALBERT (pre-trained on Masked Language Modelling) while initializing C randomly and then optimizing all parameters by maximizing the likelihood of the training data.

While plain ALBERT performs a fixed number of computational steps, it is possible to perform an arbitrary number of evaluations of the layer S. Banino et al. (2021) proposed to extend each Transformer layer with a so-called Lambda layer. More precisely, for each layer i, after S outputs a new h_i, it is then passed to the classifier and Lambda layers to get parameters $C(h_i)$ of output distributions $p(y|x,i)$ and the probability of exiting from the i-th layer $\lambda_i = \Lambda(h_i)$, which induces a generalized geometric distribution on probability of exiting from layer i equal to

$$p(i|x) = \lambda_i \prod_{j=1}^{i-1}(1-\lambda_j). \tag{1}$$

Then, having the probability distribution from each layer $p(y|x,i)$, the parameters of the model are optimized to maximize

$$\begin{aligned} L(x,y) = E_{i \sim p(i|x)}\Big[p(y|x,i)\Big] - \\ -\beta KL\Big(p(\cdot|x)||p(\cdot|\lambda)\Big) \leq p(y|x) \end{aligned} \tag{2}$$

Here, $p(\cdot|\lambda)$ is a prior distribution of exiting from each layer, parametrized by the hyperparameter λ, and $E_{i \sim p(i|x)}\Big[p(y|x,i)\Big]$ is evaluated analytically by averaging likelihoods from different layers with posterior exit probabilities. If we treat the exit layer index as a latent variable, then optimizing L from the Equation 2 could be seen as maximizing the lower bound of marginalized likelihood $p(y|x)$ (Kingma and Welling, 2014).

Note that the probability of exiting from the last layer n is normalized as $p(n|\lambda) = 1 - \sum_{i=1}^{n-1} p(i|\lambda)$ in order to make $p(i|\lambda)$ sum into 1 with a finite number of steps. The same is true for $p(i|x)$. Also note that weights of Lambda layers are shared across layers of the model.

3.1 Exit Criterion

During inference, Banino et al. (2021) proposed to sample the exit layer index from $p(i|x)$ (i.e., by sampling iteratively from a Bernoulli distribution with parameter λ_i). While a sampling-based exit criterion correlates with the variational view of PonderNet's training objective (it can be seen as performing a single sample Monte-Carlo estimation of $E_{i \sim p(\cdot|x)}\Big[p(y|x,i)\Big]$); such estimation has major variance, which introduces the randomness in the inference process of PonderNet (see Figure 2).

To overcome the issue of randomness, we propose **Q-exit**[1]: a novel deterministic criterion of performing early exit, which we used for PALBERT. Instead of sampling from the distribution $p(i|x)$ during inference, we evaluate its CDF by accumulating $p(i|x)$ from each layer. Once the CDF is greater than the threshold hyperparameter q, we perform an early exit. See Figure 1 for a schematic comparison of the sampling criterion with Q-exit. Threshold q can be seen as a trade-off between underthinking and overthinking. Therefore, q should be selected during the validation of the trained model in order to choose the best-performing value.

Based on our experiments, we found that the proposed criterion produced significantly better accuracy on various tasks compared to the original sampling criterion (see Sections 4.1, 4.4), while also being more practical than the original sampling criterion.

3.2 Lambda Layer Architecture

While the original PonderNet used a single layer MLP to obtain logit of exiting probability, we hypothesize that making the Lambda layer understand the dynamics of changing ALBERT hidden states is crucial for achieving good performance. To do so, instead of passing a single hidden state h_i from the i-th layer in Λ, we concatenate it with h_{i-1}. I.e., for PALBERT, we evaluate the probability of exiting from i-th layer as

$$\lambda_i = \Lambda([h_i, h_{i-1}]). \tag{3}$$

We used a 3 layer MLP with $\tanh$ activation for the Lambda layer to operate with more complex input. Based on the ablation study, we observed that increasing the capacity improves the accuracy of the trained model (See section 4.1). We also found it beneficial to fine-tune the Lambda layer with a different learning rate than all other parameters.

[1]**Q**-exit stands for Quantile

Method	Speed-up	SST-2	RTE	QNLI	CoLA	MRPC	MNLI	QQP	STS-B	Macro
Dev set										
ALBERT	×1.0	92.7	76.5	91.5	56.6	**90.5**	**84.8**	88.9	**90.6**	84.0
PABEE	×1.41	92.7	76.9	**91.5**	55.6	88.3	84.5	88.9	89.9	83.5
PonderNet	×1.48	91.3	74.0	88.3	51.3	87.1	81.7	87.7	88.2	81.2
PALBERT	×1.29	**93.1**	**78.3**	91.0	**58.1**	89.3	84.7	**88.9**	89.9	**84.2**
Test set										
ALBERT	×1.0	**93.4**	70.0	**92.1**	**50.5**	85.6	79.0	**84.7**	**87.4**	80.3
PABEE	×1.39	92.7	71.1	91.3	46.0	84.3	79.2	83.7	86.5	79.3
PALBERT	×1.26	93.0	**73.5**	91.7	48.6	**87.1**	**79.8**	84.4	86.5	**80.6**

Table 1: A comparison of PALBERT with recent approaches on the GLUE benchmark. Each result for the dev set is a median task score across 5 runs. We report the two metrics' mean for the MRPC, QQP, and STS-B tasks. For the MNLI task, we report the mean accuracy across matched and mismatched datasets. For the test set, we used the best model according to the dev score. In the Macro column, we present the average results across tasks. We bolded the best results and underlined the second-best results.

4 Experiments

4.1 Ablation Study

We performed an ablation study of the proposed changes in PonderNet architecture. We experimented with adding the proposed Q-exit criterion, Lambda layer architecture, and fine-tuning strategies. We also compared the proposed changes with fine-tuning vanilla ALBERT. These methods were benchmarked on SST-2, RTE, and CoLA tasks from the GLUE Benchmarking dataset (Wang et al., 2018).

For evaluation, we performed a grid hyperparameter search on an appropriate metric score on the dev split for each dataset. Following the PABEE training setup, we trained all models with a fixed learning rate until validation metrics stopped increasing for 5 epochs. We used a fixed $q = 0.5$ for all experiments on models with the Q-exit criterion.

We trained each model 5 times with the best hyperparameters and reported the mean and std values. A full list of the methods' hyperparameter ranges can be found in Table 3.

See Table 2 for the full list of the results of our ablation study. Based on these experiments, PonderNet architecture is seen as performing significantly worse than vanilla ALBERT fine-tuning. At the same time, the deterministic Q-exit criterion dramatically improves PonderNet accuracy when compared to a random sampling of the exit layer. A more complex Lambda layer that can handle hidden state changes' dynamics can further improve model accuracy when compared to the original PonderNet.

4.2 Understanding the Threshold of Q-exit

As noted previously in Section 3.1, we treat the threshold value q of the Q-exit criterion as a trade-off between underthinking and overthinking, where increasing q forces a model to evaluate more layers, and vice versa.

Therefore, it is necessary to find the best-performing threshold for each task where a model has the highest accuracy. To do so, we evaluated trained PALBERT models from the ablation study (see Section 4.1) on dev splits of tasks with different values of q. We then averaged obtained metrics and reported the mean and std values for various thresholds (See Figure 3 for the results).

We observed that exiting models with $q = 0.5$ shows the best overall performance for different tasks. Making q greater than 0.5 leads to a reduction in accuracy and can often force models to evaluate all 12 layers of ALBERT-Base.

We associate such behavior of trained models with the fact that the huge probability mass of trained posterior probability $p(i|x)$ is concentrated near the last layers of models (see Figure 2). We hypothesize that the reason for this is that the parameterization of prior probability $p(i|\lambda)$ as geometric distribution with normalized last layer, proposed with PonderNet (Banino et al., 2021), leads to a huge prior probability of exiting on the last layers (See Section 3). For MRPC, we observe a huge variance in the probabilities of exiting from different models on the first layers, which we believe leads to poor performance on this task. Note that these plots could be seen as an estimation of proba-

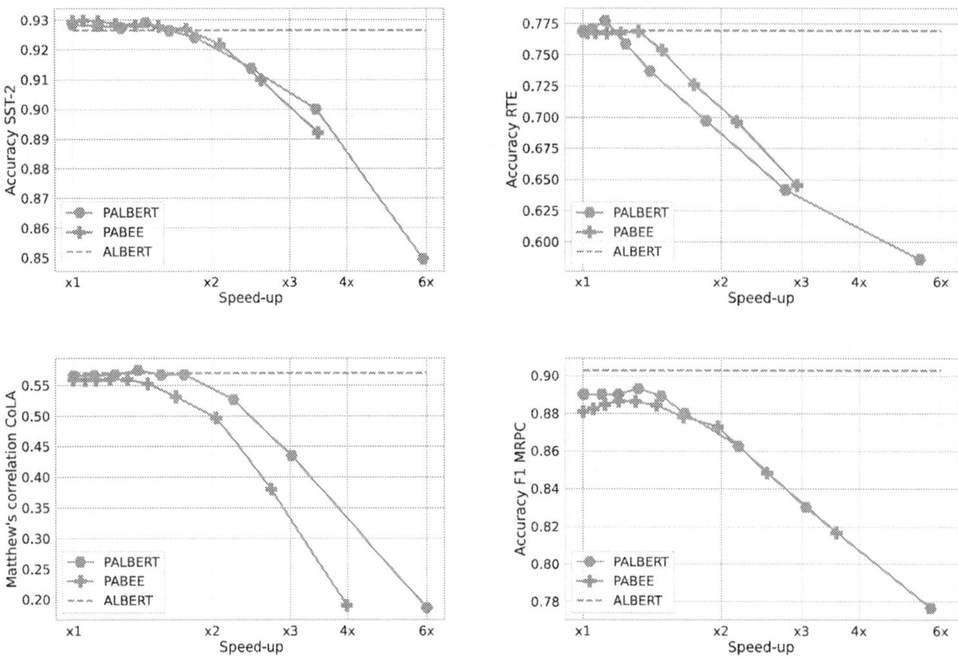

Figure 4: A comparison between PALBERT and PABEE models on CoLA and SST-2 tasks. We varied the threshold value of Q-exit for PALBERT and the patience hyperparameter for PABEE to obtain the plots of task scores of inference increasing in speed. 1x stands for plain ALBERT inference without performing an early exit. The horizontal line corresponds to plain ALBERT fine-tuning. See Section 4.3 for the analysis of these plots.

bilities of exiting from each layer with vanilla PonderNet sampling exit criterion. For the RTE task, layers $i \in [1; 10]$ have approximately the same probability of exiting with total probability mass close to 0.5, introducing huge variance in model outputs.

It is also notable that PALBERT, with a large threshold value q that performs constant exit on the last layer, has better accuracy than vanilla ALBERT fine-tuning for the SST-2 task.

4.3 Speed Analysis

While making $q < 0.5$ improves inference speed, it can also lead to underthinking and lower accuracy (see Figure 4). We compared PALBERT using different threshold values q to PABEE with different patience values t, which stands for the number of layers necessary to output the same result in a row to perform an early exit. We trained a PABEE model following the setup from the ablation study (see Section 4.1). We evaluated task scores for the specified hyperparameters as well as the increase in speed when compared to vanilla ALBERT inference of a full model with 12 layers.

Overall, we observed that PALBERT mostly produced higher scores on different tasks while also being slightly faster than PABEE. For the CoLA and MRPC datasets, PALBERT performed significantly better. The proposed method outperformed PABEE by a large margin while achieving the same increase in speed.

We observed questionable results for the SST-2 dataset: the best score for the PABEE model is slightly higher than for PALBERT. However, it was obtained with a negligible increase in speed, because the best-performing patience for this setup is 11 layers (while the whole model has only 12 layers).

Furthermore, unlike PALBERT, PABEE performed significantly worse than plain ALBERT fine-tuning on the CoLA and RTE tasks. We hypothesize that the reason for this is that separate classifiers for each layer C_i in PABEE were not able to train well enough on such small datasets as CoLA and RTE. Therefore, we can assume that performing an early exit to avoid overthinking is not the main feature of fine-tuning a well-performing

Method				SST-2	RTE	CoLA
ALBERT				92.7 ± 0.3	77.0 ± 1.9	57.0 ± 2.1
PonderNet				91.1 ± 0.6	73.5 ± 1.9	50.8 ± 2.2
Q-exit	Lambda LR	3-Layer Lambda	hidden concat.			
+	-	-	-	92.2 ± 0.3	77.3 ± 1.4	55.7 ± 0.9
+	+	-	-	92.7 ± 0.4	77.3 ± 1.4	56.5 ± 1.2
+	+	+	-	92.6 ± 0.3	77.0 ± 1.4	56.3 ± 2.4
+	+	-	+	**93.0 ± 0.3**	76.5 ± 1.6	56.9 ± 1.9
+	+	+	+	92.9 ± 0.2	**77.8 ± 1.2**	**57.4 ± 1.7**

Table 2: An ablation study of the proposed PALBERT architecture. "Lambda LR" corresponds to fine-tuning the Lambda layer with its own learning rate, "3-layer Lambda" refers to making the Lambda layer have three MLP layers instead of one, and "hidden concat." stands for concatenation of two hidden states as input to the Lambda layer.

model. Instead, it might be possible to simply focus on improving the training process (e.g., by adding auxiliary tasks on each layer).

4.4 GLUE Experiments

Finally, we compared PALBERT with different baseline models on all GLUE tasks.

We re-implemented PABEE according to the original work (Zhou et al., 2020) and used a fixed patience value $t = 6$. We also compared PALBERT with PonderNet architecture adapted for ALBERT fine-tuning. We trained 5 models with the best hyperparameters across the hyperparameter search and reported the median task score on the dev set. We evaluated the test scores on the best models, selected based on their dev scores.

See Table 1 for the full list of results. We observed that PALBERT significantly outperformed PABEE on a wide range of tasks. Vanilla PonderNet with the sampling exit criterion performed the worst. Vanilla ALBERT outperformed PABEE on most tasks and is comparable to PALBERT, while the latter has the higher score averaged across all tasks (see Macro column in Table 1).

PABEE showed the highest increase in speed and is faster than vanilla ALBERT fine-tuning $\times 1.41$ times. PALBERT is still $\times 1.29$ times faster than vanilla ALBERT, while also significantly outperforming PABEE on most tasks.

Note that for tasks with a small dataset (e.g., CoLA, RTE), PABEE is performing poorly. We hypothesize that this is caused by several independent classifiers at each layer C_i failing to train well enough, whereas PALBERT was capable of utilizing knowledge sharing between layers.

Parameter	Values range
Learning rate	[1e-5, 2e-5, 3e-5, 5e-5]
Batch size	[16, 32, 128]
Lambda learning rate	[1e-5, 2e-5, 3e-5]
β	[0.5]
λ	[0.1]
Optimizer	[Adam]
Classifier dropout	[0.1]

Table 3: Hyperparameter search ranges used in all of our experiments. Vanilla ALBERT and PABEE only used batch size and learning rate parameters, while the PonderNet model avoids finding the best Lambda layer learning rate. Weight β of KL used in Equation 2 has a fixed value of 0.5, while prior exit probability distribution parameter λ is fixed to 0.1 and following original PonderNet (Banino et al., 2021).

5 Conclusion and Future Work

In this paper, we proposed improving the PonderNet architecture in order to perform an early exit using a fine-tuned ALBERT model with the novel Q-exit criterion and a revisited Lambda layer architecture. While PALBERT outperformed some recent State-of-The-Art methods used for early exit, there is a clear direction for further improvement of this method, as it was not capable of outperforming plain ALBERT on some GLUE tasks.

We believe that PALBERT could benefit from the development of new parameterization of the prior distribution on exiting from each layer since it directly affects the resulting posterior distribution used to perform an early exit (see Figure 2).

In addition, adding more auxiliary tasks could also make it possible to improve PALBERT further. This way, training of PALBERT can be made more

PABEE-like by making independent classifiers on each layer of the model or adding self-distillation across layers.

Finally, there is still no theoretical justification for the Q-exit threshold value. Although we observed that $q = 0.5$ performed best, it is without a clear explanation as to why that is so. We hypothesize that bringing more insights into developing deterministic exit criteria could further improve the proposed method.

References

Andrea Banino, Jan Balaguer, and Charles Blundell. 2021. Pondernet: Learning to ponder. In *8th ICML Workshop on Automated Machine Learning (AutoML)*.

Diederik P. Kingma and Max Welling. 2014. Auto-Encoding Variational Bayes. In *2nd International Conference on Learning Representations, ICLR 2014, Banff, AB, Canada, April 14-16, 2014, Conference Track Proceedings*.

Zhenzhong Lan, Mingda Chen, Sebastian Goodman, Kevin Gimpel, Piyush Sharma, and Radu Soricut. 2020. Albert: A lite bert for self-supervised learning of language representations. In *International Conference on Learning Representations*.

Weijie Liu, Peng Zhou, Zhiruo Wang, Zhe Zhao, Haotang Deng, and Qi Ju. 2020. Fastbert: a self-distilling BERT with adaptive inference time. In *Proceedings of the 58th Annual Meeting of the Association for Computational Linguistics, ACL 2020, Online, July 5-10, 2020*, pages 6035–6044. Association for Computational Linguistics.

Surat Teerapittayanon, Bradley McDanel, and H. T. Kung. 2016. BranchyNet: Fast inference via early exiting from deep neural networks. In *Proceedings of the 23rd International Conference on Pattern Recognition*, pages 2464–2469. IEEE.

Ashish Vaswani, Noam Shazeer, Niki Parmar, Jakob Uszkoreit, Llion Jones, Aidan N Gomez, Łukasz Kaiser, and Illia Polosukhin. 2017. Attention is all you need. In *Advances in Neural Information Processing Systems*, pages 5998–6008.

Alex Wang, Amapreet Singh, Julian Michael, Felix Hill, Omer Levy, and Samuel R. Bowman. 2018. Glue: A multi-task benchmark and analysis platform for natural language understanding. Cite arxiv:1804.07461Comment: https://gluebenchmark.com/.

Ji Xin, Raphael Tang, Jaejun Lee, Yaoliang Yu, and Jimmy Lin. 2020. DeeBERT: Dynamic early exiting for accelerating BERT inference. In *Proceedings of the 58th Annual Meeting of the Association for Computational Linguistics*, pages 2246–2251, Online. Association for Computational Linguistics.

Wangchunshu Zhou, Canwen Xu, Tao Ge, Julian McAuley, Ke Xu, and Furu Wei. 2020. Bert loses patience: Fast and robust inference with early exit. In *Advances in Neural Information Processing Systems*, volume 33, pages 18330–18341. Curran Associates, Inc.

Wei Zhu. 2021. LeeBERT: Learned early exit for BERT with cross-level optimization. In *Proceedings of the 59th Annual Meeting of the Association for Computational Linguistics and the 11th International Joint Conference on Natural Language Processing (Volume 1: Long Papers)*, pages 2968–2980, Online. Association for Computational Linguistics.

Towards Improving Selective Prediction Ability of NLP Systems

Neeraj Varshney, Swaroop Mishra, Chitta Baral
Arizona State University
{nvarshn2, srmishr1, cbaral}@asu.edu

Abstract

It's better to say "I can't answer" than to answer incorrectly. This selective prediction ability is crucial for NLP systems to be reliably deployed in real-world applications. Prior work has shown that existing selective prediction techniques fail to perform well, especially in the out-of-domain setting. In this work, we propose a method that improves probability estimates of models by calibrating them using prediction confidence and difficulty score of instances. Using these two signals, we first annotate held-out instances and then train a calibrator to predict the likelihood of correctness of the model's prediction. We instantiate our method with Natural Language Inference (NLI) and Duplicate Detection (DD) tasks and evaluate it in both In-Domain (IID) and Out-of-Domain (OOD) settings. In (IID, OOD) settings, we show that the representations learned by our calibrator result in an improvement of $(15.81\%, 5.64\%)$ and $(6.19\%, 13.9\%)$ over *MaxProb* –a selective prediction baseline– on NLI and DD tasks respectively.

1 Introduction

In real-world applications, AI systems often encounter novel inputs that differ from their training data distribution. Prior work has shown that even state-of-the-art models tend to make incorrect predictions on such inputs (Elsahar and Gallé, 2019; Miller et al., 2020; Koh et al., 2021; Hendrycks et al., 2021). This raises reliability concerns and hinders their adoption in real-world safety-critical domains like biomedical and autonomous robots. *Selective prediction* addresses these concerns by enabling systems to abstain from making predictions when they are likely to be incorrect. Avoiding incorrect predictions allows them to maintain high task accuracy and thus makes them more reliable.

Hendrycks and Gimpel (2017) proposed '*MaxProb*' that uses the maximum softmax probability across all answer candidates as the confidence estimate to selectively make predictions. While performing reasonably well in the *in-domain* setting, *MaxProb* and other existing selective prediction techniques fail to translate that performance in the *out-of-domain* setting (Varshney et al., 2022b; Kamath et al., 2020).

In this work, we propose a selective prediction method that improves probability estimates of models in both in-domain and out-of-domain settings by learning strong representations via calibration. Specifically, we calibrate models' outputs using a held-out dataset and use the calibrator as confidence estimator for selective prediction. To this end, we first argue that *"all instances are not equally difficult and the model is not equally confident in all its predictions"* and then through extensive experiments, we show that prediction confidence is positively correlated with correctness while difficulty score is negatively correlated (5.2). We leverage the above finding to calibrate models' outputs using these two signals.

For computing the difficulty scores, we use a *model-based* technique (3.1) because human perception of difficulty may not always correlate well with machine interpretation. To calibrate a model, we annotate instances of a held-out dataset conditioned on the model's predictive correctness (computed using difficulty score and prediction confidence) and then train a calibrator using these instances. This annotation score represents the likelihood of correctness of the model's prediction. Finally, the trained calibrator predicts this likelihood value for test instances and is used as the confidence estimator for selective prediction.

To evaluate the efficacy of our method, we conduct comprehensive experiments in In-Domain (IID) and Out-of-Domain (OOD) settings for Natural Language Inference (NLI) and Duplicate Detection (DD) tasks. We also compare its performance with existing calibration techniques. On the NLI task, our method achieves 15.81% and 5.64% im-

Proceedings of the 7th Workshop on Representation Learning for NLP, pages 221 - 226

provement on AUC of *risk-coverage* curve over *MaxProb* in IID and OOD setting respectively. Furthermore, on the DD task, it achieves 6.19% and 13.9% improvement in IID and OOD setting respectively. Finally, we hope that our work will facilitate development of more robust and reliable AI systems making their wide adoption in real-world applications possible.

2 Selective Prediction

Selective prediction enables a system to abstain on instances where it is likely to be incorrect i.e it consists of a *selector* (g) that determines if the system should output the prediction. Usually, g comprises of a prediction confidence estimator $\tilde{g}$ and a threshold th that controls the abstention level:

$$g(x) = \mathbb{1}[\tilde{g}(x)) > th]$$

A selective prediction system makes trade-offs between $coverage$ and $risk$. For a dataset D, coverage at a threshold th corresponds to the fraction of answered instances (where $\tilde{g} > th$) and risk is the error on those answered instances.

With the decrease in th, coverage will increase, but the risk will usually also increase. The overall selective prediction performance across all thresholds is measured by the area under *risk-coverage curve* (El-Yaniv et al., 2010). **Lower the AUC, the better the system** as it represents lower average risk across all thresholds.

3 Method

We propose to train a confidence estimator that can assign higher scores to correctly predicted instances than incorrectly predicted ones. To this end, we leverage a held-out dataset and annotate it's instances conditioned on the model's predictive correctness. Specifically, we infer the model on the held-out dataset and annotate instances with a score such that correctly predicted instances get assigned a higher score than incorrectly predicted instances. This annotation score models the likelihood of the prediction being correct and is computed using the model's prediction confidence and difficulty level of the instance. Finally, a calibrator (regression model) is trained using this annotated held-out dataset and used as the confidence estimator for selective prediction.

We detail each component of our method and the intuition behind it in the following subsections.

3.1 Difficulty Score Computation

To compute difficulty score of an instance, we evaluate it after every training epoch and subtract the aggregated softmax probability assigned to the ground-truth answer from 1 i.e. for an instance i, difficulty score d_i is calculated as:

$$s_i = \frac{\sum_{j=1}^{E} c_{ji}}{E}$$

$$d_i = 1 - s_i$$

where the model is trained till E epochs and c_{ji} is prediction confidence of the correct answer given by the model after j^{th} training epoch. Note that c_{ji} is probability assigned to the correct answer not the maximum probability across all answer candidates. The intuition behind this procedure is that the *instances that can be consistently answered correctly from the early stages of training are inherently easy and should receive lower difficulty score than the ones that require a large number of training steps.* A similar method has been explored in Swayamdipta et al. (2020) for analyzing "training dynamics" but here we use it to quantify difficulty of the held-out instances.

3.2 Annotation Score Computation

We define annotation score for the held-out instances as a function of *softmax probability* outputted by the model and the *difficulty score*. We show that softmax score is positively correlated while difficulty score is negatively correlated with the predictive correctness i.e the system is more likely to be correct if the softmax score is high and difficulty score is low. Furthermore, in order to justifiably separate the scores for correct and incorrect prediction scenarios in the range 0 to 1, we push the scores above 0.5 in case of correct and below 0.5 in case of incorrect scenarios. Concretely, we use the following functions to compute this:

$$AS_1 = \begin{cases} 0.5 + \frac{maxProb}{2}, & \text{if correct} \\ 0.5 - \frac{maxProb}{2}, & \text{otherwise} \end{cases}$$

$$AS_2 = \begin{cases} 0.5 + \frac{s_i}{2}, & \text{if correct} \\ 0.5 - \frac{s_i}{2}, & \text{otherwise} \end{cases}$$

$$AS_3 = \begin{cases} 0.5 + \frac{max(s_i, maxProb)}{2}, & \text{if correct} \\ 0.5 - \frac{min(s_i, maxProb)}{2}, & \text{otherwise} \end{cases}$$

AS_1 uses only softmax, AS_2 uses only difficulty score and AS_3 uses a combination of both. These annotation strategies assign a relatively higher score when the model's prediction is correct and a lower score when it is incorrect. This gold score ranges from 0 to 1 as both s_i and $maxProb$ lie in the same range and better captures the likelihood of correctness unlike the categorical labels (1 for correct and 0 for incorrect) used in typical calibration approaches. **Note that this annotation computation is only required for training the calibrator and not at test time.** Therefore, difficulty score of the test instances need not be computed.

Both difficulty score and annotation score computation procedures are generic and are widely applicable since NLP systems usually make probabilistic predictions for all kinds of tasks ranging from Classification to Question Answering.

3.3 Calibration

Equipped with annotation scores, we extract syntactic features, namely, lengths, Semantic Textual Similarity (STS) value, number of common words between given sentences, and presence of negation words / numbers from the held-out instances to train the calibrator model. These features along with maxProb and prediction outputted by the model serve as inputs for the calibrator. Finally, we use a simple random forest implementation of Scikit-learn (Pedregosa et al., 2011) to train our calibrator that learns strong representations for the inputs. We note that these syntactic features are general and applicable for all language understanding tasks and any regression model can be used as the calibrator. We compare our method with other calibration techniques described in Section 4.1.

4 Experimental Setup

4.1 Calibration Baselines

Kamath et al. (2020) study a calibration-based selective prediction technique for Question Answering datasets where they annotate a held-out dataset such that correctly predicted instances are assigned class label '1' and incorrect ones are assigned label '0'. Then, a calibrator is trained using this annotated binary classification dataset using features such as input length and probabilities of top 5 predictions. The softmax probability assigned to class '1' by this calibrator is used as the confidence estimator for selective prediction. We refer to this approach as **Calib C**. We also train a transformer-based model for calibration (**Calib T**) that leverages the entire input text for this classification task instead of the syntactic features (Garg and Moschitti, 2021).

Our proposed calibration method differs from these approaches as we quantify the correctness on a continuous scale (instead of categorical labels '1' and '0') using prediction confidence and difficulty of the instances and use explicitly provided general syntactic features described in Section 3.3 for training. Our annotation procedure provides more flexibility for the calibrator to look for fine-grained features distinguishing various annotation scores. We note that our simplest annotation strategy (AS_1) that does not incorporate difficulty score is similar to Calib R method described in Varshney et al. (2022b) but our calibration method uses more general syntactic features.

Note that for fair estimation of abilities of the proposed method, we compare it with other calibration-based techniques only. Other techniques such as Monte-Carlo dropout (Gal and Ghahramani, 2016) and Error Regularization (Xin et al., 2021) are complementary and can further improve our performance.

4.2 Datasets

We conduct experiments with Natural Language Inference and Duplicate Detection datasets and compare the performance of various calibration techniques in in-domain and out-of-domain settings.

NLI Datasets: SNLI (Bowman et al., 2015), MNLI (Williams et al., 2018) (Matched and Mismatched), and Stress Test (Naik et al., 2018) (Competence, Distraction, and Noise).

Duplicate Detection Datasets: QQP (Iyer et al., 2017) and MRPC (Dolan and Brockett, 2005).

For NLI task, we train 3-way classification model (NLI has three labels) on SNLI and evaluate the selective prediction performance on SNLI (IID) and MNLI, Stress Test (OOD) datasets. For the DD task, we train model on MRPC and evaluate on MRPC (IID) and QQP (OOD) datasets. We use BERT-BASE model (Devlin et al., 2019) with a linear layer on top of [CLS] token representation for training the model for these tasks. We train these models with the default learning rate of $5e-5$ for 3 epochs.[1] We use the same experimental setup as (Varshney et al., 2022b) for calibration methods.

[1] See Appendix for details

Method	SNLI	MNLI			Stress Test			
		Matched	Mismatched	Avg	Competence	Distraction	Noise	Avg
MaxProb (AUC)	2.78	14.00	14.44	14.22	47.87	26.49	20.34	31.57
Calib T (%)	-181.2	-129.55	-127.86	-128.69	-48.65	-81.3	-91.17	-68.93
Calib C (%)	+8.97	+2.15	-1.36	+0.40	-3.75	**+8.27**	-0.80	+0.55
Proposed (%)	**+15.81**	**+2.35**	**+2.04**	**+2.19**	**+8.01**	+6.60	**+0.22**	**+5.64**

Table 1: Comparing percentage improvement of various calibration approaches on AUC of risk-coverage curve (over MaxProb) in in-domain (SNLI) and out-of-domain settings (MNLI, Stress Test) for NLI task.

Method	MRPC	QQP
MaxProb (AUC)	6.13	40.46
Calib T (%)	-148.87	+2.21
Calib C (%)	-0.82	+2.0
Proposed (%)	**+6.19**	**+13.9**

Table 2: Comparing % improvement of various calibration approaches on AUC of risk-coverage curve in IID (MRPC) and OOD (QQP) settings for DD task.

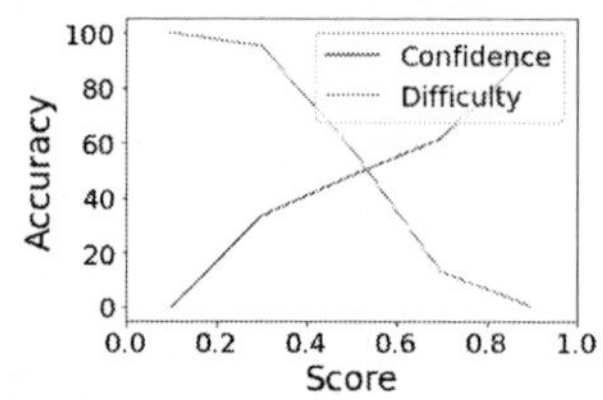

Figure 1: Trend of Model Accuracy with Confidence and Difficulty score for the NLI task.

5 Results and Analysis

5.1 MaxProb Struggles in OOD Setting

First rows in Table 1 and 2 show the AUC values achieved by MaxProb in NLI and DD tasks respectively. Note that in selective prediction, low AUC values of risk-coverage curves are preferred. We find that MaxProb performs well in the IID setting as it achieves low AUC values (2.78 on SNLI and 6.13 on MRPC). However, it fails to translate that in the OOD setting (AUC of 14.22 on MNLI, 31.57 on Stress Test, and 40.46 on QQP). This implies that the model makes a significant number of incorrect predictions with relatively high MaxProb and thus needs to be calibrated.

For calibration methods, we compare the performance improvement achieved over MaxProb w.r.t the minimum possible AUC.

5.2 Proposed Method Outperforms All

Our method shows a clear benefit over existing calibration techniques as it leads to a considerable improvement in all the cases. The proposed method achieves 15.81% and 6.19% improvement in the IID setting on SNLI and MRPC respectively. Furthermore, it achieves 2.19% on MNLI, 5.64% on Stress Test, and 13.9% on QQP in the OOD setting. *Calib T considerably degrades performance in both IID and OOD settings.* However, *Calib C results in a minor improvement in the IID setting* (8.97% for SNLI) *but does not consistently improve in the OOD setting* (especially on MNLI Mismatched and Competence Stress Test). We attribute this to the limited signal that is given to the calibrator by annotating the held-out dataset with categorical labels '1' and '0'. Thus, it learns weak representations.

Comparing Annotation Functions: We find that *the improvement using our method comes from using AS_3 as the annotation score* which outperforms AS_1 and AS_2. This is expected as it leverages useful signals provided by both maxProb and difficulty score for annotation computation.

Relationship With Predictive Correctness: To further analyze our method, we plot the relationship of predictive correctness with prediction confidence and difficulty score in Figure 1. It shows that prediction confidence is positively correlated while the difficulty score is negatively correlated with correctness. This further justifies our annotation score computation procedure.

6 Conclusion and Future Work

We proposed a selective prediction method that calibrates the model outputs using prediction confidence and difficulty level of the instances. Through comprehensive experiments, we demonstrated that it achieves considerable improvement over MaxProb on NLI and Duplicate Detection tasks in both IID and OOD settings. We hope that our work will facilitate development of more robust and reliable AI systems making their wide adoption in real-world applications possible.

Acknowledgements

We thank the anonymous reviewers for their insightful feedback. This research was supported by DARPA SAIL-ON and DARPA CHESS programs.

References

Samuel R. Bowman, Gabor Angeli, Christopher Potts, and Christopher D. Manning. 2015. A large annotated corpus for learning natural language inference. In *Proceedings of the 2015 Conference on Empirical Methods in Natural Language Processing*, pages 632–642, Lisbon, Portugal. Association for Computational Linguistics.

Jacob Devlin, Ming-Wei Chang, Kenton Lee, and Kristina Toutanova. 2019. BERT: Pre-training of deep bidirectional transformers for language understanding. In *Proceedings of the 2019 Conference of the North American Chapter of the Association for Computational Linguistics: Human Language Technologies, Volume 1 (Long and Short Papers)*, pages 4171–4186, Minneapolis, Minnesota. Association for Computational Linguistics.

William B Dolan and Chris Brockett. 2005. Automatically constructing a corpus of sentential paraphrases. In *Proceedings of the Third International Workshop on Paraphrasing (IWP2005)*.

Ran El-Yaniv et al. 2010. On the foundations of noise-free selective classification. *Journal of Machine Learning Research*, 11(5).

Hady Elsahar and Matthias Gallé. 2019. To annotate or not? predicting performance drop under domain shift. In *Proceedings of the 2019 Conference on Empirical Methods in Natural Language Processing and the 9th International Joint Conference on Natural Language Processing (EMNLP-IJCNLP)*, pages 2163–2173, Hong Kong, China. Association for Computational Linguistics.

Yarin Gal and Zoubin Ghahramani. 2016. Dropout as a bayesian approximation: Representing model uncertainty in deep learning. In *international conference on machine learning*, pages 1050–1059. PMLR.

Siddhant Garg and Alessandro Moschitti. 2021. Will this question be answered? question filtering via answer model distillation for efficient question answering. In *Proceedings of the 2021 Conference on Empirical Methods in Natural Language Processing*, pages 7329–7346, Online and Punta Cana, Dominican Republic. Association for Computational Linguistics.

Dan Hendrycks, Steven Basart, Norman Mu, Saurav Kadavath, Frank Wang, Evan Dorundo, Rahul Desai, Tyler Zhu, Samyak Parajuli, Mike Guo, et al. 2021. The many faces of robustness: A critical analysis of out-of-distribution generalization. In *Proceedings of the IEEE/CVF International Conference on Computer Vision*, pages 8340–8349.

Dan Hendrycks and Kevin Gimpel. 2017. A baseline for detecting misclassified and out-of-distribution examples in neural networks. *Proceedings of International Conference on Learning Representations*.

Shankar Iyer, Nikhil Dandekar, and Kornél Csernai. 2017. First quora dataset release: Question pairs. *data. quora. com*.

Amita Kamath, Robin Jia, and Percy Liang. 2020. Selective question answering under domain shift. In *Proceedings of the 58th Annual Meeting of the Association for Computational Linguistics*, pages 5684–5696, Online. Association for Computational Linguistics.

Pang Wei Koh, Shiori Sagawa, Henrik Marklund, Sang Michael Xie, Marvin Zhang, Akshay Balsubramani, Weihua Hu, Michihiro Yasunaga, Richard Lanas Phillips, Irena Gao, Tony Lee, Etienne David, Ian Stavness, Wei Guo, Berton Earnshaw, Imran Haque, Sara M Beery, Jure Leskovec, Anshul Kundaje, Emma Pierson, Sergey Levine, Chelsea Finn, and Percy Liang. 2021. Wilds: A benchmark of in-the-wild distribution shifts. In *Proceedings of the 38th International Conference on Machine Learning*, volume 139 of *Proceedings of Machine Learning Research*, pages 5637–5664. PMLR.

John Miller, Karl Krauth, Benjamin Recht, and Ludwig Schmidt. 2020. The effect of natural distribution shift on question answering models. In *International Conference on Machine Learning*, pages 6905–6916. PMLR.

Swaroop Mishra and Anjana Arunkumar. 2021. How robust are model rankings: A leaderboard customization approach for equitable evaluation. In *Proceedings of the AAAI Conference on Artificial Intelligence*, volume 35, pages 13561–13569.

Aakanksha Naik, Abhilasha Ravichander, Norman Sadeh, Carolyn Rose, and Graham Neubig. 2018. Stress test evaluation for natural language inference. In *Proceedings of the 27th International Conference on Computational Linguistics*, pages 2340–2353, Santa Fe, New Mexico, USA. Association for Computational Linguistics.

Fabian Pedregosa, Gaël Varoquaux, Alexandre Gramfort, Vincent Michel, Bertrand Thirion, Olivier Grisel, Mathieu Blondel, Peter Prettenhofer, Ron Weiss, Vincent Dubourg, et al. 2011. Scikit-learn: Machine learning in python. *the Journal of machine Learning research*, 12:2825–2830.

Pedro Rodriguez, Joe Barrow, Alexander Miserlis Hoyle, John P. Lalor, Robin Jia, and Jordan Boyd-Graber. 2021. Evaluation examples are not equally informative: How should that change NLP leaderboards? In *Proceedings of the 59th Annual Meeting of the Association for Computational Linguistics and the 11th International Joint Conference on Natural Language Processing (Volume 1: Long Papers)*, pages 4486–4503, Online. Association for Computational Linguistics.

Swabha Swayamdipta, Roy Schwartz, Nicholas Lourie, Yizhong Wang, Hannaneh Hajishirzi, Noah A. Smith, and Yejin Choi. 2020. Dataset cartography: Mapping and diagnosing datasets with training dynamics. In *Proceedings of the 2020 Conference on Empirical Methods in Natural Language Processing (EMNLP)*, pages 9275–9293, Online. Association for Computational Linguistics.

Neeraj Varshney, Swaroop Mishra, and Chitta Baral. 2022a. Ildae: Instance-level difficulty analysis of evaluation data. *arXiv preprint arXiv:2203.03073*.

Neeraj Varshney, Swaroop Mishra, and Chitta Baral. 2022b. Investigating selective prediction approaches across several tasks in iid, ood, and adversarial settings. *arXiv preprint arXiv:2203.00211*.

Adina Williams, Nikita Nangia, and Samuel Bowman. 2018. A broad-coverage challenge corpus for sentence understanding through inference. In *Proceedings of the 2018 Conference of the North American Chapter of the Association for Computational Linguistics: Human Language Technologies, Volume 1 (Long Papers)*, pages 1112–1122, New Orleans, Louisiana. Association for Computational Linguistics.

Ji Xin, Raphael Tang, Yaoliang Yu, and Jimmy Lin. 2021. The art of abstention: Selective prediction and error regularization for natural language processing. In *Proceedings of the 59th Annual Meeting of the Association for Computational Linguistics and the 11th International Joint Conference on Natural Language Processing (Volume 1: Long Papers)*, pages 1040–1051, Online. Association for Computational Linguistics.

Appendix

A Related Work

Instance-level difficulty analysis has recently received considerable attention. Varshney et al. (2022a) explore five different applications of difficulty analysis of evaluation data such as conducting efficient yet accurate evaluations with fewer instances and estimating OOD performance reliably. Rodriguez et al. (2021) incorporate item response theory based difficulty quantification and analyze ranking reliability of leaderboards. Mishra and Arunkumar (2021) study robustness of model rankings by weighting instances based on their difficulty score. Swayamdipta et al. (2020) analyze the behavior of model on individual instances during training (*training dynamics*) and categorize training instances into three different difficulty regions.

B Experimental Details

We use batch size of 32 on Nvidia V100 16GB GPUs for our experiments. We train these models with the default learning rate of $5e-5$ for 3 epochs. In Calib T approach, we use BERT-BASE model as the calibrator and train it using the annotated held-out dataset. For training this calibrator, we use the default learning rate of $5e-5$. In the proposed approach, we use a simple random forest implementation of Scikit-learn (Pedregosa et al., 2011) to train the calibrator. Note that more advanced regression models could be used to further improve the performance of our approach. However, we leave that for future work as the focus of this paper is to show efficacy of our proposed approach on the selective prediction task.

C Features of Training Calibrator

We extract syntactic features, namely, lengths, Semantic Textual Similarity (STS) value, number of common words between given sentences, and presence of negation words / numbers from the held-out instances to train the calibrator model. These features along with maxProb and prediction outputted by the model serve as inputs for the calibrator.

For the NLI task, we compute these features for premise and hypothesis sentences i.e. STS value, number of common words, etc. between premise and hypothesis sentences.

Similarly, for the DD task, we compute these features for the given two sentences.

On Target Representation in Continuous-output Neural Machine Translation

Evgeniia Tokarchuk
Language Technology Lab
University of Amsterdam
e.tokarchuk@uva.nl

Vlad Niculae
Language Technology Lab
University of Amsterdam
v.niculae@uva.nl

Abstract

Continuous generative models proved their usefulness in high-dimensional data, such as image and audio generation. However, continuous models for text generation have received limited attention from the community. In this work, we study continuous text generation using Transformers for neural machine translation (NMT). We argue that the choice of embeddings is crucial for such models, so we aim to focus on one particular aspect: target representation via embeddings. We explore pretrained embeddings and also introduce knowledge transfer from the discrete Transformer model using embeddings in Euclidean and non-Euclidean spaces. Our results on the WMT Romanian-English and English-Turkish benchmarks show such transfer leads to the best-performing continuous model.

1 Introduction & Related work

Discrete neural models represent the majority of systems used in sequence-to-sequence tasks (Sutskever et al., 2014; Vaswani et al., 2017). Despite the promising advantages of continuous-output models in terms of efficiency and expressivity, literature has awarded them relatively little attention. While past work focuses on continuous training objectives, we remark that the choice of word representations is essential.

Continuous-output NMT was first studied by Kumar and Tsvetkov (2019). They study regularized probabilistic loss functions, even though their results show that by far the biggest gain comes from switching to pretrained fastText (Bojanowski et al., 2017) embeddings from word2vec (Mikolov et al., 2013). Bhat et al. (2019) follow up with a study of margin-based losses. However, to the best of our knowledge, there is no comprehensive study on token-level representation and their impact on the continuous NMT performance.

In our work, we attempt to fill the gap and give insights about target representation in continuous-output NMT by highlighting an analogy between target representations and the output layer of a discrete model. We propose, as a knowledge transfer strategy, pretraining word representations with a discrete translation model. On two different language pairs, namely Romanian-English (Ro→En) and English-Turkish (En→Tr), we find that this strategy outperforms externally-trained representations, even from massive pretrained language models. Moreover, we find, somewhat surprisingly, that high dimensionality not only does not help, but can even substantially hurt, and that taking into account the natural spherical geometry of the cosine objective can lead to better performance with smaller dimensionality.

2 Continuous-output NMT

NMT seeks to translate a sequence of tokens $\boldsymbol{x}_{1:N} = (x_1, ..., x_N)$ from the source language to a sequence $\boldsymbol{y}_{1:T} = (y_1, ..., y_T)$ in the target language using a neural model:

$$\boldsymbol{x}_{1:N} \rightarrow \boldsymbol{y}_{1:T}(\boldsymbol{x}_{1:N}) = \underset{\boldsymbol{y}_{1:T}}{\operatorname{argmax}}\, p(\boldsymbol{y}_{1:T}|\boldsymbol{x}_{1:N}). \quad (1)$$

The probabilistic model above is typically implemented by sequence-to-sequence deep neural models (Sutskever et al., 2014; Bahdanau et al., 2015; Vaswani et al., 2017), using the decomposition

$$p(\boldsymbol{y}_{1:T}|\boldsymbol{x}_{1:N}) = \prod_{i=1}^{T} p(y_i \mid \boldsymbol{y}_{1:i-1}, \boldsymbol{x}_{1:N}). \quad (2)$$

In a **discrete model**, the conditional token probabilities in eq. (2) are categorical distributions over a fixed vocabulary $\mathcal{V}_{\text{tgt}}$,

$$\begin{aligned} p(y_i \mid \boldsymbol{y}_{1:i-1}, \boldsymbol{x}_{1:N}) &= \frac{\exp \boldsymbol{e}_{y_i}^\top \boldsymbol{W} \boldsymbol{h}_i}{\sum_{j=1}^{|\mathcal{V}_{\text{tgt}}|} \exp \boldsymbol{e}_{y_j}^\top \boldsymbol{W} \boldsymbol{h}_i} \\ &= \frac{\exp \boldsymbol{h}_i \cdot \boldsymbol{w}(y_i)}{\sum_{v \in \mathcal{V}_{\text{tgt}}} \exp \boldsymbol{h}_i \cdot \boldsymbol{w}(v)}, \end{aligned} \quad (3)$$

where $\boldsymbol{h}_i \in \mathbb{R}^d$ is the model output for position i, (a function of $\boldsymbol{x}$ and the Transformer weights $\boldsymbol{\theta}$), and

Proceedings of the 7th Workshop on Representation Learning for NLP, pages 227 - 235
May 26, 2022 ©2022 Association for Computational Linguistics

$\boldsymbol{w}(v) \in \mathcal{W}$ is the embedding of vocabulary token v, *i.e.*, the vth row of $\boldsymbol{W}$. Typically, $\mathcal{W} = \mathbb{R}^d$ and $\boldsymbol{W}$ is randomly initialized and learned jointly with $\boldsymbol{\theta}$. The log-probability of the gold token is typically referred as the *cross-entropy loss*, and has the value:

$$L_{\text{D}}(\boldsymbol{\theta},\boldsymbol{W}) = -\sum_{i=1}^{T} \log p(y_i \mid \boldsymbol{y}_{1:i-1}, \boldsymbol{x}_{1:N})$$
$$= \sum_{i=1}^{T} \left(-\boldsymbol{h}_i \cdot \boldsymbol{w}(y_i) + \log \sum_{v \in \mathcal{V}_{\text{tgt}}} \exp \boldsymbol{h}_i \cdot \boldsymbol{w}(v) \right).$$

In a **continuous model**, the output space is not limited to a discrete vocabulary but instead gives mass to the entire space $\mathcal{W}$, and we interpret the notation $p(y_i|\boldsymbol{y}_{1:i-1},\boldsymbol{x})$ to mean $p(\boldsymbol{w}(y_i)|\boldsymbol{y}_{1:i-1},\boldsymbol{x})$. A common parametrization uses the cosine similarity,

$$p(\boldsymbol{w}(y_i)|\boldsymbol{y}_{1:i-1},\boldsymbol{x}) \propto \exp \frac{\boldsymbol{h}_i \cdot \boldsymbol{w}(y_i)}{\|\boldsymbol{h}_i\| \|\boldsymbol{w}(y_i)\|}. \tag{4}$$

Here, the distribution is over a continuous space, so the normalizer is an integral $\int_{\mathcal{W}} \mathrm{d}\boldsymbol{v} \exp \frac{\boldsymbol{h}_i \cdot \boldsymbol{v}}{\|\boldsymbol{h}_i\| \|\boldsymbol{v}\|}$. By a symmetry argument, it can be shown that the normalizer does not depend on $\boldsymbol{h}$ and is therefore a constant, yielding the **cosine distance loss**:

$$L_{\text{C}}(\boldsymbol{\theta}) = -\sum_{i=1}^{T} \log p(\boldsymbol{w}(y_i)|\boldsymbol{y}_{1:i-1},\boldsymbol{x})$$
$$= \text{const} + \sum_{i=1}^{T} \left(1 - \frac{\boldsymbol{h}_i \cdot \boldsymbol{w}(y_i)}{\|\boldsymbol{h}_i\| \|\boldsymbol{w}(y_i)\|} \right). \tag{5}$$

The cosine loss is an intuitive choice with a history of use in NLP (Subramanian et al., 2018; Wieting et al., 2019). Its probabilistic interpretation we give has roots in directional statistics (Mardia et al., 2000), and corresponds to a Langevin distribution (also known as vMF) with fixed scale. Kumar and Tsvetkov (2019) studied more general Langevin distributions for NMT. Even though these more flexible formulations provide useful modelling extensions, the impact of the loss seems less than the impact of embeddings.

Unlike the discrete model, where the embeddings $\boldsymbol{w}(\cdot)$ can be learned from scratch, in a continuous model, this is not an option because the trivial solution of setting them all to the same (nonzero) value and learning to always output that value as $\boldsymbol{h}_i$ leads to the minimal loss of zero. *Therefore, for continuous-output NMT, good pretrained token representations are essential!*

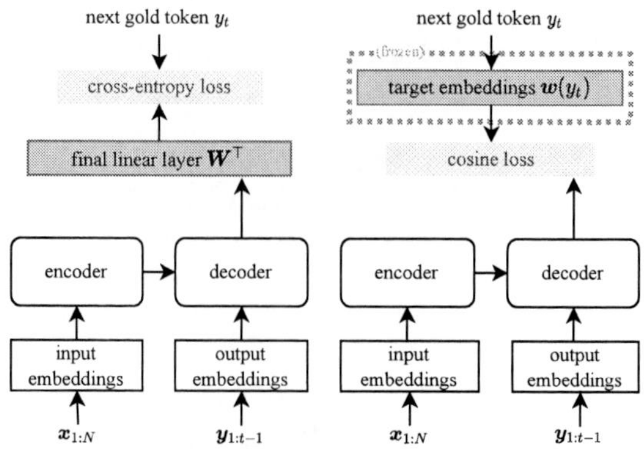

Figure 1: Illustration of the parallels between the discrete (left) and continuous (right) Transformers.

Model architecture. We build our continuous model on top of the Transformer (Vaswani et al., 2017) encoder-decoder model, which powers most state-of-the-art NMT models. In contrast, previous work uses recurrent models (Bahdanau et al., 2015). The encoder is unchanged, while the decoder is slightly reorganized, as shown in figure 1. We re-interpret the output layer $\boldsymbol{W}$ as the target embeddings, which only needs to be applied to the gold token during training. The target embeddings are frozen and set to one of the choices discussed in §3.

3 Target Embeddings

3.1 Euclidean Representations

fastText. Following Kumar and Tsvetkov (2019) we use `fastText` (Bojanowski et al., 2017) target embeddings. We experiment with two different variants. The first is the publicly-available CommonCrawl pretrained `fastText` model (Mikolov et al., 2018; Grave et al., 2018). These models contain subword information and we use the provided API to extract vectors for every subword in the preprocessed MT training data. For comparison, we also train `fastText` models entirely from scratch on the preprocessed MT training data.

mBART. Since the work of Kumar and Tsvetkov (2019), large language models proved highly effective at generating contextualized vector representations for a variety of downstream tasks. We therefore consider extracting target representations from mBART (Tang et al., 2021). For further adaptation to MT, we use the fine-tuned NMT many-to-many mBART-large many-to-many model (Tang et al., 2021) from the huggingface Transformers library (Wolf et al., 2020). A natural thought would be to extract the mBART input embeddings for subwords occuring in the MT data. However, we found that mBART input embeddings are less adequate that mBART model outputs, especially for subwords that are common in multiple languages, and lead to the poor performance. We refer to the appendix D for details. Therefore, we propose encoding every subword type $v \in V$ by processing `[target-lang] v` through the mBART decoder, and using the last hidden activations.

MT-transfer. Using our observation of the parallel between the linear output layer of a discrete MT model $\boldsymbol{W}$ and the target embeddings in a continuous one (figure 1), we propose a novel knowledge transfer strategy. We train a Transformer-base model (baseline) on the preprocessed MT parallel data, choose the best checkpoint on development set, and use the output layer weights as target embeddings.

3.2 Non-euclidean Representations

Both embedding methods discussed so far assume that the tokens live in an Euclidean space, like most NLP models. However, this assumption is receiving increasing scrutiny (Nickel and Kiela, 2017; Bronstein et al., 2017; Tifrea et al., 2019). Indeed, since the cosine distance is a function of *directions* only, it may be suboptimal to use embeddings that encode information in vector lengths. We consider two methods for learning embeddings on the surface of the sphere, $\boldsymbol{w}(y) \in \mathbb{S}^{d-1} \subseteq \mathbb{R}^d$, where

$$\mathbb{S}^{d-1} := \{\boldsymbol{u} \in \mathbb{R}^d : \|\boldsymbol{u}\| = 1\}. \qquad (6)$$

Spherical Text Embeddings (JoSe). Meng et al. (2019) propose learning directional embeddings on the unit sphere using Riemannian optimization, reporting improved performance on word similarity tasks, where cosine similarity is typical. Since continuous MT models also rely on cosine similarity, we expect similar results. We train spherical embeddings using the code released by Meng et al. (2019) on the target-side monolingual data of each MT language pair, after BPE tokenization. The released pretrained JoSe model does not apply, due to lack of subword information.

Spherical MT embeddings. As a spherical counterpart of the MT transfer learning insight, we propose training a baseline Transformer model with decoder input and output embeddings constrained to $\mathbb{S}^{d-1}$. We employ Riemannian optimization (Gabay, 1982; Udriste, 1994; Bonnabel, 2013); specifically, Riemannian Adam (Becigneul and Ganea, 2019) for the last hidden layer $\boldsymbol{W}$ as well as the other embeddings, and regular (Euclidean) Adam (Kingma and Ba, 2015) for all other parameters. Riemannian Adam is provided in `geoopt` (Kochurov et al., 2020). To our knowledge, this is the first instance of non-euclidean embeddings trained with an MT objective.

3.3 Dimensionality Reduction

While high-dimensional vectors can be richer, computational costs increase with dimension, and distances can be harder to tell apart (Aggarwal et al., 2001; Beyer et al., 1999).

To explore the impact of the target dimension, for the embeddings trained only on MT data, we retrain the embeddings for every dimensionality we consider. For external embeddings, we use PCA: in the case of `fastText`, we use the provided `reduce_model.py` script. For mBART, we apply cosine kernel PCA (Schölkopf et al., 1997) from `scikit-learn` (Pedregosa et al., 2011). Dimensionality reduction on the sphere is non-trivial and a possible avenue for future work.

4 Experiments

We experiment using the publicly available WMT 2016 Ro→En dataset with 612K parallel training sentences, and the WMT 2018 En→Tr dataset with 207K parallel training sentences. We compute BLEU (Papineni et al., 2002) using `sacrebleu` (Post, 2018)[1] on `newsdev2016` and `newstest2016` for both Ro→En and En→Tr. Detailed information about data is collected in appendix A.

All experiments and implementation are based on fairseq (Ott et al., 2019) framework. We use 6-layers Transformer base model as a baseline. For continuous model, encoder and decoder embeddings size are set to 512 (they are not initialized with pretrained embeddings), and output layer size depends on the target embeddings dimensionality. We choose the best model checkpoint based on development BLEU. For generation, we rely on the top-1 nearest neighbor search (greedy) using cosine similarity, the details are discussed in appendix C.

4.1 Results & Analysis

Table 1 shows the BLEU along with the BERTScore (Zhang et al., 2020) results of continuous output NMT models with different target embeddings. Since BERTScore is based on semantic similarity, it is suitable to assess the continuous model

[1]BLEU+case.mixed+numrefs.1+smooth.exptok.13a+version.1.5.1

embeddings	dim.	Ro→En dev16 BLEU	Ro→En dev16 BSc	Ro→En test16 BLEU	Ro→En test16 BSc	En→Tr dev16 BLEU	En→Tr dev16 BSc	En→Tr test16 BLEU	En→Tr test16 BSc	En→Tr test17 BLEU	En→Tr test17 BSc
discrete	-	33.0	65.6	31.6	64.9	12.0	69.3	12.2	69.2	12.2	69.8
+beam=5	-	33.7	66.6	32.3	66.1	12.7	70.4	12.8	70.5	13.0	71.0
Trained on target monolingual data											
JoSe (𝕊)	100	29.6	43.3	27.4	43.1	2.7	54.1	2.9	54.7	3.3	55.9
JoSe (𝕊)	50	29.9	50.9	28.2	51.8	9.7	64.0	9.4	63.9	9.9	64.7
fastText	512	26.4	47.0	25.4	47.9	3.5	52.8	3.3	54.1	3.3	52.7
fastText	300	27.2	51.4	26.6	52.1	9.1	64.0	9.0	63.9	9.5	64.7
fastText	100	29.3	57.1	28.6	57.2	9.2	62.6	9.2	62.6	9.4	63.1
fastText	50	29.3	56.4	28.6	56.5	9.2	63.1	9.2	63.1	9.4	63.8
Trained on bilingual data											
MT-transfer	512	29.7	56.4	28.7	57.2	10.9	67.9	10.7	67.8	11.3	68.6
MT-transfer	100	**32.2**	**63.0**	**30.9**	**62.9**	8.5	61.8	8.2	61.5	8.9	62.3
MT-transfer	50	31.7	62.3	30.6	62.3	8.5	60.8	8.6	60.7	8.9	61.4
MT-transfer (𝕊)	512	30.4	61.0	29.0	60.9	10.3	67.1	9.8	66.8	10.2	67.6
MT-transfer (𝕊)	100	30.8	61.0	29.7	60.9	**11.4**	**68.6**	**11.2**	**68.1**	**11.6**	**69.1**
MT-transfer (𝕊)	50	31.3	60.9	30.0	60.9	9.2	63.3	9.1	62.8	9.5	63.5
Pretrained on external data											
fastText	300	27.5	55.1	27.0	55.7	9.2	62.6	9.1	62.1	9.3	63.0
fastText$_{\text{PCA}}$	100	29.6	59.4	28.6	59.0	9.1	63.0	9.3	62.8	9.5	63.5
mBART-MT	1024	24.9	48.6	24.6	49.5	0.0	29.5	0.0	29.6	0.0	29.5
mBART-MT$_{\text{PCA}}$	512	29.5	58.9	28.7	59.5	9.5	65.6	8.9	64.5	9.2	65.2
mBART-MT$_{\text{PCA}}$	100	28.9	57.1	27.9	58.0	9.7	65.1	9.2	64.5	9.8	65.3
mBART-MT$_{\text{PCA}}$	50	27.3	54.2	26.4	54.1	8.2	61.8	7.9	61.4	8.5	62.2

Table 1: BLEU and BERTscore (BSc), in percentages, on newstest and newsdev. Spherical models are denoted by 𝕊.

performance. We re-scale BERTScore using baseline, to provide more human-readable outputs. The BERTScores agrees with the BLEU score both on Ro→En and En→Tr. Contrary to past work (Kumar and Tsvetkov, 2019; Bhat et al., 2019), when upgrading to state-of-the-art Transformer models with BPE, continuous models do not catch up to the discrete counterpart. We attribute this to the highly tuned Transformer architecture, and find that our exploration manages to shrink the gap considerably. We next analyze the various dimensions of variation in the choice of target representation.

MT knowledge transfer. On both tasks, the best performing continuous model uses embeddings learned by a discrete MT model. Bilingual data contains valuable information about the target language, but external mBART embeddings lag behind MT-transfer, perhaps since the latter are fine-tuned to the target language and domain. This finding prompts promising directions for hybrid embeddings via fine-tuning or adaptation.

Geometry. Spherical embeddings (JoSe and MT-transfer(𝕊)) prove useful compared to the euclidean embeddings, and tend to scale well to smaller dimensions and datasets. MT-transfer(𝕊) is the best continuous model for En→Tr.

Dimensionality. Throughout, we record the best performance with embeddings slightly smaller than the standard values used in discrete models. This is most pronounced for mBART-MT, with which En→Tr training fails entirely for $d = 1024$. According to our findings, the smaller dimensionality of the target embeddings benefits the model's performance. However, it might no longer hold for large-scale MT datasets.

External pretraining. Surprisingly, we find no clear indication that large-scale external pretraining with fastText or mBART is superior to leaning only on the task data, even when compared to monolingual embeddings, and even on the lower-resource language pair. However, we cannot use the full contextualization abilities of mBART, because we are limited to selecting one embedding

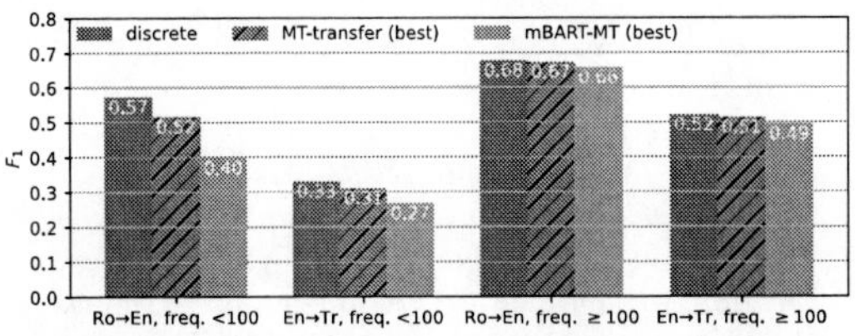

Figure 2: Word-level F_1 score by training frequency.

	Output
Src.	În Bucuresti se vor inregistra 26 de grade la amiaza.
Ref.	Bucharest will register 26 degrees at noon.
discrete	Bucharest will register 26 degrees at noon.
MT-transfer	There will be 26 degrees at afternoon in Bucharest.
mBART-MT	There will be 26 degrees in Bucharest at evening.
Src.	horă și rock cu vioară și chitară
Ref.	Hora and rock with a violin and guitar
discrete	Hora and rock with both a violin and guitar
MT-transfer	Hora, rock with vivid and chitar
mBART-MT	Resolution and rock with its shadow and furniture

Table 2: Translation examples. Words with training frequency < 100 are highlighted.

vector per target subword. Better transfer of contextual representations from large language models remains an open question.

Rare words. One might expect external pretraining to benefit words that occur rarely in the MT training data, via transfer. Figure 2 reveals the opposite trend. Even the best continuous model struggles for words with frequency under 100, but mBART-MT degrades much more for such rare words. For more common words, the gap is small. Some examples of sentences with the rare words are shown in Table 2. More examples can be found in Appendix E.

Length. We find continuous models to struggle more with shorter sentences. For Turkish target sentences longer than 10 words, the difference in average sentence BLEU between the discrete and the best continuous model is 1.04; for sentences with $\leq$10 words it is 2.48. Ro→En exhibits a similar trend. This suggests future work should focus on the representations of rare words and short sentences.

5 Conclusion

In this work, we investigated the importance of target representations for continuous NMT in two language pairs. We find that our proposed strategy to transfer embeddings from a discrete Transformer model outperforms all other embedding choices. We pinpoint the impact of properties like dimensionality and geometry, and provide further insight into the errors made by continuous models. Our proposed transfer strategy is effective despite using much less data compared to large pretrained models. We believe that further research into combining external data with MT-transfer embeddings may be necessary for improving continuous model performance. Even though our model performance is behind the discrete model, we argue that this work can be seen as a stepping stone for building strong and reliable continuous model for text generation.

Acknowledgments

We thank all the members of the UvA Language Technology Lab for their constant feedback on our work. Special thanks to Ali Araabi and Amir Soleimani for their useful comments on the manuscript, and to Nicola De Cao for the insightful discussions on the topic. Finally, we want to thank anonymous reviewers for their valuable input and suggestions. Vlad Niculae is partially supported by the Hybrid Intelligence Centre, a 10-year program funded by the Dutch Ministry of Education, Culture, and Science through the Netherlands Organisation for Scientific Research (`https://hybrid-intelligence-centre.nl`).

References

Charu C Aggarwal, Alexander Hinneburg, and Daniel A Keim. 2001. On the surprising behavior of distance metrics in high dimensional space. In *Proceedings of the International Conference on Database Theory*. Springer.

Dzmitry Bahdanau, Kyung Hyun Cho, and Yoshua Bengio. 2015. Neural machine translation by jointly learning to align and translate. In *Proceedings of the International Conference on Learning Representations*.

Gary Becigneul and Octavian-Eugen Ganea. 2019. Riemannian adaptive optimization methods. In *International Conference on Learning Representations*.

Kevin Beyer, Jonathan Goldstein, Raghu Ramakrishnan, and Uri Shaft. 1999. When is "nearest neighbor" meaningful? In *International conference on database theory*, pages 217–235. Springer.

Gayatri Bhat, Sachin Kumar, and Yulia Tsvetkov. 2019. A margin-based loss with synthetic negative samples for continuous-output machine translation. In *Proceedings of the 3rd Workshop on Neural Generation and Translation*, pages 199–205, Hong Kong. Association for Computational Linguistics.

Piotr Bojanowski, Edouard Grave, Armand Joulin, and Tomas Mikolov. 2017. Enriching word vectors with subword information. *Transactions of the Association for Computational Linguistics*, 5:135–146.

Silvere Bonnabel. 2013. Stochastic gradient descent on riemannian manifolds. *IEEE Transactions on Automatic Control*, 58(9):2217–2229.

Michael M. Bronstein, Joan Bruna, Yann LeCun, Arthur Szlam, and Pierre Vandergheynst. 2017. Geometric deep learning: Going beyond euclidean data. *IEEE Signal Processing Magazine*, 34(4):18–42.

Daniel Gabay. 1982. Minimizing a differentiable function over a differential manifold. *Journal of Optimization Theory and Applications*, 37(2):177–219.

Edouard Grave, Piotr Bojanowski, Prakhar Gupta, Armand Joulin, and Tomas Mikolov. 2018. Learning word vectors for 157 languages. In *Proceedings of the International Conference on Language Resources and Evaluation (LREC 2018)*.

Jeff Johnson, Matthijs Douze, and Hervé Jégou. 2019. Billion-scale similarity search with GPUs. *IEEE Transactions on Big Data*, 7(3):535–547.

Diederik P. Kingma and Jimmy Ba. 2015. Adam: A method for stochastic optimization. In *Proceedings of the International Conference on Learning Representations*.

Max Kochurov, Rasul Karimov, and Serge Kozlukov. 2020. Geoopt: Riemannian optimization in PyTorch.

Taku Kudo and John Richardson. 2018. SentencePiece: A simple and language independent subword tokenizer and detokenizer for neural text processing. *CoRR*, abs/1808.06226.

Sachin Kumar and Yulia Tsvetkov. 2019. Von Mises-Fisher loss for training sequence to sequence models with continuous outputs. In *Proceedings of the International Conference on Learning Representations*.

Kanti V Mardia, Peter E Jupp, and KV Mardia. 2000. *Directional statistics*, volume 2. Wiley Online Library.

Yu Meng, Jiaxin Huang, Guangyuan Wang, Chao Zhang, Honglei Zhuang, Lance Kaplan, and Jiawei Han. 2019. Spherical text embedding. *Advances in Neural Information Processing Systems*, 32.

Tomás Mikolov, Kai Chen, Greg Corrado, and Jeffrey Dean. 2013. Efficient estimation of word representations in vector space. In *Proceedings of the International Conference on Learning Representations*.

Tomas Mikolov, Edouard Grave, Piotr Bojanowski, Christian Puhrsch, and Armand Joulin. 2018. Advances in pre-training distributed word representations. In *Proceedings of the International Conference on Language Resources and Evaluation (LREC 2018)*.

Maximillian Nickel and Douwe Kiela. 2017. Poincaré embeddings for learning hierarchical representations. In *Advances in Neural Information Processing Systems*, volume 30.

Myle Ott, Sergey Edunov, Alexei Baevski, Angela Fan, Sam Gross, Nathan Ng, David Grangier, and Michael Auli. 2019. fairseq: A fast, extensible toolkit for sequence modeling. In *Proceedings of the 2019 Conference of the North American Chapter of the Association for Computational Linguistics (Demonstrations)*, pages 48–53, Minneapolis, Minnesota. Association for Computational Linguistics.

Kishore Papineni, Salim Roukos, Todd Ward, and Wei-Jing Zhu. 2002. Bleu: a method for automatic evaluation of machine translation. In *Proceedings of the 40th Annual Meeting of the Association for Computational Linguistics*, pages 311–318, Philadelphia, Pennsylvania, USA. Association for Computational Linguistics.

F. Pedregosa, G. Varoquaux, A. Gramfort, V. Michel, B. Thirion, O. Grisel, M. Blondel, P. Prettenhofer, R. Weiss, V. Dubourg, J. Vanderplas, A. Passos, D. Cournapeau, M. Brucher, M. Perrot, and E. Duchesnay. 2011. Scikit-learn: Machine learning in Python. *Journal of Machine Learning Research*, 12:2825–2830.

Matt Post. 2018. A call for clarity in reporting BLEU scores. In *Proceedings of the Third Conference on Machine Translation: Research Papers*, pages 186–191, Brussels, Belgium. Association for Computational Linguistics.

Bernhard Schölkopf, Alexander Smola, and Klaus-Robert Müller. 1997. Kernel principal component analysis. In *Proceedings of the International Conference on Artificial Neural Networks*, Berlin, Heidelberg. Springer Berlin Heidelberg.

Rico Sennrich, Barry Haddow, and Alexandra Birch. 2016. Neural machine translation of rare words with subword units. In *Proceedings of the 54th Annual Meeting of the Association for Computational Linguistics (Volume 1: Long Papers)*, pages 1715–1725, Berlin, Germany. Association for Computational Linguistics.

Sandeep Subramanian, Adam Trischler, Yoshua Bengio, and Christopher J Pal. 2018. Learning general purpose distributed sentence representations via large scale multi-task learning. In *Proceedings of the International Conference on Learning Representations*.

Ilya Sutskever, Oriol Vinyals, and Quoc V. Le. 2014. Sequence to sequence learning with neural networks. In *Advances in Neural Information Processing Systems*, Cambridge, MA, USA. MIT Press.

Yuqing Tang, Chau Tran, Xian Li, Peng-Jen Chen, Naman Goyal, Vishrav Chaudhary, Jiatao Gu, and Angela Fan. 2021. Multilingual translation from denoising pre-training. In *Findings of the Association for Computational Linguistics: ACL-IJCNLP 2021*, pages 3450–3466, Online. Association for Computational Linguistics.

Alexandru Tifrea, Gary Becigneul, and Octavian-Eugen Ganea. 2019. Poincare Glove: Hyperbolic word embeddings. In *Proceedings of the International Conference on Learning Representations*.

Constantin Udriste. 1994. *Convex Functions and Optimization Methods on Riemannian Manifolds*, volume 297. Springer Science & Business Media.

Ashish Vaswani, Noam Shazeer, Niki Parmar, Jakob Uszkoreit, Llion Jones, Aidan N. Gomez, Łukasz Kaiser, and Illia Polosukhin. 2017. Attention is all you need. In *Advances in Neural Information Processing Systems*, Red Hook, NY, USA. Curran Associates Inc.

John Wieting, Taylor Berg-Kirkpatrick, Kevin Gimpel, and Graham Neubig. 2019. Beyond BLEU:training neural machine translation with semantic similarity. In *Proceedings of the 57th Annual Meeting of the Association for Computational Linguistics*, pages 4344–4355, Florence, Italy. Association for Computational Linguistics.

Thomas Wolf, Lysandre Debut, Victor Sanh, Julien Chaumond, Clement Delangue, Anthony Moi, Pierric Cistac, Tim Rault, Remi Louf, Morgan Funtowicz, Joe Davison, Sam Shleifer, Patrick von Platen, Clara Ma, Yacine Jernite, Julien Plu, Canwen Xu, Teven Le Scao, Sylvain Gugger, Mariama Drame, Quentin Lhoest, and Alexander Rush. 2020. Transformers: State-of-the-art natural language processing. In *Proceedings of the 2020 Conference on Empirical Methods in Natural Language Processing: System Demonstrations*, pages 38–45, Online. Association for Computational Linguistics.

Tianyi Zhang, Varsha Kishore, Felix Wu, Kilian Q. Weinberger, and Yoav Artzi. 2020. Bertscore: Evaluating text generation with BERT. In *Proceedings of the International Conference on Learning Representations*.

A Data

We follow a standard pre-processing pipeline: all training sentences are tokenized and truecased using moses. We apply BPE (Sennrich et al., 2016) segmentation with 40K merge operations for Ro→En and 16K for En→Tr. Where necessary, we apply the SPM (Kudo and Richardson, 2018) model provided by the mBART pretrained model. The training data statistics are collected in Table 3.

Validation set `newsdev2016` and test set `newstest2016` for Ro→En contains 1999 sentences. Validation set `newsdev2016` and test set `newstest2016` for En→Tr contains 1999 sentences. En→Tr validation set `newsdev2016` contains 1001 sentences, test set `newstest2016` contains 3000 sentences and `newstest2017` contains 3007 sentences.

	Ro→En	En→Tr
# train sentences	612K	207k
# running tokens (tgt)	16.6M	4.6M
target vocab. size	25k	12K

Table 3: Training data statistics

B Hyperparameters

For all models, the learning rate is set to $5 \cdot 10^{-4}$ and the effective batch size set to 64k tokens. Warm-up steps are 10K for Ro→En and 4k for En→Tr. We use dropout 0.3 for all our models. We train model with the Adam optimizer (Kingma and Ba, 2015).

C Generation

To find the closest token on each generation step, we use the cosine similarity between output of the model and target embeddings.

$$\tilde{y}_i = \underset{v \in V_{tgt}}{\operatorname{argmin}} d(\boldsymbol{h}_i, \boldsymbol{w}(v)) \qquad (7)$$

where $\tilde{y}_t$ is the token predicted by the model, and $d(\cdot)$ is the cosine distance between the model output and the token embeddings of the token in target vocabulary.

The complexity of the NN search for NMT depends on vocabulary size, the sequence length and the vector dimensions. To speed up search, we use the `faiss` (Johnson et al., 2019) library for fast nearest neighbors search. However, instead of approximation, we use exact search, which nevertheless boosts the computation speed. Investigation of the different variants of the approximate nearest neighbors search is out of the scope of this paper.

D mBART embeddings

As we mentioned in §3.1, the straightforward way to utilize the mBART embeddings is to extract the input embeddings matrix. The extracted embeddings matrix contains 250K vocabulary types. We filter embeddings to keep only the tokens, which is observed in training MT data. After filtering, the vocabulary consists of 27,508 types. However, the performance of continuous models using these embeddings drop dramatically on Ro→En (17.0 BLEU on the development set, which is 16.7 BLEU worse than a discrete model). We hypothesize that this might be due to the multilingual ambiguity of the token embeddings in the input matrix. For the filtered embeddings matrix, the 3 nearest neighbors for the word "_neighbor" are: "_neighborhood", "_mondat", "_mbr". For mBART-MT, obtained as discussed in §3.1, the 3 nearest neighbors for the word "_neighbor" are: "friend", "_companion" and "_mentor".

E Examples

We provide sentence examples of the best performing model for each embeddings type in table 4 on the next page.

	Output
Src.	În Bucuresti se vor inregistra 26 de grade la amiaza.
Ref.	Bucharest will register 26 degrees at noon.
discrete	Bucharest will register 26 degrees at noon.
JoSe ($\mathbb{S}$)	There will be 26 degrees at afternoon in Bucharest.
fastText	There will be 26 degrees in Bucharest at afternoon.
MT-transfer	There will be 26 degrees at afternoon in Bucharest.
MT-transfer($\mathbb{S}$)	There will be 26 degrees in Bucharest at the afternoon.
fastText (pretrained)	There will be 27 degrees in Bucharest in the afternoon.
mBART-MT	There will be 26 degrees in Bucharest at evening.
Src.	The other undergraduates giggled.
Ref.	Diğer lisans öğrencileri kıkırdadı.
discrete	Diğer lisans öğrencileri de oldukça yavaş gitti.
JoSe ($\mathbb{S}$)	Diğer başka leme eğitim aları da zevkler.
fastText	Diğer mezunlar da karmaşıklaştırıldı.
MT-transfer	Diğer mezunlar ise hediye ediliyorlar.
MT-transfer ($\mathbb{S}$)	Diğer mezunlar ise bıkmış durumda.
fastText (pretrained)	Diğer mezunlar ise relayor.
mBART-MT	Diğer lisans öğrencileri beenhard.

Table 4: Translation examples for Ro→En and En→Tr. Continuous models have a tendency to select synonyms or near-synonyms (noon and afternoon, öğrencileri and mezunlar.)

Zero-shot Cross-lingual Transfer is Under-specified Optimization

Shijie Wu, Benjamin Van Durme, Mark Dredze
Department of Computer Science
Johns Hopkins University
shijie.wu@jhu.edu, vandurme@jhu.edu, mdredze@cs.jhu.edu

Abstract

Pretrained multilingual encoders enable zero-shot cross-lingual transfer, but often produce unreliable models that exhibit high performance variance on the target language. We postulate that this high variance results from *zero-shot cross-lingual transfer solving an under-specified optimization problem.* We show that any linear-interpolated model between the source language monolingual model and source + target bilingual model has equally low source language generalization error, yet the target language generalization error reduces smoothly and linearly as we move from the monolingual to bilingual model, suggesting that the model struggles to identify good solutions for both source and target languages using the source language alone. Additionally, we show that zero-shot solution lies in non-flat region of target language error generalization surface, causing the high variance.

1 Introduction

Pretrained multilingual encoders like Multilingual BERT (mBERT; Devlin et al., 2019) and XLM-RoBERTa (XLM-R; Conneau et al., 2020) facilitate zero-shot cross-lingual transfer (Wu and Dredze, 2019; Hu et al., 2020) — training the model on one language then using it on another language without additional task-specific training data. While the generalization performance on the source language has low variance, on the target language the variance is much higher with zero-shot cross-lingual transfer (Keung et al., 2020; Wu and Dredze, 2020), making it difficult to compare different models in the literature. Similarly, pretrained monolingual encoders also have unstable performance during fine-tuning (Devlin et al., 2019; Phang et al., 2018).

Why are these models so sensitive to the random seed? Many theories have been offered: catastrophic forgetting of the pretrained task (Phang et al., 2018; Lee et al., 2020; Keung et al., 2020), small data size (Devlin et al., 2019), impact of random seed on task-specific layer initialization and data ordering (Dodge et al., 2020), the Adam optimizer without bias correction (Mosbach et al., 2021; Zhang et al., 2021), and a different generalization error with similar training loss (Mosbach et al., 2021). However, none of these factors fully explain the high generalization error variance of zero-shot cross-lingual transfer on target language but low variance on source language.

We offer a new explanation for high variance in target language performance: *the zero-shot cross-lingual transfer optimization problem is under-specified.* Based on the well-established linear interpolation of 1-dimensional plot and contour plot (Goodfellow et al., 2014; Li et al., 2018), we empirically show that any linear-interpolated model between the monolingual source model and bilingual source and target model has equally low source language generation error. Yet the target language generation error surprisingly reduces smoothly and linearly as we move from a monolingual model to a bilingual model. To the best of our knowledge, no other paper documents this finding.

This result provides a new answer to our mystery: only a small subset of the solution space for the source language solves the target language on par with models with actual target language supervision; the optimization could not find such a solution with existing condition (without target language supervision), hence an under-specified optimization problem. If target language supervision were available, as it was in the counterfactual bilingual model, the optimization would find the smaller subset. By comparing both mBERT and XLM-R, we find that the generalization error surface of XLM-R is flatter than mBERT, contributing to its better performance compared to mBERT. Thus, zero-shot cross-lingual transfer has high variance, as the solution found by

Code is available at https://github.com/shijie-wu/crosslingual-nlp.

Proceedings of the 7th Workshop on Representation Learning for NLP, pages 236 - 248

zero-shot cross-lingual transfer lies in the non-flat region of the target language generalization error surface. Small turbulence on the parameter space would lead to big generalization error difference, hence the high variance.

2 Existing Hypotheses (Related Work)

Prior studies have observed fine-tuning variance with pretrained encoder, and have offered various hypotheses to explain this behavior. Catastrophic forgetting – when neural networks trained on one task forget that task after training on a second task (McCloskey and Cohen, 1989; Kirkpatrick et al., 2017) —has been credited as the source of high variance in both monolingual fine-tuning (Phang et al., 2018; Lee et al., 2020) and zero-shot cross-lingual transfer (Keung et al., 2020). Mosbach et al. (2021) wonder why preserving cloze capability is important. However, in zero-shot cross-lingual transfer, deliberately preserving the multilingual cloze capability with regularization improves performance but does not eliminate the zero-shot transfer gap (Aghajanyan et al., 2021; Liu et al., 2021).

Small training data size often seems to have higher variance in performance (Devlin et al., 2019), but Mosbach et al. (2021) found that when controlling the number of gradient updates, smaller data size has the similar variance as larger data size.

In the pretraining-then-fine-tune paradigm, random seeds impact the initialization of task-specific layers and data ordering during fine-tuning. Dodge et al. (2020) show development set performance has high variance with respect to seeds. Additionally, Adam optimizer without bias correction—an Adam (Kingma and Ba, 2014) variant (inadvertently) introduced by the implementation of Devlin et al. (2019)—has been identified as the source of high variance during monolingual fine-tuning (Mosbach et al., 2021; Zhang et al., 2021). However, in zero-shot cross-lingual transfer, while different random seeds lead to high variance in target languages, the source language has much smaller variance in comparison even with standard Adam (Wu and Dredze, 2020).

Beyond optimizers, Mosbach et al. (2021) attributes high variance to generalization issues: despite having similar training loss, different models exhibit vastly different development set performance. However, in zero-shot cross-lingual transfer, the development or test performance variance is much smaller on the source language compared to target language.

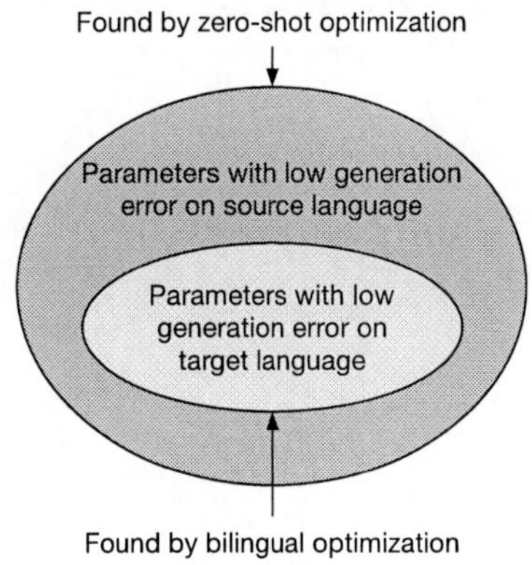

Figure 1: zero-shot cross-lingual transfer is an under-specified optimization problem. With the existing condition, the optimization could not find the solution that we really want.

3 Under-specified Optimization

Existing hypotheses do not explain the high variance of zero-shot cross-lingual transfer: much higher variance on generalization error of the target language compared to the source language. We propose a new explanation: *zero-shot cross-lingual transfer is an under-specified optimization problem.*[1] As in Fig. 1, optimizing a multilingual model for a specific task using only source language annotation allows choices of many good solutions in terms of generalization error. However, unbeknownst to the optimizer, these solutions have wildly different generalization errors on the target language. In fact, a small subset has similar low generalization error as models trained on target language. Yet without the guidance of target data, the zero-shot cross-lingual optimization could not find this smaller subset. As we will show in §5, the solution found by zero-shot transfer lies in a non-flat region of target language generalization error, and small turbulence in the parameter space causes big difference in generalization error, causing its high variance.

3.1 Linear Interpolation

We test this hypothesis via a linear interpolation between two models to explore the neural network parameter space. Consider three sets of neural network parameters: θ_{src}, θ_{tgt}, $\theta_{\{src,tgt\}}$ for a model

[1]This explanation provides deeper insight on the common belief that no target data causes high variance. We provide evidence on how these two factors interact.

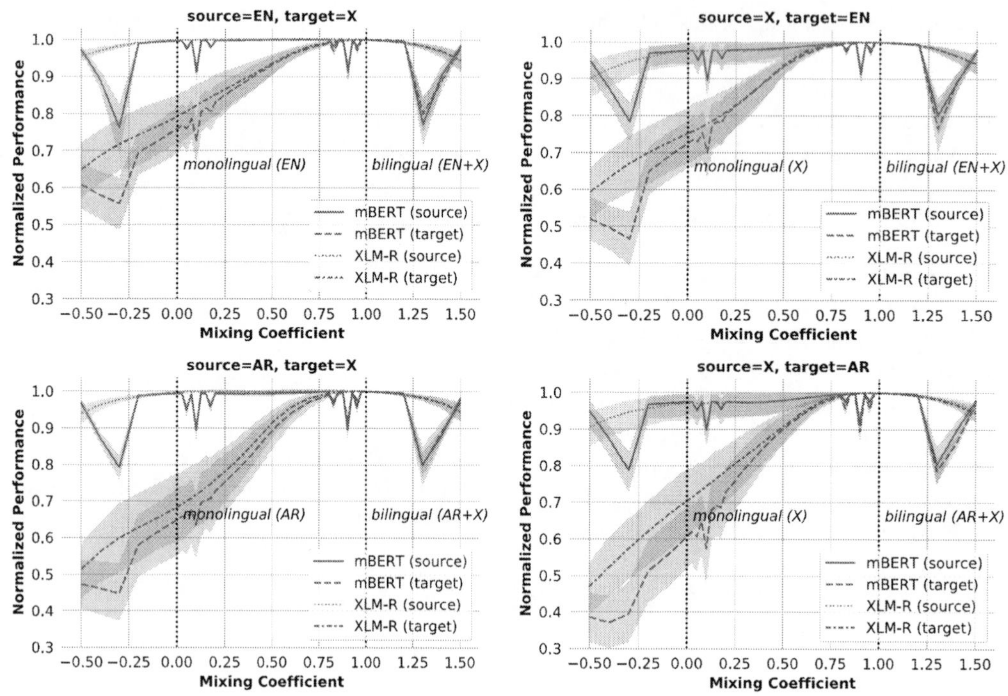

Figure 2: Normalized performance of a linear interpolated model between a monolingual and bilingual model. A single plot line shows the performance normalized by the matching bilingual model and aggregated over eight language pairs and four tasks, with the shaded region representing 95% confidence interval. The x-axis is the linear mixing coefficient α in Eq. (1) and Eq. (2), with $\alpha = 0$ and $\alpha = 1$ representing source language monolingual model and source + target bilingual model, respectively. Each subfigure title indicates the source and target languages. Across all experiments, the source language dev performance stays consistently high (red and purple lines) during interpolation while the target language dev performance starts low and increases smoothly and linearly as it moves towards the bilingual model (gray and blue lines). App. D break down this figure by tasks.

trained on task data for the source language only, target language only and both languages, respectively. This includes both task-specific layers and encoders.[2] Note all three models have the same initialization before fine-tuning, making the bilingual model a counterfactual setup if the corresponding target language supervision were available. We obtain the 1-dimensional (1D) linear interpolation of a monolingual (source) task trained model and bilingual task trained model with

$$\theta(\alpha) = \alpha\theta_{\{src,tgt\}} + (1-\alpha)\theta_{src} \quad (1)$$

or we could swap source and target by

$$\theta(\alpha) = \alpha\theta_{\{src,tgt\}} + (1-\alpha)\theta_{tgt} \quad (2)$$

where α is a scalar mixing coefficient (Goodfellow et al., 2014). Additionally, we can compute a 2-dimensional linear interpolation as

$$\theta(\alpha_1, \alpha_2) = \theta_{\{src,tgt\}} + \alpha_1\delta_{src} + \alpha_2\delta_{tgt} \quad (3)$$

where $\delta_{src} = \theta_{src} - \theta_{\{src,tgt\}}$, $\delta_{tgt} = \theta_{tgt} - \theta_{\{src,tgt\}}$, α_1 and α_2 are scalar mixing coefficients (Li et al., 2018).[3] Finally, we can evaluate any interpolated models on the development set of source and target languages, testing the generalization error on the same language and across languages.

The performance of the interpolated model illuminates the behavior of the model's parameters. Take Eq. (1) as an example: if the linear interpolated model performs consistently high for our task on the source language, it suggests that both models lie within the same local minimum of source language generalization error surface. Additionally, if

[2]We also experiment with interpolating the encoder parameters only and observe similar findings. On the other hand, interpolating the task-specific layer only has a negligible effect.

[3]Li et al. (2018) use two random directions and they normalize it to compensate scaling issue. In this setup, we find δ_{src} and δ_{tgt} have near identical norms, so we do not apply additional normalization. As these two directions are not random, we find that it spans around 55°. We plot the norm ratio and angle of these two vectors in App. B.

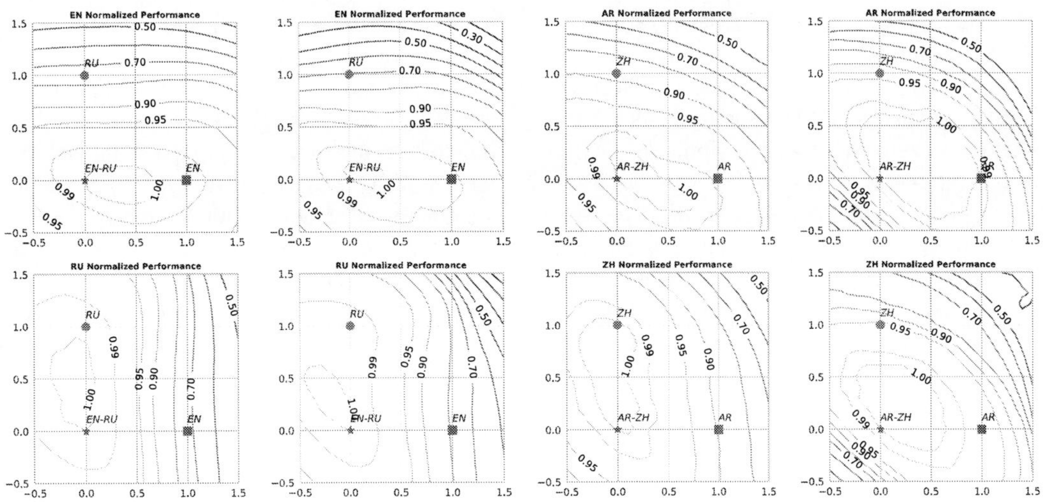

(a) EN-RU NER w/ mBERT (b) EN-RU NER w/ XLM-R (c) AR-ZH XNLI w/ mBERT (d) AR-ZH XNLI w/ XLM-R

Figure 3: Normalized performance of 2D linear interpolation between bilingual model and monolingual models. The x-axis and the y-axis are the α_1 and α_2 in Eq. (3), respectively. By comparing mBERT and XLM-R, we observe that XLM-R has flatter target language generalization error surface compared to mBERT. Different language pairs and tasks combination shows similar trends and additional figures can be found in App. E

the linear interpolated model performs vastly differently on the target language, it would support our hypothesis. On the other hand, if the linear interpolated model performance drops on the source language, it suggests that both models lie in different local minimum of source language generalization error surface, suggesting the zero-shot optimization searching the wrong region.

4 Experiments

We consider four tasks: natural language inference (XNLI; Conneau et al., 2018), named entity recognition (NER; Pan et al., 2017), POS tagging and dependency parsing (Zeman et al., 2020). We evaluate XNLI and POS tagging with accuracy (ACC), NER with span-level F1, and parsing with labeled attachment score (LAS). We consider two encoders: base mBERT and large XLM-R. For the task-specific layer, we use a linear classifier for XNLI, NER, and POS tagging, and Dozat and Manning (2017) for dependency parsing.

To avoid English-centric experiments, we consider two source languages: English and Arabic. We choose 8 topologically diverse target languages: Arabic[4], German, Spanish, French, Hindi, Russian, Vietnamese, and Chinese. We train the source language only and target language only monolingual model as well as a source-target bilingual model.

We compute the linear interpolated models as described in §3.1 and test it on both the source and target language development set. We loop over $\{-0.5, -0.4, \cdots, 1.5\}$ for α, α_1 and α_2.[5] We report the mean and variance of three runs by using different random seeds. We normalized both mean and variance of each interpolated model by the bilingual model performance, allowing us to aggregate across tasks and language pairs. Details of fine-tuning can be found in App. A.

5 Results

In Fig. 2, we observe that interpolations between the source monolingual and bilingual model have consistently similar source language performance. In contrast, surprisingly, the target language performance smoothly and linearly improves as the interpolated model moves from the zero-shot model to bilingual model.[6] The only exception is mBERT, where the performance drops slightly around 0.1 and 0.9 locally. In contrast, XLM-R has a flatter slope and smoother interpolated models.

Fig. 3 further demonstrates this finding with a

[4]Arabic is only used when English is the source language.

[5]We additionally select 0.025, 0.05, 0.075, 0.125, 0.15, 0.175, 0.825, 0.85, 0.875, 0.925, 0.95, and 0.975 for α due to preliminary experiment.

[6]We also show the variance of the interpolated models in App. C. The source language has much lower variance compared to target language on the monolingual side of the interpolated models, echoing findings in Wu and Dredze (2020).

2D linear interpolation. The generalization error surface of the target language of XLM-R is much flatter compared to mBERT, perhaps the fundamental reason why XLM-R performs better than mBERT in zero-shot transfer, similar to findings in CV models (Li et al., 2018). As we discuss in §3, these two findings support our hypothesis that zero-shot cross-lingual transfer is an under-specified optimization problem. As Fig. 3 shows, the solution found by zero-shot transfer lies in a non-flat region of target language generalization error surface, causing the high variance of zero-shot transfer on the target language. In contrast, the same solution lies in a flat region of source language generalization error surface, causing the low variance on the source language.

6 Discussion

We have presented evidence that zero-shot cross-lingual transfer is an under-specified optimization problem, and the cause of high variance on target language but not the source language tasks during cross-lingual transfer. This finding holds across 4 tasks, 2 source languages and 8 target languages. Training bigger encoders addresses this issue indirectly by producing encoders with flatter cross-lingual generalization error surfaces. However, a more robust solution may be found by introducing constraints into the optimization problem. There are a few potential solutions.

Few-shot cross-lingual transfer is a potential way to further constrain the optimization problem. Zhao et al. (2021) finds that it is important to first train on source language then fine-tune with the few-shot target language example. Through the lens of our analysis, this finding is intuitive since fine-tuning with a small amount of target data provides a guidance (gradient direction) to narrow down the solution space, leading to a potentially better solution for the target language. The initial fine-tuning with the source data is also important since it provides a good starting point. Additionally, Zhao et al. (2021) observes that the choice of shots matters. This is expected as it significantly impacts the quality of the gradient direction.

Similarly, silver target data is a potential way to further constrain the optimization problem. While Yarmohammadi et al. (2021) finds that jointly training with gold source data and silver target data benefits cross-lingual transfer, a pipeline fine-tuning approach like few-shot cross-lingual transfer is also worth exploring.

Unsupervised model selection like Chen and Ritter (2020) and optimization regularization like Aghajanyan et al. (2021) have been proposed in the literature to improve zero-shot cross-lingual transfer. Through the lens of our analysis, both solutions attempt to constrain the optimization problem.

As none of the existing techniques fully constrain the optimization, future work should study the combination of existing techniques and develop new techniques on top of it instead of studying one technique at a time.

Acknowledgments

This research is supported in part by ODNI, IARPA, via the BETTER Program contract #2019-19051600005. The views and conclusions contained herein are those of the authors and should not be interpreted as necessarily representing the official policies, either expressed or implied, of ODNI, IARPA, or the U.S. Government. The U.S. Government is authorized to reproduce and distribute reprints for governmental purposes notwithstanding any copyright annotation therein.

This research is supported by the following open-source softwares: NumPy (Harris et al., 2020), PyTorch (Paszke et al., 2017), PyTorch lightning (Falcon, 2019), scikit-learn (Pedregosa et al., 2011), Transformer (Wolf et al., 2019).

References

Armen Aghajanyan, Akshat Shrivastava, Anchit Gupta, Naman Goyal, Luke Zettlemoyer, and Sonal Gupta. 2021. Better fine-tuning by reducing representational collapse. In *International Conference on Learning Representations.*

Yang Chen and Alan Ritter. 2020. Model selection for cross-lingual transfer using a learned scoring function. *arXiv preprint arXiv:2010.06127.*

Alexis Conneau, Kartikay Khandelwal, Naman Goyal, Vishrav Chaudhary, Guillaume Wenzek, Francisco Guzmán, Edouard Grave, Myle Ott, Luke Zettlemoyer, and Veselin Stoyanov. 2020. Unsupervised cross-lingual representation learning at scale. In *Proceedings of the 58th Annual Meeting of the Association for Computational Linguistics*, pages 8440–8451, Online. Association for Computational Linguistics.

Alexis Conneau, Ruty Rinott, Guillaume Lample, Adina Williams, Samuel Bowman, Holger Schwenk, and Veselin Stoyanov. 2018. XNLI: Evaluating cross-lingual sentence representations. In *Proceedings of the 2018 Conference on Empirical Methods* in Natural Language Processing, pages 2475–2485, Brussels, Belgium. Association for Computational Linguistics.

Jacob Devlin, Ming-Wei Chang, Kenton Lee, and Kristina Toutanova. 2019. BERT: Pre-training of deep bidirectional transformers for language understanding. In *Proceedings of the 2019 Conference of the North American Chapter of the Association for Computational Linguistics: Human Language Technologies, Volume 1 (Long and Short Papers)*, pages 4171–4186, Minneapolis, Minnesota. Association for Computational Linguistics.

Jesse Dodge, Gabriel Ilharco, Roy Schwartz, Ali Farhadi, Hannaneh Hajishirzi, and Noah Smith. 2020. Fine-tuning pretrained language models: Weight initializations, data orders, and early stopping. *arXiv preprint arXiv:2002.06305*.

Timothy Dozat and Christopher D Manning. 2017. Deep biaffine attention for neural dependency parsing. In *International Conference on Learning Representations*.

WA Falcon. 2019. Pytorch lightning. *GitHub. Note: https://github.com/PyTorchLightning/pytorch-lightning*, 3.

Ian J Goodfellow, Oriol Vinyals, and Andrew M Saxe. 2014. Qualitatively characterizing neural network optimization problems. *arXiv preprint arXiv:1412.6544*.

Charles R. Harris, K. Jarrod Millman, Stéfan J van der Walt, Ralf Gommers, Pauli Virtanen, David Cournapeau, Eric Wieser, Julian Taylor, Sebastian Berg, Nathaniel J. Smith, Robert Kern, Matti Picus, Stephan Hoyer, Marten H. van Kerkwijk, Matthew Brett, Allan Haldane, Jaime Fernández del Río, Mark Wiebe, Pearu Peterson, Pierre Gérard-Marchant, Kevin Sheppard, Tyler Reddy, Warren Weckesser, Hameer Abbasi, Christoph Gohlke, and Travis E. Oliphant. 2020. Array programming with NumPy. *Nature*, 585:357–362.

Junjie Hu, Sebastian Ruder, Aditya Siddhant, Graham Neubig, Orhan Firat, and Melvin Johnson. 2020. Xtreme: A massively multilingual multi-task benchmark for evaluating cross-lingual generalisation. In *International Conference on Machine Learning*, pages 4411–4421. PMLR.

Phillip Keung, Yichao Lu, Julian Salazar, and Vikas Bhardwaj. 2020. Don't use English dev: On the zero-shot cross-lingual evaluation of contextual embeddings. In *Proceedings of the 2020 Conference on Empirical Methods in Natural Language Processing (EMNLP)*, pages 549–554, Online. Association for Computational Linguistics.

Diederik P Kingma and Jimmy Ba. 2014. Adam: A method for stochastic optimization. *arXiv preprint arXiv:1412.6980*.

James Kirkpatrick, Razvan Pascanu, Neil Rabinowitz, Joel Veness, Guillaume Desjardins, Andrei A Rusu, Kieran Milan, John Quan, Tiago Ramalho, Agnieszka Grabska-Barwinska, et al. 2017. Overcoming catastrophic forgetting in neural networks. *Proceedings of the national academy of sciences*, 114(13):3521–3526.

Cheolhyoung Lee, Kyunghyun Cho, and Wanmo Kang. 2020. Mixout: Effective regularization to finetune large-scale pretrained language models. In *International Conference on Learning Representations*.

Hao Li, Zheng Xu, Gavin Taylor, Christoph Studer, and Tom Goldstein. 2018. Visualizing the loss landscape of neural nets. In *Advances in Neural Information Processing Systems*, volume 31. Curran Associates, Inc.

Zihan Liu, Genta Indra Winata, Andrea Madotto, and Pascale Fung. 2021. Preserving cross-linguality of pre-trained models via continual learning. In *Proceedings of the 6th Workshop on Representation Learning for NLP (RepL4NLP-2021)*, pages 64–71, Online. Association for Computational Linguistics.

Michael McCloskey and Neal J. Cohen. 1989. Catastrophic interference in connectionist networks: The sequential learning problem. *Psychology of Learning and Motivation*, 24:109–165.

Marius Mosbach, Maksym Andriushchenko, and Dietrich Klakow. 2021. On the stability of fine-tuning BERT: Misconceptions, explanations, and strong baselines. In *International Conference on Learning Representations*.

Xiaoman Pan, Boliang Zhang, Jonathan May, Joel Nothman, Kevin Knight, and Heng Ji. 2017. Cross-lingual name tagging and linking for 282 languages. In *Proceedings of the 55th Annual Meeting of the Association for Computational Linguistics (Volume 1: Long Papers)*, pages 1946–1958, Vancouver, Canada. Association for Computational Linguistics.

Adam Paszke, Sam Gross, Soumith Chintala, Gregory Chanan, Edward Yang, Zachary DeVito, Zeming Lin, Alban Desmaison, Luca Antiga, and Adam Lerer. 2017. Automatic differentiation in pytorch.

Fabian Pedregosa, Gaël Varoquaux, Alexandre Gramfort, Vincent Michel, Bertrand Thirion, Olivier Grisel, Mathieu Blondel, Peter Prettenhofer, Ron Weiss, Vincent Dubourg, Jake Vanderplas, Alexandre Passos, David Cournapeau, Matthieu Brucher, Matthieu Perrot, and Édouard Duchesnay. 2011. Scikit-learn: Machine learning in python. *Journal of Machine Learning Research*, 12(85):2825–2830.

Jason Phang, Thibault Févry, and Samuel R Bowman. 2018. Sentence encoders on stilts: Supplementary training on intermediate labeled-data tasks. *arXiv preprint arXiv:1811.01088*.

Thomas Wolf, Lysandre Debut, Victor Sanh, Julien Chaumond, Clement Delangue, Anthony Moi, Pierric Cistac, Tim Rault, Rémi Louf, Morgan Funtowicz, Joe Davison, Sam Shleifer, Patrick von Platen, Clara Ma, Yacine Jernite, Julien Plu, Canwen Xu, Teven Le Scao, Sylvain Gugger, Mariama Drame, Quentin Lhoest, and Alexander M. Rush. 2019. Huggingface's transformers: State-of-the-art natural language processing. *ArXiv*, abs/1910.03771.

Shijie Wu and Mark Dredze. 2019. Beto, bentz, becas: The surprising cross-lingual effectiveness of BERT. In *Proceedings of the 2019 Conference on Empirical Methods in Natural Language Processing and the 9th International Joint Conference on Natural Language Processing (EMNLP-IJCNLP)*, pages 833–844, Hong Kong, China. Association for Computational Linguistics.

Shijie Wu and Mark Dredze. 2020. Do explicit alignments robustly improve multilingual encoders? In *Proceedings of the 2020 Conference on Empirical Methods in Natural Language Processing (EMNLP)*, pages 4471–4482, Online. Association for Computational Linguistics.

Mahsa Yarmohammadi, Shijie Wu, Marc Marone, Haoran Xu, Seth Ebner, Guanghui Qin, Yunmo Chen, Jialiang Guo, Craig Harman, Kenton Murray, et al. 2021. Everything is all it takes: A multipronged strategy for zero-shot cross-lingual information extraction. *arXiv preprint arXiv:2109.06798*.

Daniel Zeman, Joakim Nivre, Mitchell Abrams, Elia Ackermann, Noëmi Aepli, Hamid Aghaei, Željko Agić, Amir Ahmadi, Lars Ahrenberg, Chika Kennedy Ajede, Gabrielė Aleksandravičiūtė, Ika Alfina, Lene Antonsen, Katya Aplonova, Angelina Aquino, Carolina Aragon, Maria Jesus Aranzabe, Hórunn Arnardóttir, Gashaw Arutie, Jessica Naraiswari Arwidarasti, Masayuki Asahara, Luma Ateyah, Furkan Atmaca, Mohammed Attia, Aitziber Atutxa, Liesbeth Augustinus, Elena Badmaeva, Keerthana Balasubramani, Miguel Ballesteros, Esha Banerjee, Sebastian Bank, Verginica Barbu Mititelu, Victoria Basmov, Colin Batchelor, John Bauer, Seyyit Talha Bedir, Kepa Bengoetxea, Gözde Berk, Yevgeni Berzak, Irshad Ahmad Bhat, Riyaz Ahmad Bhat, Erica Biagetti, Eckhard Bick, Agnė Bielinskienė, Kristín Bjarnadóttir, Rogier Blokland, Victoria Bobicev, Loïc Boizou, Emanuel Borges Völker, Carl Börstell, Cristina Bosco, Gosse Bouma, Sam Bowman, Adriane Boyd, Kristina Brokaitė, Aljoscha Burchardt, Marie Candito, Bernard Caron, Gauthier Caron, Tatiana Cavalcanti, Gülşen Cebiroğlu Eryiğit, Flavio Massimiliano Cecchini, Giuseppe G. A. Celano, Slavomír Čéplö, Savas Cetin, Özlem Çetinoğlu, Fabricio Chalub, Ethan Chi, Yongseok Cho, Jinho Choi, Jayeol Chun, Alessandra T. Cignarella, Silvie Cinková, Aurélie Collomb, Çağrı Çöltekin, Miriam Connor, Marine Courtin, Elizabeth Davidson, Marie-Catherine de Marneffe, Valeria de Paiva, Mehmet Oguz Derin, Elvis de Souza, Arantza Diaz de Ilarraza, Carly Dickerson, Arawinda Dinakaramani, Bamba Dione, Peter Dirix, Kaja Dobrovoljc, Timothy Dozat, Kira Droganova, Puneet Dwivedi, Hanne Eckhoff, Marhaba Eli, Ali Elkahky, Binyam Ephrem, Olga Erina, Tomaž Erjavec, Aline Etienne, Wograine Evelyn, Sidney Facundes, Richárd Farkas, Marília Fernanda, Hector Fernandez Alcalde, Jennifer Foster, Cláudia Freitas, Kazunori Fujita, Katarína Gajdošová, Daniel Galbraith, Marcos Garcia, Moa Gärdenfors, Sebastian Garza, Fabrício Ferraz Gerardi, Kim Gerdes, Filip Ginter, Iakes Goenaga, Koldo Gojenola, Memduh Gökırmak, Yoav Goldberg, Xavier Gómez Guinovart, Berta González Saavedra, Bernadeta Griciūtė, Matias Grioni, Loïc Grobol, Normunds Grūzītis, Bruno Guillaume, Céline Guillot-Barbance, Tunga Güngör, Nizar Habash, Hinrik Hafsteinsson, Jan Hajič, Jan Hajič jr., Mika Hämäläinen, Linh Hà Mỹ, Na-Rae Han, Muhammad Yudistira Hanifmuti, Sam Hardwick, Kim Harris, Dag Haug, Johannes Heinecke, Oliver Hellwig, Felix Hennig, Barbora Hladká, Jaroslava Hlaváčová, Florinel Hociung, Petter Hohle, Eva Huber, Jena Hwang, Takumi Ikeda, Anton Karl Ingason, Radu Ion, Elena Irimia, Ọlájídé Ishola, Tomáš Jelínek, Anders Johannsen, Hildur Jónsdóttir, Fredrik Jørgensen, Markus Juutinen, Sarveswaran K, Hüner Kaşıkara, Andre Kaasen, Nadezhda Kabaeva, Sylvain Kahane, Hiroshi Kanayama, Jenna Kanerva, Boris Katz, Tolga Kayadelen, Jessica Kenney, Václava Kettnerová, Jesse Kirchner, Elena Klementieva, Arne Köhn, Abdullatif Köksal, Kamil Kopacewicz, Timo Korkiakangas, Natalia Kotsyba, Jolanta Kovalevskaitė, Simon Krek, Parameswari Krishnamurthy, Sookyoung Kwak, Veronika Laippala, Lucia Lam, Lorenzo Lambertino, Tatiana Lando, Septina Dian Larasati, Alexei Lavrentiev, John Lee, Phng Lê Hồng, Alessandro Lenci, Saran Lertpradit, Herman Leung, Maria Levina, Cheuk Ying Li, Josie Li, Keying Li, Yuan Li, KyungTae Lim, Krister Lindén, Nikola Ljubešić, Olga Loginova, Andry Luthfi, Mikko Luukko, Olga Lyashevskaya, Teresa Lynn, Vivien Macketanz, Aibek Makazhanov, Michael Mandl, Christopher Manning, Ruli Manurung, Cătălina Mărănduc, David Mareček, Katrin Marheinecke, Héctor Martínez Alonso, André Martins, Jan Mašek, Hiroshi Matsuda, Yuji Matsumoto, Ryan McDonald, Sarah McGuinness, Gustavo Mendonça, Niko Miekka, Karina Mischenkova, Margarita Misirpashayeva, Anna Missilä, Cătălin Mititelu, Maria Mitrofan, Yusuke Miyao, AmirHossein Mojiri Foroushani, Amirsaeid Moloodi, Simonetta Montemagni, Amir More, Laura Moreno Romero, Keiko Sophie Mori, Shinsuke Mori, Tomohiko Morioka, Shigeki Moro, Bjartur Mortensen, Bohdan Moskalevskyi, Kadri Muischnek, Robert Munro, Yugo Murawaki, Kaili Müürisep, Pinkey Nainwani, Mariam Nakhlé, Juan Ignacio Navarro Horñiacek, Anna Nedoluzhko, Gunta Nešpore-Bērzkalne, Lng Nguyễn Thị, Huyền Nguyễn Thị Minh, Yoshihiro Nikaido, Vitaly Nikolaev, Rattima Nitisaroj, Alireza Nourian, Hanna Nurmi, Stina Ojala, Atul Kr. Ojha,

Adédayọ Olúòkun, Mai Omura, Emeka Onwuegbuzia, Petya Osenova, Robert Östling, Lilja Øvrelid, Şaziye Betül Özateş, Arzucan Özgür, Balkız Öztürk Başaran, Niko Partanen, Elena Pascual, Marco Passarotti, Agnieszka Patejuk, Guilherme Paulino-Passos, Angelika Peljak-Łapińska, Siyao Peng, Cenel-Augusto Perez, Natalia Perkova, Guy Perrier, Slav Petrov, Daria Petrova, Jason Phelan, Jussi Piitulainen, Tommi A Pirinen, Emily Pitler, Barbara Plank, Thierry Poibeau, Larisa Ponomareva, Martin Popel, Lauma Pretkalniņa, Sophie Prévost, Prokopis Prokopidis, Adam Przepiórkowski, Tiina Puolakainen, Sampo Pyysalo, Peng Qi, Andriela Rääbis, Alexandre Rademaker, Taraka Rama, Loganathan Ramasamy, Carlos Ramisch, Fam Rashel, Mohammad Sadegh Rasooli, Vinit Ravishankar, Livy Real, Petru Rebeja, Siva Reddy, Georg Rehm, Ivan Riabov, Michael Rießler, Erika Rimkutė, Larissa Rinaldi, Laura Rituma, Luisa Rocha, Eiríkur Rögnvaldsson, Mykhailo Romanenko, Rudolf Rosa, Valentin Roșca, Davide Rovati, Olga Rudina, Jack Rueter, Kristján Rúnarsson, Shoval Sadde, Pegah Safari, Benoît Sagot, Aleksi Sahala, Shadi Saleh, Alessio Salomoni, Tanja Samardžić, Stephanie Samson, Manuela Sanguinetti, Dage Särg, Baiba Saulīte, Yanin Sawanakunanon, Kevin Scannell, Salvatore Scarlata, Nathan Schneider, Sebastian Schuster, Djamé Seddah, Wolfgang Seeker, Mojgan Seraji, Mo Shen, Atsuko Shimada, Hiroyuki Shirasu, Muh Shohibussirri, Dmitry Sichinava, Einar Freyr Sigurðsson, Aline Silveira, Natalia Silveira, Maria Simi, Radu Simionescu, Katalin Simkó, Mária Šimková, Kiril Simov, Maria Skachedubova, Aaron Smith, Isabela Soares-Bastos, Carolyn Spadine, Steinþór Steingrímsson, Antonio Stella, Milan Straka, Emmett Strickland, Jana Strnadová, Alane Suhr, Yogi Lesmana Sulestio, Umut Sulubacak, Shingo Suzuki, Zsolt Szántó, Dima Taji, Yuta Takahashi, Fabio Tamburini, Mary Ann C. Tan, Takaaki Tanaka, Samson Tella, Isabelle Tellier, Guillaume Thomas, Liisi Torga, Marsida Toska, Trond Trosterud, Anna Trukhina, Reut Tsarfaty, Utku Türk, Francis Tyers, Sumire Uematsu, Roman Untilov, Zdeňka Urešová, Larraitz Uria, Hans Uszkoreit, Andrius Utka, Sowmya Vajjala, Daniel van Niekerk, Gertjan van Noord, Viktor Varga, Eric Villemonte de la Clergerie, Veronika Vincze, Aya Wakasa, Joel C. Wallenberg, Lars Wallin, Abigail Walsh, Jing Xian Wang, Jonathan North Washington, Maximilan Wendt, Paul Widmer, Seyi Williams, Mats Wirén, Christian Wittern, Tsegay Woldemariam, Tak-sum Wong, Alina Wróblewska, Mary Yako, Kayo Yamashita, Naoki Yamazaki, Chunxiao Yan, Koichi Yasuoka, Marat M. Yavrumyan, Zhuoran Yu, Zdeněk Žabokrtský, Shorouq Zahra, Amir Zeldes, Hanzhi Zhu, and Anna Zhuravleva. 2020. Universal dependencies 2.7. LINDAT/CLARIAH-CZ digital library at the Institute of Formal and Applied Linguistics (ÚFAL), Faculty of Mathematics and Physics, Charles University.

Tianyi Zhang, Felix Wu, Arzoo Katiyar, Kilian Q Weinberger, and Yoav Artzi. 2021. Revisiting few-sample BERT fine-tuning. In *International Conference on Learning Representations*.

Mengjie Zhao, Yi Zhu, Ehsan Shareghi, Ivan Vulić, Roi Reichart, Anna Korhonen, and Hinrich Schütze. 2021. A closer look at few-shot crosslingual transfer: The choice of shots matters. In *Proceedings of the 59th Annual Meeting of the Association for Computational Linguistics and the 11th International Joint Conference on Natural Language Processing (Volume 1: Long Papers)*, pages 5751–5767, Online. Association for Computational Linguistics.

A Fine-tuning Experiments Detail

We follow the implementation and hyperparameter of Wu and Dredze (2020). We optimize with Adam (Kingma and Ba, 2014). The learning rate is `2e-5`. The learning rate scheduler has 10% steps linear warmup then linear decay till 0. We train for 5 epochs and the batch size is 32. For token level tasks, the task-specific layer takes the representation of the first subword, following previous work (Devlin et al., 2019; Wu and Dredze, 2019). Model selection is done on the corresponding dev set of the training set. We fine-tune each model using a single Quadro RTX 6000 and it takes less than one hour except for XNLI.

During fine-tuning, the maximum sequence length is 128. We use a sliding window of context to include subwords beyond the first 128 for NER and POS tagging. At test time, we use the same maximum sequence length with the exception of parsing, where the first 128 words instead of subwords of a sentence were used. We ignore words with POS tags of `SYM` and `PUNCT` during parsing evaluation. For NER, the prediction of `BIO` was post-processed to make sure a valid span is produced.

All datasets we used are publicly available: NER[7], XNLI[8][9], POS tagging and dependency parsing[10]. For POS tagging and dependency parsing, we use the following treebanks: Arabic-PADT, German-GSD, English-EWT, Spanish-GSD, French-GSD, Hindi-HDTB, Russian-GSD, Vietnamese-VTB, and Chinese-GSD. Data statistic can be found in Tab. 1.

B Norm Ratio and Angle of δ_{src} and δ_{tgt}

Fig. 4 plots the relationship between $||\delta_{src}||/||\delta_{tgt}||$ and angle between δ_{src} and δ_{tgt}. We observe most δ_{src} and δ_{tgt} have similar norms, and the angle between them is around 55°.

[7]`https://www.amazon.com/clouddrive/share/d3KGCRCIYwhKJF0H3eWA26hjg2ZCRhjpEQtDL70FSBN`

[8]`https://dl.fbaipublicfiles.com/XNLI/XNLI-MT-1.0.zip`

[9]`https://dl.fbaipublicfiles.com/XNLI/XNLI-1.0.zip`

[10]`https://lindat.mff.cuni.cz/repository/xmlui/handle/11234/1-3424`

	XNLI	NER	POS tagging Parsing
en-train	392703	20000	12543
en-dev	2490	10000	2002
ar-train	392703	20000	6075
ar-dev	2490	10000	909
de-train	392703	20000	13814
de-dev	2490	10000	799
es-train	392703	20000	14187
es-dev	2490	10000	1400
fr-train	392703	20000	14449
fr-dev	2490	10000	1476
hi-train	392703	5000	13304
hi-dev	2490	1000	1659
ru-train	392703	20000	3850
ru-dev	2490	10000	579
vi-train	392703	20000	1400
vi-dev	2490	10000	800
zh-train	392703	20000	3997
zh-dev	2490	10000	500

Table 1: Number of examples.

C Normalized Variance of Linear Interpolated Models

Fig. 5 plots the normalized variance of linear interpolated models.

D Break Down of Normalized Performance of Linear Interpolated Models by Tasks

Fig. 6 (NER), Fig. 7 (Parsing), Fig. 8 (POS), and Fig. 9 (XNLI) plot the normalized performance of linear interpolated models break down by task. We observe similar findings as Fig. 2.

E Additional 2D Linear Interpolation

Fig. 10 plots additional 2D linear interpolation. We observe similar findings as Fig. 3.

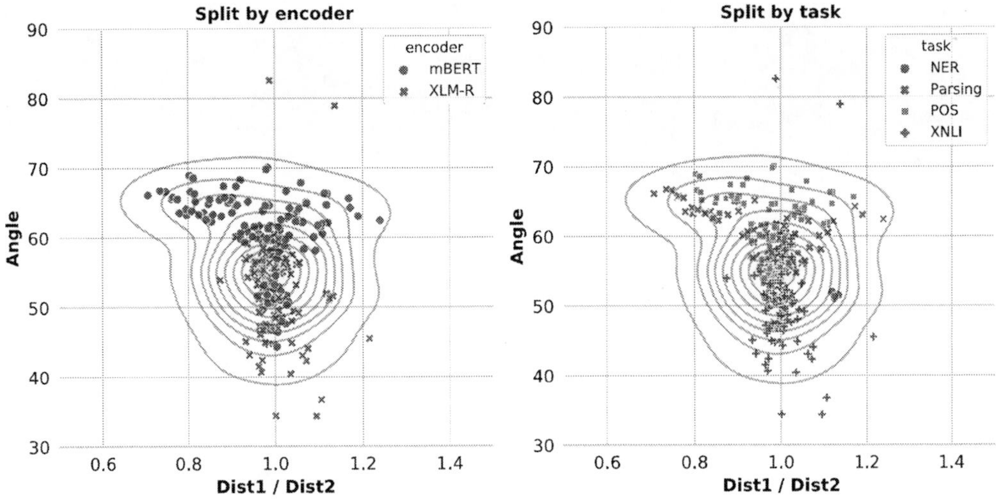

Figure 4: $\|\delta_{src}\|/\|\delta_{tgt}\|$ v.s. angle between δ_{src} and δ_{tgt}. Most δ_{src} and δ_{tgt} have similar norms, and the angle between them is around 55°.

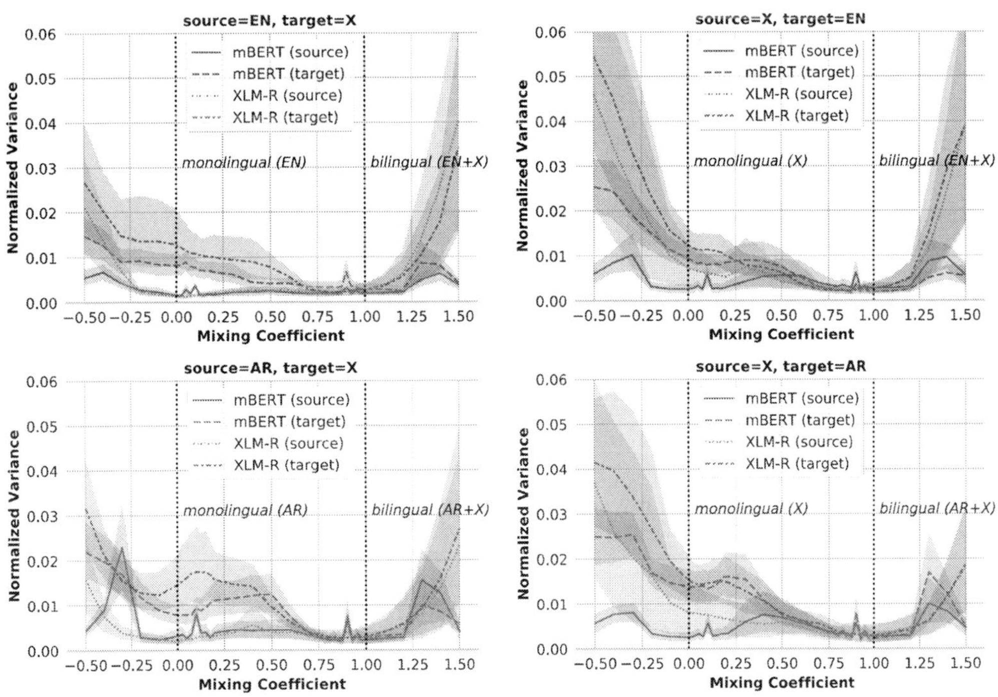

Figure 5: Normalized variance of linear interpolation between monolingual model and bilingual model. The source language has much lower variance compared to target language on the monolingual side of the interpolated models.

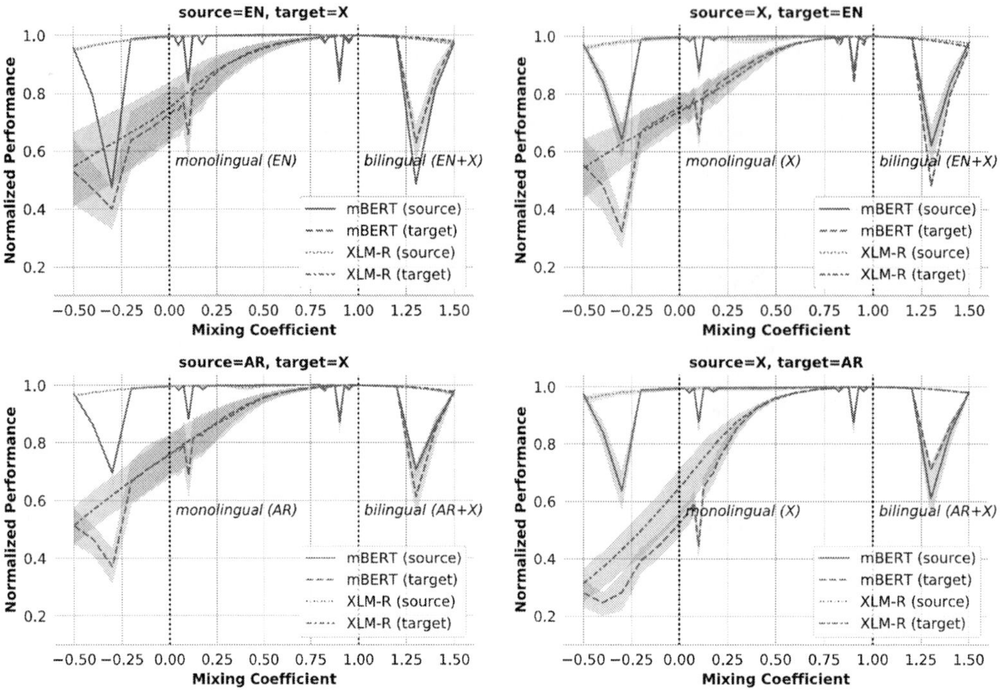

Figure 6: Normalized NER performance of linear interpolated model between monolingual and bilingual model

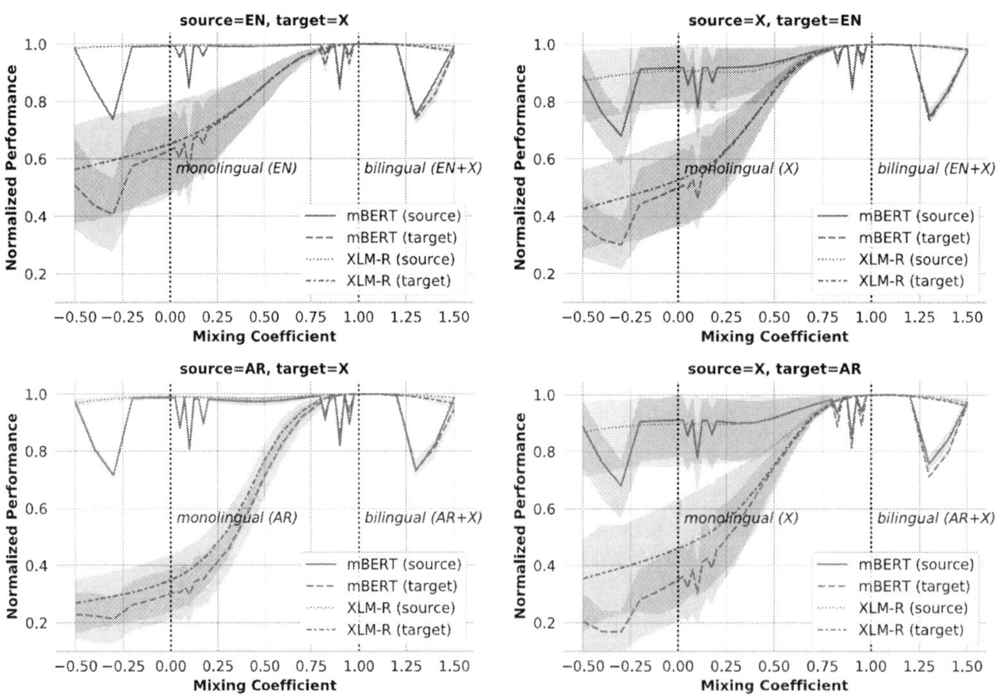

Figure 7: Normalized Parsing performance of linear interpolated model between monolingual and bilingual model

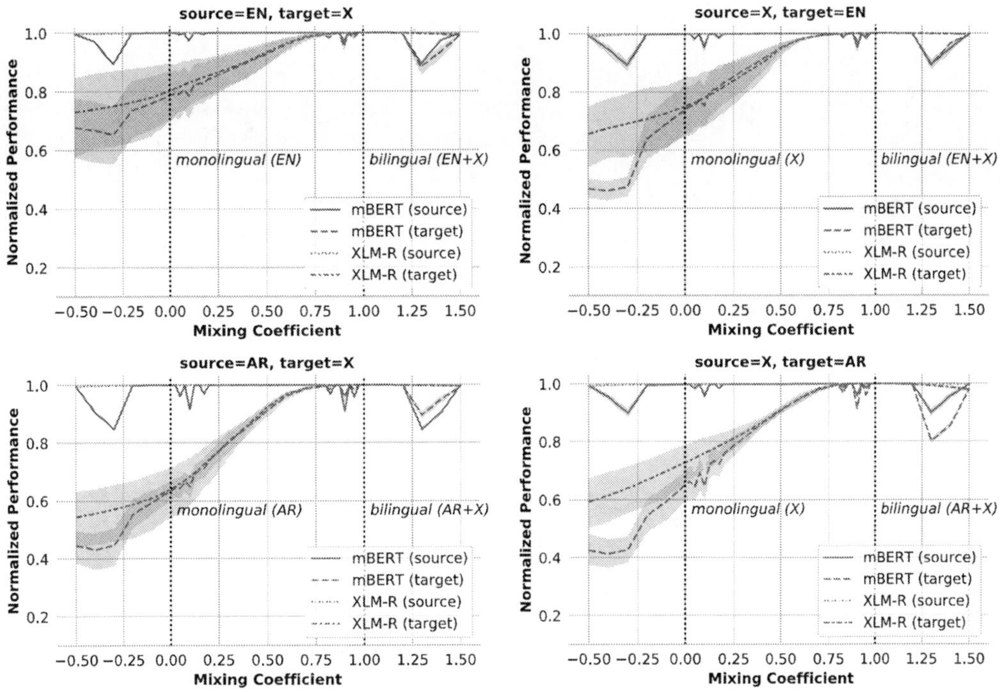

Figure 8: Normalized POS performance of linear interpolated model between monolingual and bilingual model

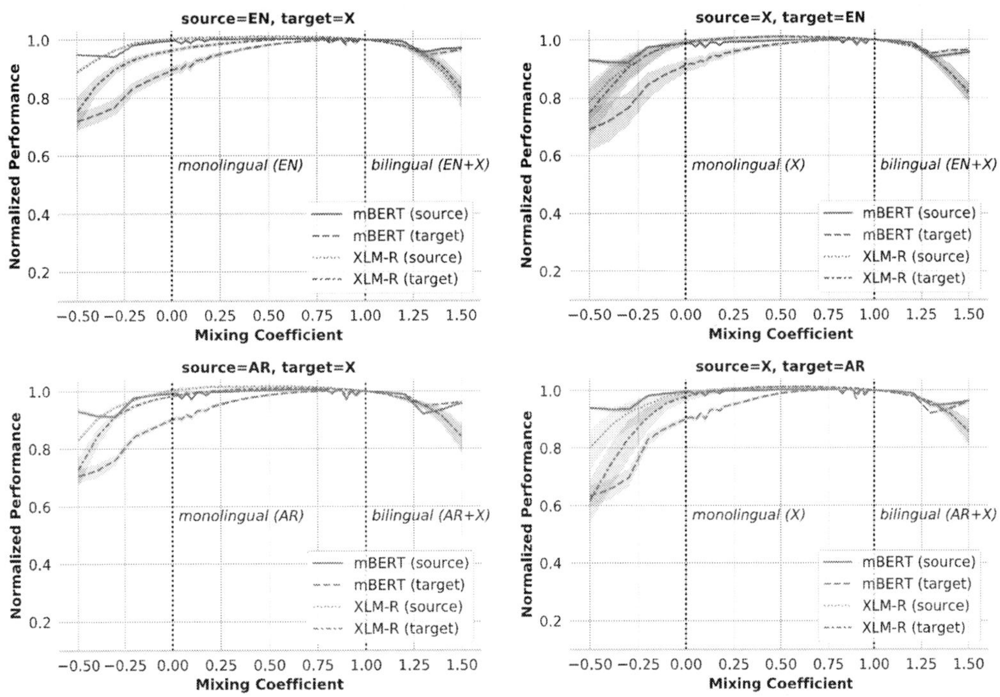

Figure 9: Normalized XNLI performance of linear interpolated model between monolingual and bilingual model

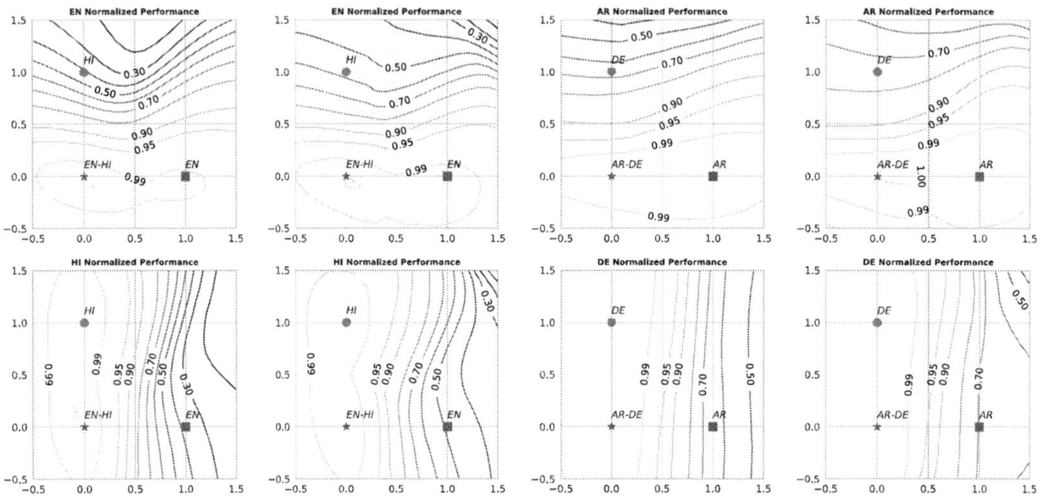

(a) EN-HI Parsing w/ mBERT (b) EN-HI Parsing w/ XLM-R (c) AR-DE POS w/ mBERT (d) AR-DE POS w/ XLM-R

Figure 10: Additional normalized performance of 2D linear interpolation between bilingual model and monolingual models

Same Author or Just Same Topic? Towards Content-Independent Style Representations

Anna Wegmann, Marijn Schraagen and Dong Nguyen
Department of Information and Computing Sciences
Utrecht University
Utrecht, the Netherlands
a.m.wegmann, m.p.schraagen, d.p.nguyen@uu.nl

Abstract

Linguistic style is an integral component of language. Recent advances in the development of style representations have increasingly used training objectives from *authorship verification (AV)*: Do two texts have the same author? The assumption underlying the AV training task (same author approximates same writing style) enables self-supervised and, thus, extensive training. However, a good performance on the AV task does not ensure good "general-purpose" style representations. For example, as the same author might typically write about certain topics, representations trained on AV might also encode content information instead of style alone. We introduce a variation of the AV training task that controls for content using conversation or domain labels. We evaluate whether known style dimensions are represented and preferred over content information through an original variation to the recently proposed STEL framework. We find that representations trained by controlling for conversation are better than representations trained with domain or no content control at representing style independent from content.

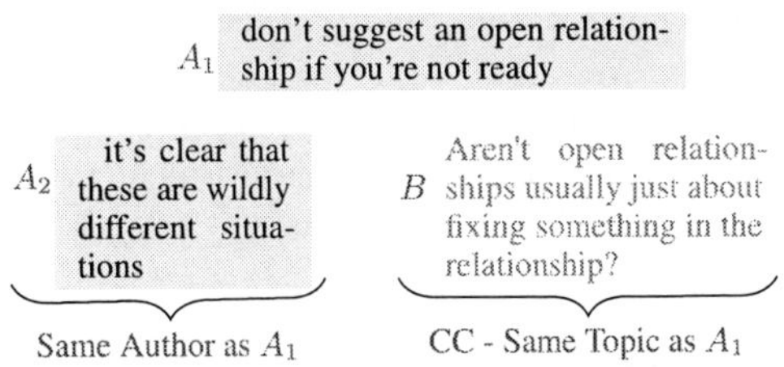

Figure 1: **Contrastive Authorship Verification (CAV) Setup and Content Control (CC) Variable.** The CAV task is to match A_1 with the utterance A_2 that was written by the same author. Contrary to the traditional authorship verification task (AV), this is complemented by a third "constrastive" utterance that was written by a different author (B). In addition to the CAV variation to AV, we experiment with content control (CC) by selecting B and A_1 to have the same approximate content with the help of a topic proxy. As topic proxies we use conversation and domain information.

1 Introduction

Linguistic style (i.e., how something is said) is an integral part of natural language. Style is relevant for natural language understanding and generation (Nguyen et al., 2021; Ficler and Goldberg, 2017) as well as the stylometric analysis of texts (El and Kassou, 2014; Goswami et al., 2009). Applications include author profiling (Rao et al., 2010) and style preservation in machine translation systems (Niu et al., 2017; Rabinovich et al., 2017).

While authors are theoretically able to talk about any topic and (un-)consciously choose to use many styles (e.g., designed to fit an audience (Bell, 1984)), it is typically assumed that there are combinations of style features that are distinctive for an author (sometimes called an author's idiolect). Based on this assumption, the *authorship verification* task (AV) aims to predict whether two texts have been written by the same author (Coulthard, 2004; Neal et al., 2017; Martindale and McKenzie, 1995). Recently, training objectives based on the AV task have been used to train style representations (Boenninghoff et al., 2019b; Hay et al., 2020; Zhu and Jurgens, 2021). Training objectives on AV are especially promising because they do not require any additional labeling when author identifiers are available. Similar to the distributional hypothesis, the assumption underlying the AV training task (same author approximates same writing style) enables extensive self-supervised learning.

Style and content are often correlated (Gero et al., 2019; Bischoff et al., 2020): For example, people might write more formally about their professional career but more informally about personal hobbies. As a result, style representations might encode spurious content correlations (Poliak et al., 2018), especially when their AV training objective does not control for content (Halvani et al., 2019;

Proceedings of the 7th Workshop on Representation Learning for NLP, pages 249 - 268

Sundararajan and Woodard, 2018). Current style representation learning methods either use no or only limited control for content (Hay et al., 2020) or use domain labels to approximate topic (Boenninghoff et al., 2019a). Zhu and Jurgens (2021) work with 24 domain labels (here: product categories) for more than 100k Amazon reviews to improve generalizability. However, using a small set of labels might be too coarse-grained to fully represent and thus control for content. In this paper, we use "content" and "topic" to refer to different concepts. We assume same content (fulfilled if two utterances are paraphrases of each other) implies same topic (e.g., two utterances that discuss personal hobbies), while same topic does not necessarily imply same content.

Approach. We introduce two independent variations to the AV task (see Figure 1): adding a contrastive sentence (CAV setup) and addressing content correlation with a topic proxy (CC). We train several siamese BERT-based neural networks (Reimers and Gurevych, 2019) to compare style representations learned with the new variations to the AV task. We train on utterances from the platform Reddit but our approach could be applied to any other conversation dataset as well. While previous work mostly aimed for learning representations that represent an author's individual style (Boenninghoff et al., 2019b; Hay et al., 2020; Zhu and Jurgens, 2021), we aim for general-purpose style representations. As a result, we evaluate the generated representations on (a) whether known style dimensions (e.g. formal vs. informal) are present in the embedding space (Section 4.2) and preferred over content information (Section 4.3) and (b) whether sentences written by the same author are closer to each other even when they have different content (Section 4.1).

Contribution. With this paper, we (a) contribute an extension of the AV task that aims to control for content (CC) with conversation labels, (b) introduce a novel variation of the AV setup by adding a contrastive utterance (CAV setup), (c) compare style representations trained with different levels of content control (CC) on two task setups (AV and CAV), (d) introduce a variation of the STEL framework (Wegmann and Nguyen, 2021) to evaluate whether representations prefer content over style information and (e) demonstrate found stylistic features via agglomerative clustering. We find that representations trained on the conversation topic proxy are better than representations trained with domain or no content control at representing style independent from content. Additionally, combining the conversation topic proxy with the CAV setup leads to better results than combining it with the AV setup. We show that our representations are sensitive to stylistic features like punctuation and apostrophe types such as ' vs. ' using agglomerative clustering. We hope to further the development of content-controlled style representations. Our code and data are available on GitHub.[1]

2 Related Work

Recently, deep learning approaches have been used in authorship verification (Shrestha et al., 2017; Litvak, 2019; Boenninghoff et al., 2019a; Saedi and Dras, 2021; Hay et al., 2020; Hu et al., 2020; Zhu and Jurgens, 2021). Training on transformer architectures like BERT has been shown to be competitive with other neural as well as non-neural approaches in AV and style representation (Zhu and Jurgens, 2021; Wegmann and Nguyen, 2021). AV methods have controlled for content by restricting the feature space to contain "content-independent" features like function words or character n-grams (Neal et al., 2017; Stamatatos, 2017; Sundararajan and Woodard, 2018). However, even these features have been shown to not necessarily be content-independent (Litvinova, 2020).

Semantic sentence embeddings are typically trained using supervised or self-supervised learning (Reimers and Gurevych, 2019). For supervised learning, models are often trained on manually labelled natural language inference datasets (Conneau et al., 2017). For self-supervised learning, *contrastive* learning objectives (Hadsell et al., 2006) have been increasingly used. Contrastive objectives push semantically distant sentence pairs apart and pull semantically close sentence pairs together. Different strategies for selecting sentence pairs have been used, e.g., same sentences as semantically close vs. randomly sampled as semantically distant sentences (Giorgi et al., 2021; Gao et al., 2021). Reimers and Gurevych (2019) also experiment with a *triplet loss*, which pushes an anchor closer to a semantically close sentence and pulls the same anchor apart from a semantically distant sentence. Semantic representations are typically first evaluated on the task that they have been

[1] https://github.com/nlpsoc/Style-Embeddings

trained on, e.g., binary tasks for binary contrastive objectives and triplet tasks (similar to Figure 1) for triplet objectives (Reimers and Gurevych, 2019). Semantic representations are often also evaluated on the STS benchmark (Cer et al., 2017) or semantic downstream tasks like semantic search, NLI (Bowman et al., 2015; Williams et al., 2018) or SentEval (Conneau and Kiela, 2018).

Typically, objective functions that are known from semantic embedding learning have been used (Hay et al., 2020; Zhu and Jurgens, 2021) with AV training tasks to learn style representations. Zhu and Jurgens (2021) address possible spurious correlations by sampling half of the different and same author utterances from the same and the other half from different domains (e.g., subreddits for `Reddit`). Style representations are often trained and evaluated on the AV task (Boenninghoff et al., 2019a; Zhu and Jurgens, 2021; Bischoff et al., 2020).

3 Style Representation Learning

We describe the new Contrastive Authorship Verification setup (CAV) and our approach to content control (CC) in Section 3.1. Then we describe the generation of training tasks (Section 3.2) and the hyperparameters for model training (Section 3.3).

3.1 Training Task

The authorship verification (AV) task is the task of predicting whether two texts are written by the same or different authors. In the following, we introduce two independent variations to the AV task: Adding (1) contrastive information with the CAV setup and (2) content control via topic proxies.

CAV setup. We introduce an adaption of the Authorship Verification task — the Contrastive Authorship Verification setup (CAV, Figure 1): Given an anchor utterance A_1 and two other utterances A_2 and B, the task is to identify which of the two sentences were written by the same author as A_1. Using a contrastive AV setup adds learnable information to the task (namely the contrast between A_2 and B w.r.t. A_1) and enables the use of learning objectives that require three input sentences and have been successful in semantic embedding learning (Reimers and Gurevych, 2019). We experiment with both CAV and AV setups for style representation learning. In the future, it is also possible to adapt this setup to include several instead of just one contrastive "negative" different author utterance (similar to contrastive semantic learning, e.g., in Gao et al. (2021)). One task with the CAV setup, which consists of three utterances (A_1, A_2, B), can be split up into two AV tasks: (A_1, A_2) and (A_1, B). We compare the CAV and AV setups during evaluation (Section 4).

Content Control (CC). Models optimized for AV have been known to make use of semantic information (Sari et al., 2018; Sundararajan and Woodard, 2018; Potha and Stamatatos, 2018) and to perform badly in cross-topic settings (Halvani et al., 2019; Bischoff et al., 2020). Recent studies use AV tasks to train style representations and address possible correlations by controlling for domain (Zhu and Jurgens, 2021; Boenninghoff et al., 2019b). However, it is unclear to what extent these domain labels are better (or worse) than other ways of controlling for content. We compare three different levels of content control by approximating content with the help of a topic proxy. We sample the utterance pairs written by different authors (B and A_1 for CAV, c.f. Figure 1) (i) from the same *conversation*, (ii) from the same *domain* (e.g., subreddit for `Reddit` as in Zhu and Jurgens (2021)) or (iii) *randomly* (as a baseline, similar to Hay et al. (2020)). Our newly proposed use of the same conversation "topic proxy" is inspired by semantic sentence representation learning, where conversations have previously been used as a proxy for semantic information encoded in utterances (Yang et al., 2018; Liu et al., 2021). We test to what extent the three different topic proxies are contributing to content-independent style representations during evaluation (Section 4.3).

3.2 Task Generation

We use a 2018 `Reddit` sample with utterances from 100 active subreddits[2] extracted via `ConvoKit` (Chang et al., 2020)[3]. Per subreddit, we sample 600 conversations with at least 10 posts (which we call utterances). All subreddits are directed at an English audience, which we infer from the subreddit descriptions.

Generation. We removed all invalid utterances[4]. Then, we split the set of authors into a non-

[2]`https://zissou.infosci.cornell.edu/convokit/datasets/subreddit-corpus/subreddits_small_sample.txt`

[3]MIT license

[4]Utterance of only spaces, tabs, line breaks or of the form: `""`, `" [removed] "`, `"[ removed ]"`, `"[removed]"`, `"[ deleted ]"`, `"[deleted]"`, `" [deleted] "`

CC level	Data Split	Setup # AV	Setup # CAV	Uttterance #	Author #	Author ma	(A_1, A_2) co	(A_1, A_2) do	(A_1, B) co	(A_1, B) do
	train set	420,000	210,000	546,757	194,836	9	0.27	0.56	1.00	1.00
Conversation	dev set	90,000	45,000	116,451	41,848	8	0.26	0.55	1.00	1.00
	test set	90,000	45,000	116,621	41,902	8	0.27	0.55	1.00	1.00
	train set	420,000	210,000	544,587	240,065	9	same pairs		0.01	1.00
Domain	dev set	90,000	45,000	116,490	50,939	8	as		0.02	1.00
	test set	90,000	45,000	116,586	51,182	8	conversation		0.02	1.00
	train set	420,000	210,000	548,082	270,079	9	same pairs		0.00	0.01
No	dev set	90,000	45,000	117,149	57,352	8	as		0.00	0.01
	test set	90,000	45,000	117,434	57,726	8	conversation		0.00	0.02

Table 1: **Data Split Statistics.** Per content control (CC) level, we display the number of tasks per setup (# CAV, # AV), unique utterances and authors for each split. We also show the maximum number of times an author occurs as A_1's author (ma) and the fraction of same author (A_1, A_2) and utterance pairs of different authors (A_1, B) that occur in the same conversation (co) and domain (do).

overlapping 70% train, 15% development and 15% test author split. For each CC level (conversation, domain, no) and each author split, we generated a set of training tasks, i.e., nine sets in total (see Table 1).

First, we generated the tasks for the train split of the dataset with conversation content control. We sampled 210k distinct utterances A_1 from the train author split. We use a weighted sampling process to not overrepresent authors that wrote more utterances than others. The maximum time one author wrote A_1 is 9 (c.f. "ma" in Table 1). Then, for each utterance A_1, we randomly sampled an utterance B that was part of the same conversation as A_1 but written by a different author. Then, for all 210k (A_1, B)-pairs, an utterance A_2 was sampled randomly from all utterances written by the same author as A_1 and for which $A_1 \neq A_2$ holds. We equivalently sampled 45k tasks for the dev and test.

For the domain and no CC level, we reuse A_1 and A_2, to keep as many correlating variables constant as possible. Thus, we only resampled 210k utterances B written by a different author from A_1 by sampling from the same domain or randomly.

We make sure that each combination of (A_1, A_2, B) occurs only once. Thus there are no repeating CAV tasks.[5] However, it is possible that some utterances occur more than once across tasks. In total, we generate 210k train, 45k dev and 45k test tasks for each CC level (see Table 1), corresponding to a total of 420k, 90k and 90k AV-pairs when splitting the CAV task into (A, SA) and (A, DA) pairs (c.f. Section 3.1).

3.3 Training

We use the `Sentence-Transformers`[6] python library (Reimers and Gurevych, 2019)[7] to fine-tune several siamese networks based on (1) 'bert-base-uncased', (2) 'bert-base-cased' (Devlin et al., 2019) and (3) 'roberta-base' (Liu et al., 2019). We expect those to perform well based on previous work (Zhu and Jurgens, 2021; Wegmann and Nguyen, 2021). We compare using (a) contrastive loss (Hadsell et al., 2006) with the AV setup (Section 3.1) tasks and (b) triplet loss (Reimers and Gurevych, 2019) with the CAV setup (Figure 1). The binary contrastive loss function uses a pair of sentences as input while the triplet loss expects three input sentences. For the loss functions, we experiment with three different values for the margin hyperparameter (i) 0.4, (ii) 0.5, (iii) 0.6. We train with a batch size of 8 over 4 epochs using 10% of the training data as warm-up steps. We use the Adam optimizer with the default learning rate (0.00002). We leave all other parameters as default. We use the BinaryClassificationEvaluator on the AV setup with contrastive loss and the TripletEvaluator on the CAV setup with triplet loss from `Sentence-Transformers` to select the best model out of the 4 epochs. The BinaryClassificationEvaluator calculates the accuracy of identifying similar and dissimilar sentences, while the TripletEvaluator checks if the distance between A and SA is smaller than

[5]Due to the sampling process, there might be same author (A_1, A_2) pairs that occur twice. However, this remains unlikely due to the high number of authors and utterances. Overall, the share of repeating pairs remains lower than 1%.

[6]`https://sbert.net/`

[7]with Apache License 2.0

Training Task Setup	CC level	AV Conversation AUC ±σ	AV Domain AUC ±σ	AV No AUC ±σ	CAV Conversation acc ±σ	CAV Domain acc ±σ	CAV No acc ±σ
RoBERTa base		.53	.57	.61	.53	.58	.63
AV	**Conversation**	**.69** ± .02	.70 ± .02	.71 ± .02	**.68** ± .02	.69 ± .02	.70 ± .02
	Domain	.68 ± .01	**.71** ± .01	.73 ± .02	.67 ± .01	**.70** ± .01	.73 ± .00
	No	.58 ± .01	.63 ± .02	**.79** ± .00	.59 ± .01	.66 ± .01	**.78** ± .00
CAV	**Conversation**	**.69** ± .00	.70 ± .00	.71 ± .00	**.68** ± .00	.69 ± .00	.70 ± .00
	Domain	.68 ± .00	.70 ± .00	.72 ± .00	**.68** ± .00	**.70** ± .00	.72 ± .01
	No	.58 ± .00	.63 ± .03	.77 ± .00	.59 ± .00	.65 ± .00	.77 ± .00

Table 2: **Test Results.** Results for 6 different fine-tuned RoBERTa models on the test sets. We display the accuracy of the models for the contrastive authorship verification setup (CAV) and the AUC for the authorship verification task (AV) with different content control approaches (CC). We display the standard deviation (σ). Best performance per column is boldfaced. Models generally outperform others on the CC level they have been trained on.

the distance between A and DA. We use cosine distance as the distance function.

4 Evaluation

We evaluate the learned style representations on the Authorship Verification task (i.e., the training task) in Section 4.1. Then, we evaluate whether models learn to represent known style dimensions via the performance on the STEL framework (Wegmann and Nguyen, 2021) in Section 4.2. Last, we evaluate representations on their content-independence with an original manipulation of STEL (Section 4.3).

4.1 Authorship Verification

We display the AV and CAV performance of trained models in Table 2. On the development sets, RoBERTa models consistently outperformed the cased and uncased BERT models. Also, different margin values only led to small performance differences (Appendix A). Consequently, in Table 2, we only display the performance of the six fine-tuned RoBERTa models on the test sets using the three different content controls (CC) and two different task setups (AV and CAV setups) with constant margin values of 0.5.

AV performance is usually calculated with either (i) AUC or (ii) accuracy using a predetermined threshold (Zhu and Jurgens, 2021; Kestemont et al., 2021). We use cosine similarity to calculate the similarity between sentence representations. Thus, there is no clear constant default threshold to decide between same and different author utterances. A threshold could be fine-tuned on the development set, however for simplicity we use AUC to calculate AV performance instead.We use accuracy for the CAV task — here no threshold is necessary (cosine similarity is calculated between A_1, A_2 and A_1, B and the highest similarity utterance is chosen). This makes the performance scores on the test sets less comparable across setups – however, comparability of the CAV and AV performance scores are limited in any case as the AV vs. CAV setups are fundamentally different. Performance scores can be compared across the same column, i.e., within the same AV and CAV setup. We aggregate performance with mean and standard deviation for three different random seeds per model parameter combination.[8]

Overall, the AV & CAV training task setup (rows in Table 2) lead to similar performance on the test sets. As a result, we do not distinguish between them in this section's discussion. Generally, the representations tested on the CC level they were trained on (diagonal) outperform other models that were not trained with the same CC level. For example, representations trained with the conversation CC level, perform better on the test set with the conversation CC than representations trained with the domain or no CC.

Tasks with the conversation label are hardest to solve. For all models, the performance is lowest on the conversation test set and increases on the domain and further on the random test set. This is in line with our assumption that the conversation test set has semantically closer different author utterance (A_1, B)-pairs that make the AV task harder due to reduced spurious content cues (Section 3.1).

Representations trained with the conversation CC might encode less content information.

[8] We used seeds 103-105. A total of 5 out of 18 models did not learn. We re-trained those with different seeds.

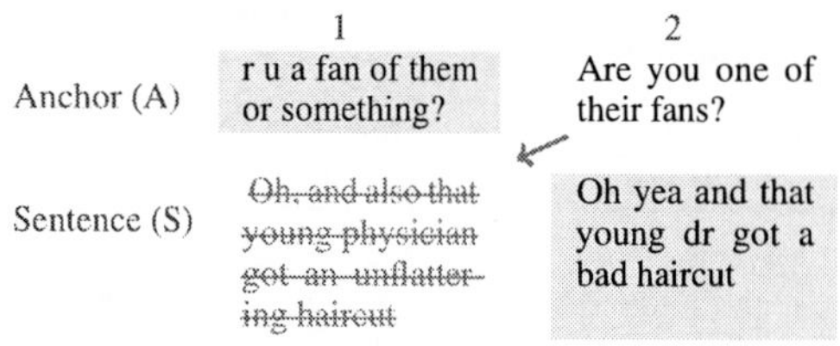

Figure 2: **STEL-Or-Content Task.** We take the original STEL instances (figure without manipulations) and move A2 to the sentence position with the different style (here: the more formal A2 replaces the more formal S1). These resulting triple tasks can test if a model prefers style over content cues.

The average performance across the three CC levels is slightly higher for the models trained with domain than conversation CC level and lowest for no CC. Across the three test sets with the different CC levels, the standard deviation in performance is biggest for models trained without CC and smallest for models trained with the conversation CC. Representations trained with domain or no CC might latch on to more semantic features because they are more helpful on the no and domain CC test sets. Models learned with the conversation CC might in turn learn more content-agnostic representations. Overall, a representation that performs well on the AV task alone might do so by latching on to content (not style) information. As a result, a good AV performance alone might not be indicative of a good representation of style. We further evaluate the quality of style representations and their content-independence in Sections 4.2 and 4.3.

4.2 STEL Task

We calculate the performance of the representations on the STEL framework (Wegmann and Nguyen, 2021)[9]. Here, models are evaluated on whether they are able to measure differences in style across four known dimensions of style (formal vs. informal style, complex vs. simple style, contraction usage and number substitution usage). Models are tested on 1830 tasks of the same setup: Two "sentences" S1 and S2 have to be matched to the style of two given "anchor" sentences A1 and A2. The task is binary. Sentences can either be matched without reordering (A1-S1 & A2-S2) or with reordering (A1-S2 & A2-S1). For example, consider the sentences in Figure 2 before alterations. The correct solution to the task is to reorder the sentences, i.e., to match A1 with S2 because they both exhibit a more informal style and A2 with S1 because they both exhibit a more formal style. The STEL sentence pairs (S1, S2) and (A1, A2) are always paraphrases of each other (in contrast to A_1 and B for the AV task which are only chosen to be about the same approximate topic, c.f. 3.1). The anchor pairs and sentence pairs are randomly matched and are thus otherwise expected to have no connection in content or topic. Representations can thus not make use of learned content features to solve the task.

We display the STEL results for the RoBERTa models in Table 3. **STEL performance is comparable across all fine-tuned models — for all different CC levels and AV & CAV setups.** Surprisingly, the overall STEL performance for the fine-tuned models is lower than that of the original RoBERTa base model (Liu et al., 2019). Thus, models may have 'unlearned' some style information. In the remainder of this subsection, we analyze possible reasons for this STEL performance drop.

Performance stays approximately the same or improves for the formal/informal and the contraction dimensions but drops for the complex/simple and the nb3r substitution dimensions. Based on manual inspection, we notice nb3r substitution to regularly appear in specific conversations and for specific topics. Future work could investigate whether the use of nb3r substitution is less consistent for one author than other stylistic dimensions. As the nb3r dimension of STEL only consists of 100 instances, future work could increase the number of instances. Further, we perform an error analysis to investigate the STEL performance drop in the complex/simple dimension. We manually look at consistently unlearned (i.e., wrongly predicted by the fine-tuned but correctly predicted by the original RoBERTa model) or learned (i.e., wrongly predicted by the RoBERTa model and correctly predicted by the fine-tuned model) STEL instances (see details in Appendix B.1). We find several problematic examples where the correct solution to the task is at least ambiguous. We display two such examples in Table 4. The share of examples with problematic ambiguities is higher for the unlearned (50/55) than for the newly learned STEL instances (29/41).

[9]https://github.com/nlpsoc/STEL, with data from Rao and Tetreault (2018); Xu et al. (2016) and with permission from Yahoo for the "L6 - Yahoo! Answers Comprehensive Questions and Answers version 1.0 (multi part)": https://webscope.sandbox.yahoo.com/catalog.php?datatype=l. Data and code available with MIT License with exceptions for proprietary Yahoo data.

		all		formal, n $= 815$		complex, n $= 815$		nb3r, n $= 100$		c'tion, n $= 100$	
		o	o-c	o	o-c	o	o-c	o	o-c	o	o-c
				acc$\pm\sigma$	acc$\pm\sigma$	acc$\pm\sigma$	acc$\pm\sigma$	acc$\pm\sigma$	acc$\pm\sigma$	acc$\pm\sigma$	acc$\pm\sigma$
org		**.80**	.05	.83	.09	**.73**	.01	**.94**	**.13**	**1.0**	.00
A	c	.71	.35	.83 $\pm$ .02	.64 $\pm$ .00	.57 $\pm$ .02	.13 $\pm$ .04	.61 $\pm$ .02	.04 $\pm$ .01	.91 $\pm$ .10	.00 $\pm$ .01
A	d	.73	.28	.84 $\pm$ .01	.56 $\pm$ .04	.69 $\pm$ .05	.05 $\pm$ .02	.61 $\pm$ .02	.03 $\pm$ .02	.98 $\pm$ .03	.00 $\pm$ .00
A	n	.72	.22	**.85** $\pm$ .01	.46 $\pm$ .04	.57 $\pm$ .01	.03 $\pm$ .01	.62 $\pm$ .04	.05 $\pm$ .02	.98 $\pm$ .01	.00 $\pm$ .00
C	c	.71	**.42**	.81 $\pm$ .02	**.69** $\pm$ .02	.59 $\pm$ .01	**.24** $\pm$ .02	.65 $\pm$ .09	.03 $\pm$ .01	.99 $\pm$ .02	**.04** $\pm$ .02
C	d	.71	.32	.82 $\pm$ .01	.61 $\pm$ .02	.57 $\pm$ .01	.12 $\pm$ .01	.64 $\pm$ .05	.03 $\pm$ .01	.99 $\pm$ .01	.01 $\pm$ .01
C	n	.71	.24	**.85** $\pm$ .00	.50 $\pm$ .02	.56 $\pm$ .01	.04 $\pm$ .01	.59 $\pm$ .03	.06 $\pm$ .01	.98 $\pm$ .04	.00 $\pm$ .00

Table 3: **STEL and STEL-Or-Content Results.** We display STEL accuracy across 4 style dimensions (n =number of instances) for the same RoBERTa models as in Table 2: Per task setup (AV - A, CAV - C) and content control level (conversation - c, domain - d, none - n), the performance on the original (o) and the STEL-Or-Content task instances (o-c) are displayed. Per column, the best performance is boldfaced. For the fine-tuned RoBERTa models, performance generally increases on the STEL-Or-Content task compared to the original RoBERTa model (org).

Generally, the number of complex/simple STEL instances with ambiguities is surprisingly high for both the learned as well as the unlearned instances, consistent with the lower performance of the models in this category. Several of the found ambiguities should be relatively easy to correct in the future (e.g., spelling mistakes or punctuation differences).

4.3 Content-Independence of Style Representations

We tested whether models are able to distinguish between different authors (in Section 4.1) and represent styles when the content remains the same (Section 4.2). However, we have not tested whether models learn to represent style independent from content.

Different approaches have been used to test whether style representations encode unwanted content information, including (a) comparing performance on the AV task across domain (Boenninghoff et al., 2019b; Zhu and Jurgens, 2021), (b) assessing performance on function vs. content words (Hay et al., 2020; Zhu and Jurgens, 2021) and (c) predicting domain labels from utterances using their style representations (Zhu and Jurgens, 2021). However, these evaluation methods have limitations: Domain labels usually come from a small set of coarse-grained labels and function words have been shown to not necessarily be content-independent (Litvinova, 2020). Additionally, next to content, AV might include other spurious features that help increase performance without representing style.

To test if models learn to prefer style over content, we introduce a variation to the STEL framework — the *STEL-Or-Content* task: From one original STEL instance (Section 4.2), we take the sentence that has the same style as A2 and replace it with A2. In Figure 2, this leads to S1 being replaced by A2. The new task is to decide whether A1 matches with the new S1 (originally A2) or with S2. The task is more difficult than the original STEL task as S2 is written in the same style as A1 but has different content and the new S1 is written in a different style but has the same content. The representations will have to decide between giving 'style or content' more weight. This setup is similar to the CAV task (Figure 1). The main differences to the CAV task are (i) that we do not use same author as a proxy for same style but instead use the predefined style dimensions from the STEL framework and (ii) that we control for content with the help of paraphrases (instead of using ony a topic proxy).

We display the STEL-Or-Content results in Table 3. The performance for the new task is low (< 0.5 which corresponds to a random baseline). However, the task is also very difficult as lexical overlap is usually high between the anchor and the false choice (i.e., the sentence that was written in a different style but has the same content). Nevertheless, performance should only be considered in combination with other evaluation approaches (Sections 4.1 and 4.2) as on this task alone models might perform well because they punish same content information.

Models trained on the CAV task with the conversation CC level are the best at representing style independent from content. The performance increases from an accuracy of 0.05 for the original RoBERTa model to up to $0.42\pm.01$ for the representation trained with the CAV task and the

Agg.	GT	Anchor 1 (A1)	Anchor 2 (A2)	Sentence 1 (S1)	Sentence 2 (S2)	Ambiguity
un	✓	TDL Group announced in March 2006, in response to a request [...]	[...] storm names Alberto Helene Beryl Isaac Chris [...]	Palestinian voters in the Gaza Strip [...] were eligible to participate in the election.	1. Palestinian voters in the Gaza Strip [...] were eligible to participate in the election.	A1/A2 have different content
l	✗	[...] 51 Phantom [...] received nominations in that same category.	[...] 1 phantom [...] received nominations in the same category.	[...] the Port Jackson District Commandant could exchange with all military land with buildings on the harbor.	[...] the Port Jackson District Commandant could communicate with all military installations on the harbour.	A2 spelling mistake, S1 sounds unnatural

Table 4: **STEL Error Analysis.** For the complex/simple STEL dimension, we display examples of ambiguous instances that were learned (l) or unlearned (un) the fine-tuned RoBERTa models. A ground truth (GT) of ✓ means that S1 matches with A1 and S2 with A2 in style, while ✗ means S1 matches with A2 and S2 with A1.

conversation CC. This 'CAV conversation representation' did not just learn to punish same content cues because of its performance on the AV task and the STEL framework: (1) On the AV task, the representation performed comparably on all three test sets. If the model had learned to just punish same content cues, we would expect a clearer difference in performance as confounding same content information should be more prevalent for the random than the conversation test set. (2) The representation performed comparably to the other representations on the STEL framework, where style information is needed to solve the task but content information cannot be used.

C #	Consistent	Example
3	no last punct.	I am living in china, they are experiencing an enormous baby boom
4	punctuation / casing	huh thats odd i'm in the 97% percentile on iq tests, the sat, and the act
5	' vs '	I assume it's the blind lady?
7	linebreaks	I admire what you're doing but [...] I know I'm [...]

Table 5: **Clusters for RoBERTa Trained on CAV with Conversation Content Control.** We display one example for 4 out of 7 clusters. We mention noticeable consistencies within the cluster (Consistent).

5 Style Representation Analysis

We want to further understand what the style representations learned to be similar styles. We take the best-performing style representation (RoBERTa trained on the CAV task with the conversation CC and seed 106) and perform agglomerative clustering on a sample of 5.000 CAV tasks of the conversation test set resulting in 14,756 unique utterances. We use 7 clusters based on an analysis of Silhouette scores (Appendix C). Out of all utterance pairs that have the same author, 46.2% appear in the same cluster. This is different from random assignments among 7 clusters[10] which corresponds to 20.1% ± .00. As authors will have a certain variability to their style, a perfect clustering according to general linguistic style would not assign all same author pairs to the same cluster.

In Table 5, we display examples for 4 out of 7 clusters. We manually looked at a few hundred examples per cluster to find consistencies. We found clear consistencies within clusters in the punctuation (e.g., 97% of utterances have no last punctuation mark in Cluster 3 vs. an average of 37% in the other clusters), casing (e.g., 67% of utterances that use *i* instead of *I* appear in Cluster 4), contraction spelling (e.g., 22 out of 27 utterances that use *didnt* instead of *didn't* appear in Cluster 4), the type of apostrophe used (e.g., 90% of utterances use ' vs ' in Cluster 5 vs. an average of 0% in the other clusters) and line breaks within an utterance (e.g., 72% of utterances in Cluster 7 include line breaks vs. an average of 22% in the other clusters). We mostly found letter-level consistencies — likely because they are easiest to spot manually. We expect representations to also capture more complex stylometric information because of their performance on the AV and STEL tasks (Section 4). Future work could analyze whether and what other stylistic consistencies are represented by the models.

For comparison we also cluster with the base RoBERTa model (see Appendix D). The only three interesting RoBERTa clusters (i.e., clusters 2,3,4

[10]Calculated mean and standard deviation of 100 random assignments of utterances to the 7 clusters of the same size.

that contain more than three elements and not as many as 86.7% of all utterances), seem to mostly differ in utterance length (average number of characters are 15 in Cluster 2 vs. in 1278 in Cluster 3) and in the presence of hyperlinks (84% of utterances contain 'https://' in Cluster 4 vs. an overall average of 2%). Average utterance lengths are not as clearly separated by the clusters of the trained style representations.

6 Limitations and Future Work

We propose several directions for future research:

First, conversation labels are already inherently available in conversation corpora like `Reddit`. However, it remains a difficulty to transfer the conversation CC to other than conversation datasets. Moreover, even when using the conversation CC, content information might still be useful for AV: If one person writes "my husband" and another writes "my wife" within the same conversation, it is highly unlikely that those utterances have been generated by the same person. With the recent advances in semantic sentence embeddings, it might be interesting to train style representations on CAV tasks with a new content control level: Two utterances could be labelled as having the same content if their semantic embeddings are close to each other (e.g., when cosine similarity is above a certain threshold).

Second, for the `STEL`-Or-Content task, the so-called "triplet problem" (Wegmann and Nguyen, 2021) remains a potential problem. Consider the example in Figure 2. Here, the `STEL` framework only guarantees that A1 is more informal than A2 and S2 is more informal than S1. Thus, in some cases A2 can be stylistically closer to A1 than S2. However, we expect this case to be less prevalent: A2 would need to be already pretty close in style to A1, or both S2 and S1 would need to be substantially more informal or formal than A1. In the future, removing problematic instances could alleviate a possible maximum performance cap.

Third, the representation models may learn to represent individual stylistic variation as we use utterances from the same individual author as positive signals (c.f. Zhu and Jurgens (2021)). However, because the representation models learn with same author pairs that are generated from thousands of authors, it is likely that they also learn consistencies along groups of authors that use similar style features (e.g., demographic groups based on age or education level, or subreddit communities). Future work could explore how different CC levels and training tasks influence the type of styles that are learned.

7 Conclusion

Recent advances in the development of style representations have increasingly used training objectives from authorship verification (Hay et al., 2020; Zhu and Jurgens, 2021). However, representations that perform well on the Authorship Verification (AV) task might do so not because they represent style well but because they latch on to spurious content correlations. We train different style representations by controlling for content (CC) using conversation or domain membership as a proxy for topic. We also introduce the new Contrastive Authorship Verification setup (CAV) and compare it to the usual AV setup. We propose an original adaptation of the recent `STEL` framework (Wegmann and Nguyen, 2021) to test whether learned representations favor style over content information. We find that representations that were trained on the CAV setup with conversation CC represent style in a way that is more independent from content than models using other CC levels or the AV setup. We demonstrate some of the learned stylistic differences via agglomerative clustering — e.g., the use of a right single quotation mark vs. an apostrophe in contractions. We hope to contribute to increased efforts towards learning general-purpose content-controlled style representations.

Ethical Considerations

We use utterances taken from 100 subcommunities (i.e., subreddits) of the popular online platform `Reddit` to train style representations with different training tasks and compare their performance. With our work, we aim to contribute to the development of general style representations that are disentangled from content. Style representations have the potential to increase classification performance for diverse demographics and social groups (Hovy, 2015).

The user demographics on the selected 100 subreddits are likely skewed towards particular demographics. For example, locally based subreddits (e.g., canada, singapore) might be over-represented. Generally, the average `Reddit` user is typically more likely to be young and male.[11] Thus, our representations might not be representative of (English) language use across different social groups. However, experiments on the set of 100 distinct subreddits should still demonstrate the possibilities of the used approaches and methods. We hope the ethical impact of reusing the already published `Reddit` dataset (Baumgartner et al., 2020; Chang et al., 2020) to be small but acknowledge that reusing it will lead to increased visibility of data that is potentially privacy infringing. As we aggregate the styles of thousands of users to calculate style representations, we expect it to not be indicative of individual users.

We confirm to have read and that we abide by the ACL Code of Ethics.

Acknowledgements

We thank the anonymous ARR reviewers for their helpful comments. This research was supported by the "Digital Society - The Informed Citizen" research programme, which is (partly) financed by the Dutch Research Council (NWO), project 410.19.007. Dong Nguyen was supported by the research programme Veni with project number VI.Veni.192.130, which is (partly) financed by the Dutch Research Council (NWO).

References

Jason Baumgartner, Savvas Zannettou, Brian Keegan, Megan Squire, and Jeremy Blackburn. 2020. The Pushshift Reddit dataset. In *Proceedings of the International AAAI Conference on Web and Social Media*, pages 830–839, Atlanta, USA. Association for the Advancement of Artificial Intelligence.

Allan Bell. 1984. Language style as audience design. *Language in Society*, 13(2):145–204.

Sebastian Bischoff, Niklas Deckers, Marcel Schliebs, Ben Thies, Matthias Hagen, Efstathios Stamatatos, Benno Stein, and Martin Potthast. 2020. The importance of suppressing domain style in authorship analysis. *arXiv preprint 2005.14714*.

Benedikt Boenninghoff, Steffen Hessler, Dorothea Kolossa, and Robert M. Nickel. 2019a. Explainable authorship verification in social media via attention-based similarity learning. In *2019 IEEE International Conference on Big Data (Big Data)*, pages 36–45.

[11]https://www.journalism.org/2016/02/25/reddit-news-users-more-likely-to-be-male-young-and-digital-in-their-news-preferences/

Benedikt Boenninghoff, Robert M. Nickel, Steffen Zeiler, and Dorothea Kolossa. 2019b. Similarity learning for authorship verification in social media. In *ICASSP 2019 - 2019 IEEE International Conference on Acoustics, Speech and Signal Processing (ICASSP)*, pages 2457–2461.

Samuel R. Bowman, Gabor Angeli, Christopher Potts, and Christopher D. Manning. 2015. A large annotated corpus for learning natural language inference. In *Proceedings of the 2015 Conference on Empirical Methods in Natural Language Processing*, pages 632–642, Lisbon, Portugal. Association for Computational Linguistics.

Daniel Cer, Mona Diab, Eneko Agirre, Iñigo Lopez-Gazpio, and Lucia Specia. 2017. SemEval-2017 task 1: Semantic textual similarity multilingual and crosslingual focused evaluation. In *Proceedings of the 11th International Workshop on Semantic Evaluation (SemEval-2017)*, pages 1–14, Vancouver, Canada. Association for Computational Linguistics.

Jonathan P. Chang, Caleb Chiam, Liye Fu, Andrew Wang, Justine Zhang, and Cristian Danescu-Niculescu-Mizil. 2020. ConvoKit: A toolkit for the analysis of conversations. In *Proceedings of the 21th Annual Meeting of the Special Interest Group on Discourse and Dialogue*, pages 57–60, 1st virtual meeting. Association for Computational Linguistics.

Alexis Conneau and Douwe Kiela. 2018. SentEval: An evaluation toolkit for universal sentence representations. In *Proceedings of the Eleventh International Conference on Language Resources and Evaluation (LREC 2018)*, Miyazaki, Japan. European Language Resources Association (ELRA).

Alexis Conneau, Douwe Kiela, Holger Schwenk, Loïc Barrault, and Antoine Bordes. 2017. Supervised learning of universal sentence representations from natural language inference data. In *Proceedings of the 2017 Conference on Empirical Methods in Natural Language Processing*, pages 670–680, Copenhagen, Denmark. Association for Computational Linguistics.

Malcolm Coulthard. 2004. Author identification, idiolect, and linguistic uniqueness. *Applied linguistics*, 25(4):431–447.

Jacob Devlin, Ming-Wei Chang, Kenton Lee, and Kristina Toutanova. 2019. BERT: Pre-training of deep bidirectional transformers for language understanding. In *Proceedings of the 2019 Conference of the North American Chapter of the Association for Computational Linguistics: Human Language Technologies, Volume 1 (Long and Short Papers)*, pages 4171–4186, Minneapolis, Minnesota. Association for Computational Linguistics.

Sara El Manar El and Ismail Kassou. 2014. Authorship analysis studies: A survey. *International Journal of Computer Applications*, 86(12).

Jessica Ficler and Yoav Goldberg. 2017. Controlling linguistic style aspects in neural language generation. In *Proceedings of the Workshop on Stylistic Variation*, pages 94–104, Copenhagen, Denmark. Association for Computational Linguistics.

Tianyu Gao, Xingcheng Yao, and Danqi Chen. 2021. SimCSE: Simple contrastive learning of sentence embeddings. In *Proceedings of the 2021 Conference on Empirical Methods in Natural Language Processing*, pages 6894–6910, Online and Punta Cana, Dominican Republic. Association for Computational Linguistics.

Katy Gero, Chris Kedzie, Jonathan Reeve, and Lydia Chilton. 2019. Low level linguistic controls for style transfer and content preservation. In *Proceedings of the 12th International Conference on Natural Language Generation*, pages 208–218, Tokyo, Japan. Association for Computational Linguistics.

John Giorgi, Osvald Nitski, Bo Wang, and Gary Bader. 2021. DeCLUTR: Deep contrastive learning for unsupervised textual representations. In *Proceedings of the 59th Annual Meeting of the Association for Computational Linguistics and the 11th International Joint Conference on Natural Language Processing (Volume 1: Long Papers)*, pages 879–895, Online. Association for Computational Linguistics.

Sumit Goswami, Sudeshna Sarkar, and Mayur Rustagi. 2009. Stylometric analysis of bloggers' age and gender. In *Proceedings of the International AAAI Conference on Web and Social Media (Volume 3)*, pages 214–217.

Raia Hadsell, Sumit Chopra, and Yann LeCun. 2006. Dimensionality reduction by learning an invariant mapping. In *IEEE Computer Society Conference on Computer Vision and Pattern Recognition - Volume 2 (CVPR'06)*, pages 1735–1742.

Oren Halvani, Christian Winter, and Lukas Graner. 2019. Assessing the applicability of authorship verification methods. In *Proceedings of the 14th International Conference on Availability, Reliability and Security (ARES '19)*, New York, NY, USA. Association for Computing Machinery.

Charles R. Harris, K. Jarrod Millman, Stéfan J. van der Walt, Ralf Gommers, Pauli Virtanen, David Cournapeau, Eric Wieser, Julian Taylor, Sebastian Berg, Nathaniel J. Smith, Robert Kern, Matti Picus, Stephan Hoyer, Marten H. van Kerkwijk, Matthew Brett, Allan Haldane, Jaime Fernández del Río, Mark Wiebe, Pearu Peterson, Pierre Gérard-Marchant, Kevin Sheppard, Tyler Reddy, Warren Weckesser, Hameer Abbasi, Christoph Gohlke, and Travis E. Oliphant. 2020. Array programming with NumPy. *Nature*, 585(7825):357–362.

Julien Hay, Bich-Lien Doan, Fabrice Popineau, and Ouassim Ait Elhara. 2020. Representation learning of writing style. In *Proceedings of the Sixth Workshop on Noisy User-generated Text (W-NUT 2020)*, pages 232–243, Online. Association for Computational Linguistics.

Dirk Hovy. 2015. Demographic factors improve classification performance. In *Proceedings of the 53rd Annual Meeting of the Association for Computational Linguistics and the 7th International Joint Conference on Natural Language Processing (Volume 1: Long Papers)*, pages 752–762, Beijing, China. Association for Computational Linguistics.

Zhiqiang Hu, Roy Ka-Wei Lee, Lei Wang, Ee-peng Lim, and Bo Dai. 2020. Deepstyle: User style embedding for authorship attribution of short texts. In *Web and Big Data*, pages 221–229, Cham. Springer International Publishing.

Mike Kestemont, Enrique Manjavacas, Ilia Markov, Janek Bevendorff, Matti Wiegmann, Efstathios Stamatatos, Benno Stein, and Martin Potthast. 2021. Overview of the cross-domain authorship verification task at PAN 2021. In *Proceedings of the Working Notes of CLEF 2021*, pages 1743–1759, Bucharest, Romania.

Marina Litvak. 2019. Deep dive into authorship verification of email messages with convolutional neural network. In *5th International Conference on Information Management and Big Data*, pages 129–136, Lima, Peru. Springer International Publishing.

Tatiana Litvinova. 2020. Stylometrics features under domain shift: Do they really "context-independent"? In *22nd International Conference on Speech and Computer*, pages 279–290, Cham. Springer International Publishing.

Che Liu, Rui Wang, Jinghua Liu, Jian Sun, Fei Huang, and Luo Si. 2021. DialogueCSE: Dialogue-based contrastive learning of sentence embeddings. In *Proceedings of the 2021 Conference on Empirical Methods in Natural Language Processing*, pages 2396–2406, Online and Punta Cana, Dominican Republic. Association for Computational Linguistics.

Yinhan Liu, Myle Ott, Naman Goyal, Jingfei Du, Mandar Joshi, Danqi Chen, Omer Levy, Mike Lewis, Luke Zettlemoyer, and Veselin Stoyanov. 2019. RoBERTa: A robustly optimized BERT pretraining approach. *arXiv preprint 1907.11692*.

Colin Martindale and Dean McKenzie. 1995. On the utility of content analysis in author attribution: "the federalist". *Computers and the Humanities*, 29(4):259–270.

Tempestt Neal, Kalaivani Sundararajan, Aneez Fatima, Yiming Yan, Yingfei Xiang, and Damon Woodard. 2017. Surveying stylometry techniques and applications. *ACM Computing Surveys*, 50(6).

Dong Nguyen, Laura Rosseel, and Jack Grieve. 2021. On learning and representing social meaning in NLP: a sociolinguistic perspective. In *Proceedings of the 2021 Conference of the North American Chapter of the Association for Computational Linguistics: Human Language Technologies*, pages 603–612, Online. Association for Computational Linguistics.

Xing Niu, Marianna Martindale, and Marine Carpuat. 2017. A study of style in machine translation: Controlling the formality of machine translation output. In *Proceedings of the 2017 Conference on Empirical Methods in Natural Language Processing*, pages 2814–2819, Copenhagen, Denmark. Association for Computational Linguistics.

F. Pedregosa, G. Varoquaux, A. Gramfort, V. Michel, B. Thirion, O. Grisel, M. Blondel, P. Prettenhofer, R. Weiss, V. Dubourg, J. Vanderplas, A. Passos, D. Cournapeau, M. Brucher, M. Perrot, and E. Duchesnay. 2011. Scikit-learn: Machine learning in Python. *Journal of Machine Learning Research*, 12:2825–2830.

Adam Poliak, Jason Naradowsky, Aparajita Haldar, Rachel Rudinger, and Benjamin Van Durme. 2018. Hypothesis only baselines in natural language inference. In *Proceedings of the Seventh Joint Conference on Lexical and Computational Semantics*, pages 180–191, New Orleans, Louisiana. Association for Computational Linguistics.

Nektaria Potha and Efstathios Stamatatos. 2018. Intrinsic author verification using topic modeling. In *Proceedings of the 10th Hellenic Conference on Artificial Intelligence*, SETN '18, New York, NY, USA. Association for Computing Machinery.

Ella Rabinovich, Raj Nath Patel, Shachar Mirkin, Lucia Specia, and Shuly Wintner. 2017. Personalized machine translation: Preserving original author traits. In *Proceedings of the 15th Conference of the European Chapter of the Association for Computational Linguistics: Volume 1, Long Papers*, pages 1074–1084, Valencia, Spain. Association for Computational Linguistics.

Delip Rao, David Yarowsky, Abhishek Shreevats, and Manaswi Gupta. 2010. Classifying latent user attributes in Twitter. In *Proceedings of the 2nd International Workshop on Search and Mining User-Generated Contents*, SMUC '10, page 37–44, New York, NY, USA. Association for Computing Machinery.

Sudha Rao and Joel Tetreault. 2018. Dear sir or madam, may I introduce the GYAFC dataset: Corpus, benchmarks and metrics for formality style transfer. In *Proceedings of the 2018 Conference of the North American Chapter of the Association for Computational Linguistics: Human Language Technologies, Volume 1 (Long Papers)*, pages 129–140, New Orleans, Louisiana. Association for Computational Linguistics.

Nils Reimers and Iryna Gurevych. 2019. Sentence-BERT: Sentence embeddings using Siamese BERT-networks. In *Proceedings of the 2019 Conference on Empirical Methods in Natural Language Processing and the 9th International Joint Conference on Natural Language Processing (EMNLP-IJCNLP)*, pages 3982–3992, Hong Kong, China. Association for Computational Linguistics.

Chakaveh Saedi and Mark Dras. 2021. Siamese networks for large-scale author identification. *Computer Speech & Language*, 70:101241.

Yunita Sari, Mark Stevenson, and Andreas Vlachos. 2018. Topic or style? Exploring the most useful features for authorship attribution. In *Proceedings of the 27th International Conference on Computational Linguistics*, pages 343–353, Santa Fe, New Mexico, USA. Association for Computational Linguistics.

Prasha Shrestha, Sebastian Sierra, Fabio González, Manuel Montes, Paolo Rosso, and Thamar Solorio. 2017. Convolutional neural networks for authorship attribution of short texts. In *Proceedings of the 15th Conference of the European Chapter of the Association for Computational Linguistics: Volume 2, Short Papers*, pages 669–674, Valencia, Spain. Association for Computational Linguistics.

Efstathios Stamatatos. 2017. Masking topic-related information to enhance authorship attribution. *Journal of the Association for Information Science and Technology*, 69(3):461–473.

Kalaivani Sundararajan and Damon Woodard. 2018. What represents "style" in authorship attribution? In *Proceedings of the 27th International Conference on Computational Linguistics*, pages 2814–2822, Santa Fe, New Mexico, USA. Association for Computational Linguistics.

Pauli Virtanen, Ralf Gommers, Travis E. Oliphant, Matt Haberland, Tyler Reddy, David Cournapeau, Evgeni Burovski, Pearu Peterson, Warren Weckesser, Jonathan Bright, Stéfan J. van der Walt, Matthew Brett, Joshua Wilson, K. Jarrod Millman, Nikolay Mayorov, Andrew R. J. Nelson, Eric Jones, Robert Kern, Eric Larson, C J Carey, İlhan Polat, Yu Feng, Eric W. Moore, Jake VanderPlas, Denis Laxalde, Josef Perktold, Robert Cimrman, Ian Henriksen, E. A. Quintero, Charles R. Harris, Anne M. Archibald, Antônio H. Ribeiro, Fabian Pedregosa, Paul van Mulbregt, and SciPy 1.0 Contributors. 2020. SciPy 1.0: Fundamental Algorithms for Scientific Computing in Python. *Nature Methods*, 17:261–272.

Anna Wegmann and Dong Nguyen. 2021. Does it capture STEL? A modular, similarity-based linguistic style evaluation framework. In *Proceedings of the 2021 Conference on Empirical Methods in Natural Language Processing*, pages 7109–7130, Online and Punta Cana, Dominican Republic. Association for Computational Linguistics.

Adina Williams, Nikita Nangia, and Samuel Bowman. 2018. A broad-coverage challenge corpus for sentence understanding through inference. In *Proceedings of the 2018 Conference of the North American*

Chapter of the Association for Computational Linguistics: Human Language Technologies, Volume 1 (Long Papers), pages 1112–1122, New Orleans, Louisiana. Association for Computational Linguistics.

Wei Xu, Courtney Napoles, Ellie Pavlick, Quanze Chen, and Chris Callison-Burch. 2016. Optimizing statistical machine translation for text simplification. *Transactions of the Association for Computational Linguistics*, 4:401–415.

Yinfei Yang, Steve Yuan, Daniel Cer, Sheng-yi Kong, Noah Constant, Petr Pilar, Heming Ge, Yun-Hsuan Sung, Brian Strope, and Ray Kurzweil. 2018. Learning semantic textual similarity from conversations. In *Proceedings of The Third Workshop on Representation Learning for NLP*, pages 164–174, Melbourne, Australia. Association for Computational Linguistics.

Jian Zhu and David Jurgens. 2021. Idiosyncratic but not arbitrary: Learning idiolects in online registers reveals distinctive yet consistent individual styles. In *Proceedings of the 2021 Conference on Empirical Methods in Natural Language Processing*, pages 279–297, Online and Punta Cana, Dominican Republic. Association for Computational Linguistics.

A Results on the Development Set

A.1 Hyperparameter Tuning

We evaluated contrastive (on the AV training setup), triple (on the CAV training setup) and online contrastive loss (on the AV training setup) using implementations from `Sentence-Transformers`. We experiment with the loss hyperparameter "margin" with values of 0.4, 0.5, 0.6 for the uncased BERT model (Devlin et al., 2019) on the domain training data. Results are displayed in Figure 6. Contrastive and triplet loss perform better than online contrastive loss. The margin value only has a small influence on the performance scores. Based on these results, we decided to run all further models only with the contrastive and triplet loss functions and a margin value of 0.5.

	conversation		domain		no	
	CAV	AV	CAV	AV	CAV	AV
	acc	auc	acc	auc	acc	auc
c 0.4	0.63	0.63	**0.68**	**0.68**	**0.71**	**0.71**
c 0.5	0.63	0.63	**0.68**	**0.68**	**0.71**	**0.71**
c 0.6	0.62	0.63	**0.68**	**0.68**	**0.71**	**0.71**
t 0.4	0.63	0.62	0.68	0.67	0.70	0.70
t 0.5	**0.64**	**0.64**	**0.68**	**0.68**	0.70	0.70
t 0.6	0.63	0.63	0.67	0.67	0.70	0.70
c-on 0.4	0.58	0.58	0.64	0.64	0.67	0.67
c-on 0.5	0.58	0.58	0.64	0.64	0.67	0.67
c-on 0.6	0.58	0.58	0.64	0.64	0.67	0.67

Table 6: **Hyperparameter-tuning results on the dev AV and CAV datasets with varying content control.** Results for BERT uncased trained on the contrastive authorship verification tasks (CAV). With different loss functions (contrastive - c, triple - t, contrastive online - c-on) and margin values (0.4, 0.5, 0.6). For each dev set (conversation, domain and no content control), we display the accuracy of the models for the CAV task and the AUC for the authorship verification task (AV). For each dev set and CAV/AV setup, the best performance is boldfaced. contrastive and triple loss behave comparable. The margin value only has a small influence.

		conv		sub		no	
		CAV	AV	CAV	AV	CAV	AV
		acc	AUC	acc	AUC	acc	AUC
-	bert	0.52	0.51	0.59	0.57	0.64	0.61
	BERT	0.53	0.52	0.59	0.57	0.63	0.60
	RoBERTa	0.53	0.53	0.58	0.57	0.63	0.61
c	bert c 0.5	0.65	0.66	0.66	0.67	0.68	0.68
	bert t 0.5	0.65	0.66	0.66	0.67	0.67	0.68
	BERT c 0.5	0.66	0.67	0.67	0.68	0.69	0.70
	BERT t 0.5	0.66	0.67	0.67	0.68	0.68	0.69
	RoBERTa c 0.5	**0.69**	**0.70**	0.70	0.71	0.70	0.72
	RoBERTa t 0.5	0.68	0.69	0.69	0.70	0.70	0.70
s	bert c 0.5	0.63	0.63	0.68	0.68	0.71	0.71
	bert t 0.5	0.64	0.64	0.68	0.68	0.70	0.70
	BERT t 0.5	0.65	0.65	0.68	0.68	0.71	0.71
	BERT c 0.5	0.64	0.65	0.69	0.69	0.71	0.72
	RoBERTa c 0.5	0.67	0.68	**0.71**	**0.72**	0.73	0.74
	RoBERTa t 0.5	0.68	0.68	0.70	0.70	0.72	0.73
r	bert c-0.5	0.55	0.54	0.63	0.62	0.76	0.76
	bert t-0.5	0.55	0.54	0.62	0.61	0.74	0.75
	BERT c 0.5	0.57	0.56	0.64	0.63	0.76	0.77
	BERT t 0.5	0.58	0.56	0.64	0.62	0.75	0.75
	RoBERTa c 0.5	0.59	0.58	0.65	0.64	**0.77**	**0.78**
	RoBERTa t 0.5	0.59	0.57	0.65	0.63	**0.77**	0.77

(a) CAV and AV Performance

		conv		sub		no	
		AV		AV		AV	
		thr	acc	thr	acc	thr	acc
-	bert	0.82	0.51	0.70	0.55	0.69	0.58
	BERT	0.86	0.51	0.85	0.55	0.85	0.58
	RoBERTa	0.96	0.52	0.97	0.55	0.97	0.58
c	bert c 0.5	0.72	0.61	0.73	0.62	0.73	0.63
	bert t 0.5	0.27	0.61	0.27	0.62	0.29	0.63
	BERT c 0.5	0.24	0.62	0.28	0.63	0.26	0.64
	BERT t 0.5	0.72	0.62	0.73	0.63	0.73	0.64
	RoBERTa c 0.5	0.72	**0.64**	0.72	0.64	0.73	0.65
	RoBERTa t 0.5	0.30	0.63	0.31	0.64	0.32	0.64
s	bert c 0.5	0.73	0.59	0.73	0.63	0.73	0.65
	bert t 0.5	0.16	0.60	0.19	0.63	0.19	0.64
	BERT t 0.5	0.20	0.61	0.27	0.63	0.23	0.65
	BERT c 0.5	0.74	0.60	0.74	0.64	0.72	0.66
	RoBERTa c 0.5	0.72	0.63	0.72	**0.65**	0.72	0.67
	RoBERTa t 0.5	0.22	0.63	0.24	**0.65**	0.19	0.66
r	bert c-0.5	0.76	0.53	0.77	0.58	0.74	0.69
	bert t-0.5	0.14	0.53	0.37	0.57	0.24	0.68
	BERT c 0.5	0.40	0.54	0.35	0.59	0.23	0.69
	BERT t 0.5	0.74	0.54	0.76	0.59	0.74	0.69
	RoBERTa c 0.5	0.80	0.56	0.77	0.60	0.74	**0.71**
	RoBERTa t 0.5	0.38	0.55	0.34	0.59	0.19	0.66

(b) Details on the AV results

Table 7: **(Dev) Results.** We display the accuracy of the models for the contrastive authorship verification (CAV) setup and the AUC for the authorship verification (AV) setup on each dev set (conversation, domain and no). We show results for 18 fine-tuned models: BERT uncased (bert), RoBERTa and BERT cased trained with the conversation, domain and no content control. With different loss functions (contrastive - c, triple - t) and margin values (0.4, 0.5, 0.6). For the AV task, we also display the optimal threshold according to AUC (thr) and its matching accuracy. Generally, RoBERTa models perform the best with increasing performance from conversation to domain to random. Accuracies for< CAV are higher than for AV. Models perform the best on the task they have been trained on. Contrastive and Triple loss seem to behave comparable. Best performance per dev set and CAV/AV task is boldfaced.

A.2 Detailed Results on the Development Sets

We display the performance of further fine-tuned models on the dev sets in Table 7. RoBERTa (Liu et al., 2019) generally performs better than the uncased and cased BERT model (Devlin et al., 2019). Performance for the triplet and contrastive loss functions are comparable. We only use RoBERTa models in the main paper and both contrastive and triplet loss as a result.

train data	model	all		formal		complex		nb3r		c'tion	
		STEL	o-c	STEL	o-c	STEL	o-c	STEL	o-c	STEL	o-c
-	BERT uncased (bert)	0.75	0.03	0.76	0.05	0.70	0.00	**0.93**	0.09	1.00	0.00
	BERT cased (BERT)	**0.78**	0.05	0.80	0.10	**0.71**	0.00	0.92	**0.11**	1.00	0.00
conv.	bert c 0.5	0.68	0.21	0.72	0.40	0.59	0.07	0.73	0.06	1.00	0.01
	bert t 0.5	0.68	0.30	0.71	0.52	0.61	0.15	0.72	0.05	0.99	0.06
	BERT c 0.5	0.73	0.32	0.83	0.62	0.60	**0.19**	0.67	0.06	1.00	0.00
	BERT t 0.5	0.73	**0.37**	0.79	**0.66**	0.63	0.15	0.74	0.05	1.00	**0.15**
domain	bert c 0.4	0.70	0.12	0.76	0.26	0.61	0.01	0.72	0.02	1.00	0.00
	bert c 0.5	0.69	0.13	0.74	0.27	0.59	0.01	0.68	0.05	1.00	0.00
	bert c 0.6	0.70	0.13	0.76	0.26	0.61	0.01	0.72	0.04	1.00	0.00
	bert c-on 0.4	0.65	0.02	0.67	0.03	0.60	0.00	0.69	0.02	0.84	0.00
	bert c-on 0.5	0.65	0.02	0.67	0.03	0.60	0.00	0.69	0.02	0.84	0.00
	bert c-on 0.6	0.65	0.02	0.67	0.03	0.60	0.00	0.69	0.02	0.84	0.00
	bert t 0.4	0.71	0.15	0.78	0.31	0.59	0.01	0.78	0.05	1.00	0.00
	bert t 0.5	0.68	0.18	0.74	0.37	0.58	0.03	0.72	0.06	1.00	0.00
	bert t 0.6	0.69	0.22	0.76	0.44	0.58	0.04	0.69	0.06	1.00	0.00
	BERT c-0.5	0.73	0.23	0.82	0.48	0.61	0.02	0.77	0.03	1.00	0.00
	BERT t-0.5	0.71	0.28	0.81	0.56	0.57	0.06	0.80	0.04	1.00	0.00
random	bert c 0.5	0.69	0.09	0.77	0.20	0.58	0.01	0.68	0.02	0.98	0.00
	bert t 0.5	0.70	0.13	0.75	0.26	0.61	0.03	0.79	0.06	1.00	0.00
	BERT c-0.5	0.72	0.21	**0.84**	0.44	0.55	0.02	0.75	0.07	1.00	0.01
	BERT t-0.5	0.73	0.23	**0.84**	0.48	0.59	0.03	0.68	0.05	1.00	0.00

Table 8: **Results on STEL and STEL-Or-Content.** We display STEL accuracy for different language models and methods. The performance on the set of STEL and STEL-Or-Content (o-c) task instances is displayed. The best performance is boldfaced. Performance for the trained models goes down for the original STEL framework in the complex/simple and nb3r substitution dimension. Performance generally increases for the STEL-Or-Content task.

B Details on STEL results

We display the STEL results on further trained models in Table 8. Interestingly, cased BERT seems to be the better choice for the contraction STEL dimension.

aggregate		unlearned f/i	unlearned c/s	learned f/i	learned c/s
CC	conversation	21	34	62	22
	domain	13	34	62	24
	no	21	44	67	24
setup	AV	8	9	61	11
	CAV	6	14	55	14
-	all	1	4	48	8

Table 9: **Error Analysis STEL Results.** For the formal/informal (f/i) and complex/simple (c/s) STEL dimension, we display the number of instances that were unlearned and learned by all RoBERTa models in an aggregate. We use three different aggregates: (i) all models trained with a given CC level, (ii) all models trained with a certain task setup and (iii) all models.

	unlearned	learned
no ambiguity	$\frac{5}{55} \approx 9\%$	$\frac{12}{41} \approx 29\%$
typo simple	$\frac{21}{55} \approx 38\%$	$\frac{13}{41} \approx 32\%$
typo complex	$\frac{11}{55} \approx 20\%$	$\frac{6}{41} \approx 15\%$
error grammar simple	$\frac{15}{55} \approx 27\%$	$\frac{9}{41} \approx 22\%$
error grammar complex	$\frac{5}{55} \approx 9\%$	$\frac{3}{41} \approx 7\%$
changed content	$\frac{5}{55} \approx 9\%$	$\frac{3}{41} \approx 7\%$
word as/more complex	$\frac{16}{55} \approx 29\%$	$\frac{11}{41} \approx 27\%$
naturalness	$\frac{7}{55} \approx 13\%$	$\frac{3}{41} \approx 7\%$

Table 10: **Categories Error Analysis STEL Results.** For the six fine-tuned RoBERTa models, we manually looked at the common learned as well as the unlearned simple/complex examples. We put the examples in the displayed ambiguity classes.

n	avg. silhouette
2	0.23
3	0.21
4	0.23
5	**0.27**
6	**0.27**
7	0.26
8	0.23
9	0.19
10	0.20
11	0.19
12	0.18
13	0.19
14	0.17
15	0.16
16	0.16
17	0.16
18	0.17
19	0.17
20	0.17
21	0.16
22	0.16
23	0.15
24	0.15
25	0.15
26	0.15
30	0.15
40	0.15
50	0.15
100	0.13
150	0.13
200	0.12

Table 11: **Silhouette values.** We experiment with different numbers of clusters for one fine-tuned RoBERTa model (R CAV CONV 106). It was on the CAV task with conversation CC. The highest Silhouette score is reached for cluster sizes of 5–7.

B.1 Error Analysis RoBERTa STEL results

In Table 9, we display the number of learned and unlearned STEL instances across different aggregates for the RoBERTa models. We combine all such unique STEL instances across the aggregates and annotate if they contain ambiguities. In Table 10, we display the results. Overall, the learned STEL instances contain fewer ambiguities. However, they still show considerable amounts of ambiguities.

C Details on cluster parameters

We use agglomerative clustering for the RoBERTa model trained on the CAV setup with a margin of 0.5 and conversations as CC with seed 106 (R CAV CONV 106). We experiment with different numbers of clusters and display the results in Table 11. The highest Silhouette scores are reached for cluster sizes of 5, 6, 7. We select a cluster size of 7 for evaluation.

D Details on the cluster analysis

We give more examples of the seven clusters in Table 12. Refer to our Github repository for the complete clustering. We did not find obvious consistencies for clusters 1, 2 and 6. That does, however, not mean that more nuanced stylistic consistencies are not present. We recommend using a higher number of clusters, possibly different clustering algorithms and testing out statistics for known style features to pinpoint more consistencies.

Out of all utterance pairs that have the same author, 46.2% appear in the same cluster for the style embedding model. This is different from a random distribution among 7 clusters[12] which corresponds to $20.1\% \pm .00$. As authors will have a certain variability to their style as well (e.g., Zhu and Jurgens (2021)), a perfect clustering according to writing

[12]Calculated mean and standard deviation of 100 random assignments of utterances to the 7 clusters, with the same number of elements in each cluster.

style would not assign all same author pairs to the same cluster. For the RoBERTa base model the fraction of same author pairs in the same cluster is closer to the random distribution (75.4% vs. 76.1% for the random distribution[13]). The fraction of utterance pairs that appear in the same domain are close to the random distribution for both the style embedding model (23.6% vs. 20.1%) and the RoBERTa base model (77.6% vs. 76.0%). The percentage for the RoBERTa base models is a lot higher as the first cluster contains almost 90% of all utterances. Random assignment of utterances across the 7 clusters, that keeps the clustering size would already lead to 76.0% same author pairs appearing in the same cluster (almost all of them in the first). Results are similar for utterance pairs that appear in the same conversation.

[13]The share is high for RoBERTa base because the first cluster already contains 86.7% of all utterances.

C	#	Consistency	Example 1	Example 2	Example 3
1	4065	citing previous comments, standard punctuation, URLs	Yes. Proportionally, this kid's feet are absolutely enormous.	> Please delete your account. Says the no life who always shits on anything Kanye or anti-Drake I can promise you that capitalism is very much alive in Norway.	[This should help.](YOUTUBE-LINK)
2	4016	short sentences?	Nice catch! Well done. cookies are in the back of this Grammar party. You can have two.	You can mute them we've been told!	Came here to post this only to find it's already the top voted comment. This is a good sub.
3	2165	no last punctuation mark	I am living in china, they are experiencing an enormous baby boom	Seems like sarcasm. But could also be Poe	[...] The earth probably has two or more degrees of symmetry, but less than infinite (like a sphere), but I'm honestly not too concerned about the minutiae of it
4	1794	punctuation / casing	huh thats odd i'm in the 97% percentile on iq tests, the sat, and the act	Its not a problem if you a got a full game. Whats the problem if a game didnt get expansions?	Fair point, I didnt know that. Just at glance I kind of went 'woah that doesnt seem right'
5	1555	' instead of ' apostrophe	I assume it's the blind lady?	Oh I wasn't really dismissing them. I'm saying Ford will try their own thing compared to Fiat	It's 4am in Brussels and I am still hyped
6	781	similar to 1?	Well, as your neighbors, I'd say Fuck you.. But we're not like that, see? We want to be part of the alliance, not part of the 'fuck you, we cant be competitive with jobs or innovate any more, so we're going to run massive tariffs against all our friendly nations	Hah, thus the one calf larger than the other issue. I have it too ;)	[So you are saying that current encryption falls apart as long as the quantum computer is large enough](URL). (for reference, the current highest qubit is 50)'
7	380	linebreaks	I admire what you're doing but [...] I know I'm in the minority. [...]	75% of the problems I run into are solved by [...] I work in live streaming.	All the suggestions others have given are excellent. RS7 makes the most sense to me. But [...] Meanwhile, [...]

Table 12: **Clustering - fined-tuned RoBERTa model.** We display examples for each cluster of the 7 clusters that resulted from the agglomerative clustering of 14,756 randomly sampled texts with the RoBERTa model fine-tuned on the CAV setup with the conversation CC. We mention noticeable consistencies (Consistency) within the cluster and give three examples each. Consistencies that are not as clear are marked with a '?'.

C	#	Consistency	Example 1	Example 2	Example 3
1	12798	wide variety	Just googled it, looks like a great device for the price! If I weren't so impatient I would have bought this online. Great battery life!	This is exactly why i believe iphone 5 body was perfect example of good balance with design(timeless) and utility	[...] The earth probably has two or more degrees of symmetry, but less than infinite (like a sphere), but I'm honestly not too concerned about the minutiae of it
2	1110	short utterances	here we go!!	And her good posture.	Not in California.
3	310	long utterances	I've never had the pleasure of seeing Neil live but I got on a big kick a few years ago after buying one of his live albums (can't remember which one) where I listened to all his live albums and then wanted to see as many of his live performance I could find on YouTube. [...]	> but the movie has the superior ending I think. [...] [...]	So .... heavily influenced by the social economics ... but still voluntary, got it. [...] Then how about this. [...] Everyone still keeps their child that way, you even promote child birth. No sterilization, no stigmatization of poor people, no poor people stuck with child with heavy needs requiring care that they can't pay for.
4	232	URLs	`https://youtu.be/GmULc5VANsw`	[This](`https://np.reddit.com/r/MakeupAddiction/comments/25hkqi/how_to_tell_if_your_foundationprimer_is_silicone/`) might help!	I thought there was 51 stars because of Puerto Rico `https://en.m.wikipedia.org/wiki/51st_state`

Table 13: **Clusters for RoBERTa base.** We display examples for 4 out of 7 clusters as a result of the agglomerative clustering of 14756 randomly sampled texts from the conversation test set. We mention noticeable consistencies (Consistency) within the cluster and give three examples each.

E Computing Infrastructure

The training of 23 RoBERTa (Liu et al., 2019), 13 uncased BERT and 6 cased BERT models (Devlin et al., 2019) took about 846 GPU hours with one RTX6000 card with 24 GB RAM on a Linux computing cluster. Further analysis and clustering of two RoBERTa models took about 24 GPU hours. We used a machine with 32 GB RAM and 8 intel i7 CPUs using Ubuntu 20.04 LTS without GPU access to generate the training data.

We used `Sentence-Transformers` 2.1.0 (Reimers and Gurevych, 2019) and `numpy` 1.18.5 (Harris et al., 2020), `scipy` 1.5.2 (Virtanen et al., 2020) and `scikit-learn` 0.24.2 (Pedregosa et al., 2011).

We use previous work, including code and data, consistent with their specified or implied intended use (Reimers and Gurevych, 2019; Chang et al., 2020; Wegmann and Nguyen, 2021). The `ConvoKit` open-source Python framework invites NLP researchers and 'anyone with questions about conversations' to use it (Chang et al., 2020). The `SentenceTransformers` Python framework can be used to compute sentence / text embeddings.[14] We comply with asking permission for part of the dataset for `STEL` and citing the specified works (Wegmann and Nguyen, 2021). Wegmann and Nguyen (2021) state the intended use of developing improved style(-sensitive) measures.

F Intended Use

We hope our work will inform further research into style and its representations. We invite researchers to reuse any of our provided results, code and data for this purpose.

[14]`https://sbert.net/`

WeaNF: Weak Supervision with Normalizing Flows

Andreas Stephan
University of Vienna
andreas.stephan@univie.ac.at

Benjamin Roth
University of Vienna
benjamin.roth@univie.ac.at

Abstract

A popular approach to decrease the need for costly manual annotation of large data sets is weak supervision, which introduces problems of noisy labels, coverage and bias. Methods for overcoming these problems have either relied on discriminative models, trained with cost functions specific to weak supervision, and more recently, generative models, trying to model the output of the automatic annotation process. In this work, we explore a novel direction of generative modeling for weak supervision: Instead of modeling the output of the annotation process (the labeling function matches), we generatively model the input-side data distributions (the feature space) covered by labeling functions. Specifically, we estimate a density for each weak labeling source, or labeling function, by using normalizing flows. An integral part of our method is the flow-based modeling of multiple simultaneously matching labeling functions, and therefore phenomena such as labeling function overlap and correlations are captured. We analyze the effectiveness and modeling capabilities on various commonly used weak supervision data sets, and show that weakly supervised normalizing flows compare favorably to standard weak supervision baselines.

1 Introduction

Currently an important portion of research in natural language processing is devoted to the goal of reducing or getting rid of large labeled datasets. Recent examples include language model fine-tuning (Devlin et al., 2019), transfer learning (Zoph et al., 2016) or few-shot learning (Brown et al., 2020). Another common approach is weakly supervised learning. The idea is to make use of human intuitions or already acquired human knowledge to create weak labels. Examples of such sources are keyword lists, regular expressions, heuristics or independently existing curated data sources, e.g. a movie database if the task is concerned with TV shows. While the resulting labels are noisy, they provide a quick and easy way to create large labeled datasets. In the following, we use the term labeling functions, introduced in Ratner et al. (2017), to describe functions which create weak labels based on the notions above.

Throughout the weak supervision literature generative modeling ideas are found (Takamatsu et al., 2012; Alfonseca et al., 2012; Ratner et al., 2017). Probably the most popular example of a system using generative modeling in weak supervision is the data programming paradigm of Snorkel (Ratner et al., 2017). It uses correlations within labeling functions to learn a graph capturing dependencies between labeling functions and true labels.

However, such an approach does not directly model biases of weak supervision reflected in the feature space. In order to directly model the relevant aspects in the feature space of a weakly supervised dataset, we investigate the use of density estimation using normalizing flows. More specifically, in this work, we model probability distributions over the input space induced by *labeling functions*, and combine those distributions for better weakly supervised prediction.

We propose and examine four novel models for weakly supervised learning based on normalizing flows (**WeaNF-***): Firstly, we introduce a **standard** model **WeaNF-S**, where each labeling function is represented by a multivariate normal distribution, and its **iterative** variant **WeaNF-I**. Furthermore **WeaNF-N** additionally learns the **negative** space, i.e. a density for the space where the labeling function does not match, and a **mixed** model, **WeaNF-M**, where correlations of sets of labeling functions are represented by the normalizing flow. As a consequence, the classification task is a two step procedure. The first step estimates the densities, and the second step aggregates them to model label prediction. Multiple alternatives are discussed and analyzed.

Proceedings of the 7th Workshop on Representation Learning for NLP, pages 269 - 279
May 26, 2022

We benchmark our approach on several commonly used weak supervision datasets. The results highlight that our proposed generative approach is competitive with standard weak supervision methods. Additionally the results show that smart aggregation schemes prove beneficial.

In summary, our contributions are i) the development of multiple models based on normalizing flows for weak supervision combined with density aggregation schemes, ii) a quantitative and qualitative analysis highlighting opportunities and problems and iii) an implementation of the method[1]. To the best of our knowledge we are the first to use normalizing flows to generatively model labeling functions.

2 Background and Related Work

We split this analysis into a weak supervision and a normalizing flow section as we build upon these two areas.

Weak supervision. A fundamental problem in machine learning is the need for massive amounts of manually labeled data. Among others, weak supervision provides a way to counter the problem. The idea is to use human knowledge to produce noisy, so called weak labels. Typically, keywords, heuristics or knowledge from external data sources is used. The latter is called distant supervision (Craven and Kumlien, 1999; Mintz et al., 2009). In Ratner et al. (2017), data programming is introduced, a paradigm to create and work with weak supervision sources programmatically. The goal is to learn the relation between weak labels and the true unknown labels (Ratner et al., 2017; Varma et al., 2019; Bach et al., 2017; Chatterjee et al., 2019). In Ren et al. (2020) the authors use iterative modeling for weak supervision. Software packages such as SPEAR (?), WRENCH (?) and Knodle (Sedova et al., 2021) allow a modular use and comparison of weak supervision methods. A recent trend is to use additional information to support the learning process. Chatterjee et al. (2019) allow labeling functions to assign a score to the weak label. In Ratner et al. (2018) the human provided class balance is used. Additionally Awasthi et al. (2020); Karamanolakis et al. (2021) use semi-supervised methods for weak supervision, where the idea is to use a small amount of labeled data to steer the learning process.

Normalizing flows. While the concept of normalizing flows is much older, Rezende and Mohamed (2016) introduced the concept to deep learning. In comparison to other generative neural networks, such as Generative Adversarial networks (Goodfellow et al., 2014) or Variational Autoencoders (Kingma and Welling, 2014), normalizing flows provide a tractable way to model high-dimensional distributions. So far, normalizing received rather little attention in the natural language processing community. Still, Tran et al. (2019) and Ziegler and Rush (2019) applied them successfully to language modeling. An excellent overview over recent normalizing flow research is given in Papamakarios et al. (2021). Normalizing flows are based on the change of variable formula, which uses a bijective function $g : Z \to X$ to transform a base distribution Z into a target distribution X:

$$p_X(x) = p_Z(z) \left| \det \left(\frac{\partial g(z)}{\partial z^T} \right) \right|^{-1}$$

where Z is typically a simple distribution, e.g. multivariate normal distribution, and X is a complicated data generating distribution. Typically, a neural network learns a function $f : X \to Z$ by minimizing the KL-divergence between the data generating distribution and the simple base distribution. As described in Papamakarios et al. (2021) this is achieved by minimizing negative log likelihood

$$\log p_X(x) = \log p_Z(f(x)) + \log \left| \det \left(\frac{\partial f(x)}{\partial x^T} \right) \right|$$

The tricky part is to design efficient architectures which are invertible and provide an easy and efficient way to compute the determinant. The composition of bijective functions is again bijective which enables deep architectures $f = f_1 \circ \cdots \circ f_n$. Recent research focuses on the creation of more expressive transformation modules (Lu et al., 2021). In this work, we make use of an early, but well established model, called RealNVP (Dinh et al., 2017). In each layer, the input x is split in half and transformed according to

$$y_{1:d} = x_{1:d} \quad (1)$$

$$y_{d+1:D} = x_{d+1:D} \odot \exp\left(s(x_{1:d})\right) + t\left(x_{1:d}\right) \quad (2)$$

where $\odot$ is the pointwise multiplication and s and t neural networks. Using this formulation to realize

[1] https://github.com/AndSt/wea_nf

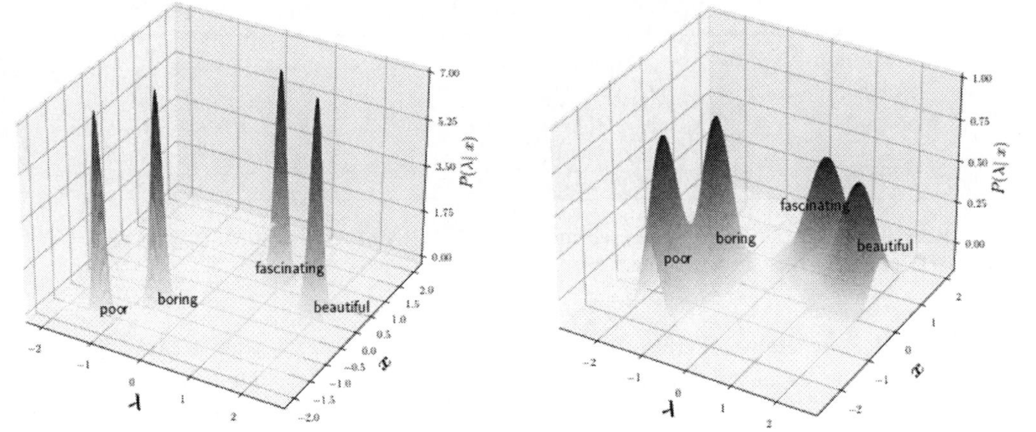

(a) Schematic view of the densities estimated by **WeaNF-S/I**. The concatenated input $[\boldsymbol{x}; \boldsymbol{\lambda}]$ is fed into the flow to learn the probability $P(x|\lambda)$. The graph shows the posterior $P(\lambda|x)$.

(b) **WeaNF-N** and **WeaNF-M** aim to smoothen the probability space, aiming to generalize more robustly to instances not directly matched by labeling functions.

Figure 1: Schematic overview of **WeaNF-***. The $X-$axis represents the labeling function embedding $\boldsymbol{\lambda}$, the $Y-$axis the text input $\boldsymbol{x}$. The $Z-$axis represents the learned density related to a labeling function. In this example we use the task sentiment analysis and keyword search as labeling functions. Blue denotes a negative sentiment and red a positive sentiment.

a layer f_i, it is easy and efficient to compute the inverse and the determinant.

Normalizing flows were used for semi-supervised classification (Izmailov et al., 2019; Atanov et al., 2020) but not for weakly supervised learning, which we introduce in the next chapter.

3 Model Description

In this section the models are introduced. The following example motivates the idea. Consider the sentence s, "The movie was fascinating, even though the graphics were poor, maybe due to a low budget.", the task sentiment analysis and labeling functions given by the keywords "fascinating" and "poor". Furthermore, "fascinating" is associated with the class POS, and "poor" with the class NEG. We aim to learn a neural network, which translates the complex object, text and a possible labeling function match, to a density, in the current example $P(s|\text{fascinating})$ and $P(s|\text{poor})$. We combine this information using basic probability calculus to make a classification prediction.

Multiple models are introduced. The standard model *WeaNF-S* naively learns to represent each labeling function as a multivariate normal distribution. In order to make use of unlabeled data, i.e. data where no labeling function matches, we iteratively apply the standard model *(WeaNF-I)*. Based on the observation that labeling functions overlap, we derive *WeaNF-N* modeling the negative space, i.e. the space where the labeling function does not match and the mixed model, *WeaNF-M*, using a common space for single labeling functions and the intersection of these. Furthermore, multiple aggregation schemes are used to combine the learned labeling function densities. See table 1 for an overview.

Before we dive into details, we introduce some notation. From the set of all possible inputs $\mathcal{X}$, e.g. texts, we denote an input sample by x and its corresponding vector representation by $\boldsymbol{x}$. The set of t labeling functions is $T = \{\lambda_1, \ldots, \lambda_t\}$ and the classes are $Y = \{y_1, \ldots, y_c\}$. Each labeling function $\lambda : \mathcal{X} \to \emptyset \cup \{y\}$ maps the input to a specific class $y \in Y$ or abstains from labeling. In some of our models, we also associate an embedding with each labeling function, which we denote by $\boldsymbol{\lambda} \in \mathbb{R}^h$. The set of labeling functions corresponding to label y is T_y.

WeaNF-S/I. The goal of the standard model is to learn a distribution $P(x|\lambda)$ for each labeling function λ. Similarly to Atanov et al. (2020) in semi-supervised learning, we use a randomly initialized embedding $\boldsymbol{\lambda} \in \mathbb{R}^h$ to create a representation for each labeling function in the input space. We concatenate input and labeling function vector and provide it as input to the normalizing flow, thus

	$P(y\|x) \propto$	WeaNF-S/I	WeaNF-N	WeaNF-M
Maximum	$\max_{\lambda \in T_y} P_\theta(x\|\lambda)$	√		√
Union	$\sum_{\lambda \in T_y} P(\lambda\|x)$		√	
NoisyOr	$1 - \prod_{\lambda \in T_y} (1 - P(\lambda\|x))$		√	
Simplex	$P\left(\left[\boldsymbol{x}; \frac{1}{\|T_y\|} \sum_{\lambda \in T_y} \boldsymbol{\lambda}\right]\right)$			√

Table 1: Overview over the used aggregation schemes. Note that $P(\lambda|x)$ is only accessible with WeaNF-N (see equation 4). Bold symbols denote vector representations.

learning $P([\boldsymbol{x}; \boldsymbol{\lambda}_i])$, where $[\cdot]$ describes the concatenation operation. A standard RealNVP (Dinh et al., 2017), as described in section 2 is used. See appendix B.1 for implementational details. In order to use the learned probabilities to perform label prediction, an aggregation scheme is needed. For the sake of simplicity, the model predicts the label corresponding to the labeling function with the highest likelihood, $y = \arg\max_{y \in Y} \max_{\lambda \in T_y} P(x|\lambda)$.

Additionally, to make use of the unlabeled data, i.e. the data points where no labeling function matches, an iterative version WeaNF-I is tested. For this, we use an EM-like (Dempster et al., 1977) iterative scheme where the predictions of the model trained in the previous iteration are used as labels for the unlabeled data. The corresponding pseudo-code is found in algorithm 1.

Algorithm 1 Iterative Model (WeaNF-I)

```
Require: X_l ∈ R^{n_l×d}, corresponding matches
    λ_l ∈ {0,1}^{n_l×t}, unmatched X_u ∈ R^{n_u×d}
  F = train_flow(X_l, λ_l)
  for i = 1, ..., r do
      (λ_u)_i = arg max_λ F((X_u)_i; λ)
      X = concat(X_l, X_u), λ = concat(λ_l, λ_u)
      F = train_flow(X, λ)
  end for
```

Negative Model. In typical classification scenarios it is enough to learn $P(x|y)$ to compute a posterior $P(y|x)$ by applying Bayes' formula twice, resulting in

$$P(y|x) = \frac{P(x|y)P(y)}{P(x|y)P(y) + P(x|\neg y)P(\neg y)} \quad (3)$$

where the class prior $P(y)$ is typically approximated on the training data or passed as a parameter. This is not possible in the current setting as often two labeling functions match simultaneously. In order to learn $P(\lambda|x)$, we explore a novel variant that additionally learns $P(x|\neg\lambda)$. The learning process is similar to $P(x|\lambda)$, so a second embedding $\tilde{\boldsymbol{\lambda}}$ is introduced to represent $\neg\lambda$. We optimize $P([\boldsymbol{x}; \boldsymbol{\lambda}]$ and $P\left(\left[\boldsymbol{x}; \tilde{\boldsymbol{\lambda}}\right]\right)$ simultaneously. In each batch I, the positive sample pairs $(x_i, \lambda_i)_{i \in I}$ and negative pairs (x_i, λ_j), sampled such that $(x_i, \lambda_j) \notin \{(x_i, \lambda_i)\}_{i \in I}$, are used to train the network. The number of negative samples per positive sample is an additional hyperparameter. Now Bayes' formula can be used as in equation 3 to obtain

$$P(\lambda|x) = \frac{P(x|\lambda)P(\lambda)}{P(x|\lambda)P(y) + P(x|\neg\lambda)P(\neg\lambda)}. \quad (4)$$

The access to the posterior probability $P(\lambda|x)$ provides additional opportunities to model $P(y|x)$. After initial experimentation we settled on two options. A simple addition of probabilities neglecting intersection probability, equation 5, which we call Union, and the NoisyOr formula, equation 7, which has previously shown to be effective in weakly supervised learning (Keith et al., 2017):

$$P(y|x) \propto \sum_{\lambda \in T_y} P(\lambda|x) \quad (5)$$

$$P(y|x) = P(\{\vee_{\lambda \in T_y} \lambda\}|x) \quad (6)$$

$$= 1 - \prod_{\lambda \in T_y} (1 - P(\lambda|x)) \quad (7)$$

Mixed Model. It was already mentioned that it is common that two or multiple labeling functions hit simultaneously. While WeaNF-N provides access to a posterior distribution which allows to model these interactions, the goal of the mixed model WeaNF-M is to model these intersections explicitly already in the density of the normalizing flow. More specifically, we aim to learn $P(x|\{\lambda_i\}_{i \in I})$ for arbitrary index families I. Once again, the embeddings space is used to achieve this

Dataset	#Classes	#Train / #Test samples	#LF's	Coverage(%)	Class Balance
IMDb	2	39741 / 4993	20	0.60	1:1
Spouse	2	8530 / 1187	9	0.30	1:5
YouTube	2	1440 / 229	10	1.66	1:1
SMS	2	4208 / 494	73	0.51	1:6
Trec	6	4903 / 500	68	1.73	1:13:14:14:9:10

Table 2: Some basic statistics describing the datasets. Coverage is computed on the train set by #matches / #samples.

goal. For a given sample x and a family I of matching labeling functions, we uniformly sample from the simplex of all possible combinations and obtain $\boldsymbol{\lambda}_I = \sum_{i \in I} \alpha_i \boldsymbol{\lambda}_i, \alpha_i \geq 0, \sum_{i \in I} \alpha_i = 1$. Afterwards we concatenate the weighted sum of the labeling function embeddings $\boldsymbol{\lambda}_I$ with the input x and learn $P([\boldsymbol{x}; \boldsymbol{\lambda}_I])$. Now that the density is able to access the intersections of labeling functions, we derive a new direct aggregation scheme. By σ_y we denote the simplex generated by the set of boundary points $\{\boldsymbol{\lambda}\}_{\lambda \in T_y}$. It is important to think about this simplex, as it theoretically describes the input space where the model learns the density related to class y. We use the naive but efficient variant which just computes the center of the simplex:

$$P(y|x) \propto P\left(\left[\boldsymbol{x}; \frac{1}{|T_y|} \sum_{\lambda \in T_y} \boldsymbol{\lambda}\right]\right) \quad (8)$$

Implementation. In practice, sampling of data points has to be handled on multiple occasions. Empirically and during the inspection of related implementations, e.g. the Github repository accompanying Atanov et al. (2020), we found that it is beneficial if every labeling function is seen equally often during training. It supports preventing a biased density towards specific labeling functions. When training WeaNF-N, the negative space is much larger than the actual space, so an additional hyperparameter controlling the amount of negative samples is needed. WeaNF-M aims to model intersecting probabilities directly. Most intersections occur too rarely to model a reasonable density. Thus we decided to only take co-occures into account which occur more often than a certain threshold. See appendix A.3 to get a feeling for the correlations in the used datasets.

4 Experiments

In order to analyze the proposed models experiments on multiple standard weakly supervised classification problems are performed. In the following, we introduce datasets, baselines and training details.

4.1 Datasets

Within our experiments, we use five classification tasks. Table 2 gives an overview over some key statistics. Note that these might differ slightly compared to other papers due to the removal of duplicates. For a more detailed overview of our preprocessing steps, see appendix A.1.

The first dataset is **IMDb** (Internet Movie Database) and the accompanying sentiment analysis task (Maas et al., 2011). The goal is to classify whether a movie review describes a positive or a negative sentiment. We use 10 positive and 10 negative keywords as labeling functions. See Appendix A.2 for a detailed description.

The second dataset is the **Spouse** dataset (Corney et al., 2016). The task is to classify whether a text holds a spouse relation, e.g. "Mary is married to Tom". Here, 90% of the samples belong to the no-relation class, so we use macro-F_1 score to evaluate the performance. As the third dataset another binary classification problem is given by the **YouTube** Spam (Alberto et al., 2015) dataset. The model has to decide whether a YouTube comment is spam or not. For both, the Spouse and the YouTube dataset, the labeling functions are provided by the Snorkel framework (Ratner et al., 2017).

The **SMS** Spam detection dataset (Almeida et al., 2011), we abbreviate by SMS, also asks for spam but in the private messaging domain. The dataset is quite skewed, so once again macro-F_1 score is used. Lastly, a multi-class dataset, namely **TREC-6** (Li and Roth, 2002), is used. The task is to classify questions into six categories, namely Abbreviation, Entity, Description, Human and Location. The labeling functions provided by (Awasthi et al., 2020) are used for the SMS and the TREC dataset. We

	IMDb	Spouse(F_1)	YouTube	SMS (F_1)	Trec
MV	56.84	49.87	81.66	56.1	61.2
MV + MLP	73.20	29.96	**92.58**	92.41	53.27
DP + MLP	67.79	57.05	88.79	84.40	43.00
WeaNF-S	73.06	52.28	89.08	86.71	67.4
WeaNF-I	**74.08**	**57.96**	89.08	**93.54**	**67.8**
WeaNF-N (NoisyOr)	72.96	54.60	90.83	79.63	54.8
WeaNF-N (Union)	71.98	50.83	91.70	83.48	60.2
WeaNF-M (Max)	70.16	55.16	85.15	88.23	49.8
WeaNF-M (Simplex)	63.53	56.91	86.03	76.29	25.4

Table 3: Comparison of baselines to our model variants. The numbers reflect accuracies, or F_1-scores, where explicitly mentioned. Names in parenthesis describe the aggregation mechanism.

took the preprocessed versions of the data available within the Knodle weak supervision programming framework (Sedova et al., 2021).

4.2 Baselines

Three baselines are used. While there are many weak supervision systems, most use additional knowledge to improve performance. Examples are class balance (Chatterjee et al., 2019), semi-supervised learning with very little labels (Awasthi et al., 2020; Karamanolakis et al., 2021) or multi-task learning (Ratner et al., 2018). To ensure a fair comparison, only baselines are used that solely take input data and labeling function matches into account. First we use majority voting (MV) which takes the label where the most rules match. For instances where multiple classes have an equal vote or where no labeling function matches, a random vote is taken. Secondly, a multi-layer perceptron (MLP) is trained on top of the labels provided by majority vote. The third baseline uses the data programming (DP) paradigm. More explicitly, we use the model introduced by Ratner et al. (2018) implemented in the Snorkel (Ratner et al., 2017) programming framework. It performs a two-step approach to learning. Firstly, a generative model is trained to learn the most likely correlation between labeling functions and unknown true labels. Secondly, a discriminative model uses the labels of the generative model to train a final model. The same MLP as for second baseline is used for the final model.

4.3 Training Details

Text input embeddings are created with the SentenceTransformers library (Reimers and Gurevych, 2019) using the *bert-base-nli-mean-tokens* model. They serve as input to the baselines and the normalizing flows. Hyperparameter search is performed via grid search over learning rates of $\{1e-5, 1e-4\}$, weight decay of $\{1e-2, 1e-3\}$ and epochs in $\{30, 50, 100, 300, 450\}$, and label embedding dimension in $10, 15, 20$ times the number of classes. Additionally, the number of layers is in $\{6, 8\}$, and the negative sampling value for WeaNF is in $\{2, 3\}$. The full set up ran 30 hours on a single GPU on a DGX 1 server.

5 Analysis

The analysis is divided into three parts. Firstly, a general discussion of the results is given. Secondly, an analysis of the densities predicted by WeaNF-N is shown and lastly, a qualitative analysis is performed.

5.1 Overall Findings

Table 3 exposes the main evaluation. The horizontal line separates the baselines from our models. For WeaNF-N and WeaNF-M, no iterative schemes were trained. This enables a direct comparison to the standard model WeaNF-I.

Interestingly, the combination of Snorkel and MLP's is often not performing competitively. In the IMDb data set there is barely any correlation between labeling functions, complicating Snorkel's approach. The large number of labeling functions e.g. Trec, SMS, could also complicate correlation based approaches. Appendix A.3 shows correlation graphs.

As indicated by the bold numbers, the WeaNF-I is the best performing model. Only on the YouTube dataset, an iterative scheme could not improve the results. Related to this observation, in Ren

Labeling Function	Example	Dataset	$P(x\|\lambda)$	Label (λ)	Gold	Prediction
won .* claim	...won ... call ...	SMS	↑	Spam	Spam	Spam
.* I'll .*	sorry, **I'll** call later	SMS	↑	No Spam	No Spam	No Spam
.* i .*	**i** just saw ron burgundy captaining a party boat so yeah	SMS	↓	No Spam	No Spam	No Spam
(explain|what) .* mean .*	**What** does the abbreviation SOS **mean** ?	Trec	↑	DESCR	ABBR	DESCR
(explain|what) .* mean .*	What are Quaaludes ?	Trec	↑	DESCR	DESCR	DESCR
who.*	**Who** was the first man to ... Pacific Ocean ?	Trec	↓	HUMAN	HUMAN	HUMAN
check .* out .*	**Check out** this video on YouTube:	YouTube	↑	Spam	Spam	Spam
#words < 5	subscribe my	YouTube	↑	Spam	Spam	No Spam
.* song .*	This **Song** will never get old	YouTube	↓	No Spam	No Spam	No Spam
.* dreadful .*	...horrible performance .... annoying	IMDb	↑	NEG	NEG	NEG
.* hilarious .*	...liked the movie...funny catch-phrase...WORST...low grade...	IMDb	↑	POS	NEG	POS
.* disappointing .*	don't understand stereotype ... goofy ..	IMDb	↓	NEG	NEG	POS
.* (husband|wife) .*	...Jill.. she and her **husband**...	Spouse	↑	Spouses	Spouses	Spouses
.* married .*	... asked me to marry him and I said yes!	Spouse	↑	Spouses	No Spouses	Spouses
family word	Clearly excited, Coleen said: 'It's my eldest **son** Shane and Emma.	Spouse	↓	No Spouses	No Spouses	No Spouses

Table 4: Examples selected from the 10 most likely (↑) and 10 most unlikely (↓) combinations of sentences and labeling functions, using the density $P(x|\lambda)$ provided by WeaNF-I. Labeling function matches are bold. We observe that the flow often generalizes to unmatched examples. We slightly simplified some rules and shortened some texts in order to fit the page size.

	IMDb	Spouse	YouTube	SMS	Trec
Acc	72.38	74.04	78.17	88.71	72.63
P	5.93	5.1	38.95	23.3	13.65
R	37.53	39.31	55.01	44.34	61.07
F_1	10.25	9.02	45.61	30.55	22.31
Cov	4.31	5.74	19.31	3.01	4.39

Table 5: Evaluation of the labeling function prediction $P(\lambda|x)$. Precision, Recall and F_1 score are computed via the weighted average of the statistics of all labeling functions. Coverage is computed as #matches/#all possible matches.

Dataset	Labeling Fct.	Cov(%)	Prec	Recall
IMDb	*boring*	5.8	13.12	26.87
Spouse	family word	9. 0	16.53	35.96
YouTube	*song*	23.58	56.72	70.73
SMS	won *call*	0.81	66.67	1.0
Trec	how.*much	2.4	60.0	75.0

Table 6: Statistics for the labeling functions obtaining the highest F_1 score for the prediction $P(\lambda|x)$, using the WeaNF (NoisyOr) model.

Dataset	Labeling Fct.	Cov(%)	Prec	Recall
IMDb	*imaginative*	0.42	0.77	52.38
Spouse	spouse keyword	14.5	0	0
YouTube	person entity	2.62	6.45	33.33
SMS	I .* miss	0.6	0	0
Trec	what is .* name	2.2	2.26	100

Table 7: Same as table 6, but here the labeling functions obtaining the lowest F_1 score are shown. Only those are taken into account which occur more often than 10 times in the test set.

et al. (2020) the authors achieve promising results using iterative discriminative modeling for semi-supervised weak supervision.

WeaNF-N outperforms the standard model in three out of five datasets. We observe that these are the datasets with a large amount of labeling functions. Possibly, this biases the model towards a high value of $P(x|\neg\lambda)$ which confuses the prediction.

The simplex aggregation scheme only outperforms the maximum aggregation on two out of five datasets. We infer that the probability density over the labeling function input space is not smooth enough. Ideally, the simplex method should always have a high confidence in the prediction of a labeling function λ if its confident on the non-mixed embedding $\boldsymbol{\lambda}$ which is what Max is doing.

5.2 Density Analysis

We divide into a global analysis and a local, i.e. a per-labeling function, analysis. Table 5 provides some global statistics, table 6 and 7 subsequently show statistics related to the best and worst performing labeling function estimations. In the local analysis a labeling function is predicted if $P(\lambda|x) \geq 0.5$. The WeaNF-N model is used because it is the only model with direct access to $P(\lambda|x)$.

It is important to mention that in the local analysis, a perfect prediction of the matching labeling function is not wanted, as this would mean that there is no generalization. Thus, a low precision might be necessary for generalization, and a the recall would indicate how much of the original semantic or syntactic meaning of a labeling function is retained.

Interestingly, while the overall performance of WeaNF-N is competitive on the IMDb and the Spouse data sets, it is failing to predict the correct labeling function. One explanation might be that these are the data sets where the texts are substantially longer which might be complicated to model for normalizing flows. In table 7 typically the worst performing approximation of labeling function matches seems to be due to low coverage. An exception is the the Spouse labeling function.

5.3 Qualitative Analysis

In table 4 a number of examples are shown. We manually inspected samples with a very high or low density value. Note that density values related to $P(x|\lambda), \lambda \in T_y$ are functions f taking arbitrary values which only have to satisfy $\mathbb{E}_{x:\lambda(x)=y}[f(x)] = 1$.

We observed the phenomenon that either the same labeling functions take the highest density values $P(x|\lambda)$ or that a single sample often has a high likelihood for multiple labeling functions. In the table 4 one can find examples where the learned flows were able to generalize from the original labeling functions. For example, for the IMDb dataset, it detects the meaning "funny" even though the exact keyword is "hilarious".

6 Conclusion

This work explores the novel use of normalizing flows for weak supervision. The approach is divided into two logical steps. In the first step, normalizing flows are employed to learn a probability distribution over the input space related to a labeling function. Secondly, principles from basic probability calculus are used to aggregate the learned densities and make them usable for classification tasks. Motivated by aspects of weakly supervised learning, such as labeling function overlap or coverage, multiple models are derived each of which uses the information present in the latent space differently. We show competitive results on five weakly supervised classification tasks. Our analysis shows that the flow-based representations of labeling functions successfully generalize to samples otherwise not covered by labeling functions.

Acknowledgements

This research was funded by the WWTF through the project "Knowledge-infused Deep Learning for Natural Language Processing" (WWTF Vienna Research Group VRG19-008), and by the Deutsche Forschungsgemeinschaft (DFG, German Research Foundation) - RO 5127/2-1.

References

T C Alberto, J V Lochter, and T A Almeida. 2015. TubeSpam: Comment Spam Filtering on YouTube. In *2015 IEEE 14th International Conference on Machine Learning and Applications (ICMLA)*, pages 138–143.

Enrique Alfonseca, Katja Filippova, Jean-Yves Delort, and Guillermo Garrido. 2012. Pattern Learning for Relation Extraction with a Hierarchical Topic Model. In *Proceedings of the 50th Annual Meeting of the Association for Computational Linguistics (Volume 2: Short Papers)*, pages 54–59, Jeju Island, Korea. Association for Computational Linguistics.

Tiago A Almeida, J M G Hidalgo, and A Yamakami. 2011. Contributions to the study of SMS spam filtering: new collection and results. In *DocEng '11*.

Andrei Atanov, Alexandra Volokhova, Arsenii Ashukha, Ivan Sosnovik, and Dmitry Vetrov. 2020. Semi-Conditional Normalizing Flows for Semi-Supervised Learning.

Abhijeet Awasthi, Sabyasachi Ghosh, Rasna Goyal, and Sunita Sarawagi. 2020. Learning from Rules Generalizing Labeled Exemplars.

Stephen H Bach, Bryan Dawei He, Alexander Ratner, and Christopher Ré. 2017. Learning the Structure of Generative Models without Labeled Data. *CoRR*, abs/1703.0.

Tom B Brown, Benjamin Mann, Nick Ryder, Melanie Subbiah, Jared Kaplan, Prafulla Dhariwal, Arvind Neelakantan, Pranav Shyam, Girish Sastry, Amanda Askell, Sandhini Agarwal, Ariel Herbert-Voss, Gretchen Krueger, Tom Henighan, Rewon Child, Aditya Ramesh, Daniel M Ziegler, Jeffrey Wu, Clemens Winter, Christopher Hesse, Mark Chen,

Eric Sigler, Mateusz Litwin, Scott Gray, Benjamin Chess, Jack Clark, Christopher Berner, Sam McCandlish, Alec Radford, Ilya Sutskever, and Dario Amodei. 2020. Language Models are Few-Shot Learners.

Oishik Chatterjee, Ganesh Ramakrishnan, and Sunita Sarawagi. 2019. Data Programming using Continuous and Quality-Guided Labeling Functions. *CoRR*, abs/1911.0.

D Corney, M-Dyaa Albakour, Miguel Martinez-Alvarez, and Samir Moussa. 2016. What do a Million News Articles Look like? In *NewsIR@ECIR*.

Mark Craven and Johan Kumlien. 1999. Constructing Biological Knowledge Bases by Extracting Information from Text Sources. In *Proceedings of the Seventh International Conference on Intelligent Systems for Molecular Biology*, pages 77–86. AAAI Press.

A P Dempster, N M Laird, and D B Rubin. 1977. Maximum likelihood from incomplete data via the EM algorithm. *JOURNAL OF THE ROYAL STATISTICAL SOCIETY, SERIES B*, 39(1):1–38.

Jacob Devlin, Ming-Wei Chang, Kenton Lee, and Kristina Toutanova. 2019. BERT: Pre-training of Deep Bidirectional Transformers for Language Understanding.

Laurent Dinh, Jascha Sohl-Dickstein, and Samy Bengio. 2017. Density estimation using Real NVP.

Ian J Goodfellow, Jean Pouget-Abadie, Mehdi Mirza, Bing Xu, David Warde-Farley, Sherjil Ozair, Aaron Courville, and Yoshua Bengio. 2014. Generative Adversarial Networks.

Pavel Izmailov, Polina Kirichenko, Marc Finzi, and Andrew Gordon Wilson. 2019. Semi-Supervised Learning with Normalizing Flows.

Giannis Karamanolakis, Subhabrata Mukherjee, Guoqing Zheng, and Ahmed Hassan Awadallah. 2021. Self-Training with Weak Supervision.

Katherine Keith, Abram Handler, Michael Pinkham, Cara Magliozzi, Joshua McDuffie, and Brendan O'Connor. 2017. Identifying civilians killed by police with distantly supervised entity-event extraction. In *Proceedings of the 2017 Conference on Empirical Methods in Natural Language Processing*, pages 1547–1557, Copenhagen, Denmark. Association for Computational Linguistics.

Diederik P Kingma and Max Welling. 2014. Auto-Encoding Variational Bayes.

Xin Li and Dan Roth. 2002. Learning Question Classifiers. In *COLING 2002: The 19th International Conference on Computational Linguistics*.

Cheng Lu, Jianfei Chen, Chongxuan Li, Qiuhao Wang, and Jun Zhu. 2021. Implicit Normalizing Flows. In *International Conference on Learning Representations*.

Andrew L Maas, Raymond E Daly, Peter T Pham, Dan Huang, Andrew Y Ng, and Christopher Potts. 2011. Learning Word Vectors for Sentiment Analysis. In *Proceedings of the 49th Annual Meeting of the Association for Computational Linguistics: Human Language Technologies*, pages 142–150, Portland, Oregon, USA. Association for Computational Linguistics.

Mike Mintz, Steven Bills, Rion Snow, and Daniel Jurafsky. 2009. Distant supervision for relation extraction without labeled data. In *Proceedings of the Joint Conference of the 47th Annual Meeting of the ACL and the 4th International Joint Conference on Natural Language Processing of the AFNLP*, pages 1003–1011, Suntec, Singapore. Association for Computational Linguistics.

George Papamakarios, Eric Nalisnick, Danilo Jimenez Rezende, Shakir Mohamed, and Balaji Lakshminarayanan. 2021. Normalizing Flows for Probabilistic Modeling and Inference.

Alexander Ratner, Stephen H Bach, Henry R Ehrenberg, Jason Alan Fries, Sen Wu, and Christopher Ré. 2017. Snorkel: Rapid Training Data Creation with Weak Supervision. *CoRR*, abs/1711.1.

Alexander Ratner, Braden Hancock, Jared Dunnmon, Frederic Sala, Shreyash Pandey, and Christopher Ré. 2018. Training Complex Models with Multi-Task Weak Supervision.

Nils Reimers and Iryna Gurevych. 2019. Sentence-BERT: Sentence Embeddings using Siamese BERT-Networks. In *Proceedings of the 2019 Conference on Empirical Methods in Natural Language Processing*. Association for Computational Linguistics.

Wendi Ren, Yinghao Li, Hanting Su, David Kartchner, Cassie Mitchell, and Chao Zhang. 2020. Denoising Multi-Source Weak Supervision for Neural Text Classification. *Findings of the Association for Computational Linguistics: EMNLP 2020*.

Danilo Jimenez Rezende and Shakir Mohamed. 2016. Variational Inference with Normalizing Flows.

Anastasiia Sedova, Andreas Stephan, Marina Speranskaya, and Benjamin Roth. 2021. Knodle: Modular Weakly Supervised Learning with PyTorch.

Shingo Takamatsu, Issei Sato, and Hiroshi Nakagawa. 2012. Reducing Wrong Labels in Distant Supervision for Relation Extraction. In *Proceedings of the 50th Annual Meeting of the Association for Computational Linguistics (Volume 1: Long Papers)*, pages 721–729, Jeju Island, Korea. Association for Computational Linguistics.

Dustin Tran, Keyon Vafa, Kumar Krishna Agrawal, Laurent Dinh, and Ben Poole. 2019. Discrete Flows: Invertible Generative Models of Discrete Data.

Paroma Varma, Frederic Sala, Ann He, Alexander Ratner, and Christopher Ré. 2019. Learning Dependency Structures for Weak Supervision Models.

positive	negative
beautiful	poor
pleasure	disappointing
recommendation	senseless
dazzling	second-rate
fascinating	silly
hilarious	boring
surprising	tiresome
interesting	uninteresting
imaginative	dreadful
original	outdated

Table 8: Keywords used to create rules for the IMDb dataset.

Zachary M Ziegler and Alexander M Rush. 2019. Latent Normalizing Flows for Discrete Sequences.

Barret Zoph, Deniz Yuret, Jonathan May, and Kevin Knight. 2016. Transfer Learning for Low-Resource Neural Machine Translation.

A Additional Data Description

A.1 Preprocessing

A few steps were performed, to create a unified data format. The crucial difference to other papers is that we removed duplicated samples. There were two cases. Either there were very little duplicates or the duplication occurred because of the programmatic data generation, thus not resembling the real data generating process. Most notably, in the spouse data set 60% of all data points are duplicates. Furthermore, we only used rules which occurred more often than a certain threshold as it is impossible to learn densities on only a handful of examples. The threshold is In order to have unbiased baselines, we ran the baseline experiments on the full set of rules and the reduced set of rules and took the best performing number.

A.2 IMDb rules

The labeling functions for the IMDb dataset are defined by keywords. We manually chose the keywords. We defined them in such a way that their meaning has rather little semantic overlap. The keywords are shown in table 8.

A.3 Labeling Function Correlations

In order to use labeling functions for weakly supervised learning, it is important to know the correlation of labeling functions to i) derive methods to combine them and ii) help to understand phenomena of the model predictions.

Thus we decided to add correlation plots. More specifically, we use the Pearson Correlation coefficient.

B Additional Implementationial Details

B.1 Architecture

As mentioned in section 3, the backbone of our flow is RealNVP architecture, which we introduced in section 2. With sticking to the notation in formula 2 the network layers to approximate the functions s and t are shown below

```
s = nn.Sequential(
    nn.Linear(dim, hidden_dim),
    nn.LeakyReLU(),
    nn.BatchNorm1d(hidden_dim),
    nn.Dropout(0.3),
    nn.Linear(hidden_dim, dim),
    nn.Tanh()
)
t = nn.Sequential(
    nn.Linear(dim, hidden_dim),
    nn.LeakyReLU(),
    nn.BatchNorm1d(hidden_dim),
    nn.Dropout(0.3),
    nn.Linear(hidden_dim, dim),
    nn.Tanh()
)
```

Hyperparameters are the depth, i.e. number of stacked layers, and the hidden dimension.

B.2 WeaNF-M Sampling

For the mixed model WeaNF-M the sampling process becomes rather complicated.

Next up, the code to produce the convex combination $\alpha_1, \ldots, \alpha_t$ is shown. The input tensor takes values in $\{0, 1\}$ and has shape $b \times t$ where b is the batch size and t the number of labeling functions.Note that some mass is put on every labeling functions. We realized that this bias imrpoves performance.

```
def weight_batch(self, batch_y: torch.Tensor):
    """Returns weighting array forming convex sum.
    Shape: (batch_dim, num_rules)
    """
    batch_y = batch_y.float()
    batch_y += 0.1 * torch.ones(batch_y.shape)
    batch_y = batch_y * torch.rand(batch_y.shape)
    row_sum = batch_y.sum(axis=1, keepdims=True)
    nbatch_y = batch_y / row_sum
    return nbatch_y
```

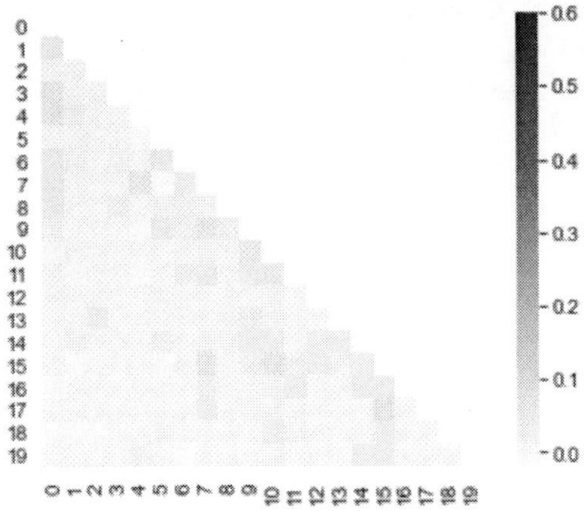

(a) IMDb

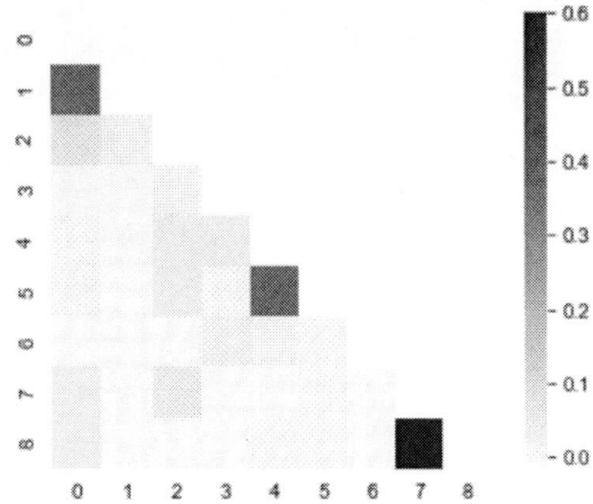

(b) Spouse

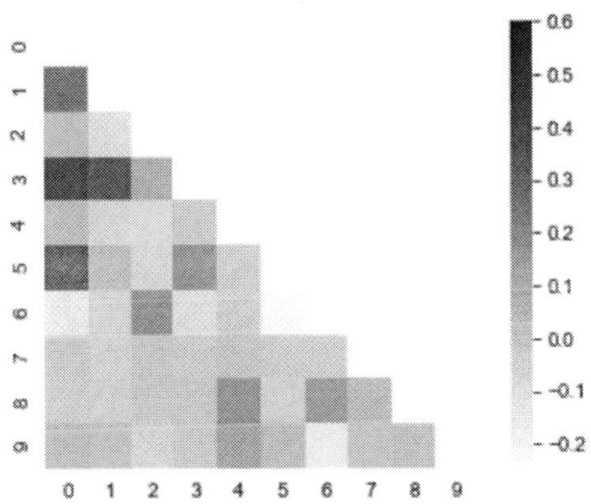

(c) YouTube

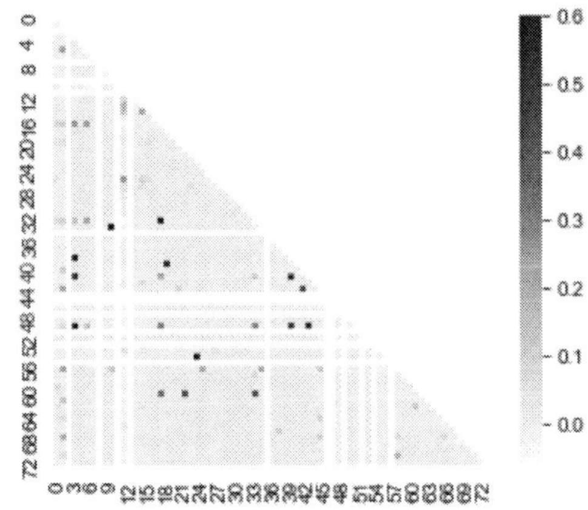

(d) SMS

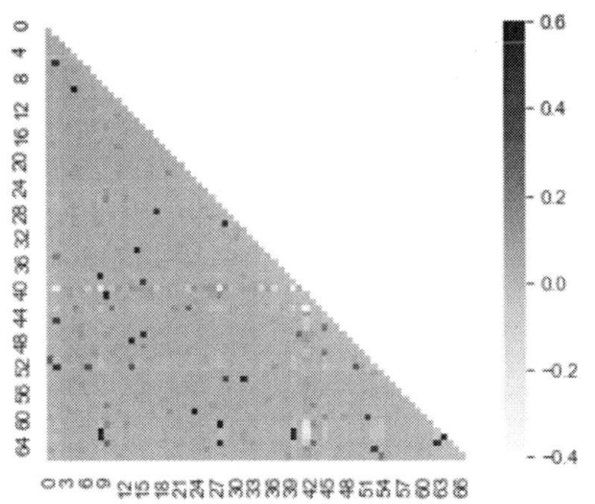

(e) Trec

Author Index

Association for Computational Linguistics
209 N. Eighth Street
Stroudsburg, Pennsylvania 18360

ISBN 978-1-7138-6750-0

CURRAN ASSOCIATES INC.
proceedings
.com